Aristophanes and the Defin

Aristophanes and the Definition of Comedy

◆

M. S. SILK

UNIVERSITY PRESS

This book has been printed digitally and produced in a standard specification in order to ensure its continuing availability

OXFORD
UNIVERSITY PRESS

Great Clarendon Street, Oxford OX2 6DP

Oxford University Press is a department of the University of Oxford.
It furthers the University's objective of excellence in research, scholarship,
and education by publishing worldwide in

Oxford New York

Auckland Cape Town Dar es Salaam Hong Kong Karachi
Kuala Lumpur Madrid Melbourne Mexico City Nairobi
New Delhi Shanghai Taipei Toronto
With offices in
Argentina Austria Brazil Chile Czech Republic France Greece
Guatemala Hungary Italy Japan South Korea Poland Portugal
Singapore Switzerland Thailand Turkey Ukraine Vietnam

Oxford is a registered trade mark of Oxford University Press
in the UK and in certain other countries

Published in the United States
by Oxford University Press Inc., New York

Oxford is a registered trade mark of Oxford University Press
in the UK and in certain other countries

Published in the United States
by Oxford University Press Inc., New York

© M. S. Silk 2000

The moral rights of the author have been asserted

Database right Oxford University Press (maker)

Reprinted 2005

All rights reserved. No part of this publication may be reproduced,
stored in a retrieval system, or transmitted, in any form or by any means,
without the prior permission in writing of Oxford University Press,
or as expressly permitted by law, or under terms agreed with the appropriate
reprographics rights organization. Enquiries concerning reproduction
outside the scope of the above should be sent to the Rights Department,
Oxford University Press, at the address above

You must not circulate this book in any other binding or cover
And you must impose this same condition on any acquirer

ISBN 0-19-925382-X

Contents

Prologue

I Aristophanes' comic writing is exhilarating and surprising; complex, perhaps disconcertingly; much written about in recent years; much illuminated; effectively undervalued; misread, because much of the discussion, much of the illumination, even, is off-centre. Aristophanes is one of the world's great writers: *discuss*. In the pages that follow, I propose to do precisely this: to define Aristophanes' literary greatness, and to do so by focusing on the issue that seems to me to lie at the heart of his work: the definition of comedy.

And whose definition would that be? My title has a multiple point. In the first place, Aristophanes' work may be seen to have something of a defining force for posterity in its realization of comedy and the possibilities of comedy. Then again, Aristophanes himself gives every sign of a preoccupation with the question: what *is* comedy?—or, perhaps, what *should* it be? And again, my own attempt to deal with these two related topics leads me to try to shed some light on Aristophanes' question—at least, his first question—in a wider perspective. That is, both through explicit arguments in Chapters 2, 7, and 8, and implicitly through the book as a whole, I hope to add something to the theory of Comedy (with a capital C) myself.

A writer whose work can support such questions, and a writer whose work has itself a defining quality for posterity, must be a great writer indeed: *discuss*. One returns, then, and inevitably, to the first aim of this book (inseparable, as it seems to me, from the other): the elucidation of the quality and qualities of Aristophanes' writing. In search of this elucidation, the book will be literary-critical in the strictest sense. We may need to discriminate between Aristophanes and others, and—inseparable again—we shall certainly need to consider where his own strengths and weaknesses lie and why some of his moments, his inclinations, his plays, are more satisfying than others. In this connection let me make clear that I do not share, and see no reason to share, the coy embarrassment about value judgements that permeates the modern (and especially postmodern) academy. Such embarrassment is in some ways peculiarly characteristic of classical studies, where a curious convergence has taken place between traditional historicist philology (which tries to take values for granted) and post-structural relativism (which tries to take them to pieces). While I have learned a great deal from spokesmen and spokeswomen of both persuasions, I take both of their underlying philosophies to be misguided. I have discussed some of these issues elsewhere.[1] Suffice it here to note that judgements of value are implicit in every consequential act of reading a literary work—if only because reading it commits us to some kind of provisional decision that it is worth reading, *and* because judgements of value are implicit in all acts of interpretation (without which reading is impossible), *and* because the whole notion of 'literature' is (as theorists like Eagleton and Macherey rightly insist) inextricably implicated in notions of value,[2] *and* because (as classicists, above all others, must be aware) the literature available to us is almost always pre-sifted on one or other evaluative ground. The question is only: should we tolerate issues of value to lurk beneath the surface (or surface randomly)—or should we subject them to the open scrutiny they deserve?

I take it as axiomatic, furthermore, that literature, from Homer to Gabriel García Márquez, is a continuum and literary experience, in turn, a whole, such that one inevitably does—and should relish the fact that one does—interpret one point on the continuum in the light of another. Dispassionate historicism (whether old or quasi-relativist new)[3] is indispensable, but as a means, not an end. For a writer like Aristophanes—for a writer who, as we say, 'matters'—it is not enough. Generally, it is minor and limited art that invites discussion in purely historical terms. Art and artists that count for more have something challenging to say to generations and cultures beyond their age, and demand wider

[1] Esp. in 'Pindar meets Plato: theory, language, value, and the classics', in S. J. Harrison (ed.), *Texts, Ideas, and the Classics* (Oxford, forthcoming).

[2] See e.g. P. Macherey and E. Balibar, 'Literature as an ideological form', in R. Young (ed.), *Untying the Text* (London 1981) 79–99, and T. Eagleton, *The Ideology of the Aesthetic* (Oxford 1990).

[3] On which see, briefly, my remarks in M. S. Silk (ed.), *Tragedy and the Tragic: Greek Theatre and Beyond* (Oxford 1996) 3–4.

perspectives for their interpretation. Indeed it is such art and such artists that help to create the wider perspectives in the first place. It does not follow, however, that the artists in question are uniquely equipped, or even especially well equipped, to interpret the products of their own creativity; and here, as elsewhere, it is a fact of life that authors' intentions (where known or recoverable) are interesting to know, but that interpretations based on them (or on speculations about them) are—if this is their sole claim to authority—arbitrary.[4]

A great and *challenging* writer: *discuss*. All significant artists must be challenging. They change us (whoever 'we' may be) by challenging us. They surprise us into enlarging our categories of experience—which, in Aristophanes' case, includes the experience of comedy itself. The challenge, in his case, is implicit in the problematic of definition.

This book is aimed at readers with an intelligent interest in Aristophanes and readers with an intelligent interest in the possibilities of comedy *tout court* (and I hope the two categories will often coincide). It contains, as will have become obvious, a fair amount of theorizing—though not necessarily theorizing of a very fashionable kind: Kierkegaard figures in my bibliography as well as Bakhtin, Adorno as well as Aristotle, Leavis as well as Derrida. I do not assume familiarity with any particular theory, however. Nor do I assume any knowledge of Greek (though Chapters 3 and 4, in particular, focus on issues of, or bound up with, language). Nor do I assume familiarity with the minutiae of Greek culture or literature or with any technical particulars of Greek dramatic form or theatrical history or dramaturgy. Parts II

[4] In A's case, one must be esp. vigilant against regressive 'logic' like (premise), 'one of his aims must have been to entertain and impress spectators who were not especially intelligent or learned', so that (conclusion) we had better 'reject some over-subtle interpretations which modern scholars have put forward from time to time' (an infelicitous opening salvo in a generally valuable book: D. M. MacDowell, *Aristophanes and Athens* (Oxford 1995) 3). Any work is or means whatever its relationships prompt it to be or mean—where 'relationships' subsumes relationships between elements of the work, relationships of its elements with the linguistic and other external codes presupposed, and relationships between the work (or its elements) and other works—including works not yet composed (cf. T. S. Eliot, 'Tradition and the individual talent', in *The Sacred Wood* (London 1920) 47–59). Interpretations (subtle or otherwise) should be rejected as and if incompatible with these relationships—not on the basis of some extra-interpretative diagnosis of a work's level. Works can, of course, operate on more than one level in any case. On intentionalism, see further below, p. 42 with n. 1.

and III of this Prologue contain some relevant material in the form of a summary résumé and a chronological chart, which, between them, should assist the reader who finds any of the chapters that follow less than self-explanatory. However, I do assume that those who come to this book will probably come with some sense of what an Aristophanic comedy is (as also with some sense of what literature is and does), and my account of Aristophanes is certainly not comprehensive, if only because I do not provide systematic expositions of individual plays, nor am I equally concerned, even, with all of the extant eleven, but primarily with the Old Comedies—the first nine of the eleven—in which the characteristics and qualities that concern me most are most evident.

Aristophanes as a *writer*: here too there is something to discuss, especially against the background of important recent work on the oral and performative modalities of classical Attic culture and drama.[5] Aristophanes is poet, playwright, writer. Unlike 'poet' or 'playwright', however, 'writer' suggests the modern condition of writerly self-consciousness and mission, which seems to me precisely to give the word a special aptness as applied to Aristophanes—'so may I be victorious, so may I be thought a true artist'[6]—notwithstanding the undoubted importance of orality and performance in Aristophanes' Athens. Drama, needless to say, is more than words: the words of drama imply performance, and (in the case of ancient Greek drama) performance in a very particular theatrical space and context. It does not follow, though, that an emphasis on words is illegitimate or inappropriate. It seems to me, rather, a wholly necessary and appropriate complement to the current—and, in itself, welcome—stress on the stagecraft and the semiotics of drama as performed. The reason why Aristophanes still matters to us as a living force—the reason why he is of more than merely historical interest—is his words. The

[5] See e.g.: R. Thomas, *Literacy and Orality in Ancient Greece* (Cambridge 1992); G. Nagy, *Poetry as Performance: Homer and Beyond* (Cambridge 1996); O. Taplin, *The Stagecraft of Aeschylus* (Oxford 1977); D. Wiles, *The Masks of Menander* (Cambridge 1991); S. Goldhill and R. Osborne (eds.), *Performance Culture and Athenian Democracy* (Cambridge 1999).

[6] *Nub.* 520, tr. Sommerstein: cf. below, p. 46. In case it needs saying, rejection of intentionalism does not entail signing up to the post-structuralist prejudice—summed up in M. Foucault's classic, but flawed, 'What is an author?' (e.g. in J. V. Harari (ed.), *Textual Strategies* (Ithaca, NY 1979) 141–60)—that author-talk is factitious and that discussion of authors' achievements is 'therefore' inappropriate.

words are, after all, what survives; words have an element of stability that theatrical performance—even a single original performance—must always lack;[7] the Greeks themselves ranked words ahead of other competing or associated media (ahead of music, ahead of spectacle);[8] and if, in Aristophanes' particular case, one wanted confirmation of the propriety of focusing on a verbal text, one could find it in the incontrovertible fact that, unlike most Greek dramatists that we know of, Aristophanes himself preferred to write the book and leave the producing/directing to someone else.[9] And if calling Aristophanes 'a writer'

[7] And performance (if known) is no less subject than words to variability of interpretation. There is at least one area, though, where inference about 'the' production is bound to be determinative on any reading of the words: ascription of lines to speakers, which is sometimes unclear now but must have been unambiguous once (for a straightforward instance see Sommerstein on *Nub.* 1105). On the general questions at issue here, see further: Taplin, *Stagecraft*, 1–60; D. Wiles, 'Reading Greek performance', *G&R* 34 (1987) 136–51; S. Goldhill, 'Reading performance criticism', in I. McAuslan and P. Walcot (eds.), *Greek Tragedy* (Oxford 1993) 1–11; S. Goldhill, *Reading Greek Tragedy* (Cambridge 1986) 281–6.

[8] Wiles, *Masks*, 210: 'Aristophanes wrote in an age which valued the author above all other theatrical artists.' Words and music: see esp. Pratinas, 1. 6–7 *PMG* (τὰν ἀοιδὰν κατέστασε Πιερὶς βασίλειαν· ὁ δ' αὐλὸς | ὕστερον χορευέτω· καὶ γάρ ἐσθ' ὑπηρέτας), and Pl. *Rep.* 398d (τήν γε ἁρμονίαν καὶ ῥυθμὸν ἀκολουθεῖν δεῖ τῷ λόγῳ). Both passages imply the normal, as well as normative, privileging of words in the classical period. Words and spectacle: contrast the cultural prestige of word-artists (poets, orators, philosophers) with the limited recognition of visual artists. In classical, as in later, Greece, visual art is essentially seen as a craft, without a Muse or inspiration (cf. P. A. Murray, 'Poetic genius and its classical origins', in Murray (ed.), *Genius: The History of an Idea* (Oxford 1989) 22–5). This contrast is one-sidedly articulated, but not invented, by Aristotle, for whom the theatrical 'visual design' (*opsis*: on the term see M. S. Silk, 'The "six parts of tragedy" in Aristotle's *Poetics*', *PCPS* 40 (1994) 109 with n. 7) notoriously comes bottom in importance out of the 'six parts' (*Poet.* VI). One might very pertinently add Aristotle's own gloomy admission that most Greeks (οἱ ἄνθρωποι) regard the poet-composer (*poiêtês*) as composer of words in verse (*metra*) (not, as Aristotle himself would wish, as composer of 'fictions', *muthoi*: *Poet.* I and IX).

[9] See below, p. 17. A's reasons were not necessarily the same at all times. The simplest explanation is spelled out at *Eq.* 515–16: he found directing tough. Most critics and commentators explain away the tendency by recourse to special factors, e.g. those only applicable, if at all, to certain stages of his career. Note esp. the *fable convenue* that he was too young to put on plays when he began writing them: see e.g. the discussion (with bibliog.) in MacDowell, *Aristophanes and Athens*, 34–41); contrast the welcome simplicity of A. Lesky, *A History of Greek Literature*, tr. J. Willis and C. de Heer (London 1966) 426–7. In the history of Greek drama as a whole, we might see here a significant step in a development away from a stereotypical original *Gesamtkunst*, where an Aeschylus wrote *and* directed *and* acted, towards increasing specialization, with the professionalization of acting another major development here. By not directing his own plays, A is in any case subverting the special (authorial) significance of the first production. Further

makes him sound a bit like figures, even, of the modern writerly age like Brecht or Beckett, like T. S. Eliot or Lorenz Hart, like Woody Allen or García Márquez—then, well and good: these are all, incidentally, among the figures of the modern age—among various figures of various ages—to whose work we shall be appealing, for one reason or another, in the discussions to come. In associating Aristophanes in this way with modern writerliness, one should not, indeed, dissociate him from his fellow poets of the Attic Old Comedy and his primary situation within the culture of the Athenian city-state, the *polis*. Of course it is important to have a sense of his membership of the Old Comic club,[10] and (among much else) salutary to consider how much of the portfolio of demonstrable Aristophanic qualities was actually unique to Aristophanes in his time. On this last limited point, indeed, we must report (on admittedly limited evidence) that there is no sign elsewhere in Old Comedy of his underlying dynamic—of which his preoccupation with tragedy is one, main, diagnostic feature.[11] And (on the larger issue) the fact that Aristophanic art, like all art, is a product of a particular culture and is implicated in the particularities of its institutions, social and political, in no way exempts us from the challenge of coming to terms with its relationships and its significance on a bigger stage.

II After which, it is only appropriate to say something about Aristophanes' immediate context—literary, cultural, social, political—as part of the promised résumé. Aristophanes is the best-known poet of the Old Comedy, which (like the other forms of Attic drama, tragedy, satyr-play, and later versions of comedy itself) is a verse form, performed by masked actors and chorus. 'Old Comedy' itself is an ancient but inexact term, which roughly

evidence of A's own orientation towards the written word may be found in the presumption that he sanctioned the circulation of the unperformed (and 'unperformable'?) *Clouds* II (see below, p. 15): so rightly K. J. Dover, *Aristophanes, Clouds* (Oxford 1968), p. xcviii.

[10] See below, pp. 13–14.

[11] Below, pp. 48–53. It is obviously possible, even likely, that the large imbalance of evidence for A, as against the rest of Old Comedy (see below, p. 14), serves to make us see as distinctively Aristophanic what was actually generic. However, it seems clear that A was consistently an innovator, so that 'generic' might often only mean a feature popularized by A himself: see the discussions in D. Harvey and J. Wilkins (eds.), *The Rivals of Aristophanes* (forthcoming).

covers the comic drama of the fifth century BC,[12] and more specifically the comic output of the eighty-odd years from the institutionalization of comedy at Athens (traditionally dated to 486) to the end of the Peloponnesian War (404). The last two of Aristophanes' extant eleven plays lie outside this period. The first nine (from *Acharnians*, 425, to *Frogs*, 405) belong to its last phase, as do his earliest, lost, plays (427/6).

During these last decades of the Old Comedy, performances of comic drama (along with the other dramatic forms, including tragedy) took place at two annual state festivals in honour of the god Dionysus, the City Dionysia and the Lenaea, at the Theatre of Dionysus on the Acropolis. A set number of comic poets (probably five) submitted, normally, a single play in open competition. The costs of each production (chiefly the expense of training and dressing the chorus) were borne by a state-appointed citizen of suitable means (known as a *khorêgos*). The competitions were decided by an elaborately appointed panel of judges whose verdicts (it is clear) were taken seriously by the poets; how far they corresponded with audience reactions (and so tell us about ancient taste) and how far, in any case, they tell us anything about dramatic or poetic qualities perceptible to us is debatable.[13] The chorus numbered twenty-four, the speaking actors three (perhaps sometimes more), along with silent supernumeraries. In Aristophanes' time, at the Lenaea (though not yet at the Dionysia) the leading actor in each play competed for a separate prize; these 'protagonists' were effectively professionals; the chorus, and presumably the other actors, were amateurs.

The chorus performed on a large circular dancing-floor (*orkhêstra*), surrounded by the audience on three sides; the actors performed on a raised stage, with a two-storey building (*skênê*) behind it, or appeared (usually only when playing divinities) on a crane (*mêkhanê*) suspended above the stage, or were 'wheeled out' across the stage on a platform (*ekkuklêma*). Whether and how often actors usurped the *orkhêstra*, or chorus-members the stage,

[12] i.e. *Attic* comic drama: there was also an independent tradition of comic drama, associated chiefly with Epicharmus, in Sicily: see below, pp. 69–70.

[13] Known results are included in the chart below, pp. 18–21. Modern commentators tend to pay unnecessary deference to them and to the whole process (see e.g. A. W. Pickard-Cambridge, *The Dramatic Festivals of Athens*², rev. J. Gould and D. M. Lewis (corr. edn., Oxford 1988) 95–9). For all we know, verdicts may have been as erratic, even inexplicable, as modern awards of Hollywood Oscars.

is unclear.[14] Masks might be generic (old men, young men, slaves, etc.) or distinctive ('portrait masks'), in representation of particular individuals. Comic masks tended to give an impression of distortion and male costumes, likewise, to be 'distorted' by padding and by the attachment (or exposure) of a leather phallus: how uniformly is, again, unclear.[15] All performers (actors and chorus) were men.

Performance itself included song and dance (usually combined and mostly, though not entirely, choral), speech (from the actors and the chorus leader), and an intermediate kind of verbal delivery, generally called 'recitative' or 'chant' (common both in choral sections and between actors). With very occasional and special exceptions, all words (sung, chanted, or spoken) were in verse, the commonest metre being the iambic trimeter (a rising rhythmic form roughly akin to the staple of most canonical English verse).[16] The tonal range of language involved was enormous—both in Aristophanes and in other Old Comic poetry—all the way from frank obscenity to high style. Musical accompaniment for songs was chiefly on the unaccompanied *aulos* (conventionally mistranslated 'flute'). The music itself (like Greek music in general) an audience from the modern Western world would find rhythmically complex, melodically alien, and harmonically minimal. Acting styles and stage movements would tend to

[14] See e.g. K. J. Dover, *Aristophanic Comedy* (London 1972) 19, E. Csapo and W. J. Slater, *The Context of Ancient Drama* (Ann Arbor 1995) 268, and below, pp. 207–8 n. 3.

[15] Arist. *Poet.* v refers to 'the comic mask' as 'ugly and distorted' (*αἰσχρόν τι καὶ διεστραμμένον*), but is presumably generalizing from contemporary (late Middle?) comedy. Vase paintings certainly suggest distortion, both for masks and costumes (see e.g. the sample in O. Taplin, *Comic Angels* (Oxford 1993)), though modern authorities are probably too ready to extrapolate from such evidence. Visual art in any age is liable to establish its own generalizing conventions: modern visual symbols for public toilets put all 'men' in trousers, all 'women' in skirts; 'the most obvious feature of Greek art is that men are mostly naked or partially naked, whereas women are usually clothed' (A. Stewart, *Art, Desire, and the Body in Ancient Greece* (Cambridge 1997) 24). On the phallus see L. M. Stone, *Costume in Aristophanic Poetry* (Salem 1984) 72–126.

[16] e.g. (*Ach.* 500) *to gár dikaíon oíde kaí trugôidía* (where -*ôi*- is a diphthongal single syllable), cf. e.g. (Keats) 'Fade fár awáy, dissólve, and quíte forgét' (etc.): in both cases the accentual marks indicate notional underlying rhythm (quantitative in Greek, 'stress', essentially, in English). Greek verse is properly analysed into patterns of syllables, ⏑ (light), – heavy, and × (indeterminate, 'anceps'): for the terminology see W. S. Allen, *Accent and Rhythm* (Cambridge 1973) 53–62; in general, M. L. West, *Greek Metre* (Oxford 1982).

involve the kind of bold, externalized stylization appropriate to performance from masked actors in a large outdoor theatre whose capacity exceeded 15,000 (equivalent, maybe, to a tenth of the total—both sexes, all ages—citizen population of the time). Audiences covered the social spectrum from high state officials to the collectivity of ordinary citizens (the *dêmos*), from artists and intellectuals to peasant farmers, from women to children to slaves. Visiting foreigners attended the Dionysia, though not the Lenaea, and the Dionysia in particular was a magnificent public occasion, and, necessarily, an occasion fraught with potential political significance, in terms of self-understanding and self-projection on the part of the articulate spokesmen of the *polis*. How, and how far, that potential was realized by Aristophanes is a matter of interpretation.[17]

In Aristophanic Old Comedy and (to judge from the fragments of other poets of the genre) in Old Comedy as a whole, there are recurrent structural features: a spoken introductory scene ('prologue'), the chorus's entrance song (*parodos*), a formal debate (agon), a sequence in the form of a direct address by the chorus to the audience (the parabasis or 'approach'), and a concluding scene (*exodos*) which often contains or promises a *kômos* (the 'party', from which the name of 'comedy' is itself derived).[18] There may be additional unclassifiable scenes ('episodes') and songs, especially in the later part of the play. The technical terms cited here are all Greek in origin (though agon, in particular, is simply a modern appropriation of the Greek word for 'contest'). The agon and parabasis tend to have elaborate structures of their own.

Old Comedy as a whole was expansive and unpredictable. Different plays might involve very different kinds of material and treatment—from mythological burlesque or some kind of social confrontation to topical presentations which might have a prominent satirical element (like *Clouds*) or not (like *Peace*), and which—whether satirical or not—might be fairly described as 'political' in a narrow sense (like *Knights*) or not (like *Frogs*).

[17] See below, pp. 301–49. Unconvincing attempts have been made to detect typical differences between Lenaean ('Athenian') and Dionysian ('Panhellenic') plays; see e.g. C. F. Russo, *Aristofane autore di teatro*² (Florence 1984) 3–21; *contra*, e.g., Pickard-Cambridge, *Festivals*, 39–41, and MacDowell, *Aristophanes and Athens*, 16.

[18] Below, p. 78 n. 116.

These labels will require closer scrutiny at a later stage, but it is worth spelling out here that if we survey the evidence for Old Comic plots and plot material overall, it is clearly false to suppose (as often implied) that 'political satire', or indeed satire as such, was a determinative requirement of the genre. At the very least, however, it is apparent that 'comic politics' was a prominent feature of Aristophanes' plays of the 420s, much of it directed against Cleon, the most powerful politician of the day. From various references in these same plays it is inferred that Cleon retaliated against Aristophanes himself with public denunciations and threats of legal action.[19] This impression of direct political engagement may or may not be all it seems. Nevertheless, comic involvement in democratic debate—of which this kind of real-life agon would be an extreme example—is unquestionably one of the distinctive features of Old Comedy, albeit not necessarily the most distinctive feature of Aristophanic comedy itself.

Such involvement is equally one of various features of Old Comedy which can be seen to take on a reduced significance or scope in the wake of Athens' sobering defeat in the Peloponnesian War. That defeat is followed by a series of momentous political developments, which begin with civil war and democratic restoration, and end, inside seventy years, with Athens a conquered city in a Macedonian empire under Philip, then Alexander. By the time of the death of Alexander in 323, a century after Aristophanes' arguments with Cleon, a drastic cultural reorientation has taken place, and all the distinctive features of Old Comedy have gone. The New Comedy—Menandrian comedy of manners—disclaims (among much else) the public stance and the interest in topicality, the tonal range and the expansive unpredictability, the agon and the parabasis and the traditional use of a chorus: the chorus is now removed from the action and restricted to interludes. These developments—broadly speaking—begin in a transi-

[19] Supposedly in response to *Babylonians* and to *Knights*: see, succinctly, MacDowell, *Aristophanes and Athens*, 42–5, 175–6. Apart from A's 'testimony', the only supporting evidence is statements in the ancient *Vitae* and scholia (e.g. schol. on *Ach.* 378), which themselves may have been derived, in whole or part, from the text. Cleon and A apart, there is some (much-contested) evidence for legislation restricting the scope of comic satire before and after this period: see F. S. Halliwell, 'Comic satire and freedom of speech in classical Athens', *JHS* 111 (1991) 48–70, MacDowell, *Aristophanes and Athens*, 42–5, and cf. the chronology below, pp. 19–20, under years 440–437 and 415.

tional period, conventionally labelled Middle Comedy, to which Aristophanes' last two extant plays, *Ecclesiazusae* and *Plutus*, and especially the latter, clearly belong: the evidence about certain of his last plays is still more revealing.[20]

The cultural reorientations of the fourth century may be traced back to a nexus of tensions and developments in the fifth. From the standpoint of an Old Comic poet concerned with the possibilities of comedy, Athens in the closing decades of the fifth century is in cultural, as also in political, turmoil. This city of great intellectual explorers—the tragedian Euripides, the historian Thucydides, the philosopher Socrates—is also the city famous for its religious traditions, its great religious festivals and movements, and (in tragedy, in particular) its religious poetry. The student of classical Attic literature and society soon learns to see the city as a cultural hot-house, where new forms and configurations grow up, and perhaps wither, with startling rapidity, and where resistance to the new can often be new and exciting itself. A hundred years before Aristophanes' first phase of comic politicking, Athens was a small conservative agricultural community; by the 420s Athens is an outward-looking power and a centre of political, intellectual, and artistic creativity; and in different ways Aristophanic comedy can be shown to acknowledge both of these realities.

The innovations themselves make up a formidable list. This hundred-year period sees the establishment of the peculiar Attic form of direct democracy, and it is in this same period that Athens invents, or hosts the development of, the dramatic forms—comedy, tragedy, satyr-play—and a wealth of prose forms, notably historiography, philosophy and oratory; and these literary developments may be seen to follow, more or less, the trajectory of the progressive democratization of the state. Attic drama, equally, may be seen to be the heir to the earlier poetic traditions of Greece: lyric poetry (meaning *song*), high and low, and epic poetry, narrative and didactic; and—to use a revealing, if perhaps tendentious, recategorization of that same range of earlier material—poetry of praise, poetry of blame.[21] Tragedy, the earliest of

[20] See below, pp. 51–2.

[21] See variously J. Herington, *Poetry into Drama* (Berkeley 1985); G. F. Else, *The Origin and Early Form of Greek Tragedy* (Cambridge, Mass. 1965); R. Rosen, *Old Comedy and the Iambographic Tradition* (Atlanta 1988); G. Nagy, *The Best of the Achaeans* (Baltimore 1979) 211–75. The identification of Greek 'praise poetry'

the new cultural forms, is, in its heyday, incontestably the most prestigious of them, but from the second half of the fifth century, even the supremacy of tragedy comes into question with the rise of prose thought. This last development is critical. From the 450s Athens becomes a centre for philosophers and philosophy, and 427 (the year of Aristophanes' first play) is the landmark date when the influential Sicilian sophist Gorgias visits the city. Through a cluster of separate challenges to existing tradition, the sophistic movement—a configuration of independent thinkers and teachers, whose very name (partly thanks to their chief enemy, Plato) still drips with connotations of subversive irresponsibility—helps to establish philosophical argument as a prime concern for modern man. More specifically, the sophists proclaim the word, language, the power and the study of language, as the source of intellectual enlightenment and control. Here begins linguistic science. Here, above all, begins oratory as a prestigious art-form with, soon, its own supporting science (rhetorical theory) and its own self-evident claim to a major place in the life of an open, democratic society.

Articulate verbalizing is not just a dominant form of late fifth-century political practice: it is an intense preoccupation of the whole culture. Athens in this generation is truly 'the city of words'.[22] Since the world of archaic Greece, poets above all others—'wise' ones, *sophoi*—had spoken both to and for the community.[23] This role was inherited by drama, and most directly by tragedy, with its complex articulating and mediating of the traditions, the aspirations, the values, and the tensions of the newly democratic state. For all such 'serious' poetry in the traditional high style (which looks back, ultimately, to Homer) it is myth—meeting point of religious belief and socio-cultural practice—that serves as vehicle. By the time the Peloponnesian War is at an end, and Old Comedy is giving way to its successor forms, tragedy, mythic poetry, and poetry in general are themselves giving way in prestige and significance to the challenge of

and 'blame poetry' was originally due to M. Detienne, *Les Maîtres de vérité dans la grèce archaïque* (Paris 1967) 16–27.

[22] The title of ch. 3 in Goldhill's *Reading Greek Tragedy*, and, more recently, of ch. 5 in D. T. Steiner, *The Tyrant's Writ: Myths and Images of Writing in Ancient Greece* (Princeton 1994).

[23] On poetic *sophia*, see below, pp. 46–7 n. 11.

philosophy and oratory, a process which only intensifies with time. There is a momentous dissociation of sensibility here, and Aristophanes, in the last third of the century, is both an observer and a participant in this crisis.[24]

'Crisis', of course, is an irresistible label for developments in this period outside the sphere of thought and art. From 431 Athens is at war, and remains at war for most of the rest of the century. To the inevitable challenges of war are added special tensions between overpopulated town and ravaged country, and between the new radical democratic leadership, assumed by men like Cleon, and the traditions of aristocracy which had survived the democratization of the state. Needless to say, any of these developments, and those in the artistic–intellectual sphere too, may be perceived—by us or by a comic playwright in Aristophanes' Athens—as associated developments, indeed may be bundled together, in terms of familiar polarities, as new/old, good/bad (or bad/good). However, anyone who comes to Aristophanic comedy, or to this book, equipped with, for instance, the stereotype (to be found in some discussions) that our poet backs everything traditional and 'conservative' and opposes everything innovative and 'modern', should be swiftly disabused.

III By comparison with his fellow poets of the Old Comedy, Aristophanes has been well treated by time. For Aristotle, in the *Poetics*, half a century or so after the poet's death, Aristophanes is the representative poet of comedy, and by the time of Plutarch (first century AD) he is the representative poet, still, of Old Comedy—though Aristotle's dramatic norms virtually constitute a prescription for Menandrian New Comedy, while Plutarch's preference for Menander is explicit.[25] Old Comic outspokenness may have commended itself to Horace in the Augustan age, but Aristophanes' survival among the reading publics of later antiquity and Byzantium was surely due not to this, but to such incidental educational advantages as his repositories of once

[24] With this sketch of Greek literary-cultural history, compare and contrast M. S. Silk, 'Language, poetry and enactment', *Dialogos* 2 (1995) 109–11, T. Cole, *The Origins of Rhetoric in Ancient Greece* (Baltimore 1991), B. Gentili, *Poesia e pubblico nella Grecia antica*[2] (Rome 1995) 155–211.

[25] Arist. *Poet.* III; Plut. *Moral.* 853a–854d.

topical but now antiquarian allusion and his impeccably Attic Greek.[26] At all events, he survived.

Aristophanes' career covers a roughly forty-year span from 427 to *c*.386. The scholars of later antiquity knew of forty-four plays attributed to him, of which four (all now lost) were declared spurious. From a fragmentary inscription, we do know of at least one other possible Aristophanic comedy,[27] and simple arithmetic suggests that if it was normally open to a comic poet to submit two plays a year, one at the Lenaea, one at the City Dionysia, the total public output of a writer with a forty-year career could have been considerably in excess of forty. Nevertheless, a strike rate of eleven out of forty compares favourably even with the best surviving tragedian, Euripides (eighteen[28] out of ninety-two), and contrasts with the substantial loss of the work of all the other comic poets, from whom only one other complete play (Menander's *Dyscolus*) is extant. From the other Old Comic writers, however, as also from Aristophanes' lost plays themselves, thousands of fragments, long or short, do survive as quotations in other ancient sources or as bits of ancient copies preserved on papyrus in the dry Egyptian sands.[29]

The forty-four known plays are listed below in English alphabetical order, with Greek names following. The four reportedly spurious plays are square-bracketed. English names given are those by which the plays are referred to in the text of this book (with alternative translations in brackets).[30] The list contains

[26] See Hor. *Sat.* 1. 4. 1 ff. and (for A's place in the educational canon) J. Henderson, *Aristophanes: Lysistrata* (Oxford 1987), pp. lviii–lxi.

[27] *IG* II² 2321]*ΑΝΤΟΠΡΕΣ*[? = Ὀδομαντοπρέσβεις (see *PCG* iii. 2. 226).

[28] i.e. discounting *Rhesus* as non-Euripidean, but including the satyr-play *Cyclops*.

[29] If we put end to end every surviving scrap of Old Comedy, we seem to possess (very roughly): (*a*) 15,000 lines' worth of Aristophanic plays; (*b*) 1,000, of Aristophanic fragments; (*c*) 3,000 (including about 1,000 of Eupolis/Cratinus), of fragments of other Old Comedy poets. These figures include *all* surviving remains: i.e. (*a*) subsumes all eleven plays (including the two 'Middle Comedies'); and (*b*) and (*c*) subsume *all* known fragments of Old Comedy poets (including, again, fragments that might, or even clearly do, belong to the early fourth century). The figures are artificial in another sense: a 'line' is not a constant (single verse lines may be of very different lengths) and, for the purpose of the calculation, 100 one-word fragments may be counted as twenty or thirty lines. In addition to fragments there are numerous testimonia, bearing on one or more of the lost plays.

[30] For several plays (extant and lost) there are no universally agreed 'English' names. I use the best-established or the most natural English, Some of the best-established, however, are in Latin or Latinized Greek. In the notes extant plays are

several doublets—that is, a given name was used twice. In the case of *Aeolosicon*, both plays are lost. In the case of the two *Dramas* (which themselves have alternative names), one was spurious, but again both are lost. In three cases, one play does in fact survive, but the surviving plays, *Peace* I, *Plutus* II, and *Thesmophoriazusae* I, are generally known for convenience simply as *Peace*, *Plutus*, and *Thesmophoriazusae*, and are so designated in this book. Finally, there is the special case of *Clouds*, cited in the ancient lists as two separate plays. In fact, a play of this name was produced (in 423, but not to the judges' taste), then revised (*c*.417), but never produced in its revised form. *Clouds* I (first, unrevised, version) is lost; *Clouds* II (second, revised, version) survives. Here too it is conventional to refer simply to *Clouds* (albeit, in this case, often with specific discussion of the issues involved). The list in full:[31]

Acharnians Ἀχαρνῆς
Aeolosicon I and II Αἰολοσίκων
Amphiaraus Ἀμφιάραος
Anagyrus Ἀνάγυρος
Babylonians Βαβυλώνιοι
Banqueters Δαιταλῆς
Birds Ὄρνιθες
Clouds I and II Νεφέλαι
Cocalus Κώκαλος
Daedalus Δαίδαλος

generally referred to by conventional—Latin—abbreviations: *Ach.* (*Acharnians*), *Eq.* (*Equites*: *Knights*), *Nub.* (*Nubes*: *Clouds*), *Vesp.* (*Vespae*: *Wasps*), *Pax* (*Peace*), *Av.* (*Aves*: *Birds*), *Lys.* (*Lysistrata*), *Thes.* (*Thesmophoriazusae*), *Eccl.* (*Ecclesiazusae*), *Pl.* (*Plutus*).

[31] The Greek names given are those by which the plays were known in later antiquity. These may or may not be authorial. At *Nub.* 554 A refers to *Knights* as Ἱππῆς, as we would, but at 529 to his *Banqueters* (Δαιταλῆς) by the names of two of the play's characters. The very existence of alternative titles in the case of the two Δράματα plays points to a state of uncertainty in—later—antiquity itself. We know of alternative titles also for (e.g.) *Lysistrata*: see Henderson, *Lysistrata*, p. xv. The logic of our title is often obvious, esp. when the plays are named after the chorus (which most plays with plural names—from *Acharnians* to *Women Campers* — will be), but, as the *Banqueters* point indicates, 'obvious' still may or may not mean 'original'. On the vagaries and uncertainties of names of literary works in antiquity, see E. Nachmanson, *Der griechische Buchtitel* (Göteborg 1941). The assumption that titles recorded in the *Didaskaliai* (3rd-cent. BC inscriptional lists of dramatic data) are based on authoritative official records (see e.g. K. Dover, *Aristophanes, Frogs* (Oxford 1993) 56) may or may not be sound, but (even if sound) 'authoritative' still does not necessarily mean 'authorial' in a modern sense.

Danaids Δαναΐδες
[*Dionysus Shipwrecked* Διόνυσος ναυαγός]
Dramas or *Centaur* Δράματα ἢ Κένταυρος
[*Dramas* or *Niobus* Δράματα ἢ Νίοβος]
Ecclesiazusae Ἐκκλησιάζουσαι (*Women in Assembly*)
Farmers Γεωργοί
Frogs Βάτραχοι
Fryers Ταγηνισταί
Gerytades Γηρυτάδης
Heroes Ἥρωες
[*Islands* Νῆσοι]
Knights Ἱππῆς (*Cavalry, Horsemen*)
Lemnian Women Λήμνιαι
Lysistrata Λυσιστράτη
Merchant Ships Ὁλκάδες
Old Age Γῆρας
Peace I and II Εἰρήνη
Phoenician Women Φοίνισσαι
Plutus I and II Πλοῦτος (*Wealth*)
[*Poetry* Ποίησις]
Polyidus Πολύιδος
Preview Προάγων (*Proagon*)
Seasons Ὧραι
Storks Πελαργοί
Telemessians Τελεμησσῆς
Thesmophoriazusae I and II Θεσμοφοριάζουσαι
Triphales Τριφάλης ('Mister Three-Prick')
Wasps Σφῆκες
Women Campers Σκηνὰς καταλαμβάνουσαι

The extant plays, with dates of first production,[32] are:

[32] Production—not necessarily composition. It is widely assumed, without discussion, that except for special cases (like posthumous productions of Eur. *Bacch.* and Soph. *OC*, or speculative scenarios about the genesis of the (?) Aeschylean *PV*), the first theatrical production of a Greek play indicates its date of composition—i.e. that the play would be composed for the coming year's competition. No doubt, something like this often happened; and, no doubt, one may accept that the assumption is likely to hold good for the final version of any play, esp. the final version of a more or less topical comedy. However, it defies belief that Greek dramatists never anticipated Horace's advice to write a draft and put it away for later (*AP* 388–9: see variously Brink and Rudd ad loc.)—or, if not a whole draft, then sketches, speeches, ideas, images, songs, quotable quotes, jokes, single lines, or scenes. Perhaps A's tinkering with *Clouds*, after the production, is only an unusual, and unusually visible, version of what more commonly went on in the years *before* a production.

Acharnians 425
Knights 424
Clouds 423/*c*.417
Wasps 422
Peace 421
Birds 414
Lysistrata 411
Thesmophoriazusae 411
Frogs 405
Ecclesiazusae *c*.392
Plutus 388

This tally represents a reasonable cross-section from Aristophanes' known output, including, as it does, both early and late plays, but the selection is obviously biased towards the earlier part of his career. Of the extant plays, eight belong to the first twenty-odd years, three to the second; and five of the first eight (if we include *Clouds*) belong to the 420s. One overall effect of the selection as we have it is that plays dealing with topical and public matters predominate.

Greek playwrights generally directed ('produced') their own plays.[33] Aristophanes is unusual. He is known to have directed *Knights*, *Plutus*, and (possibly) *Wasps*, and known *not* to have directed *Acharnians*, *Birds*, *Lysistrata*, and *Frogs*—together with the lost plays, *Banqueters* (427), *Babylonians* (426), *Amphiaraus* (414), *Cocalus* (387), *Aeolosicon* II (386), and, probably, *Preview* (422).[34] We have no information about his other plays, including *Clouds* (i.e. *Clouds* I: *Clouds* II was never staged), *Peace*, *Thesmophoriazusae*, and *Ecclesiazusae*.

As a point of reference for the résumé just offered and the discussions to come, the datable details of Aristophanes' career may be usefully set out in the context of events at Athens from the institutionalization of tragedy to the deaths of Menander and the last of the canonical Attic orators: a roughly 240-year span from the late sixth to the early third centuries BC. In the chart that follows, some dates (including the very first) are conventional, and

[33] Direction (of performers), rather than (or as well as) production (of the dramatic concept) is indicated by the Greek terminology, *didaskalos* (and cognates), and most obviously the compound *khorodidaskalos*. Cf. Csapo and Slater, *Context*, 39–40, and below, p. 46 n. 10.

[34] On *Wasps* and *Preview*, see MacDowell, *Aristophanes and Athens*, 34. For data on the rest, see Pickard-Cambridge, *Festivals*, 84–6.

a few (not just those marked *c.* for 'circa') may be inexact or controversial. All of Aristophanes' datable plays (as well as some by other playwrights) are included: all Aristophanic plays are in bold; all lost plays are in brackets. Of the undated Aristophanic plays: *Anagyrus*, *Heroes*, *Seasons*, *Women Campers* may be ascribed to the years 421–412; *Daedalus*, *Dramas/Centaur*, *Peace* II, *Polyidus*, *Triphales* to 415–405; *Aeolosicon* I, *Fryers*, *Lemnian Women*, *Old Age*, *Phoenician Women*, *Storks*, *Thesmophoriazusae* II to 409–389; the date of *Danaids* is beyond conjecture.[35]

ARISTOPHANES: CHRONOLOGY AND CONTEXT

*c.*534	Traditional date for institutionalization of tragedy at Dionysia
525/4	Birth of Aeschylus
508/7	Democratic reforms of Cleisthenes
*c.*500	Comic poet Epicharmus *fl.* in Sicily
499	Aeschylus' first production
496/5	Birth of Sophocles
490/79	Persian Wars
486	Institutionalization of comedy at City Dionysia (March/April): comic poet Chionides wins first recorded victory
484	Aeschylus' first victory
*c.*480	Birth of Euripides
*c.*480	Birth of Antiphon, earliest of 'the ten (Attic) orators'
472	Aeschylus' *Persians*
472	Attested victory by comic poet Magnes
469	Birth of Socrates
468	Sophocles' first victory
467	Aeschylus' *Seven against Thebes*
462/1	Democratic reforms of Ephialtes
*c.*460	Birth of Thucydides
458	Aeschylus' *Oresteia*
456	Death of Aeschylus
456/5	Philosopher Anaxagoras settles in Athens
455	Euripides' first production
*c.*453	First victory by comic poet Cratinus

[35] For evidence and discussion of the dating of A's plays, see P. Geissler, *Chronologie der altattischen Komödie*² (Zurich 1969), *PCG* iii. 2 (under the various titles), J. van Leeuwen, *Prolegomena ad Aristophanem* (Leiden 1908), A. H. Sommerstein, *Aristophanes: Acharnians*² (Warminster 1984) 3–5, 25. Documentation about the other items in the chart may be found in *OCD*³; *PCG*; Csapo and Slater, *Context*; Pickard-Cambridge, *Festivals*.

450	First victory by comic poet Crates
c.450	First visit of sophist Protagoras to Athens
c.450	**Birth of Aristophanes**
449	Institution of prize for best tragic actor
c.445	First victory by comic poet Telecleides
443+	Political ascendancy of Pericles as *stratêgos*
441	Euripides' first victory
c.440	Productions of comedy introduced at Lenaea (January/February)
440	'Decree of Morychides' limiting scope of comic satire
438	Euripides' *Alcestis* (and *Telephus*)
437	'Decree of Morychides' repealed
437/6	Trial of Anaxagoras for impiety
c.434	Institution of prize for best comic actor at Lenaea
431	Euripides' *Medea*
431	Outbreak of Peloponnesian War with Sparta
430	Outbreak of plague at Athens
c.430	(Cratinus' *Dionysalexandrus*)
429	First play by comic poet Eupolis
429	First victory by comic poet Phrynichus
429	Death of Pericles; rise of Cleon as popular leader
c.429	Birth of Plato
428	Euripides' *Hippolytus*
427	Arrival in Athens of Gorgias, popularizer of rhetoric
427	(**Banqueters**, second), Aristophanes' earliest play
426	(**Babylonians**, first, Dionysia): ? Cleon brings indictment for *adikia*
425	**Acharnians**, first, Lenaea (beat Cratinus' *Victims of the Storm* and Eupolis' *New Moons*)
424	**Knights**, first, Lenaea (beat Cratinus' *Satyrs* and Aristomenes' *Porters*)
424	(? **Farmers**, Dionysia)
423	(? **Merchant Ships**, Lenaea)
423	(**Clouds I**, third, Dionysia) (beaten by Cratinus' *Wineflask* and Ameipsias' *Connus*)
c.423	? Death of Cratinus
422	(**Preview**, first, Lenaea), **Wasps**, second, Lenaea (Leucon's *Ambassadors* third)
422	Death of Cleon
421	(Eupolis' *Maricas*)
421	**Peace**, second, Dionysia (beaten by Eupolis' *Flatterers* with Leucon's *Members of the Clan* third)
421	Peace of Nicias with Sparta

420	(Eupolis' *Autolycus*)
c.417	**Clouds II** (revised version of **Clouds I**): not performed
416	First victory of tragedian Agathon (victory celebration = setting of Plato's *Symposium*)
415	Euripides' *Trojan Women*
415	Dispatch of Athenian expedition to Sicily
415	? Proposal of Syracosius to restrict satire on named individuals
414	(**Amphiaraus**, Lenaea)
414	**Birds**, second, Dionysia (beaten by ? Ameipsias' *Revellers*, with Phrynichus' *Hermit* third)
413	War resumed by Sparta
413	Destruction of Athenian expedition in Sicily
412	Euripides' *Helen*
c.412	Eupolis' last play (*Demes*)
c.412	Death of Eupolis
411	**Lysistrata**, Lenaea
411	Oligarchic revolution of the 'Four Hundred'
411	**Thesmophoriazusae I**, Dionysia
410	Restoration of democracy
c.410	First victory by Plato Comicus
409	Sophocles' *Philoctetes*
409	Euripides *Phoenissae*
408	Euripides' *Orestes*
408	(**Plutus I**)
408/7	(? **Gerytades**)
406	Death of Euripides
406	Death of Sophocles
405	**Frogs**, first, Lenaea (beat Phrynichus' *Muses* and Plato Comicus' *Cleophon*)
405	Euripides' *Bacchae* and *Iphigenia at Aulis* produced posthumously
404	Surrender of Athens: end of Peloponnesian War
404	Imposition of oligarchy ('Thirty Tyrants')
403	Civil war and restoration of democracy
c.402	(**Telemessians**)
401	Sophocles' *Oedipus at Colonus* produced posthumously
c.400	Death of Agathon
c.400	Death of Thucydides
399	Execution of Socrates
399/90	? Plato's first dialogues
c.392	**Ecclesiazusae**
388	**Plutus II**
387	(**Cocalus**, first?, Dionysia)

386	(? **Aeolosicon II**)
c.386	**Death of Aristophanes**
384	Birth of Aristotle
c.380	? Plato's *Symposium* (presents 'Aristophanes' in 416)
359	Philip becomes king of Macedon
347	Death of Plato
342/1	Birth of Menander
338	Macedonian victory over Athens at Chaeronea
336	Death of Philip: succeeded by Alexander
c.330	Aristotle's *Poetics*
323	Death of Alexander
322	Death of Aristotle
c.321	Menander's first play
316	Menander's *Dyscolus*
292/1	Death of Menander
c.290	Death of Dinarchus, last of the 'ten orators'

IV Finally, some practical points.

Greek is normally quoted in the Greek alphabet. Where Greek words are transliterated, I use ^ for eta/omega (long e/o).

Translation: where text is quoted, I normally quote in Greek and English, but where any bit of text is quoted a second time, I generally quote only in English (with a cross-reference to the first, fuller, quotation, as necessary). All Greek in the text is accompanied by a translation, usually in verse. My translations are not cribs. Some are 'closer' than others, but many avoid privileging the 'literal' sense in the ordinary way that translations do, because much of the time I am quoting Aristophanes' Greek in a literary-critical spirit to support a claim about its form, or tone, or style, or effect. In such cases I have privileged the point at issue: that is, I have aimed to offer a translation that suggests the form, or tone, or style, or effect of the Greek, if necessary at the cost of some adjustment of the 'literal' sense. I make no apology for this—the misrepresentation involved is arguably less—but I would recommend readers without Greek to consult another translation (e.g. Sommerstein's) *as well*, if they wish to see what an 'ordinary' translation looks like.

Texts and abbreviations: unless otherwise indicated, the Greek text of Aristophanes follows the Budé edition by Coulon (for the plays) and *PCG* (for the fragments). Texts of other Greek sources usually follow LSJ^9 and LSJ $Supp^2$. In the notes 'Aristophanes' is frequently abbreviated 'A' (or, in lexicographical citations, 'Ar.' as in LSJ). Other abbreviations of ancient authors and works broadly follow *OCD*³ or else LSJ/*Supp*. For a full list of bibliographical abbreviations used, see p. 437 below.

Secondary literature: this book is not a survey or an introduction, in which a detailed 'guide to further reading' would be appropriate. Any reader in need of an introduction is advised to consult MacDowell, *Aristophanes and Athens*, and the essays in E. Segal, *Oxford Readings in Aristophanes* (Oxford 1996), together with Segal's own introduction (pp. xi–xxi).

Dates: three-digit dates (425 etc.) are BC, and four-digit dates AD, unless otherwise specified. Occasionally 'BC' or 'AD' is added for the sake of clarity.

Acknowledgements: this book contains material from several previously published essays and articles. In all cases earlier material has been revised; in general it has been excerpted, expanded, or indeed (in some instances) confronted. Most of the earlier material has gone into Chapters 2, 4, 5, and 8, and is acknowledged, as appropriate, ad loc.; the book as a whole, as well as most of its specifics, is new. The earlier material is drawn from: (*a*) 'Aristophanes as a lyric poet', *Yale Classical Studies* 26 (1980) 99–151 (see Chapter 4); (*b*) 'The autonomy of comedy', *Comparative Criticism* 10 (1988) 3–37 (see Chapter 2); (*c*) 'Pathos in Aristophanes', *Bulletin of the Institute of Classical Studies* 34 (1988) 78–111 (see Chapter 8); (*d*) 'The people of Aristophanes', in C. B. R. Pelling (ed.), *Characterization and Individuality in Greek Literature* (Oxford 1990) 150–73 (see Chapter 5 and, very briefly, 6); (*e*) 'Aristophanic paratragedy', in A. H. Sommerstein *et al.* (eds.), *Tragedy, Comedy and the Polis* (Bari 1993) 477–504 (see Chapter 8); (*f*) 'Putting on a Dionysus show: Aristophanes' comic kinship with the Broadway balladeers', *Times Literary Supplement* for 28 August 1998 (see Chapters 4 and 6). My thanks, for permission to use this material, to: Cambridge University Press [(*a*) and (*b*)]; *Bulletin of the Institute of Classical Studies* [(*c*)]; *Oxford University Press* [(*d*)]; Levante Editori [(*e*)]; The Times Supplements Ltd [(*f*)]. Some other comedy-related material has been referred to, rather than reused: (*g*) 'Style, voice and authority in the choruses of Greek drama', *Drama* (Stuttgart) 7 (1999) 1–26; (*h*) 'Aristophanes versus the rest: comic poetry in Old Comedy', in Harvey and Wilkins, *Rivals of Aristophanes*; (*i*)

'Space and solitude in Aristophanes', *Pallas* (Toulouse) 55 (2001) (forthcoming). I am greatly indebted to the staff of OUP for their helpfulness, advice, efficiency, and meticulous attention to detail. On a more personal note, my thanks to all—students, colleagues, performers and directors, audiences of papers, friends, those near and dear—who have advised me or helped shape my views over the years.

I

Three Openings

First, *Plutus*:

ΚΑΡΙΩΝ *ὡς ἀργαλέον πρᾶγμ' ἐστίν, ὦ Ζεῦ καὶ θεοί,*
δοῦλον γενέσθαι παραφρονοῦντος δεσπότου.
ἢν γὰρ τὰ βέλτισθ' ὁ θεράπων λέξας τύχῃ,
δόξῃ δὲ μὴ δρᾶν ταῦτα τῷ κεκτημένῳ,
μετέχειν ἀνάγκη τὸν θεράποντα τῶν κακῶν. 5
τοῦ σώματος γὰρ οὐκ ἐᾷ τὸν κύριον
κρατεῖν ὁ δαίμων, ἀλλὰ τὸν ἐωνημένον.
καὶ ταῦτα μὲν δὴ ταῦτα· τῷ δὲ Λοξίᾳ,
ὃς θεσπιῳδεῖ τρίποδος ἐκ χρυσηλάτου,
μέμψιν δικαίαν μέμφομαι ταύτην, ὅτι 10
ἰατρὸς ὢν καὶ μάντις, ὥς φασιν, σοφὸς
μελαγχολῶντ' ἀπέπεμψέ μου τὸν δεσπότην,
ὅστις ἀκολουθεῖ κατόπιν ἀνθρώπου τυφλοῦ,
τοὐναντίον δρῶν ἢ προσῆκ' αὐτῷ ποεῖν.
οἱ γὰρ βλέποντες τοῖς τυφλοῖς ἡγούμεθα, 15
οὗτος δ' ἀκολουθεῖ, κἀμὲ προσβιάζεται,
καὶ ταῦτ' ἀποκρινόμενος τὸ παράπαν οὐδὲ γρῦ.
ἐγὼ μὲν οὖν οὐκ ἔσθ' ὅπως σιγήσομαι,
ἢν μὴ φράσῃς ὅ τι τῷδ' ἀκολουθοῦμέν ποτε,
ὦ δέσποτ', ἀλλά σοι παρέξω πράγματα. 20

CARIO Zeus and you other gods, how hard it is
To be the slave of a demented master.
Suppose the servant gives him good advice,
And his owner then decides to ignore it—
The servant has to share the consequences. 5
It's heaven's will: a man's body belongs
Not to himself, but to the one who's bought him.
But that's as may be. It's Loxias,
Who from his golden tripod prophesies,
That's actually to blame—because 10
A wise healer and seer they call him,
And yet he sent my master home so mad
That now he's following a blind man,

The opposite of what he ought to do.
Those of us with sight lead those without; 15
But he follows, and drags me along as well,
And not so much as a squeak from him in front.
Well, I for one will not stay silent.
Unless you tell me why we're following
Him, master, I'll give you trouble. 20

Master (as yet silent) and slave (speaking). The master is determinedly following a blind man, and Cario, the slave with him, has no idea why. These essential points of the situation we gather (with or without the aid of stage action) by lines 13 and 19. The verbal approach to these points is oblique: the speech opens with a generalization (1–2) which prompts a rather more reflective generality (3–5) and then another (6–7), in a pattern which is repeated in miniature at 14–15. Oblique but smooth: the writing has an obvious discipline and coherence. The texture is fairly even, and the diction, in particular, covers a fairly narrow range. The most distinctive sequence is 8–9, where first 'Loxias' as conventional equivalent for Apollo and then the elevated idiom patently evokes the idiom of tragedy, in conformity, one infers, with the dignity of the subject.[1] Even so, the range from this high point to (say) the 'trouble' in 20[2] is not much greater than one might find within a speech in a Euripidean tragedy. That is, lines 8–9 do not impinge as disconnected from the rest, and one obvious reason for this is a more pervasive tragedy-derived flavour associated, above all, with the prevailing sententiousness of the whole: 'general reflection' and 'tragic rhesis' go together.[3] And granted that the slave is to some degree talking the language of tragedy, his talk is still broadly 'in character'. From his words we readily recognize a consistent type: a grumbling, honest, street-wise servant. The evenness of the texture, and correlatively of the portrayal, allows the gentle humour of the situation to establish

[1] See P. Rau, *Paratragodia* (Munich 1967) 162 (though 'Loxias' is not exclusively, as Rau asserts, 'poetischer Name des Apoll': cf. Hdt. 1. 91). The Greek in 9 is elevated by the compounds θεσπιῳδεῖ and χρυσηλάτου and by the tragic-compatible rhythm.

[2] παρέχειν πράγματα: (e.g.) Hdt. 1. 155, Aesch. fr. 78a 13 (sat.), Men. *Epitr.* 930.

[3] As in a celebrated monograph by H. F. Johansen, *General Reflection in Tragic Rhesis* (Copenhagen 1959). The passage, or at least the situation presupposed, might claim tragic resonances in other ways: the sight of a blind old man at the start of the play recalls the opening of Soph. *OC*.

itself cumulatively by easy stages that correspond to a natural sequence of exposition and implied response: the master (to the alarm of his slave) is *mad* (2), because (to the bafflement of his slave) he's *following a blind man* (13), and (to the exasperation of his slave) he *won't say why* (19).

The easy coherence of the elements is their most apparent quality, and what they cohere around is a more or less lifelike action. Our attention is at no point directed away from the action to a tragic original or to anything else. More generally, we are not to be distracted—and it would jar if we *were* distracted—by any perceived difference between the slave's talk about himself, his talk about his master, and his talk about life. The modulation from narrative monologue to dramatic address is, again, such as to minimize any sense of discontinuity: *he* does this, *he* makes me do it too—well, *I* won't do it, unless *you* tell me . . . Behind all this coherence, though not as yet explained to the audience any more than to the slave, is an 'impossible' premise concerning a blind god of wealth. However, the consequential action attached to this premise strikes us as broadly logical, and the psychology and the whole spirit broadly realist. This sort of formula—impossible premise, logical consequences—is familiar from the fiction of our own age: no, a man can't be turned into a beetle, but just suppose he were—what would happen?[4] The formula is often, and quite inaccurately, applied to Aristophanic comedy as a whole. Let us therefore note how right the formula seems *here*: in response to what will indeed prove to be an impossible premise, the specific behaviour of the master, in action, and the slave, in words, will itself prove to be equally and appropriately logical and coherent.

Plutus is a late play, Aristophanes' last extant play, and the realist qualities of its opening lines are those that the world will presently learn to associate with Menandrian New Comedy. The contrast with the qualities apparent in the first lines of Aristophanes' last extant Old Comedy, *Frogs*, could hardly be greater:

ΞΑΝΘΙΑΣ εἴπω τι τῶν εἰωθότων, ὦ δέσποτα,
ἐφ' οἷς ἀεὶ γελῶσιν οἱ θεώμενοι;

[4] The theme of Kafka's *Metamorphosis* (*Die Verwandlung*, 1916): see below, p. 261, and on the categorization of such works cf. C. Brooke-Rose, *A Rhetoric of the Unreal* (Cambridge 1981) 66–7.

ΔΙΟΝΥΣΟΣ νὴ τὸν Δί' ὅ τι βούλει γε, πλὴν 'πιέζομαι'.
τοῦτο δὲ φύλαξαι· πάνυ γάρ ἐστ' ἤδη χολή.
ΞΑ. μηδ' ἕτερον ἀστεῖόν τι;
ΔΙ. πλήν γ' ὡς 'θλίβομαι'. 5
ΞΑ. τί δαί; τὸ πάνυ γέλοιον εἴπω;
ΔΙ. νὴ Δία
θαρρῶν γε· μόνον ἐκεῖν' ὅπως μὴ 'ρεῖς—
ΞΑ. τὸ τί;
ΔΙ. μεταβαλλόμενος τἀνάφορον ὅτι χεζητιᾷς.
ΞΑ. μηδ' ὅτι τοσοῦτον ἄχθος ἐπ' ἐμαυτῷ φέρων,
εἰ μὴ καθαιρήσει τις, ἀποπαρδήσομαι; 10
ΔΙ. μὴ δῆθ', ἱκετεύω, πλήν γ' ὅταν μέλλω 'ξεμεῖν.
ΞΑ. τί δῆτ' ἔδει με ταῦτα τὰ σκεύη φέρειν,
εἴπερ ποήσω μηδὲν ὧνπερ Φρύνιχος
εἴωθε ποιεῖν καὶ Λύκις κἀμειψίας
σκεύη φέρουσ' ἑκάστοτ' ἐν κωμῳδίᾳ; 15
ΔΙ. μή νυν ποήσῃς· ὡς ἐγὼ θεώμενος,
ὅταν τι τούτων τῶν σοφισμάτων ἴδω,
πλεῖν ἢ 'νιαυτῷ πρεσβύτερος ἀπέρχομαι.
ΞΑ. ὢ τρισκακοδαίμων ἄρ' ὁ τράχηλος οὑτοσί,
ὅτι θλίβεται μέν, τὸ δὲ γέλοιον οὐκ ἐρεῖ. 20

XANTHIAS Shall I tell them one of the usual jokes, master,
The ones that always get the audience laughing?
DIONYSUS Yes, anything you like—except 'I'm all *squeezy*'.
Not that one: it makes me feel too sick.
XAN. Anything but that one?
DIO. Oh—and 'I'm all *squashy*'. 5
XAN. Well, what about something really droll?
DIO. Right you are,
Only mind it's not the one—
XAN. Yes?—
DIO. Where you waggle your pole and say you *need a shit*.
XAN. What about, 'unless someone gets
All this weight off me, I'll start *farting it off*'? 10
DIO. Please—not till I'm supposed to throw up anyway.
XAN. So what was the point of my carrying all these bags,
If I can't do what Phrynichus always does
And Lycis always does and Ameipsias always does,
When they put baggage-boys in *their* comedies?[5] 15
DIO. Well, don't. When I'm in the audience
And I see any of that sophisticated stuff,
It puts years on me.

[5] Text as codd.; interpretation as Stanford ad loc.

XAN. So—thrice wretched is this neck of mine:
It's all *squashed*, and it still can't do its joke. 20

A very different slave—and master: Xanthias and the god of drama, Dionysus. The two share a dialogue that, so far, consists of one extended piece of humour: which jokes—viz. scatological jokes—Xanthias *shouldn't* say to entertain the audience. A short list of these is duly provided by the speakers, more or less in order of ascending rudeness. Coming from *Plutus*, we might be tempted to say that the main effect of this protracted joke is to retard the dramatic action—to retard it almost for the duration of the joke, in that only the repeated references to Xanthias and baggage even bear on the action, which can hardly get far while the two are talking in this vein. It is not until later that we learn that Xanthias and Dionysus are on a journey to the Underworld, via the house of Heracles, though an audience would see that the two are on a journey and that Dionysus himself is grotesquely dressed in Heraclean accoutrements. In *Plutus*, certainly, Cario's monologue may take a while to get to what is evidently its point, but only because it starts with a general version of the particular situation as the speaker sees it.

From the perspective of *Plutus*, in any case, one would be bound to find another aspect of the *Frogs* opening more problematic still. Instead of any mild situational humour or any restrained ease, *Frogs* proceeds by violence: a violence that destroys, in particular, the very integrity of the 'illusion' that we tend to associate with dramatic action as such. And indeed the two characters' earnest discussion of Xanthias' lines, audience responses, other comedies, and *this* comedy, is not only prolonged, but actually begins—and so begins to 'violate the illusion'— even before that illusion and the dramatic action with which we associate it have been verbally established in the first place. The dialogue comes close to supplanting any illusion at all. But then (it might be said), the very basis of the scene—an eccentric-looking god and his extremely Athenian slave carrying the bags—is hardly such as to promote the kind of fictional credibility we can and do attach to the slave (and his silent master) in *Plutus*.

All of which serves to show how distinct the worlds of Aristophanic Old Comedy and Middle Comedy are, and how inappropriate the perspectives of *Plutus* are for a play like *Frogs,* how limiting and how limited. The *Frogs* passage contradicts not some, but virtually all, of the norms one might extrapolate from *Plutus*. Witness the exuberant range of its language, farts at one end and a hint of paratragedy ('thrice wretched', 19)[6] at the other. And witness the unpredictable image of life that the language creates. If the slave in *Plutus* behaves more or less like a real slave, what are we to say of his counterpart in *Frogs,* who is indeed—like a real slave in real life—preoccupied with his baggage duties and his physical pains, and addresses his master as a slave would (ὦ δέσποτα, 1), yet in the same breath speaks like the actor playing himself ('tell them')? And the master is hardly more predictable than the slave. He too is ready to concern himself with the actor's lines; and though a god, he too uses coarse language ('shit', 8, above all) that is seemingly unrelatable to anything one might predicate of his equivalent 'real-life' persona. The way he says 'shit' and his slave 'thrice wretched' incidentally seems to present us with an inversion of opposites: at these moments the god-master is talking low, the man-slave talking (or at least hinting at talking) high. And far from growing out of a character's 'natural' responses to a situation, the humour of this passage seems to possess a determinative authority to which the characters' responses are themselves subordinate. One notes that the exuberant effrontery of the getting-it-both-ways (what-are-we-*not*-going-to-say?) joke is flaunted—irrespective of the speaker—by a prominent articulation of the forbidden catchwords, whereby each, on its first mention, is placed climactically at the end of the syntactic unit and the verse line.[7] Again, one notes that one overriding joke accommodates others *en route,* notably the pleasantry that an immortal god should be subject to ageing by exposure to corny routines (18) and the running joke *ex silentio* that Dionysus' absurd and unexplained get-up is ignored both by Xanthias and by Dionysus himself.[8]

[6] Not in the Greek adjective (on the 'prosaic' distribution of which see LSJ s.v.), but in the cast of the line (cf. e.g. ὦ πολλὰ τλᾶσα καρδία καὶ χεὶρ ἐμή, Eur. *Alc.* 837), with the familiar kind of tragic appeal to τοὐμὸν ἄθλιον δέμας (Soph. *OT* 1388) 'degraded' to a crick in the τράχηλος. This kind of passing evocation should, but does not, figure in Rau, *Paratragodia*, where the lines of paratragedy are drawn too restrictively.

[7] πιέζομαι ('squeezy') 3; so 5, 8, 10.

[8] The first stage reaction to Dionysus' Heraclean costume is from Heracles himself (implicitly at 39, explicitly at 45–7).

The exuberance, the stylistic range from the tragic to the obscene, the unpredictabilities, the seeming indifference to the continuities of 'action' and 'illusion', all serve to differentiate the *Frogs* passage sharply from its equivalent in *Plutus*. Negatively, these features are almost as alien to that play as they are to the New Comedy of Menander, to the model of tragic drama constructed by Aristotle, and to the long tradition of Western dramatic expectations which derives from Aristotelian-Menandrian canons. Positively, though, do the distinctive features of this *Frogs* passage have any collective rationale? Some encouragement to think that they do is provided by a glance at the next section of dialogue in *Frogs*:

ΔΙ. εἶτ' οὐχ ὕβρις ταῦτ' ἐστὶ καὶ πολλὴ τρυφή,
ὅτ' ἐγὼ μὲν ὢν Διόνυσος, υἱὸς σταμνίου,
αὐτὸς βαδίζω καὶ πονῶ, τοῦτον δ' ὀχῶ,
ἵνα μὴ ταλαιπωροῖτο μηδ' ἄχθος φέροι;
ΞΑ. οὐ γὰρ φέρω 'γώ;
ΔΙ. πῶς φέρεις γὰρ ὅς γ' ὀχεῖ; 25
ΞΑ. φέρων γε ταυτί.
ΔΙ. τίνα τρόπον;
ΞΑ. βαρέως πάνυ.
ΔΙ. οὔκουν τὸ βάρος τοῦθ' ὃ σὺ φέρεις ὄνος φέρει;
ΞΑ. οὐ δῆθ' ὅ γ' ἔχω 'γὼ καὶ φέρω, μὰ τὸν Δί' οὔ.
ΔΙ. πῶς γὰρ φέρεις, ὅς γ' αὐτὸς ὑφ' ἑτέρου φέρει;
ΞΑ. οὐκ οἶδ' · ὁ δ' ὦμος οὑτοσὶ πιέζεται. 30
ΔΙ. σὺ δ' οὖν ἐπειδὴ τὸν ὄνον οὐ φῄς σ' ὠφελεῖν,
ἐν τῷ μέρει σὺ τὸν ὄνον ἀράμενος φέρε.
ΞΑ. οἴμοι κακοδαίμων· τί γὰρ ἐγὼ οὐκ ἐναυμάχουν;
ἦ τἄν σε κωκύειν ἂν ἐκέλευον μακρά.

DIO. What an outrage, what impertinence,
For me, Dionysus, son of—Juice,
To struggle along on foot and let him ride,
So he can have a rest from carrying the luggage!
XAN. Aren't I carrying anything?
DIO. How can you?—you're riding. 25
XAN. Well, I've got *this*.
DIO. How?
XAN. Up to here.
DIO. Well, anything you've got, the donkey's got.
XAN. Not what I've got here, he hasn't.
DIO. Well, how can you be carrying? You're being carried.

XAN. The one thing I know is: my shoulder's all *squeezed*. 30
DIO. Well, if the donkey's not doing anything for you,
You lift him up and carry *him*.
XAN. Just my luck: why didn't I join the fleet?
Then I could have told you where to go.

The continuation involves a second comic routine, structured around a pseudo-sophistic argument, introduced by Dionysus: should a slave carrying bags while riding a donkey be said to be (*a*) carrying or (*b*) being carried? At the same time, the routine accommodates a set of less elevated touches from Xanthias: phallus innuendo (26, 28), word play (26), and a grand climactic recapitulation of the first and feeblest of the forbidden jokes of the opening (30).[9] We now observe that the whole scene up to this point accommodates not only an inversion of high and low, but a complementary pattern whereby Xanthias introduces and largely sustains the physical low humour, as Dionysus does the more intellectual high humour. Underlying the inversion, then, is a confrontation of opposites, which (as the play proceeds) can be seen to prefigure the play's eventual concern with the opposition of Aeschylus and Euripides—physical Aeschylus versus intellectual Euripides—and Dionysus' initial alignment with the latter. In this opposition, Euripides represents sophistication and indeed *sophistic*-ation, and one of his own characters' most inimitable moments of sophistic logic-chopping will duly be used against him when Dionysus eventually reverses his position: 'my *tongue* swore—but I'll choose Aeschylus.'[10] In these opening lines, then, whether we realize it or not, we are already thinking towards Euripides.

If the second comic routine prefigures the great issue of the play, so too, of course, does the first. A play that is to deal with playwrights and how they write is introduced by an extended joke about—playwrights and how they write. (For the prefiguration, as for the joke itself, it is basic that Dionysus is not merely a god, but the god of drama.) More pointedly, we might say that *Frogs*' intense concentration on words is prefigured by both of the

[9] For the word play see Stanford on 26–7. The phallic implications in ταυτί (26: cf. αὐτὸ τοῦτο *Vesp.* 1062: below, p. 392) and ὅ γ' (28)—without which the two remarks are inconsequential—are not considered by comm.

[10] *Ran.* 1471 ἡ γλῶττ' ὀμώμοκ', Αἰσχύλον δ' αἱρήσομαι (cf. 102 γλῶτταν δ' ἐπιορκήσασαν ἰδίᾳ τῆς φρενός): Eur. *Hipp.* 612 ἡ γλῶσσ' ὀμώμοχ', ἡ δὲ φρὴν ἀνώμοτος. On the reputation of the *Hipp.* line see Barrett ad loc.

extended routines, and more emphatically by their conjunction; and belatedly it might occur to us to note the artificiality of saying that this kind of opening retards the action: it would be truer to say, it *is* the action. Between the introductory comic routines and the play that they introduce, certainly, there is a relationship of a distinctive kind.

The second routine, meanwhile, serves to remind us of other significant, and in themselves familiar, features of Aristophanes' writing. In 22, 'Dionysus, son of . . .', we expect '. . . Zeus'. But instead of *Dios*, or equivalent, we get *stamniou*, genitive of a pseudo-name based on *stamnos* ('wine-jar').[11] The trick belongs to the group that later antiquity categorized as jokes *para prosdokian*, 'contrary to expectation'. Here, the sudden, unpredictable joke has the effect of deflating the tone of the speaker, Dionysus, rather as his scatologies did before: as such, it belongs to the inversional pattern of the opening. At the same time, it adds to the growing presence of unpredictabilities, which are such a feature of the scatological sequence itself.

In 33, 'Why didn't I join the fleet?', we find something seemingly different in kind. *Frogs* was written for performance in the year 405, some months after the naval battle of Arginusae. Given a desperate shortage of manpower, the city offered freedom to any slave who volunteered to serve at sea; and a freed slave could deal on equal terms with his ex-master, if he chose. The allusion reaches outside the stage-world to the particularities of the real Athens of the day, in a way immensely characteristic of Aristophanic Old Comedy. What we might bear in mind is, once again, the unpredictability of this particular, or indeed any particular, topical allusion. The allusion, we might say, is unpredictable because it is so specific: it involves a sudden refocusing onto a very specific (albeit momentous) event, one of incalculable multitudes of events from public experience. Contrast the generalities of *Plutus*. No one, indeed, could literally predict that Cario, talking aloud about *his* individual problem with *his* individual master, would begin by reflecting on masters and slaves in society in general. Nevertheless, the connection is close and, one feels, all of a piece with the play's underlying concentration on 'the action'. Here in *Frogs* the momentary disconnection of a topical allusion is

[11] For other resonances of the joke, see I. Lada-Richards, *Initiating Dionysus: Ritual and Theatre in Aristophanes' Frogs* (Oxford 1999) 14, 37 n. 72.

equally of a piece with the underlying norms of *this* writing. If the opening of *Frogs* is anything to go by, the principle of logical development which seems to have a determinative force in the case of *Plutus*—the principle which Aristotle has taught us to value as 'organic' development—has, at the very least, no such central significance here.

Beneath the rich diversity and seemingly boundless freedom of Aristophanes' writing in *Frogs* we begin to sense an underlying coherence: not only between the opening of the play and what follows, but between the very elements of which the diversity is composed. Coherence, that is, of a very particular kind is itself a characteristic element of Aristophanic Old Comedy as a whole; and it will be one of the aims of this book to explore and interpret it, in contradistinction, implicitly or explicitly, to the quite different kind of coherence that is familiar from most Western literature since Aristophanes' day and that is prefigured in late Aristophanes itself. For the moment let us bring the qualities of *Frogs* into sharper focus by looking at another opening, the opening of Aristophanes' earliest extant play, *Acharnians*:[12]

ΔΙΚΑΙΟΠΟΛΙΣ *ὅσα δὴ δέδηγμαι τὴν ἐμαυτοῦ καρδίαν,*
ἥσθην δὲ βαιά, πάνυ δὲ βαιά, τέτταρα·
ἃ δ' ὠδυνήθην, ψαμμακοσιογάργαρα.
φέρ' ἴδω, τί δ' ἥσθην ἄξιον χαιρηδόνος;
ἐγῷδ' ἐφ' ᾧ γε τὸ κέαρ εὐφράνθην ἰδών, 5
τοῖς πέντε ταλάντοις οἷς Κλέων ἐξήμεσεν.
ταῦθ' ὡς ἐγανώθην, καὶ φιλῶ τοὺς ἱππέας
διὰ τοῦτο τοὔργον· ἄξιον γὰρ Ἑλλάδι.
ἀλλ' ὠδυνήθην ἕτερον αὖ τραγῳδικόν,
ὅτε δὴ 'κεχήνη προσδοκῶν τὸν Αἰσχύλον, 10
ὁ δ' ἀνεῖπεν· εἴσαγ', ὦ Θέογνι, τὸν χορόν.
πῶς τοῦτ' ἔσεισέ μου δοκεῖς τὴν καρδίαν;
ἀλλ' ἕτερον ἥσθην, ἡνίκ' ἐπὶ Μόσχῳ ποτὲ
Δεξίθεος εἰσῆλθ' ᾀσόμενος Βοιώτιον.
τῆτες δ' ἀπέθανον καὶ διεστράφην ἰδών, 15
ὅτε δὴ παρέκυψε Χαῖρις ἐπὶ τὸν ὄρθιον.
ἀλλ' οὐδεπώποτ' ἐξ ὅτου 'γὼ ῥύπτομαι

[12] A much-discussed sequence—see: K. J. Dover, *Greek and the Greeks* (Oxford 1987) 224–36; W. G. Arnott, 'Comic openings', *Drama* 2 (1993) 14–32 at 19–22; G. W. Dobrov, 'The poet's voice in the evolution of dramatic dialogism', in Dobrov (ed.), *Beyond Aristophanes* (Atlanta 1995) 47–97 at 58–61; L. Edmunds, 'Aristophanes' *Acharnians*', *YCS* 26 (1980) 26, 33; Silk, 'Versus the rest'.

οὕτως ἐδήχθην ὑπὸ κονίας τὰς ὀφρῦς
ὡς νῦν, ὁπότ' οὔσης κυρίας ἐκκλησίας
ἑωθινῆς ἔρημος ἡ πνὺξ αὑτηί, 20
οἱ δ' ἐν ἀγορᾷ λαλοῦσι κἄνω καὶ κάτω
τὸ σχοινίον φεύγουσι τὸ μεμιλτωμένον.
οὐδ' οἱ πρυτάνεις ἥκουσιν, ἀλλ' ἀωρίαν
ἥκοντες, εἶτα δ' ὠστιοῦνται πῶς δοκεῖς
ἐλθόντες ἀλλήλοισι περὶ πρώτου ξύλου, 25
ἀθρόοι καταρρέοντες· εἰρήνη δ' ὅπως
ἔσται προτιμῶσ' οὐδέν· ὦ πόλις πόλις.

DICAEOPOLIS Count the heartaches I've had since last year.[13]
And grains of joy? *Four*.
But worries: *sandstormillions*![14]
Let's see, what's brought me any happitude?
I know one thing I saw that did entrance my heart: 5
The five talents fell out when Cleon puked
Lit me up: thank the knights for that!
What they did, they did right by Greece.
But then there was a 'tragic accident':
Me waiting, open mouth, for Aeschylus, 10
And the man calls out: '*Theognis*, your turn.'
Imagine how that shook me.
Another 'treat' was when Dexitheus
Came on after Moschus to sing a Boeotian air.[15]
And this year I dropped dead *and* got a crick in
the neck[16] 15
From watching Chaeris stoop for the high notes.[17]
But never since I first learned to wash
Have I been so stung to the brows of my eyes

[13] 'In how many ways have I been *hurt*!' δέδηγμαι, though an expressive idiom, is demonstrably not a live metaphor in the context of psychological pain (*pace* e.g. Arnott, 'Comic openings', 17): ἐμὲ . . . ἔδακε λύπη Hdt. 7. 16a, δάκνομαι ψυχήν Thgn. 910, λύπῃ καρδίαν δηχθήσομαι Eur. *Alc.* 1100 (likewise *Il.* 5. 493, Hes. *Op.* 451, Pind. *Pyth.* 8. 87, Aesch. *Pers.* 846, Ar. *Nub.* 12, Xen. *Cyr.* 1. 4. 13, Arist. *Soph. El.* 182^b 33); for the criteria involved in distinguishing live and 'dead' metaphor, see M. S. Silk, *Interaction in Poetic Imagery* (Cambridge 1974) 27–56, 82. Given the familiarity of the idiom, any interpretation like 'bitten my own heart with rage' (Sommerstein) is out of the question. Rau, *Paratragodia*, 185, unconvincingly discusses the line as a possible case of paratragedy.

[14] In the Greek there is no 'storm' in 3 or 'grains' in 2, but A's 'sand: infinity' equation is too remote from modern colloquial associations of ideas to carry unsupported. On my policy in translating, see above, p. 21.

[15] Allusion obscure: lengthy discussion, but imponderable conclusions, in Starkie ad loc. and M. Landfester, 'Aristoph. *Ach.* 13 f.', *RhM* 113 (1970) 93–4.

[16] On 15 cf. Arnott, 'Comic openings', 19.

[17] 'High notes' is ὄρθιος ('a traditional melody of very high pitch', LSJ s.v.).

As I am now. A full assembly due
To meet at dawn, and here's the Pnyx deserted, 20
And they'll be chattering in the square, or charging
Up and down to dodge the painted rope.
Even the Presidents aren't here. They'll turn up late,
And when they do come, just imagine
The jostling for the front seats, 25
All streaming in. And as for peace,
They couldn't give a damn. O City city.

Acharnians opens with a welter of topical allusions, different from *Frogs* in degree, but from *Plutus* in kind. If the opening of *Frogs* makes it clear that Aristophanes is a great humorist, the opening of *Acharnians* can only be the work of a great poet, for all the 'prosaic' associations of most of its topical references. We register at once the rich immediacy of the writing: the bustle and diversity of a many-sided community is captured by a largely staccato articulation (six sentences in the first eight lines)[18] and a startling range of tone. The inevitable obscurity (for us) of various of the allusions seems a small price to pay—and the lucid generalities of *Plutus* seem dearly bought by comparison. On the one side we have the expansive sensuousness of physical language (associated not least with the verbs) which serves to energize the presentation of satirical targets ('puked', ἐξήμεσεν, 6; 'stoop', παρέκυψε, 16), the present scene ('jostling', ὠστιοῦνται, 24; 'streaming', καταρρέοντες, 26), and the speaker's own feelings ('aches', δέδηγμαι, 1; 'lit', ἐγανώθην, 7).[19] Expansive too are the Joycean coinages in 3 and 4; the wicked pun on 'tragic' in 9; and the bathos in 15.[20] At the same time we have a finely controlled tonal movement, whose

[18] Depending on what one counts as a sentence, six at least: my translation adds to the number.

[19] ἐγανώθην ('glowed') belongs to the first of two similar-looking word groups: (*a*) γάνος, γανόω, γανάω, denoting physical brightness, (*b*) γάνυμαι, denoting psychological gladness (see LSJ s.vv.). In post-classical Greek, prose and verse, (*a*) words are often used in sense (*b*). In the classical period (where both groups are usually restricted to verse) there are a few instances that imply the influence of (*b*) on (*a*), of which the present passage, Pl. *Rep.* 411a, and Aesch. fr. 78c. 55 (not in LSJ) are the clearest, but it is not clear how far the usage was standard (LSJ's interpretations of γανάω in *Od.* 7. 128, γάνος in Aesch. *Agam.* 579, and γανόω in Anacr. 444 *PMG* (= 13A Bergk) are gratuitous).

[20] On χαιρηδόνος see Rau, *Paratragodia*, 185; for the τραγῳδικόν pun cf. Men. *Epitr.* 1125 (and R. L. Hunter, *The New Comedy of Greece and Rome* (Cambridge 1985) 118–21).

most marked feature is a series of poeticisms. The pattern begins at once. From a neutral tone in 1, the level rises suddenly in 2, then drops abruptly with the bathetic specificity of 'four'.[21] A similar manoeuvre takes place three lines later: a rise to the elevated 'entrance my heart' (*κέαρ εὐφράνθην*, 5)[22] and a rapid drop to the coarse physicality of Cleon vomiting the five talents (6). There follows another ascent, but now with a difference. The new peak of tonal prominence is not a passing word or phrase, but a complete sentence and recognizable quotation from Euripides, which (after a more gradual ascent) provides a first climax: 'right by Greece' (*ἄξιον γὰρ Ἑλλάδι*, 8).[23] And following a protracted low sequence, there is a similar ascent from the sharp everyday detail of the jostling and the painted rope to the more decisive climactic invocation, again very obviously tragic in tone, 'O City city' (*ὦ πόλις πόλις*, 27).[24]

What the 'Greece' of 8 and the 'city' of 27 also have in common is a direct reference to the community of Athens and (beyond the city-state) the looser community of Greece itself. That is, in the mouth of an as yet anonymous individual, the two quotations constitute an appeal to that world whose richness is demonstrated, and celebrated, by the very texture of the speech in question. And plainly the quotations share a laconic dignity which informs our response to the anxieties at the heart of Dicaeopolis' speech, which is the concern with war and peace. His nuggets of good news or bad news, laughable or not, constitute an ascending series whose climax comes with the long, urgent sentence, 'But never since . . .' (17).[25] This series runs quite independently of the sequence of

[21] *βαιά* is a verse word (i.e. not in *Attic* prose: LSJ s.v.), whose poeticism is transferred onto 'joy' in my English. On 2, cf. Rau, *Paratragodia*, 185. Dover, *Greek and the Greeks*, 227, considers the possibility that *τέτταρα* here is a colloquialism.

[22] *κέαρ* is a high-verse archaism (see LSJ s.v. *κῆρ*); *εὐφραίνω* is tonally non-specific; but the elevated tone of the two items, *εὐφράνθην ἰδών*, in combination is sufficiently indicated by their occurrence at Pind. *Ol.* 9. 62: *εὐφράνθη τε ἰδὼν ἥρως*. Dicaeopolis is momentarily just such a *hêrôs*.

[23] From *Telephus*: see p. 39 n. 29 below. The ascent to *ἄξιον* is via *ἐγανώθην* (n. 19 above). Dover, *Greek and the Greeks*, 229, speculates that *ἄξ. γὰρ Ἑλλ.* is a phrase that 'has passed into general use'. If true (and there is no supporting evidence for it), this would not affect the present argument.

[24] The phrase is attested at Soph. *OT* 629, and similar invocations occur in tragedy elsewhere (Rau, *Paratragodia*, 185). My English equivalent, 'O City city' (*sic*), comes from Eliot, 'The Waste Land', 259.

[25] The run of the whole sequence indicates that (*pace* interpreters: see e.g.

poeticisms, but the two eventually converge, and their point of convergence is that urgent sentence's already climactic end: 'And as for peace . . . O City city.'[26] A sense of urgency is indeed perceptible from the very start of the speech. Until 17, however, no justification or explanation for this urgency is given or even hinted at, and at 17 it only comes in the form of a prolonged outburst whose rationale is itself delayed. When that rationale is at last spelled out and when, along with it, the justification for such an urgent tone is made explicit, a powerful emphasis results.[27] 'And as for peace . . . O City city': the whole organization of the speech so far leads up to this moment, and the evocative quality of the writing here gains a decisive force from the contrast with the seeming pleasantries that precede it. In consequence, this appeal to the collective has a comic power and a comic poignancy that we cannot have expected and will certainly not find easy to define.

What is 'comic' power and 'comic' poignancy? Any sort of adequate answer will require a good deal of discussion—of moods, of stylistic mechanisms, of character and structure, of the meaning of 'comic' and 'comedy', and of Aristophanes' claim to be a 'serious' writer. In advance of this discussion, we can usefully underline the significance of associating these items in a single list—and, not least, associating the other, more 'literary'-seeming, items with 'seriousness'.

In catching our glimpse of the coherence of Aristophanic comedy, we begin to acknowledge not merely the connectedness of its diverse elements, but, inevitably, their connection with wider issues, including those we associate with 'serious' literature.

Edmunds, '*Acharnians*', 26, 33) the obscure 'treat' in 13 must be ironic, i.e. that Dexitheus has been responsible for one of Dicaeopolis' many 'heartaches'. The structure of the sequence from 9, then, is not an alternating series of joys and sorrows, but a short series of sorrows culminating in the present one at 17: i.e. a simple instance of a *Priamel* (on which see below, pp. 150–1). Despite the pseudo-precise plurality of *τέτταρα* (2), Dicaeopolis can only recall *one* piece of good news (4–8).

[26] Strictly speaking, the 'point' of convergence is the whole sequence (*εἰρήνη* to *πόλις πόλις*). The *εἰρήνη* sentence is plain, but there is nothing in it which is alien to elevated verse (for the construction with *ὅπως* see the parallels in W. W. Goodwin, *Syntax of the Moods and Tenses of the Greek Verb* (rev. edn.; London 1929) 123; for *προτιμάω* thus, those in LSJ s.v. II), while its metrical features have a tragic strictness in contradistinction to (e.g.) the violation of the law of the final cretic in 24 or the second-foot anapaest in 23.

[27] Emphasis from postposition (as in hyperbaton and in 'retrospective imagery': see Silk, *Interaction*, 67–9, 167–72).

Discussion of Aristophanes has generally focused on certain aspects of his plays—notably their humour, their formal and theatrical techniques, their claim to 'seriousness'—as separate aspects. If one thing is missing, it is any sustained attempt to identify his greatness as a writer of comic poetry in a way that *places* these and other aspects in relation to each other. This sounds like a plea for a synthesis of present knowledge. Not so, or only partly so. What is really needed is a reconsideration of relationships and, in some instances, a reconsideration of what we think we 'know' in the first place. It is symptomatic that discussions of Aristophanes' *writing* do not commonly lead, as ours has begun to lead, to consideration of his 'seriousness'. Seriousness, on the contrary, is discussed under a separate, circumscribed heading, often associated with the question: is Aristophanic comedy 'political'? Aristophanes' seriousness can and should be discussed, but the nature of the seriousness in question must—again—be reconsidered.

A satisfying treatment of Aristophanic comedy in all its aspects, all duly 'placed' in relation to each other, is an ideal that no one book can hope to achieve. The aim of this book is to initiate the required reconsideration, and if we look back to the opening of *Acharnians*, a way in suggests itself. Our analysis of that opening began with linguistic features and ended (seemingly in different territory) with the collectivity of Athens. One element, however, was common to that beginning and that end: tragedy. Even from our *Plutus* passage it could be gathered that tragedy means something for Aristophanes, though from *Plutus* alone one would never suspect what that something might be. Putting the three openings together, and the *Acharnians* and *Frogs* passages in particular, we can observe striking variations in the ways the tragic presence seems to make itself felt. In *Plutus* a concentration of tragic tone elevates a momentary topic—Apollo at Delphi—in conformity with a conventional estimate of its dignity, while a more pervasive tragic flavour ensures that this moment of concentration is not dislocating; and this tragic flavour (we could add) also ensures that our overall sense of the comic speaker and *his* dignity is more positive than it might otherwise have been. In *Frogs*, on the other hand, we find a strictly localized evocation of tragedy enforcing a speaker's grotesqueness and the incongruity of a given situation ('thrice wretched . . .'). More significantly, we may now be struck by the way that in *Frogs* the forthcoming opposition of two *tragedians* is prefigured—by the opposition of Xanthias and Dionysus, of physical language and intellectual sophistries—on *comic* ground. In *Acharnians*, conversely, the comic appeal for peace is itself mediated in tragic language.

The variety, and still more the significance, of these tragic evocations is confirmed if we stay with *Acharnians* and look briefly beyond the opening lines. We may note, to begin with, that the very first tragic quotation in the play ('they did right by Greece', 8)[28] is a quotation from Euripides' lost *Telephus*; that the very last tragic quotation, near the end of the play, is likewise a quotation from *Telephus*;[29] and that between these two quotations—between the point where Dicaeopolis begins to turn our thoughts towards peace and the point where he establishes peace on his own—there is a long sequence of allusions to, and appropriations of, this same *Telephus*, through which Dicaeopolis succeeds in defending his private treaty against the successive assaults of the chorus of old Acharnian charcoal-burners and General Lamachus.[30] When cornered by the old men, he counters with an imitation of a famous hostage scene in Euripides' play: there, Telephus got himself a hearing by holding the infant son of Agamemnon hostage; here, Dicaeopolis does the same by threatening death to a basket of Acharnian charcoal (326–46). Suddenly called upon to defend his conduct in a public oration, and in need of (as we might say) a suitable image, Dicaeopolis pays a visit to a mildly exasperated Euripides to borrow the pitiable beggar's outfit in which Telephus had himself appeared in Euripides' play. Now equipped to stir his hearers' pity as well as sustain his own inspiration,[31] Dicaeopolis begins his speech (497 ff.):

[28] i.e. the first identifiable quotation, as opposed to the first discernible evocation of tragic idiom.

[29] Eur. fr. 720 (*Ach.* 8) and 705a (*Ach.* 1188) Nauck-Snell respectively.

[30] For a list of *Telephus* appropriations in this sequence, see Rau, *Paratragodia*, 19–42. It is infelicitous to talk of 'parody' here (e.g. 'Dicaeopolis parodies Euripides' *Telephus*': S. Goldhill, *The Poet's Voice* (Cambridge 1991) 209). 'Writers on Aristophanes commonly use "parody" in a loose sense to cover all sorts of pastiche and allusion': L. P. E. Parker, *The Songs of Aristophanes* (Oxford 1997) 6. See below, pp. 351–2.

[31] Pity: *Ach.* 383–4, 413 (τοὺς βασιλεύοντας ῥάκι' ἀμπισχών, ἵν' ἐλεινοὶ | τοῖς ἀνθρώποις φαίνοιντ' εἶναι, *Ran.* 1063–4). Inspiration: *Ach.* 447, 484.

μή μοι φθονήσητ', ἄνδρες οἱ θεώμενοι,
εἰ πτωχὸς ὢν ἔπειτ' ἐν Ἀθηναίοις λέγειν
μέλλω περὶ τῆς πόλεως, τρυγῳδίαν ποιῶν.
τὸ γὰρ δίκαιον οἶδε καὶ τρυγῳδία. 500
ἐγὼ δὲ λέξω δεινὰ μέν, δίκαια δέ.
οὐ γάρ με νῦν γε διαβαλεῖ Κλέων . . .

Condemn me not, you in the audience,
If, whiles I am a beggar, among us Athenians
I talk affairs of state in a comedy.
You see, comedy has a sense of duty too. 500
And what I have to say is bold, but right.
And this time Cleon can't accuse me . . .[32]

The great oration begins in a famously astonishing mixture of *personae*—the character Dicaeopolis (now a beggar), the actor playing him (in a comedy), the poet Aristophanes himself (the 'me' who is at odds with Cleon)—and in a mixed idiom that once again involves tragic quotations from *Telephus*.[33] The implications are remarkable. In the most punningly literal sense imaginable, tragedy—Euripidean tragedy—is shown to be needed if the vital quest which the comic 'hero' is there to pursue is to succeed. And this moment of supreme dependency on tragedy is chosen for the supremely untragic ('illusion'-breaking) assertion of comedy's own capacities. Comedy can deal with affairs of state, because comedy *too* has a 'sense of duty': it knows *to dikaion*—'what is right'. The word play with Dicaeopolis' own name is very marked: plainly *Dikaio-polis* ('Citizen Right') is supremely fitted to offer the assertion.[34] And the point of the assertion is no less plain.

[32] 'whiles . . . beggar': Shakespeare, *King John*, II. i. 593. *λέγειν . . . περί*: 'talk *about*', but (given the context) with a hint of 'speak *for*', i.e. in a life-or-death struggle (*περὶ πτόλιος . . . μαχήσεται*, *Il.* 18. 265).

[33] Italicized in my translation: Eur. fr. 703 Nauck-Snell. On the much-discussed question of the 'identity' of Dicaeopolis here, cf. the summary in MacDowell, *Aristophanes and Athens*, 42–3.

[34] His name was revealed to the audience not long before (line 406), at the beginning of the Euripides scene. For an additional possibility that *Dik*-aiopolis recalls a charge of *a-dikia* brought by Cleon, see O. Taplin, 'Tragedy and trugedy', *CQ* 33 (1983) 331. Edmunds, '*Acharnians*', 1, argues that *Δικ.* is literally 'he of just city', not 'he who is just in/to the city', but e.g. *ἀδύπολις* at Soph. *OT* 510 is 'dear to the city' (not 'of a dear city') and *ὀρθόπολις* at Pind. *Ol.* 2. 8 is 'uprighter of the city' *or* 'of an upright city'. Presumably the compound implies either or both. The ambiguity is noted in principle by e.g. A. M. Bowie, *Aristophanes: Myth, Ritual and Comedy* (Cambridge 1993) 24 n. 29. Greek *δίκαιον* itself covers 'as it should be' in a range of senses—'right', 'fair', 'honest', 'reasonable', 'acceptable' (see K. J. Dover, *Greek Popular Morality in the Time of Plato and Aristotle* (Berkeley 1974)

'Comedy has a sense of duty *too*' is only worth saying because it contradicts a prejudice that comedy has *no* 'sense of duty', unlike other literary media, and (in particular) unlike that other medium that we are in the process of alluding to. 'Be patient with me, now you see me before you like Telephus in the tragedy. You see, like tragedy, comedy has a sense of duty of its own.' *Too* means 'like tragedy',[35] and the relationship is made still more obvious by a brilliant verbal *coup*. 'Comedy' in lines 499 and 500 is not the normal *kômôidia*, but a punning formation, *trugôidia* ('wine-song'): '*trygedy* too': the effect is oddly—humorously—disconcerting.[36] It is hardly surprising that this passage commonly figures in scholarly discussions of the 'seriousness' of Aristophanic comedy—or that such discussions, faced with such a passage, seem often unsure of their ground. Whatever else may be said about Dicaeopolis' speech (and its continuation), it is apparent that the claim to 'seriousness' here is the opposite of straightforward and that it is both dependent on, and complicated by, a seeming consciousness of tragedy and *its* 'seriousness'.

If 'comedy *too*' implies that comedy sometimes can or does occupy tragic ground, the more fundamental corollary is that comedy normally has its own territory. Aristophanes' consciousness of tragedy presupposes a sense of difference between tragedy and his own medium, such that any comic use of tragedy opens up the possibility of new modes of comedy itself. What Dicaeopolis points us towards, then, is not merely an Aristophanic preoccupation with tragedy, but an Aristophanic interest in new alignments of comedy *vis-à-vis* the 'serious' drama of Euripides and his fellow-tragedians. Over his whole career, Aristophanes has, in fact, a special relationship with tragedy. In a kind of applied theory he strives to define the limits and the scope of comedy and sees in tragedy an essential point of reference. This will prove to be an immensely fruitful, exciting, if also problematic, enterprise.

170–1, 180–94): hence my 'duty', as well as 'right', at the cost of repetition in the Greek.

[35] Rightly, Taplin, 'Trugedy', 332, and Goldhill, *Poet's Voice*, 194–5. Translators generally say 'even comedy' here, missing the point.

[36] For further discussion of this 'trygedy', see Taplin, 'Trugedy' (*sic*!), 331–3, A. T. Edwards, 'Aristophanes' comic poetics', *TAPA* 121 (1991) 157–79, at 157–63, and below, pp. 78 n. 116, 432–4.

2
Comedy and Tragedy

Aristophanes often talks about comedy. His choruses, that is, and sometimes his characters too, present views on other works by Aristophanes himself, or on the work of other playwrights—

> So what was the point of my carrying all these bags,
> If I can't do what Phrynichus always does
> And Lycis always does and Ameipsias always does,
> When they put baggage-boys in *their* comedies?
>
> (*Frogs* 12–15)—

or views on the comedy to which the words belong or on comedy in general:

> Condemn me not, you in the audience
> If, whiles I am a beggar, among us Athenians
> I talk affairs of state in a comedy.
> You see, comedy has a sense of duty too.
>
> (*Acharnians* 497–500)

For a variety of reasons the comments tend to resist any straightforward interpretation. If they are, or seem to be, direct, conscious, authorial statements, which comment on the work as if from outside it, they thereby acquire the notoriously problematic status associated with all authorial statements of intent. The conscious author can only be an interpreter like the rest of us. We value him for his work, not for his views of it: 'never trust the artist, trust the tale'.[1] If, conversely, such comments are, or seem to be, an 'ordinary' part of the play, they are subject to all the ordinary problems of literary interpretation: should we privilege *this* part of a play against *another* part which, perhaps, contradicts

[1] D. H. Lawrence, *Studies in Classic American Literature* (1924): A. Beal, *D. H. Lawrence, Selected Literary Criticism* (London 1956) 297. On intentions, see the summary discussions and bibliographical references in Silk, *Interaction*, 59–63, Goldhill, *Reading Greek Tragedy*, 283, along with (e.g.) J. T. Shawcross, *Intentionality and the New Traditionalism* (Philadelphia 1991).

it? should we privilege any part of a play against any other part? can any part of a play ever be taken 'at face value'? In a comedy full of jokes and comic configurations, it may well be peculiarly perverse to take even the simplest statement at face value. In the *Frogs* passage can we trust Xanthias as a guide to the practice of Aristophanes' contemporaries and rivals, Phrynichus, Lycis and Ameipsias? *Do* they 'always' do it? And what *exactly* is the 'it' that they do?

Then again, Aristophanes' comments on comedy are often difficult for *us* to deal with, because they presuppose a culture whose literary perspectives are—to us—almost inconceivably narrow. In cultural terms, classical Greece was largely self-sufficient and robustly confident in its self-sufficiency, as only a delimited, coherent culture can be. Whatever foreign influences there may have been in an earlier age, the Greek poets of Aristophanes' time look across to a handful of contemporaries and back to a handful of predecessors, all part of one single Greek continuum. For them, and for Aristophanes himself, literature begins with Homer and consists largely of a few major writers in each of a few different media or genres, most of which belong exclusively to the world of the Greek city-state. For practical purposes no sense of alternative versions of literature in other societies or other languages exists; and given the modest size of the Greek societies and the modest time-scale between even Homer and Aristophanes, the corpus of literature is itself bound to be small, coherent, delimited and manageable: such as to give a new writer a sense of direction, without deterring him from 'making it new' himself.[2] To a writer in the continuum the tradition he is part of has an absolute authority; and being part of an absolute is, to him, an incalculable advantage: the sense of being part of an absolute was, no doubt, one of the factors that made the great achievements of Greek literature possible. However, to a literary critic or theorist or interpreter within the continuum, the lack of perspective is a limitation of equivalent dimensions, and the more decisively so in an age when critical awareness, critical conceptualization, critical terminology, are in their infancy. The categories and the theoretical experience available to a Dicaeopolis

[2] 'Make it new' was Ezra Pound's slogan ('Tching prayed on the mountain and | wrote MAKE IT NEW | on his bath tub': *Canto* 53) and the title of a collection of his essays published in 1934.

called upon to talk about literature are rudimentary—a point which needs no great substantiation. Suffice it to say that it is not until two generations after Aristophanes' death that the first major work of literary theory, Aristotle's *Poetics*, even comes to be written. Furthermore, the categories available for a Dicaeopolitan disquisition on comedy would be even more restricted than literary categories in general. In an institutional sense, the medium of comedy in Dicaeopolis' Athens is still new, too new to have attracted much serious attention, still too new, therefore, for even Aristotle to give it much serious attention a century later.[3]

The upshot is that, in his comments on comedy, Aristophanes' terms of reference frequently possess a marvellous sensuous immediacy or imagistic range of suggestion, but seldom any technical basis or systematic quality; and that interpretations we may wish to put on his comments may imply distinctions or relationships whose applicability is impossible to gauge, or a precision that Aristophanes himself had no opportunity to consider. Dicaeopolis talks about comedy's 'sense of duty'. Many of the world's writers, no doubt, write with some sort of 'sense of duty'. Brecht or Beckett, García Márquez or Jane Austen, Ben Jonson or Virgil, Demosthenes or Euripides: each, we might think, writes with some sort of 'sense of duty'—each, perhaps, with a different sort. We might find it helpful to ask: given these points of reference, what (if any) 'sense of duty' do *we* ascribe to Aristophanic comedy? Is it most like Brecht's? Or . . . ? Is it perhaps a bit like . . . , but also a bit like . . . ? And if like . . . , how

[3] Chiefly because a new artistic medium 'is likely to piece itself together out of motifs, styles, means of circulation that had belonged to some medium not thought of as art proper' (D. Craig, *Marxists on Literature* (Harmondsworth 1975) 160; cf. Aristotle, *Poet.* v). As is well known, the *Poetics* apparently included a second book on comedy, subsequently lost (R. Janko, *Aristotle on Comedy* (London 1984) 63–6). There is, however, very little reason to credit that lost book with any consequential theory of comedy remotely as impressive as Aristotle's extant theory of tragedy. This is certainly the case if (following Janko) we regard the quaint little treatise known as the *Tractatus Coislinianus* as its epitome (Janko's rewarding study of the treatise tends to evade its striking mediocrity). If on the other hand we deny the Aristotelian link, it is very hard to explain why any Aristotelian pearls of wisdom on comedy were ignored by all of subsequent antiquity. I presume that all or most of what Aristotle in fact said on the subject was perfunctory—and maybe *Tract. Coisl.* reflects it—and that there were no pearls there to be ignored anyway. At all events there is precious little sign of an intelligent interest in comedy in *Poetics* as we have it (cf. below, pp. 53–64).

like . . . ? And whether or not we could agree on an answer, the discussion might well be illuminating: that is, it might well illuminate Aristophanes (as well as . . .). It would be quite different to ask: what sort of 'sense of duty' does Aristophanes himself seem to ascribe to Aristophanic comedy? Quite different, and not especially illuminating, given that Aristophanes has no knowledge of most of the other writers listed, or of the particular stances which their works variously, and perhaps uniquely, embody, or of the range of stances which between them they represent. This in no way prevents Aristophanes from producing work that, as it happens, looks forward to one or more of these possible stances, but it inevitably prevents him from describing his own achievement as—in principle—we can, and above all it gives him no interest in trying to do so.[4]

Given such problems, one will, no doubt, do well to avoid any very specific interpretation of single passages and concentrate instead on what seem to be Aristophanes' underlying aspirations or ideals.[5] Admittedly, we shall find that, if conceived as supports for a theory of what comedy should ideally aspire to, many of Aristophanes' comments are essentially negative: *don't* do what Phrynichus and Lycis and Ameipsias 'always' do, but instead do . . . *what*? Even so, there are a variety of more positive messages (most of them recurring in several plays), of which three of special interest stand out: comedy should be *original*, should be *sophisticated*, and should be what we will find it difficult not to call *serious*. Aristophanes' own comedy (we are often assured) is all of these things, and (it is implicit or sometimes explicit) comedy in general should be too.

The exact vocabulary used varies, but originality is often designated by the adjective *kainos*, 'new'. In the parabasis of *Wasps* the choral spokesman tells us that the audience's distaste for *Clouds* the previous year was due to the author's crop of

[4] The point is implicit in a fundamental principle of language which J. Lyons, *Semantics* (2 vols., Cambridge 1977) i. 248 has felicitously labelled 'cultural salience': 'every language is integrated with the culture in which it operates; and its lexical structure . . . reflects those distinctions which are (*or have been*) important in the culture' (my italics). Newly revealed distinctions, almost inevitably, have no language ready to express them.

[5] With the sketch that follows compare (and contrast): A. H. Sommerstein, 'Old Comedians on Old Comedy', *Drama* 1 (1992) 14–33; M. L. Chirico, 'Per una poetica di Aristofane', *La Parola del Passato* 45 (1990) 95–115; J. M. Bremer, 'Aristophanes on his own poetry', *Entr. Hardt* 38 (1993) 125–65.

'brand-new ideas' (*kainotatas . . . dianoias*, 1044), while in the parabasis of *Clouds* itself the spokesman (here as author) assures the audience that 'I always use my skills to introduce new modes [of comedy]' (*kainas ideas*, 547).[6] 'Sophisticated' is commonly *dexios*. The spokesman in *Clouds* continues: 'new modes, all different and all sophisticated' (*pasas dexias*, 548). His counterpart in *Acharnians* had already made the claim, with due apologies for self-advertisement: 'Ever since our director[7] has been in charge of comic choruses, he's never approached the audience to say how sophisticated [*dexios*] he is. But *now* . . .' (628–30).[8]

For seriousness there is no one particular word. Alongside *dikaios*, with its aura of rights and duties, which Aristophanes uses in *Acharnians* (500–1) and elsewhere,[9] we find, for instance, the vocabulary of didactic instruction. The author purports to have something to communicate. He 'teaches', *didaskei*.[10] In *Acharnians* the claim is that his is 'the best instruction' (*ta beltista didaskôn*, 658), in *Frogs* that his chorus has the task of giving the city 'good advice and teaching' (*xumparainein kai didaskein*, 686–7). And elsewhere, less specifically, we learn that he has 'made our art great' and 'built it up to towering dimensions' (*epoiêse tekhnên megalên . . . kàpurgôs' oikodomêsas*, *Peace* 749). He is *sophos*, an 'artist' (*Clouds* 520).[11] He hopes to have much to say

[6] Likewise *Vesp.* 1053, fr. 543 *PCG* (see Kassel–Austin ad loc.), cf. *Pax* 54, *Thes.* 967, besides various passages where *kainos* is not itself used, but a commendation of originality is implicit (as in *Ran.* 12–15 above). Cf. also the use of the word of jokes, *Eccl.* 926–7. External testimony to A's quest for innovation may be found in Cratinus fr. 342 (below, p. 416): so Dover, *Aristophanic Comedy*, 214.

[7] *didaskalos*. Oddly, of course, A was generally *not* his own *didaskalos*, and indeed had apparently never yet been one (above, p. 17).

[8] 'Approached' (παρέβη), sc. in the parabasis. *dexios* likewise at *Vesp.* 65, 1059, *Ran.* 1114. The word is also used, correlatively, of the ideal audience (or the actual audience flattered as ideal): *Eq.* 233, *Nub.* 521, 527.

[9] *Ach.* 645, 655, 661; *Eq.* 510.

[10] Uses of *didask-* referring to the director (as *Ach.* 628 above) are not directly relevant to the notion of comic 'teaching', though W. G. Arnott, 'A lesson from the *Frogs*', *G&R* 38 (1991) 18–19, argues interestingly that the former would have helped to fortify the latter.

[11] The poet's claim to *sophia* is a traditional one and much discussed in recent times: see the bibliography in Goldhill, *Poet's Voice*, 168 n. 2. In lexicographical terms, the σοφός word group (including σοφιστής) has a range of active denotations from 'wise' to 'clever' to 'skilled', and is associated with art in general and poetry in particular from *c.*600 (σοφίη thus in Solon 13. 52; according to Isoc. *Antid.* 313, Solon was called σοφιστής himself). Contrary to a long-standing piece of methodological *naïveté* on the part of some commentators, σοφ-, in such applications,

that is 'amusing' (*geloia*) and much that is—literally—'serious' (*spoudaia*) (*Frogs* 389–90).

The positive implication of all these claims is still unclear. The 'great art', to judge from the parabasis in *Peace*, supposedly involves rejection of traditional comic routines ('he got his rivals to stop having fun with rags . . . he outlawed hungry Heracleses . . . he got rid of slaves on the run . . .', 739–48)—but quite apart from the fact that such routines appear elsewhere in Aristophanes' own comedies, we are not given much indication of what it is that is supposed to have replaced these 'lowbrow buffooneries' (748).[12] As far as 'seriousness' is concerned, we are indeed given an elusive impression of some kind of confrontation with public causes like peace or public figures like Cleon—on the strength of which in *Wasps* Aristophanes proclaims himself a true Heracles, a 'deliverer from evil' and a 'cleanser of the land';[13] but 'elusive' is the operative word, and even here there is very little indication of what the confrontation is supposed to have amounted to. The *Peace* parabasis is another case in point. After his castigation of 'buffooneries', the spokesman goes on to assert that Aristophanes avoids satirizing (*kômôidôn*) petty, private individuals (751), but, on the contrary, assails the great, like Cleon, 'the Jag-Toothed One himself' (754). We are treated to a wonderfully grotesque description of this monstrous opponent (753–8), almost identical with earlier tirade in *Wasps* (1031–5), but the obvious inference that the author especially relished this particular piece of satirical imagery, again, adds little to our theoretical comprehension of the 'great art' itself.

It seems then that Aristophanes' characterizations of his comic practice or his comic ideals are in the end calculated to frustrate

implies the wisdom as well as the skill: rightly, e.g., H. Maehler, *Die Auffassung des Dichterberufs im frühen Griechentum bis zur Zeit Pindars* (Göttingen 1963) 94; wrongly, e.g. W. J. Verdenius, *Commentaries on Pindar*, i (Leiden 1987) 111. See further p. 48 n. 19 below.

[12] *βωμολοχεύματ' ἀγεννῆ*. Likewise with A's claim that *Vesp.* (though *μηδὲν . . . λίαν μέγα*) is *κωμῳδίας . . . φορτικῆς σοφώτερον* (*Vesp.* 56, 66) and the claim at *Nub.* 537 that his comedy (*Nub.* in particular) is 'respectable' (*σώφρων*)—which is also followed by a list of proscribed routines. Here, as in the *Pax* passage, the items conspicuously include what A himself *does* do (see Sommerstein on *Pax* 740–5 and *Nub.* 537–43), which is no doubt a separate—jokey—point. Even the crude jokes proscribed at the start of *Ran.* are of course used as jokes *there*.

[13] *Vesp.* 1030 *Ἡρακλέους ὀργήν τιν' ἔχων . . .* , 1043 *ἀλεξίκακον, τῆς χώρας τῆσδε καθαρτήν*: cf. Sommerstein and MacDowell on 1043.

us: they are uncommunicative, almost as repeated instances of a conventional formula are uncommunicative. Yet there is one large qualification to be made. Again and again, the phraseology that Aristophanes uses recalls his own characterizations of tragedy, not least, though not always, the tragedy of Euripides. If Aristophanes strives to be original (*kainos*), Euripides is *the* original writer *par excellence*, the master of 'artistic originality' (*kaina prospherôn sopha*, *Thesmophoriazusae* 1130).[14] In *Frogs* (1107) Aeschylus is implicitly the poet of 'the traditional' (*ta palaia*), Euripides of 'the original' (*ta kaina*).[15] If Aristophanes is *dexios*, 'sophisticated', this is also a possible designation for Aeschylus and Euripides in *Frogs* (1370), but particularly for the *sophisticated* innovator Euripides, the *poiêtês dexios* that Dionysus yearns for (66–71).[16] If (according to *Peace*) Aristophanes 'instructs' (*didaskei*) his public, it is, however, the Aeschylus of *Frogs* who is adamant that poets must have the role of 'instructor' (*didaskalos*, 1055)—and one notes in passing that the 'poets' in question are not explicitly restricted to writers of tragedy.[17] If (according to *Peace*) Aristophanes made the 'art' of comic poetry 'great' (*megalê*), even 'toweringly' great (*epurgôse*), this again recalls a characterization that will be used of Aeschylus in *Frogs*: he (says the chorus) was the 'first of all the tragedians to build the towering phrase' (*purgôsas rhêmata*, 1004), whereas Euripides is subsequently accused of 'stripping tragic art of its greatness' (1494–5).[18] And if Aristophanes is a true artist (*sophos*), so too are all great tragedians, Aeschylus and Euripides among them (*sophoin androin*, *Frogs* 896), because for fifth-century writers the word *sophos* is, above all others, the catchword for the artistic leadership of society, to which poets in general aspire.[19]

[14] *sophos* here with connotations of ingenuity, as much as grand 'art'. The phrase (and the line to which it belongs) is a quotation from Eur. himself (*Med.* 298).

[15] Cf. Dover ad loc.

[16] *dexios* of tragedy: also *Ran.* 762, 1121. Of Eur. in particular: also *Ran.* 1009, cf. *Thes.* 9.

[17] τοῖς μὲν γὰρ παιδαρίοισιν | ἐστὶ διδάσκαλος ὅστις φράζει, τοῖσιν δ' ἡβῶσι ποιηταί—i.e. the poet should have the role for adults (rightly, Dover) that 'teachers' (*didaskaloi*) have for children.

[18] τά τε μέγιστα παραλιπόντα | τῆς τραγῳδικῆς τέχνης: below, p. 366. A's phraseology, τέχνην μεγάλην . . . οἰκοδομήσας (*Pax* 749), is closely paralleled by Pherecrates 100 *PCG*, τέχνην μεγάλην ἐξοικοδομήσας, said of Aeschylus (by himself). The relative chronology of Pherecrates' play (*Κραπαταλοί*) and *Peace* is unknown (cf. n. 21 below).

[19] See p. 46 n. 11 above. The contest in *Frogs* is an agon in *sophia* (882) to

Comedy *too* . . . So many Aristophanic roads (it does begin to seem) lead to tragedy. And if the route is sometimes indirect, we can put this down (perhaps) to the non-availability of conceptual short-cuts and (certainly) to the very pervasiveness of Aristophanes' preoccupation with tragedy. It is not, indeed, that explicit interest in tragedy was anything new for a comic writer. The admittedly meagre fragments and attestations of Aristophanes' predecessors still contain allusions to tragedy, to Aeschylus, to Sophocles and to Euripides, including—in a passage of Cratinus which will need our attention later—a barb aimed at Aristophanes himself, the (supposed) follower of Euripides.[20] We find samples of paratragedy and at least one apparent instance of a tragedian—Euripides—as a character in a play.[21] Yet Aristophanes' engagement with tragedy is so marked, so prolonged, and above all so complex and even paradoxical (as Cratinus' sally about him serves to suggest) that it is hard to imagine that any other comic poet before him possessed—or was possessed by—an interest in tragedy of quite the same kind.

The prolonged engagement seems in fact to have lasted a good twenty years, beginning with *Acharnians* (425 BC), where Euripides lends Dicaeopolis his stage properties and his lines in the cause of peace, and ending with *Frogs* (405 BC), where Euripides competes with Aeschylus before the god of tragedy, Dionysus, himself.[22] Between these plays comes *Thesmophoriazusae* (411 BC), in which yet another stage Euripides enlists his own plays in contention with the women of Athens. Other plays, now lost, had the same overt concern with tragedy, as we can gauge from surviving fragments and the implications of the titles: a second *Thesmophoriazusae* and two plays in which Euripides seems again to have figured, *Preview* and (perhaps) *Dramas* or *Centaur*.[23] All of

establish which tragedian is more *sophos* in the art of poetry (780): see Dover, *Frogs*, 12–14.

[20] e.g. Crates 28 *PCG*, Cratinus 276 *PCG* (tragedy); Teleclides 15 *PCG* (Aeschylus); Cratinus 17 *PCG* (Sophocles); Teleclides 41–2 *PCG* (on Euripides); Cratinus 342 *PCG* (Euripides and A: see p. 416 below).

[21] See respectively e.g. Cratinus 115 *PCG* and Callias 15 *PCG* (Diog. Laert. 2. 18), where, however, the speaker supposed to be Euripides is female. Aeschylus was a character in the *Κραπαταλοί* of A's older contemporary Pherecrates (n. 18 above), but the play itself may well not pre-date A's own career.

[22] We know of no play outside this period with any substantial tragic presence.

[23] There was also *Phoenician Women* (above, p. 16), apparently a burlesque of Eur.'s play of the same name—but (*pace* Silk, 'Paratragedy', 477) interest in

these plays, again, are known or reasonably presumed to date from somewhere in the twenty-year span.[24] It is striking that we know of only one Aristophanic play with a prominent interest in art or literature which is *not* centred on tragedy,[25] whereas (so far as we can judge) none of Aristophanes' predecessors seem to have had any such clearly defined pattern of interest, nor indeed any of his contemporaries either.[26]

Aristophanes is concerned with tragedy because he is concerned with the possibilities of comedy. The tragedy that concerns him (our impression is bound to be) includes more than its fair share of Euripides. We have provisionally to assume that Aristophanes has a specific, though not an exclusive, interest in Euripides—and we will find it difficult here to forget Cratinus' joke about a supposed community of interest between the two playwrights. However, we, who have a wider and a longer view, must, inevitably and properly, subsume Aristophanes' concerns and his sense of comic possibilities within a more capacious frame of reference. We begin the task, of course, with a particular piece of historical knowledge denied to Aristophanes himself. We know, as he could not know, the implications of his career, in the sense that we know the aftermath of his own late dramatic ventures, of which *Plutus* is one, though not the final one. Our handbooks tell of a 'long-standing convergence' between tragedy and comedy, the result of

tragedy as such should be distinguished from burlesque of tragic-mythic subjects (cultivated by e.g. Strattis, who shows none of A's interest in tragedy and the tragic *per se*: see Silk, 'Versus the rest', n. 20). For the contents of the second *Thes.*, see the summary in G. Norwood, *Greek Comedy* (London 1931) 252–3. According to schol. *Vesp.* 61c (*PCG* iii. 2. 158, test. iv) Eur. was a character in *Dramas* and *Preview*. Whether the *Δράματα* in question was the Aristophanic *Centaur* or the spurious *Niobus* (above, pp. 14–16) is unclear.

[24] See above, pp. 18–20.

[25] *Gerytades*, in which we meet a delegation of assorted poets in Hades (fr. 156 *PCG*). For the date of the play (above, p. 20), cf. Geissler, *Chronologie*, 61 ff., and Kassel–Austin in *PCG* iii. 2. 101. The pertinent-sounding *Poetry* and *Dramas* or *Niobus* are presumed spurious (above, p. 16). Other comedies did have, or may have had, incidental literary presences (like the dithyrambic poet in *Av.* 904–52) or interests which could only be called 'literary' in a very extended sense (like the verse oracles in *Eq.*). In *Banqueters* an 'old-versus-new' educational debate is at one point expressed in terms of Homer-versus-rhetoric, as in *Nub.* it is at one point expressed as Aesch.-versus-Eur. (1364–72). The wider issue is not affected.

[26] Cratinus, for instance, wrote no known play centred on tragedy, but did write one about Archilochus and Homer, one about comedy, and one (apparently) about music (Ἀρχίλοχοι, Πυτίνη, Εὐνεῖδαι respectively). On Old Comedy and tragedy, see further Silk, 'Versus the rest', and cf. Dover, *Frogs*, 25–8, and n. 23 above.

which is Menandrian New Comedy, known to us from the extant *Dyscolus*, from other fragments large and small, and from the Roman imitations that mediate this new comedy of manners to the Western world. It is this tradition that eventually produces the comic drama of Shakespeare, Molière and Chekhov, and this same tradition that helps to institutionalize an association between all drama and what we have already referred to as *realist* principles and *Aristotelian* canons—however much Shakespeare, in particular, may transcend those principles and those canons.

The many actual developments that correspond to our tidy formula of 'convergence' are, no doubt, considerably more complicated, but the overall pattern is irrefutable. On the tragic side, we have Euripides' notable experiments with themes of intrigue and adventure, with less-than-heroic levels of experience, with the portrayal of all-too-human emotions, and with a variety of what *we* are wont to see as comic techniques or effects,[27] unrelated though these might often be to the general run of Old Comedy in Euripides' own time. Within Old Comedy itself, on the other hand, we can point to Crates, who seems to have rejected the prevalent satire of specific individuals in favour, perhaps, of some kind of social comedy; to Pherecrates, who is known to have experimented with fictions involving love interests and family relationships; and to Aristophanes himself, whose extraordinary career includes one late play (*Cocalus*) which, according to an ancient source, 'introduced rape and recognition and all the other features picked up by Menander'.[28] The evidence of his fourth-century plays, *Ecclesiazusae* and, especially, *Plutus*, together with this ancient testimony to his last work of all, leaves no doubt that Aristophanes played an active role in the converging process. The

[27] Eur.'s role in the development of New Comedy was well understood in antiquity: see esp. Satyrus, *Vita*, VII. 1. On his use of 'comic' elements cf.: B. Seidensticker, *Palintonos Harmonia* (Göttingen 1982); Goldhill, *Reading Greek Tragedy*, 244–64; O. Taplin, 'Fifth-century tragedy and comedy: a *synkrisis*', *JHS* 106 (1986) 163–6.

[28] Crates: see M. G. Bonanno, *Studi su Cratete comico* (Padua 1972) 19–54. Pherecrates: see esp. the fragments of *Κοριαννώ* (73–84 *PCG*), named after a courtesan (Athen. 13. 567c), and Anon. *de Com.* iii. 29 ff. Koster. *Cocalus*: see *Vit. Ar.* (*PCG* iii. 2. 3). For a lucid account of the development from Old to New Comedy, see E. W. Handley, 'Comedy', in P. E. Easterling and B. M. W. Knox (eds.), *The Cambridge History of Classical Literature*, i: *Greek Literature* (Cambridge 1985) 398–414, to which Wiles, *Masks*, provides an illuminating counterpoint.

narrowing of horizons to a world of social behaviour and domestic relationships between more or less ordinary people—the elimination, in effect, of some of the most distinctive characteristics of Old Comedy as a genre—is partly the work of Old Comedy's most renowned exponent. And so too is the process whereby what we can now see as Aristotelian-realist principles become a familiar norm for comic drama, and indeed for fictional literature as a whole.

With Euripides in mind, and Aristophanes' relationship with tragedy as well, we might usefully put down a marker here, in advance of a fuller discussion to come, that, up to and including *Frogs*, and contrary to many modern misstatements, Aristophanes is never hostile to Euripides *tout court*, but is content to seem ambivalent about the great tragedian's experiments. For even if Euripides *has* 'stripped tragic art of its greatness' (*Frogs* 1494–5), he is *still* among 'the true artists' (*Frogs* 896), and has it in him *also* (not least) to be a prime aid for a *bona fide* Aristophanic quest (Dicaeopolis' quest for peace in *Acharnians*). Given, however, that Euripides' experiments are never presented as approximations to Aristophanic Old Comedy itself,[29] the natural inference is that Euripides, the great experimenter, holds a special interest for Aristophanes, beyond all other tragedians, precisely because he is an experimenter. It is not simply that he is a fashionable influence or a fashionable target, but that, as an experimenter, he is himself uniquely committed to the definition, or redefinition, of his own art. In this sense—because of this commitment—he matters above all to the comic poet.

Given Aristophanes' special interest in tragedy and a uniquely committed tragedian, given his seeming ambivalence towards this tragedian, and given his active role in the eventual, momentous process of convergence with tragic drama, our urgent need is for some point of reference which can help us evaluate this set of relationships. We propose a literary-theoretical point of reference.[30] The question that arises from Aristophanes' preoccupation with tragedy—put in its most innocent form—is this: do we find it natural or inevitable for a *comic* writer to have such a response to *tragedy*? And the question is surely imponderable, unless we know the answer to a more nakedly theoretical question: what is the

[29] So, rightly, Seidensticker, *Palintonos Harmonia*, 209.

[30] The following argument is based on Silk, 'Autonomy'.

relationship between comedy and tragedy as such? Although it is not common for this question to be posed in such abstract terms, there is no doubt what the common answer to it will be: tragedy and comedy constitute—do they not?—a pair of natural opposites. Aristophanes' interest in tragedy—one perhaps thinks—will have something to do with the attraction, or repulsion, of opposites. Talk of *convergence* between tragedy and comedy in Greek literary history makes it sound—perhaps?—as if two opposites are in question; and convergence between opposites is no doubt feasible.

The world, certainly, thinks that tragedy and comedy are opposites and that this opposition is a fact of life, or of language, for ancient Greece as for the modern West. For our age, as for earlier ages, the fundamental pattern of the opposition is laid out in Aristotle's *Poetics*. Tragedy (the Aristotelian argument runs) is a dramatic *mimêsis*, and so too is comedy (*Poetics* I), but whereas tragedy deals with people who are 'better than us' or 'people of substance' (*spoudaious*), comedy deals with people who are 'worse than us' or 'low', 'trivial' (*phaulous*) (*Poetics* II). Aristophanes had voiced thoughts about the need to be 'serious' as well as to 'amuse' (*Frogs* 389–90); it is now asserted, in the same words, but without reference to Aristophanes, that comedy's business is with 'the amusing', 'the laughable' (*to geloion*), whereas tragedy has 'serious concerns' (*ta spoudaia*) (*Poetics* IV).[31] It is further suggested, though the thought is not fully articulated, that where tragedy deals in painful matters and, correspondingly, appeals to emotions such as pity and fear, comedy is painless and evokes (presumably) laughter (*Poetics* V–VI).[32] It follows that a tragedy properly ends in misfortune, but a comedy in reconciliation: 'Orestes and

[31] In *Poet.* II, then, *spoudaios* is opposed to *phaulos*, but in IV to *geloios*. The two oppositions might seem to be independent, but in IV (1448^{b}26, 37) are in effect run together in a discussion of the spiritual prehistory of drama, whereby the prototype of tragedy is Homeric epic and of comedy is the 'Homeric' 'iambic' satire, *Margites*. The evident tidiness of this schema, however, is spoiled, again in IV, by the claim that the actual *source* of tragedy is the dithyramb, and of comedy the phallic song. The expected implication would be that the dithyramb, like epic, is an elevated form, whereas the phallic song, like satire, is vulgar; but instead Aristotle ascribes 'ludicrous diction' (*lexis geloia*), and so a low status, to (apparently) the dithyrambic prototype itself.

[32] The sub-Aristotelian theory of comedy adumbrated in *Tract. Coisl.* involves a more specific contrast at this point, as at various others (see Janko, *Aristotle on Comedy*, 151–60).

Aegisthus walk off as friends, and no one is killed by anyone' (*Poetics* XIII).

On this Aristotelian basis, assumed to be, as it purports to be, in line with canonical Greek practice, all subsequent Western theory has been founded, most explicitly in the shape of a series of syntheses, late Greek, Graeco-Roman or Renaissance,[33] but explicitly or implicitly in all ages. 'Thanks to the Greeks', wrote Northrop Frye, 'we can distinguish tragedy from comedy in drama, and so we still tend to assume that each is the half of drama that is not the other half.'[34] Frye's tone is reproachful, but it is still implicit in his reproach that tragedy and comedy are, as Aristotle said they were, two opposite types of drama—that they are, as Samuel Johnson put it in succinct neo-Aristotelian terms, 'two modes of imitation . . . intended to promote different ends by contrary means'.[35] The opposition is rarely argued, but widely assumed. It is assumed now, as it has been assumed in the past. It is assumed by literary theorists and equally by scholars and critics of Greek literature, in their dealings with comedy, with tragedy, and with both. In the relationship between Greek tragedy and Greek comedy, for instance, we are said to be faced with two 'fascinatingly related *yet opposed* ways of approaching through art the world and the truth'; we learn that in his theatrical experiments Euripides engineers 'a fusion *and contrast* of comic and tragic effects'; and that Euripides, though not its only exponent, is the supreme Greek master of this 'attunement of *opposite* tensions (*palintonos harmoniê*), comic and tragic'.[36]

[33] On these see: A. P. McMahon, 'Seven questions on Aristotelian definitions of tragedy and comedy', *HSCP* 40 (1929) 97–198; Seidensticker, *Palintonos Harmonia*, 14–19, 249–60; Janko, *Aristotle on Comedy*, 48–52, 153–60; G. Zanker, *Realism in Alexandrian Poetry* (London 1987) 137–46, 151–3; M. T. Herrick, *Comic Theory in the Sixteenth Century* (Urbana 1964). The ancient theory may be traced back, beyond Aristotle, to Plato (cf. Seidensticker, *Palintonos Harmonia*, 14–15; Zanker, *Realism*, 137, 151); it is first set out as a theory by Aristotle; its fuller forms come later. On Aristotle's own version of the opposition, cf. S. Halliwell, *Aristotle's Poetics* (London 1986) 266–76.

[34] N. Frye, *Anatomy of Criticism* (Princeton 1957) 13.

[35] *Preface to Shakespeare* (1765), in W. Raleigh (ed.), *Johnson on Shakespeare* (rev. edn., Oxford 1925) 16.

[36] The quotations (with my italics) belong to three important, and very different, discussions: Taplin, '*Synkrisis*', 173; Goldhill, *Reading Greek Tragedy*, 263 (Arrowsmith's words, quoted approvingly); Seidensticker, *Palintonos Harmonia*, 11 ('eine spannungsreiche "gegenstrebige Harmonie" . . . von Komik und Tragik', alluding to Heraclit. 51).

It is certainly true that tragedy and comedy are different; that their differences tend to include (as Dr Johnson put it) 'different ends'; and that, in particular, tragic and comic drama or (still more particularly) Greek *tragôidia* and *kômôidia* have some contrasting features.[37] None of this, however, makes tragedy and comedy—or even, of course, *tragôidia* and *kômôidia*—a pair of opposites. It is also true—it is part of my own argument—that for Aristophanes himself contemporary tragedy is not merely distinct from his own drama, but does in various ways represent the alternative pole of a contrastive system from which he constantly takes his bearings. However, this only reinforces the need to scrutinize the relationship between comedy and tragedy *as such*. Only from such a scrutiny can it be seen that, irrespective of Aristophanes' perception of tragedy, and irrespective of the impression created by the convergence of Greek comedy with tragedy, *his* relationship with tragedy is special, individual, significant—and *not* a corollary of some essential condition of comedy itself.

The traditional, Aristotelian or Aristotelian-based, assumption that tragedy and comedy are opposites is false and, for reasons that will become clear, pernicious. It has bedevilled the appreciation of comedy in general and Aristophanes in particular, and it needs to be fully examined and exposed before we can take our discussion of Aristophanic comedy any further. The examination will inevitably involve anticipating some details of our discussion of Aristophanes himself. More important: it inevitably involves appeal to the long and wide perspective which is not available to Aristophanes, but is available to us: the continuum of literary and literary-theoretical experience to which Aristophanes and Greek tragedy, but also comedy as a whole and tragedy as a whole, properly belong. And given this perspective, the examination will also serve to introduce various theoretical issues—Aristotelian and other—which in due course it will be our business to confront.

[37] Discussed and stressed most recently, in respect of Greek drama, by Taplin, '*Synkrisis*', with qualifications in Taplin, 'Comedy and the tragic', in Silk, *Tragedy and the Tragic*, 188–202 (with which cf. the response, ibid., by B. Gredley, 'Comedy and tragedy—inevitable distinctions', 203–16). Taplin himself, however, insists that in earlier and later fifth-century tragedy the opposition is less marked ('*Synkrisis*', 165–6, 172) and that various of the most apparent points of contrast cease to be operative when Aristophanic Old Comedy makes way for Menandrian New (ibid. 174).

Consider, then, the specifics of the Aristotelian, or Aristotelian-based, opposition. Many of them amount to one general principle: *tragedy is high, but comedy is low*. So said many theorists for many centuries, and most insistently during the Renaissance. Thus Scaliger in 1561: 'Comedy employs characters from rustic or low city life . . . The language is that of everyday life. Tragedy, on the other hand, employs kings and princes . . . The language is grave, polished, removed from the colloquial.'[38] Yet sometimes, as Horace noted, comedy raises her voice (and tragedy drops hers).[39] In particular, the style of some comedy (for instance, the elevated lyrics in Aristophanes' *Frogs* or *Thesmophoriazusae*) is very high in part, and the style of much other comedy (from the sandstormillions of metaphors and exotic word-formations in Aristophanes to the epigrammatic dialogue of Oscar Wilde) is only misleadingly described as everyday. Likewise the characters of comedy are not necessarily trivial in status (*Frogs* begins with a slave, but also a god) nor indeed necessarily trivial in stature: do we look up to Aristophanes' Lysistrata less than to Aeschylus' feeble Agamemnon or Shakespeare's very foolish fond old Lear? True it may have been that from Menander to the eighteenth century, and broadly under Aristotelian influence, assumptions akin to Scaliger's were generally borne out in comic dramatic practice. But that consideration in no way makes the assumptions themselves true, *tout court*. A theorist may prefer to concentrate on the specific distortions or deformations of dramatic character, and maintain, with Molière's Dorante, that the purpose of comedy is 'to dramatize the faults of mankind'.[40] Or prefer to suppose that what is distorted or deformed is not the character represented but its representation, so that comedy (supposedly unlike tragedy) itself deforms; many no doubt assume, probably erroneously, that Aristotle himself meant this.[41] Either way, the argument fails.

[38] J. C. Scaliger, *Poetics*: B. F. Dukore (ed.), *Dramatic Theory and Criticism* (New York 1974) 140.

[39] *Ars Poetica*, 93–8.

[40] *La Critique de l'école des femmes* (1663), Scene VI. Aristotle (*Poet.* V) had spoken of human 'error' (ἁμάρτημα) and 'deformity' (αἶσχος), without making it clear whether either involved what we would think of as any moral failing.

[41] *Poet.* V, referring back to II, begins: 'Comedy, as we have said, is a depiction of inferior people (μίμησις φαυλοτέρων)'. The earlier passage involves the virtually synonymous phrase, χείρους . . . μιμεῖσθαι . . . τῶν νῦν. Both passages refer to the object, not the accuracy, of the depiction; and the same is true of the comment associating comedy and deformity in *Poet.* V. However, judgements about accuracy

Are more faults—or worse faults—dramatized in *Frogs* than in *Agamemnon*? Is Aristophanes' Aeschylus more 'deformed' than Aeschylus' Clytemnestra? Are there worse faults (or more faults) or worse deformations (or more deformations) in Shakespearean comedy than in Shakespearean tragedy?

Alternatively, then: *tragedy appeals to emotional responses such as pity and fear, but comedy makes us laugh*. The principle has a more modern, less Aristotelian version: *tragedy is emotional, comedy is intellectual*. For English students of comedy this formula was apparently sanctified by Meredith's spokesmanship of 'thoughtful laughter'[42] and, before that, by Dryden's suggestion that comedy 'works on the judgement and fancy',[43] and many theorists still seem to believe it: 'tragedy plays on our emotions, it involves us and demands our sympathy for the protagonist; comedy appeals to our intellect, we observe critically and laugh at the victim.'[44] The trouble is first that some of the most canonically tragic tragedies are in the most obvious sense *thought*-provoking. One thinks perhaps of Sophocles' *Oedipus*

are made elsewhere in the treatise ('Sophocles said *he* portrayed people as they ought to be, but that Euripides portrayed them as they were', XXV).

[42] 'The test of true comedy is that it shall awaken thoughtful laughter': George Meredith, *An Essay on Comedy and the Uses of the Comic Spirit* (1897) (originally a lecture 'On the Idea of Comedy . . .' given in 1877), in W. Sypher (ed.), *Comedy* (New York 1956) 47.

[43] In his preface to *An Evening's Love* (1671).

[44] D. L. Hirst, *Tragicomedy* (London 1984), p. xi. The basis of this antithesis is ancient, although in antiquity the formula 'comedy : thought : : tragedy : feeling' was not fully spelled out. 'Tragedy:feeling' derives from Aristotle's *katharsis* ('by rousing pity and fear tragedy effects a *katharsis* of such emotions', *Poet.* VI); 'comedy:thought', ultimately, from Aristotle's thoughts on the intellectuality of jokes (*Rhet.* 3. 11. 6), combined with the definition in the opening sentence of Donatus (?), *De Comoedia* (4th cent. AD?): 'Comedy is a story dealing with the various modes of public and private behaviour, *from which one learns* what is practical in life and what, on the other hand, is to be avoided' ('comoedia est fabula . . . instituta continens affectuum . . . *quibus discitur* . . .', *CGF* 67 Kaibel). On the huge influence of Donatus' treatise on later centuries, see McMahon, 'Seven questions', 126–7. The association of comedy and thought seems to have crystallized, at least in Britain, in the eighteenth century: see especially James Beattie, *Essays on Poetry and Music*[3] (London 1779) 181–91, and cf. Horace Walpole's celebrated inversion, 'life is a comedy to him that thinks and a tragedy to him that feels' (letter to the Countess of Upper Ossory, 16 Aug. 1776). Bergson's theory of laughter presents a classic modern version of the antithesis ('its appeal is to intelligence . . . it is incompatible with emotion': p. 75 below). As far as A's own assumptions are concerned, it is worth adding that *Eccl.* 1155–6 in effect divides audiences schematically into thinkers (*τοῖς σοφοῖς μέν*) and laughers (*τοῖς γελῶσι δ' ἡδέως*).

Tyrannus and Nietzsche's characterization of its 'marvellous tangle of a trial, slowly unravelled by the judge, bit by bit, for his own undoing'[45]— quite apart from the (more deviant?) way that (say) the recognition scene in Euripides' *Electra* compels its audience to call to mind the equivalent scene in Aeschylus' *Choephori*[46]—or indeed the sense in which all literary fiction is liable to have some 'philosophical' credentials (as Aristotle himself saw), in that it deals in general truths.[47] And then, various kinds of straightforwardly comic comedy are themselves associated with emotion—at which point we take issue again with one of the premises of Aristotle's theory. Much comic drama (from Aristophanes to modern 'alternative' comedy) sets out to shock by violating audience taboos. On the screen, in particular, comedy is often associated with excitement (comedy thrillers) or fear (horror comedies)—and the association with excitement, at least, is prefigured on the ancient stage by the delayed recognitions and the desperate last-minute deceptions of New Comedy. Above all, in the theatre as in the cinema, comedy may be associated with the sympathetic emotions and with pathos. One thinks of Falstaff ('I do begin to perceive that I am made an ass'),[48] of Chaplin walking uncertainly off the screen with one of his heroines, and (as we shall see) of Aristophanes' old wasps looking back to their youthful prowess.[49] As such instances show, it is not necessarily the case that in comedy we 'laugh at the victim', if indeed we necessarily laugh at all.

Very obviously, then: *comedy has a happy ending, unlike tragedy*. This familiar Aristotelian principle is no doubt more often applicable than not, as is the closely related idea that comedy is painless and tragedy painful. However, it is also true that many

[45] Friedrich Nietzsche, *The Birth of Tragedy* (*Die Geburt der Tragödie*, 1872), IX.

[46] Cf. e.g. Goldhill, *Reading Greek Tragedy*, 247–50.

[47] *Poet.* IX. Even Heath, who seeks, improbably, to deny any intellectual 'intention' to the Greek (though only the Greek) tragedians, feels obliged to grant that (e.g.) *Antigone* 'can and does prompt readers [and spectators?] to serious reflection on moral and intellectual questions', because it 'does involve fundamental issues of a religious, moral, and political nature': M. Heath, *The Poetics of Greek Tragedy* (London 1987) 76, 73.

[48] *The Merry Wives of Windsor*, V. v.

[49] Below, pp. 389–92. Arguably, too, intellectual humour is itself not strictly intellectual, but experiential. Cf. E. Bentley, *The Life of the Drama* (London 1965) 229–30, on the joke: 'Why do we laugh at jokes? The point of the joke can be explained, but the explanation is not funny. The intellectual content is not the essence. What counts is the experience which we call "getting the joke".'

comedies, from Aristophanes' *Clouds* to Molière's *Misanthrope*, have sour triumphs which one would never identify as happy endings unless one thought one had to. Many, again, have a selectively happy outcome, from which one character or set of characters is excluded: our earliest extant comic play, Aristophanes' *Acharnians*, is an example.[50] Some even end with a death, as do Shakespeare's *Love's Labour's Lost*, Goldoni's *Venetian Twins*, and again—arguably—Aristophanes' *Clouds*.[51] In any case, all manner of non-comic works, ancient and modern, end 'happily'—including some tragedies, like Aeschylus' *Eumenides*;[52] some epics; many lyric poems; many novels—on the strength of which, indeed, Northrop Frye was disposed to call such works comedy too, while medieval Christendom, similarly converting a supposedly necessary condition for comedy into a sufficient condition, duly attached the name 'comedia' (or *Commedia*) to works of Christian redemption like Dante's.[53]

Still more obviously, then: *tragedy is a type of serious drama, where comedy (with or without laughter) seeks merely to amuse.* Dante aside, this principle has an obvious superficial plausibility. However, it is easy to point to amusing scenes or characters in tragedy, even if the amusement often has a black edge: the porter in *Macbeth*, the foot-shuffling guard in *Antigone*, the cross-dressing in *Bacchae*, are cases in point. And more fundamentally—and without unduly pre-empting discussion yet to come—let us note that comic drama has repeatedly given its audiences some impression of 'seriousness', ever since Dicaeopolis in *Acharnians* first claimed a 'sense of duty' for Aristophanic comedy. We

[50] The pattern is referred to by Aristotle in *Poet.* XIII. In the Renaissance the favourite examples were Plautine: 'There are, on the other hand, many comedies which end unhappily for some of the characters. Such are *Miles Gloriosus*, *Persa*, and *Asinaria*' (Scaliger: Dukore, *Dramatic Theory*, 141).

[51] On *Clouds* see below, p. 360. Mike Leigh's *Abigail's Party* (1977) is another, recent, example.

[52] The earliest extant example (458 BC): Aristotle himself was well aware that tragedies often did end like this (*Poet.* XIII).

[53] Frye, *Anatomy*, 43–8. The famous letter ascribed to Dante and addressed to Can Grande della Scala (*c.*1318?) also refers to the 'low' style of the *Commedia* by way of confirming the propriety of its title, but it is surely the movement from the 'horror' of the beginning to the joyous end which is decisive (*pace* e.g. H. A. Kelly, *Tragedy and Comedy from Dante to Pseudo-Dante* (Berkeley 1989)). Medieval definitions of 'comedia' concentrate on the happy end (as does that by Vincent of Beauvais in the 13th cent.: *Speculum Doctrinale*, 109). Even in the Renaissance a solemn work on the subject of Christian redemption could be called a comedy as (e.g.) was *Christus Triumphans* ('comoedia apocalyptica') by John Foxe (1556).

can take our pick from a spectrum of instances—from the overt didacticism of a Shaw to the 'unobtrusive moral subtlety' of a Menander.[54] We can note too that 'seriousness' is by any standards an elusive commodity ('drama is made serious', said J. M. Synge, 'by the degree in which it gives the nourishment, not very easy to define, on which our imaginations live');[55] and (on the other side) that much acknowledged comedy, from Menander onwards, is barely capable of inducing actual laughter; and that some acknowledged comic playwrights, even, have turned this fact into a principle in its own right ('nor is the moving of laughter always the end of comedy; that is rather a fowling for the people's delight': Ben Jonson);[56] and that the Anglo-French 'sentimental comedy' of the eighteenth century is not even concerned to be amusing (but instead 'to introduce a joy too exquisite for laughter that can have no spring but in delight': Steele);[57] and, above all (as we know from our long and wide perspective), that the propensity to amuse is a central characteristic of a great range of artworks or proto-artworks, including not merely verbal dramas, but also verbal jokes, mimes without words, music (with or without words), films (with or without), and cartoons (which sometimes have words, but nowadays tend to be virtually or actually wordless).

It is this last consideration that begins to make it obvious why 'comedy' is not and cannot be a proper opposite of 'tragedy'. There is a full and fully perceptible measure of continuity between all the comic phenomena just listed. There is, for instance, a full measure of continuity between Woody Allen acting in a film comedy and Woody Allen as a stand-up comedian telling jokes; and so too there is continuity between Woody Allen joking, in or out of a film, and any one of us making a joke in ordinary conversation. But while there is a tragic 'equivalent', no doubt, to the Woody Allen film, there is surely none to the stand-up comedian or his, or indeed our, jokes. It follows that while we may distinguish between the various manifestations of comedy and the comic, we should distinguish them only as manifestations

[54] D. M. Bain, *Menander, Samia* (Warminster 1983), p. xix.
[55] Preface to *The Tinker's Wedding* (1907).
[56] *Timber: or Discoveries* (*c*.1620): *Ben Jonson*, ed. C. H. Herford and P. and E. Simpson, viii (Oxford 1947) 643.
[57] Preface to *The Conscious Lovers* (1723).

of this comic continuum. And that, on this basis, it is arbitrary to limit 'comedy' to the sphere of drama. The name might, with some plausibility, be applied to the whole continuum or to any part of it.[58]

In fact, at the risk of seeming temporarily to reinstate the tragedy–comedy opposition at a more fundamental level, one must declare that comedy is accidentally dramatic, whereas tragedy is essentially dramatic—'by nature', as Aristotle might have said. Tragedy, as generally understood, has certain characteristics which, in combination, are found largely or only in drama: notably, concentrated action, heightening (often associated with the concentration), and a cumulative logic. Visual art is too static: a Rembrandt or a Michelangelo may be moving or majestic, but not tragic. Miniatures are too short: there is no such thing as a tragic epigram or a tragic sonnet. Narrative fiction, like the *Iliad* or *Anna Karenina*, may have something of a tragic quality, but even the *Iliad* and *Anna Karenina* are too discursive or too tolerant of the unheightened to persuade us to push out the generic boundary and think of them *as* tragedy.[59] Yet there *is*

[58] Cf. Sypher, *Comedy*, 209: 'As we move "up" the scale of comic action, the mechanisms become more complex, but no more "comic"'—though (e.g.) 'embodiments' would be more to the point than 'mechanisms'. Theoretical attempts to set up barriers between parts of the comic continuum usually involve assertion rather than argument. Among the notable exceptions are Pirandello's *L'umorismo* (pp. 75–6 below) and Freud's *Der Witz und seine Beziehung zum Unbewussten* (1905) (cited as S. Freud, *Jokes and their Relation to the Unconscious*, trans. J. Strachey, Penguin Freud Library, vi, ed. A. Richards (Harmondsworth 1976)). In this important discussion Freud maintained a dogged struggle to mark off jokes from 'the comic', despite his perception of overlap (e.g. 'what is a joke to me may be merely a comic story to other people', 150) and of some never fully specified relatedness (e.g. 'a comparison . . . between jokes and a closely related type of the comic may confirm our assumption that . . .', 232) and his apparent incapacity to articulate the distinction except in closed terminology (e.g. pleasure in jokes is derived 'from an economy in expenditure upon inhibition', pleasure in the comic 'from an economy in expenditure upon ideation (upon cathexis) 302). For a perverse attempt to separate jokes in life from jokes in plays, see S. Langer, *Feeling and Form* (New York 1953) 344–5.

[59] With novels and even paintings, however, it is not hard to find loose allusions, with 'tragic' effectively used to mean 'sad'. Cf. e.g. Wordsworth's 'gay or tragic pictures' ('The Excursion', IV. 562) or, in more detail, Yeats ('The Tragic Theatre', 1910, in *Uncollected Prose by W. B. Yeats*, ed. J. P. Frayne and C. Johnson, ii (London 1975) 389): 'when we look at the faces of the old tragic paintings, whether it is in Titian or in some painter of medieval China, we find there sadness and gravity, a certain emptiness even as of a mind that waited the supreme crisis (and indeed it seems at times as if the graphic art, unlike poetry which sings the crisis itself, were the celebration of waiting).' This seems a confirmation, rather than a

such a thing as a comic miniature (a joke) and comic visual art (a cartoon) and a comic novel, just as there is such a thing as a comic drama: all of these entities lie within the range of comedy. Tragedy, then, is a dramatic genre, whereas 'comedy' (contrary to the supposition of most theorists in most eras) is evidently something wider altogether.

Before we pursue the theoretical implications of that last point, it is only fair to acknowledge that the name 'comedy' (or its equivalents in other modern languages) is not, as a matter of fact, normally applied with equal freedom to *all* points on the comic continuum. Nor indeed was the Greek name *kômôidia* so applied.[60] This is undeniable; and one reason for our insistence on restricting the application of 'comedy' in this way is continued deference to the prestige of the familiar opposition. Given that tragedy *is* a dramatic genre, we remember to call comedy a dramatic genre too.[61] However, it is also true that the usage of our 'comedy' and Greek *kômôidia* (or 'revel-song') is extended in a way to which 'tragedy' and Greek *tragôidia* ('goat-song'?)[62] present no equivalent. In line with the unmistakable continuity between comic drama and the telling of jokes, we use the vocabulary of 'comedy', 'comic', and 'comedian' for jokes and

contradiction, of the principle that there are no tragic miniatures. If tragedy *is* to be related to any other art, it will most readily be to the cumulative art of music, as Nietzsche saw. But it would be more feasible to argue, as Nietzsche does, that spoken tragedy embodies the spirit of music than that wordless music aspires to the condition of tragedy (cf. M. S. Silk and J. P. Stern, *Nietzsche on Tragedy* (Cambridge 1981), esp. 229–30, 249–51, 262–3).

[60] We are not concerned here with one-off comparisons, like the characterization offered by 'Longinus' of (parts of) the *Odyssey* as 'a sort of comedy of manners' (οἱονεὶ κωμῳδία τίς ἐστιν ἠθολογουμένη, *Subl.* 9. 15). Nor with the helpless use of a phrase like 'a kind of comic entertainment' (κωμικῆς παιδιᾶς . . . τρόπος) used by Sosibius (3rd cent. BC: *FGH* 595 F7 = Athen. 14. 621d) for the primitive performances of the Spartan *deikelistai* (κωμῳδία itself similarly at Athen. 10. 445a–b)—any more than with Herodotus' (similar?) use of τραγικός for the lyric ritual of hero worship at Sicyon (Hdt. 5. 67: on which see A. W. Pickard-Cambridge, *Dithyramb, Tragedy and Comedy*², rev. T. B. L. Webster (Oxford 1962) 132–47 and 101–7 respectively).

[61] Though even here it is true of (e.g.) contemporary English usage that 'comedy' is freely used to label dramatic, semi-dramatic, or barely dramatic new work of a comic kind on radio or television, whereas outside the theatre newly composed serious drama is seldom, if ever, called 'tragedy'. Hence the phrases 'radio tragedy' or 'television tragedy' sound absurd, whereas the expressions 'radio comedy' and 'television comedy' (with a variety of applications) are commonplace.

[62] *kômôidia* is derived from *kômos*, 'revel' or 'party', and *tragôidia*, conventionally, from *tragos*, 'goat': see below, p. 78 with n. 116.

jokers, and so (*mutatis mutandis*) did the Greeks. The verb *kômôidein* is used, like a genre term, of the 'ridiculing' practised by the comic dramatist: the Athenians, said one hostile witness, did not allow their dramatists to 'ridicule the *dêmos*' (*kômôidein* . . . *ton* . . . *dêmon*); and Aristophanes, according to his own testimony, was accused of doing just that.[63] But the same verb is used by Plato of the backbiting indulged in by the ill-educated ('whether drunk or sober') and the satirical barbs of the witty, of Socrates making fun of Gorgias and Meletus making fun of Socrates; by Lysias of an accuser's distortions in a lawsuit; by Aristotle of the critical sallies of a pair of forgotten *littérateurs*.[64] And in Aristophanes himself the adjective *kômôidikos* is used of a young girl's jokes against an old woman, and the scurrilous coinage *kômôido-loikhôn* of a flatterer and his *bons mots*.[65]

Again, modern theoretical discussions of comedy often, and usually without comment, turn from drama to the joke—from the 'comic in character' to the 'comic in words'[66]—and so too did their ancient counterparts. Witness Plato, discussing the dangerous effects of exposure to literature: 'Doesn't the same principle apply to humour [*to geloion*], if in comic drama [*en mimêsei* . . . *kômôidikêi*] or for that matter in private conversation [*idiâi*] you enjoy jokes you would be ashamed to make [*gelôtopoiôn*] yourself?'[67] Witness again, on a different scale, the discussion of comedy in a later treatise, the *Tractatus Coislinianus*. This gets under way with a definition of *kômôidia* as a dramatic *mimêsis* ('an imitation of an action that is ridiculous'), and concludes with the phases of Greek comic drama ('Old Comedy has a preponderance

[63] Ps.-Xen. *Ath. Pol.* 2. 18 and Ar. *Ach.* 631 (*κωμῳδεῖ τὴν πόλιν ἡμῶν καὶ τὸν δῆμον καθυβρίζει*).

[64] Pl. *Rep.* 395e *κακηγοροῦντάς τε καὶ κωμῳδοῦντας ἀλλήλους καὶ αἰσχρολογοῦντας, μεθύοντας ἢ καὶ νήφοντας*, ibid. 452d *ἐξῆν τοῖς τότε ἀστείοις πάντα ταῦτα κωμῳδεῖν* (where *οἱ ἀστεῖοι* are the people who invent *τὰ ἀστεῖα*, expounded by Aristotle, *Rhet.* 3. 10–11), *Gorg.* 462e (*δια-κωμῳδεῖν*), *Apol.* 31d (*ἐπι-κωμῳδεῖν*); Lys. 24. 18; Arist. *Poet.* 1458^{b}32 and (*δια-κωμῳδεῖν*) 1458^{b} 6 (*pace* comm., there is no reason to suppose that either of the critics mentioned—Ariphrades and Euclides—is some obscure comic poet: cf. Lucas ad locc.).

[65] *Eccl.* 889 ('jokes' like *θανάτῳ μέλημα*, 905); *Vesp.* 1318 ('arselicking', more or less: see J. Henderson, *The Maculate Muse: Obscene Language in Attic Comedy*^{2} (Oxford 1991) 167).

[66] Bergson, *Le Rire* (p. 75 n. 103 below: Sypher, *Comedy*, 144): 'the comic in words follows closely on the comic in situation and is finally merged, along with the latter, in the comic in [dramatic] character'.

[67] *Rep.* 606c: on the sense of *ἰδίᾳ* see Shorey's note in the Loeb edition.

of the ridiculous. New Comedy abandons this'). Between the two, however, we find an inventory of mechanisms of 'laughter' (*gelôs*), consisting largely of types of joke which could be quite independent of drama ('. . . repetition . . . diminutives . . .'), and are indeed so treated by other late-antique sources.[68] Like Plato and like us, the author of the treatise acknowledges, by implication, that comedy is not necessarily a dramatic genre or, indeed, a genre in any strict sense at all.

Genres, along with more diffuse entities such as modes, have been subjected to an unusually patient and informed discussion by Alastair Fowler. His *Kinds of Literature* can serve as a suitable point of reference. Genres, as Fowler says, are not fixities. They change, because 'every literary work changes the genre it relates to'. Yet they are realities, and historically based realities. That is, they arise and reach a characteristic state in specifiable cultures at specifiable periods; they change, more or less, as new instances in each period are created; and they commonly change most of all when new instances are created in cultures and periods removed from the genre's presumed source. Fowler himself seeks to define the historical basis more narrowly. 'Genre' means a group of works 'belonging integrally . . . to the culture of a particular society', and when the members of that culture identify the works as belonging to a particular genre, they are in effect identifying an element of their culture: they—and we, looking back to the works of their culture—are interpreting, rather than classifying. Relatable groups which belong to different cultures and periods, such as Attic tragedy and Elizabethan tragedy, are to be thought of as belonging to a single mode, but not a single genre.[69]

The justification for this view of genre, however, is evidently the perceived degree of likeness normally associated with the instances belonging to any one culture and period as against those belonging to others. Attic tragedy has its characteristics; Elizabethan tragedy has its characteristics; modern tragedy (perhaps) has its characteristics; but they are not necessarily the same characteristics. In Fowler's own words: 'there is a good deal to say

[68] *Tract. Coisl.*, pp. 24, 40, 24–36 Janko. Hermog. *περὶ μεθόδου δεινότητος* 34 (*περὶ τοῦ κωμικῶς λέγειν* , 451. 11 Rabe) has a very similar list of mechanisms, but with a mixture of exemplifications from comic drama, from oratory, and (in one case) from life ('non ex scriptore sed e vitae usu fictum', *CGF* 82 Kaibel). For other versions of the list see Janko, *Aristotle on Comedy*, 24–37, 164–6.

[69] A. Fowler, *Kinds of Literature* (Oxford 1982) 23, 133, 37–52, 135.

about Attic tragedy, Elizabethan tragedy, perhaps even modern tragedy, but not much that makes sense about all tragedy'. And he adds: 'without some historical localization, discussion of genre tends towards the vacuous'. One gathers, then, that not only is discussion about instances of a genre (in Fowler's sense of the word) distinguishable from discussion about instances of a mode (in his sense): mode-talk is suspect, as genre-talk is not. As before, however, the basis for that conclusion, evidently, is perceived likenesses or unlikenesses between the instances. So Fowler feels able to commend the use of the supposed mode-word 'tragedy' to cover both Attic and Elizabethan serious drama: 'the changes that brought the Attic to the English form . . . certainly confused classical critics. All the same . . . through all the changes . . . there is an impressive coherence in the modal grouping.' On a matter of detail, again, he is able to note that 'Ibsen has shown us that tragedy is not [i.e. not necessarily] about kings', yet that 'we should not conclude from changes in tragedy's matter [i.e. specifiable matter] that it has none'. And on comparable grounds Fowler is happy to allow that 'some closely related societies (French, Italian, British) recognize roughly similar principal modes such as comic, tragic, pastoral'.[70]

This 'recognizing' may be done by the historical societies in question, but the actual recognition of the 'modal' similarities themselves is clearly up to Fowler and the rest of us: *we* are the ones who must see that they *are* similarities. Likewise (one is left to infer) it is for us to recognize the supposedly more impressive similarities between instances of a given genre (in Fowler's sense): this must be so, or else none of us (Fowler or anyone else) would have any way of knowing that they *are* more impressive. Identification, whether modal or generic, is a matter of interpreting, and we are to be the interpreters. But if so, it must also be for us, as part of our interpretative function, to decide which sets of similarities are in fact the more impressive sets. And it follows, despite Fowler's arguments, that our interpretations, based on perceived likenesses and unlikenesses, are not, after all, limited to historically based identifications and may, if need be, override them.[71]

[70] Ibid. 47, 135, 65, 133.

[71] It also follows a fortiori that more mechanically historicist arguments like that of Heath—who is wholly 'sceptical of broader [sc. transcultural] generic [etc.] categories, believing that poetics can only be profitable as a historical enquiry into the workings of a particular system of conventions in a given historical and cultural

By common perception, including Fowler's own perception, Elizabethan and Attic tragedy have profound likenesses, such that their overall grouping produces an 'impressive coherence'. In specific cases, indeed, the consequential likenesses perceived between an Attic and an Elizabethan play may be as impressive as those different likenesses perceived between one of these plays and other plays from its own culture. For instance, Euripides' *Electra* or Sophocles' *Electra* arguably have as much in common with some English revenge plays as they do with, say, Aeschylus' *Persians*.[72] We do not conclude that there are three genres of tragedy here: Attic, Elizabethan, and transcultural revenge. We conclude that Attic and Elizabethan tragedy, which share many likenesses including those perceptible between their revenge plays, form a generic continuum which, as it happens, is transcultural.

By the same argument, we might interpret as a genre the numerous instances of the comedy of manners from Menander to Molière (and beyond), on the grounds of their perceived likenesses. But if so, and by the same argument, we would find it difficult to interpret as a genre a group of instances drawn partly from the Menandrian comedy of manners and partly from the early comedies of Aristophanes, notwithstanding the fact that all these instances belong to what is, by comparison, a single culture and a single period, and share an unchallenged right to a single label, *kômôidia*, and notwithstanding the fact that Aristophanic comedy (or at any rate its earlier instances) itself seems to be, by any standards, a genre. Tragedy, then, is recognizably a genre, whereas comedy—even in its earliest Western phase—looks uncomfortably like something wider.

context' (*Poetics*, 1)—are doomed from the start. There is certainly no way of eliminating our own interpretative-identificatory role. Even if we pretend that 'genre' *must* presuppose what Fowler calls 'the culture of a particular society', who else but us, after all, can ever decide where 'the culture of a particular society' begins and ends? Do the English Romantic poets who produced a dozen and more sub-Shakespearean tragedies belong to 'the same' culture as Shakespeare himself? Is the culture that spawned Nonnus' epic *Dionysiaca* 'the same' culture as the one that gave birth to the Homeric epics twelve centuries before? Is the culture of Menander 'the same' as the culture of Aristophanes? These are questions which someone—*us*—still has to answer; and it can only be us, in whatever age 'we' happen to live, if only because (though not only because) only we aftercomers have the perspective to decide such questions.

[72] Cf. the spread in J. Kerrigan, *Revenge Tragedy: Aeschylus to Armageddon* (Oxford 1996).

The perceived likenesses of a genre constitute what Fowler calls a 'generic repertoire'. Every genre has a characteristic, though not necessarily invariable, repertoire—as tragedy does, with its cumulative dramatic form, concentrated action, heightening, its great fall, its sense of an ending, and so on. Members of genres resemble one another as members of families do: they have common sets of characteristics, but *each* member need not be expected to have *each* characteristic in the set. And at this point Fowler invokes, in suitably modified form, the Wittgensteinian principle of family resemblances.[73]

Genres are historically based: modes come out of them. Modes are the perceived character of what were once (and may still be) genres, when that character is embodied in other genres.[74] If we perceive something of tragedy in *Anna Karenina*, we continue to think of the book as a novel, but as a novel in the tragic mode: the generic repertoire of tragedy is partly present, but not fully determinative. One could, and to some extent does, say the equivalent in respect of *comic* elements in non-dramatic works: we perceive something of 'comedy', but . . . The trouble is, one would have to say it with such frequency as to discredit the procedure, and one would find oneself saying it up to, and beyond, the perimeters of literature and art—as with the joke and the cartoon.

In passing, Fowler touches on what he calls 'archetypes'. These are 'psychological rather than literary types', and 'they appear just as much in other media, other fields of discourse, other arts'.[75] In Fowler's terminology, then, what we customarily call 'comedy' is presumably an archetype. He does indeed use the word of Northrop Frye's famous four 'mythic' types, of which comedy was one. In Frye's schema, however, the four types were said to be comedy, romance, tragedy, and satire (corresponding symbolically to spring, summer, autumn, and winter), with each type subsuming works of diverse eras and genres.[76] Frye's 'romance' and 'satire' are not our concern. But if the present argument is sound, Frye's treatment of 'comedy' has an independent justification which his parallel treatment of 'tragedy' lacks.

[73] Fowler, *Kinds*, 55–74, 156–9, 40–4.

[74] See Fowler's very constructive discussion: ibid. 55–6, 106–11, 167–9.

[75] Ibid. 151; cf. his discussion of 'permanent' potentialities of literature, ibid. 235–55.

[76] Ibid. 150; Frye, *Anatomy*, 131–239.

Genres are historically based entities. As such, they develop; and it is appropriate here to draw attention to a common but widely neglected pattern in the historical development of most genres, a pattern neglected, indeed, even by the historically minded Fowler himself. In his list of the various possible constituents of the generic repertoire, from 'external structure' to 'reader's task', Fowler includes 'occasion'. 'Many kinds', he writes, 'used to have a characteristic occasion, at least initially.' Examples given are such minor types as the epithalamium, but he adds: 'occasion has been a feature of other kinds too. Attic tragedy was partly determined by festival requirements; and several of Shakespeare's plays have a large festal element.' Then he concludes by returning to the minor concerns of the masque, the epitaph, and the modern poetry-reading.[77] One would not gather from these remarks that there is actually a consideration of fundamental importance here: the austere vocabulary of 'occasion' and 'occasional' is not, perhaps, best fitted to reveal the fact.

Many of our generic categories—including most of our main generic categories—are Greek in origin; and most of the Greek genres began as *performative* entities, whose original character was variously dependent on an external performative context, and whose original definition must be treated as virtually equivalent to that context. The paean was a song sung in honour of the god Apollo at a gathering of Apollo's worshippers. The epithalamium was a celebratory song sung outside the bridal chamber at a wedding ceremony. Tragedy was a kind of drama performed in honour of, and at a specific festival of, the god Dionysus. At its earliest—formative and *per*formative—stage, it is likely, though not actually necessary, that a genre also has a full set of *textual* characteristics with which its audiences, and authors, learn to associate it, and by which it can be identified. What it is necessarily identified by is its *context*. Most textual characteristics will be secondary—chronologically and, at this stage, logically too. A paean, no doubt, will always have had such minimal textual characteristics as reference or allusion to the god in whose honour it was to be sung (though no such reference or allusion was ever part of the characteristic textual repertoire of tragedy as we have it). But in general, the characteristics of each genre will

[77] Fowler, *Kinds*, 67; the topic crops up again at ibid. 152–3, but nothing said there has a particular bearing on the present discussion.

have accrued in the course of time. In this way the paean, the epithalamium, and tragedy duly did acquire their characteristic textual repertoires, and in these and other Greek genres, over long periods, the repertoire was both extensive and remarkably settled.[78]

Comedy, however, despite a comparable contextual identity, was different, as the development from Aristophanes to Menander so clearly shows. To restate the point: while Aristophanes' earlier plays, from *Acharnians* to *Frogs*, show the kind and degree of resemblance to each other that one would expect of a Greek genre, late Aristophanic comedy, such as *Plutus*, is conspicuously different, and Menandrian comedy of manners, which *Plutus* prefigures, still more so. In particular, then, the prominent characteristics of Aristophanes' earlier drama—its discontinuities, 'sense of duty', obscenity, satire, slapstick, high poetry, one-off jokes, featured song and dance—mean that it could *never*, on textual grounds, be regarded as 'the same genre' as the decorous and homogeneous drama of Menander. By any reasonable standards of perceived likeness, what antiquity itself—revealingly—decided to separate into 'Old' and 'New' comedy are two different entities.[79] However, the *kômôidia* of Aristophanes, early and late, and of Menander is still all one *kômôidia*, whatever the differences in textual repertoire, because its performative context defines it as *kômôidia*.

Even before the time of Aristophanes, furthermore, comic drama was already quite diverse. We know relatively little of Greek comedy between its institutionalization at Athens (486 BC) and the start of Aristophanes' own career, but in Athens we do know of those noteworthy experiments of Crates and Pherecrates;[80] and before them we know of Epicharmus, whose distinctive type of comic drama was on view in Sicily early in the fifth century at the time when comedy was first institutionalized in Attica. The genealogical relation between the Sicilian and Attic forms is unclear, but various differences between them are

[78] For a rather different treatment of some of these issues, see L. E. Rossi, 'I generi letterari e le loro leggi scritte e non scritte nelle letterature classiche', *BICS* 18 (1971) 69–94.

[79] With or without 'Middle Comedy': on the ancient history of the bipartite/tripartite categorization see Janko, *Aristotle on Comedy*, 244, together with the material discussed at 40–1 and 242–50.

[80] Above, p. 51.

striking. The apparent absence of song, of a chorus, and of personal satire in Epicharmus' plays; their length (perhaps four times shorter than Aristophanes'); Epicharmus' penchant for narrative speech, allegory, and mythological burlesque: all this suggests the scale of the difference.[81]

These plays are clearly 'comedy' and were clearly so regarded by various observers, including Aristotle ('[the invention of] *kômôidia* is claimed . . . by the Megarians of Sicily, on the grounds that Epicharmus came from there').[82] Yet the performative context of these plays was different from that of their Attic counterparts. Accordingly, it seems, they had their own local contextual label, *dramata*, and Aristotle and others seem to have felt hesitant about applying the Attic label, *kômôidiai*, to them directly.[83] But with or without Epicharmus, it is obvious that comedy—meaning comic drama—was special. Greek genres in general, and tragedy in particular, do not present anything like this picture of diversity and eccentric development.[84] And the Greeks' own contextual labelling (we can now see) serves partly to reflect this unusual textual situation, but partly to conceal it.

Compare and contrast the subsequent histories of tragedy and comedy. Tragedy, which seems to have its generic repertoire when we first meet it in Aeschylus, keeps it throughout the period of classical and post-classical Greece, and seems also to keep it thereafter. Tragic drama reappears sporadically, in a very few cultures, in sufficiently clear relationship to Greek tragedy to permit discussions, from the Renaissance to George Steiner, to be visibly discussions of the same thing, and to make it feasible for Steiner, like many of his predecessors, to argue persuasively that tragedy is a serious dramatic form, but that not all serious drama is tragedy: tragedy has specific textual properties by which we

[81] See Pickard-Cambridge, *Dithyramb*, 230–88.

[82] *Poet.* III (cf. V). For the Sicilian Theocritus, Epicharmus simply 'invented *kômôidia*' (*ὁ τὰν κωμῳδίαν εὑρὼν Ἐπίχαρμος*, *Epigr.* 18 Gow = *AP* IX. 600). Similarly Anon. *de Com.* (test. 9, *CGF* 89 Kaibel) and others. At *Tht.* 152e Plato includes Epicharmus among *τῶν ποιητῶν οἱ ἄκροι τῆς ποιήσεως ἑκατέρας* with the phrase *κωμῳδίας μὲν Ἐπίχαρμος*—but this turns out to mean, not 'purveyor of comedy', but 'spiritual founder of comedy', as is shown by the continuation, *τραγῳδίας δὲ Ὅμηρος* (cf. Pl. *Rep.* 595b–c).

[83] That is, *kômôidiai* in the plural: Pickard-Cambridge, *Dithyramb*, 276–7; Kaibel in *RE* vi. 36.

[84] One ancient genre (*vel sim.*) that does is Roman *satura*, distinct from, but often associated with, comedy.

continue to recognize it in its various transcultural embodiments.[85]

The history of comedy continues to be very different. Menandrian-Roman comedy of manners is revived in the Renaissance. In the medieval West, in the meantime, the word 'comedia' (and vernacular equivalents) is retained for some categories of broadly 'optimistic' literature, without special reference to drama, and generally without any reference to a wealth of more or less disregarded popular forms, dramatic and otherwise. Comedy of manners, once revived, is variously modified, in the direction of something itself more various (as with Shakespeare) or less (as with the constrictions of eighteenth-century 'sentimental comedy'). And then in the nineteenth and especially the twentieth centuries, after a series of theoretical and practical reinterpretations (perhaps in that order), comedy begins to display its diversity in new ways that, very properly, attract increasing critical attention. It maintains itself as uncomplicated comic theatre, prolifically, from Feydeau to Neil Simon *et al.* At the same time, and more disturbingly, it expands into a range of 'serious' drama which is frequently perceived as, and even labelled by its authors, tragicomedy. So Beckett used the word of *Waiting for Godot* in his English version; Strindberg of *Creditors*; Ibsen, retrospectively, of *The Wild Duck*; so Dürrenmatt called *The Old Lady's Visit* 'eine tragische Komödie', and Ionesco *The Chairs* 'farce tragique'.[86]

These were hardly the first wide-scale experiments with tragicomic drama: that distinction belongs to the sixteenth and seventeenth centuries, which produced the 'mixed tragedies' of Cinthio and the pastoral drama of Guarini and Fletcher.[87] Nevertheless, the modern perception, understandably, is that, for all its well-known Renaissance antecedents, tragicomedy is itself peculiarly modern. An imposing list of quotations could be mustered, from Schelling ('the combination of opposites, especially tragic and comic, is the fundamental principle of modern drama') to

[85] G. Steiner, *The Death of Tragedy* (New York 1961).

[86] All designations in the published versions, except for the Ibsen, which the author came up with when discussing a Copenhagen performance in 1898: Henrik Ibsen, *Samlede Verker*, ed. F. Bull, H. Koht, and D. A. Seip, x (Oslo 1932) 38.

[87] The name 'tragicomedy', but little else, was derived from Plautus (see p. 81 n. 131 below). Cinthio used 'tragicomedia' of his *Altile* (1543). The seminal tragicomedy in the pastoral mode was Guarini's *Il Pastor Fido* (1583).

Victor Hugo ('the drama . . . which in the same breath moulds . . . tragedy and comedy is the salient characteristic . . . of the literature of today'), from Thomas Mann ('the essential achievement of modern art is that it has ceased to recognize the categories of the tragic and the comic or the dramatic classifications, tragedy and comedy, and sees life as tragicomedy') to Anouilh (' "I play everything . . ., tragedy and comedy." "And you never get them mixed up . . .?" "Never used to in the old days. But with the plays we get served up these days . . ." ').[88] And—what concerns us most—the modern perception is also that this modern tragicomedy represents an expansion of the flexible comic, not of its supposed, tragic, opposite. Dürrenmatt's motto, 'we can achieve the tragic out of comedy', is representative.[89] As early as 1772, indeed, Goldsmith saw sentimental comedy in these terms. This 'new species of dramatic composition' presented 'the virtues of a private life' and the 'distresses . . . of mankind', and 'in this manner . . . the comic poet is invading the province of the tragic muse'.[90]

Meanwhile, alongside modern comic theatre and tragicomedy, comedy proliferates in cinematic drama, in non-dramatic fiction and elsewhere, and is shown to be worthy of serious intellectual scrutiny in its diverse proto-artistic manifestations, such as the joke (scrutinized by Freud) and the carnival (scrutinized by

[88] Schelling, *Philosophie der Kunst* (1802–3), in Friedrich Schelling, *Sämtliche Werke* (Stuttgart 1859) v. 718; Hugo, Preface to *Cromwell* (1827); Mann, Preface to Joseph Conrad, *The Secret Agent*, trans. as *Der Geheimagent* by E. W. Freissler (Berlin 1926): Thomas Mann, *Altes und Neues* (Stockholm 1953) 501; Anouilh, *Le Rendez-vous de Senlis* (1937), Act 3 (Philémon and Isabelle): Jean Anouilh, *Pièces roses* (Paris 1942) 186. The peculiar modernity of tragicomedy is denied by Seidensticker (*Palintonos Harmonia*, 10, 35, and *passim*), because he reads tragicomedy back into Euripides *et al.* Such a recategorization is not without precedent, though the usual beneficiary was formerly Shakespeare: 'Shakespeare is always a writer of tragicomedy', Yeats ('The tragic theatre', 1910, in W. B. Yeats, *Essays* (London 1924) 297); 'Shakespeare's plays are not in the rigorous or critical sense either tragedies or comedies, but compositions of a distinct kind', Johnson (in Raleigh, *Johnson on Shakespeare*, 15). See further p. 96 n. 188 below.

[89] Friedrich Dürrenmatt, 'Theaterprobleme' (1954), in Dürrenmatt, *Theater-Schriften und Reden*, ed. E. Brock-Sulzer (Zurich 1966) 122.

[90] In 'A Comparison between Sentimental and Laughing Comedy': *The Miscellaneous Works of Oliver Goldsmith* (London 1806), iv. 459. Cf. J. L. Styan, *The Dark Comedy* (Cambridge 1968) 43: 'the conventions of the comic stage readily admit an admixture of seemingly extraneous elements like the tragic and the pathetic, whereas tragedy has its fabric dangerously stretched to admit the comic or the farcical.'

Bakhtin).[91] And yet, notwithstanding such theoretical advances and such manifold opportunities for critics and theorists to respond to the range of comic art, and comic proto-art, modern theory has remained quaintly respectful towards the notion that comedy is 'really'—'still'—a dramatic form, like tragedy. The spurious opposition with tragedy has had a hypnotic effect, and critical or theoretical perceptions, striking as they may be, are not properly absorbed.

As a particular, and particularly important, example of hypnosis, consider further the belief that comic characters and their behaviour are in some way deformed. By the Renaissance this principle had been firmly moralized,[92] so that deformations had become object lessons and comedy, accordingly, by 'dramatizing the faults of mankind',[93] had become the correction of vice. In Sidney's words: 'comedy is an imitation of the common errors of our life', and these are represented 'in the most ridiculous and scornful sort that may be; so as it is impossible that any beholder can be content to be such a one'.[94] It is implicit in this whole tradition of thought that the comic dramatist and his audience are above the particular 'errors' depicted and hence above those persons represented as being subject to them. Comic laughter, then, is essentially ridicule and connotes superiority: the audience (in Hobbes's famous words) apprehend 'some deformed thing in another, by comparison whereof they suddenly applaud themselves' in an experiential moment of 'sudden glory'.[95]

This view of comedy was opposed on one front by Samuel Johnson, reflecting in 1751 'that every dramatic composition which raises mirth is comic; and that, to raise mirth, it is by no means universally necessary that the personages should be either mean or corrupt'.[96] Part of his precept was put into practice by

[91] See below pp. 75–6.

[92] The beginning of the moralizing process is visible in antiquity: cf. Donatus, 'from which one learns', p. 57 n. 44 above. It may even go back to the Hellenistic period: cf. S. Halliwell, 'Ancient interpretations of ὀνομαστὶ κωμῳδεῖν in Aristophanes', *CQ* 34 (1984) 84.

[93] Molière: above, p. 56.

[94] Philip Sidney, *An Apology for Poetry* (1595), in *Elizabethan Critical Essays*, ed. G. G. Smith (Oxford 1904), i. 176–7. Unlike Aristotle's 'errors' (p. 56 n. 40 above), Sidney's are unequivocally moral.

[95] *Leviathan* (1651), i. 6. Cf. e.g. Quintil. 6. 3. 7 (with reference to laughter as such): 'a derisu non procul abest risus' ('le rire n'est pas loin de la risée'). The tradition goes back to Plato (*Phlb.* 49d–50a).

[96] *The Rambler*, 125.

Beaumarchais, whose *Marriage of Figaro*, produced in 1784, pointedly challenged assumptions of social superiority by satirizing the aristocracy: 'except for the Count and his agents, everyone in the play behaves as he ought to'.[97] A different challenge comes from a succession of thinkers in France and Germany: from Sébastien Mercier, advocate of sentimental drama, who declares in 1773 that 'laughter and tears . . . are not separate from each other';[98] from Jean Paul Richter, who, in his *Introduction to Aesthetics* (1804), senses that *humour*, as a newly identified species of the comic, has some relation to seriousness and to the sympathetic emotions, and far from involving any glorious comparison between our individual selves and others, sets all individuals ('the finite') against the ideal and 'recognizes no individual folly, no fools, but only folly and a mad world'.[99] By transcending the individual, then, this tolerant humour implies a particular view of life. It is perhaps (Jean Paul reflects) a peculiarly romantic, therefore modern, version of the comic, and 'the one and only Shakespeare' (an honorary romantic for so many German theorists) excels in it; but then again it may be that 'all comic poetry must become romantic—that is, humorous'.[100] One might have thought that English critics, with the example of Shakespeare in front of them, would be eager to take the point. Hazlitt, for one, was determined not to: 'the fault, then, of Shakespeare's comic muse is, in my opinion, that it is too good-natured and magnanimous', for 'we sympathize with his characters oftener than we laugh at them'.[101] And in France, nearly a century later, Bergson

[97] Preface to *Le Mariage de Figaro*.

[98] *Du Théâtre ou nouvel essai sur l'art dramatique*, v.

[99] In which respect humour is taken to differ from 'the comic', which involves only contrasts between finite and finite: *Jean Pauls Sämtliche Werke*, ed. E. Berend, xi (Weimar 1935) 111–12, in the course of a largely metaphysical account of 'der Humor'. The 'folly' passage runs: 'Es gibt für ihn keine einzelne Thorheit, keine Thoren, sondern nur Thorheit und eine tolle Welt.' Hobbes's theory is specifically rejected on p. 108.

[100] Ibid. xi. 113–14, Shakespeare's 'Romantic' qualities included the sense of infinite openness epitomized in the title of a Goethe essay, 'Shakespeare und kein Ende'. Cf. then the openness of comedy itself: below, pp. 91–3.

[101] William Hazlitt, *Lectures on the English Comic Writers* (1819), Lecture II, following Schlegel's third 'Lecture on Dramatic Art' (*Vorlesungen über dramatische Kunst und Literatur*, 1808): 'The comic writer must . . . take care to avoid anything calculated to excite . . . sympathy with the situation of his characters': *A. W. Schlegel's Vorlesungen über dramatische Kunst und Literatur*, ed. G. V. Amoretti (2 vols., Bonn 1923) i. 31.

could still win new generations of admirers for the neo-classical view, majestically reformulated in his essay, *Laughter* (1900). Comic laughter and all laughter (Bergson hardly distinguishes)[102] is seen as a kind of natural mechanism developed by the human species to protect its social groups from the dangers of individual inflexibility: laughter is laughter *at*, and it has a purpose. Physical ineptitude, temperamental obstinacy, and outmoded fashion are its targets; and, as such, laughter, in Bergson's classic phrases, is 'above all a corrective', 'a sort of social gesture' which 'pursues a utilitarian aim of general improvement', 'its appeal is to intelligence, pure and simple', 'its function is to intimidate by humiliating', it is 'incompatible with emotion', it would 'fail in its object if it bore the stamp of sympathy or kindness'.[103] In this discussion, almost imperceptibly, 'the comic' in art is narrowed to the comic drama, and the particular tradition of comic drama which best fits Bergson's thesis, the comedy of manners, epitomized for him by Molière. And underpinning this narrow view of comedy, barely perceptible, is the unconsidered opposition with tragedy.

Since Bergson the ridicule-superiority view of the comic has been repeatedly challenged. In 1905 Freud made the indispensable distinction between 'purposeful' (in effect, aggressive) and 'innocent' jokes,[104] noting also that 'comparison of another person with ourself' is neither the only basis for 'comic pleasure' nor, when it is the basis, necessarily entails any feeling of superiority.[105] In 1908 Pirandello gave a definitive shape to the aesthetic of humour initiated by Jean Paul a century before.[106] Humour, he argued, was not the property of any one age or culture, but 'the result of a very special natural disposition' and a very special sense of life. What earlier theory had represented as a comparison, he reinterpreted as 'a perception of the opposite': 'I see an old lady . . .

[102] Cf. p. 63 n. 66 above.

[103] *Le Rire: essai sur la signification du comique* in the standard (and splendid) English translation by C. Brereton and F. Rothwell (*Laughter: An Essay on the Meaning of the Comic*): Sypher, *Comedy*, 187, 73, 64, 188, 180, 187.

[104] Freud, *Jokes*, 132–62. Freud himself (140) distinguishes two kinds of 'purpose', the hostile and the obscene, and only associates the hostile explicitly with aggression, but an aggressive element in the obscene is apparent even from his own discussion (cf. for instance his remarks on 'sexual aggression' on 141).

[105] Ibid. 256. His analyses of Falstaff and Don Quixote (ibid. 296–7) are noteworthy in this connection.

[106] Luigi Pirandello, *L'umorismo*, quoted as *On Humor* from the transl. by A. Illiano and D. P. Testa (Chapel Hill 1974).

all dolled-up like a young girl . . . I perceive that she is the opposite of what a respectable old lady should be.' This 'perception' (he proposed) was a feature of all comedy. The distinguishing feature of humour, which Jean Paul had identified as a contrast between the finite and the ideal, he took to be an additional 'feeling of the opposite', not necessarily sympathetic, but arguably associated with a bitter or 'perplexed' interest in the case ('perhaps she is distressed by it, and does it only because . . .').[107] A generation after Pirandello, Bakhtin offered a different perspective on the comic comparison, and the possibilities of transcending it, through his discussion of carnival humour, as represented in the popular rituals and spectacles of the Middle Ages and subsequently embodied in various literary works, notably those of Rabelais: 'carnival . . . is a special condition of the entire world'; 'carnival celebrated temporary liberation from the prevailing truth and from the established order'; it marked 'the suspension of all hierarchical rank'; it involved 'a special form of free and familiar contact' between people 'usually divided by the barriers of caste, property, profession and age'; carnival is distinct from 'modern negative satire' in which the satirist 'places himself above the object of his mockery'; its laughter is 'the laughter of all the people' and 'universal in scope'; it ensures that 'the entire world is seen in its comic aspect'.[108]

Yet notwithstanding these and other related contributions to the theory of comedy, belief in ridicule dies hard. 'The more sophisticated forms of humour', writes Arthur Koestler, 'evoke mixed, and sometimes contradictory, feelings; but whatever the mixture, it must contain one ingredient whose presence is indispensable: an impulse, however faint, of aggression.'[109] The

[107] *On Humor*, 91, 113, 116, 130–1. It is apparent from Pirandello's discussion that 'humour' must be a species of 'the comic', not something separate from it, and as so often, the gain represented by his specific insights seems to be much greater than anything achieved by even his strenuous endeavours to territorialize and partition comedy: cf. below, p. 93.

[108] M. Bakhtin, *Tvorchestvo François Rabelais i Narodnaya Kul'tura Srednevekov'ya i Renessansa* (written in 1940 and eventually published in Moscow in 1965), quoted here from the transl. by H. Iswolsky, *Rabelais and his World* (Cambridge, Mass. 1968) 7, 10–12. Jean Paul had already perceived the 'great equality' engendered by the medieval feast of fools (*Sämtliche Werke*, xi. 118–19). Bakhtin's otherwise generous acknowledgement of Jean Paul (*Rabelais*, 41–2) misses this point.

[109] A. Koestler, *The Act of Creation* (London 1964) 52.

phrasing makes it sound as if the aggression may be so faint as to be undetectable. What then prompts this insistence on it? Not so much (one infers) any of Koestler's impressively varied perspectives in art, psychology, or science. And not ignorance either: though he chooses, for instance, to ignore the contrary implications of Freud's theory of the joke, he is evidently well acquainted with it.[110] The basis of his argument emerges clearly enough: 'it is the aggressive element . . . which turns pathos into bathos, tragedy into comedy.'[111] The old opposition is simply too insidiously powerful to resist.

The general belief in ridicule (and much else) is propped up by the old opposition between tragedy and comedy. The question arises: what props up that opposition? What is it that makes it *still* so hard to resist? There seem to be a number of factors.

In the first place, the acknowledged fact that tragedy and comic drama do often have points of contrast. This does not actually make them determinative opposites, any more than (say) tobacco (which is bitter to the taste, popular with adults, etc.) is made determinatively opposite to milk chocolate (which is sweet to the taste, popular with children etc.) by virtue of such points of contrast. However, it gives the opposition a superficial plausibility.

Second, the fact that the opposition goes back to ancient Greece, where Western literature begins, and where Western perceptions of literature begin.

Third, the fact that it was Aristotle who articulated the opposition. The subsequent conversion of the opposition into a formula, in accordance with the schematic tendencies of later antiquity, would not have commended itself to neo-classical Europe without the *imprimatur* of his *Poetics*; and even today the *Poetics* probably carries more weight, for good or ill, than any other single literary-theoretical document, past or present.

Fourth, the auditory parallelism of the names *kômôidia* and *tragôidia* in Greek, and likewise of their Latin and vernacular European derivatives and counterparts ever since. Once again, such a phenomenon in itself shows nothing. In Greek, as in many languages, it is common for antonyms to lack parallel form,[112]

[110] *Der Witz* is quoted or referred to by Koestler, *Creation*, at pp. 55, 59, 86.

[111] *Creation*, 52.

[112] e.g. not one of the ten Pythagorean pairs of opposites listed by Aristotle in

while, conversely, parallel form itself may well imply some other relationship or none at all. Thus—to take the most obviously pertinent instances—*kômôidia* and *tragôidia* belong to a larger set of *-ôidia* nouns, among which there is at least one pair of opposites (*khorôidia*, 'group song'; *monôidia*, 'solo song');[113] then again, various items that are relatable, but clearly not relatable by any principle of opposition (e.g. *humnôidia*, 'hymn-singing'; *thrên-ôidia*, 'dirge-singing');[114] and again, other items that hardly involve much relationship at all.[115] And certainly there is nothing in the stem elements of our two words—'revel song' and 'goat song'—to suggest any kind of pairing whatsoever: *revel* and *goat* make a very unlikely couple.[116]

Fifth, the long-fashionable linguistic superstition that language is not merely a system of differences (as it self-evidently is), but of oppositions, and is problematic without oppositions. The superstition is no more than that.[117] Even in the immediate vicinity of

Metaphysics A 5 (986ª) has parallel form: *πέρας καὶ ἄπειρον, περιττὸν καὶ ἄρτιον, ἓν καὶ πλῆθος, δεξιὸν καὶ ἀριστερόν, ἄρρεν καὶ θῆλυ, ἠρεμοῦν καὶ κινούμενον, εὐθὺ καὶ καμπύλον, φῶς καὶ σκότος, ἀγαθὸν καὶ κακόν, τετράγωνον καὶ ἑτερόμηκες.*

113 See Plato, *Leg.* 764d–e.

114 Cf. esp. Aesch. *Agam.* 990–1: *τὸν δ' ἄνευ λύρας ὅμως ὑμνῳδεῖ | θρῆνον Ἐρινύος.*

115 e.g. *prosôidia*, which on its first occurrence apparently means 'address' (Aesch. fr. 299 *TGF*), seems, in this sense, tenuously related to most of the other members of the set.

116 The voluminous literature on the origins of comedy and tragedy offers no hint of any relationship, oppositional or other, between the elements *kôm-* and *trag-* in themselves: see discussions and bibliography in Pickard-Cambridge, *Dithyramb*, 149–66, 225–6; Csapo and Slater, *Context*, 89–101; G. A. Privitera, 'Origini della tragedia e ruolo del ditirambo', *Stud. Ital. Fil. Cl.* 84 (1991) 184–95; Silk and Stern, *Nietzsche on Tragedy*, 142–50; Handley, 'Comedy', 110–18. We do not know, even, which of the forms *kômôidia*/*tragôidia* is earlier, nor which was the earliest compound formation in the *-ôidia*/*-ôidos* series (though *-ôidos* doubtless comes before *-ôidia*: Pickard-Cambridge, *Dithyramb*, 149). Else, *Origin*, 114, considers the possibility that *tragôid-* was formed on the analogy of one of the other members of its series. O. Szemerényi, 'The origins of Roman drama and Greek tragedy', *Hermes* 103 (1975) 300–32, at 319–30, argues that *tragôid-* is the product of folk etymology. It is at least certain that the old attempt to derive *tragôidia* from *trugôidia* is absurd; the latter is a 'degraded' derivative of the former: Pickard-Cambridge, *Dithyramb*, 106–7; Taplin, 'Trugedy', 332–3; Else, *Origin*, 111 n. 18; P. Ghiron-Bistagne, 'Un calembour méconnu d'Aristophane', *REG* 86 (1973) 285–7. By comparison, the etymology of *kômôidia* (from *kômos*: Szemerényi, 'Origins' 321) is uncontroversial.

117 Lyons, *Semantics*, i. 270: 'From its very beginnings structural semantics (and indeed structural linguistics in general) has emphasized the importance of relationships of paradigmatic opposition. Trier himself opens his major work (1931) with the challenging statement that every word that is pronounced calls forth its opposite . . . in the consciousness of the speaker and hearer; and this statement

'tragedy' and 'comedy', such concepts as 'epic' and 'lyric'—*pace* Nietzsche—are not opposites and have no opposites,[118] and yet readers and critics of epic and lyric still cope.

And sixth, snobbery: the snobbery that has led many theorists (of whom Bergson is among the most illustrious) to equate comedy with the sophisticated comic drama of Molière or Shakespeare in tacit contradistinction to the sophisticated tragic drama of France or England, and so ignore the vulgarities of jokes and joking, organized and spontaneous, that have (no doubt) always figured in France, in England, and in all Western cultures in which theorizing about comedy has taken place.[119] Yet the effect of this attitude, ironically enough, is not to enhance the status of (even) Molière's or Shakespeare's comedy. Quite the contrary: the logic of such manoeuvres is to keep all comedy, including sophisticated comedy, firmly in its place.[120]

For (sad to say) the assumed opposition between tragedy and comedy is not a neutral one: it is not felt to be an opposition between equals. If it presupposed only a contrast between (say) emotion and intellect, things might have been otherwise. But given reference to contrasts like high against low, the opposition seems to have been endowed from the first with an evaluative implication which it has never lost. Comedy deals in low subjects (maybe); therefore it must be low art. Comedy represents

can be matched with similar assertions by other structural semanticists . . . Trier's statement . . . appears to imply that every word in the vocabulary has an opposite'. Lyons's own discussion is an effective antidote.

[118] Nietzsche, *Birth of Tragedy*, V–VIII; cf. Silk and Stern, *Nietzsche on Tragedy*, 152–3, 282.

[119] Cf. Frye, *Anatomy*, 22, on Matthew Arnold's 'touchstones' for the highest class of literature (in 'The Study of Poetry'): '[Arnold's] demotion of Chaucer and Burns to Class Two . . . seems to be affected by a feeling that comedy and satire should be kept in their proper place'.

[120] The modern theoretical preoccupation with tragicomedy has done nothing to shake the theorists' faith in the opposition. However the tragicomic is construed, its elements are still taken to be the traditional opposites. This was the pattern in the first tragicomic age, the Renaissance, with its quest for what Battista Guarini called 'a third perfect genre' which would mix tragedy's 'publicly responsible character, serious action, terror and commiseration' with comedy's 'private character, private business, laughter and wit' (*Compendio della poesia tragicomica* (1599): Dukore, *Dramatic Theory*, 150). It was equally the case in the second, as Schelling's flat assertion (quoted above, p. 71), reminds us: 'the combination of opposites, especially tragic and comic, is the fundamental principle of modern drama'. If anything, interest in the combination has served to further distract attention from the actual character of the elements combined.

distorted characters (maybe); therefore it must be distorted art. In *Poetics* IV, Aristotle offers some thoughts on the different sensibilities of (on the one hand) the writers who pointed the way towards comedy and (on the other) the precursors of its presumed opposite. The spiritual ancestors of the tragedians were the 'nobler' spirits; the forerunners of the comic poets were men of a 'meaner' disposition. And a corresponding principle (one gathers) was at work when tragedy and comedy themselves saw the light of day: writers were drawn to one or the other 'by their natural inclinations'.[121] Tragedy's nobler subject-matter, then, attracts the better sort of person, and a chain of damaging, and hugely influential, correlations is complete. But then again, it may be that comedy is also the victim of a deep-seated puritanical prejudice in favour of suffering as against joy, solemnity as against merriment. 'Sorrow is better than laughter . . . the art of fools is in the house of mirth', declared the author of Ecclesiastes.[122] Homer was wrong to show the gods as being under the influence of laughter, said Plato.[123] Christ never laughed, according to at least one early Father of the Church.[124] In a wholly perfect world, laughter (apparently) would cease to exist. Hence Baudelaire's bland suggestion that Paradise would have no humour in it, because 'the comic disappears at the level of absolute knowledge and power'; so 'laughter is Satanic' and 'the comic is an element of damnation and of diabolic origin'.[125]

But the particular contrast that has done most damage to the standing of comedy is surely that between the serious and the amusing, simply because in everyday life such a contrast almost invariably carries an implication that seriousness is preferred. 'I was only joking', we say—but never, 'I was only being serious'. And Byron said, 'And if I laugh at any mortal thing, 'Tis that I may not weep'[126]—but not, 'And if I weep . . ., 'Tis that I may not

[121] *οἱ μὲν σεμνότεροι . . . οἱ δὲ εὐτελέστεροι . . . κατὰ τὴν οἰκείαν φύσιν.*

[122] Eccl. vii. 3–4.

[123] *Rep.* 389a. 'How do you make God laugh? Tell him your future plans': Woody Allen, quoted in *The Independent* (London), Magazine Section, 7 Oct. 1989. The joke relies partly on this sense that no perfect being can be so imperfect as to laugh, however much our own imperfection might give grounds for amusement at our own expense.

[124] John Chrysostom, LVII. 69 Migne.

[125] Charles Baudelaire, 'De l'essence du rire' (1855): *Curiosités esthétiques*, ed. H. Lemaitre (Paris 1962) 245, 250, 246.

[126] *Don Juan*, IV. 4: seemingly derived from Petrarch, *Rime* 102 (Sonetto LXX), 'Pero, s'alcuna volta i'rido o canto . . .'.

laugh'. Laughing and joking in life are generally conceived of as playing, and we tend to believe (with Aristotle) that play is not an end, but a means to a serious purpose (*to spoudazein*), just as we assume (with the animal behaviourists) that animal play is subordinate to 'serious, real action'.[127] Once the terms of the covert analogy are spelled out, it is obvious that no true equivalence exists between 'serious' tragedy and 'serious' living: both tragedy and comedy, in or out of drama, are in this sense equally *play*ful. But 'serious' is opposite to 'frivolous' or 'trivial' as well as to 'funny', and the ambiguity goes back to Aristotle, whose *spoudaios* is opposite to *phaulos*, as well as to *geloios*.[128] Thanks in part to this ambiguity, it seems, we have learnt to misapply the preference for seriousness in life to art; and tragedy, which in Aristotle's terms presents 'serious action',[129] is regarded as itself more 'serious', closer to the norm, more reflective of the real. Accordingly, we not only pair tragedy and comedy: we pair them *in that order*. We tend to follow that order in any straightforward use of the pairing, and we tend to retain it in any secondary usage, as we already find Plato doing when he spoke of 'the whole tragedy and comedy of life'.[130] We perpetuate the order also in the label 'tragicomedy', and notwithstanding an abortive experiment in classical Attic comedy (appropriately enough),[131] no one seems to have made

[127] See Arist. *EN* 10. 6. 6 (1176^{b}) σπουδάζειν δὲ καὶ πονεῖν παιδιᾶς χάριν ἠλίθιον φαίνεται καὶ λίαν παιδικόν· παίζειν δ' ὅπως σπουδάζῃ, κατ' Ἀνάχαρσιν, ὀρθῶς ἔχειν δοκεῖ, and Gregory Bateson (and others) summarized by E. Goffman, *Frame Analysis* (New York 1974) 41. Aristophanic audiences no doubt tended to share Aristotle's assumption, hence the equation between joking and triviality occasionally voiced by Aristophanic characters (e.g. *Nub.* 296, cf. *Vesp.* 650), notwithstanding the comic irony of such self-deprecation. Among those to have taken play more 'seriously' in modern times are Johan Huizinga ('culture as play': *Homo Ludens* (Haarlem 1938)) and Hans-Georg Gadamer ('Play as the clue to ontological explanation', in *Truth and Method* (New York 1982) 91–118). For Greek antiquity, a few scattered advocacies of γέλως against σπουδή, from Simonides to Lucian, are noted by R. B. Branham, 'The wisdom of Lucian's Tiresias', *JHS* 109 (1989) 159–60.

[128] See p. 53 n. 31 above. The ambiguity in the Greek is made worse, arguably, by the fact that *spoudaios* can *also* stand as opposite to *ponêros*, 'morally bad' (e.g. Xen. *HG* 2. 3. 19, cf. Isoc. *Panath.* 185).

[129] Tragedy is *mimêsis praxeôs spoudaias* (*Poet.* VI).

[130] *Phlb.* 50b.

[131] *Kômôido-tragôidia* was used as the title of a play by the comic writer Alcaeus (?early 4th cent. BC: ii. 9–10 *PCG*) and also by a later comedian, Anaxandrides (mid-4th cent.: ii. 249–50 *PCG*). On the ascription of a third play with this title to the Sicilian Dinolochus, see *CGF* 149 Kaibel (testim. and fr. 3). The earliest known use of the more familiar compound is as 'tragicomoedia' in Plautus'

much effort to get the order reversed. 'To speak of theatre is to speak first of tragedy': in linguistic terms, we make 'tragedy' the marked form within the opposition.[132]

We privilege tragedy over comedy. We think: 'tragedy is the positive and comedy is the negative'.[133] We think: 'it is impossible to set the limits of the ludicrous until the serious has first been defined . . . We can discuss tragedy (which deals directly with the serious) without reference to comedy, but, when talking about comedy, must always refer to the standards of seriousness which give it its essential definition.'[134] We should reflect that for this last proposition to have any plausibility, all comedy would have to share Aristophanic comedy's preoccupation with its tragic counterpart: 'comedy has a sense of duty *too*'.

Through a great variety of theoretical orientations, theorists seem to be assuring us that there is something secondary, special, perhaps inexplicable, about comedy. 'Comic fancy', says Bergson, 'is a strange plant'[135]—whereas tragic fancy, no doubt, grows to order in every garden. In the innovatory sociological world of Erving Goffman's 'frame analysis', humour seems to involve frame-breaking rather than frame-making in its own right.[136] Is there even something perverse about comedy? One might infer as much from Freud, whose impressive discussion of jokes subsides into a claim that the comic, and all humour, involves a painless regression to an infantile state of pleasure at an 'expenditure which is too large': in our pursuit of the 'lost laughter of childhood', we are 'repudiating adult reality and serving an illusion'.[137]

prologue to his *Amphitruo*, 59 and 63. Whether or not Plautus took the word from his lost Greek model for the play (often assumed to have been a 'Middle Comedy', i.e. mid-4th cent.) is not known, but the form is not attested in Greek. See further Seidensticker, *Palintonos Harmonia*, 20–4.

[132] F. I. Zeitlin, *Playing the Other* (Chicago 1996) 349, and (on 'marked' forms) e.g. Lyons, *Semantics*, i. 305–11.

[133] W. Kerr, *Tragedy and Comedy* (New York 1967) 20.

[134] R. W. Corrigan, *Comedy: Meaning and Form*² (San Francisco 1981) 9–10. Contrast Plato (*Leg.* 816d–e): 'it is impossible to comprehend *ta spoudaia* without [*ta*] *geloia* or any of a pair of opposites without the other' (but as part of an argument whereby *both* comedy *and* tragedy are dismissed as deleterious to the philosopher's ideal state).

[135] In Sypher, *Comedy*, 102–3.

[136] Note e.g. Goffman's commendation of Bergson in the course of discussing 'primary frameworks' (*Frame Analysis*, 38–9).

[137] Freud, *Jokes*, 289, 302, 249, and 'Der Humor' (1927) (cited as S. Freud, 'Humour', tr. J. Strachey, Penguin Freud Library, xiv, ed. A. Dickson (Harmondsworth 1985) 425–33, at 432).

From a quite different starting-point Northrop Frye arrives at the conclusion that comedy's happy endings symbolize a hope of rebirth and renewal and, thereby, a conviction that it is 'death that is somehow unnatural, even though it always happens'.[138] It is Frye too who argues that in comedy 'actions are twisted to fit the demands of a happy ending', whereas tragedy, to which comedy is ostensibly opposite, is (apparently) free from any comparable distortion.[139]

The belief in comic distortion, of course, is fundamental to the extensive Aristotelian tradition of comic theory. But within or beyond the confines of that tradition, this belief is surely a corollary of a no less fundamental conviction: that comedy presupposes comparison, whereas serious art, such as tragedy, does not. In the Aristotelian tradition, comedy consists in 'the comparison of some eccentricity with a norm'.[140] Freud at one point allows himself the thought that 'we derive comic pleasure in general from a comparison', and adds: 'every such comparison . . . involves a certain degradation'.[141] The idea of comparison is still implicit in Jean Paul's contrast between finite and ideal and again in Pirandello's 'perception of the opposite'; and it is not challenged by his additional 'feeling of the opposite'. Even in Bakhtin's theory of carnival humour its presence can be felt. During carnival, Bakhtin tells us, 'the entire world is seen in its comic aspect', as if there was in truth a 'comic aspect' and carnival spoke that truth. But then that truth, it seems, constitutes only a 'temporary liberation from the prevailing truth', as if the prevailing truth is a temporarily hidden term of comparison, and as if comedy's truth is not real enough truth to be true once carnival is over.

Comedy, unlike tragedy, is supposed to be based on a comparison. But what grounds are there for the supposition? When we delight in Laurel and Hardy, the one 'so fat' and the other 'so stupid',[142] and in Stan's benign smile and sublime unawareness of

[138] N. Frye, *A Natural Perspective* (New York 1965) 122.

[139] *Anatomy*, 206.

[140] B. Aikin-Sneath, *Comedy in Germany in the First Half of the Eighteenth Century* (Oxford 1936) 13, summing up the rationalist theory of Johann Christoph Gottsched and his age.

[141] *Jokes*, 272–3.

[142] Characterizations by Spike Milligan in a BBC television tribute to Laurel and Hardy.

the havoc some well-meant action of his is about to cause his friend, the one thing we are not doing is discrediting the smile, the sublime unawareness, or even the prospective havoc by comparing them with our 'serious' world to their disadvantage. Arguably we make no comparison at all. Alternatively, if we do, we do so no more than we do when watching the right and inevitable progression of Oedipus to his doom, or the wrong and unnecessary progression of Lear to his. And when we exchange the world of Laurel and Hardy for the light of day, we are certainly no more aware of a reassertion of prevailing experiential truths than when we leave the worlds of Oedipus or Lear. That is: in a very extended sense of the word 'comparison', it may be said that *all* response to experience and *all* articulation of this response in language or any other medium involves comparison, a placing of one experience against another, one thought against another, a distinguishing of one time, place, quality, identity, entity, from another. Does comedy involve this any more than tragedy involves it? Or indeed any more than any other product of experience, or incitement to experience, involves it? 'Man is the only animal that laughs and weeps', says Hazlitt, 'for he is the only animal that is struck with the difference between what things are and what they ought to be.'[143] Comparison (it follows) must underlie grief as much as it underlies amusement, and so too it must also underlie most feelings that are likely to generate art, or be generated by art, from perplexity to indignation, from curiosity to fear, from achievement to loss, from tolerance to intolerance. Pure love, perhaps, is absolute, and does not presuppose comparison. If so, it cannot be love of things as we know them, because things as we know them are always imperfect, or, even if we are beguiled into thinking them perfect, they are surrounded by other things which are seen to be less perfect than themselves. In so far as comedy does involve comparison, therefore, there is still nothing specially or distinctively comparative about it or the responses associated with it.

Our feelings, from perplexity to love, are responses to the truth as we see it. If (with Bakhtin) we may speak of truth, we may say that comedy, as the product of a response to experience, can speak

[143] *Lectures on the English Comic Writers*: the opening sentence of Lecture I. Once again, though, much laughter is only 'comparative' in a very extended sense, e.g. the laughter of hysteria, or of babies being tickled, or of friends greeting.

truth—comedy *too*, as Aristophanes puts it. And this is hardly a novel suggestion. Perhaps the single most remarkable feature of the history of comic theory is that the idea of comic truth first establishes itself in antiquity, in the heyday of belief in comic distortion and at a time when belief in the opposition with tragedy (serious, therefore truthful, tragedy) was both fully operative and at least more speciously plausible than it is today.

The idea of comic truth appears in the ancient world as a conception of comic realism. This variant of comic theory clearly presupposes the lifelike qualities of Menandrian comedy of manners, and it is no coincidence that its earliest attestation should be a Hellenistic scholar's famous question: 'O Menander, O life, which of you imitated the other?'[144] Elsewhere, though, unqualified assertions are the norm: we find a Graeco-Roman intellectual of the same era apparently responding to comic drama in general as to 'a mirror of everyday life', and Cicero, at the end of the Hellenistic age, offering a composite description of comedy as 'an imitation of life, a mirror of custom, a reflection of truth'.[145] Any possibility of conflict with the more familiar classical argument that associates comedy with ridicule and distortion is now reduced by a certain shift of emphasis onto the 'low' qualities of the characters and the life represented: here, perhaps, begins the belief, still strong in our own day, that low life, whether socially or morally low, is somehow more 'real' than other kinds. At all events, it is as a mirror of *everyday* life that comedy first stakes a formal claim to truth.

It cannot be said that much intelligence is applied to the task of working out this claim in antiquity or in the Renaissance, when serious theorizing resumes, or indeed until the turn of the nineteenth century. Then, after centuries of deference to the now established principle that 'comedy feigns in a verisimilar manner',[146] the Western world is suddenly face to face with

[144] Aristophanes of Byzantium (Syrian. *Comm. in Hermog.* 2. 23. 6 Rabe): see R. Pfeiffer, *History of Classical Scholarship* (Oxford 1968) 190–1.

[145] Livius Andronicus ('cotidianae vitae speculum') and Cicero ('imitationem vitae, speculum consuetudinis, imaginem veritatis'), quoted by Donatus, *De Comoedia* (*CGF* 67 Kaibel). Horace's robust question, 'ridentem dicere verum | quid vetat?' (*Sat.* 1. 1. 24–5), is similarly unqualified. See further the discussions of associated material by Janko, *Aristotle on Comedy*, 49–51, and Zanker, *Realism*, 133–50.

[146] Francesco Robortello, *Explicatio eorum omnium quae ad Comoediae artificium pertinent* (1548): Dukore, *Dramatic Theory*, 126.

notions like Jean Paul's, that the humorist may be, in one sense, purveying distortion, yet is, in another sense, reflecting reality, because what he actually sees is 'a mad world'.[147] The relationship between humour and reality, thus, is made more complex, and not, or not necessarily, so prejudicial. A generation later, this relationship is reconsidered by Kierkegaard, who offers what is still, in some ways, the most sustained piece of thinking on the subject that we have. In his *Concluding Unscientific Postscript* (1846) the existential philosopher of religion constructs a cosmology of experience, within which humour and the comic have an important place. There are 'three spheres of existence: the aesthetic, the ethical, the religious'. In the gaps between them are 'two boundary zones': 'irony, constituting the boundary between the aesthetic and the ethical', and 'humour, as the boundary that separates the ethical from the religious'.[148] As these quotations suggest, Kierkegaard's discussion is abstract, in the tradition of Jean Paul; but, unlike the thoughts of Jean Paul, his belong to a formidable intellectual construct, essentially independent of literary-theoretical reference and not easily translated into it. The thoughts, none the less, are arresting, sometimes, perhaps, gratuitously so ('prayer expresses the highest pathos of the infinite, and yet it is comical'), but more often rewardingly so: 'existence itself . . . is both pathetic and comic in the same degree'; 'the comical is always the mark of maturity'; the humorist has 'an essential conception of the suffering in which life is involved' and 'comprehends the profundity of the situation'.[149]

At the root of the comic, Kierkegaard tells us (momentarily recalling Jean Paul), is 'the contradiction between the infinite and the finite', which means that 'the comic is present everywhere', because 'wherever there is life, there is contradiction'. At one stage, Kierkegaard uses this principle to subvert the opposition with tragedy: 'what lies at the root of both the comic and the tragic . . . is the discrepancy, the contradiction, between the infinite and the finite.' At another, however, he uses it to reassert the

[147] Above, p. 74.

[148] Søren Kierkegaard, *Afsluttende uvidenskabelig Efterskrift*, cited from the transl. by D. F. Swanson and W. Lowrie, *Concluding Unscientific Postscript* (Princeton 1941) 448.

[149] Ibid. 83, 84, 250, 400–1. In Kierkegaard's usage 'humour' and 'the comic' are not systematically contrasted.

opposition: 'the tragic and the comic are . . . both . . . based on contradiction; but the tragic is the suffering contradiction, the comic, the painless contradiction.'[150] At which point one notes that a limitation is put on the humorist's 'conception of suffering': he has the 'essential conception', but goes on to 'revoke the suffering in the form of the jest'. That is, the humorist 'comprehends the profundity of the situation, but at the same moment it occurs to him that it is doubtless not worthwhile to attempt an explanation. This revocation is the jest.'[151] In an apparently unexplained reversal of the 'maturity' earlier associated with the comic, this limitation is further translated into a startling anticipation of Freud's infantilism: 'precisely because the pleasantry of humour consists in revocation', it often constitutes 'a regression to childhood'; humour involves 'a childlike hope and a childlike wish that everything might be made up for'.[152] One is reminded of Frye's version of comic wish-fulfilment, as well as of Freud. And when Kierkegaard eventually converts his map into a hierarchy, one is not surprised to learn that although (still very strikingly) 'the different existential stages take rank in accordance with their relationship to the comical', this is 'not in the sense that the comical is the highest stage'. That 'highest stage' (as the 'religious individual' can perceive, after, and partly through, his 'discovery of the comical') is the religious itself, wherein suffering is not revoked: 'for religiosity is the purest pathos'.[153]

It must, after all, now seem to the literary theorist, if not, perhaps, to the existential philosopher, that this massive argument amounts to a reassertion of the old opposition in a new form. Although Kierkegaard gives the comic a very distinctive weight, and even goes so far as to deny (against Aristotle and most of the rest of the world) that seriousness is 'a good in and for itself',[154] the opposition and its inherent limiting force seem somehow to survive. Intellect ('essential conception') versus emotion ('purest pathos'), painless versus painful: the old antitheses are subjected to an extraordinary reinterpretation, yet they survive. Does the humorist actually 'revoke' anything, as Kierkegaard says he does? And if he does, what *is* it that he revokes? Does he, perhaps (as Pirandello was to suggest), retain an interest through his 'feeling

[150] Ibid. 82–3, 413, 459; 82–3; 459 (transl. slightly modified).
[151] Ibid. 400–1.
[152] Ibid. 491, 489.
[153] Ibid. 463, 413.
[154] Ibid. 468.

of the opposite'? Is it in fact the pressure of the old, negative opposition that leads Kierkegaard to his conclusion? The ambivalence of his argument can serve as a splendid formula for many subsequent essays in the philosophy of comedy. Even this brief account of it says enough to suggest how a case for comic truth might be made—and, equally, how the perennial opposition with tragedy serves to confuse the issue.

Comedy is generally treated—even, eventually, by Kierkegaard—as a sort of gigantic exception. I suggest it is a sort of norm. It is not, indeed, a norm in any evaluative sense; and there is no reason to question the consensus that grants a special, almost absolute, distinction to a select group of non-comic works, from the *Iliad* to *Anna Karenina*, via the tragedies of Sophocles, Racine, and Shakespeare. Few observers have wished to challenge the consensus, on practical or theoretical grounds;[155] and it is no coincidence that, whereas the word 'tragedy' carries with it expectations of achievement, as opposed to (say) 'soap-opera', which carries the opposite, the word 'comedy' has no specifiable evaluative implications of any kind. 'Tragedy', then, is crypto-evaluative, upwards, and 'soap-opera' crypto-evaluative, downwards; and characterizations like 'poor tragedy' or 'fine soap-opera' have more than a flavour of self-contradiction. 'Comedy', by comparison, is neutral: a comedy may be poor or fine or neither.

The normality of comedy lies elsewhere: in its correspondence with, and proximity to, the diversities of life. This normality may be inferred from a number of considerations, most of them already discussed. First: 'the comic rhythm . . . is capable of the most

[155] The most notable exception is Schiller, who (in his *Naive and Sentimental Poetry*) used an idiosyncratic reinterpretation of the familiar ideas of comic realism and comic intellectuality to reach the conclusion that the comic writer ('whose genius is particularly nourished by actual life') aims distinctively at 'the highest aim for which man strives', which is dispassion: *Über naive und sentimentalische Dichtung* (1795–6), in Friedrich Schiller, *Sämtliche Werke*, ed. E. von den Hellen *et al.* (16 vols., Stuttgart 1904–5), xii. 198, 236. Within the Hegelian tradition, F. T. Vischer gave comedy notional primacy on the different ground that it contains 'the sublime and the tragic within itself' and represents 'pure freedom of consciousness': *Aesthetik oder Wissenschaft des Schönen* (16 vols., Stuttgart 1846–57), v. 1443–5. Schiller's discussion is introduced by the remarkable (and unsubstantiated) statement, 'It has often been disputed which of the two, tragedy or comedy, deserves precedence' ('Es ist mehrmals darüber gestritten worden, welche von beiden, die Tragödie oder die Komödie, vor der andern den Rang verdiene', *Sämtliche Werke*, xii. 197).

diverse presentations'.[156] That is, comedy manifests itself in a uniquely extensive range of works of art and proto-art from drama to the joke and the cartoon, and in uniquely variable ways. This is why one cannot readily conceive of perfect comedy, as one might (and Aristotle and Nietzsche did) conceive of perfect tragedy.[157]

Second: 'there never will be civilization where comedy is not possible'.[158] That is, comedy is present and popular in all ages, albeit not necessarily in dramatic form. ('Humour at present seems to be departing from the stage', wrote Goldsmith in 1772.)[159] Tragedy, by extreme contrast, needs specific conditions in which to grow and flourish. In Dürrenmatt's words, it requires a 'world order' and a 'true community', and, as Susanne Langer once pointed out, not just any community or any world order: 'tragedy is a mature art form, that has not arisen in all parts of the world, not even in all great civilizations. Its conception requires a sense of individuality which some religions and some cultures . . . do not generate.'[160]

Third: irrespective of the level of achievement represented by any one of its specific manifestations, comedy is seen to be a 'natural' human creation in its own right, without reference to other human creations, on a variety of grounds from the social to the metaphysical. Even from the partial theories of Freud and Bergson an acceptable 'naturalist' defence of comedy might be constructed, especially if we supplement Freud's theory of the joke with his later perception of communal festivity as licensed release from social stress.[161] One might reasonably include in such a defence Susanne Langer's derivation of comedy from 'sheer vitality' and the 'pure sense of life' which belongs to 'the basic

[156] Langer, *Feeling and Form*, 346.

[157] *Poet.* XIII; *Birth of Tragedy*, XXI–XXII: cf. Silk and Stern, *Nietzsche on Tragedy*, 228. Within drama one might indeed conceive of a perfect comedy of manners, which is different—and the difference is the point.

[158] Meredith: Sypher, *Comedy*, 32.

[159] Goldsmith, *Works*, iv. 461.

[160] Dürrenmatt, *Theater-Schriften*, 123–4; Langer, *Feeling and Form*, 334. Cf. F. M. Cornford, *The Origin of Attic Comedy* (Cambridge 1914) 186: 'tragedy is the exceptional phenomenon that calls for some special explanation', because 'true tragedy has very rarely made its appearance at all.'

[161] In *Massenpsychologie und Ich-Analyse* (1921) (cited as S. Freud, *Group Psychology and the Analysis of the Ego*, tr. J. Strachey, Penguin Freud Library, xii, ed. A. Richards (Harmondsworth 1985) 95–178, at 163–4). Freud's thesis is taken up and particularized by C. J. Barber, *Shakespeare's Festive Comedy* (Princeton 1959) 3–8.

rhythm of animal existence'.[162] In the wake of Freud, Langer relates this rhythm in turn to 'the strain of maintaining a vital balance amid the alien and impartial chances of the world', and suggests that the 'illusion of life' which the comic writer creates is 'the oncoming future fraught with dangers and opportunities, that is, with physical or social events occurring by chance and building up the coincidences with which individuals cope according to their lights': comedy, therefore, is 'an image of human vitality holding its own in the world amid the surprises of unplanned coincidence'.[163] Much comedy, we may add, and perhaps (by this criterion) the most readily explicable comedy of all, amounts to the celebration of coincidence: obvious examples are the glorious ingenuities of farce and the relish for puns which so appalled Dr Johnson in Shakespeare ('a quibble, poor and barren as it is, gave him such delight that he was content to purchase it by the sacrifice of reason, propriety and truth').[164]

Picking up Langer's 'coping', rather than her 'coincidences', we might also subsume under this third heading the much-discussed tendency of comedy to work towards solidarity between individuals. Theorists acknowledge it in different ways. 'Laughter is always the laughter of a group', said Bergson; Freud reflected on the joker's need to communicate his jokes and the role of the 'third person' in this process; Northrop Frye contrasted the 'pathos' of the 'exclusion of an individual' from a social group with the tendency of comic fiction to construct a newly integrated social order.[165] We may observe that even when it approximates to 'negative' ridicule, comedy still necessarily presupposes some co-operative solidarity with its audience, albeit at the expense of a victim; and that the comedy which is furthest from the negative, and which is epitomized by Bakhtin's 'carnival', calls for a solidarity that is social, but more than merely social, a solidarity that is in principle '*universal* in scope', whereby 'the *entire* world is

[162] *Feeling and Form*, 332, 330.

[163] Ibid. 331. By a process of questionable logic, however, Langer's eventual conclusion about the worth of such 'images' is that 'in comedy there is a general trivialization of the human battle', whereas tragedy 'exhibits an exactly opposite tendency to general exaggeration of issues and personalities' (349).

[164] Raleigh, *Johnson on Shakespeare*, 24. Freud noted that such verbal jokes, when (in his terms) 'innocent', show the purest possible innocence: *Jokes*, 133.

[165] Bergson, in Sypher, *Comedy*, 64; Freud, *Jokes*, 191–211, esp. 195–6; Frye, *Anatomy*, 39, 43–4.

seen in its comic aspect'.[166] Implicit in this third consideration, then, is the claim that there is a legitimate comic response to life, which all individuals are, in principle, able to share; and as the example of Bakhtin serves to remind us, that 'legitimate response' would subsume, or would be correlative to, the 'truth' that we might wish to ascribe to comedy, as to other modes of art.

Fourth: comedy overlaps into life, as perhaps no other mode of art does. It does so very obviously through the close connection, in fact the continuum, between art-comedy and the common joke. The overlap is apparent in other ways too. Bakhtin noted: 'carnival is not a spectacle seen by the people, they live in it'; 'carnival does not know footlights, [that is] . . . it does not acknowledge any distinction between actors and spectators'; accordingly, carnival 'belongs to the borderline between art and life'.[167] In this connection we may ponder the significance of the way that Aristophanic (and some other) comic drama can break its illusion and establish a complicity between actors and spectators, then return to the illusion as if nothing has happened. In a sense nothing *has* happened. There is no real breach, because actually or potentially the complicity was always there; and comedy is not wholly containable within the aesthetic sphere in the first place. 'Shall I tell them one of the usual jokes?', says Xanthias to Dionysus at the start of *Frogs*. The point is not only that this sort of 'breaking frame' is in itself comic, but that the frame it 'breaks', being comic too, is already open—open to, and open like, the life outside it. All in all, we may say with Bergson: 'the comic belongs neither altogether to art, nor altogether to life.'[168]

And fifth: unlike other modes of art, and certainly unlike the genre of tragedy, comedy evokes the freedom we associate with living. Modern theorists insistently link comedy and freedom, and in a great variety of contexts; and that variety seems to be corroboration of the point by itself. Comedy is seen to flourish under conditions of political freedom, freedom of movement, freedom of thought: 'I look upon humour to be almost of English growth . . . And what appears to me to be the reason of it is the

[166] Above, p. 76.

[167] *Rabelais*, 7.

[168] Sypher, *Comedy*, 148. I was wrong, however, to suggest (in Silk, 'Autonomy', 25) that the relation between laughter in life and laughter at art is special: (*a*) the relation between tears in life and tears at art is no different; (*b*) much comedy involves no laughter; (*c*) much laughter in life is unrelated (p. 84 n. 143 above).

great freedom . . . which the common people of England enjoy' (Congreve); ' the comic spirit thrives only on the open heath. One finds it wherever there is inward freedom, among the young at university . . . for example, or outward freedom, as in the very largest cities' (Jean Paul).[169] Comedy aims to free obstinate individuals from their anti-social rigidities (Bergson); it has a 'liberating' effect on the individual psyche (Freud); and through carnival it offers 'liberation from the prevailing truth' to those imprisoned within the social hierarchy (Bakhtin).[170] On a broad socio-political plane, Dürrenmatt invites us to use comedy against 'the tyrants of this planet' and declares that 'man's freedom manifests itself in laughter'.[171] Within the comic work itself, the author may, by the vision of an inclusive community, construct 'a kind of . . . pragmatically free society' (Frye) or, conversely perhaps, create unfettered spirits like Falstaff, living out their 'free existence' on an essentially individual basis (Hegel).[172]

But the relation between comedy and freedom is nowhere more obvious than with comedy's 'diverse presentations', to which this discussion repeatedly returns. 'Humour', said Ionesco with his own experiments in mind, 'is freedom.'[173] With such freedom, it might be thought, the old opposition with tragedy comes into view again. On such grounds, Dürrenmatt, for one, contrasts 'tragedy, the strictest genre in art' with comedy's 'unformed world'.[174] But the point is not that comedy is free, where tragedy is constrained (and, incidentally, where epic is constrained and where many other literary kinds are constrained). The point is that comedy is *free, if desired, to be constrained*: free even to be like tragedy, as Greek New Comedy, with its psychological realism and organic development, is like Euripides. Or it is free to be free like Aristophanic comedy, where all things seem to be possible, and

[169] Congreve, letter to John Dennis, 'Concerning humour in comedy' (1695); and Jean Paul, *Sämtliche Werke*, xi. 125. In antiquity a link was often made between satirical Old Comedy and 'free speech' (*libertas* or *parrhêsia*: e.g. Horace, *Sat.* 1. 4. 1–5, and *AP* 281–2, and Plut. *Mor.* 711–12), but not between free speech and comedy as such.

[170] Bergson, above, p. 75; Freud, 'Humour', 428; Bakhtin, *Rabelais*, 10.

[171] *Theater-Schriften*, 128.

[172] Frye, *Anatomy*, 169; Hegel, *Vorlesungen über die Aesthetik* (1835), in *Sämtliche Werke*, ed. H. Glockner (20 vols., Stuttgart 1927–30), xiii. 207 (cf. the Hegelian Vischer, p. 88 n. 155 above).

[173] Eugène Ionesco, *Notes and Counter-Notes*, tr. D. Watson (London 1967) 46.

[174] *Theater-Schriften*, 120.

what are supposed to be incompatible opposites are found freely coexisting or freely exchanged. Indeed, Aristophanes is even free to advertise his 'secondary' dependence on tragedy, and free to recreate 'reality' in the very act of being 'secondary'. In *Acharnians* Dicaeopolis' defence of his outrageous conduct in making a private peace with the Spartans is elevated by explicit borrowings from Euripides, and so encompasses a grotesque kind of hybrid eloquence through which his case is accepted. Yet it is the marvellous ingenuity of the hybrid that becomes the new and satisfying object of our amusement, not its dependence on Euripides—despite the fact that Euripides was literally sought out in person to provide the necessary assistance.

Yet for all its freedom and diversity, comedy is still identifiable as such without reference to any particular historical period. The label is not vacuous, as (say) 'lyric' is liable to be when so used. And comedy is surely more of a readily identifiable entity than those facets of the comic continuum into which theorists periodically attempt to partition it. Humour, farce, burlesque and the rest are important realities, of which any discussion of comedy must repeatedly take account. But the realities in question are seldom such that we can think of them as 'kinds' of literature (or of art) in their own right, because they show up—repeatedly—within the same comedies, and are often hard to distinguish from one another.[175] Comedy itself is different. As a mode of art (an 'archetype', in Fowler's terms), it is indeed not recognizable by a cluster of fixed textual features, yet it remains recognizable. It has its repertoire of 'family' characteristics.

First: comedy tends to amuse. Any version of comedy may *also*, at some point or at all points, be 'serious' in some sense of that word, but it still tends to amuse. This characteristic effect may be associated with feelings of triumph or joy. If such feelings actually supplant amusement, we become reluctant to apply the name 'comedy' to the product, even if we are mindful of Wittgenstein, even if there is a historical justification for the name, and even though any such attested widening of nomenclature is in some degree (as argued) corroboration of comedy's own diversity. 'Sentimental comedy' and Dante's 'comedy' are cases in point.

[175] Cf. Styan, *Dark Comedy*, 43. The list of not properly distinguishable subtypes should include humour—*pace* Jean Paul, Pirandello, and Freud (above, pp. 74 n. 99, 75–6, 61 n. 58).

At all events, triumph in itself is not comic: no one mistakes triumphal odes for comedy.[176]

Second: whereas many literary types offer images of loss, comedy (including, certainly, Dante's) offers projections of survival, which is not quite the same as having 'happy endings', though most comic *dramas* do have such endings, and though survival in comic drama often calls forth a celebration. Many jokes (though fewer comic dramas) are about death, but they tend to involve the survivors, or else they involve the dead in some kind of continuing existence (in worldly conversation before the Pearly Gates, or whatever). One comic drama that corresponds closely to the pattern is Aristophanes' *Frogs*, where we find *both* the dead in 'continuing existence' *and* the 'survivors' Xanthias and Dionysus, and, at the heart of the play, the latter's quest to add to the number of survivors one deceased poet. Nor is it only the dead in and around Pluto's palace who vociferously assert their propensity to exist: even the corpse in transit to Hades notoriously does so.[177] In a very literal sense comedy is pro-life.

Third: as that last point suggests, comedy tends towards the material and away from the metaphysical. Brecht notes that, compared with other drama, the 'tone' of dramatic comedy is always 'more materialistic'.[178] Bakhtin says: 'laughter degrades and materializes'.[179] And Kierkegaard: 'the religiosity of hidden awareness is *eo ipso* inaccessible to comic apprehension'.[180] Or as Woody Allen put it: 'not only is there no God, but try getting a plumber on weekends.'[181] This materialism is the common implication of various ideas already considered: the notion of

[176] Not even Hobbes, quite (above, p. 73)—though J. K and F. S. Newman, in *Pindar's Art* (Hildesheim 1984), did their best to assimilate the comic and the Pindaric 'komic' (p. x and *passim*).

[177] *Ran.* 173–7.

[178] In a note on *Die Dreigroschenoper* (1931): *Brecht on Theatre*, ed. J. Willett (New York 1964) 46.

[179] *Rabelais*, 20, generalizing from the specific instance of medieval and Rabelaisian 'grotesque realism'. As a characterization of all 'laughter', however, 'degradation' is less than felicitous: cf. the sensible remarks by Bergson (in Sypher, *Comedy*, 141). One is uncomfortably reminded of Aristotle's *phaulos* (p. 53 above), which is supposed to apply to all *kômôidia*. On the whole, Freud rightly tries to restrict his equivalent concept ('Herabsetzung') to caricature, parody, travesty, and obscenity (*Jokes*, 261, 286), despite the comment quoted above, p. 82.

[180] *Postscript*, 465.

[181] Woody Allen, *Getting Even* (London 1973) 33.

comic realism which is first voiced in Hellenistic Greece; Baudelaire's contention that 'laughter is Satanic', from which he infers the corollary, 'it is therefore profoundly human';[182] and, not least, Jean Paul's principle of the humorous world of the finite, set against the ideal.[183] A related point is made by Pirandello, who draws attention to the way that comedy ('humour') stays closer than most art to life's specific embodiments: 'art generally abstracts and concentrates; that is, it catches and represents the essential and characteristic ideality of both men and things. Now it seems to the humorist that all this oversimplifies nature and tends to make life too reasonable or at least too coherent.'[184] Specific embodiment is not at all peculiar to comedy, but it is nevertheless peculiarly important for its own special 'truth'. And Pirandello's articulation of this point is surely one of the possible counters to the old complaint that comedy distorts reality.

It is by the combination of characteristics, not by any single one of them, that we identify comedy, although if there is one by which we are likely to try, it will be the tendency to amuse. Yet even amusement is not a decisive criterion. Consider Terence's *Heauton Timorumenos* (*The Self-Tormentor*) and Beckett's *Waiting for Godot*. The former is a comedy, the latter a hybrid with some comic components. Much of the *Heauton* is concerned with the troubled Menedemus, the 'self-tormentor' of the title, and his officious neighbour Chremes, who insists on forcing his boundlessly wise humanity on Menedemus ('homo sum') but is shown to be 'only wise next door'.[185] Given this orientation, much of the play is only faintly amusing and its capacity to amuse is certainly slighter than that of *Godot* with all its extravagant knockabout and word play. But the *Heauton* is wholly earthbound and its sights are fixed on survival, up to and including its familiar closing note,

[182] Above, p. 80: Baudelaire, *Curiosités esthétiques*, 250.

[183] Above, p. 74. Jean Paul adds: 'the comic cannot exist without sensuousness ... [and whereas] the serious always emphasizes the general ... and spiritualizes things ... the comic writer ... fastens our mind ... upon physical detail' (*Sämtliche Werke*, xi. 125–6). The principle is challenged to no purpose by K. S. Guthke, *Modern Tragicomedy* (New York 1966) 49–50. In favour of the idea that comedy 'is quite capable of treating the relation of man to the universe', Guthke can only offer tragedies with comic elements like *Lear* and hybrids like Ionesco's.

[184] Pirandello, *On Humor*, 142–3.

[185] Terence, *Heauton*, 75–9 and 922–3. Cf. H. D. Jocelyn, 'Homo sum', *Antichthon* 7 (1973) 14–46.

'Oh, and I want you to forgive my slave.'[186] The preoccupation of Beckett's dialogue with time and the future, the tramps' threats to leave each other, motifs of suicide and crucifixion and *God*-ot, produces both a powerful sense of loss and an impression of a beyond that might redeem the loss, despite the very fact that any specifiable beyond is lost too: 'I have lived through this long day and I can assure you it is very near the end of its repertory.'[187] *Godot*, accordingly, however comic in part, is not comic as a whole.[188]

The briefest scrutiny of comedy's three characteristics suffices to confirm that, in the literary sphere, comedy is indeed unlike tragedy, but not determinatively unlike it: not, that is, its opposite. In none of the three cases is the feature in question confined to comedy or its absence confined to tragedy; in one case, furthermore, tragedy's own lack of the feature is not absolute. With amusement: works that are not comedy—including (as we have pointed out) even some works of canonical Greek tragedy—can amuse,[189] while the general absence of amusement is as characteristic of epic poetry and some other literary types as it is of tragedy. With survival and loss: projections of survival are common to many genres, ancient and modern, from epithalamia to whodunits, and are generally characteristic of another broad category of literary expression, romance; while in tragedy not everything is loss, especially at the Greek fountainhead, where (quite apart from plays like *Eumenides*) the tragic chorus regularly offers a model of survival in itself.[190] The observation prompts the thought that in the Greek world the purest images of loss are to be found not in tragedy, but in such genres as the epitaph and the lyric dirge (the *thrênos*). As for the material and the metaphysical:

[186] A representative instance of Frye's inclusive 'free society': Terence, *Heauton*, 1066–7.

[187] Vladimir, in Samuel Beckett, *Waiting for Godot* (London 1956) 86.

[188] Likewise *The Tempest*, with its supernatural overtones ('You are three men of sin . . . and my fellows | Are ministers of fate . . .', III. iii), is generally perceived as tragicomedy, notwithstanding its original label of comedy. On the complexity of this play, see e.g. M. C. Bradbrook, *The Growth and Structure of Elizabethan Comedy*[2] (London 1973) 204–6.

[189] For some obvious instances, see above, p. 59. Equally obvious instances occur in the other 'serious' Greek genres: e.g. *Od.* 6. 56–149 (Nausicaa, Alcinous, Odysseus), Pind. *Pyth.* 9 (see Silk, *Interaction*, 170–1).

[190] Nietzsche's insight: Silk and Stern, *Nietzsche on Tragedy*, 266–8; M. S. Silk, 'Notions of the chorus in the nineteenth century', *Drama* 7 (1999) 199–200.

from the *Iliad* to *Paradise Lost*, epic poetry is hardly less metaphysical than tragedy; and is (say) the non-comic novel appreciably less material than the comic?

Tragedy is not *per se* comedy's opposite; and comedy is not dependent on tragedy or on any 'serious' norm outside itself, except in particular cases where a 'serious' original is appropriated or parodied or otherwise presupposed. That is: comedy, in itself, is no more dependent on any 'serious' point of reference than any other form of art commonly is.[191] And even when it is visibly dependent, as in Dicaeopolis' paratragic defence in *Acharnians*, it is free to do as Dicaeopolis does: use tragic norms to help create a new comic self-sufficiency. Comedy, then, is free to depend or not: it is, and always was, autonomous. And this being so, Aristophanes' preoccupation with tragedy is seen to have a particular significance. It betokens, not a response to an inevitable relationship, not even an unusually intense response to an inevitable relationship, but, on the contrary, a special attempt to create a relationship. As such, it implies a search for identity: Aristophanic comedy is working out its own definition.

It is with this conclusion in mind that various issues raised during the foregoing discussions must be pursued, more systematically or more specifically, in the chapters that follow: Aristophanes' diversity of style, in speech and in song; pathos, humour, and satire; the high and the low; the metaphysical and the material; truth and reality; logic and discontinuity; Aristophanes and Euripides; generic expectation and literary hybrids. And (thinking back to Aristophanes' own claims for his comic poetry) however hard it may be to be quite sure about a Greek writer's originality, we shall at least find plenty of evidence for Aristophanes' sophistication and much occasion to discuss his 'seriousness' and the meaning of 'seriousness' in relation to his own comedy.

[191] And one should avoid dependency talk (just as much as oppositionality talk, p. 54 above), however sophisticated: 'the inverted commas of comic inversion' (Goldhill, *Poet's Voice*, 222).

3

Language and Style

Aristophanes is a master of words and a great poet, and the two attributes, while not synonymous, are—*pace* Aristotle—closely related.[1] In no other area, however, has discussion of Aristophanes been so hesitant. To judge from the received opinions about his work, it might well be said of him, as Eliot said of Milton, that 'while it must be admitted that [he] is a very great poet indeed, it is something of a puzzle to decide in what his greatness consists'.[2] If we suggest, provisionally, that as a poet Aristophanes is certainly as great as any of the Greek tragedians, we must at once add that his poetry is certainly not great in the way that any of their poetry might be said to be great. World literature, no doubt, does not provide us with much other comic poetry to help us get our bearings here, even if it has given us an abundance of comic verse. There is, again, a piece of long-standing sceptical wisdom, which goes back at least as far as Horace, to the effect that 'comic poetry' is a contradiction in terms.[3] None of this need deflect us from our contention: Aristophanes is a master of words and a great poet.

Words certainly occupy a position of dominance within Aristophanes' creative world. Witness our earlier examples: the open-

[1] *Poet.* IX: 'a poet [*poiêtês*, maker] should be [a poet by virtue of] making plot-structures, rather than verses'. See further Halliwell, *Aristotle's Poetics*, 344–9.

[2] The opening words of 'Milton' (1936): T. S. Eliot, *On Poetry and Poets* (London 1957) 138 (where the essay is retitled 'Milton I'). There exists no satisfactory overview of A's style. Part of the problem is that the more thoughtful discussions tend to deal with strictly delimited aspects, e.g. J. Taillardat, *Les Images d'Aristophane*² (Paris 1965); Dover, *Greek and the Greeks*, 224–36, 'The style of Aristophanes' (actually on levels of language, cf. p. 117 n. 50 below); A. López Eire, *La lengua coloquial de la comedia aristofánica* (Murcia 1996)—or else deal only with aspects but also go beyond style (and often are most valuable when they do): thus H.-J. Newiger, *Metapher und Allegorie. Studien zu Aristophanes* (Munich 1957); Rau, *Paratragodia*; Henderson, *Maculate Muse*; B. Zimmermann, *Untersuchungen zur Form und dramatischen Technik der Aristophanischen Komödien* (3 vols., Königstein and Frankfurt 1984–7).

[3] 'quidam comoedia necne poema | esset quaesivere': Hor. *Sat.* 1. 4. 45–6.

ing of *Acharnians*, with its rich variety of verbal effects; and, even more obviously, the opening of *Frogs*, with its joke as action—forbidden words about forbidden words. Along with his age, Aristophanes is intrigued by words, but (more than that) at such moments he makes words not merely his instruments, or his subjects, but almost his actors. And if no such verbal richness impinged on us in our third example, the opening of *Plutus*, we may treat the fact as a small symptom—but one of many in late Aristophanes—of a shift towards Aristotelian values, towards a use of words as a strictly mediating instrument of more-than-verbal action, towards such a sense of words as is aptly summed up in a famous anecdote about Menander and a comedy in progress. 'Oh, yes,' that most Aristotelian of comic artists remembers to say, 'I've written the play, the plot's worked out—all I have to do is put the lines in.'[4]

In *Frogs* and *Acharnians*, and the plays between, Aristophanes does everything imaginable to ensure that words compel our attention. He plies us with language-jokes, like those at the start of *Frogs*. He lectures us about local speech variations, warns off rivals who plagiarize his comparisons, deflates the modish fashions for *-ikos* adjectives and *-sis* abstract nouns.[5] He mimics the speech patterns of barely intelligible foreigners and the quaint features of nominally intelligible non-Attic Greeks: the Megarian farmer who sells his daughters and the Spartan ambassador who sings of the Persian wars do so in versions of Megarian and Laconian Doric.[6] And over and over again he fills the air with verbal presences evocative of earlier and contemporary literature—evocative of all and any literature, from the old epic to the New Dithyramb, from oratory to oracles, from sophistic quibbles to Aesopian fables—but, above all, evocative of tragedy.[7] The

[4] Plut. *Moral.* 347e; cf. Silk, 'Six parts', 113.

[5] See fr. 706 *PCG*; *Nub.* 559 (with Dover ad loc.); *Eq.* 1378–80 (with Neil ad loc.) and *Nub.* 1172–3; and *Nub.* 317–18 (with Dover).

[6] See esp. *Ach.* 100–15, *Av.* 1678–82, *Thes.* 1001–225 (foreigners), *Ach.* 729–835 (Megarian), *Lys.* 1247–72 (Spartan). From Homer onwards (where Trojans talk like Achaeans), most Greek literature ignores linguistic *differentiae*. The idea that comedy might be different is registered by *Tract. Coisl.*, p. 38 Janko (cf. Janko's comm.: *Aristotle on Comedy*, 223–5). More generally, see C. W. Müller, K. Sier, and J. Werner (eds.), *Zum Umgang mit fremden Sprachen in der griechisch-römischen Antike* (Stuttgart 1992) and S. C. Colvin, *Dialect in Aristophanes and the Politics of Language in Ancient Greek Literature* (Oxford 1999).

[7] e.g. *Pax* 1280–1 (epic), *Av.* 1372–409 (New Dith.), *Thes.* 383–432 (oratory, cf. 382), *Eq.* 197–201 (oracles), *Nub.* 1427–9 (sophistry), *Av.* 471–5 (fables).

preoccupation with tragedy that characterizes the plays is to a large extent made manifest in an endless appropriation of tragic language. This paratragedy—and likewise the *para*-epic and the *para*-all-the-rest—sometimes involves parodic satire, but generally involves something more revealing of Aristophanes' deepest orientations. That is: the use of tragedy represented by (say) the exhilarating send-up of Euripidean monody in *Frogs* (1331 ff.),

> ὦ νυκτὸς κελαινοφαὴς ὄρφνα . . .
>
> O night's gloom, black-lit . . .

is ultimately less characteristic and less significant than the 'creative' presences already discussed and represented by the admittedly unspectacular instance at *Acharnians* 27:

> . . . προτιμῶσ' οὐδέν· ὦ πόλις πόλις.
>
> They couldn't give a damn. O City city.[8]

On a larger scale the dominance of words is evident in the confrontations around which so many of the plays are organized, confrontations that again and again crystallize into battles where two rival parties strive to persuade a third. To clear the way for these *agônes*, physical conflict regularly gives way to verbal eristics, and Aeschylus versus Euripides (*Frogs*), head-woman Lysistrata versus head-man Commissioner (*Lysistrata*), Sausage-Seller versus Paphlagon (*Knights*), son Bdelycleon versus father Philocleon (*Wasps*), all become contests of words, superseding *stasis* in Hades, a siege of the Acropolis, death-threats and a cavalry charge, and an old man's desperate attempts to escape confinement.

In *Acharnians*, Dicaeopolis' hopes of success in the good cause of peace depend on his chance to use words—λέγειν—'among us Athenians' (498). In *Clouds*, Strepsiades' less worthy hopes of evading his debts are stirred by the prospect of 'learning to talk' (βουλόμενος μαθεῖν λέγειν, 239)—of becoming, indeed, 'miles the best talker in Greece' (τῶν Ἑλλήνων εἶναί με λέγειν ἑκατὸν σταδίοισιν ἄριστον, 430). In Dicaeopolis' case the use of words 'among us Athenians' means exercising the legitimate skills of the public orator. In *Clouds* these same skills attract a strong negative valuation, freely admitted by Strepsiades himself (443–51):

[8] See below, p. 139 n. 86 and above, pp. 34–7.

εἴπερ τὰ χρέα διαφευξοῦμαι,
τοῖς τ' ἀνθρώποις εἶναι δόξω
θρασύς, εὔγλωττος, τολμηρός, ἴτης,
βδελυρός, ψευδῶν συγκολλητής,
εὑρησιεπής, περίτριμμα δικῶν,
κύρβις, κρόταλον, κίναδος, τρύμη,
μάσθλης, εἴρων, γλοιός, ἀλαζών,
κέντρων, μιαρός, στρόφις, ἀργαλέος,
ματιολοιχός.

If I can beat my debts
And make men think me
Bold, glib, confident, cavalier,
Shocking, a mint of lies,
A coiner of phrases, a smooth lawyer,
A tablet of stone, a drum, fox, needle's eye,
A lash, dry wit, man of oil, charlatan,
An old lag, villain, twister, a pain,
A quibble-licker.

The facility with words that Strepsiades seeks (and which—*exemplum sui*—his own 'speech' embodies) is the facility advertised and purveyed by the sophists in the name of 'persuasion', and what is foregrounded in *Clouds* is not only words, but the whole apparatus, real or supposed, of contemporary sophistic word-mongering. When Strepsiades fails to achieve his ambition and transfers it to his son Pheidippides, the two competing controllers of the young man's fate are both *Logoi*, 'words' or (as English usage requires) 'arguments', Right and Wrong. On any reading, part of what *Clouds* is about is the power of words, as symbolized by Socrates, by his meteorological deities (in their first incarnation), and above all by Wrong. In *Clouds* this power is seen as sinister. Elsewhere word-mongering is more commonly represented as laughable excess—hence the ridicule of dithyrambic poetry in *Birds* and pretentious hymnody (as practised by Agathon's servant) in *Thesmophoriazusae*.[9] One way or the other, an attentive reading of Aristophanes might sometimes lead us to conclude that *any* distinctive use of language is suspect: witness (for instance) *Frogs*, where, for most of the long contest between the poets, there is apparently little to choose between the insubstantiality of Euripides, whose 'tongue' produces words that

[9] *Av.* 1372 ff.; *Thes.* 39 ff.

answer to nothing, and the bloated turgidity of Aeschylus, whose 'lungs' breathe forth a weight of language that resists examination.[10] At such moments Aristophanes seems almost to prefigure the notion of language as alienation, which will lead Epicurus, at the end of the fourth century, to deny the value of any but plain words as a means of mediating reality, or (in a more extreme case) which led Epicurus' greater predecessor, Plato, to question the mediating capacity of words as such, thus anticipating a whole series of modern arguments, of which Nietzsche's remains the most notable, that language is a 'prison-house' and that truth must be sought outside it.[11] But all this is only *seems*. Against such negative testimony we must set the celebration, even glorification, of the richness and variety of language (and—precisely *through* language—of life) that is writ large in all the manifold 'critiques' under discussion, those in *Frogs* and *Clouds* included. There is more to say about both plays, but for the moment the general point can stand.

A writer's characteristic use of words we call his, or her, style. A writer's style may be stable or else, less commonly, mobile.[12] In stable writing there is a broadly predictable consistency of usage in respect of the main areas of style—diction, imagery, sound and rhythmic patterns, schematic conformations, word-order, syntax—but especially within those groups of features that are hierarchically dominant within the style in question. Some writers follow, or create, a homogeneous idiom: a reader can feel it impressionistically, and can articulate the impression, with whatever refinements, as and if required. The main characters in Wilde's *The Importance of Being Earnest* all use a particular version of upper-class British English idiom of a given era, an idiom which is fluent, precise, and ample (in particular, by colloquial standards, syntactically ample), and which is at all times informed by, and in effect dominated by, an irresistible superficial wit. Act II:

[10] γλῶσσα . . . πλευμόνων *Ran.* 827–9; cf. below, pp. 197–8.

[11] Epicurus: Diog. Laert. 10. 13, Epicur. *Ep. Hdt.* 38 and *de Nat.* 28. 5 Vogliano. Plato: e.g. *Crat.* 440c–d. Nietzsche: first in 'Über Wahrheit und Lüge im aussermoralischen Sinne' (1873), in Nietzsche, *Werke, Kritische Gesamtausgabe*, ed. G. Colli and M. Montinari (Berlin 1967–), ii. 2. 367 ff. 'Prison-house': F. Jameson, *The Prison House of Language* (Princeton 1972).

[12] This distinction is my own, as is the theory that follows.

CECILY — Do you suggest, Miss Fairfax, that I entrapped Ernest into an engagement? How dare you? This is no time for wearing the shallow mask of manners. When I see a spade, I call it a spade.

GWENDOLEN — I am glad to say that I have never seen a spade. It is obvious that our social spheres have been widely different.

At no point in the dialogue, needless to say, does Cecily ever get near enough to any demotic name-calling to risk undermining the given stability, if only because (as Gwendolen's *bon mot* implies) the stability in question entails an established system of decorum with awesome socio-linguistic presuppositions, which no speaker would dare challenge, and which imply a sense of fixed distance—distance from unmediated experience and distance from other socio-linguistic groups.

The style of Homer's *Iliad*, with its concrete immediacy and its formulaic stylization,[13] is broadly stable—irrespective of the possible plurality of hands (or voices) that comprise this author. A broad stability is likewise ascribable to the famous indirectness ('perverse and pedantick' or yet sublime) of *Paradise Lost*;[14] to the evenly ornate language of Bacchylides' choral lyrics; to the concentrated abstractions of Aristotle (though one would surely have contrasted the idiom of his exoteric dialogues, had they survived, with that of his esoteric treatises); to the Attic grace of Menander, whose language 'gives a single impression and maintains its uniformity by means of locutions that are ordinary, everyday and in general use'.[15] On the other hand, it is apparent that the language of Oscar Wilde's servants differs from that of their masters; that the characteristic style of the narrator of the *Iliad* is distinguishable from that of his characters and that, among his characters, the language of Achilles is slightly, but demonstrably, distinct from that of his peers;[16] and that one might detect comparable distinctions within Milton's *Paradise Lost* (if only because 'the language of rebellion cannot be the same with that of

[13] M. S. Silk, *Homer, The Iliad* (Cambridge 1987) 16–27, 54–69.

[14] 'Perverse . . .': Samuel Johnson, *Lives of the English Poets*, ed. A. Waugh (2 vols., London 1906), i. 132. 'Indirectness': C. B. Ricks, *Milton's Grand Style* (Oxford 1963) 147–50.

[15] Plut. *Moral.* 853d.

[16] R. P. Martin, *The Language of Heroes: Speech and Performance in the Iliad* (Ithaca 1989) 146–205.

obedience')[17] and within Menander (whose Greek 'can still appeal to modern critics, as it did to ancient ones, by its air of aptness to character').[18]

In such distinctions we glimpse an alternative and more complex kind of stability, one that is not absolute but is based on differential organization and, in general, differential decorum. This differential stability is commonplace in the modern novel, if only because narration and direct speech commonly present a marked stylistic contrast. It is especially common, and well-understood, in Greek literature. We soon learn to expect that in any tragedy the sung lyrics will be in one idiom (an ornate idiom roughly like Bacchylides'), the spoken dialogue in another (less ornate), and the chanted recitative in an intermediate idiom (closer to the lyrics, though still recognizably an idiom of its own). The sources of tragic differentiation are fairly constant—they depend on specialized metres and metrical patterns, specialized features of diction and word-formation, and dialect differences (whereby the lyrics, in particular, are characterized by a superficial 'Doric' colouring); more important is that the differentiations themselves are preserved, and that these relationships remain broadly constant within—as, indeed, between—given plays. All Greek tragedies are stylistically (and otherwise) elevated; but their differentiated segments are elevated in different degrees, if not in different ways. In other genres, some individual works have an individual version of such an organization. Hesiod's *Works and Days*, with a hexametric epic idiom akin to Homer's, offers at least two distinct forms of that idiom: it begins with a proem in incantatory style, full of parallelisms and richer than anything in the 'didactic' sections that follow.[19] Ancient oratory operated on the basis of a more elaborate version of the Hesiodic principle. As the rhetoricians constantly reminded their readers, a speech was to be composed in set parts, from the prooemium to the epilogue, each with its appropriate style.[20]

In some Platonic dialogues, notably *Symposium*, differentiation is by speaker: Plato's Diotima philosophizes in semi-abstract

[17] Johnson, *Lives*, i. 120.

[18] E. W. Handley, *The Dyskolos of Menander* (London 1965) 13.

[19] 'The lines [of the proem, 1–10] are rather stylized', says West ad loc., with some understatement.

[20] See e.g. J. F. D'Alton, *Roman Literary Theory and Criticism* (London 1931) 121–2.

Socratic dialectic; Plato's Aristophanes 'commits himself wholeheartedly to the particular';[21] Plato's Agathon struts his stuff in sophistic word play. Compare and contrast *Republic*, where—as if by some idiosyncratic reversal of the Hesiodic principle—we find a closing section of distinctive stylistic intensity, which deserves our attention here because of the contrast it will be seen to present with Aristophanes' modes of expression. Against the earlier run of dialogue and dialectic, Plato offers us one of his narrative 'myths' concerning the deep mysteries of life and death, for whose climax on this occasion he creates a special idiom as far from the ordinary Socratic as could be imagined. The creative idiom, indeed, is as far from ordinary Greek as could be imagined, eliminating for a few eerie moments that plethora of particles, articles, and prepositions that abound in virtually all forms of the language and, for good measure, eliminating verbs as well. 'At the still point of a turning world' we stand, with ordinary activity, and ordinary relationship, absent (10. 617d):

σφᾶς οὖν, ἐπειδὴ ἀφικέσθαι, εὐθὺς δεῖν ἰέναι πρὸς τὴν Λάχεσιν. προφήτην οὖν τινὰ σφᾶς πρῶτον μὲν ἐν τάξει διαστῆσαι, ἔπειτα λαβόντα ἐκ τῶν τῆς Λαχέσεως γονάτων κλήρους τε καὶ βίων παραδείγματα, ἀναβάντα ἐπί τι βῆμα ὑψηλὸν εἰπεῖν· Ἀνάγκης θυγατρὸς κόρης Λαχέσεως λόγος. ψυχαὶ ἐφήμεροι, ἀρχὴ ἄλλης περιόδου θνητοῦ γένους θανατηφόρου.

Now when they arrived, they had to go before Lachesis straight away. A minister first stood them in line, then took assignments and patterns of lives from the lap of Lachesis, and went up to a high platform and said: 'This is the word of Lachesis, maiden daughter of Necessity. Transient souls, now is the start of another cycle of mortal generation laden with death.'

But literally, word for word, and in their precise order, the minister's words run: 'Necessity's maiden daughter Lachesis' word. Souls transient, other cycle's mortal generation's death-laden start.'[22] On reflection, the *modus operandi* here is not, after all, so different from what we find in *Symposium*. It is true that the mythic narrative differs from the predominant style of the dialogue, but it is only one section of that narrative that is strikingly distinct, and in that most striking section we actually revert to the *Symposium* principle of stylistic differentiation by speaker. It is

[21] K. J. Dover, 'Aristophanes' speech in Plato's *Symposium*', *JHS* 86 (1966) 47.
[22] For fuller discussion of the passage, see Silk, 'Pindar meets Plato'.

simply that the speaker, unusually, is an unearthly *prophêtês*, a spokesman of things beyond earthly knowledge, and speaks accordingly.

These examples, whether commonplace like the oratorical or exceptional like the Platonic, are all examples of differential stability. Qualifications, of course, are called for. In characterizing 'a style' as sophistic or ornate we are using a necessary shorthand. Plainly, a good deal of analysis and comparison would be needed to make such labels entirely plausible. Again, when we see the predominant style in a Homeric epic or a Platonic dialogue as 'more or less' undifferentiated, we are appealing to a necessary simplification. Kirk suggested that Homer's Greek accommodates (*inter alia*) a 'catalogue' style, a 'majestic' style, a 'decorated lyrical' style, an 'aphoristic style', and in a similar vein Thesleff ascribed to Plato no fewer than ten different styles from the 'colloquial' to the 'ceremonious'.[23] Such differentiations (if plausible) are appropriate to a different kind of discussion. So too is the distinction between a mode of differentiation that operates within a single work and one that is operative generically. With oratory or tragedy, the mode is generic: the kind of differential stability we see in one play by Euripides is not very different from the kind we see in another play by Sophocles. In the given case of Plato, the mode to some extent varies between works. Nevertheless, styles that are differentially stable constitute a distinct and significant group. They stand together against styles that are stable overall. Equally, they stand together—but also together with styles that have this absolute stability—against those styles which are not consistently stable at all, but are—in whole or in part—*mobile*.

There are no doubt moments of stylistic mobility in much of the world's literature, including some of the instances already cited. Take Plato: it is arguable that the use of a special language for the *prophêtês* in *Republic* x, though explicable in terms of differential stability, is itself so special—so *ad hoc*, so extreme—as to make any suggestion of stability seem forced. Or Menander: 'though it is common for Menander to use characteristic mannerisms of speech to differentiate between characters, particularly striking language may be turned on and off as the dramatic

[23] G. S. Kirk, *The Songs of Homer* (Cambridge 1962) 162–78; H. Thesleff, *Studies in the Styles of Plato* (Helsinki 1967).

emphasis requires.'[24] Or even Homer—for even a model of stability like the *Iliad*, with all its formulaic fixities, has hints of instability, as deeper analysis reveals an 'oscillation between the fixed and the free'.[25] Nevertheless, there is a clear distinction to be drawn between any of these authors or works and the kind of work that can accommodate (for instance) this from Beckett (*Waiting for Godot*, I. 31–2):

POZZO He imagines that when I see him indefatigable, I'll regret my decision. Such is his miserable scheme. As though I were short of slaves! Atlas, Son of Jupiter! Well, that's what I think. Anything else? *Vaporizer.*

VLADIMIR You want to get rid of him?

POZZO Remark that I might just as well have been in his shoes and he in mine. If chance had not willed otherwise. To each his due.

VLADIMIR You waagerrim?

POZZO I beg your pardon?

VLADIMIR You want to get rid of him?

POZZO I do. But instead of driving him away as I might have done, I mean instead of simply kicking him out on his arse, in the goodness of my heart I am bringing him to the fair, where I hope to get a good price for him.

Here the stylistic range of the main speaker, Pozzo, varies instantly and unpredictably between the portentously formal ('indefatigable') and the bathetically banal ('vaporizer'), the literary ('Atlas, son of Jupiter') and the colloquial ('that's what I think'), the old-world polite ('remark') and the contemporary coarse ('on his arse').

Or take a simpler instance, from Woody Allen:[26]

'It's for you.'
The voice on the other end was Sergeant Reed of Homicide.
'You still looking for God?'
'Yeah.'
'An all-powerful Being? Great Oneness, Creator of the Universe? First Cause of all things?'
'That's right.'
'Somebody with that description just showed up at the morgue. You better get down here right away.'

[24] S. M. Goldberg, *The Making of Menander's Comedy* (London 1980) 63.
[25] Silk, *Iliad*, 24 (cf. 55–6, 65–7).
[26] *Getting Even*, 145–6.

It was Him all right, and from the looks of Him it was a professional job.
'He was dead when they brought Him in.'
'Where'd you find Him?'
'A warehouse on Delancey Street.'
'Any clues?'
'It's the work of an existentialist.'

Here the idiom oscillates between two incompatible mid-century norms, one from the realm of the philosophical-theological treatise, the other from the world of the crime thriller. The oscillating (be it noted) belongs both to the words of the narrator ('Him', but 'professional job') and, more blatantly, to those of Sergeant Reed: 'First Cause of all things', but 'showed up at the morgue'; 'warehouse on Delancey Street', but 'existentialist'. Any possibility that, given so much oscillating, oscillation might itself become the source of an admittedly eccentric type of stability is precluded, partly by the seeming randomness of the particular switches, but particularly by the sense that the two norms coexist at an impossible distance from each other, never forming a single mode, never meeting, except in the punning '*looking for* God' and '*work of an* existentialist', where the puns, as puns, draw attention to the separateness of their two spheres of reference, rather than marrying them.

Or, again, consider this harsher collocation of styles from Eliot (*Coriolan* I):

Now come the virgins bearing urns, urns containing
Dust
Dust
Dust of dust, and now
Stone, bronze, stone, steel, stone, oakleaves, horses' heels
Over the paving.
That is all we could see. But how many eagles!
  and how many trumpets!
(And Easter Day, we didn't get to the country,
So we took young Cyril to church. And they rang a bell
And he said right out loud, *crumpets*.)
  Don't throw away that sausage,
It'll come in handy. He's artful. Please, will you
Give us a light?
Light

Light
Et les soldats faisaient la haie? ILS LA FAISAIENT.

The voice—whether one, two, or several, we are not required to ponder—begins in high-literary style ('virgins *bearing* urns', 'Dust/Dust/Dust *of* dust'), drops dramatically (in both senses) to the bathetic depths of 'young Cyril', 'crumpets' (rhyming over-insistently with the still lofty 'trumpets') and 'give us a light', and then, through a sardonic play on that last word, recalls the high style of 'Dust/Dust' in 'Light/Light', before switching, with another drastic dislocation of language and (therefore) tone, to French: '*Et les soldats* . . .'

And as a classic English paradigm, one might consider those few pages of *Hamlet* (II. i–III. ii) that encompass the hero's brief evocation of sub-Virgilian melodrama ('With eyes like carbuncles, the hellish Pyrrhus . . .'), his reversion to prose ('You could, for a need, study a speech of some dozen or sixteen lines . . .?'), and then to poetry ('What's Hecuba to him or he to Hecuba?'), and more poetry ('To be or not to be . . .'), and heightened prose ('Get thee to a nunnery: why wouldst thou be a breeder of sinners?'), and ordinary prose ('Speak the speech, I pray you, as I pronounced it to you . . .'), then poetry again ('No, let the candied tongue lick absurd pomp'), then racy prose with obscene innuendo:

— Lady, shall I lie in your lap?
— No, my lord.
— I mean my head upon your lap?
— Ay, my lord.
— Do you think I meant *count*ry matters?
— I think nothing, my lord.
— That's a fair thought to lie between maids' legs.
— What is, my lord?
— Nothing.[27]

Contrast the straightforward stability that marks the end of the play (v. ii), where all characters share a common stylistic decorum—Horatio ('Flights of angels sing thee to thy rest'), the

[27] For the obscene sense of 'nothing', see N. F. Blake, *Shakespeare's Language: An Introduction* (London 1983) 50, and cf. E. Partridge, *Shakespeare's Bawdy* (rev. edn., London 1968) s.vv. 'circle', 'O', 'ring'. Johnson's distress at the 'blanket' image in *Macbeth* (*The Rambler*, 168: Raleigh, *Johnson on Shakespeare*, 203–5) is occasioned by a much milder, but characteristic, instance of the same mobility.

ambassador ('The ears are senseless that should give us hearing'), the dying Hamlet himself ('Absent thee from felicity awhile'). Elsewhere in Shakespeare, again, a differential stability characterizes the writing: noble Prince Hal greets the prostrate figure of Falstaff in verse ('Death hath not struck so fat a deer today'); grotesque Falstaff stumbles to his feet in prose ('to counterfeit dying, when a man thereby liveth, is to be no counterfeit') (*Henry IV, Part I*, v. iv).

In ancient literature there are few developed analogues to these modern specimens of mobility. It is representative that in Greek tragedy there is no equivalent to Shakespeare's mobilities of style, and noteworthy that Euripides' supposedly tragicomic experiments nowhere engender any appreciable stylistic heterogeneity of the kind under discussion. Euripides' tragedy remains a model of differential stability, no less than the tragedy of his predecessors. In Euripides, as in most Greek—and most ancient—literature, stability rules: decorum and distance are fundamental. The stylistic level at which Euripides' dialogue is pitched may be, overall, a few degrees 'lower' than theirs, or perhaps the range in question is in any case wider. But the differences between his lyrics, his recitative, and his dialogue are as evident as those in Aeschylean or Sophoclean drama, dependent as they indeed are on precisely the same sets of characteristic features.[28] The closest ancient approximations to the modern versions of mobility are provided by the Roman satirists (not least, Petronius), and first and foremost by Aristophanes. Quite unlike the Greek tragedians, he practises a mobility of language which equals, and in some ways even exceeds, anything we have seen in our English exemplars. Let us recall the opening of *Frogs* (19–20)—

> *ὦ τρισκακοδαίμων ἄρ' ὁ τράχηλος οὑτοσί,*
> *ὅτι θλίβεται μέν, τὸ δὲ γέλοιον οὐκ ἐρεῖ*
>
> So—thrice wretched is this neck of mine:
> It's all 'squashed', and it still can't do its joke—

[28] Eur.'s occasional use of 'colloquialisms' (P. T. Stevens, *Colloquial Expressions in Euripides* (Wiesbaden 1976)) does nothing to affect the point: the 'colloquialisms' in question are not low vulgarisms, but 'ordinary', still tragic-compatible, idioms; and in Euripidean lyric, even the 'semi-comic' Phrygian in *Orestes* sings in consistently 'articulate, high-flown, typical' lyric idiom (M. L. West, *Euripides, Orestes* (Warminster 1987) 277).

where a hint of high style in *ὦ τρισκακοδαίμων* rapidly makes way for the coarse pleasantry that was first featured a few lines earlier. And in the opening lines of *Acharnians* we may recall the extraordinary range of idiom that confronts us—from exotic coinages to moments of sensuous description, from painful puns to (as so often) tragic resonances.[29]

Mobility in such instances presupposes diversity of stylistic technique, as well as variability of stylistic level—in fact the kind of diversity that makes passages like *Peace* 774–95 possible:

Μοῦσα, σὺ μὲν πολέμους ἀπ-
ωσαμένη μετ' ἐμοῦ
τοῦ φίλου χόρευσον, 775
κλείουσα θεῶν τε γάμους
ἀνδρῶν τε δαῖτας
καὶ θαλίας μακάρων· σοὶ
γὰρ τάδ' ἐξ ἀρχῆς μέλει. 780
ἢν δέ σε Καρκίνος ἐλθὼν
ἀντιβολῇ μετὰ τῶν παίδων χορεῦσαι,
μήθ' ὑπάκουε μήτ' ἔλ- 785
θῃς συνέριθος αὐτοῖς,
ἀλλὰ νόμιζε πάντας
ὄρτυγας οἰκογενεῖς, γυλιαύχενας ὀρχηστὰς
νανοφυεῖς, σφυράδων ἀποκνήσματα, μηχανοδίφας. 790
καὶ γὰρ ἔφασχ' ὁ πατὴρ ὃ παρ' ἐλπίδας
εἶχε τὸ δρᾶμα γαλῆν τῆς
ἑσπέρας ἀπάγξαι. 795

Lady, I pray thee, cast out war
And, sweetheart, dance with me instead
And hail, as thou hast hailed before,
Heroes' feasts, gods new-wed,
Felicity among the blest.
Mind you, if Carcinus turns up and pest-
ers you to dance with his boys, ignore
The lot,
Seek not
To be seen dead

[29] Above, pp. 29, 35–6. Stanford was on the right lines in associating A with Rabelais, Shakespeare, and Joyce, against the 'homogeneous and disciplined' styles of Homer, Sophocles, and Plato—even if his formulation effectively ignores the factor of *differential* stability (Plato, 'homogeneous'?) and introduces an unfortunate implication of *in*discipline (W. B. Stanford, *Aristophanes, The Frogs* (London 1963), p. xlii).

With
Fighting-cock stay-at-homes,
Hedgehog-necked poky-formed
Gimmick-grabbing knobs of dancing goat-turd.

You heard Dad's tragedy croaked,
When they eventually booked the play?—
And he blamed the cat : 'she choked
My drama speechless yesterday.'

This lyric stanza[30] begins in the manner of elevated choral lyric with a reminiscence of Stesichorus, marked not only by the phraseology, but also by the lofty dactylo-epitrite metre (for us associated definitively with the splendours of the victory-ode).[31] Yet no sooner is the idiom established than it changes. The invocation to the Muse ('Lady') implies the voice of a lofty artist, and a lofty artist might indeed bid his Muse get the dancers going—as the poet Alcman once did, and as Aristophanes himself was to do in *Frogs*; or might declare that the Muse bids *him* dance, as Euripides' chorus once did; or might say, as another Euripidean chorus said, that his dance is dear to the Muses, or that the Muses themselves love to dance, either on their own or (say) with Apollo, as Sappho and Simonides did.[32] But no lofty artist would tell the Muse to join in a dance *with* him. Though not quite an invitation

[30] The ode of the parabasis and, in form, a cletic hymn: on its technical aspects see Olson ad loc., Parker, *Songs*, 6–10, 276–8, Zimmermann, *Untersuchungen*, ii. 181–3; however, the literary-stylistic aspects of the song have hardly been acknowledged. (C. Kugelmeier, *Reflexe früher und zeitgenössischer Lyrik in der alten attischen Komödie* (Stuttgart 1996) 84–9, and elsewhere, is effectively concerned with Stesichorus, rather than with A's song.) As elsewhere, but very obviously here, my transl. aims to convey the force, effect, and movement of the original, at the cost of (several times) expanding or departing from the Greek; even so, I have not always contrived to locate the movement in the corresponding place, and I have only been able to hint at the metre.

[31] Stesich. 33 *PMG*: precise appreciation of the opening lines is hindered by uncertainty about how much of the A is straight Stesichorus. In ascribing *πολέμους ἀπωσαμένη* to Stesich., however, Page (in *PMG*) is possibly wrong, and in ascribing *μετ' ἐμοῦ* likewise (followed by e.g. Kugelmeier, *Reflexe*, 24, 84) certainly wrong (rightly, Parker, *Songs*, 7): the jovial 'relationship' set up between poet and Muse is Aristophanic, as my analysis indicates. The rhythm of A's composite is dactylic at first (–⏑⏑–⏑⏑–× | –⏑⏑–⏑⏑–), then in its subsequent variations largely follows tragic precedents (cf. West, *Greek Metre*, 132–3, on the use of the ithyphallic, as in 775, and the Aristophanean, as in 785).

[32] Respectively Alcm. 27 *Μῶσ' . . . τίθη χορόν*, Ar. *Ran.* 674; Eur. *HF* 686 *Μούσας αἵ μ' ἐχόρευσαν*; Eur. *El.* 874–5 *ἁμέτερον . . . Μούσαισι χόρευμα φίλον*; Sapph. 208 *PLF*, Simon. 73 *PMG*.

to be Ginger to his Fred, the command 'dance with me' (*μετ' ἐμοῦ χόρευσον*), especially with a casual endearment ('sweetheart': *τοῦ φίλου*) tacked on, evokes a very different context—perhaps of family relationship, more likely of erotic love.[33]

The switch of idiom now becomes programmatic for the whole stanza. First, we find ourselves back with the lofty tones of the beginning, ('And hail . . .': *κλείουσα* . . .),[34] then at once in a plain sequence ('Mind you . . .': *ἢν δέ σε* . . .), not exactly coarse or vulgar in tone, but once again alien to high lyric and in general redolent of ordinary conversation: one notes in particular the everyday presence of 'Carcinus', name of a real-life individual, the celebrated tragedian father of three equally celebrated terpsichorean sons.[35] Then, with 'Seek not' (*συνέριθος* . . .),[36] high style returns once more, only again to disappear at once in favour of the ordinary ('To be seen dead': *ἀλλὰ νόμιζε πάντας*), which in its turn makes way for something quite new.

Without warning, the entire character of the writing changes to a distinctive and violent idiom of abuse, starkly consisting of clotted-compound appositional phrases, improbably mediated, in Aristophanes' Greek, through a new all-dactylic rhythm, with the rich mixture introduced by a metaphor of a distinctive, transformational, type (think of them as *ὄρτυγας*, fighting-*birds*),[37] and the heavy compounds poised between the high and the low, the familiar (high *or* low) and the outlandish.[38] Deliciously, given

[33] For the dancing, cf. daughter to mother at Eur. *Tro.* 332–3 *χόρευε, μᾶτερ,* . . . *μετ' ἐμέθεν* and groom to bride at Ar. *Av.* 1759–61 *ὦ μάκαιρα* . . . *συγχόρευσον*. For the endearment (*φίλου*, '[me your] lover', transferred in the English to '[you, my] sweetheart'), note that though substantival *φίλος* and (after Homer) *οἱ φίλοι* are very common throughout prose and verse, the sg. *ὁ φίλος* is rare in high verse (Soph. *Aj.* 680 is one such occurrence) and chiefly occurs in comedy and philosophical generalizations, a disproportionate number of them proverbial in character. Thus: Ar. *Thes.* 346 *προδιδοῦσ' ἑταίρα τὸν φίλον* and *Eccl.* 897–9 *στέργειν* . . . *τὸν φίλον ᾧπερ ξυνείην* (both erotic); Arist. *Pol.* 1287^{b}33 *ὅ γε φίλος ἴσος καὶ ὅμοιος* and *EN* 1166^{a}31 *ἔστι γὰρ ὁ φίλος ἄλλος αὐτός* (cf. R. Strömberg, *Greek Proverbs* (Göteborg 1954) 76), cf. Arist. *EE* 1238^{a}16, 1241^{a}13, 1245^{a}29–30, *EN* 1170^{b}7.

[34] Lofty tones signalled by the epic form *κλείουσα* and the verse-word *δαῖτας*: see LSJ s.vv. *κλέω* (A) and *δαίς*. The absence of definite articles in the seven-noun sequence from *θεῶν* to *ἀρχῆς* confirms the shift.

[35] In the Greek NB also *ἀντιβολεῖν* in the sense 'beg' (LSJ s.v. I. 5). On Carcinus and sons, see *Vesp.* 1498 ff. and below, p. 432.

[36] *συνέριθος* is restricted to high verse and Plato (LSJ s.v.). For Plato and verse usage cf. Silk, *Interaction*, 39, 220–1.

[37] In Greek, *quails*, i.e. little birds kept as pets but chiefly for fighting (see Dunbar on *Av.* 704–7).

[38] (*a*) *οἰκογενής* (lit. 'home-born') is an ordinary prosaic formation, unattested in

the concurrent switch to dactylic rhythm, the compounds carry a new resonance. Through their morphological or phraseological-rhythmical resemblance to a variety of familiar Homeric shapes, 'stay-at-homes', 'hedgehog-necked', 'poky-formed', and 'gimmick-grabbing' evoke the bizarrely different world of heroic epic, a world of lofty compound adjectives like διογενής ('born-of-Zeus'), ἐριαύχην ('arch-necked'), εὐρυφυής ('wide-formed'), ἀργυροδίνης ('silver-swirling').[39] After which, we begin a new sentence, with a sudden switch of tone from the abusive to the confidential (καὶ γάρ . . .: 'You heard . . .')—and the idiom changes once more. Simple colloquial Greek reappears, replete with little words (particles, articles, prepositions), and no elevation,[40] and a very specific topical allusion, articulated to the point of a sharp satirical climax on the last phrase. Carcinus' play (apparently) wasn't ready, because (absurd excuse) the cat (in Greek, 'weasel' or 'polecat') throttled it: it was accordingly, *speechless*.

The whole sequence is extraordinary, and yet more extraordinary is that the sequence is repeated, almost note for note, in the

classical high verse (cf. LSJ s.v.). ἀλεκτορίδες οἰκ. is Aristotle's similar phrase for birds raised on the premises (*HA* 558[b]20). Contrast Pindar's lofty ἐνδομάχας ἀλέκτωρ, *Ol.* 12. 14. The point of the compound here (as of Pindar's) is that birds remote from the wild are lacking in competitive aggression. (*b*) γυλιαύχην, (*c*) νανοφυής, and (*d*) μηχανοδίφης are all eccentric neologisms, whose separate elements are ordinary or low: see the spread of evidence in LSJ s.vv. γυλιός (in whatever sense: on the interpretation, see E. K. Borthwick, 'The dances of Philocleon and the sons of Carcinus in Aristophanes' *Wasps*', *CQ* 18 (1968) 50), νᾶνος, μηχανή, and compound adjectives like μακραύχην, μονοφυής. Compounds in -διφ- are the exclusive province of Old Comedy (Ar. *Nub.* 192, *Av.* 1424, Cratin. 2) and post-classical authors: see the data in Headlam–Knox on Herod. 3. 54. On the sense of διφάω see Hes. *Op.* 374 and West ad loc.

[39] Rhythmically, 788–9, ὄρτυγας . . . , is like an abbreviated epic verse (dact. hex. cat.) 790–1, νανοφυεῖς . . . , a regular dact. hex. The sequences recall the epic for another reason, evoking a distinctive idiom of less-than-heroic reproach, marked by similar, if less intensive, clusters of disparaging compounds: cf. *Il.* 3. 39 Δύσπαρι, εἶδος ἄριστε, γυναιμανές, ἠπεροπευτά, 5. 31 Ἆρες Ἄρες βροτολοιγέ, μιαιφόνε, τειχεσιπλῆτα, Hes. *Op.* 196 (of envy) δυσκέλαδος, κακόχαρτος ὁμαρτήσει στυγερώπης; sim. Pind. *Nem.* 8. 33 (dactylo-epitrites), Ar. *Eq.* 1068 (parachresmody, dact. hex.). Such clusterings build on the pattern of one-off 'compound adjectives . . . coined for insults in the *Iliad*' (West on Hes. *Op.* 39, q.v.); instances outside *Il.* include (all dact. hexx.) *Od.* 18. 79, Hes. *Op.* 373 and *Scut.* 266, *h.Herm.* 436, Hippon. 128. 1. For the *reductio ad absurdum* of the type, see D. L. Page, *Further Greek Epigrams* (Cambridge 1981) 475–7 (Hellenistic elegiacs).

[40] Some of the vocabulary is used in e.g. tragedy, but not distinctively so: παρ' ἐλπίδα Aesch. *Agam.* 900 (and Pind. *Ol.* 13. 83)—but also Thuc. 4. 62. 3 and Aen. Tact. 23. 3.

metrically equivalent antistrophe immediately afterwards. Thus we have our Stesichorean high-lyrical opening,

> *τοιάδε χρὴ Χαρίτων δα-*
> *μώματα καλλικόμων*
>
> Hymns of praise the deep-haired Graces taught him (796–7)[41]

followed by the switch to ordinary (albeit very loaded) phraseology:

> *τὸν σοφὸν ποιητὴν*
> *ὑμνεῖν*
>
> A true artist should deliver . . . (798–9).[42]

Then, as in the earlier stanza, the pattern is repeated twice,[43] until—as in the earlier stanza—ordinary Greek is juxtaposed to outlandish. Corresponding to the satire on the Carcinus family is a sally at the expense of the gormandizing brothers and fellow-tragedians, Morsimus and Melanthius (808–13):

> *ἀδελ-*
> *φός τε καὶ αὐτός, ἄμφω*
> *Γοργόνες ὀψοφάγοι, βατιδοσκόποι Ἅρπυιαι,*
> *γραοσόβαι μιαροί, τραγομάσχαλοι ἰχθυολῦμαι.*
>
> One brother
> And the other
> On the job,
> Both
> Tea-time Medusas,
> Cod-swooping Harpies,
> Fish-slitting armpits of scare-crone goat-pong.

[41] Stesich. 35. 1 *PMG*, marked (*inter alia*) by ellipse of the article and high-style compound *καλλικόμων* (cf. the spread of usage in LSJ s.v.). For 'deep-haired' cf. Tennyson, 'Oenone', 173–4 ('her deep hair | Ambrosial').

[42] Note the definite article, as well as the prosaic *ποιητής* (not in high verse: the closest is Astydam. Min. 4. 2 *TGF*, which is satyric (cf. '*Trag.*' *Adesp.* 646a 36 *TGF*); an alleged use in Eur. fr. 663 Nauck is not credible).

[43] From the high-lyrical *χελιδὼν . . . κελαδῇ* (both words quoted from Stesich.: fr. 34 *PMG*) to ordinary topical *Μόρσιμος* and *Μελάνθιος* (800–1, 802–3); and from high-lyrical *ὄπα γηρύσαντος* (archetypal verse-words (cf. LSJ s.vv. *ὄψ* A and *γηρύω*), the former archetypically without article) to the ordinary idiom of *τραγῳδῶν* (with article back) (804–5, 806): *τρ.*, like *ποιητής*, belongs to prose/comedy but not high verse (an occurrence on an iambic 'exercice de versification' on a 5th/4th-cent. vase (*CEG* ii. 902) is no exception).

Once more the two dactylic lines are stacked with cheerily offensive heavy compounds, introduced (again) by a transformational metaphor ('Medusas'), with the metaphorical noun accompanied by a relatively commonplace compound, *ὀψοφάγοι* ('tea-time', literally 'titbit-eating').[44] What follows differs from the strophe only in the sense that the exaggerated features are, if anything, yet more exaggerated: a second mythological transformation ('Harpies') and new depths of compounded extravagance.[45] However, in place of the satire that concludes the strophe, the antistrophe offers, first another touch of coarseness, then a last moment of high style, and thus an extra stylistic collision (815–18):

> ὧν καταχρεμψαμένη μέγα καὶ πλατὺ
> Μοῦσα θεὰ μετ' ἐμοῦ ξύμ-
> παιζε τὴν ἑορτήν.
>
> Give them a fat gob
> Of spit, my lady Muse, but scorn
> Not me, please,
> This pious morn.[46]

Notwithstanding this and other variations, the two stanzas display an astonishing degree of correspondence. There could be no better illustration of Aristophanes' stylistic virtuosity or the control he exercises over it, and it is that virtuosity, but also that control, on which his disconcerting mobility depends.

As our specimen passage from *Plutus* suggested,[47] Aristophanes' late drama tends towards a homogeneity of style. By contrast, his earlier plays—the Old Comedies from *Acharnians*

[44] Cf. the spread of usage of the compound in LSJ s.v.

[45] As before, the tone of the first elements in each compound is neutral or commonplace (cf. LSJ s.vv. *βατίς* ('skate', here transl. 'cod'), *γραῦς, τράγος, ἰχθῦς*), but the second is more variable: *-σκόπος* is equivocal (cf. e.g. high *τερασκόπος*, prosaic *τερατοσκόπος*: LSJ s.vv.); *γραοσόβαι* is a one-off compound from ordinary *σοβέω*; *ἰχθυολῦμαι* recalls the isolated, and elevated, *παιδολυμάς* of Aesch. *Cho.* 605; *τραγομάσχαλοι* (which puns maliciously on *τραγῳδῶν*, 806) involves the ordinary-to-low *μασχάλη*, 'armpit' (LSJ s.v.). In the transl. the armpittery has been reformulated to make 'armpits' a parallel trope to the 'knobs' of 791 and '*goat*-pong' (*τραγο-*) to the 'goat-turd' (*σφυράδων*) of 790; 'scare-crone' comes from Sommerstein.

[46] *Μοῦσα θεά* is the only bit of high style here, but *ξυμπαίζειν* and *ἑορτή* (common to all registers of the language: LSJ s.vv.) accommodate themselves to the earlier elevation. 'This pious morn': Keats, 'Ode on a Grecian Urn', st. 4.

[47] Above, pp. 24–6.

to *Peace*, and *Peace* to *Frogs*—are paradigms of stylistic mobility. At the same time, however, like all surviving Greek plays of the fifth century, these same plays defer to the principle of differential stability in the way that the division of a play into performatively distinct sections of speech, recitative, or song is enforced by stylistic means. The performative sectionalization has strong metrical implications, in that certain metres are used only, or largely, in one performative mode. Speech is normally conducted in iambic trimeters, the commonest metre of Attic comedy (as of Attic drama as a whole). Anapaestic metres (to take another common group) are not associated with speech, but with song and, especially, with recitative. The catalectic anapaestic tetrameter[48] is associated particularly with the first section of the parabasis, so much so that the section can even be announced in the play itself in such terms (*Acharnians* 627):

> ἀλλ' ἀποδύντες τοῖς ἀναπαίστοις ἐπίωμεν.
>
> Let's strip for action and attack the anapaests.[49]

Such an association of metre and function is generally identified as a formal phenomenon, but it is equally a stylistic one. A switch of metre (as to anapaests) is inevitably a stylistic switch, because a cast of words based on one recurring shape is bound to differ from one based on others. But in any case Aristophanes' metrical groupings are also, very definitely, associated with contrasting stylistic levels, with the effect that the idiom of the ordinary iambic trimeters is 'lowest'—meaning, presumptively, closest to 'that of actual life'—whereas the linguistic features of the recitative metres are broadly 'higher', and those of the lyrics 'highest' of all.[50] 'Height' in this sense is established negatively—by the characteristic absence or reduced presence of 'low' features—and positively, by the characteristic presence, to whatever degree, of 'high' features. At the 'highest' point of the recitative

[48] ⏑⏑–⏑⏑–⏑⏑–⏑⏑–⏑⏑–⏑⏑–⏑⏑–– (with or without contractions).

[49] Likewise *Eq.* 504, *Pax* 735, *Av.* 684.

[50] The quoted phrases belong to H. Richards, *Aristophanes and Others* (London 1909) 119, who called levels 'strata' and who, though without either adequate methodology or comprehensive data, offered a useful account of 'The diction of Aristophanes' (ibid. 116–59); cf. Silk, 'Lyric poet', 119–22. Richards's 'diction', however, covers only the lexicon, not linguistic features as a whole. A project for a fuller linguistic analysis of A's levels is sketched by Dover, *Greek and the Greeks*, 224–36.

scale stand the anapaests; and, accordingly, any representative anapaestic sequence carries (for instance) relatively little of Aristophanes' abundant obscenity, and is liable to carry, instead, specific features not attested in comic iambics (unless in clearly paratragic contexts), but attested in high poetry outside the comic sphere—in tragedy, epic, and lyric. Thus the anapaests that follow the stripping-for-action in *Acharnians* begin (628):

> *ἐξ οὗ γε χοροῖσιν ἐφέστηκεν τρυγικοῖς ὁ διδάσκαλος ἡμῶν . . .*
>
> Ever since our director *has been in charge of comic choruses* . . .

but literally,

> . . . *has choruses directed comic* . . .

Here the given phrase has a slight, but perceptible, high-poetic cast, not because of the diction as such, but by virtue of the word-order. The words in question comprise a noun–adjective phrase, separated by a verb, as is commonplace in high poetry, but not in ordinary Greek speech patterns, as represented in (*inter alia*) comic iambics.[51] Such diagnostic contrasts, multiplied many times in the course of a single play, constitute a major source of the differential stability that may properly be ascribed to Aristophanes.

And yet Aristophanic verse, however stable in this sense, remains also strikingly and defiantly mobile; and this is so, partly because style is more than a matter of levels, partly because even within each Aristophanic level, though there are tendencies, there are no restrictions, and partly because Aristophanic comedy ultimately operates on what one can only call a popular basis. Specifically, it works on a principle of democratic inclusiveness, to which the logic of decorum and distance is inapplicable. As our earlier instances from *Acharnians* showed, Aristophanes' 'ordinary' speech can 'rise'; and as our *Peace* examples have shown, his song (though more 'elevated' overall) can and does 'fall'—only to 'rise' and 'fall', but without any decorous predictability, again. At

[51] e.g. the only instances earlier in *Ach.* occur at 229–31 in lyric (*σχοῖνος . . . ἀντεμπαγῶ ὀξύς*) 303 in recitative (*λόγους λέγοντος . . . μακρούς*), and 445 (*πυκνῇ . . . μηχανᾷ φρενί*) and 572 (*βοῆς ἤκουσα πολεμιστηρίας*), both of which are paratragic (Rau, *Paratragodia*, 33, 41). (Instances involving the definite article are different and not counted.) By contrast, one quickly finds examples in Homer (*Il.* 1. 1–2 *μῆνιν ἄειδε . . . οὐλομένην*), Pindar (*Ol.* 1. 10–11 *ἀφνεὰν ἱκομένους . . . ἑστίαν*), Euripides (*Med.* 7 *γῆς ἔπλευσ' Ἰωλκίας*).

bottom (*mot juste*), Aristophanic comedy rests on a 'low', colloquial, popular substrate, which is, however, anything but an exclusive, embattled confrontational space. This substrate dominates the iambic trimeters that are the staple of all the plays, but also underlies all the varieties of differentiated expression, and all these varieties may at any point revert to it.[52] With an immediacy that more decorous writing cannot attain, Aristophanes' poetry responds to and draws strength from the specifics of the audience's own socio-linguistic experience. Its world is the world of known people, with their known particularities and known names, from Carcinus to Cleon. Its world is the world of known particulars, from war and peace to gobs of spit. And through its relationship with this world it allows us to glimpse—not for the first time, perhaps, and certainly not for the last—a series of correlations: between the low, the popular, the topical, the particular, the immediate. We may relate these Aristophanic realities, in turn, to fundamental theory and to fundamental corollaries of the comic; and (or but) we may, in any case, provisionally conclude that while the differential stability that exists within Aristophanes' comedy guarantees the low (and its equivalents) a voice, it is only his mobility that allows the low to make its decisive contribution throughout the various compartments—but now no longer compartments—which that kind of stability entails.

The combination of mobile and differentially stable is rare. Among our examples, the nearest analogue is Shakespeare: not the comic Shakespeare especially, but, for instance, the Shakespeare of *Hamlet*, a tragedy, whatever its complexities, albeit to some a hybrid which is 'not in the rigorous or critical sense' a tragedy at all.[53] What Aristophanes' drama least resembles, among our examples, is the even, homogeneous comic texture of Oscar Wilde. And what late Aristophanes does, and then what Menander does more, is shift the comic norm substantially in the direction of that kind of homogeneity. Such a shift involves the progressive elimination of *both* Aristophanes' differential stability *and* his mobility. In this sense Aristophanes' eventual

[52] 'The substratum of Aristophanic language is presumably colloquial': K. J. Dover, in M. Platnauer (ed.), *Fifty Years (and Twelve) of Classical Scholarship* (Oxford 1968) 126. Cf. López Eire, *Lengua coloquial*.

[53] Johnson: Raleigh, *Johnson on Shakespeare*, 15.

abandonment of (for instance) the parabasis is ultimately relatable to, and not merely coincident with, the attenuation of the stylistic diversity seen in the openings of *Acharnians* and *Frogs*—in favour of the 'classical' restraint epitomized by the opening of *Plutus*. And for those of us who in the modern age associate stylistic mobility with the heterodox experiments of Eliot, or Beckett, or indeed Shakespeare, it is salutary to note that there is no necessary correlation between mobility and experiment: in its time, and from the standpoint of Aristophanic Old Comedy, the predominant idiom of *Plutus* must have represented heterodoxy and experiment, however 'natural' in the light of later developments (and indeed other ancient norms) its greater homogeneity may now seem to us.

Putting mobility to one side for the moment, let us consider the question: what are the specifics of Aristophanes' style? Faced with this question, we need first to clarify another fundamental, though rarely discussed, theoretical issue. When we speak of 'the style' of a work, an author, a genre, this implies an expectation of something more than a multiplicity of stylistic features. And if the work, author, or genre is substantial enough and significant enough to justify scrutiny, the expectation will prove to be well founded. It is indeed common for 'the style' of a work (etc.) to impinge on us as an accumulation of various discrete, momentary, details. Nevertheless, closer scrutiny will generally reveal a logic underlying the details, whereby they are seen to be related both to each other and, ultimately, to other aspects of the work (etc.) in question. In this spirit one espouses an interpretation of Homer that relates the intense stylization of the language to the massively ritualistic character of the life portrayed; or the observation (so unmistakable, it can almost be taken as a *datum*) that the dislocations and alarming juxtapositions of Eliot's 'Coriolan' or (still more unmistakably) Eliot's 'Waste Land' are symptoms of the eclectic heterogeneity ('I can connect nothing with nothing') that the poet identifies in contemporary life; or the argument that the elevation of Greek tragic idiom is the corollary of an aristocratic-heroic ethos integral to tragedy, at least in its Greek form.[54] And if

[54] Silk, *Iliad*, 100–2; Eliot, 'The Waste Land', 301–2; M. S. Silk, 'Tragic language: the Greek tragedians and Shakespeare', in Silk, *Tragedy and the Tragic*, 464 and 490–1 n. 24. There is, of course, nothing new about such 'holistic' readings: cf. e.g. Dionysius Hal., *On Thucydides*.

the style of an author, a work, or a genre can actually be shown to lack such a logic, and actually is a mere assemblage of details or devices, it will surely be a failure. The interpreter's need to find and articulate the logic, therefore, is a critical duty in the fullest sense. For Aristophanes, indeed, one will not find the kind of intellectual coherence of style and outlook that is implicit in the relatively Aristophanic mobility of Eliot. In the end, though, one will find a coherence, and one more akin to that embodied in the very un-Aristophanic idioms of Homer and of Greek tragedy. And the identification of the specific features of Aristophanes' style is the first step towards this end.

Aristophanes (it must by now be obvious) is a writer of considerable stylistic diversity, whose mobility indeed presupposes a diverse range of stylistic levels, techniques, and effects for him to be mobile with and between. Within this diversity, none the less, certain stylistic features can be shown to be especially significant. The first is physicality—physicality as we saw it in the verbal energy and sharp detail of Dicaeopolis' opening monologue in *Acharnians*:

> *τοῖς πέντε ταλάντοις οἷς Κλέων ἐξήμεσεν*
>
> . . . .
>
> *οἱ δ' ἐν ἀγορᾷ λαλοῦσι κἄνω καὶ κάτω*
> *τὸ σχοινίον φεύγουσι τὸ μεμιλτωμένον.*
>
> The five talents fell out when Cleon puked
>
> . . . .
>
> And they'll be chattering in the square, or charging
> Up and down to dodge the painted rope . . .

Here, the predisposition of all comedy towards the material, towards the 'specific embodiment', is given poetic form—here as almost everywhere in Aristophanes, in a rich variety of different guises.[55]

Take a few more instances from *Acharnians*. Alongside the rich immediacy of the opening monologue we can set this (186–92):

> ΔΙ. *ἀλλὰ τὰς σπονδὰς φέρεις;*
> ΑΜ. *ἔγωγέ, φημι, τρία γε ταυτὶ γεύματα.*
> *αὗται μέν εἰσι πεντέτεις. γεῦσαι λαβών.*

[55] 'Specific embodiment': above, p. 95. The materiality of A's writing is acknowledged in a variety of ways, from Plato's portrayal of A in *Smp.* to Newiger's treatment of Aristophanic 'allegory' (*Metapher und Allegorie*).

ΔΙ. αἰβοῖ.
ΑΜ. τί ἐστιν;
ΔΙ. οὐκ ἀρέσκουσίν μ᾽ ὅτι
ὄζουσι πίττης καὶ παρασκευῆς νεῶν.
ΑΜ. σὺ δ᾽ ἀλλὰ τασδὶ τὰς δεκέτεις γεῦσαι λαβών.
ΔΙ. ὄζουσι χαὖται . . .

DICAEOPOLIS Got the treaties?
AMPHITHEUS Got three samples.
This one's a five-year: take a sip.
DIC. Nasty!
AMPH. What's the problem?
No joy here:
Smells of pitch and naval preparations.
AMPH. Try the ten-year—have a sip.
DIC. Smells as well . . .

Vines and wine, here and elsewhere in Aristophanes, connote peace. More specifically, the passage relies in the first place on the ambiguity of the word *σπονδαί*, 'drink-offerings' as well as 'treaty'. Dicaeopolis is offered three versions of a peace-treaty with Sparta, each of a different duration; and—or *that is*—he is offered three sample vintages, each of a different year. Abstract issues of peace and war are dramatized concretely through the metonymic word play. Then again, 'smells of pitch and naval preparations' embodies an idiom, to be discussed in its own right shortly, in which the concrete 'smells', the semi-abstract 'preparations', and the equivocal 'pitch' combine to produce a sensuous effect of a sharply distinctive kind.[56]

More straightforward in point of technique, and more intensely physical in its effect, is Dicaeopolis' vision of fulfilment in his phallic song (*Acharnians* 271–5):

πολλῷ γάρ ἐσθ᾽ ἥδιον, ὦ Φαλῆς Φαλῆς,
κλέπτουσαν εὑρόνθ᾽ ὡρικὴν ὑληφόρον
τὴν Στρυμοδώρου Θρᾷτταν ἐκ τοῦ φελλέως,
μέσην λαβόντ᾽, ἄραντα, κατα-
βαλόντα καταγιγαρτίσαι.

Yes, how much sweeter, my Lord Prick, to catch
Strymodorus' Thratta, ready and ripe,

[56] 'Pitch: used both for caulking ships and for flavouring inferior wines': Sommerstein ad loc. On the idiom, see below, pp. 145–7.

Sneaking wood from the fell, tackle her,
Toss her and tumble her down, and press her grape.

The closing metaphor (suggestive again of the association between wine and peace) is novel and, as is usual with novel metaphor, operates with a powerful sensuous charge.[57] The passage then continues with a still more straightforward, yet hardly less powerful, metonymic cluster, with each component *pars pro toto*, symbolic specific instance of a more general condition (276–9):

Φαλῆς Φαλῆς,
ἐὰν μεθ' ἡμῶν ξυμπίῃς, ἐκ κραιπάλης
ἕωθεν εἰρήνης ῥοφήσεις τρύβλιον·
ἡ δ' ἀσπὶς ἐν τῷ φεψάλῳ κρεμήσεται.

Lord Prick, Prick,
Drink with me now and, come the morning,
You have a cup of peace to stop your headache:
I'll hang my shield up in the fire's embers.

Sensuous physicality is not the only characteristic of Aristophanes' imagery, but it is its single most prominent characteristic. Accordingly, one of his favourite kinds of image is the transformation, whose physical shock-effect is almost pure: 'Tea-time Medusas' (*Peace* 810). This kind of image has an instantaneous quality. It is bold, perhaps racy, certainly explicit, short, and sharp; its obvious grammatical prerequisite is a nominal base; noun is transformed to noun, thing to thing: the *haecceitas* ('thisness') is fundamental.[58] Instances abound, from the earlier plays,

[57] On the metaphor, the passage, and the translation, see below, pp. 181–7. On the sensuous and other functions of metaphor, see M. S. Silk, 'Metaphor and metonymy: Aristotle, Jakobson, Ricoeur, and others', in G. Boys-Stones (ed.), *Metaphor and Allegory* (Oxford, forthcoming).

[58] Racy: the transformation is arguably a popular kind of image, esp. in certain forms: cf. W. B. Stanford, *Aeschylus in his Style* (Dublin 1942) 94, on the 'metaphorical identification of persons with inanimate objects', and H. W. Prescott, 'Criteria of originality in Plautus', *TAPA* 63 (1932) 112–13, on 'Plautinities in Plautus' that turn out to be Greek in provenance (with ref. to e.g. Anaxandrides, 35 *PCG*). Nominal base: cf. C. Brooke-Rose, *A Grammar of Metaphor* (London 1958), esp. 17–25. *Haecceitas*: as in the usage of the 13th-cent. Christologist, John Duns Scotus, who exercised a notable influence on G. M. Hopkins. 'This . . . Scotist concept of *haecceitas* defines the thisness that constitutes an existent, that makes this being *be*': J. F. Cotter, *Inscape: The Christology and Poetry of Gerard Manley Hopkins* (Pittsburgh 1972) 125–6.

ἔχε νυν ἐπὶ τούτοις τουτονὶ τὸν ὀκλαδίαν
καὶ παῖδ' ἐνόρχην, ὅσπερ οἴσει τόνδε σοι·
κἄν που δοκῇ σοι, τοῦτον ὀκλαδίαν ποίει

On that condition take this folding chair
And a boy with balls: make him carry it—
Or else make *him* a *folding chair* instead

(*Knights* 1384–6),

to the later,

νὴ τοὺς θεούς, Μίδας μὲν οὖν, ἢν ὦτ' ὄνου λάβητε

God's truth, you'll each be *Midas*—with an ass's ear

(*Plutus* 287),

but the type is especially characteristic of the earlier. The short, sharp shocks occur not only in ones, but also, quite often, in clusters, as again at *Peace* 810–11 ('Medusas . . . Harpies . . .') or, more elaborately, as at *Acharnians* 936–9, where Dicaeopolis is busy converting the informer Nicarchus into

πάγχρηστον ἄγγος . . .,
κρατὴρ κακῶν, τριπτὴρ δικῶν,
φαίνειν ὑπευθύνους λυχνοῦ-
χος καὶ κύλιξ
τὰ πράγματ' ἐγκυκᾶσθαι

. . . an all-purpose container:
A dish for dirt,
A prosecutions pot,
A lamp to bring the state accounts to light,
A tray for trouble-making—

where sensuousness is hugely intensified by sound.

The most aggressively physical feature of Aristophanic poetry is obscenity. In view of the ubiquitousness of obscenities in the plays, lengthy exemplification is hardly necessary. A few moments from *Acharnians*, once again, will serve to suggest the range and physical relish of Aristophanes' maculate imagination, from Dicaeopolis' attempts to keep himself occupied during his solitary wait at the assembly (30)—

στένω, κέχηνα, σκορδινῶμαι, πέρδομαι

Sighing, yawning, stretching, farting—

to the scene in which the Megarian farmer seeks to pass his daughters off to Dicaeopolis as piglets, and the pair create a classic routine around the equivocal word *χοῖρος* ('pig' and 'cunt': 729–96)—to the elaborate verbal tableau (rich in sound-effects again) through which Dicaeopolis, now triumphant, confronts his crippled opponent, the man of war, Lamachus (1214–21):

ΛΑ. *λάβεσθέ μου, λάβεσθε τοῦ σκέλους· παπαῖ,*
προσλάβεσθ', ὦ φίλοι.
ΔΙ. *ἐμοῦ δέ γε σφὼ τοῦ πέους ἄμφω μέσου*
προσλάβεσθ', ὦ φίλαι.
ΛΑ. *εἰλιγγιῶ κάρα λιθῷ πεπληγμένος*
καὶ σκοτοδινιῶ.
ΔΙ. *κἀγὼ καθεύδειν βούλομαι καὶ στύομαι*
καὶ σκοτοβινιῶ.

LAM. Get my leg
Off the ground—
Boys, get me up.
DIC. Grab my cock,
Hand it round—
Girls, get it up!
LAM. My head, my head aches
from a stone-on-brain encounter,
Whirling in the dark.
DIC. My hard, my hard-on
seeks a stay-in-bed encounter,
Shagging in the dark.[59]

It is a predisposition of comedy, we recall, not only to 'materialize', but even to 'degrade', and at such moments Aristophanes could hardly be a more literal exponent of this principle. Aristophanic obscenity continues to embarrass or irritate some—especially, perhaps, some of those whose preferred hunting-ground is political satire. Yet it is the same instinct for the material that produces these 'degradations' as also underlies Old Comedy's concern with a particular community and all its urgent realities, including political realities ('O City, city': *Acharnians* 27)

[59] For the *σκέλους/πέους* association in the first quatrain, cf. *Pax* 898 *πὺξ ὁμοῦ καὶ τῷ πέει*, and schol. ad loc., *παρὰ προσδοκίαν οὖν ἀντὶ τοῦ τῷ σκέλει*. The importance (and not merely the abundance) of obscenity in A is definitively established by Henderson, *Maculate Muse* (whatever reservations one may have about various of his interpretations, large and small).

in the here and now. The further implications of this materiality will appear in due course.

Several of the passages already before us embody another significant Aristophanic trait: accumulation. First and foremost, this means lists:

> Sighing, yawning, stretching, farting . . .
>
> Fighting-cock stay-at-homes,
> Hedgehog-necked poky-formed
> Gimmick-grabbing knobs of dancing goat-turd . . .[60]

The common feature of such lists is juxtaposition. Items are conjoined paratactically (ABC . . .), without subordination, and with sequential accumulation as the only visible organizing principle. Outside lists, paratactic-accumulative instincts come to the fore again in a relish for heavy compounds ('stay-at-homes', 'hedgehog-necked'). Strikingly, these include a number of multiple compounds like the one that—in seeming criticism of the very phenomenon under discussion—Euripides applies to Aeschylus in *Frogs*, *κομποφακελορρήμονα* ('fancy-phrase-trusser') or the ones Aeschylus applies back, *στωμυλιοσυλλεκτάδη* ('Old trendy-word-catcher') and *ῥακιοσυρραπτάδη* ('Old used-clothes stitcher').[61] Like lists, all such compounds minimize syntactic complication, in line with a general syntactic simplicity in Aristophanic writing as a whole.[62]

The paratactic list, ABC . . ., is a kind of parallel structure ('A is parallel to B, and . . .'), and parallel structures are another ubiquitous feature of Aristophanes' style in their own right. Recall Lamachus and Dicaeopolis—

[60] *Ach.* 30 and *Pax* 788–90: above, pp. 124 and 111–14. A list of A's lists is offered by E. S. Spyropoulos, *L'Accumulation verbale chez Aristophane* (Thessaloniki 1974)—but many examples (and any significant literary interpretation) are missing.

[61] *Ran.* 839–42. *στωμυλιο-* connotes not just empty, but fashionable, talk (cf. *στωμύλλειν* at *Nub.* 1003 and *στωμυλεῖται* at *Eq.* 1376), while *ῥακιο-* points not just to Eur.'s supposed fondness for heroes in rags (*Ran.* 1060 ff.), but perhaps also to his supposed willingness to recycle his own ideas (as in his prologues, *Ran.* 1198 ff.: cf. Goldhill, *Poet's Voice*, 216, and Sommerstein on *Ran.* 1198–1247). Many of the multiple compounds in the plays are included in a list of comic coinages (*vel sim.*) in W. J. M. Starkie, *The Acharnians of Aristophanes* (London 1909), pp. l–lii.

[62] 'Der Satzbau ist ohne Verwicklung': W. Schmid and O. Stählin, *Geschichte der griechischen Literatur*, I. iv (Munich 1959) 427, without further discussion.

λάβεσθέ μου, λάβεσθε τοῦ σκέλους . . .
προσλάβεσθ', ὦ φίλοι.
ἐμοῦ δέ γε σφὼ τοῦ πέους . . .
προσλάβεσθ', ὦ φίλαι.

Get my leg . . .
Boys, get me up.
Grab my cock . . .
Girls, get it up!—

and the elaborate correspondence of detail between the choral stanzas in *Peace* ('Lady . . .'—'Hymns . . .'), each with its high-lyrical opening, its successive switches, its satire on named fellow-performers, its accumulation of heavy compounds, and the rest. Both of these instances involve passages of sung lyric. Many others occur in recitative, often in agonistic sequences. Witness the matching insults of the two Arguments in *Clouds* (908–9)—

ΑΔΙΚ. τυφογέρων εἶ κἀνάρμοστος.
ΔΙΚ. καταπύγων εἶ κἀναίσχυντος.

WRONG You old twit, something's gone inside your brain.
RIGHT You crude git, someone's cock's inside your bum—

or those of Paphlagon-Cleon and Sausage-Seller in *Knights* (294–5):

ΠΑ. διαφορήσω σ', εἴ τι γρύξει.[63]
ΑΛ. κοπροφορήσω σ', εἰ λαλήσεις.

PAPH. Make a sound and I'll tear you to bits.
S.-S. Say a word, and you'll be in the shits.

At *Knights* 1164–9 Paphlagon and Sausage-Seller compete more subtly in iambic dialogue for the favour of master Demos:

ΠΑ. ὁρᾷς; ἐγώ σοι πρότερος ἐκφέρω δίφρον.
ΑΛ. ἀλλ' οὐ τράπεζαν· ἀλλ' ἐγὼ προτεραίτερος.
ΠΑ. ἰδοὺ φέρω σοι τήνδε μαζίσκην ἐγὼ
ἐκ τῶν ὀλῶν τῶν ἐκ Πύλου μεμαγμένην.
ΑΛ. ἐγὼ δὲ μυστίλας μεμυστιλημένας
ὑπὸ τῆς θεοῦ τῇ χειρὶ τἠλεφαντίνῃ.

PAPH. A chair for you: I got in first.
S.-S. You missed the table: I got in firster.

[63] Text as Neil (*et al.*), q.v.

PAPH. I offer you a barley-cake
Made of flour we won that day in Pylos.
S.-S. And I've got finger-bread for you,
Breadfulled by Our Lady's ivory finger.

The essence of the competition at this moment is balance, but implicit, as much as formal, balance: first, in the one-line offerings, Paphlagon's chair versus Sausage-Seller's table; then, in the two-liners, Paphlagon's cake versus Sausage-Seller's bread, each with its improbable, supposedly sacral, associations.[64] And not only are the competitors' offerings balanced one against the other: they are also contrasted in a way that foreshadows Sausage-Seller's eventual victory. The 'political' package represented by Paphlagon's bribes is unique; Sausage-Seller's package is, as he might say, more unique still—hence his strikingly one-off expressions, προτεραίτερος ('firster') and μεμυστιλημένας ('breadfulled').[65] Parallelisms, then, are constructed both between the agonists and between the elements of each.

Lysistrata 456–61, again from a sequence of iambic dialogue, is a very different instance. Our heroine calls up her troops to drive off the foe:

> ὦ ξύμμαχοι γυναῖκες, ἐκθεῖτ' ἔνδοθεν,
> ὦ σπερμαγοραιολεκιθολαχανοπώλιδες,
> ὦ σκοροδοπανδοκευτριαρτοπώλιδες,
> οὐχ ἕλξετ', οὐ παιήσετ', οὐκ ἀράξετε,
> οὐ λοιδορήσετ', οὐκ ἀναισχυντήσετε;
> παύσασθ', ἐπαναχωρεῖτε, μὴ σκυλεύετε.
>
> Girls, get over here and make it quick.
> All you down-the-market swede-and-cabbage women,
> All you at-the-roadhouse bread-and-garlic women!
> Get them, slap them harder, give them a beating,
> Give them a shout-down, show them how you play bad.
> Stop now! Sound the retreat: no stripping bodies!

Lists, multiple compounds, parallel structures, go together. The organization of the passage repays analysis. The whole sequence, in the first place, is line-stopped: each trimeter verse ends with an appreciable pause and no consequential enjambement. Contrast,

[64] ὀλαί (= Homeric οὐλαί) were sprinkled on the victim's head before sacrifice. 'Our Lady' is Athena, whose statue in the Parthenon was part-ivory.
[65] μυστιλῶμαι as passive 'seems to be unique' (Neil ad loc.).

for instance, Lysistrata's moment of military command with a superficially comparable sequence in Sophocles (*Oedipus Coloneus* 897–903, Theseus speaking):

> *οὔκουν τις ὡς τάχιστα προσπόλων μολὼν*
> *πρὸς τούσδε βωμοὺς πάντ' ἀναγκάσει λεὼν*
> *ἄνιππον ἱππότην τε θυμάτων ἄπο*
> *σπεύδειν ἀπὸ ῥυτῆρος, ἔνθα δίστομοι*
> *μάλιστα συμβάλλουσιν ἐμπόρων ὁδοί,*
> *ὡς μὴ παρέλθωσ' αἱ κόραι, γέλως δ' ἐγὼ*
> *ξένῳ γένωμαι τῷδε, χειρωθεὶς βίᾳ;*

Fagles's verse translation misrepresents the flow of the passage thus:

> Quickly, one of you, to the altars!
> Force our people to break off the rites,
> make a dash for it, all of them,
> foot-soldiers, cavalry, full gallop—
> go where the two highways meet, hurry!—
> before the girls are past that point
> and I'm a mockery to my enemy here,
> easy game for the first rough hand.[66]

A considerable misrepresentation, this, which effectively eliminates any significant enjambement and produces instead a tense and insistent sequence of unitary-rhythmic statements and qualifications. In its actual fluidity, whereby the rhythmic units are assumed, rather than asserted, and the syntactic-semantic organization is correspondingly allowed an independent life, the passage might be better rendered (*exempli gratia*) like this:

> One of you serving men, quick, go
> To the altars and call each worshipper
> From sacrifice and bid him run or ride
> At full speed to where the two roads meet,
> Before the girls have made it, and our friend
> Leaves me a victim and a laughing-stock.

There is in fact only a single coincidence of rhythm and sentence-structure before the final resolution.

In Aristophanic comedy, as in Fagles's (as opposed to the real) Sophocles, the single verse is often not so much a point of

[66] Sophocles, *The Three Theban Plays*, tr. R. Fagles (London 1982) 324.

departure as a unit in a series; and this insistence on the serial unit implies an instinct for parallelism, which duly engenders further parallel structuring on top. So, in Lysistrata's speech, a single opening verse of command is followed by a parallel pair, each consisting of monosyllabic address and multiple compounds whose parallelism is further enforced by sound-patterning at the beginning and end. The next two lines constitute another parallel pair, each line consisting of miniature accumulations of imperatives (aurally enforced), followed by another single-line set of imperative verbs to match the opening command.[67] These last three lines, furthermore, embody an additional parallelism. Within each line the sequence of verb forms is such that a rhythmic climax comes at the end. Each miniature series follows the 'law of increasing members' ('Friends, Romans, countrymen . . .'), so that the final member of each series is rhythmically the most considerable.[68] Elaborate as it is, there is something irresistible about the sequence and its momentum. And the same instinct that leads Aristophanes to associate one accumulative resource with another leads him to construct such analytically complex, yet natural-seeming, structures of parallel elements throughout his works.

It is fully in line with Aristophanes' method that parallel structure should be enforced by additional sound-effects in Lysistrata's speech:

ὦ σπερ-: 'All you . . . swede-and- . . .'
ὦ σκορ-: 'All you . . . bread-and- . . .'

In the same way, parallelism in the Lamachus/Dicaeopolis interchange is enforced by assonance on the keywords σκέλους/πέους ('leg'/'cock'); in the Nicarchus transformations by alliteration

[67] In the Greek, additionally, the opening and closing verses (456, 461) have the parallel feature of simple imperatives, 459–60 that of negative questions plus future verbs, with consequent internal rhyme, while the parallelism of 457–8 is enforced by alliteration (ὦ σπερ-/ὦ σκορ-) and rhyme (-νοπώλιδες/-τοπώλιδες), with additional semantic parallelism between σπερμ- and σκοροδο-: both elements qualify the women (not their produce: cf. Henderson ad loc.). Market women are a tough *seed* (LSJ s.v. σπέρμα II. 3); 'roadhouse' (boarding-house) women are, like fighting cocks, toughened by garlic. σπ. and σκ. belong, obviously, to the same semantic field (σκόροδον . . . ἀπὸ σπέρματος . . . βλαστάνει, Thphr. *HP* 7. 2. 1).

[68] 'Das Gesetz der wachsenden Glieder': O. Behagel, 'Beziehungen zwischen Umfang und Reihenfolge von Satzgliedern', *Ind. Forsch.* 25 (1909) 139. Cf. L. P. Wilkinson, *Golden Latin Artistry* (Cambridge 1963) 175–8.

(and more) for the opening items, *κρατὴρ κακῶν/τριπτὴρ δικῶν* ('dish for dirt'/'prosecutions pot') and in the *Clouds* insults by aural play on *τυφογέρων/καταπύγων* ('old twit'/'crude git').[69]

Given that such sound-patterns are well suited to linking the words that carry the pattern, it is no surprise that the use of aural links should be common in Aristophanes.[70] We find, for instance, a messenger rushing on towards the end of *Acharnians* to call Lamachus to war in a series of such linked phrases—so much so that within six lines (1071–6) he has invoked *μάχαι καὶ Λάμαχοι* ('fights and Lamachites'), *τοὺς λόχους καὶ τοὺς λόφους* ('plumes and platoons'), *Χοᾶς καὶ Χύτρους* ('Pitchers and Pots').[71] In fully fledged lists, too, it is often the case that links are supported by sound patterning. *Birds* 429–30 is a good example:

πυκνότατον κίναδος,
σόφισμα, κύρμα, τρῖμμα, παιπάλημ' ὅλον.

he's a real trickster,
All skill, swag, spice, sophistry.[72]

[69] In the Nicarchus passage at *Ach.* 937, besides the obvious *κ- κ-* that links the first pair and the *κρ- -κων τρ- -κων* that links both pairs, note the parallelism between *κρᾱ- κᾰ-* and *τρῑ- δῐ-* (where, as the sole inexactness in the pattern, voiced *δ-* stands in for unvoiced *τ-*). The aural sequence is resolved at the end of the sentence by more patterning in *κύ-λιξ . . . ἐγ-κυ-κᾶσθαι* (*Ach.* 939: above, p. 124). At *Nub.* 908–9 (above, p. 127) accentual and phraseological similarity, together with homoeoteleuton, outweighs a difference in metrical shape: – ⏑ ⏑ – / ⏑ ⏑ – –.

[70] For the common linking functions of sound-patterns, see my discussions in *Interaction*, 173–87, 224–8, and 'Assonance, Greek' in *OCD*³, 193–4. The inclination of classical scholars to associate such patterns (esp. when alliterative) with emotional or mimetic effects (often loosely lumped together as 'expressive' effects: see, classically, Fraenkel on Aesch. *Agam.* 268) is not helpful. Sometimes, of course, an alliterative link will *also* involve an 'expressive' effect (usually a sensuous charge): in A, note, e.g. *Nub.* 407 *ῥοίβδου καὶ . . . ῥύμης*, *Ach.* 353 *βάλλειν καὶ βοᾶν*, *Pax* 898 *πὺξ ὁμοῦ καὶ τῷ πέει*.

[71] With the first two cf. *μαχῶν καὶ Λαμάχων* in the phallic song (*Ach.* 269–70) and *τῶν λόφων καὶ τῶν λόχων* at *Ach.* 575.

[72] Word-final patterning in Greek, word-initial in the English. The first three *-μα* words are metonyms ('things for the people associated with the things'), and *κύρμα* (lit. 'booty') and *τρῖμμα* ('bits', as in a concoction of ground spices and meal (LSJ s.v. II. 1), too fine to get a handle on) are metaphorical as well. *παιπάλημα*, however, is only attested of people (LSJ s.v.), so is presumably standard—colloquial?—usage (likewise *κίναδος*). LSJ's conversion of *κύρμα* to 'swindler', *τρῖμμα* to 'knave', and *παιπ.* to 'metaphor', are characteristic misinterpretations (from which recent comm. ad loc. are not exempt) in the face of heightened usage: see my comments in *Interaction*, 33, 82–4, and 'LSJ and the problem of poetic archaism: from meanings to iconyms', *CQ* 33 (1983) 303–30.

In these and other cases (one might argue) the relish for parallel structures—from alliterative links to agonistic fencing—is essentially a *popular* one: the comic poet's formal instincts, like so much else, are close to immediate experience—in this instance, patterns of linguistic usage, such as are experienced, and immediately available, in popular forms elsewhere.[73] The popular affinity of various of his other favoured stylistic means—from obscenities to transformations—is likewise apparent.[74]

Accumulation as a stylistic phenomenon has a further set of implications that are most unmistakable, perhaps, in the case of lists. Whatever the overt mood of a list, one tends to sense a kind of exuberance in it that is associated, precisely, with its accumulative quality. In the first instance, this manifests itself as a matter of phraseological triumph, as in the *Birds* line just quoted: *σόφισμα, κύρμα . . .* ('All skill, swag . . .'). Often there is a satirical gusto, as in *Knights* 47–9, where the target is Paphlagon-Creon:

> *ὑποπεσὼν τὸν δεσπότην*
> *ᾔκαλλ', ἐθώπευ', ἐκολάκευ', ἐξηπάτα*
> *κοσκυλματίοις ἄκροισι*
>
> he fell at Master's feet,
> Fondling, fawning, wheedling, hoaxing him,
> With scraps of old leather.[75]

Then again, one finds a natural-seeming association between lists and the good things of life, as if the form, quite simply, connoted *plenty*. *Peace* is especially rich in examples. Thus 999–1003:

> *καὶ τὴν ἀγορὰν ἡμῖν ἀγαθῶν*
> *ἐμπλησθῆναι, 'κ Μεγάρων σκορόδων,*
> *σικύων πρῴων, μήλων, ῥοιῶν,*
> *δούλοισι χλανισκιδίων μικρῶν·*
> *κἀκ Βοιωτῶν γε . . .*

[73] See my discussion in 'Lyric poet', 128 (citing proverbs like Zen. *Paroem.* 1. 73, magic refrains like Theocr. 2. 17, folk songs like *Carm. Pop.* 2 *PMG*). Cf. below, pp. 162 n. 4, 165 n. 9, 166 n. 11.

[74] Obscenities: see Henderson, *Maculate Muse*, 1–35, esp. 31 on 'the popular idiom' (and cf. his comments on 'social rules', 240–2). Transformations: p. 123 n. 58 above.

[75] Here, and often (cf. *Av.* 430 above), the list and the verse line coincide, as if accumulation and the integrity of the recurrent rhythmic unit go together: cf. above, p. 128, on *Lys.* 456–61.

And make our market-place
Full of good things: from Megara, garlic,
Spring cucumber, pomegranate, apple,
Woollens (for the servants), undersized;
And from Boeotia . . .[76]

These 'good things' (*ἀγαθά*) are of course dependent on peace. So too, evidently, is freedom of action—whence the urgency of taking possession of Peace herself. Compare 338–42:

ἀλλ' ὅταν λάβωμεν αὐτήν, τηνικαῦτα χαίρετε
καὶ βοᾶτε καὶ γελᾶτ'· ἤ-
δη γὰρ ἐξέσται τόθ' ὑμῖν
πλεῖν, μένειν, κινεῖν, καθεύδειν,
εἰς πανηγύρεις θεωρεῖν . . .

When we get her, then you can cheer
And shout and laugh. Then you can
Take a trip, stay at home, have a shag, have a sleep,
Visit the festivals . . .

Here, in particular, the simple directness of the listings is richly evocative of a truly 'innocent'—Goethean-'naive'—wholeness. We are not far from the blues singer's celebration of immediate, aggregated satisfactions: 'Gimme a pigfoot and a bottle of beer . . .'[77]

And not only the pleasures themselves but the natural responses to them are wont to be listed in the same spirit. The passage just quoted is preceded by this (335–6):

ἥδομαι γὰρ καὶ γέγηθα καὶ πέπορδα καὶ γελῶ
μᾶλλον ἢ τὸ γῆρας ἐκδὺς ἐκφυγὼν τὴν ἀσπίδα.

I'm so much
Better, happier, fartier, laughier,
Freed of that shield,
Than if I'd sloughed my old age off.[78]

[76] *μικρῶν* here surely (as comm. have failed to see) involves a recessive joke. The good news for the servants (slaves) is that they should be getting woollens; the less good news is that the woollens are undersized—i.e. *μ.* = '*too* small', as at Hdt. 5. 9 (*μικρὸς καὶ ἀδύνατος*), Ar. *Nub.* 1017. After the Megara list, a Boeotia list follows (1004–5); cf. a list of Boeotian *ἀγαθά* at *Ach.* 873–80, and of Athenian *ἀγαθά* at fr. 581 *PCG*.

[77] 'Gimme a Pigfoot', Bessie Smith (1933).

[78] The transl. of *Pax* seeks to convey the exuberance partly by coinages (like 'fartier') Aristophanic in kind, but absent from this bit of Greek (which has 'I fart' etc.). For similar lists cf. *Pax* 291 and *Plut.* 288.

It is no doubt symptomatic of Aristophanes' 'degraded' physicality that farting should become a metonym for contentment—but then the satisfying relish of the new whole is equally indicative of how misleading an appeal to 'degradation' can be.

The relish expressed in articulating the connection between peace and plenty is made to accommodate an additional sense of tenderness when the list comprises lost country sweets, now back in view again. *Peace* 571–9:

> ἀλλ' ἀναμνησθέντες, ὦνδρες,
> τῆς διαίτης τῆς παλαιᾶς,
> ἥν παρεῖχ' αὕτη ποθ' ἡμῖν,
> τῶν τε παλασίων ἐκείνων
> τῶν τε σύκων, τῶν τε μύρτων,
> τῆς τρυγός τε τῆς γλυκείας
> τῆς ἰωνιᾶς τε τῆς πρὸς
> τῷ φρέατι, τῶν τ' ἐλαῶν,
> ὧν ποθοῦμεν . . .
>
> Remembering
> The old life once
> Peace rendered us:
> Fruit-loaf,
> Fresh figs, myrtle,
> Sweet young wine,
> A bed of violets
> By the well, the olive trees
> We miss . . .

Such an evocation of rural felicities almost gives one the feel of a Keatsian caress—

> But in embalmed darkness guess each sweet
> Wherewith the seasonable month endows
> The grass, the thicket, and the fruit-tree wild;
> White hawthorn, and the pastoral eglantine;
> Fast fading violets covered up in leaves;
> And mid-May's eldest child,
> The coming musk-rose—[79]

[79] 'Ode to a Nightingale', st. 5. The enchantments in Keats's chief source are less emotive: 'I know a bank whereon the wild thyme blows, | Where ox-lips and the nodding violet grows | Quite over-canopied with luscious woodbine, | With sweet musk-roses, and with eglantine' (*A Midsummer Night's Dream*, II. i). Shakespeare's *nodding* violet has—romantically—become a doomed collection of *fast-fading* violets.

though, in this instance at least, Aristophanes' 'sweets' are less realized. *His* well and *his* trees are situated somewhere between Keats's particularizings and the easier generalities of the modern song-writer:

I'll be seeing you
In all the old familiar places
That this heart of mine embraces
All day through—
In that small café,
The park across the way,
The children's carousel,
The chestnut tree,
The wishing-well.[80]

The relish we can discern in Aristophanes' lists is equally apparent in his multiple compounds. When Aeschylus is called a 'fancy-phrase-trusser' (*κομποφακελορρήμονα*, *Frogs* 839) or Lysistrata summons up her 'swede-and-cabbage-women' (*σκοροδοπανδοκευτριαρτοπώλιδες*, *Lysistrata* 458), the gusto is palpable, irrespective of the satirical or non-satirical function of the new composite. The accumulative-creative force that transmits itself to, and through, such outlandish formations is a wholly exuberant one, as Aristophanes himself confirms. *Peace* 520–2 (Trygaeus addressing the goddess):

ὦ πότνια βοτρυόδωρε, τί προσείπω σ' ἔπος;
πόθεν ἂν λάβοιμι ῥῆμα μυριάμφορον
ὅτῳ προσείπω σ';

Our Lady of the Vine: what do I call you?
Where can I find a hundred-gallon word
To greet you with?

For such a colossally exuberant moment only a colossally exuberant word-formation will do. It is very much in line with that logic that Aristophanes' biggest attested compound is, as much as any actual list, an accumulation of good things. *Ecclesiazusae* 1168 ff. (banquet time):

[80] 'I'll Be Seeing You': Irving Kahal (lyrics) and Sammy Fain (1938). On the poetic qualities of the 'festive imagery' of *Peace*, compare and contrast the chapter of that name in C. Moulton, *Aristophanic Poetry* (Göttingen 1981) 82–107.

τάχα γὰρ ἔπεισι
λοπαδοτεμαχοσελαχογαλεο- . . .

Here it is on its way to the table,
Dishy-slicy-sharky-dogfishy- . . .[81]

and so on for another sixty-seven syllables. Like the serial jokes at the start of *Frogs*, which are pursued with a similar relish, the compound (it would seem) is almost infinitely extendible.

Aristophanes' writing is irredemably physical, accumulative—and discontinuous. Discontinuity, indeed, might be taken to be a corollary of the essential mobility of his style. After all, it is certainly writ large in collocations like (*Peace* 774 ff.)

. . . among the blest.
Mind you, if Carcinus turns up . . .

Given a diverse range of stylistic elements, techniques and tones, intermittent collisions of incompatible items ('blest'/'mind you') are readily available. Aristophanes' style does, of course, comprise a great range of techniques and tones, his use of which makes the style as a whole unstable. What makes it discontinuous is that collisions are not intermittent (let alone avoided, as they would be within a differentially stable system): they are a common, even a ubiquitous, feature. It would (that is) be possible, within a mobile style, to modulate from one key to another *gradually*, as for instance Eliot at one point does (albeit briefly) in the passage from 'Coriolan'—

Dust of dust . . .
Don't throw away that sausage . . .
Please, will you
Give us a light?
Light
Light—

where the incompatibles are the biblical-poetic (as 'Dust of dust') and the banal-colloquial ('Don't . . . sausage'), and where, at the given moment, a transition is made from the colloquial to the poetic, via the repetition of 'light'; it is also apparent that the incompatible elements are deployed in blocks. This is not how

[81] Text as (and transl. based on) Sommerstein. The gargantuan compound may also allude to contemporary dithyrambery: see Ussher ad loc. and cf. esp. Philox. 836 (e) 13 *PMG*.

Aristophanes usually works. He does not favour transitions or indeed blocks: instead, he *switches*. He does so persistently, and not only from one tone or register to another. His switches take a great variety of guises, seeming to require only that there is a norm of some kind, established or assumed, from which he can create an instant departure. A number of familiar Aristophanic manoeuvres—familiar, but widely, and unhelpfully, discussed in isolation from each other—have this decisive feature in common. Coinages: you have a norm of possible Greek, which suddenly gives way to the impossible (*Acharnians* 4):

> φερ' ἴδω, τί δ' ἥσθην ἄξιον χαιρηδόνος;
>
> Let's see, what's brought me any *happitude*?

Obscenity: you have a norm of acceptably polite Greek from which bursts out the sudden explosive unacceptable (*Acharnians* 30):

> στένω, κέχηνα, σκορδινῶμαι, πέρδομαι
>
> Sighing, yawning, stretching, *farting*.

Paratragedy: you have a norm of unelevated Greek, which suddenly turns tragic (*Acharnians* 5):[82]

> ἐγῷδ' ἐφ' ᾧ γε τὸ κέαρ εὐφράνθην ἰδών
>
> I know one thing I saw that *did entrance my heart*.

Para prosdokian: a 'straight' sequence interrupted by a sudden explosive joke (*Frogs* 21–3):[83]

> εἶτ' οὐχ ὕβρις ταῦτ' ἐστὶ καὶ πολλὴ τρυφή,
> ὅτ' ἐγὼ μὲν ὢν Διόνυσος, υἱὸς Σταμνίου,
> αὐτὸς βαδίζω καὶ πονῶ
>
> What an outrage, what impertinence,
> For me, Dionysus, son of—*Juice*,
> To struggle along on foot.

[82] The *gradual* ascent towards a paratragic climax at *Ach.* 26–7 is thus unusual and significant: see above, pp. 36–7, and below, p. 351.

[83] 'The instances of comic surprise in Aristophanes are legion': Starkie, *Acharnians*, p. lxvii. For the record, the ancient theorists who established the principle of humour *para prosdokian* tended to interpret it very narrowly, as e.g. did Demetrius (*Eloc.* 152), who classified it as merely one among many mechanisms of 'charm' (ibid. 137–62).

'Violation of the illusion': you have a norm of stage discourse within a self-sufficient fictive world, and someone on stage, suddenly, violates it by stepping out from his world into ours, or out from his perception of his world into ours.[84] At *Acharnians* 416–17 Dicaeopolis explains the threat facing him from the old Acharnians who, of course, comprise the chorus of the play:

> δεῖ γάρ με λέξαι τῷ χορῷ ῥῆσιν μακράν·
> αὕτη δὲ θάνατον, ἢν κακῶς λέξω, φέρει.
>
> I have to make a long speech to the *chorus*,
> And if I fail, it means my death.

And metaphor, so common in Aristophanes, and so often (and the significance of the point is now apparent) in the form of short, sharp transformations. This type of image illustrates with great clarity the principle that imagery, especially metaphor, embodies a disruption of an established terminology (the tenor) by a new and unpredicted terminology (the vehicle).[85] Like the sudden obscenity, then, the transformation is a converging point of two Aristophanic tendencies, the physical and the discontinuous. *Knights* 1384–6:

> ἔχε νυν ἐπὶ τούτοις τουτονὶ τὸν ὀκλαδίαν
> . . . .
> κἄν που δοκῇ σοι, τοῦτον ὀκλαδίαν ποίει.
>
> On that condition take this folding chair
> . . . .
> Or else make him a *folding chair* instead.

In all these cases, the principle is of a sudden switch *from* a norm *to* something incompatible with it—and then a switch back again. The characteristic effect, then, is disruptive and momentary. It is not, indeed, that Aristophanes' paratragedies (and the rest) are never sustained. One can of course point to sequences of sustained paratragedy—like the parody of Euripides that begins at *Frogs* 1331–2,

[84] In other connections 'violation of the illusion' is an unhelpful way of characterizing the phenomenon (cf. above, p. 91). Here the label has the virtue of making the kinship of mechanisms apparent.

[85] On the frequency of metaphor in A, witness the size of Taillardat's book, *Images* (pp. 553)—which is mostly concerned with metaphorical 'images', but actually misses many relevant usages altogether. On metaphor as disruptive of terminology, see Silk, *Interaction*, 12, 27, 87.

ὦ νυκτὸς κελαινοφαὴς ὄρφνα,
τίνα μοι δύστανον ὄνειρον . . .

O night's gloom, black-lit,
What is this unhappy apparition . . .?—[86]

and sequences of sustained obscenity—like *Peace* 868–74,

ΟΙ. ἡ παῖς λέλουται καὶ τὰ τῆς πυγῆς καλά.
ὁ πλακοῦς πέπεπται, σησαμῆ ξυμπλάττεται.
καὶ τἄλλ' ἁπαξάπαντα· τοῦ πέους δὲ δεῖ.
ΤΡ. ἴθι νυν ἀποδῶμεν τήνδε τὴν Θεωρίαν
ἀνύσαντε τῇ βουλῇ.
ΟΙ. τίς αὑτηί; τί φῄς;
αὕτη Θεωρία 'στὶν ἣν ἡμεῖς ποτε
ἐπαίομεν Βραυρωνάδ' ὑποπεπωκότες;

SLAVE The girl's washed; her bum looks gorgeous.
The cake's baked, there are sesame-biscuits setting.
It's all there: only the cock's missing.
TRYGAEUS Right, let's get a move on: let's give
Holiday back to the Council.
SLAVE This one?
Is she the 'Holiday' we used to have in the old days,
When we shagged our way to Brauron after a few drinks?[87]

and sustained 'violations of illusion', like the opening of *Frogs* ('Shall I tell them one of the usual jokes . . .?'),[88] and sustained metaphors, as at *Frogs* 939–41:

ἀλλ' ὡς παρέλαβον τὴν τέχνην παρὰ σοῦ τὸ πρῶτον εὐθὺς
οἰδοῦσαν ὑπὸ κομπασμάτων καὶ ῥημάτων ἐπαχθῶν,
ἴσχνανα μὲν πρώτιστον αὐτὴν καὶ τὸ βάρος ἀφεῖλον . . .

When I took over tragedy from you,
Swollen and overweight with bombast,
The first thing that I did was slim it down . . .

In few of these passages are the 'sustained' disruptions total (obscenity rarely consists of uninterrupted series of rude words, and so on), but in any case such passages are still exceptional.

From coinages to metaphors, then, we have a set of familiar, if

[86] On this passage see Silk, 'Paratragedy', 482–3.

[87] Note the characteristic parallelisms in the opening lines. For the translation 'Holiday' for *Theôria*, see below, p. 240 n. 74.

[88] Above, pp. 27–8.

seemingly very diverse, embodiments of that sudden disruption which subverts the continuity of the writing. All (it will be agreed) are highly characteristic of earlier Aristophanes, less characteristic of his final phase, and (in general) even less characteristic of the comedy of manners which that final phase prefigures. It is worth adding to the list one other, more specialized, mechanism of disruption, in fact a facet of poetic imagery, which illustrates the discontinuous propensities of Aristophanic style with particular clarity. Much imagery, in Greek and in other poetry, is interactive: that is, whereas all imagery involves a temporary conjunction of its two terminologies, tenor and vehicle, interactive imagery involves some kind of additional engagement or fusion between the two.[89] Such engagement takes various forms, several of which serve broadly to prepare or introduce the disruptive terminology of the vehicle:

> How bravely thou becomest thy *bed*, fresh lily,
> And whiter than the sheets.
>
> But when the melancholy fit shall *fall*
> *Sudden from heaven* like a weeping cloud . . .[90]

Rather as if the disruptive force of the vehicle were valued as and for itself, Aristophanes makes little use of such softening devices. On the contrary, he favours the type of interaction that tends, above all, to maximize disruption. This is achieved by *intrusion*, whereby terminology belonging to the tenor, the 'real' subject, intrudes at the expense of some part of the vehicle, as if the terms of the image were summarily reversed. Thus:

> See, see, King Richard doth himself appear
> As doth the blushing *discontented* sun

(where any actual 'discontent' must belong to the king, not the sun). Or again:

> But when the melancholy fit shall fall
> Sudden from heaven like a *weeping* cloud

(where it is the melancholic who does any 'weeping'). Or again:

[89] See Silk, *Interaction*.

[90] Shakespeare, *Cymbeline*, II. ii, and Keats, 'On Melancholy', st. 2: examples from Silk, *Interaction*, 87–8 and 97. On preparatory/introductory interaction, see ibid. 87–103 and 150–4.

He hath no eyes, the dust hath blinded them.
Comb down his hair; look, look—it stands upright
Like lime-twigs set to catch *my* winged *soul*

(where a more banal, non-interactive sequence might run: 'Like lime-twigs set to catch their winged prey').[91]

For intrusion to exist, the vehicle—and therefore the whole image—must be more than momentary. It must be sustained enough to become a miniature norm in its own right, which is then disrupted by the unpredictable intrusion of the tenor terminology. Hence one finds it in similes (as in the three English examples just cited) or long metaphors, for instance those of an allegorical character. Consider Lysistrata's wool-working politics, as offered to a sceptical Commissioner, at *Lysistrata* 572–8:

ΛΥ. κἂν ὑμῖν γ' εἴ τις ἐνῆν νοῦς,
ἐκ τῶν ἐρίων τῶν ἡμετέρων ἐπολιτεύεσθ' ἂν ἅπαντα.
ΠΡ. πῶς δή; φέρ' ἴδω.
ΛΥ. πρῶτον μὲν χρῆν, ὥσπερ πόκον, ἐν βαλανείῳ
ἐκπλύναντας τὴν οἰσπώτην ἐκ τῆς πόλεως, ἐπὶ κλίνης
ἐκραβδίζειν τοὺς μοχθηροὺς καὶ τοὺς τριβόλους ἀπολέξαι,
καὶ τούς γε συνισταμένους τούτους καὶ τοὺς πιλοῦντας ἑαυτοὺς
ἐπὶ ταῖς ἀρχαῖσι διαξῆναι καὶ τὰς κεφαλὰς ἀποτῖλαι.

LYS. And if you had more sense,
You'd manage politics the way we handle wool.
COM. Meaning what?
LYS. First, bath the city, like a fleece,
And wash the dung off. Put it on a bunk,
Beat the *criminals* out and pick off the burrs.
Any bits *banding together* or matted together
In *search of power*—card them, prise out their *heads*.

The intrusions begin with two that are particularly striking because they belong to, and therefore disrupt, seeming parallel structures. 'Beat the criminals out' is an acceptable vehicle-tenor sequence, but not in this allegorical (i.e. vehicle-dominant) context. 'Pick off the burrs' is acceptable vehicle terminology, and presupposes an equivalent sequence before it ('Beat the [say] bits

[91] Shakespeare, *Richard II*, III. iii, Keats, loc. cit., and Shakespeare, *II Henry VI*, III. iii: Silk, *Interaction*, 140–2. On intrusion, see ibid. 138–49. The pivotal effects noted below, pp. 186 n. 59 and 398 n. 101, involve the kind of 'softening' that A does not usually favour.

of dirt out and pick off the burrs'). 'Beat the criminals out' and 'pick off the burrs' are thus, in the ordinary way of things, incompatible. If 'pick off the burrs', then (e.g.) 'beat the bits of dirt out'; if 'beat the criminals out', then (e.g.) 'pick off the troublemakers'. The configuration is repeated in the next line: 'banding together' and 'matted together' are structurally parallel, but the one is in tenor terminology, the other in vehicle. From that last vehicle item we then switch harshly to the tenor, 'in search of power', which goes with the 'banding', but not the 'matted', then back to the vehicle ('card them') and once again, very harshly, a mixture of vehicle ('prise out') and tenor ('heads') in forced parallel to the pure vehicle, 'card'. The harshness is very much to the point, conveying as it does the unsentimental quality of the particular advice, but more fundamentally it simply (or not simply) reflects Aristophanes' discontinuous mode of expression. In terms of local effect, the intrusions carry a largely explanatory function: they tell us what the detail of the image 'means' in 'real' terms.[92]

Contrast the metaphor at *Knights* 919–22:

> ἁνὴρ παφλάζει, παῦε παῦ',
> ὑπερζέων· ὑφελκτέον
> τῶν δᾳδίων, ἀπαρυστέον
> τε τῶν ἀπειλῶν ταυτηί.
>
> He's bubbling! Stop him
> Boiling over. I'll pull
> Some of the firewood out, and use
> My hand to skim his *threats* off.[93]

'Paphlagon' is equally 'Paphlagonian (slave)' and 'bubbler', and the Paphlagonian's frenzy of promises and menaces is duly represented in the metaphorical terms of the 'bubbling' (παφλάζει) that his name evokes. Image and intrusion are so structured that the late switch from cauldrons and hot water to 'threats' has, paradoxically, something of the effect of a sensuous inversion that realizes the image as a whole.[94]

[92] Regarding the detail of the *Lys.* image, cf. Moulton, *Poetry*, 49–58. On explanatory intrusion, see Silk, *Interaction*, 139–41. For intrusion in multiple parallel structure (not a common phenomenon—not, at least, attested in the corpus of poetry dealt with in *Interaction*), cf. *Eq.* 528 and 496 (below, pp. 143, 153) and the simpler structures, as at *Pax* 565, discussed below, pp. 145–6.

[93] Text as Sommerstein. For ταυτηί as 'hand' see Sommerstein ad loc.

[94] On 'realizing' (enacting) intrusion, cf. Silk, *Interaction*, 139–41, 144–6.

Whatever the variations in form or function, the sense of rupture remains constant. *Knights* (which presents a striking number and range of intrusions) offers a particularly notable instance. Parabasis: in praise of Aristophanes' great predecessor, and contemporary, Cratinus, who (526–8)

> πολλῷ ῥεύσας ποτ' ἐπαίνῳ
> διὰ τῶν ἀφελῶν πεδίων ἔρρει, καὶ τῆς στάσεως παρασύρων
> ἐφόρει τὰς δρῦς καὶ τὰς πλατάνους καὶ τοὺς ἐχθροὺς προθελύμνους.
>
> Bursting his banks with overflowing *popularity*,
> Flooded the *honest* plains, and, torn from where they were standing,
> Oak trees, plane trees, *opponents*, bore downstream, uprooted.

The passage mobilizes three formally contrasting intrusions in quick succession, each of them independently disruptive: hence a cumulative effect of violence, once again, as stylistic correlative of the image in question.[95]

Knights, again, has instances associated with the play's basic allegory. Old man Demos is the figurative equivalent of the People of Athens, his slaves correspond to the politicians, and Paphlagon, the master's pet slave, to Cleon. The language of the play includes sequences that are figurative (Paphlagon, slaves, and master), sequences that are non-figurative (Cleon, politicians, and people), and sequences that move from one to the other.[96] Where the movement involves a separation of the two into formally self-contained compartments, no sense of intrusion is produced. Thus (64–6 and 74–6):

[95] ἐπαίνῳ and ἐχθρούς are clearly (intrusive) tenor terms, with no literal application within the semantic field of rivers, banks, floods. For ἐχθ. = 'opponent in competition', cf. Pind. *Pyth.* 8. 86 (and see further Silk, 'Versus the rest', n. 11). ἀφελής is grossly misinterpreted by comm., LSJ, and translators (most recently Henderson in the new Loeb) as 'even', 'broad', 'open'—as if the word could be used in its own right (as a vehicle term) of 'plains'—undeterred by the fact that it is 'unexampled in this sense' (Neil ad loc.): the scholia ad loc. are confused, but less so. See further Silk, loc. cit., and Pearson on Soph. fr. 723. 'Honest' is a shade or two more complimentary than the Greek (cf. Thgn. 1211 ἀφελῶς παίζουσα: 'simplement, directement, inconsidérément', van Groningen ad loc.), but the transl. needs a word of exclusive and clear-cut tenor application. 'Honest plains' is like Keats's 'weeping cloud' or Pindar's ἀδὺ κλάϊθρον (*Pyth.* 1. 8, of sleep), tenor adjective + vehicle noun: see Silk, *Interaction*, 142, 145.

[96] Discussed by e.g. Newiger, *Metapher und Allegorie*, 11–49, but not in literary-stylistic terms. Sommerstein has some helpful ad loc. comments (as e.g. on *Eq.* 60: n. 97 below).

κᾆτα μαστιγούμεθα
ἡμεῖς· Παφλαγὼν δὲ περιθέων τοὺς οἰκέτας
αἰτεῖ, ταράττει, δωροδοκεῖ . . .

ἀλλ' οὐχ οἷόν τε τὸν Παφλαγόν' οὐδὲν λαθεῖν·
ἐφορᾷ γὰρ αὐτὸς πάντ'. ἔχει γὰρ τὸ σκέλος
τὸ μὲν ἐν Πύλῳ, τὸ δ' ἕτερον ἐν τἠκκλησίᾳ.

We get flogged, while Paphlagon
Does his tour of the household,
Making demands, starting trouble, taking bribes . . .

Nothing we do is hidden from Paphlagon.
His eyes are everywhere. *He's got one foot*
In Pylos and the other in the Assembly.

At other times the movement takes place as a true intrusive switch within a single structure, for instance when the other servants complain of Paphlagon (58–60):

ἡμᾶς δ' ἀπελαύνει κοὐκ ἐᾷ τὸν δεσπότην
ἄλλον θεραπεύειν, ἀλλὰ βυρσίνην ἔχων
δειπνοῦντος ἑστὼς ἀποσοβεῖ τοὺς ῥήτορας.

Us he pushes away, and no one else
Is allowed to wait on master; at dinner
He cracks a whip to scare off any *politicians.*[97]

The effect of disruptive intrusion, so characteristic, then, of Aristophanes' usage within his extended images, may also arise outside the sphere of imagery proper; and it is revealing to see how commonly, and how variously, Aristophanes does in fact make it arise. At *Peace* 637 a moment of humour *para prosdokian* produces the effect. Hermes explains how the demagogues expelled Peace from the countryside and specifically

τήνδε μὲν δικροῖς ἐώθουν τὴν θεὸν κεκράγμασιν

Thrust the goddess back with two-pronged *shouts.*[98]

[97] 'One would expect either "the flies" or "the other servants"': Sommerstein ad loc. A similar switch at *Vesp.* 923 impinges as an unconscious joke at the speaker's expense. A canine prosecutor charges the dog Labes with stealing cheese (alluding allegorically to Cleon's treatment of Laches for misconduct): 'So don't you let him off—*ὡς ὄντ' αὖ πολὺ* | *κυνῶν ἁπάντων ἄνδρα μονοφαγίστατον*—In any case, of all the dogs | He's much the greediest *man* alive'.

[98] Open to analysis as a (drastically compressed) metonymy: 'with two-pronged ⟨pitchforks and loud⟩ shouts'.

Earlier in the same play a comparable, if more elaborate, effect is engendered by complementary distribution of paired adjectives and nouns. Hermes inspects the troops (564–5):

> *ὦ Πόσειδον, ὡς καλὸν τὸ στῖφος αὐτῶν φαίνεται*
> *καὶ πυκνὸν καὶ γοργὸν ὥσπερ μᾶζα καὶ πανδαισία.*
>
> God, what a magnificent mass of men,
> Packed as close and awesome to the eye
> As *cake and Easy Street.*

It is *cakes* that might be 'close-packed' but it is *Easy Street* that would be fabulously 'awesome' to behold.[99]

Taken as a unit on its own, *μᾶζα καὶ πανδαισία*, 'cake and Easy Street', illustrates another relatable, and highly characteristic, Aristophanic manoeuvre: a conjunction—or rather, disjunction—of concrete and abstract (in either order) in a simple parallel structure calculated to sharpen the sense of transference from one dimension to another. 'An afternoon of nurses and rumours', wrote Auden.[100] Aristophanes' disjunctions are less sinister, but no less disconcerting, witness *Knights* 874:

[99] Cf. Milton, *PL* VII. 502–3, 'air, water, earth, | By fowl, fish, beast, was flown, was swum, was walked': a 'figure of correlative distribution', Wilkinson, *Artistry*, 214. The word *γοργός* is like *δεινός*, 'awesome', esp. frighteningly (*γ. ὁπλίτης φανεὶς κτείνεις μ'*, Eur. *Andr.* 458–9), but also impressively: at Xen. *Eq.* 10. 17 we hear of the *γαυριώμενος* horse that men call *θυμοειδῆ καὶ σοβαρὸν καὶ ἅμα ἡδύν τε καὶ γοργὸν ἰδεῖν*. As Xen.'s last phrase suggests, the word also connotes *looks*—i.e. 'awesome to look at', but also, often, 'with awesome eyes'—a connotation duly activated at *Pax* 565 by *Γοργόνας* in 561 (and perhaps, historically, due to the real or else seeming connection with *Γοργώ*). When used of eyes, *γ.* connotes, in turn, 'flashing', but such connotations are wrongly converted into a denotation by some comm., e.g. Mastronarde on Eur. *Pho.* 146 (who extracts 'with *bright and* terrifying eyes' from *ὄμμασι γοργός*) and Henderson on *Pax* 565 itself (whose transl., in the new Loeb, has 'lustrous'): contrast Bond on Eur. *HF* 131 ff. For an interesting, if one-sided, discussion of the word, see G. P. Shipp, *Modern Greek Evidence for the Ancient Greek Vocabulary* (Sydney 1979) 198–200. *πανδαισία*: the word is misrepresented by (among others) LSJ and Olson ('a feast . . .'), though their citations are adequate. *πανδ.* is semi-abstract and has connotations of the fabulous: Sommerstein's 'feast of plenty' is on the right lines, but in context too concrete. The sense is given by Harpocrat. p. 201 Keaney (= Isae. fr. 100), *πανδαισία· τὸ πάντα ἔχειν ἄφθονα καὶ μηδὲν ἐλλείπειν ἐν τῇ δαιτί.* Hdt. 5. 20. 4 (*ὦ Πέρσαι, οἴκατε πανδαισίῃ τελείῃ ἱστιῆσθαι*) reads like an ironic allusion to perfection.

[100] 'In Memory of W. B. Yeats' (1940). Cf. Catullus 44. 15 'otioque et urtica' (I owe the example to Guy Lee) and García Márquez, *Love in the Time of Cholera*, tr. E. Grossman (New York 1988) 154, 'women degraded by arthritis and resentment'. 'Tea and sympathy' (title of a play by Robert Anderson, 1957) is equivalent, though now virtually proverbial, therefore weakened.

εὐνούστατόν τε τῇ πόλει καὶ τοῖσι δακτύλοισιν

Devoted to *my country and my toes.*

At *Knights* 803 the more concrete member of the pair is actually the vehicle of an image, and the more abstract virtually its tenor equivalent—

ὁ δὲ δῆμος

ὑπὸ τοῦ πολέμου καὶ τῆς ὁμίχλης ἃ πανουργεῖς μὴ καθορᾷ σου

You're using *war and mist* to stop the people
Seeing through your crimes—

where disjunction could be analysed as metaphorical hendiadys: 'mist *of* war'.[101] Harsh hendiadys is available as an 'explanation' of various instances where metaphor is not involved, but harshness, rather than explicability, is what impinges most immediately. Consider *Peace* 596,

τοῖς ἀγροίκοισιν γὰρ ἦσθα χῖδρα καὶ σωτηρία.

To country-folk you meant *oats and salvation*

and *Ecclesiazusae* 541,

. . . *ἐν ἀλέᾳ κατακείμενον καὶ στρώμασιν*

. . . tucked up in *warmth and blankets*

and instances like *Clouds* 13, where the odd conjunction involves two members of a longer list:

ὑπὸ τῆς δαπάνης καὶ τῆς φάτνης καὶ τῶν χρεῶν

What with *the cost and the stables and the debts.*[102]

One distinctive set of instances is based on the principle of a pair of more or less metaphorical, but wholly incompatible, *smells.*[103] Here belongs *Acharnians* 190, where the treaty

[101] Etymologically, so to speak, the phrase is thus construable as an equivalent of *νέφος πολέμοιο* (*Il.* 17. 243, Ar. *Pax* 1090, cf. Pind. *Nem.* 10. 9).

[102] Cf. e.g. *Pax* 748 . . . *κακὰ καὶ φόρτον καὶ βωμολοχεύματ' ἀγεννῆ* and ultimately the mild (and conventional Greek) kind of pairing represented by *Pax* 307 *μοχλοῖς καὶ μηχαναῖσιν* (see Platnauer and Olson ad loc.).

[103] Cf. Taillardat, *Images*, 437. The connection of several of the instances with peace (*Ach.* 190, *Eq.* 1332, *Pax* 526–38) reads like a private association of the kind once ascribed by C. Spurgeon to Shakespeare: *Shakespeare's Imagery* (Cambridge 1935), esp. 186–99.

> ὄζουσι πίττης καὶ παρασκευῆς νεῶν,
> Smells of pitch and naval preparations,

and likewise *Knights* 1332, where a rejuvenated Demos

> οὐ χοιρινῶν ὄζων, ἀλλὰ σπονδῶν
> Smells not of voting-shells, but peace,[104]

Clouds 1007, where the young man taught by Right will

> μίλακος ὄζων καὶ ἀπραγμοσύνης καὶ λεύκης φυλλοβολούσης
> Smell of convolvulus, quietism, and poplars unleaving,[105]

Peace 526, where the goddess Peace smells sweet

> . . . ὥσπερ ἀστρατείας καὶ μύρου
> . . . as demobilizing and perfume,[106]

and (more elaborately) *Clouds* 50–2, where farmer Strepsiades went to bed with his new wife

> ὄζων τρυγός, τρασιᾶς, ἐρίων, περιουσίας
> Smelling of rough wine, dried figs, sheep's wool, abundance

while (in a parallel list)

> ἡ δ' αὖ μύρου, κρόκου, καταγλωττισμάτων,
> δαπάνης, λαφυγμοῦ, Κωλιάδος, Γενετυλλίδος.
>
> She smelled of perfume, powder, deep kissing,
> Extravagance, bingeing, love-goddesses.[107]

The attentive reader of, or listener to, Aristophanes will be aware of other, related but simpler, series which involve the same effect of disruption. These include more examples of disconcerting 'smells', disconcerting now simply because, against the presupposition of their physicality, they are in fact characterized wholly as abstract. Thus *Wasps* 1058–9:

[104] Mussel-shells were used as voting tokens in the lawcourts. σπονδῶν, 'peace-treaty', has also the concrete sense 'libations'.

[105] 'Unleaving': Gerard Manley Hopkins, 'Spring and Fall' (but on the difficult φυλλοβολούσης see Dover ad loc.). ἀπραγμοσύνη denotes apoliticality, therefore (*de facto*) conservatism.

[106] Clearly said of the goddess herself, not of one of her two attendants at the expense of the other, *pace* most editors (rightly Henderson in the new Loeb).

[107] On the 'love-goddesses' see Dover ad loc.

τῶν ἱματίων
ὀζήσει δεξιότητος.

Your clothes will smell of sophistication.[108]

Then again, there are comparable jumps, not from abstract to concrete (or back), but synaesthetically from one sense to another, especially from *taste* to *sight*. Thus at *Knights* 631 we hear how the whole Council

κἄβλεψε νᾶπυ καὶ τὸ μέτωπ' ἀνέσπασεν.

Frowned and looked mustard.[109]

All these very different versions of, or relatives of, intrusion convey a sense of sudden but temporary dislocation. We may, therefore, complete this phase of our discussion by considering one further pattern: the dislocated list. As one of various converging points of different Aristophanic tendencies—in this case, discontinuity and accumulation—such a pattern too can claim a special significance. To appreciate this significance better, we need only bring to our consciousness the familiar sense that, in non-literary discourse, lists tend to be organized in some kind of strict sequence, most obviously so in practical, technical or scientific contexts: one, two, three, four . . . Aeschylus, Alcidamas, Aratus, Aristophanes . . . red, orange, yellow, green . . . first, then, now. The sequence of items (we might say, without being unduly tendentious) is organized on Aristotelian principles: according to the dictates of probability, necessity, coherence, consequential logic. When lists occur in orderly literature like (say) Greek tragedy, they may well be so structured. Take Sophocles, *Oedipus at Colonus* 1224–37:

Not to be born is best, when all is reckoned.
But once a man has seen the light of day,
The next best thing by far is to go back
Where he came from, and do it speedily.
Once youth is past . . .
. . . every affliction is present:

[108] Differently transl. below, p. 389. For abstract smells cf. *Ach.* 192, *Nub.* 398, *Lys.* 616 ff. and 943, and fr. 257 *PCG*. Comparable instances at Eupol. 176 *PCG* and Com. Adesp. 634 *PCG* may both reflect the influence of A.

[109] Cf. *Ach.* 254, *Vesp.* 455, *Pax* 1184, *Ran.* 603, *Eccl.* 292 (see Sommerstein ad loc.): Taillardat, *Images*, 216–17. Cf. García Márquez, *Love in the Time of Cholera*, 222, 'the tea . . . did taste of window', and Shakespeare, *Merchant of Venice*, I. i, 'of vinegar aspect'.

φθόνος, στάσεις, ἔρις, μάχαι
καὶ φόνοι· τό τε . . .
πύματον . . .
γῆρας . . .

Envy, confrontations, conflict, battles, blood,
. . . and last of all, old age . . .

We have here a meticulously structured logic of afflictions from 'envy' (*phthonos*) to the shedding of blood (and the aptly assonantal *phonoi*): the one leads to the other, and the items in between supply the missing links and likewise lead on, each one, to the next. At *Thesmophoriazusae* 788 we have a superficially similar list, which is nevertheless significantly different:

Everyone speaks ill of women.
To men we are one totality
Of evil, and from us it all comes:
ἔριδες, νείκη, στάσις ἀργαλέα, λύπη, πόλεμος

Conflicts, disputes, confrontation (distressing), pain, war.

The items are much the same, but by comparison with Sophocles' list they are in an unstructured sequence, so that 'pain' follows the initial 'conflicts' but precedes the final 'war', which inverts all 'logical' order.[110] Most of the Aristophanic lists already cited have

[110] Anyone familiar with the textual background of *OC* 1234–5 will see that my argument needs some amplification, because the sequence printed above depends on a crucial modern emendation. Most codd. of the Soph. have φόνοι . . . καὶ φθόνος, K has φόνοι . . . καὶ φόνος, R has φθόνοι . . . καὶ φθόνος. The inverted sequence φθόνος . . . καὶ φόνοι follows a conj. by Faehse, which is accepted by most eds.—though not by H. Lloyd-Jones and N. G. Wilson, who in the new OCT print φόνοι . . . καὶ φθόνος, and argue robustly in its favour in *Sophoclea* (Oxford 1990) 252, claiming that φθόνος is 'the worst plague of human life' and as such should occupy the climactic position at the end of the list. (They actually call it 'the emphatic position', exhibiting a common, and deeply unhelpful, confusion: Silk, *Interaction*, 68–71.) But (i) though there may (often) be a tendency in Greek writing to put the 'more vivid' item at the end of a sequence (τὰ ἐναργέστερα: so Demetr. *Eloc.* 50), φόνοι is no doubt more 'vivid' than φθόνος in any case. Then again, beginning and end are equally prominent situations for important items (Demetr. ibid. 39; cf. Silk, *Interaction*, 68–71), so that, as far as this goes, one could argue either way. (ii) φθόνος is undoubtedly fraught with negative connotations, but it misrepresents Greek usage to claim that the word, by itself, is equally fraught with the supposed momentousness, in Soph. or elsewhere—otherwise a pairing like Soph. *El.* 641 σὺν φθόνῳ τε καὶ πολυγλώσσῳ βοῇ would be unusably bathetic. (iii) The case for reversing φ./φθ. is not that φόνοι are 'worse' than φθόνος (however that might be judged), but that the organization of the passage, from τὸ νέον to πύματον . . . γῆρας, powerfully impresses on us the logic of chronological sequence which then demands to be operative throughout. And so it is—first φθόνος, then στάσεις etc.,

something of this (literally) inconsequential ordering, and, indeed, consist of items which are more obviously relatable by sideways accumulation than by linear consequence. Thus with *Clouds* 444–6:

> τοῖς τ' ἀνθρώποις εἶναι δόξω
> θρασύς, εὔγλωττος, τολμηρός, ἴτης,
> βδελυρός . . .
>
> And make men think me
> Bold, glib, confident, cavalier,
> Shocking . . .

and so on for the other sixteen items. Or compare *Acharnians* 30—

> Sighing, yawning, stretching, farting—

where the raciest item is placed at the climax of the line, but otherwise there seems no particular reason why the order of items should be one rather than another—except that the Greek shows that there is a reason after all:

> *stenô, kekhêna, skordinômai, perdomai.*

The first three items are structured on the familiar aural-rhythmic principle of 'increasing members' (⏑ – | ⏑ – ⏑ | – ⏑ – –), as effective foil for the short fart (– ⏑ –) that completes and subverts them. There is a reason, then, but in no sense an Aristotelian-logical reason.

Such 'inconsequential' lists, with or without a final climax, may also be found in literature of a more stable kind. The items, often, are not such that any specific order would impose itself (unless on essentially aural grounds):

> The grass, the thicket, and the fruit-tree wild;
> White hawthorn, and the pastoral eglantine.[111]

When there is a final climactic member of an otherwise 'inconsequential' series, the result is often a (so-called) *Priamel*. The climax is retrospectively seen as the point, and the rest as foil:

which (in Sophoclean-tragic fashion) is a sequence with causality written into it: φθόνος γὰρ στάσιος ἀρχὴν ἀπεργάζεται (Democrit. 245 Diels–Kranz). And as for the end of the sequence, φόνοι are surely 'climactic' enough, not least in tragic drama. (iv) The dislocation in codd. R and K, whether reflecting a deeper corruption or (more likely) representing a second stage of confusion, nevertheless serves to confirm what would be beyond dispute anyway: the ease of corruption between φθόν- and φόν-.

[111] Keats, above, p. 134.

Some people say: a host of cavalry
Is the loveliest thing on earth.
Some people say: an army of soldiers on foot.
Some people say: a fleet of ships.
But I say: *whatever you love best . . .*

I've been around the world in a plane,
I've settled revolutions in Spain,
The North Pole I have charted,
But *I can't get started*
With you.[112]

There is a striking instance from late Aristophanes. In *Plutus* 189–93 old Chremylus and his slave Cario are seeking to convince Wealth of the benefits he brings, and then list these benefits in alternation. The master lists dignified abstractions, the slave tangible goods. The contrast between the two lists is clear, as is the familiar *Priamel* climax, but once again neither of the lists has much in the way of consequential logic within it:

ΧΡ. τῶν μὲν γὰρ ἄλλων ἐστὶ πάντων πλησμονή·
ἔρωτος
ΚΑ. ἄρτων
ΧΡ. μουσικῆς
ΚΑ. τραγημάτων
ΧΡ. τιμῆς
ΚΑ. πλακούντων
ΧΡ. ἀνδραγαθίας
ΚΑ. ἰσχάδων
ΧΡ. φιλοτιμίας
ΚΑ. μάζης
ΧΡ. στρατηγίας
ΚΑ. φακῆς—
ΧΡ. σοῦ δ' ἐγένετ' οὐδεὶς μεστὸς οὐδεπώποτε.

CHR. Everything else a man can have too much of—
CHR./CAR. Love *bread* art *sweets*
Honour *biscuits* valour *figs*
Ambition *cake* power *soup* —
CHR. But *no one ever gets enough of you.*[113]

[112] Sappho fr. 16 *PLF* and 'I Can't Get Started' (Ira Gershwin, lyrics, and Vernon Duke: 1936).

[113] Chremylus opens (189) with a resonance of Homer (*Il.* 13. 636–7). Memorably, Rogers's transl. of the list(s) began, 'Of love, Of loaves, Of literature', with

The true dislocated list is quite different from any of these patterns, whether logical (which is not common in Aristophanes) or inconsequential (which is). It is not a feature of 'Aristotelian' writing such as tragedy. Along with the inconsequential list, it is, on the other hand, richly characteristic of Aristophanes. Its presupposition is a degree of coherence, or at least equidistance, between *some* of the items in a series (even if there is no consequential rationale to their order), which at least *one* of the items suddenly disrupts. Here as elsewhere the effect is of a switch, accentuated, often, by the sense of a parallel structure breached. At its mildest, the dislocation impinges like a simple zeugma. *Wasps* 1118–19:

τῆσδε τῆς χώρας ὕπερ
μήτε κώπην μήτε λόγχην μήτε φλύκταιναν λαβών

Who's never picked up an oar, a spear, a *blister*,
For his country.[114]

Then there are elaborate sequences like *Birds* 1534–41 (Prometheus and Peisetaerus):

ΠΡ. ὑμεῖς δὲ μὴ σπένδεσθ', ἐὰν μὴ παραδιδῷ
τὸ σκῆπτρον ὁ Ζεὺς τοῖσιν ὄρνισιν πάλιν,
καὶ τὴν Βασιλείαν σοι γυναῖκ' ἔχειν διδῷ.
ΠΕ. τίς ἐστιν ἡ Βασίλεια;
ΠΡ. καλλίστη κόρη,
ἥπερ ταμιεύει τὸν κεραυνὸν τοῦ Διὸς
καὶ τἄλλ' ἁπαξάπαντα, τὴν εὐβουλίαν,
τὴν εὐνομίαν, τὴν σωφροσύνην, τὰ νεώρια,
τὴν λοιδορίαν, τὸν κωλακρέτην, τὰ τριώβολα.

(unconscious?) evocation of a famous list in Lewis Carroll (*Through the Looking-Glass*, ch. 4): 'The time has come', the Walrus said, | 'To talk of many things: | *Of shoes—and ships—and sealing wax*—/ Of cabbages—and kings—/ And why the sea is boiling hot—/ And whether pigs have wings.' This Carroll sequence, seemingly controlled only by alliteration and rhyme, is actually itself a kind of eccentric *Priamel*, whose 'point' comes in the penultimate place. 'And why the sea is boiling hot' is meaningful as none of the other items are, because it alludes both to the maritime context of the narrative (which takes place on the sea-shore) and to the possible procedure for cooking shellfish (part of the Walrus's audience are oysters, who are about to be eaten).

[114] Cf. MacDowell ad loc. Zeugma at its simplest (say, *Thes.* 696–7 οὐ πολλὴν βοὴν | στήσεσθε καὶ τροπαῖον;) might indeed be said to be the etymon of all dislocated series.

PROM. Don't make peace, unless Zeus hands the birds
Their sceptre back and gives you Sovereignty to marry.[115]
PIS. Sovereignty? Who's she?
PROM. A lovely girl
Who guards the thunderbolt of Zeus
And everything besides: wisdom,
Law and order, common sense, *dockyards*,
Slander, *treasury officials*, a day's pay.

Here the 'ordinary' randomness of a list of abstract blessings is dislocated by the concrete, and quite unrelated, 'dockyards', that word in turn by the unrelated 'slander', and that item too by the unrelated 'treasury officials', to which—by the standards of the now prevailing norms of incoherence—the final 'day's pay' coheres sufficiently to achieve the improbable effect of a closing resolution.

The dislocation in such lists may be produced by one of the mechanisms already discussed, such as intrusion. *Knights* 527–8, discussed earlier, works this way:

and torn from where they were standing,
Oak trees, plane trees, *opponents*, bore downstream, uprooted.[116]

So too *Knights* 495–7. Sausage-Seller is primed with garlic like a fighting-cock to help him confront the enemy in a war of words. The allegory of fighting birds dominates, but is disrupted:

μέμνησό νυν
δάκνειν, διαβάλλειν, τοὺς λόφους κατεσθίειν,
χὤπως τὰ κάλλαι' ἀποφαγὼν ἥξεις πάλιν.

And don't forget:
Peck him, *ridicule* him, eat his comb,
And bite his wattles off: then come back.

Or, again, obscenity may be the disruptive factor. At *Knights* 164–7 Sausage-Seller is given a glimpse of dominion:

τούτων ἁπάντων αὐτὸς ἀρχέλας ἔσει,
καὶ τῆς ἀγορᾶς καὶ τῶν λιμένων καὶ τῆς πυκνός·
βουλὴν πατήσεις καὶ στρατηγοὺς κλαστάσεις,
δήσεις, φυλάξεις, ἐν πρυτανείῳ λαικάσεις.

[115] On the transl. of *Basileia* see below, p. 407 n. 119.
[116] Above, p. 143.

Of all these thou shalt be the lord
And of the market, harbours, Pnyx:
Walk over Council, prune the generals,
Lock them up, string them up, *get it up* in the Prytaneum.[117]

Likewise *Peace* 240–1 (Trygaeus catching sight of War):

ἆρ' οὗτός ἐστ' ἐκεῖνος ὃν καὶ φεύγομεν,
ὁ δεινός, ὁ ταλαύρινος, ὁ κατὰ τοῖν σκελοῖν;

Is he the one we all take flight from?—
Lord of terror, lord of shields, lord of *shitting down your legs*?

But then again it may be a switch *from* obscenity. At *Clouds* 1009–19 Right warns young Pheidippides against the blandishments of fashionable Wrong:

ἢν ταῦτα ποιῇς ἁγὼ φράζω
καὶ πρὸς τούτοις προσέχῃς τὸν νοῦν,
ἕξεις αἰεὶ
στῆθος λιπαρόν, χροιὰν λαμπράν,
ὤμους μεγάλους, γλῶτταν βαιάν,
πυγὴν μεγάλην, πόσθην μικράν.
ἢν δ' ἅπερ οἱ νῦν ἐπιτηδεύῃς
πρῶτα μὲν ἕξεις
χροιὰν ὠχράν, ὤμους μικρούς,
στῆθος λεπτόν, γλῶτταν μεγάλην,
κωλῆν μικράν, ψήφισμα μακρόν.

Do as I say, and stick to that,
And you shall have in perpetuity:
Glistening chest, fresh complexion,
Big shoulders, little tongue,
Big butt, short cock.
Do things the modern way instead
And you'll have, just for starters:
Pale complexion, small shoulders,
Skinny chest, big tongue,
Small butt, long *speech in the Assembly*.[118]

Given the oppositional pattern, and the contents of Right's two lists, the final item almost writes itself—'small butt, long *cock*'—

[117] *λαικάζειν* is not 'suck cocks' (recent comm. and transl., also Henderson, *Maculate Muse*, 249—a second-edn. 'corrigendum'): see Henderson, ibid. 153–4 (right *first* time).

[118] Text as Dover (q.v.). The final effect involves a typical sequence of concrete/abstract.

until Aristophanes, typically, unwrites it with (for once) a tonal switch upwards.

Perhaps the most quintessentially Aristophanic instances involve clusters of disruptive mechanisms and accumulations of disjunctions. Such is *Clouds* 50–2, with its parallel lists of 'smells', each switching from concrete to abstract, and the second going beyond the first with successive larger dislocations:

> Smelling of rough wine, dried figs, sheep's wool, abundance;
> She smelled of perfume, powder, deep kissing,
> Extravagance, bingeing, love-goddesses.[119]

Such, above all, is *Peace* 530–8. What does the goddess Peace herself smell of? Trygaeus gives Hermes an expansive answer:

ΤΡ. ταύτης δὲ βοτρύων, ὑποδοχῆς, Διονυσίων,
αὐλῶν, τραγῳδῶν, Σοφοκλέους μελῶν, κιχλῶν,
ἐπυλλίων Εὐριπίδου—

ΕΡ. κλαύσἄρα σὺ
ταύτης καταψευδόμενος· οὐ γὰρ ἥδεται
αὕτη ποιητῇ ῥηματίων δικανικῶν.

ΤΡ. κιττοῦ, τρυγοίπου, προβατίων βληχωμένων,
κόλπου, γυναικῶν διατρεχουσῶν εἰς ἀγρόν,
δούλης μεθυούσης, ἀνατετραμμένου χοῶς,
ἄλλων τε πολλῶν κἀγαθῶν.

TRYG. She smells of grapes, entertainment, Dionysia,
Flutes, tragic chorus, Sophocles' lyrics, roast thrush,
Quotes from Euripides—

HERM. You'll be for it,
Badmouthing her like that: she doesn't relish
Someone who writes for the lawcourts—

TRYG. Ivy, wine-gauze, bleating sheep,
Lap, women rushing up the field,
Slave-girl tipsy, jug knocked over:
You name it.[120]

[119] Above, p. 147.

[120] 530: I read van Leeuwen's δὲ βοτρύων: cf. Platnauer ad loc. (on whose note Olson presents no advance). 531: on τραγῳδῶν see Olson ad loc.; on κιχλῶν cf. *Ach.* 1007–12. 536: punctuation mine. κόλπου (elusively erotic: Henderson, *Maculate Muse*, 140–1) has been suspected (esp. given its position 'underneath' the similar-looking κιττοῦ), but is plausible as an isolated item in the list, with punctuation afterwards (though hardly without punctuation, as a sg. 'bosom' of pl. γυναικῶν: contrast *Ran.* 345 γόνυ πάλλεται γερόντων, where the sg. noun is integrated/protected

Here we have an exuberant list of blessings associated with Peace. The first half dozen items are reasonably coherent in an 'inconsequential' way, albeit an analyst might detect a conflation of two related lists, one to do with ordinary festivity (grapes, entertainment), the other with tragic festivals. We begin with the 'smells' (concrete) of 'grapes' (concrete), yet also of 'entertainment' (abstract). We then move to a more elaborate pattern within Trygaeus' extended accumulation of delights, as we progress logically enough from music to chorus to Sophoclean lyrics, but then switch to roast thrush (served, no doubt, at a Dionysiac banquet after the tragedy, but still involving a switch), switch back to Euripides, then again to ivy, and so on. That (say) 'Euripides' and 'ivy' have something in common (they are both *something* to do with Dionysus)[121] is not the point: the point is rather that the movement from the one item to the next is a jump, and that (representatively) the collocation of 'lawcourts' and 'ivy' in 534–5 is a shocking *iunctura* with a sharp, defamiliarizing impact. This shock is the signal for an unannounced shift away from tragedy and even from festivity as such, in favour of a series of vignettes of rural life and its fruitfulness ('sheep', 'lap', 'women'), which, however, revert back to further items (the slave-girl and the jug) at the end. At the extreme point of celebratory accumulation, all in all, dislocation seems to have become the *modus operandi* in its own right—and yet dislocation that is made to enact a richly physical sense of restored life in the round.

Ultimately, in Aristophanes' usage, the physical, the accumulative, the discontinuous, belong together. In their different ways, these three tendencies speak of the affirmation of the here and now. They betoken an exuberant acceptance of existence in all its peculiar diversity, 'with all its alien and impartial chances':[122] there is no hint of alienation here. Aristophanic poetry is not *all* physical, *all* accumulative, *all* discontinuous, or else it would be tedious, endless and unintelligible. Rather, it uses these qualities,

by sg. verb). All this, patently, is said of the goddess Peace; cf. above, p. 147 n. 106. With this dislocated list of Peace's pieces contrast a 'straight' one in the (?) spurious *Islands* (fr. 402 *PCG*).

[121] Dionysus, god of the tragic festival, was himself 'Ivy', Κισσός: Dodds on Eur. *Bacch.* 81.

[122] Langer: above, p. 90.

freely, in expression of a fully intelligible—and intelligent—vision.

Discontinuity and accumulation, it is apparent, tend to presuppose a common syntactic inclination, or rather (in the strict sense) an anti-syntactic inclination: a reluctance to subordinate words, phrases, clauses, and a preference for simple parataxis. This is how the comic poet sees, and conveys, the world: in sequences, as much as (in the Aristotelian sense) consequences; sequences of autonomous items, apprehended first and foremost in their separateness; sequences, to an extent hard for many modern sensibilities to grasp, unmediated by conceptualized and abstracted causality. The comic vision, then, privileges the physical and relates not only accumulation, but also the surprises of discontinuity, to it.

Thus defined, the comic vision quite specifically recalls the modern literary-theoretical principle of defamiliarization. This important concept, developed by the Russian Formalists in the first decades of the twentieth century, claims a validity for all art, and in particular for all poetry, by laying stress on the distinctive and surprising features of art and poetry, and then relating those features to the need to stimulate new responses to experience:

> Habitualization devours works, clothes, furniture, one's wife and the fear of war . . . And art exists that one may recover the sensation of life; it exists to make one feel things, to make the stone *stony*. The purpose of art is to impart the sensation of things as they are perceived and not as they are known. The technique of art is to make objects 'unfamiliar'.

That formulation—by Viktor Shklovsky[123]—has its own historical background and its own historical resonances. To anyone pondering the 'comic vision' of Aristophanes, it is suitably startling (defamiliarizing?) to see 'the fear of war' listed as one of the 'sensations of life' which art exists to 'impart'. Further consideration will be given in later chapters to Aristophanes' comic vision and his large themes, like war. For the moment we may content ourselves with noting how the concept of defamiliarization helps

[123] 'Art as technique' (1917), in L. T. Lemon and M. J. Reis (eds.), *Russian Formalist Criticism: Four Essays* (Lincoln, Nebr. 1965) 12. The principle was explored simultaneously, but articulated less fully and less vividly, by the founding fathers of New Criticism. Cf. e.g. I. A. Richards's suggestion that 'nearly all good poetry is disconcerting, for a moment at least': *Practical Criticism* (London 1929) 254.

to illuminate his instinct for the discontinuous, which is the defamiliarizing technique *par excellence*.

We should note also that implicit in the Formalist argument is the necessity for stylistic or phraseological originality. It is not enough to be, merely, different from the everyday. Literary cliché does not in itself defamiliarize anything. When a writer of elevated poetry says, 'Lady, I pray thee', he is doing what no everyday user of the language does, but he has not thereby made the Muse more Muse-y, as Shklovsky wants the writer to make the stone more stony. He has not thereby made anything more anything. What he has done is produce a conventional elevation which merely affirms, or reaffirms, his own membership of an exclusive club whose members use, and are expected to use, such language. However, when *Aristophanes* says, 'Lady, I pray thee', he is breaching expectation and, no sooner has he done so, than he breaches expectation again by changing idiom (μετ' ἐμοῦ τοῦ φίλου: 'and, sweetheart . . .').[124] Again and again, his juxtapositions are new, as so many of his particular usages are new—new so far as our evidence suggests, and new as his own insistence on originality might lead one to expect.[125] At the same time, his inventiveness, however diverse the writing it produces, produces writing of a particular kind, in accordance with a particular vision, and not of *any* kind. It does not, for instance, produce writing like Plato's 'souls transient', remote from any Greek norms and expressive of a particular supra-normal vision. Aristophanes' writing, by contrast, is to be seen as a drastically intensified version of its popular Greek base, to which it does in any case repeatedly return.[126]

Finally, our discussion has served to bring into relation Aristophanes' own use of language and certain of the vital characteristics of comedy we considered at a theoretical level in the previous chapter. If the comic instinct for the material and for the 'specific embodiment' that conveys it[127] is seen to be abun-

[124] *Pax* 774–5; Stesich. 33: above, pp. 111–13.

[125] 'New', meaning not absolute novelty, necessarily, but the kind or degree of novelty requisite for (live) metaphor—which is both an instance of the 'particular usages' in question and a good analogy for them as a whole.

[126] 'Intensified version of . . . popular . . . base' is equivalent to what Gerard Manley Hopkins called 'the current language heightened': letter to Robert Bridges, 15 Feb. 1879, in C. C. Abbott (ed.), *The Letters of Gerard Manley Hopkins to Robert Bridges* (London 1935) 89.

[127] Above, p. 90.

dantly in evidence in Aristophanes' stylistic usage, so too comedy's diversity and freedom are writ large in his mobility, above all. Classical tragedy and Menandrian comedy conform to laws of decorum, laws of homogeneity (absolute or differential), and laws of processive coherence, from which departure is difficult and probably destructive. Aristophanic comedy, with its own coherence, yet has at least some freedom to conform—or not. If comedy means freedom, this is comedy at its most comic.

4
The Lesson of the Lyric Poetry

With our discussion of Aristophanic language in mind and, equally, our theorizing about tragedy and comedy, it is instructive to take a closer look at Aristophanes' lyrics. What is 'lyric poetry'? To most moderns, no doubt, it means the sort of thing Keats wrote. The words of ancient Greek lyric poetry may or may not be like the words of a Keats ode—but in ancient Greece 'lyric poetry', let us not forget, means the words of songs, just as, of course, it does again in the Broadway/Tin Pan Alley world of twentieth-century popular music. 'Lyrics' are what Lorenz Hart wrote to accompany Richard Rodgers's music, and what Ira Gershwin wrote to accompany the music of his brother George.

Greek lyric poetry (it will be generally agreed) is not all equally distinguished, but in some of the victory odes of Pindar and, again, some of the choral lyrics of tragedy it includes much of the most intensified, and some of the finest, Greek poetry ever written. Given that all such poetry was originally sung, it remains a puzzle why Greek poets should have reserved their fullest exploration of verbal richness for a medium already enriched by the elements of music and, often, dance. With the music, and the dance, in large part a matter of conjecture, the puzzle is insignificant beside the impressiveness of the words themselves.[1] For us there is a puzzle of a different kind. In his lyric writing, as elsewhere, Aristophanes' words have their own impressiveness—and yet his achievement here is strikingly uneven. The explanation for this bears on our argument and needs careful formulation.

Aristophanes' use of language (to recapitulate) is diverse. One aspect of this diversity is that the level of the language varies from low to high and that, in some degree, the distinctions involved

[1] Cf. above, p. 5. On music and dance, see further: M. L. West, *Ancient Greek Music* (Oxford 1992); A. D. Barker, 'Music', in *OCD*³, 1003–12; G. Prudhommeau, *La Danse grecque antique* (Paris 1965); L. B. Lawler, *The Dance of the Ancient Greek Theater* (Iowa City 1964).

correspond with metrical *differentiae*, so that iambic dialogue (at the bottom) tends to be lower than sung lyric (at the top). As must now be apparent, however, the fact of Aristophanic mobility means that such correlations are not at all consistent. Furthermore, just as, in Aristophanes' iambics, low colloquiality is the base and (often) the point of departure, so too in the lyrics the base is a low one. However, the lyric low is still pitched differently from the dialogue low. Compare, for instance, *Frogs* 9–12, from one of our earlier discussions,

ΞΑ. μηδ' ὅτι τοσοῦτον ἄχθος ἐπ' ἐμαυτῷ φέρων,
εἰ μὴ καθαιρήσει τις, ἀποπαρδήσομαι;
ΔΙ. μὴ δῆθ', ἱκετεύω, πλήν γ' ὅταν μέλλω 'ξεμεῖν.
ΞΑ. τί δῆτ' ἔδει με ταῦτα τὰ σκεύη φέρειν . . .

XAN. What about, 'unless someone gets
All this weight off me, I'll start farting it off'?
DIO. Please—not till I'm supposed to throw up anyway.
XAN. So what was the point of my carrying all these bags . . .

with a representative sequence of low lyric from the opening of a choral song in *Wasps* (273–6):

τί ποτ' οὐ πρὸ θυρῶν φαίνετ' ἄρ' ἡμῖν
ὁ γέρων οὐδ' ὑπακούει;
μῶν ἀπολώλεκε τὰς
ἐμβάδας, ἢ προσέκοψ' ἐν
τῷ σκότῳ τὸν δάκτυλόν που,
εἶτ' ἐφλέγμηνεν αὐτοῦ
τὸ σφυρὸν γέροντος ὄντος;

Why's the old boy not out the house?
Why's he not heard us call?
Could be that he's lost his shoes
Or stubbed his toe in the dark, the way
An old man does, and sprained an ankle.

The linguistic level of the *Frogs* passage is indicated positively by the coarse vocabulary of 'farting' and 'throwing up', negatively by the absence of any feature visibly alien to ordinary speech. The *Wasps* passage is interestingly similar and interestingly different. Its idiom is plain. It has nothing ornamental about it, certainly. Yet its syntax has (by comparison with the *Frogs* passage) a modest formality that removes it from the wholly colloquial. Its vocabulary indeed is predominantly non-'poetic' ('shoes', 'stubbed', 'sprained': ἐμβάδας, προσέκοψε, ἐφλέγμηνεν) or else non-distinctive, but negatively it is marked by the absence of anything as gross as 'farting' and 'throwing up', and positively by the presence of at least one touch of discreet elevation in the phrase πρὸ θυρῶν ('out the house'), where for an instant we hear the idiom of Sophocles and Euripides, and not quite the idiom of ordinary prose, 'ordinary' Aristophanes, or (presumably) ordinary conversation.[2] The elevation (be it noted) is so slight that no significant switch to it, or from it, is, or really could be, involved; and in any case its placing right at the start of the song (therefore, so to speak, on unmarked ground) makes its occurrence even less striking than it otherwise might be.

Notwithstanding such differences between low lyric and low dialogue, it remains apparent that they share a low base. Where other, more formal or more literary, modes of Greek make their presence felt, they are to be regarded as superimpositions on this base in the lyric poetry as much as elsewhere. That is, Aristophanes the lyric poet does not belong to the well-known line that runs from Alcman to Simonides, from Pindar to the authors of those magnificent choral odes of tragedy. His lyrics may be more or less affected by that line, but he does not belong to it. His affinities[3] are rather with the tradition of low lyric that descends from folk song and Archilochus—or, presumably, from folk song *to* Archilochus—and is drawn on variously by Hipponax and, underneath the aristocratic accent, by Anacreon: a tradition that, by comparison with the 'serious' line, keeps recognizable links with popular elements.[4]

[2] Representative data for πρὸ θυρῶν (without article): Soph. *El.* 109, Eur. *Hipp.* 170, cf. *Od.* 1. 107 προπάροιθε θυράων, *Il.* 9. 473 πρόσθεν θαλάμοιο θυράων. For πρὸ τῶν θυρῶν (with): Hdt. 2. 48. 1 (θυρέων), Ar. *Vesp.* 804, Eur. *Cyc.* 635 (satyric), Men. *Grg.* 104; cf. Men. *Perik.* 299 (πρόσθε), etc. The *Hipp.* passage cited recalls the *Vesp.* context substantially (*Hipp.* 170–3 γεραιὰ . . . πρὸ θυρῶν . . . τί ποτ' ἐστί . . .), but though the relative chronology of the plays makes allusion possible (*Hipp.* 428 BC, six years before *Vesp.*), no specific allusion seems to arise. English 'out' as prep. is obsolete/dialectical: *OED* s.v.

[3] I am not speaking here of the historical origins of the lyric forms themselves, but rather (like Aristotle in *Poet.* IV) of spiritual ancestry, albeit without prejudice to historical origins proper, on which see T. McEvilley, 'Development in the lyrics of Aristophanes', *AJPh* 91 (1970) 257–76, and G. M. Sifakis, *Parabasis and Animal Choruses* (London 1971).

[4] The low tradition includes, but is wider than, *iamboi* (on the ethos of which cf. M. L. West, *Studies in Greek Elegy and Iambus* (Berlin 1974) 22–39, and Rosen, *Iambographic Tradition*—or than 'blame poetry' (above, p. 11). The *gephurismoi* of *Ran.* 416–30 presumably represent one type of popular art ('folk lyric') more or less

The ultimate affiliations of Aristophanic lyric, no less than those of Aristophanic comedy *tout court*, are, for better or worse, *popular*. Witness, in the first place, its topicality. Popular perception lives in the topical present. In the *Peace* lyric, 'Lady, I pray thee . . .' (774 ff.), allusion to Carcinus (782) betokens the comic poet's right to assert the contemporary as readily in song as he does in speech elsewhere. His simpler low lyrics often centre on such allusions. Take *Birds* 1470–5, on a (supposed) coward and shield-shedder:

> πολλὰ δὴ καὶ καινὰ καὶ θαυ-
> μάστ' ἐπεπτόμεσθα καὶ
> δεινὰ πράγματ' εἴδομεν.
> ἔστι γὰρ δένδρον πεφυκὸς
> ἔκτοπόν τι, Καρδίας ἀ-
> πωτέρω, Κλεώνυμος . . .
>
> We've flown and seen the most amazing things.
> Outside *Battle* there's a weird tree
> They call *Cleonymus* . . .[5]

Topical satire: the birds have been and seen, and report back in essentially plain Greek—without any coarseness, but in ordinary, unpretentious idiom.[6] Despite the punning, the strength of such a passage is not in verbal finesse, let alone in any lapidary verbal perfection, but in the immediate play of ideas, whose vigour is the vigour of (how often shall we find ourselves needing this phrase?) the here and now.

intact (cf. F. Graf, *Eleusis und die orphische Dichtung Athens in vorhellenistischer Zeit* (Berlin 1974) 45–6).

[5] 'Battle' for *Καρδία* (a town in the Thracian Chersonese), because καρδία, 'heart', connotes courage (not feeling, like 'heart' in English: cf. Dunbar ad loc.), and Cleonymus was a public figure alleged (see Dunbar on *Av.* 289–90) to have shown cowardice under arms.

[6] There is the -μεσθα of 1471, usually regarded as an epic/poetic form and certainly alien to prose: R. Kühner, *Ausführliche Grammatik der griechischen Sprache*, I[3], rev. F. Blass (2 vols., Hanover 1890–2), ii. 61; E. Schwyzer, *Griechische Grammatik*[2] (4 vols., Munich 1959–71), i. 670. However, the form is perhaps not so purely poetic. It is remarkably common in A himself (nine citations in G. Curtius, *Das Verbum der griechischen Sprache*, i[2] (Leipzig 1877) 94, including such very 'unpoetic' verses as *Plut.* 1160) and reappears in the *koine* (Schwyzer, *Grammatik*, i. 670 n. 3). In *Av.* 1470–2 Moulton, *Poetry*, 34, and N. W. Slater, 'Performing the city in *Birds*', in G. W. Dobrov (ed.), *The City as Comedy* (Chapel Hill 1997) 86, plausibly see what Slater calls a 'subversive appropriation' of the opening words of Sophocles' 'Ode to Man' (*Ant.* 332–3)—but the issue of stylistic level is not affected.

If a bit of satire of the Cleonymus kind can prove its popular credentials without any coarse language, one must at once add the rider that nothing is more characteristic of Aristophanes' low lyrics than the freedom with which they accommodate demotic obscenity. Take for instance *Lysistrata* 821–4, a brief duet between old woman militant and old man mock-afraid:

—τὴν γνάθον βούλει θένω;
—μηδαμῶς· ἔδεισα γάρ.
—ἀλλὰ κρούσω τῷ σκέλει;
—τὸν σάκανδρον ἐκφανεῖς.

O.W. Want me to smash your face in?
O.M. Bully! Made me cringe!
O.W. Rather I put the boot in?
O.M. Go on—show us your minge![7]

The popular basis of Aristophanes' lyric poetry as a whole is likewise attested by various of its formal characteristics: the extensive use of the simple 'systematic' grouping of rhythmical cola and the short stanza-unit, which one associates with Archilochus, Anacreon, and others, rather than the 'periodic' groupings favoured in grand choral lyric; the simpler coherence of the rhythmic constituents of Aristophanic stanzas as compared with their tragic counterparts; the use of 'patter rhythms' to suit 'vigorous dance'; and the occasional appearance of 'syllabic', rather than quantitative, rhythm, and of 'approximate responsion' between strophe and antistrophe.[8]

[7] On σάκανδρος see Henderson, *Maculate Muse*, 133. The tone of θείνω (821) is a bit of a puzzle. The verb is a verse word (cf. LSJ s.v.), and yet occurs often in A (only in the stem θεν-) in similarly/apparently low contexts: *Eq.* 640, *Vesp.* 1384, *Av.* 54, 1613, *Lys.* 364, *Ran.* 855 (contrast, perhaps, *Ach.* 564): cf. W. G. Rutherford, *The New Phrynichus* (London 1881) 10.

[8] See, respectively, A. M. Dale, *The Lyric Metres of Greek Drama*² (Cambridge 1968) 196; West, *Greek Metre*, 104; Parker, *Songs*, 22; A. M. Dale, *Collected Papers* (Cambridge 1969) 253, Parker, *Songs*, 28–9; and (on syllabic rhythm and approximate responsion) Dale, *Lyric Metres*, 56–7, 62–6, 78–9, 86, 89–91, 207; U. von Wilamowitz-Moellendorff, *Griechische Verskunst* (Berlin 1921) 470–86; West, *Greek Metre*, 105, 107, 124, 127; Zimmermann, *Untersuchungen*, ii. 118–19 on *Eq.* 303–81 and 382–456; C. Romano, *Reponsioni libere nei canti di Aristofane* (Rome 1992); Parker, *Songs*, 115–17 (sceptical). Not all authorities rush to call syllabic rhythm 'popular' (cf. Dale, *Lyric Metres*, 78), but it is hard to see what else it could be, despite its exceptional occurrence in high poetry proper. One may add that rhythms are to some extent low ('popular') or high *per se*: see Dale, *Papers*, 256 (and cf. Demetr. *Eloc.* 5 etc.) and *Lyric Metres* 54–7, 113, 147. Quick-resolution cretic-paeonics are a good example of a low rhythm: Dale, *Papers*, 253.

Then again, witness the receptiveness of Aristophanes' lyrics to that whole range of parallelisms that we have seen to be so characteristic of his style as a whole, and in particular to certain kinds of parallelism which are very specifically uncharacteristic of the lyric style of a Pindar or a Sophocles. One kind, indeed, we do find in Pindar (if not in Sophocles): the refrain. Consider, for instance, the hymn-singing initiates in *Frogs* who call on their god in short matching stanzas that end with the same one-line summons (403, 408, 413):

> Ἴακχε φιλοχορευτά, συμπρόπεμπέ με.
>
> Friend of the dance, Iacchus, be my guide.

Such a refrain involves a mode of stylization which is compatible both with the high and the low.[9] In contrast, most of the parallel structurings within the lyrics are wholly alien to the high style. Thus it is, for instance, with the iambic rhyme in *Acharnians* 1015–17,

> ἤκουσας ὡς μαγειρικῶς
> κομψῶς τε καὶ δειπνητικῶς
> αὑτῷ διακονεῖται;
>
> D'you hear him—like a master chef
> Or a *bon viveur*—ef-
> fortlessly sorting out the dinner?[10]

metrically responding to another in 1044–6 (where a whiff of high-flown verbiage adds unexpectedly to the effect of the chorus's anguish at our hero's culinary preparations):

[9] High-style refrains tend to have cultic associations: see e.g. Pind. *Paeans* 5 and 21 and, for tragedy, the remarks of E. R. Dodds, *Euripides, Bacchae*² (Oxford 1960), p. xxxviii, and Stanford, *Aeschylus*, 83–5. Low refrains probably have affinities rather with magic (cf. e.g. Theocrit. 2. 17, 22 etc., ἴυγξ, ἕλκε . . .). In 'Lyric poet', 127, I misrepresented refrains as wholly low. In 'Aristophanes' "high" lyrics reconsidered', *Maia* 49 (1997) 1–42 at 30–1 (with n. 89), G. Mathews misrepresents them the other way as wholly cultic, and compounds the error by—bizarrely—associating them with the high-style 'anadiplosis' characteristic of Euripides in operatic mode and (e.g.) parodied by A at *Ran.* 1336 φόνια φόνια: on such repetitions see Silk, 'Paratragedy', 482–3; Dover, *Frogs*, 358; W. Breitenbach, *Untersuchungen zur Sprache der Euripideischen Lyrik* (Stuttgart 1934) 195, 214–21. In tragedy, actual refrains are common only in Aeschylus; cf. n. 11 below. As the compound φιλοχορευτά suggests, the *Ran.* refrain does have high-style pretensions (but see Silk, 'Lyric poet', 112–15).

[10] In the Greek, rhyme is secured not by an extravagant overhanging word, but by the extravagant coinage δειπνητικῶς (cf. Starkie ad loc.).

> ἀποκτενεῖς λιμῷ 'μὲ καὶ
> τοὺς γείτονας κνίσῃ τε καὶ
> φωνῇ τοιαῦτα λάσκων;
>
> Me and my mates can smell the stew!
> What with that and all the beau-
> teous talk of food, you're killing us!

And thus it is again with our instance of agonistic cry and counter-cry—Lamachus and Dicaeopolis—from the end of the same play: *τοῦ σκέλους . . . τοῦ πέους . . . σκοτοδινιῶ . . . σκοτοβινιῶ* . . .—'My leg . . . My cock . . . My head aches . . . My hard-on . . .'[11]

However, if low lyric is Aristophanes' primary idiom, it does not follow that it represents an ideal type. It is the low lyrics in which (as Dover reminds us) we sometimes find the most 'tediously unsophisticated aspects of Greek comedy'. He makes the comment apropos the rival choruses of old men and old women in *Lysistrata*, and adds:

> while the two choruses are at odds, their abusive words and threats of violence go on longer than (to our taste) humorous invention can be sustained, and when they are united they devote no less than four whole stanzas to the primitive joke, 'if anyone wants to borrow anything from me, let him come to my house at once—and he'll get nothing'.[12]

This is popular vigour at its most restrictive and trivial; *entertainment* arising out of the immediate dramatic moment, and playing, perhaps, on some current resonance outside the drama—but hardly, to use the modern dichotomy, *art*. Certainly Aristophanes' special achievement as a lyric poet is not to be found here.

I first considered the nature of Aristophanes' lyric poetry in 1980, in an article which has attracted its quota of attention.[13] My concern at that time was to elucidate the variety of Aristophanes'

[11] Above, p. 125. For the popular character of the multiple assonance in all these *Ach.* examples (to which add e.g. *Lys.* 1189–91), cf. the swallow song, *Carm. Pop.* 2 *PMG*, and Silk, *Interaction*, 224–6. In tragic lyrics, much the closest parallels (few as they are) are in Aesch. (cf. Stanford, *Aeschylus*, 83–4; Silk, *Interaction*, 227)—not the only time Aesch. elevates the popular (cf., then, his use of refrains (n. 9 above)). In *Ach.* 1044–6 the 'high' point is the 'poetic' λάσκω (LSJ s.v. III).

[12] Dover, *Aristophanic Comedy*, 154, on *Lys.* 1043–71 and 1189–215.

[13] Silk, 'Lyric poet': see esp. Zimmermann, *Untersuchungen* (e.g. i. 68–9); Parker, *Songs*, 10–16; Mathews, 'Reconsidered', *passim*; C. Prato, 'I metri lirici di Aristofane', *Dioniso* 57 (1987), esp. 209, 214–15; K. J. Dover, *Entr. Hardt* 38 (1993) 200; also comments by such reviewers as R. G. Ussher, *JHS* 103 (1983) 168, and R. M. Harriott, *G&R* 29 (1982) 86–7.

lyrics, to place the various types on a high/low spectrum, and, with this spectrum in mind, to distinguish between his more and his less impressive work. In particular, I contrasted his experiments in high lyric (which had been widely acclaimed) with his hybrids (which had received little attention from earlier critics). In the high-lyric sphere (I sought to demonstrate), by his own superb standards, Aristophanes shows remarkably little inventiveness and no sign of the qualities a poet would need to establish a place within the traditions of Pindaric or tragic lyric poetry, where (perversely enough) received opinion seemed to have situated him. Conversely, by making use, in part, of tragic elements, albeit in a way alien to tragic decorum—by adding (that is) high elements to the low-lyric base—he creates a range of astonishing hybrids which represents a significant achievement and through which (we may now add) his dialectic with tragedy is conducted with particular clarity. To judge from published responses to that article, I may have succeeded in the demonstration. At all events, though the formulation of my critique of Aristophanes' high lyrics has been challenged (not, in my judgement, to much purpose), the overall argument seems not to have been queried as such.[14] Nor (apart from some points of detail) do I see any grounds for querying it now: I seek rather to re-present the case in revised form, as suits the present discussion.

[14] The challenges: (*a*) the propriety of discussing lyrics out of dramatic context (Zimmermann, *Untersuchungen*, i. 69; Parker, *Songs*, 10; see already my comments in 'Lyric poet', 105–7); (*b*) the critique of the high lyrics as such (esp. Mathews, 'Reconsidered', *passim*). Regarding (*a*): 'dramatic context' cannot make up for deficiencies elsewhere unless 'dramatic context' calls for deficient writing (see below, p. 175, and on the general issue of detachable songs, 268–70). Regarding (*b*): though Mathews, in particular, evidently supposes he is opposing my assessment, much of his challenge serves only to provide further confirmation of it, sometimes even explicitly (see e.g. below, p. 178 n. 37). I have myself modified my views on particular songs (see e.g. the more favourable assessment of *Av.* 227–62 below, pp. 191–5, compared with 'Lyric poet', 141), and have also withdrawn one of my own prominent distinctions ('realism' versus 'fantasy': below, p. 191). Mathews is right to point out that more could be said than I said about the 'hymnal/cultic' features of A's cletic hymns (below, p. 178 n. 38)—but (*pace* Mathews) this has no direct bearing on their assessment. In 'Lyric Poet', 104–5, 110–11, I duly acknowledged the generic acceptability of A's high lyrics on the level of 'Bacchylides on his dullest days', or 'Euripides at his most perfunctory', or 'the lesser Homeric hymns'. Mathews seems to me to have gone to some trouble to prove the point (along with a few, not notably successful, attempts to do more than this: see e.g. below, p. 179 n. 39). Here and overall, my general position is unchanged.

High lyrics are scattered among the extant plays, from *Acharnians* to *Frogs*. They fall into two broad groups, devotional pieces and what (for lack of a better term) we may call *exotica*. Apart from the high style itself, the groups share two common features. The first—as corollary and corroboration of the elevation—is mythological material, perhaps 'religious' in spirit (as generally in the devotional lyrics), perhaps not. The second is charm. These features apart, the difference between the two groups is readily apparent. Taken out of context, the devotional pieces would mostly have no visible, or even plausible, connection with comic drama. By contrast, the *exotica* cannot be taken out of context: they presuppose one or other of the extraordinary and often riotous situations that Aristophanes' Old Comedies bring into existence—and yet seek to divert them, briefly, into a realm of order and elegance. Both groups of instances, then, represent experiments with 'seriousness', at least in so far as 'serious' means 'not funny'; but though indeed widely praised in the past, they succeed only on a very modest level and appeal only to a very limited kind of response.

As representative of the two groups, consider the opening lyrics of *Clouds*, comprising the *parodos*, or entrance of the chorus. The context of this piece is worth a moment's attention. The chorus are summoned in elevated anapaestic recitative by their high priest, the great fraud Socrates (266),

> *ἄρθητε, φάνητ', ὦ δέσποιναι . . .*
> O Ladies, appear unto me . . .

though this grand apostrophe is somewhat undermined by a distinctly prosaic end to the line:

> *. . . τῷ φροντιστῇ μετέωροι*
> . . . in mid-air, a philosopher.[15]

The Clouds' prospective beneficiary, Strepsiades, subverts the grandeur of the moment more comprehensively. *His* response keeps the metre, but drastically lowers the tone. Clouds mean *rain*, therefore . . . (267–8):

[15] Contrast the spreads of *δέσποινα* (cultic/high poetic) and *φροντιστής* (comedy/philosophy) in LSJ s.vv. The latter was evidently a nickname of Socrates himself: Xen. *Symp*. 6. 6 *ἆρα σύ, ὦ Σώκρατες, ὁ φροντιστὴς ἐπικαλούμενος*, Pl. *Ap*. 18b, Ameips. Com. ii. 200 *PCG* (cf. Dover, *Clouds*, pp. l–li).

μήπω, μήπω γε, πρὶν ἂν τουτὶ πτύξωμαι, μὴ καταβρεχθῶ.
τὸ δὲ μηδὲ κυνῆν οἴκοθεν ἐλθεῖν ἐμὲ τὸν κακοδαίμον' ἔχοντα.

Oh please, let me wrap myself up or I'll get soaked:
Trust me to go out of the house with no cap on.

Socrates resumes, regardless, in high style (269–74):

ἔλθετε δῆτ', ὦ πολυτίμητοι Νεφέλαι . . .
ὑπακούσατε δεξάμεναι θυσίαν καὶ τοῖς ἱεροῖσι χαρεῖσαι.

O come, ye illustrious Clouds . . .
As ye rejoice in our rites, and our sacrifice, hearken!

And the Clouds duly hearken, and sing (275–90):

ἀέναοι Νεφέλαι, 275
ἀρθῶμεν φανεραὶ δροσερὰν φύσιν εὐάγητον
πατρὸς ἀπ' Ὠκεανοῦ βαρυαχέος
ὑψηλῶν ὀρέων κορυφὰς ἔπι
δενδροκόμους, ἵνα 280
τηλεφανεῖς σκοπιὰς ἀφορώμεθα
καρπούς τ' ἀρδομέναν ἱερὰν χθόνα
καὶ ποταμῶν ζαθέων κελαδήματα
καὶ πόντον κελάδοντα βαρύβρομον·
ὄμμα γὰρ αἰθέρος ἀκάματον σελαγεῖται 285
μαρμαρέαισιν αὐγαῖς.
ἀλλ' ἀποσεισάμεναι νέφος ὄμβριον
ἀθανάτας ἰδέας ἐπιδώμεθα
τηλεσκόπῳ ὄμματι γαῖαν. 290

Clouds everlasting,
Raise we to view our glittering, dew-laden form,
Forth from our father, Ocean deep-voiced,
On to the leaf-tressèd peaks of the lofty mountains,
So we may gaze at the far-away heights,
At the sacred earth whose crops we water,
At the holy rivers' roaring,
At the roaring sea deep-sounding.
Heaven's unwearied eye sparkles with glistering rays.
Cast we the watery mist
Off our immortal guise and, with eye far-seeing,
Look on the world![16]

[16] Text as Dover, here and in the antistrophe (298 ff.: below, p. 173). For a few details in the transl., cf. an equally unchallenging composition, Shelley's 'The Cloud' (1820).

Roll up, roll up, and hear 'The Singing Clouds' . . . This undeniably exotic piece of dactylic verse has been transformed by eminent readers into something inconceivably different from what it actually is: into 'one of the most beautiful lyrical passages of Attic literature', and even, simply, 'one of the most beautiful creations of Greek lyric'.[17] No responsible reading can accommodate such gratuity. Another critic, with more reason, praises the overall *dramatic* point of the chorus and its tone here. A cloud-chorus aptly symbolizes 'unworldly' thought and insubstantial philosophy, while clouds, though easily personifiable as agents of Zeus, are not 'real' deities, hence are 'suitable objects of worship for a man devoted to *καινὰ δαιμόνια* [new divinities]'. Regarding the dramatic function of the *parodos*: 'we hear the chorus singing before it appears in the theatre and it drifts into our sight with the slow majesty of clouds which have gathered on the mountains and are spreading over the land. Their opening song is formally much closer to tragedy than to comedy and this befits their status as deities responding to Socrates' invitation'[18]—and, one might add, as elaborately grand figures calculated to make it plausible that both the sophisticated (like Socrates) and the unsophisticated (like Strepsiades) should be able to find them impressive. This one can readily accept as a strength of the passage. One can also grant that the song presents an element of foil to the humorous goings-on around it, and one can certainly give credit for Aristophanes' inventiveness in metamorphosing 'clouds' into the world of religious lyricism—and for creating such unexpected 'nature poetry' in an era when, no doubt, comparable descriptions of nature are far from the minds of most writers.

But these strengths all involve the broad rationale of the song as a whole, and serve, if anything, to show up the weakness of its local organization. The piece has an assured dramatic significance and, besides this, a weird charm; in respect of its detail, however, it is conspicuous for its triteness, its inflation, its pervasive absence of point, its almost total lack of any defamiliarizing

[17] C. P. Segal, 'Aristophanes' cloud-chorus', *Arethusa* 2 (1969) 143–61, at 148, and E. Fraenkel, *Beobachtungen zu Aristophanes* (Rome 1962) 198 ('eins der schönsten Gebilde griechischer Lyrik'). Mathews, 'Reconsidered', 29, echoes these verdicts ('an archaic and formal, indeed baroque, kind of beauty'). The *parodos* is *pretty*, yes.

[18] Dover, *Clouds*, pp. lxvii–lxix. See further Segal, 'Cloud-chorus', for an interesting interpretation of the Clouds as embodiment of 'natural vitality'.

features to bring it to life. It is a piece that exhibits none of the Aristophanic qualities we have discussed at length in the previous chapter and yet none of the qualities for which good writing in the high-lyrical sphere is rightly admired. It is high-style, and so determinedly high-style that it seems to have no time or energy to be anything else. Unlike Socrates, the chorus here is made to express itself homogeneously, *without* stylistic or tonal incongruity, *with* (instead) an inert series of elevated lyric clichés.[19] It is, in short, high-lyrical pastiche, but exaggeratedly conventional in its high-lyrical features. From the chorus' apparent relationship with Socrates we might (wrongly) have constructed an expectation that their loftiness, like his, would be lowered by some stylistic incoherence, and in Strepsiades' affably boorish response to their exalted status we might (wrongly) have suspected an incitement to bring them down to earth. On the contrary: they are and remain airborne—but not, regrettably, by means of any verbal propulsion.

From the first words (275–8), elevation is established negatively by the absence of the particles and articles that characterize 'ordinary' Greek, positively by a welter of archaic-poetic lexemes and idioms.[20] Diction and dialect advertise high pretensions: βαρυαχέος ('deep-voiced'), elevated compound complete with 'Doric alpha', conveniently embodies both (278); μαρμαρέαισιν ('glistering'), statutory epic-Ionic 'rare word' (*glôtta*), completes the picture (287).[21] As part of its inheritance from Homer, high lyric is wont to employ ornamental generic epithets. Very well then: we need at least one *bona fide*, gilt-edged, banal generic epithet to help enforce an overpowering sense of literary tradition. We duly get it: mountains are 'lofty'; everything is business as usual.[22]

[19] Within (or beyond) this homogeneity there is no signal—no identificatory frame—to suggest any kind of parody: Silk, 'Lyric poet', 108–9, and 'Paratragedy', *passim*.

[20] e.g. *simplex* ἀρθῶμεν, loosely predicative φανεραί, exotic formation εὐάγητον (= ordinary εὐαγής), stock high-verse metonym δροσεράν (= ὑγράν, *vel. sim.*: 'dewy' for 'wet'), elaborate periphrasis δροσερὰν φύσιν.

[21] Doric alpha: A. Thumb and E. Kieckers, *Handbuch der griechischen Dialekte*, i² (Heidelberg 1932) 217–21. *Glôtta*: see e.g. Silk, 'Iconyms', 303. βαρυαχής: see spread in LSJ s.v. μαρμάρεος: in pre-Hellenistic Greek attested only at *Il.* 14. 273 (of ἅλα) 17. 594 (αἰγίδα) 18. 480 (ἄντυγα)—cf. v.l. at 3. 126, 22. 441 (δίπλακα)—and Hes. *Th.* 811 (πύλαι); sim. μαρμαρόεσσαν αἴγλαν Soph. *Ant.* 610. As in A, in all these μαρμ. is fem.; in most of them, too, the accompanying noun begins with an alpha; the aspiring high-style poet's deference is total.

[22] ὑψηλῶν ὀρέων (in gen. pl.), *Il.* 12. 282, *Od.* 9. 113, *h.Ap.* 145, *Lesb. Adesp.* 14

High-style writing, in lyrics and elsewhere, occasionally allows itself a measure of inflation, whereby words, or their synonyms, are repeated at short range without much sign of any structural or other significance. Very well, then. *This* bit of high-style writing deals us a whole hand of inflationary duplications: 'peaks' *and* 'heights' (κορυφάς, σκοπιάς: 279–81), 'sacred' *and* 'holy' (ἱεράν, ζαθέων: 282–3), 'far-away' *and* 'far-seeing' (τηλεφανεῖς, τηλεσκόπῳ: 281–90), 'roaring' (noun) *and* 'roaring' (adjective) (κελαδήματα, κελάδοντα: 283–4), Heaven's 'eye' *and* the Clouds' 'eye' (ὄμμα, ὄμματι: 285–90). It isn't (to restate) that successful lyric poetry never includes such items. Of course it does, but they are the hallmarks of its lyricism, not of its success. It uses them, but not in such thick quantity, all at once, and so inertly.[23]

With their uniform high style these singing Clouds are, therefore, very different from either Socrates or Strepsiades down below. Strepsiades talks (or 'chants') low, and rises, if at all, only in momentary discontinuity. Socrates veers from register to register in a way calculated to ensure that the impression of a *poseur* is always with us. These configurations recur in the anapaestic verses following (291–6):

ΣΩ. ὦ μέγα σεμναὶ Νεφέλαι, φανερῶς ἠκούσατέ μου καλέσαντος.
ᾔσθου φωνῆς ἅμα καὶ βροντῆς μυκησαμένης θεοσέπτου;
ΣΤ. καὶ σέβομαί γ', ὦ πολυτίμητοι, καὶ βούλομαι ἀνταποπαρδεῖν
πρὸς τὰς βροντάς· οὕτως αὐτὰς τετραμαίνω καὶ πεφόβημαι.

PLF (ὑψ-), *al.* In 'Lyric poet', 107, I adduced πατρός (of Ocean) and δενδροκόμους (of peaks) as likewise 'predictable'. So they are, but in the rather different sense that these generic markers echo, rely on, or recombine phrases from the epic tradition: Ὠκεανοῖο . . . θύγατρα Hes. *Th.* 265, πόντος τ' Ὠκεανοῦ τε ῥοαί ibid. 841, ὑψικόμοισιν ὄρεσσι Asius Epic. 7 Bernabé, οὔρεος . . . περὶ δρυσὶν ὑψικόμοισι *Il.* 14. 397–8, δένδρεσιν ἠϋκόμοισιν Emped. 127. 2. However, it would be better to say that the whole stanza does this. Cf. sequences like *Il.* 16. 297–8 ἀφ' ὑψηλῆς κορυφῆς ὄρεος . . . κινήσῃ νεφέλην, Hes. *Th.* 787–9 ὑψηλῆς . . . χθονὸς . . . ἱεροῦ ποταμοῖο . . . Ὠκεανοῖο, etc.

[23] It is well known that Greek poets are more tolerant of inconsequential short-term repetitions than modern poets (or critics) would like: see the representative list of instances in J. Jackson, *Marginalia Scaenica* (Oxford 1955) 220–2, and cf. the brief discussion of the issue (arising out of my 'Lyric poet') by K. J. Dover, N. Loraux, and T. Gelzer in *Entr. Hardt* 38 (1993) 200. However, many of Jackson's examples (representatively) are more ordinary words (like τόνδε . . . τάσδε etc. in Eur. *HF* 3–9: ibid. 220) or a matter of calling the same spade the same spade (like the four sets of λόγοι at Soph. *Phil.* 1267–71: ibid. 221) or indeed cross-referential or a part of a theme (as the λόγοι in Soph. *Phil.* are: see e.g. C. P. Segal, *Tragedy and Civilization* (Cambridge, Mass. 1981) 333–40 on the 'failure of *logos*' in the play).

κεἰ θέμις ἐστίν, νυνί γ' ἤδη, κεἰ μὴ θέμις ἐστί, χεσείω.
ΣΩ. οὐ μὴ σκώψει μηδὲ ποιήσεις ἅπερ οἱ τρυγοδαίμονες οὗτοι . . .

SOC. O holy ones, Clouds, to my call ye have hearkened!
Heardst thou their voice in the thunder's awesome roar?
STR. Awesome and loose-some, your sublimities!
I'm shook up inside so bad I want to fart
Back at the roar: it's thunder-box time for me!
SOC. That'll do! You're as bad as some clown from a comedy . . .

Neither the countryman's scatologies nor the philosopher's swift descent from the pretentious to the irritably colloquial[24] do anything to ruffle the composure of the ethereal chorus who resume their song with a solemn praise of Athens.[25] If the strophe exemplified Aristophanic high lyric in its exotic mode, this antistrophe (after an 'exotic' self-address) is essentially devotional (298–313):

παρθένοι ὀμβροφόροι,
ἔλθωμεν λιπαρὰν χθόνα Παλλάδος, εὔανδρον γᾶν 300
Κέκροπος ὀψόμεναι πολυήρατον·
οὗ σέβας ἀρρήτων ἱερῶν, ἵνα
μυστοδόκος δόμος
ἐν τελεταῖς ἁγίαις ἀναδείκνυται·
οὐρανίοις τε θεοῖς δωρήματα, 305
ναοί θ' ὑψερεφεῖς καὶ ἀγάλματα,
καὶ πρόσοδοι μακάρων ἱερώταται
εὐστέφανοί τε θεῶν θυσίαι θαλίαι τε
παντοδαπαῖσιν ὥραις, 310
ἦρί τ' ἐπερχομένῳ Βρομία χάρις
εὐκελάδων τε χορῶν ἐρεθίσματα
καὶ μοῦσα βαρύβρομος αὐλῶν.

[24] The colloquial reaches a peak on τρυγοδαίμονες, a low portmanteau of the comic τρυγ- (above, p. 41) and the ordinary κακοδαίμονες: cf. Starkie ad loc. In 293 there is a sublime metrically created collision between low and high in Strepsiades' epic-style correption of βούλομαι before the following fart.

[25] Lyrical praise of Athens is invariably religious praise (and not only praise of Athenian religiosity, albeit that is writ large in the antistrophe), and comic drama avoids any belittling of Athens in this respect. As was noted by V. Ehrenberg, *The People of Aristophanes*[2] (Oxford 1951) 264, the Attic hero Theseus and the Attic goddess Athena are among the few higher beings to be untouched by Old Comic degradation. On the tonal affinity between strophe and antistrophe, see Silk, 'Lyric poet', 109–110, and Parker, *Songs*, 14–15.

Rain-making maidens,
Let us be moving, Pallas' bright country to view.
Go we to see the fair land of Cecrops,
Famed for its men, and solemnities mystical,
Rites to receive the initiates, gifts
For the gods of heaven: lo, the temple
Is revealed, shrines high-roofed, sacred
Processions of the blest, garlands,
Offerings to the gods, seasonal festivals,
And, come the Spring, Dionysiac
Joy, incitement of choirs melodious, and the deep
Voice of the flute.

If this stanza, by comparison with its predecessor, is largely detachable from the comic situation, its tone is very similar to that of the strophe, and its linguistic and stylistic contents likewise. From the archetypal verse compound in the opening phrase to a spectacular cluster of poeticisms in the last few words, lyrical elevation is pervasive.[26] So too is cliché,[27] and inflation seems more evident than ever, when in 302 ff., for instance, we encounter a string of 'solemn' mysticals and 'sacred' rituals;[28] and again in 305–9 when the same divine agencies are referred to in close succession as 'gods of heaven', as 'the blest', and as (again) 'the gods', though the context would lose nothing in particularity or force (there is precious little of either), if the second and third time round the labels were omitted.

Once again, there is dramatic point to all this religiosity and especially to its orthodoxy. On the face of it,

[26] ὀμβροφόρος ('rare and poetic': Dunbar on *Av.* 1750, where the word occurs in a high-style lyric) is first attested in Aesch. *Supp.* 35 and not found in classical prose. μοῦσα as metonym (= 'music'): poetic usage (verse + Plato: LSJ s.v. II). βαρύβρομος: high-poetic compound (trag. only in lyric: LSJ s.v.). μ. βαρ.: another characteristic high-style metonym of the kind conventionally labelled 'enallage', as at Soph. *Ant.* 793–4, νεῖκος ἀνδρῶν ξύναιμον (see V. Bers, *Enallage and Greek Style* (Leiden 1974)), where a 'natural' collocation would follow the βαρύβρομον αὐλόν of Eur. *Hel.* 1351. The lack of def. art. with μοῦσα and αὐλῶν and the consequent cluster of heavy words completes the effect.

[27] See e.g. Dover on λιπαράν/εὔανδρον/πολυήρατον/γᾶν Κέκροπος in 299–300.

[28] In the Greek, five different words out of seven meaning 'sacred' or 'sacredness' or 'sacred rite', clustered around the less predictable, but equally sacred-ful, μυστοδόκος δόμος. The compound adj. in that phrase is apparently a coinage on the model of such elevated predecessors as Aesch. ἱκεταδόκος (*Supp.* 713) and πρεσβυτοδόκος (*Supp.* 667) and the more established πανδόκος (δόμοι πανδόκοι *Cho.* 662).

> it is startling that the Clouds . . . praise the Athenians for their pious worship of the traditional gods, who according to Socrates do not exist or have no power . . . Only at the end of the action is the anomaly explained: the *Clouds* . . . [contrary to Socrates' supposition] are not . . . supplanters . . . but agents of Zeus and the traditional gods, and have come to Athens ostensibly to receive Socrates' worship and give him and his pupil their divine aid, but really to make manifest and to punish the impiety of Socrates and the dishonesty of Strepsiades.[29]

And it is a necessary corollary of this as yet hidden status that, unlike Socrates, the chorus here should confine themselves to the 'traditional poetic words'[30] which generations of poets, from Homer to the tragedians, had used in representing the theosphere. But (once again) there is nothing in this dramatic logic that requires the writing itself to be so tame. On the contrary: dramatic logic would have been better served had the choral voices done something to provoke us, as they purport to have provoked the stage figures, to a sense of awe.[31] It is not as if there were any question here of a representation of inadequacy, as there is with (say) the efforts of the 'rude mechanicals' in Shakespeare's *A Midsummer Night's Dream*—

> To show our simple skill,
> That is the true beginning of our end—

efforts which are briskly described by one of their audience as 'the silliest stuff that ever I heard'.[32]

Compare the antistrophe with Euripides' *Trojan Women*, 205–11. The captive women are guessing their ultimate destinations:

> —ἢ Πειρήνας ὑδρευομένα
> πρόσπολος οἰκτρὰ σεμνῶν ὑδάτων.
> —τὰν κλεινὰν εἴθ' ἔλθοιμεν
> Θησέως εὐδαίμονα χώραν.
> —μὴ γὰρ δὴ δίναν γ' Εὐρώτα
> τάν τ' ἐχθίσταν θεράπναν Ἑλένας . . .

[29] Sommerstein on 302–10.

[30] Segal, 'Cloud-chorus', 158.

[31] The point has the more force because of the genuine impressiveness of the *Nub.* chorus in dialogue at the end of the play, which sheds significant light on the weak lyricism of this ode (see below, p. 360), though it has no bearing on the diagnostic significance of the weakness of A's lyricism as a whole.

[32] *A Midsummer Night's Dream,* III. ii (Puck), V. i (Quince), V. i (Hippolyta).

> 'Or kept a slave to draw
> Water, pitiable, from holy Pirene.'
> 'I pray I come to Theseus' land,
> Glorious, blessed.'
> 'Not, at least not, to swirling Eurotas,
> Helen's cursed abode . . .'

Not a particularly startling piece of Euripidean verse, but chosen to suggest, simply, one of the ways good lyric poetry makes something of conventions. The epithets 'holy' (*σεμνῶν*) and 'glorious', 'blessed' (*κλεινὰν . . . εὐδαίμονα*) are complimentary—and banal. Their inertia conveys, with faint irony, just how little the forces of convention have to offer the victim at a time of crisis (and the juxtaposition of 'pitiable'—*οἰκτρά*—and 'holy'—*σεμνῶν*—enforces the point). Their opposition, in turn, to the totally unwelcome 'swirling' (*δίναν*) suggests the value to the slave, nevertheless, of even the most conventional reassurance. The passage offers, then, a poignantly effective use of the stock items, compared with which Aristophanes' uncomplicated generic charm is a very slight thing indeed.

Or again, compare Aristophanes' praise of Athens with the marvellous inventiveness—in ideas *and* words—that Pindar shows in his praise of the holy island of Delos (fr. 33c):

> *χαῖρ', ὦ θεοδμάτα, λιπαροπλοκάμου*
> *παίδεσσι Λατοῦς ἱμεροέστατον ἔρνος,*
> *πόντου θύγατερ, χθονὸς εὐρεί-*
> *ας ἀκίνητον τέρας, ἅν τε βροτοὶ*
> *Δᾶλον κικλήσκοισιν, μάκαρες δ' ἐν Ὀλύμπῳ*
> *τηλέφαντον κυανέας χθονὸς ἄστρον.*
>
> Seedling dear to bright-haired Leto's brood,
> God-builded daughter of the sea, broad
> Earth's unmoving miracle, to men you are
> Delos, but to the Olympian blest
> Dark distant earth's clear star.

By comparison with the *Clouds* songs, reading these words—let alone listening to them at performance tempo—is hard work. Good writing in the elevated sphere—from Milton to Virgil to Pindar—often is hard: difficulty is often a corollary of the defamiliar and a symptom of the mature sensibility which brings intellect and feeling, as well as craftsmanship, to bear on literary tradition. Pindar's praise, at all events, as powerful as it is witty, and as intelligent as it is moving, conjoins two etymological word-plays. *Δᾶλον* (*Dâlon*), 'Delos', evokes *δῆλος* (*dêlos*), 'clear, visible'; *ἄστρον* (*astron*), 'star', evokes the old name for the island, *Ἀστερία* (*Asteria*); and the whole process of naming is seen to have a special metaphysical validation. Pindar's own appellations enact the implication: the island is a growing organism ('seedling': *ἔρνος*), yet also a construction ('-builded': *-δμάτα*), and an animate being ('daughter': *θύγατερ*), hence truly a 'miraculous' entity defying human categorization ('miracle': *τέρας*), *therefore* aptly associated with the closing paradox, 'earth's star'. And these verbal transformations are all of a piece with Delos' strange history: once a floating island, it was fixed—by a miracle—for Leto to give birth to Apollo and Artemis.[33]

Pindar's cluster of significations is verbalized in the high style, but the difference between his verbalization and Aristophanes' is as obvious as Delos. Yes, the passage contains conventional poeticisms, like *ἔρνος*, 'seedling' (= 'offspring'); but the word here *also* participates in the important sequence just discussed *and*, for good measure, serves to evoke a relevant myth of the palm-tree on Delos which Leto is said to have grasped amid the pains of labour.[34] Yes, the passage contains conventional epithets, but they are not mere tokens, like those of Aristophanes. Leto is 'bright-haired' but the 'bright' (*λιπαρο-*) belongs to, in fact initiates, a significant theme that culminates in the metaphorical 'star' of the last verse (*λιπαρο-, Δᾶλον, -φαντον, ἄστρον*). Earth is 'broad' (*εὐρείας*), which indicates that the miracle is acknowledged everywhere. Earth (again) is 'dark' (*κυανέας*), but this word, though a possible epithet of earth, is generally an epithet of the sea.[35] Yes, 'earth' is repeated (*χθονός, χθονός*), but as part of the powerful elemental sequence (in two phases, the second in effect summarizing the first), sea—earth—Olympus—earth—star, which relates earth to heaven in an inimitably Pindaric way and,

[33] On the frag. see, in general, H. W. Smyth, *Greek Melic Poets* (London 1900) 364–6.

[34] Cf. Allen-Halliday-Sikes on *h.Ap.* 117.

[35] Of the sea: Sim. 62.4 *PMG*, Soph. *Ant.* 966, Eur. *IT* 7, Xenarch. Com. 1. 7 *PCG*, Arist. *Prob.* 932ᵃ31; cf. *κυανοχαίτης*, epic title of Poseidon (*Il.* 20. 144, *Od.* 9. 536, Hes. *Th.* 278); *κυαναυθής* Bacch. 12. 124; *κυανοειδής* Eur. *Hel.* 179 (see Kannicht ad loc.), Arist. *GA* 779ᵇ33. Of land: *Od.* 12. 242–3 *γαῖα φάνεσκε* | *ψάμμῳ κυανέῃ* is an isolated instance.

in particular, defines and amplifies the grand arena in which the significance of Delos is manifest. Yes, the gods are—as usual—'on Olympus', but *this* is because it is only from Olympus that the closing description makes sense: 'the shining rock of Delos in the dark-blue sea is like a star in the sky'[36]—in which context, of course, the habitual marine associations of the 'dark' word (*κυάνεος*) come into their own.

One could say more, but the point is surely now made. Pindar's words have a creative rightness and not merely a ceremonial plausibility, though indeed they have that too. The verbal energy and the richness of his writing have no counterpart in the *Clouds parodos*.[37] More generally, our specimens of Euripides and Pindar, different though they are, present this common contrast to Aristophanes' attempt at the high style: that the quality of their writing, though inconceivable without its elevation, is not coextensive with the elevation, but on what is done with or through it. For Aristophanes, it is as if the medium is an end in itself; and this is likewise the moral of his essays in the high style elsewhere. From the strictly devotional hymn to Pallas at *Thesmophoriazusae* 1136 ff.—

> *Παλλάδα τὴν φιλόχορον ἐμοὶ*
> *δεῦρο καλεῖν νόμος εἰς χορόν,*
> *παρθένον ἄζυγα κούρην . . .*
>
> Pallas, lover of the dance,
> Custom bids me call her hither,
> Pure, maid, unwed, to our dance . . .—[38]

to the decidedly exotic song of the hoopoe to the nightingale at *Birds* 209 ff.—

[36] G. M. Kirkwood, *Selections from Pindar* (Chico, Cal. 1982) 305. Compare the image with A's purely ornamental *ὄμμα αἰθέρος* at *Nub.* 285. The only point in saying 'eye of heaven' here, rather than 'sun', is to squeeze in an extra drop of *color poeticus*.

[37] I am glad to find that my assessment of the writing of the *parodos* has been broadly accepted: see esp. Zimmermann, *Untersuchungen*, i. 68–9; Prato, 'Metri', 235–6; Parker, *Songs*, 14–15; and even Mathews (who, in the end, is obliged to sign up to 'simple but grand', 'not . . . intellectual depth or complexity'), 'Reconsidered', 29.

[38] Note the inert -*χορον*/*χορόν* and the pleonasm of *παρθένον and ἄζυγα and κούρην*. Not without reason have A's devotional lyrics been called 'perfunctory' (by Richards, *Aristophanes*, 120). In such songs A is, to some extent, simply following norms of cletic hymnography (Mathews, 'Reconsidered', 5, 29–42), but choosing the least productive norms to follow. Contrast his marvellous inventiveness in the cletic hybrid, *Pax* 774 ff. (above, pp. 111–16).

ἄγε, σύννομέ μοι, παῦσαι μὲν ὕπνου,
λῦσον δὲ νόμους ἱερῶν ὕμνων . . .

Come, consort mine, forsake thy slumber,
Let thy holy hymn-tunes loose . . .—[39]

Aristophanes presents us with the intriguing spectacle of a versatile genius who persists in an experiment to which even his own versatility is unsuited, precisely because in it the terms of his own versatility are denied.[40]

There is a qualification to be added to this picture, which is also a confirmation of it. Various of these lyrical pieces contain welcome, if isolated, moments of vigour and life, and what is characteristic of these moments is that they do not, as in Pindar, involve a working of, and through, the elevation, nor, as in the Euripides, an ironic response to it—which response (despite the irony) does not depart from its own terms. They involve, on the contrary, an effective abandonment of elevation as such. There is actually one such moment near the end of the *parodos* in *Clouds* (311–12), at the point where the chorus's sketch of holy Athens takes in the dramatic festival itself:

ἦρί τ' ἐπερχομένῳ Βρομία χάρις
εὐκελάδων τε χορῶν ἐρεθίσματα . . .

And, come the Spring, Dionysiac
Joy, *incitement* of choirs melodious . . .

One word only, but in this (frankly) anaemic sequence a moment of rich, red blood. The phrase 'incitement of choirs' (*khorôn*

[39] *Av.* 209–22: see Silk, 'Lyric poet', 100–3. There is a nice pun in 209 σύννομε (cf. Dunbar ad loc.). Mathews's attempted defence of the song ('Reconsidered', 6–15) has some interesting points of detail (e.g. on the 'rustic paradise', ibid. 8, and the thematic point of νόμους in 210, ibid. 15), but the inconsequentiality of his discussion on the critical level is summed up, ibid. 14, by a grossly inappropriate appeal to Aesch. *Agam.* 1136–45 as a supposed specimen of comparable cliché and repetitiousness to the *Av.* song. It is no answer to a critique of writer *X* for feature *y* to say, 'but I can find a place where approved author *Z* does *y* too', unless one can show that *y* has a positive force in that place—and that it *is* the same *y* (and not merely something superficially similar). In fact, the repetitions in this *Agam.* passage are hardly on A's high-lyric scale and are in any case correlative to the high emotion of the moment, to which there is no counterpart in the *Av.* song. It is also (e.g.) grotesque to identify Aesch.'s ξουθά (*Agam.* 1142) as a cliché (as Mathews does), when the most our evidence allows us to say is that the likes of Aesch. helped to make it such (for full citations and discussion of the word, see Silk, 'Iconyms', 317–19).

[40] See Silk, 'Lyric poet', 99–117, for analysis of various other high-lyric passages in plays from *Nub.* to *Ran.*

erethismata) conforms well enough to an established high-style cast of expression, familiar in tragedy and elsewhere, in and out of lyrics.[41] The noun *erethisma* itself, however, is rather different. Perhaps coined for the occasion, the word calls up a wide range of possible contexts of domestic provocation, or provoking a wild animal, or indeed heroic-mythological challenge, or the arousal of political ambition.[42] The point, though, is not that any one of these diverse contexts is called to mind specifically. It is simply that, without warning, Aristophanes confronts us with abrasive connotations from the world of daily, as well as literary, experience. To use *erethisma* of rivalry in the sphere of dramatic competition produces a rare defamiliarizing touch; and it is intriguing, to say the least, that it should be in evocation of Aristophanes' own festival, the City Dionysia, for which *Clouds* itself was originally composed, that soft conventionalities momentarily give way to something with an edge.[43]

Aristophanes' low lyrics (we have seen) may have their elevated moments—

> Me and my mates can smell the stew!
> What with that and all the *beau-*
> *teous* talk of food, you're killing us—[44]

and his high lyrics (we now see) may be invigorated by sudden touches of life from the other end of the tonal spectrum. In these momentary reversals we have the formula for his true creativity as a lyric poet. Modest virtues may be claimed for his low lyrics, for his elevated devotional conventionalities, for his *exotica*. His real achievement lies in the creation of hybrids, and, specifically, in a creative combination of low with high which in the momentary instances just cited is effected almost in passing, but which in his most impressive lyrics is fully determinative. The result is a new kind of compound (and not any mere *mixture*) which has the

[41] Cf. e.g. Eur. *IA* 576 *Φρυγίων αὐλῶν . . . μιμήματα*, Soph. *Aj.* 54 *ἄδαστα βουκόλων φρουρήματα* (and see A. A. Long, *Language and Thought in Sophocles* (London 1968) 95–104).

[42] Cf. e.g. Men. fr. 587 Koerte *χεῖρον . . . ἐρεθίσαι γραῦν ἢ κύνα*, Xen. *Cyn.* 10. 17 *ὅταν ἐρεθίζηται [ὁ ὗς ὁ ἄγριος]*, *Il.* 4. 5 (Zeus seeks *ἐρεθιζέμεν* Hera into action), Aeschin. 2. 177 *τὰς ψυχὰς τὰς φιλοτίμους καὶ λίαν ὀξείας ἐρεθίζοντες*.

[43] For other comparable departures from the high, see *Ran.* 344–50, *Lys.* 1251–9, and *Eq.* 551–64, with discussion at Silk, 'Lyric poet', 113–14, 115–16, 144; cf. below, p. 195, on *Ran.* 218.

[44] Above, p. 166.

vigour and the other positive attributes of the low, together with the formal elegance of the high, but also, and above all, offers an enlarged tonal and expressive range all round, within which the fullest exploitation of the poet's stylistic strengths is possible. The compounding, in fact, ensures that his central instinct for mobility is guaranteed adequate expression.

In our discussion of *Peace* 774 ff. we have already encountered a fully hybrid lyric, which covers the range from the high ('Lady, I pray thee, cast out war . . .') to the low ('. . . goat-turd'), along with the 'ordinary' and the topical, among much else: 'Mind you, if Carcinus turns up . . .'[45] With its rich variety of stylistic techniques and its abundant discontinuities, that remarkable song shows how readily the hybrid idiom lends itself to Aristophanes' most characteristic usages. At the same time, a different reservation is called for. The *Peace* lyric is exuberant and brilliant, but when we recall its amiable contents—the cheers for peace and the boos for rival playwrights—we must surely agree that its undoubted exuberance and brilliance are considerably in excess of its ultimate significance. It is as if, in celebration of peace and Aristophanic poetry, the sheer relish of yes-saying and no-saying becomes a satisfying end in itself. In this sense, the *Peace* lyric, *tour de force* though it is, compares relatively unfavourably with another exemplary piece that we have already glanced at: Dicaeopolis' phallic song in *Acharnians* (263–79).[46] It is time to look at this piece in its entirety. Ode to Phales, god of the phallus:

Φαλῆς, ἑταῖρε Βακχίου,
ξύγκωμε, νυκτοπεριπλάνη-
  τε, μοιχέ, παιδεραστά, 265
ἕκτῳ σ' ἔτει προσεῖπον εἰς
τὸν δῆμον ἐλθὼν ἄσμενος,
σπονδὰς ποιησάμενος ἐμαυ-
  τῷ, πραγμάτων τε καὶ μαχῶν
καὶ Λαμάχων ἀπαλλαγείς. 270
πολλῷ γάρ ἐσθ' ἥδιον, ὦ Φαλῆς Φαλῆς,
κλέπτουσαν εὑρόνθ' ὡρικὴν ὑληφόρον,
τὴν Στρυμοδώρου Θρᾶτταν ἐκ τοῦ φελλέως,
μέσην λαβόντ', ἄραντα, κατα-
  βαλόντα καταγιγαρτίσαι. 275

[45] Above, pp. 111 ff. [46] Above, pp. 122–3.

Φαλῆς Φαλῆς,
ἐὰν μεθ' ἡμῶν ξυμπίῃς, ἐκ κραιπάλης
ἕωθεν εἰρήνης ῥοφήσεις τρύβλιον·
ἡ δ ἀσπὶς ἐν τῷ φεψάλῳ κρεμήσεται.

Lord Prick, thou friend and revel-mate of Bacchus,
Hail to thee, night-wandering, boy-loving
Fornicator! Six years on, we're home.
Peace I've made, and I am free
Of fights, and fuss, and Lamachus.
Yes, how much sweeter, my Lord Prick, to catch
Strymodorus' Thratta, ready and ripe,
Sneaking wood from the fell, tackle her,
Toss her and tumble her down, and press her grape.
Lord Prick, Prick,
Drink with me now, and come the morning,
You have a cup of peace to stop your headache;
We'll hang our shield up in the fire's embers.

The song, delivered by the Athenian Everyman on the trail of peace, is tied to the plot ('I've made . . .'), and, patently, is none the worse for that. After the opening address, we start high with a formal invocation marked by asyndeton between florid compound epithets. We stand, it seems, with one foot on the high ground of poesy, where graceful periphrases spring up on all sides. In English terms one thinks of Keats:

Thou still unravish'd bride of quietness . . .

. . . thou, light-winged Dryad of the trees . . .

Close bosom-friend of the maturing sun . . .[47]

But only *one* foot on that ground, because the ardent homogeneity of a Keats ode is absent and, equally, the kind of humourless restraint, bordering on insipidity, which we have met in Aristophanes' undiluted high lyrics in *Clouds*. Such homogeneity, indeed, is precluded by Dicaeopolis' first syllables. *Φαλῆς* ('Lord Prick') points to the world of religious practice, but hardly in any literary association with traditional myth and (therefore) high poetry; this is (apparently) an imaginary god, here put in charge of a popular kind of ritual, and the name, accordingly, will have an

[47] From the opening stanzas of 'Ode on a Grecian Urn', 'Ode to a Nightingale', and 'To Autumn'.

earthy quality, albeit with no very specifiable cultic associations.[48] Given this equivocal launch, an interest quite alien to the whimsy of the *Clouds* lyrics attaches to the high epithets and their elevated message that follows—the relationship between our deity and Dionysus, god of 'the liquid fire in the grape, the sap thrusting in the young tree, the blood pounding in the veins of a young animal'.[49]

At this point we might do well to reconsider our translation and its Keatsian resonances. With its allusive virtuosity and (yet) its basic directness, Aristophanes' writing here conveys not only the familiar sense of inclusive exuberance but also an incisive street-wise punch. These are the lyrics of a song, and in modern terms they call to mind, alongside a non-musical Keats ode, a quite different range in the experiential spectrum. In Aristophanes' lyric we have something of the grown-up wit and demotic attack of the Tin Pan Alley/Broadway popular song in its classsic modern phase.

Aristophanes' song offers a sharp engagement with a whole culture from the bottom up, an almost tangible zest, a sophisticated relish for being alive at a particular time. One recalls this, then, from Lorenz Hart's 'Manhattan'—

> We'll go to Greenwich,
> Where modern men itch
> To be free—

or, at the British end of Broadway, this, from Noel Coward's improvement on Cole Porter:

> In Texas some of the men do it:
> Others drill a hole and then do it.
> Let's do it, let's fall in love.[50]

[48] On *Φ*. see Sommerstein ad loc. W. Horn, *Gebet und Gebetsparodie in den Komödien des Aristophanes* (Nuremberg 1970) 57–9 classifies the song (with *Ran.* 420–34) as 'serious pastiche' of a popular form. That τὸ φαλλικόν was a popular form is not in doubt (Arist. *Poet.* IV: see Pickard-Cambridge, *Dithyramb*, 133–51, 164–74), and some features of A's song may be conventional (e.g. the ὦ Φαλῆς Φαλῆς refrain?), but its predominant peace/war theme obviously is not, and it is gratuitous (though flattering to the popular form in question) to suppose that much else is: 'pastiche' means something other than 'based on' or 'developed from'. Compare and contrast A's song also with the phallic frags. at *Carm. Pop.* 5 (*a*) and (*b*) *PMG*; of these (*a*) is an uneventful little ditty in plain Greek, (*b*) is actually a frag. in Doric-coloured high-style iambics (τάνδε Μοῦσαν without def. art., χέω of the voice (LSJ s.v. III. 1) etc.).

[49] Dodds, *Bacchae*, p. xii.

[50] 'Manhattan': Hart (lyrics) and Richard Rodgers (1925). 'Let's Do It': Cole

In the perspective of such models a more appropriate paraphrase for the phallic song (with imaginary music to match) might go:

> No, Mister Prick,
> More war, no more!
> No fight, no fuss,
> No Lamachus.
>
> Oh, Mister Prick,
> Oh, Mister Prick,
> It's much more fun to
> Floor the girl next door
> And give her one to
> Stick . . .[51]

Alien as Aristophanes' direct obscenity is to Broadway, there is an affinity here—however effectively our poet retains, as he does, creative access to the elevated world in a way that Hart (or Coward) never could.[52] It is integrity of access—to the elevated world as well as to the true demotic—that also decisively differentiates Aristophanes from middle-range light verse in the W. S. Gilbert tradition:

> When a merry maiden marries,
> Sorrow goes and pleasure tarries.[53]

Gilbert (who had his own Aristophanic longings)[54] duly inspired B. B. Rogers, whose still familiar renderings of Aristophanes

Porter (1928), as reworked by Coward (1944) and performed at a celebrated Las Vegas concert (1955). In such instances the relish is closely associated with an exhilarating sense of word-play close to the living tongue. Cf. e.g., from the earlier world of the British Music Hall, 'I'm all airs and graces, | Correct easy paces, | So long without food I've forgot where my face is': 'Burlington Bertie from Bow' (sung by—the American-born—Ella Shields).

[51] In the opening lines there is an allusion to a line in the (cultic-equivalent, *faute de mieux*) negro spiritual 'Down by the Riverside' (credited to Paul Barnes, 1900): 'Ain't gonna study war no more . . . '

[52] Note e.g. the mawkishness of Coward's 'London Pride' (1941). P. Furia, *The Poets of Tin Pan Alley*[2] (New York 1992), is a mine of information on the demotic triumphs (and higher-style embarrassments) of the American song-writers (see e.g. the chapter on Oscar Hammerstein, 181–94).

[53] *The Gondoliers*, Act I.

[54] Since Walter Sichel's identification of Gilbert as 'the English Aristophanes' in 1911 (*W. S. Gilbert: A Century of Scholarship and Commentary*, ed. J. B. Jones (New York 1970) 69), it has become a commonplace topic in discussions of W. S. G. See A. Fischler, *Modified Rapture: Comedy in W. S. Gilbert's Savoy Operas* (Charlottesville 1991). In the operas there are intermittent allusions to A, including the notable 'I know the croaking chorus from the *Frogs* of Aristophanes' (*The Pirates of Penzance*, Act 1).

many continue to find sufficiently authentic. Here is Rogers's version of the phallic song:

> O Phales, comrade revel-roaming
> Of Bacchus, wanderer of the gloaming,
> Of wives and boys the naughty lover,
> Here in my home I gladly greet ye,
> Six weary years of absence over;
> For I have made a private treaty
> And said good-bye to toils and fusses,
> And fights, and fighting Lamachuses.
>
> Far happier 'tis to me and sweeter,
> O Phales, Phales, some soft glade in,
> To woo the saucy, arch, deceiving
> Young Thratta . . .

This rollicking balladry is a long way from Aristophanes, and not only because of the pre-modern sanitizing. John Keats and Larry Hart: if a modern portmanteau of two such different voices seems inconceivable, that is a measure *both* of Aristophanes' distance from our modern, fragmented world—Gilbertian or other—*and* of the extraordinary quality of his hybrids.

Within the phallic song it is instructive to see how swiftly one stylistic pitch makes way for another. From the florid (*νυκτοπεριπλάνητε*: 'night-wandering') we are propelled with disarming abruptness to the common (*μοιχέ, παιδεραστά*: 'boy-loving | Fornicator'),[55] and thence, via an oddly poignant allusion to a common tragic motif ('Home at last!'),[56] to the specifics, Lamachus and all: specifics, though, that issue in a universal acclamation of life. Throughout, the lyric moves at a remarkable pace and yet allows the symbols of peace, in particular, to be given a firm delineation. The part from 'Thratta' to the 'fire's embers' is a masterpiece of concrete expression; and formally and rhythmically the lyric as a whole is a joy, with the iambics conforming perfectly to the exuberant mood[57] and the rapidity of the thought (there is no pleonasm here), and the ode powerfully organized. It is

[55] Dicaeopolis' own specified sexual target is the servant girl Thratta, and in *Ach.* as a whole he is no more interested in boys than most other Aristophanic characters ever are (see K. J. Dover, *Greek Homosexuality* (London 1978) 135–53), but like any Greek god (from Zeus downwards) Lord Prick is impartial.

[56] Below, pp. 196, 396.

[57] The tribrachic resolutions in 264, 274–5, are esp. felicitous. On the metrical form of the song see Parker, *Songs*, 126–8.

structured to a triumphant climax on 269–70 (πραγμάτων . . . : 'fights . . .'), with its 'low' word-play and parallelism, and a second climax (in both senses) on 274–6, where an intensifying assonantal series (*λαβόντ', ἄραντα, καταβαλόντα*: 'tackle . . . toss . . . tumble') is released on, and so intensifies, the unexpected item (*καταγιγαρτίσαι*: 'press her grape') that follows.[58] That metaphor (aptly in the context of Dionysus and the drinking-bowl) comes from grapes, and the grapes grow, as if naturally, out of 'ready and ripe' (*ὡρικήν*).[59]

How far this sophisticated organization is due to the co-presence of the elevated is clearly a question that we need to answer. No such sophistication was apparent in the *Clouds* lyric—a vastly more elevated affair—but then again, as the phallic song proceeds, touches of elevation do continue to be felt and, in at least one instance, clearly provide phraseological opportunities from which capital is duly made.[60] Yet, one might rather feel, it is the enlargement of reference and, above all, the sense of universal experience that is the chief contribution of the elevated—a universalizing made possible in the first place by the way Aristophanes links the popular Phales to the great god Dionysus himself. At all events, a kind of phraseological neutrality, with the idiom neither obviously elevated nor obviously low, has asserted itself by the end of the piece,[61] where, however, the

[58] On which word see Starkie ad loc. and Taillardat, *Images*, 100, as against Henderson, *Maculate Muse*, 166.

[59] *ὡρικός*, of fruit ripe in season, *ὡρικὰ . . . ὥσπερ μῆλα* Crates Com. 43 *PCG*; of people in their young prime, *ὡρικὸν . . . μειράκιον* Ar. fr. 245 *PCG* (likewise the much commoner *ὡραῖος*, LSJ s.v. I. 1 and III. 2). *ὡρικήν*, thus, is interactive, and, specifically, pivotal to *καταγιγ.* (Silk, *Interaction*, 87–97), and as such a rare exception to A's usual interactive habits (above, p. 140). *ἥδιον* (271) adds additional, if faint, preparation for the sequence (of tastes, *τῶν ἡδίστων σίτων . . . καὶ . . . τῶν ἡδίστων ποτῶν* Xen. *Cyr.* 7. 5. 81; of states, *οὔ μοι ἥδιόν ἐστι λέγειν* Hdt. 2. 46. 2; for both senses, see LSJ s.v. I).

[60] 272 is notably compressed, and the strikingly uncolloquial juxtaposition of significant participles (*κλέπτουσαν εὑρόνθ'*) and the absence of an insignificant one (*οὖσαν*, with *ὡρικήν*) help to create a miniature vignette from *κλέπτουσαν* to *ἐκ τοῦ φελλέως*, with the latter phrase effectively *apo koinou* with both *Θρᾷτταν* (cf. Starkie ad loc.) and *κλέπτ.* itself. (For the meaning of *φελλεύς*, see Dover on *Nub.* 71, Bowie, *Aristophanes*, 105, and R. G. Osborne, *Demos: The Discovery of Classical Attica* (Cambridge 1985) 20.)

[61] Note, however, the 'low' metric in the trimeters at the end: 278 violates Porson's canon and has no main caesura. (These are, presumably, *sung* trimeters, like those at 271–3—so Parker, *Songs*, 126, cf. Dale, *Lyric Metres*, 76–7, 198—but the point, presumably, is unaffected.)

hanging up of 'our shield' represents a significant affirmation of the universal.

There will be those for whom the moral ethos of the song, although or because typically Aristophanic, leaves something to be desired; and it might be said that, quite apart from its sexual amorality, the sensual relish of the song is unashamedly male-chauvinist and in some ways undisguisedly wish-fulfilling. The girl, of course, is conveniently caught *in flagrante delicto*, which gives the male a pretext, and conveniently a slave,[62] which allows him to get away with it. Against that, we may suggest that such heartfelt exuberance is a persuasive counsel for its own guilt-free standpoint; particularly so, when we note that the song is in no sense an individual's self-glorification: for Dicaeopolis' wife and daughter are both present and, indeed, given supporting roles in the celebratory ritual (244–62); and the celebration itself is a religious celebration, and *therefore* (and even though the religion is, in part, low religion) can claim a kind of public, collective significance. We may note also that, for all the general self-sufficiency of the Thratta vignette, its honesty and adult wit confer on it a surprising dignity, demonstrated at once by the way that the transition to the cool wisdom and comprehensive imagery of the three verses at the end seems entirely unforced. And, for future reference, we should note that such mature suppleness and sophistication is unmistakably correlative to mobility of style. Mature, indeed. Overall, with its effortless and enviable unity of art and entertainment, sacred and profane, the song sums up the richness of the rich culture it has grown out of.

The same splendid energy is apparent in hybrid lyrics of quite different kinds. Consider the almost Brechtian combination of ironic elevation and crisp satire in the Cleon song, *Knights* 973–84:

ἥδιστον φάος ἡμέρας
ἔσται τοῖς τε παροῦσι καὶ
τοῖσιν εἰσαφικνουμένοις, 975
  ἢν Κλέων ἀπόληται.
καίτοι πρεσβυτέρων τινῶν
οἵων ἀργαλεωτάτων
ἐν τῷ δείγματι τῶν δικῶν
  ἤκουσ' ἀντιλεγόντων, 980

[62] Indicated by the name *Θρᾷττα*: see Headlam–Knox on Herodas I. I.

ὡς εἰ μὴ γένεθ' οὗτος ἐν
τῇ πόλει μέγας, οὐκ ἂν ἤ-
στην σκεύει δύο χρησίμω,
δοῖδυξ οὐδὲ τορύνη.

Sun will shine as never when
On immigrant and citizen
The day Cleon drops dead.
But down the lawcourts, where they ped-
dle justice, some old lags can sniff
Real problems, if
Mixer and mash the city's got
While he's in charge—but s'pose he's not,
Who'll stir things up then?

A paradigm of topicality given permanent form and expression. We begin with a 'timeless' phrase in the high style (and reminiscent of Euripides)[63] and move swiftly to more down-to-earth Greek and the specifics of Cleon and contemporary Athens. The stanza form (quatrains in Greek, triadic in the English) is finely calculated to create a presumption of a climax or resolution at each shorter, sharper end.[64] The first end ('The day . . .', ἦν . . .) satisfies expectations with an almost brutal directness;[65] the second ('Real . . .', ἤκουσ' . . .) a resolution neither in form nor sense, acts as a foil to the final climax ('Who'll . . .', δοῖδυξ . . .), which rounds off the last witty conceit[66] and the whole stanza with a vigorous ironic image to match the earlier dismissive metaphor of the law-bazaar where 'they peddle justice' (δείγματι τῶν δικῶν).[67] As far as positive determinants are concerned, elevation is slight. Besides the opening phrase, the level of diction and idiom is ordinary enough.[68] But as with parts of Dicaeopolis' phallic song, the idiom, though ordinary, avoids the extremes of coarseness or extravagance. In these cases at least, then, it is almost as if

[63] See Rau, *Paratragodia*, 188.

[64] In the Greek: three aeolic quatrains, each consisting of three glyconics with a pherecratean clausula.

[65] Esp. as this is the first—and only—time that Cleon is mentioned by name in the whole play. (The *character* Cleon is referred to as Paphlagon throughout.)

[66] 'Even his old partisans of the Philocleon type defend him only as a necessary evil': Neil on 977 (where καίτοι is bland irony).

[67] 'Law-bazaar' is Sommerstein's phrase: on δεῖγμα cf. Neil ad loc. δείγματι τῶν δικῶν exemplifies the kind of alliterative link discussed above, pp. 130–1.

[68] The tone of ἀργαλέος (978) is elusive: cf. Dover on *Nub.* 450.

Aristophanes were exploring a new range of flexible yet neutral expression—neither truly high nor truly low.[69]

Almost as if . . . In one crucial respect, any talk of 'neutral' expression is seriously misleading. As was implicit in the phallic song and as this *Knights* song makes apparent, the hybrid lyrics are anything but a partnership of high and low on equal terms. We must again insist that the substrate and the premise of Aristophanes' lyric poetry is low: a low base to which elements of high idiom have been fused—or (as I put it in my 1980 discussion) 'low lyrics *plus*'.[70] The essential inequality of the relationship is symptomatized by an interesting feature of the two passages just discussed, which is in fact a characteristic feature of the hybrid lyrics in general. The lyrics start high, then dip low, and usually end low. The *Knights* passage began 'Sun will shine' (ἥδιστον φάος ἡμέρας), then dipped to plain 'topical' Greek, and ended quite aggressively the same way, with diction, and to a lesser extent idiom, alien to high poetry.[71] Likewise Dicaeopolis' monody, with ornate opening and sudden drop to the verbal realm of boy-lovers and fornicators, at which level it stays, more or less, until the end. And likewise most other comparable lyrics besides.[72] In some of the nominally high lyrics there is, as we have seen in the *Clouds parodos*, a momentary—nothing more than a momentary—

[69] Though this cannot be said of the matching stanza 985–96, similar in its closing climax on the punning Δωροδοκιστί, dissimilar both in lacking the elevation and in the positive extravagance of the coined compounds ὑομουσίας (986) and Δωροδοκιστί (996) itself.

[70] 'Lyric poet', 133.

[71] Idiom: οἷος + sup. (978) is strikingly ordinary/prosaic (LSJ s.v. II. 7), while the transformational metaphors in 983–4 are probably popular in character (above, p. 123 n. 58).

[72] See the list in Silk, 'Lyric poet', 142–3. (My citation of *Ach.* 971–99 is queried by Parker, *Songs*, 16; the argument, at 'Lyric poet', 140–1, assumes the stylized εἶδες ὦ εἶδες ὦ at 971, without which, indeed, the opening is hardly high: note e.g. πόλι in 971, and cf. Neil on *Eq.* 273.) With the analogy between A's lyrics and those of Broadway/Tin Pan Alley in mind, it is intriguing to note examples in the latter of initial elevation followed by demotic dip. Cf. e.g. Ira Gershwin, in the title song from the show *Lady, Be Good!* (1924): 'Oh, sweet and lovely | Lady, be good'. Here the first line hints high, but 'Lady' is essentially vernacular, and there is sheer Aristophanic exhilaration (cf. Parker, *Songs*, 11, on *Ach.* 1037 ff.) about the unexpected way the words make the rhythmic shape, with the 'ragging' effect of a pause before 'Lady', but not—despite the punctuation—after it. Ezra Pound misquoted these lines revealingly in *Canto* 74: 'so Mr Bullington lay on his back like an ape | singing: O sweet and lovely | o Lady be good.' That extra elevating 'o' renders the effect banal. Like B. B. Rogers, even the subversive modern poet has high-style instincts. Ira's and A's are different.

appearance of the low. In the composite mode, the low is predominant, predictable, and therefore, for a time, dispensable with; whereas the high (the new *plus*), having no such status, requires a formal introduction at the outset if it is to be allowed to take part in the proceedings at all; its survival thereafter remains in doubt, whereas the reassertion of the low is inevitable. There is also a certain mischievous comic logic behind the pattern, a conjuring trick with truth and illusion, *doxa* and *epistêmê*: you purport to stake a claim to high-lyrical status, only to subvert your own pretension at the next stroke. This is, obviously, a psychological, rather than a historical, explanation. In historical terms, one would ask: low lyric *plus*? how did the 'plus' get there in the first place?—and answer, presumably: under the influence of tragedy, that *other* dramatic form that influenced comedy in so many of its aspects, thanks to its huge pre-eminence within the Athenian culture that Old Comedy fed on and, in its turn, enriched. It is tragedy, above all, that supplies the comic poet's need for elevation in his lyrics: tragedy that provides most of the specific models for elevated parody and elevated pastiche, and all of the—often less specific—prototypes for what we know as *para*tragedy;[73] and it is tragedy that helps to engender the new, irregular compounds as well.[74]

In my earlier treatment of Aristophanes' lyrics I made the case, as here, for the special significance and distinction of the hybrids, but within the hybrids as a whole I argued for a fundamental opposition between the 'realism' of such instances as those we have been considering in *Knights* and *Acharnians* and the 'fantasy' represented by, for instance, the Hoopoe's song in *Birds* and the opening of the frog song in *Frogs* (209–20):[75]

> *βρεκεκεκὲξ κοὰξ κοάξ,*
> *βρεκεκεκὲξ κοὰξ κοάξ.* 210
> *λιμναῖα κρηνῶν τέκνα,*
> *ξύναυλον ὕμνων βοὰν*
> *φθεγξώμεθ', εὔγηρυν ἐμὰν*

[73] On parody/paratragedy, see above, p. 39 n. 30, and below, p. 351 n. 2.

[74] It is apparent that, by comparison with tragedy, other serious poetry has only a minor influence on A's lyrics. See Silk, 'Lyric poetry', 134 n. 111, and note the parallels to A's cletic hymns suggested by Mathews, 'Reconsidered', 29–42; for a critical list of all conceivable parallels/sources/influences from non-tragic lyric, see Kugelmeier, *Reflexe*.

[75] 'Lyric poet', 136–7, 141.

ἀοιδάν, κοὰξ κοάξ,
ἣν ἀμφὶ Νυσήϊον 215
Διὸς Διώνυσον ἐν
λίμναισιν ἰαχήσαμεν,
ἡνίχ' ὁ κραιπαλόκωμος
τοῖς ἱεροῖσι Χύτροισι
χωρεῖ κατ' ἐμὸν τέμενος λαῶν ὄχλος.
βρεκεκεκὲξ κοὰξ κοάξ. 220

Brekekekék koák koák,
Brekekekék koák koák.[76]
Marsh sons of the streams, let us sing
In concerted hymnal clamour
Our song melodious, koák koák,
As we sang it in the marshes
Once in honour of our Lord,
Zeus' son from Nysa, Dionysus,
And a good crowd, hung over
At the Feast of Pots,
Passed through our precinct.
Brekekekék koák koák.

I would now wish to modify my earlier position on several counts. First, because neither 'realism' nor 'fantasy' are—in this connection—entirely appropriate labels;[77] also because the polarity tends to misrepresent the shifts and diversities within and between the lyrics in question; then again because in the *Frogs* passage, for one, the 'fantasy' is actually a less significant thing than even that label (limiting though it is) allows the passage to seem.

Already, even within the hybrids, we have seen not only considerable diversity, but considerable disparity in terms of achievement: witness the life-enhancing exuberance of Dicaeopolis' phallic song, the virtuoso Carcinus/Muse lyric in *Peace*, and the topical satire of *Knights*. The *Frogs* lyric is certainly different again from any of these, but then (despite some obvious similarities) it is surprisingly different from—and less rewarding than—the Hoopoe's song as well (*Birds* 227 ff.):[78]

ἐποποποποῖ, ποποποποποῖ ποποῖ,
ἰὼ ἰὼ ἰτὼ ἰτὼ ἰτὼ ἰτὼ

[76] The -ξ endings mean /-k/: see Dover on *Nub.* 390 and id., *Frogs*, 219.

[77] On realism, see below, pp. 212 ff.

[78] In 'Lyric poet', 141, I made too much of the superficial likeness between the two, overvalued the *Ran.*, and undervalued the *Av.*

ἴτω τις ὧδε τῶν ἐμῶν ὁμοπτέρων·
ὅσοι τ' εὐσπόρους ἀγροίκων γύας 230
νέμεσθε, φῦλα μυρία κριθοτράγων
σπερμολόγων τε γένη
ταχὺ πετόμενα, μαλθακὴν ἱέντα γῆρυν·
ὅσα τ' ἐν ἄλοκι θαμὰ
βῶλον ἀμφιτιττυβίζεθ' ὧδε λεπτὸν 235
ἡδομένᾳ φωνᾷ . . .[79]

Twit, twit, twit to it, twit from it!
Caw, caw, cawling all
Birds of a feather! Countless come,
Swift, soft-voiced, from countryman's acres,
Meal-farers, seed-pickers!
Come from the furrow, chirping at the clod
Thinly, with glad voice . . .

Yes, in this *Birds* passage, as in the *Frogs* lyric, we have an extraordinary moment in an extraordinary setting: Hoopoe summons the birds to Birdland, as the frogs around the infernal lake sing in response to the arrival of Dionysus. Yes, this lyric, like the one in *Frogs*, features a scatter of bizarre effects and phraseological *exotica*. Still, the *Birds* lyric's obvious exoticism (better word, indeed, than 'fantasy') offers a more substantial comic response to life than its counterpart in *Frogs*.

For a start, the *Birds* sequence impresses us with its wit: not simply the novelty of bird noises, but the way bird noise transforms itself into human sense (*ἰτώ* to *ἴτω*, 'twit' to 'to it', 228–9),[80] in imitation of the play's large transformational theme;[81] not simply the pleasant incongruity of 'unpoetic' material in 'poetic' language, but an exuberant interplay between them, whereby, for instance, the 'birds of a feather' (*ὁμοπτέρων*, 229), which are generally met with in a secondary sense,[82] are here, of course,

[79] Text as Dunbar.
[80] The same in reverse at 259–62: see Sommerstein and Dunbar ad locc.
[81] See below, pp. 286–9.
[82] LSJ s.v. *ὁμόπτερος* lists all extant classical occurrences of this high-style word, but the article is muddled. (*a*) Etymologically, the compound means 'equivalently/likewise winged', i.e., if used of birds, = 'fellow birds', as at Aesch. *Supp.* 224, where hawks are *ὁμόπτεροι* to doves (see Johansen–Whittle ad loc.). (*b*) Usually, however, the word is used in the secondary sense of 'equivalent', 'peer'; hence Hsch. *ὁμόπτεροι· ὅμοιοι* . . . Thus Strattis Com. 88 *PCG* (where *ὁμόπτεροι* = *ὁμήλικες*), Aesch. *Cho.* 174 and *Pers.* 559 (if sound), Eur. *El.* 530 and *Pho.* 328. By an attested compensation principle (see Silk, *Interaction*, 118, 130, 156), A's use appeals to the predictable normality of (*b*) and the contextually linked re-etymology

re-etymologized and 'literal'. Again, the lyric impresses us with its charm, but also its specificity, as in the 'chirping at the clod' and the surprising 'thinly' (*λεπτόν*), which is both well-observed and the more forceful because the word, though not low, steps suddenly out of an otherwise elaborate version of the high style.[83]

In the *Frogs* song, by comparison, whimsy predominates, centred on, though not confined to, the animal noises. Modern analogies, it may be, can help us place the contrast. The spirit of the *Frogs* onomatopoeia seems uncomfortably close to a *jeu d'esprit* of an Edward Lear at his most self-sufficiently childish—

> On a little piece of wood,
> Mr Spikky Sparrow stood;
>
> . . . . .
>
> Twikky wikky wikky wee
> Wikky bikky twikky tee,
> Spikky bikky bee—

where the *Birds* song is on a different plane, closer to (say) Eliot in one of his more equable moments,

> O quick quick quick, quick hear the song-sparrow,
> Swamp-sparrow, fox-sparrow, vesper-sparrow
> At dawn and dusk—

albeit sufficiently far removed from the abrasive calls of 'The Waste Land':

> Twit twit twit
> Jug jug jug jug jug jug
> So rudely forc'd.
> Tereu . . .[84]

The *Birds* lyric, in any event, points us in a different direction. If there is still something of the Edward Lear here, there is also—

available under (*a*); Pl. *Phdr.* 256e (the only known occurrence in prose) is comparable.

[83] *μαλθακὴν ἱέντα γῆρυν* (233) is a representative high-style phrase, with *simplex* verb, hyperbaton, and verse word (*γῆρυς*: LSJ s.v.); the cast of the phrase is like *πτερόεντα δ' ἵει . . . ὀιστόν* Pind. *Ol.* 9. 11–12, *ἔπος ἵησι δυσθρήνητον* Soph. *Ant.* 1210–11. *λεπτός* is not often attested of sound, but in the classical period evidently was standard usage: *φωνὴν λεπτὴν καὶ μικράν* (of a horse) Arist. *HA* $545^{a}7$, *μέλπει . . . λεπτὰν . . . ἁρμονίαν* (of a nightingale) Eur. *Phaeth.* 67–8 Diggle, likewise *λεπτόφωνος* at Arist. *HA* $538^{b}13$ (*πάντα τὰ θήλεα λεπτοφωνότερα*) and Sapph. 24 (*c*) 6 *PLF* (no context).

[84] Lear, 'Mr and Mrs Spikky Sparrow'; Eliot, 'Cape Ann' (from 'Landscapes') and 'The Waste Land', 203–6.

given the rural evocations—something of the grown-up ease of Shakespeare's song (*Love's Labour's Lost*, v. ii):

> When icicles hang by the wall,
> And Dick the shepherd blows his nail,
> And Tom bears logs into the hall,
> And milk comes frozen home in pail,
> When blood is nipp'd and ways be foul,
> Then nightly sings the staring owl:
>   To-who;
> Tu-whit, to-who, a merry note,
> While greasy Joan doth keel the pot.

But then again—Aristophanes being Aristophanes, and multifarious to the last—the detail of the *Birds* song strikes another, and quite different, note, thanks to the two invented compounds, 'meal-farers' (*κριθοτράγων*) and 'seed-pickers' (*σπερμολόγων*), the latter of which, in particular, has a technical ring to it.[85] One is reminded, suddenly, of something quite unforeseen—of neo-classical forays into the poeticization of the alien, like Bryant's depiction of the mosquito:

> Fair insect! that, with threadlike legs spread out
> And blood-extracting bill and filmy wing,
> Dost murmur, as thou slowly sails't about,
> In pitiless ears full many a plaintive thing.[86]

Like Bryant's piece, the *Birds* lyric has its whimsy and is, no doubt, too quaint to be wholly compelling; yet the frog-song, by comparison, does (on reflection) show more than a passing resemblance to the opening of the *Clouds parodos*:

> Clouds everlasting,
> Raise we to view our glittering, dew-laden form . . .

[85] See Dunbar on *σπ*. However, her suggestion that the coinage *κρ*. would sound 'poetic' is misleading. The heavy compound has a high ring to it, but *τρώγω* and its compounds and derivatives are overwhelmingly prose/comedy words (cf. the distribution in LSJ s.v.). Homer uses the verb once, *Od*. 6. 90; low lyric also, Hippon. 26. 5, 66, Sol. 38. 1 *IEG*, *Carm. Pop*. 1 *PMG*. *κριθοτράγος* and *κοτινοτράγος* (240) were perhaps formed on the analogy of *συκοτράγος*, not yet attested in the classical period, but either in fact of earlier use or extracted by back-formation from the low *συκοτραγίδης*, Arch. 250, Hippon. 167 *IEG*.

[86] William Cullen Bryant, 'To a Mosquito'.

Aristophanes' interest is no more focused on the blobs in the marsh here than it was on the froth in the sky there, and the point is worth making because, on comparing the *Clouds* and *Frogs* lyrics with the lyric in *Birds*, one identifies in the relative immediacy of the latter a refined concern with its overt subject to which those other songs offer no equivalent. The point (it is worth noting) is not dependent on considerations of humour or lack of humour—as if 'interest' and 'humour' were somehow antithetical. Indeed, of these three sequences, taken out of context, the *Clouds* lyric, which compels the least 'interest', is also the least amusing, whereas the *Frogs* lyric is no doubt the most. This, though, is because the *Frogs* lyric is essentially one extended joke—that frogs should be both personalized and lyricized. The resulting incongruity is enjoyable, but on the level of burlesque. It is symptomatic of a lack of real engagement that the frogs' portrait of themselves should spawn pleonasm, much as the Clouds' self-portrait did.[87] And once we have recovered from the pleasurable shock of amphibious onomatopoeia, we surely find the elevation all too uniform, and it seems a long wait until the first focused detail—which is also the first moment of truly low diction—in the shape of the hangover (*κραιπαλόκωμος*, 218).[88] And it is surely more than coincidence that the moment of focus and life should be associated with evocation of Dionysiac festivity, here as it was in *Clouds*.[89] Can we be surprised if some things matter to a writer, and he writes better when dealing with those that do?

Under analysis, then, the animal songs in *Frogs* and *Birds* indicate the range of Aristophanes' hybrids, not so much by defining one pole of an opposition, but by representing different points on a wide periphery—whose width three further instances will serve to confirm. *Peace* 582 ff.:

[87] Two marshes (*λιμναῖα* and *λίμναισιν*), as well as five words out of six in sequence (*ὕμνων*, *βοάν*, *φθεγξώμεθ'*, *εὔγηρυν*, *ἀοιδάν*—together with *ἰαχήσαμεν* a few words later) for the frog-song. Cf. not only the *Nub. parodos*, but also *Av.* 209–22, analysed at Silk, 'Lyric Poet', 100–3. Contrast the single duplication of *Av.* 227 ff., *εὐσπόρους* 230/*σπερμολόγων* 232, which is rather a no-nonsense use of the same name (*vel sim.*) for the same thing.

[88] The compound is in a sense tonally equivocal—high-sounding formally, but lexemically low (i.e *κῶμος* is neutral, but *κραιπαλάω*/*κραιπάλη* confined to comedy and prose: LSJ s.vv.), like *κριθοτράγων* in *Av.* (n. 85 above).

[89] See above, pp. 179–80.

χαῖρε, χαῖρ'· ὡς ἀσμένοισιν ἦλθες ἡμῖν, φιλτάτη·
σῷ γὰρ ἐδάμην πόθῳ
δαιμόνια βουλόμενος 585
εἰς ἀγρὸν ἀνερπύσαι.
ἦσθα γὰρ μέγιστον ἡμῖν κέρδος, ὦ ποθουμένη,
πᾶσιν ὁπόσοι γεωρ-
γὸν βίον ἐτρίβομεν· 590
καὶ μόνη γὰρ ὠφέλεις.
πολλὰ γὰρ ἐπάσχομεν
πρίν ποτ' ἐπὶ σοῦ γλυκέα
κἀδάπανα καὶ φίλα·
τοῖς ἀγροίκοισιν γὰρ ἦσθα χῖδρα καὶ σωτηρία . . .[90] 595

You're come, dear lady: missed you, we did, yes,
Direly, wanting to repossess
My land. Lady much-missed, you helped us live,
When you, and no one else, did give
Us farmers much—
Sweet, cost-free, welcome—once, in time of peace.
To country-folk you meant oats and salvation . . .

In elevated rapture—but in down-to-earth cretic-paeonic rhythms[91]—the farmers appproach their song like the romantic lead in a tragic reunion duet:

ὦ φίλτατον φῶς . . .
ὦ φθέγμ', ἀφίκου; . . .
ἔχω σε χερσίν; . . .

O dearest light . . .
O voice, you have come? . . .
I hold you in my arms? . . .

ὦ ποθεινὸς ἡμέρα . . .

O much-missed day . . .[92]

The passage in fact combines the specifics of the countryside (so often a stimulus to Aristophanes' inventive faculties) with this most familiar of tragic-romantic moments into a poignant whole within which the ordinary ('low') facts of rural life—crops, outlay, and all—are revalued upwards. The mechanics of this composite

[90] Text as Sommerstein, but with Dover's *καὶ μόνη γὰρ ὠφέλεις* in 590–1; cf. Parker, *Songs*, 268–73. For the lyric in full, see below, pp. 396–8. Formally the song responds to 346 ff. and 385 ff.

[91] Above, p. 164 n. 8.

[92] Soph. *El.* 1224–6; Eur. *Hel.* 623.

effect are intriguing. Besides the shifts from higher ('Dear lady . . .': φιλτάτη . . .) to lower ('cost-free . . .': κἀδάπανα . . .),[93] the lyric is constructed on a bold equation, whereby an emotive one-to-one relationship is summoned up to convey the relish of a whole community for a personified abstraction, peace. The plausibility of this manoeuvre is enhanced by an adroit use of variation in grammatical number on the part of the chorus, who oscillate between plural and conventional singular.[94] In addition, a certain personalizing urgency is established by a series of ellipses and compressions—each unremarkable in itself[95]—but such that collectively we almost feel ourselves to have entered the abrupt intimacy of (yet another analogy) a Browning monologue:

> But do not let us quarrel any more,
> No, my Lucrezia; bear with me for once:
> Sit down and all shall happen as you wish
> . . . Will it? tenderly?
> Oh, I'll content him . . .[96]

How very different is the choric introduction to the contest between the tragedians at *Frogs* 814 ff.:

> *ἦ που δεινὸν ἐριβρεμέτας χόλον ἔνδοθεν ἕξει,*
> *ἡνίκ' ἂν ὀξύλαλόν περ ἴδῃ θήγοντος ὀδόντα* 815
> *ἀντιτέχνου· τότε δὴ μανίας ὑπὸ δεινῆς*
> *ὄμματα στροβήσεται . . .*

> Yea, the loud-thundering one will feel dire anger inside him,
> When he beholds his opponent whetting his tooth, slick-talking.
> Then will his eyes
> Roll in dire madness . . .

Opening in epic hexameters, as it does, the lyric inevitably recalls the Homeric world of 'savage beasts or heroes in chariots',[97] but

[93] The representative high point here is σῷ . . . ἐδάμην πόθῳ, with poetic hyperbaton, archaic cast, and verse word δαμάζω (see LSJ s.v.), recalling expressions like ταύτης πόθῳ πόλις δαμείη (Soph. *Trach.* 431–2).

[94] ἡμῖν/ἐδάμην/ἡμῖν. For the tragic-choral convention whereby first sg. stands for pl., see M. Kaimio, *The Chorus of Greek Drama within the Light of the Person and Number Used* (Helsinki 1970) 60–103.

[95] Ellipse of ἡμᾶς 591; ἀπὸ κοινοῦ effect of δαιμόνια (with ἐδ. πόθ. as well as with βούλομ., *pace* eds.); compressed logic of explanation in the repeated γάρ (five times in a dozen lines).

[96] The opening lines of Robert Browning's 'Andrea Del Sarto'. This *Pax* lyric, oddly, is missing from an interesting discussion of poetic tones in the play by Moulton, *Poetry*, 82–107.

[97] Stanford ad loc.

well before the close of the first quatrain diction (though not metre) has made its due (improper) descent.[98] Within this distinctive range of idiom, Aristophanes presents his insight into the fundamental difference between the representatives of traditional Athens and articulate modern man. This is achieved in vividly contrasting images. There is, first, an opposition on the psychological level: 'Aeschylus is maddened by deep-felt passion . . . Euripides is cool and subtle'.[99] Then there is a parallel contrast—not schematically precise but the more interesting for that—between the idiom reserved for reference to Aeschylus (which is largely or entirely epic, or comparably elevated) and its Euripidean counterpart (which, in a perhaps surprisingly nuanced fashion, veers between something traditional-poetic and something else, flatly prosaic and modern).[100] Given this rush of stylistic activity—and as the ode proceeds, there is a welter of imagery besides—it is arguable that the very brilliance of the writing serves to distract us from its overt point. Even so, Aristophanes is certainly doing something startling and new here, something unimaginable in elevated lyric *per se*, and something quite distinct from what he attempts in any of the passages yet discussed.[101] And once more, be it noted, it is a subject close to his heart that provides the impetus.

And quite different again, *Acharnians* 692–702, the lament of the veterans of Marathon:

> *ταῦτα πῶς εἰκότα, γέροντ' ἀπολέ-*
> *σαι πολιὸν ἄνδρα περὶ κλεψύδραν,*
> *πολλὰ δὴ ξυμπονήσαντα καὶ θερμὸν ἀπο-*
> *μορξάμενον ἀνδρικὸν ἱδρῶτα δὴ καὶ πολύν,*
> *ἄνδρ' ἀγαθὸν ὄντα Μαραθῶνι περὶ τὴν πόλιν;*
> *εἶτα Μαραθῶνι μὲν ὅτ' ἦμεν, ἐδιώκομεν,*

[98] Metre: 814–15 dact. hex., 816 dact. pent., 817 lecythion, giving overall an Aeschylean impression (Parker, *Songs*, 486). Diction: e.g. the descent from grand-manner, article-free *ἐριβρεμέτας* (Homeric *hapax*, applied to Zeus, *Il.* 13. 624 (see Janko ad loc.); picked up by Pind. *Isth.* 4. 46, of lions) to *ὀξύλαλον*. This coinage likewise hints at the high style (no def. art., and e.g. Homer has *ὀξυβελής*, *Il.* 4. 126)—but (despite e.g. *λάλημα* at Soph. *Ant.* 320, Eur. *Andr.* 937) -*λαλ*- is modern and prosaic (see the spreads in LSJ s.vv. *λαλέω*, *λαλία*), as indeed is *ὀξύς* in the given sense (*ἐς τὰς τέχνας ὀξύτερος* Hp. *Aer.* 24: LSJ s.v. III. 2).

[99] Stanford, *Frogs*, 142.

[100] As encapsulated in *ὀξύλαλον* (n. 98 above).

[101] In 'Lyric Poet', 142, I put too much stress on the negative aspect of the writing.

νῦν δ' ὑπ' ἀνδρῶν πονηρῶν σφόδρα διωκόμεθα, κᾆτα πρὸς ἁλισκόμεθα.
πρὸς τάδε τις ἀντερεῖ Μαρψίας;

How can this be right?—old man grey
Ruined at the water-clock,
Who did his share of toil,
Wiped off a man's sweat hot:
Marathon man, at the city's call.
At Marathon we led the charge;
Man vile after man
Charges us now, convicts us too.
What *Seizer* can answer this?

By comparison with most of the hybrids, high colouring is considerably less in evidence, residing in the cast of the phrasing, rather than in any high-flown vocabulary:[102] here, at least, 'high' implies creative intensification, as much as conventional elevation. Once again we have the popular cretic-paeonic rhythm, this time serving to steady rising emotion associated with a series of evocative repetitions. The effect of the piece derives from an accumulation of simple touches. There is, first, a phrase of poetic cast ('old man grey'), plangently echoed ('man's sweat hot'):

γέροντ' ἀπολέσαι πολιὸν ἄνδρα . . .
θερμὸν ἀπομορξάμενον ἀνδρικὸν ἱδρῶτα . . .[103]

The opening poeticism, however, already jars against the concrete-prosaic 'water-clock' (κλεψύδραν, symbolizing the law-courts)[104]—almost ironically, as if the old men's claim to dignity were mocked by the very context of their present treatment. Then

[102] Besides points made in the text, note the double ellipse of τὴν with κλεψύδραν (cf. Starkie ad loc.) and of ἐστί with εἰκότα, γέροντ' as adj. with ἄνδρα (as Thgn. 1351; cf. LSJ s.v. γέρων), and ἱδρῶτα δή, the particle being rare after substantives in prose and comedy. (On this see J. D. Denniston, *Greek Particles*² (Oxford 1954) 213–14, who cites two other passages in A, along with eight in prose. NB that most of the eight are in Plato, who in many ways is half a poet anyway (Silk, *Interaction*, 48, 220–1), and that four others from the overall list—two in Xen. and the other two in A (*Thes.* 1228, *Eccl.* 1163)—involve the phrase ὥρα δή, which is presumably a set expression, without any bearing on the poetic status of the noun + δή idiom as a whole.)

[103] In Greek, adj. (*vel. sim*)-verb-adj.-noun; cf. e.g. Eur. *Hec.* 445–6 ποντοπόρους κομίζεις θοὰς ἀκάτους, *Hipp.* 750–1, *Med.* 1263–4. Cf. above, p. 118 with n. 51.

[104] LSJ s.v. II; see e.g. MacDowell on *Vesp.* 93.

comes a series of pointed verbal effects, from another plangent repetition, that seems to show everything falling into place ('Marathon . . . Marathon': *ὄντα Μαραθῶνι . . . Μαραθῶνι . . . ἦμεν*), to a sardonic pun: we *charged* (*ἐδιώκομεν*) in war—now we *are charged* (*διωκόμεθα*) in law, and are both (figuratively) captured and (literally) convicted (*ἁλισκόμεθα*), with the concrete ('war') senses of these verbs summed up finally in the evocative name, 'Seizer' (*Marpsias*).[105] Meanwhile, an overriding series reaches its climax. The chorus speaks for 'old man grey' (*πολιὸν ἄνδρα*), who has expended 'a man's sweat' (*ἀνδρικὸν ἱδρῶτα*)—and not just for ordinary *man*, but the *manliness* of 'Marathon man' (*ἄνδρ' ἀγαθὸν ὄντα Μαραθῶνι*)—now a passive victim of 'vile man' (*ἀνδρῶν πονηρῶν*). Throughout the stanza, the restraint in the elevation of the writing—elevation essentially tragic in affiliation—keeps the latent rhetoric under control, while the play of wit, along with the rhythm, helps to keep the focus on the emotive subject, not (operatically) on the emotion itself.

Tragedy again: with Aristophanes' remarkable variety of lyric creations—low, high, hybrid—in mind, we must look back to the question of his relationship with the 'serious' genre. Once more, it could hardly be clearer that for this comic poet, if for no one else, the tragic constitutes a very special point of reference. Within his hybrids, diverse though they are,[106] access to the idiom of tragedy is an almost unqualified gain in dignity as it is in range of feeling—whereas, judged by his extraordinary standards of writing in the hybrids, as elsewhere, the high lyrics fail to impress. In the previous chapter we explored the organic connections between

[105] Note also: ring-form to convey the scale of the veterans' efforts (*πολλὰ δὴ ξυμπονήσαντα—ἱδρῶτα δὴ καὶ πολύν*); a wry allusion back to *περὶ κλεψύδραν* in *περὶ τὴν πόλιν* (with a cumulative weight on the preposition producing almost a concrete image by ellipse: one thinks e.g. of Solon 5. 5 *IEG*, *ἔστην ἀμφιβαλὼν κρατερὸν σάκος*); and an insidious assonantal pattern (*πολιὸν . . . πολλὰ . . . πολύν . . . πόλιν*) seeming again to show everything falling, however wrongly, into place (on such assonantal 'logic', cf. M. S. Silk, 'Tragic language', in Silk, *Tragedy and the Tragic*, 480–8). On Marpsias, cf. *Il.* 22. 199–201 *ὡς δ' ἐν ὀνείρῳ οὐ δύναται φεύγοντα διώκειν . . . ὣς ὁ τὸν οὐ δύνατο μάρψαι*. Like 'Seizer' ('seize' = 'take legal possession of': no apologies for the additional anachronistic pun), the name is perhaps fabricated *ad hoc* (cf. Starkie ad loc.), then reused by Eupol. 179 *PCG*: no 'real' examples are attested for Attica in M. J. Osborne and S. G. Byrne (eds.), *A Lexicon of Greek Personal Names*, ii (Oxford 1994) s.v. The sequence of thought in the lyric (but not much else) is picked up by [Andoc.] *in Alcib.* 22: 'old men fight our battles, while young men make speeches'.

[106] For other hybrid lyrics, see Silk, 'Lyric poet', 140–4.

the various striking features of Aristophanes' language and style. Within his hybrid lyrics this interconnectedness is as apparent as anywhere. Within the high lyrics it is absent: what can all that inert ornamentation, in *Clouds* and elsewhere, have to do with the essential ways and means of Aristophanic comedy?

A writer's effectiveness cannot be bought randomly. Literary achievement is not like some basketful of miscellaneous goods acquired on a shopping spree. In any culture a high style has its own justification and its own logic, and imitation of its superficial features is not self-justifying. In the particular case of Aristophanes, superficial imitation of the tragic high style precludes his distinctive mobility and sharply limits his capacity to exercise his genius for the discontinuous, the immediate, and the topical. At this inordinate cost, it gives him access to the conventionally serious realm of the grand, the heroic, the timeless truths of myth.

'The discontinuous' and 'the topical' versus 'the timeless truths of myth': there is a fundamental opposition here between two clusters of properties, two orientations, and ultimately two visions. Yet this is not a disguised version of the opposition between tragedy and comedy, even if it is certainly an opposition in respect of which classical *Greek* tragedy and Greek *Old* Comedy occupy polar positions.

Comedy is not the opposite of tragedy, but low is the opposite of high, and whereas Aristophanic comedy (hybrids and all) is residually low, Greek tragedy is unremittingly high, as is the great mass of epic and lyric poetry that stands behind it and with it. And the ultimate target of all such poetry is universal realities that transcend the variable phenomena of the here-and-now.[107]

> *ἐπάμεροι· τί δέ τις; τί δ' οὔ τις; σκιᾶς ὄναρ*
> *ἄνθρωπος.*
>
> Creatures of a day! What are you? Not? Shadow's dream,
> Man.[108]

Pindar's famous question and answer may be very special in their stylistic detail; in their universalizing import they are wholly representative of the high-literary traditions of which—from

[107] *Ultimate* target, *pace* fashionable overemphasis on the occasionality of the Pindaric ode and the *polis*-icality of Attic tragedy—but cf. (on Pindar) below, pp. 204–5.

[108] Pind. *Pyth.* 8. 95–6: see Silk, 'Pindar meets Plato'.

Aristophanes' vantage point—tragedy constitutes the centre. The tragic world is populated not by Carcinus and Cleon or the stage Euripides, but by the gods and heroes of myth and legend, who are essentially carriers of universal metaphysical meaning. That meaning is alien to comedy. Those carriers, in themselves, are alien too—unless subjected to some kind of comic assimilation to the contemporary world—as the Dionysus of *Frogs* (or the Dionysus of Dicaeopolis' phallic song) is assimilated. (Mythological burlesque represents another, simpler kind of assimilation, and one not especially common in Aristophanes himself.)[109] The words and phrases of tragedy that bulk so large in Aristophanes' paratragic evocations are, likewise, immediate presences, available for his use once appropriated for his own (diverse) concerns and within his own (diverse) idiom:

> And as for peace,
> They couldn't give a damn. O City city.[110]

The high, essentially tragic, presences in the hybrid lyrics are appropriated on a rather different basis, but they are assimilated with equal ease. The high-pastiche lyrics, by contrast, represent an attempt to appropriate *en bloc* what cannot be assimilated, because the writer's deepest instincts are thereby repudiated. Consider the *klepsydra*, the here-and-now localized water-clock, which symbolizes the lawcourts where the old veteran of Marathon is under attack:

> How can this be right?—old man grey
> Ruined at the water-clock?

From that clock, Aristophanes can move a long way, in almost any direction, but not so far—or rather not so consistently far—that the clock itself becomes a stylistic anomaly, as it would be in the *Clouds parodos*. There the ethos is all generic unparticularization:

> . . . Ocean deep-voiced . . . lofty mountains
> . . . far-away heights
> . . . sacred earth
> . . . holy rivers . . .[111]

[109] Above, pp. 49–50 with n. 23.
[110] *Ach.* 26–7: above, pp. 34 ff.
[111] *Nub.* 278–83: above, pp. 169 ff.

Such generic markers are proper features of high lyric, epic, and tragedy, because they are timelessly appropriate, like the timeless truths of myth and—ultimately—metaphysics themselves:

> Creatures of a day! . . . Shadow's dream,
> Man.

Metaphysics is something Aristophanes cannot appropriate, and tacitly he acknowledges it. Even in his devotional lyrics he makes no attempt at the metaphysical—as opposed to the merely religious—seriousness which is characteristic of Pindar and the choral lyrics of tragedy. He may persuade his chorus to invoke

> solemnities mystical,
> Rites to receive the initiates, gifts
> For the gods of heaven . . .

but his own special god is the here-and-now phallus, personified *ad hoc*, and what one critic unsympathetically calls the 'gnomic banalities' of high lyric are conspicuous by their absence in any of his appeals to the 'gods of heaven'.[112]

Aristophanes' forays into the high style, then, have all the piquant oddity of a repeated attempt on the part of an acrobat to be a mountain-climber. That said, the significant question becomes, not how far each of his acrobatic attempts to scale his mountain is a relative, or a substantial, or a total failure, but why he should persist in the attempt at all. The answer surely lies in the nature of his preoccupation with tragedy, and his aspiration to say (in the words of his *Frogs* chorus), not only much that is 'amusing' (*geloia*), but much that is 'serious' (*spoudaia*) too.[113] Tragedy for him has all the fascination of an alternative form of existence, but also the authority of a more prestigious form. In his world, as in ours, tragedy is valued more highly than his own form of drama. In *Frogs* the search is mounted for a playwright who can help guide the city—save the city—in her hour of need. That playwright, naturally, will be a tragedian, and the fact that the rescue attempt itself should be mounted by the comic poet only accentuates the discrepancy. Tragedy is valued more highly, and, in Aristophanes' world at least, its higher valuation is unquestionably associated with the

[112] *Nub.* 302–5 (above, pp. 173–4), and Dover, *Aristophanic Comedy*, 184.
[113] *Ran.* 389–90: above, pp. 46–7.

cluster of features under discussion: its elevation, its mythologizing, its timelessness, its universality.

Some authority for this association is provided, soon enough, by Aristotle. For the spokesman for tragedy and its canons, poetry falls into two groups, according to whether its representation of life involves what is 'serious' (*spoudaion*) or—not 'comic', but for Aristotle much the same thing—'trivial' (*phaulon*).[114] In addition, though, poetry as a whole is a 'more serious' thing (*spoudaioteron*) than, for instance, history, precisely because (as the philosopher sees it: *Poetics* IX) poetry tends to express the universal and history the particular. And it is inferential, though Aristotle is not explicit, that, by *that* criterion, one particular poetic tradition, which in his time is all but defunct, must be less 'serious' than the rest: the tradition that for us reaches its zenith in Aristophanic Old Comedy and includes, as we have noted, the low lyric of Archilochus and others in the archaic period. It is this tradition that stands apart from most Greek poetry, *including* those types of comedy that replaced the Old with typical, 'universal', names, events, and concerns: not Carcinus and Cleon and the immediacies of Athens, but Chremes and Sostrata and the less time-bound questions of manners and characters and family relationships.

There is relatively little literature that consists exclusively of *either* the universal *or* the particular; and, *pace* Aristotle, the most completely satisfying works, or moments, of literature tend to be those that give scope to the expression of both. If the climactic moment in Pindar's *Pythian* 8 is the great universal question (or questions) and the great universal answer that follows—

> . . . What are you? Not? Shadow's dream,
> Man—

it is equally true that the point of departure for this nexus is a masterpiece of elevated particularity, in which the celebratory poet portrays the victorious athlete (a wrestler) and his victims in sharp successive vignettes of physical menace and evocative specificity: τέτρασι δ' ἔμπετες ὑψόθεν | σωμάτεσσι . . . ('You fell on top of four | Bodies . . .'); κατὰ λαύρας δ' . . . | πτώσσοντι . . . ('they shrink | Down alleyways . . .').[115] The same author's characteristic

[114] *Poet.* IV–V: above, pp. 53, 81.
[115] *Pyth.* 8. 81–2, 86–7: see, in more detail, Silk, 'Pindar meets Plato'.

reinterpretation of the mythopoetic links between city, or noble family, and the realm of the timeless divine would be another, very pertinent, instance on a larger scale, while a wealth of examples from Homer onwards might be enlisted to show that the Aristophanic link (to which we have repeatedly drawn attention) between particular focus and *low* style—that is, style with *access* to the low—is not an inevitable link as such. For Aristophanes, however, it remains a necessity, thanks to the inexorable logic of popular art.

When the old men in *Acharnians*, in their particular hybrid style, sing of the water-clock, we focus on the water-clock. When Dicaeopolis, in his, sings of a phallus, of an Athenian general, of a girl carrying wood, we focus on these particularities. When his *Clouds* chorus sings of the deep voice of father Ocean, we see nothing but a generalized poetic haze. In this connection we do well to ponder again the striking, and symptomatic, conjunction of particular and general, concrete and abstract, in the *Peace* song in honour of the goddess:

τοῖς ἀγροίκοισιν γὰρ ἦσθα χῖδρα καὶ σωτηρία.

To country-folk you meant oats and salvation.[116]

'Oats and salvation': the phrase epitomizes Aristophanes' principle of hybridity. Here is the particularization that points directly to the open-ended reality we call 'life', conjoined with the more generalizing word, which (in this context of tragic-romantic greeting) evokes that high-poetic context again:

ὦ φίλτατον φῶς, ὦ μόνος σωτὴρ δόμων
Ἀγαμέμνονος, πῶς ἦλθες;

O dearest light, of Agamemnon's house
Sole saviour—you have come?[117]

And if the example, 'oats and salvation', embodies a reconciliation of the tragic general with the comic particular, it also sums up the limits of the comic poet's capacity to penetrate the sphere of tragic poetry and poetic elevation as a whole.

Comic oats and tragic salvation: the specificity of the one informs the new whole. We focus on the old Acharnians' water-clock, on Dicaeopolis' phallus—and on the new hybrid whole: oats

[116] *Pax* 596: above, p. 146. [117] Soph. *El.* 1354–5.

and salvation. And when we see, hand in hand, the comic oats and the tragic salvation, we do not see them as each would be, if represented separately in the genre (*vel sim.*) in which each might be separately represented, and we were thinking about them separately. The strangeness of their coexistence in the new context means that we see them in a new perspective: the compound carries with it the germ of a new, comic, vision.

Greek culture, if any culture ever was, was a *whole* culture, the culture from which envious later ages derived their notion of the 'whole man'. And yet the Greek view of life, as eloquently articulated by Homer and his successors, is highly stratified. To restate the issue once more, and in the simplest possible way: things are seen as *either* valuable *or* trivial; and the valuable deserve a high treatment in a proper context, which will reinforce their value; and the trivial the opposite. Hence, the whole theory of decorum: 'we ought to use words worthy of things.'[118] The new hybridity challenges this vision and offers another, in which the correlations, and therefore the values, make way, however momentarily, for a more open view of life and the possibilities of life—even the possibility of moving out from the immediacies of cultural experience (the specificities of the water-clock) into unimagined realms of possibility beyond.

This last cluster of concerns will need our attention in due course. Meanwhile, the moral of Aristophanes' lyrical experiments is plain. They constitute an especially revealing set of attempts to come to terms with what he may well have seen as a higher sphere and what we (in a larger perspective) can see as a kind of tragic-Aristotelian orthodoxy. In these experiments, tragedy serves as a liberating and enlarging force—unless taken as a model, when it becomes stultifying. With this remarkable lesson in mind, we are now in a position to consider the comic poet's relationship with the tragic Other in the spheres of characterization and then structural organization.

[118] τῶν πραγμάτων πρέποι ἂν καὶ τὰς φωνὰς ἔχειν ἀξίας: 'Longinus', *Subl.* 43. 5.

5

Character and Characterization

The discontinuity that is such a feature of Aristophanes' style is equally a fundamental quality of his writing—his humour, his poetry, his drama—as a whole. In this we see a typical correlation between style and the larger aspects of literature and yet another indication of how deep the gulf really is between Aristophanes' comic domain and the world of Aristotelian stabilities, tragedy, and Menander.

The same Aristotle, whose name we repeatedly set in opposition to Aristophanic norms, laid it down as a fact of life that drama (specifically, tragic drama) consists of a set of 'elements', of which the most important is 'plot structure' (μῦθος) and the second most important, 'character' or 'characters' (ἦθος, ἤθη), and few subsequent theorists have contested the importance of these two broad aspects of dramatic writing in general.[1] In Aristophanes' plays both are, in significant part, conceived and realized in accordance with the principle of discontinuity. In the first place—and, for convenience, reversing Aristotle's order of priorities—we can show that Aristophanes' presentation of people has this principle written into it.[2]

We can best begin with a new set of representative instances, from *Thesmophoriazusae*. This play is a striking mixture of (*inter alia*) broad comedy and devotional lyrics. Some of the broad comedy and all of the devotional lyrics are carried by one set of people, the women at the Thesmophoria—some of them in the chorus, some ostensibly among 'the characters'.[3] The women

[1] Arist. *Poet.* VI. On plots and plot structures see below, pp. 256 ff. (and on the question of challenges to their status, p. 259). The importance of character has not been challenged as such, despite disagreements about its possible primacy (to which Aristotle's arguments in *Poet.* VI are already implicit testimony) and radical reinterpretations of what character is (cf. below, pp. 222–3 n. 30).

[2] The argument that follows incorporates a modified version of parts of Silk, 'People'.

[3] Except for the possibility that the 'Lady Herald' may be the chorus leader (cf. Dover, *Aristophanic Comedy*, 166–7, Russo, *Aristofane*, 302–3), it is customary to

combine two main roles. They are humorous figures, aggressive assailants of Euripides, and they are devotional figures, pious hymn-singers who celebrate the gods in five separate choral songs. The questions we need to consider here are these: what sort of relationship is there between the two roles, and what sort of entities are the women who play them?

The two central characters of *Thesmophoriazusae* are clever Euripides and his dumb and docile relative Mnesilochus.[4] Early in the play Euripides concocts a plan to get a man disguised as a woman to infiltrate the women's festival. Euripides cannot go himself. His fellow dramatist Agathon has the wit and the performing skills required, and Euripides asks him to do the job. When Agathon refuses, Mnesilochus offers his services instead—although (on the evidence of his bumbling performance to date) he patently lacks any qualification for such a delicate mission (209–13):

ΕΥ. ὦ τρισκακοδαίμων, ὡς ἀπόλωλ'.
ΜΝ. Εὐριπίδη,
ὦ φίλτατ', ὦ κηδεστὰ μὴ σαυτὸν προδῷς.
ΕΥ. πῶς οὖν ποίησω δῆτα;
ΜΝ. τοῦτον μὲν μακρὰ
κλάειν κέλευ', ἐμοὶ ὅ τι βούλει χρῶ λαβών.
ΕΥ. ἄγε νυν . . .

EU. What an appalling bit of luck!—I've had it.
MN. My dear chap—cousin!—don't give up so soon.
EU. What can I do?

assume that the two groups are wholly separate. But what distinguishes e.g. 531–2 (traditionally ascribed to the chorus) from 533–9 (ascribed to the anonymous 'First Woman')? The groups share the same alignment and the same virtual anonymity: two of the women (we learn incidentally) have typical names (*Μίκα* 760, *Κρίτυλλα* 898), but then so do *choral* individuals elsewhere (*Δράκης Lys.* 254, *Νικοδίκη Lys.* 321, etc.). Need it be assumed that the groups are wholly separate in fact? The possibility that they are not is raised (though no more) by H. Hansen, 'Aristophanes' *Thesmophoriazusae*: theme, structure, and production', *Philologus* 120 (1976) 165–85, at 176.

[4] The name 'Mnesilochus' is not used in the text, but derives from the scholia. This notwithstanding, it is both convenient and harmless (Homerists use the name 'Homer' the same way), whereas the alternatives (the favourite English alternatives are 'Kinsman' and 'Inlaw') are frigid and distracting (e.g. 'Inlaw' in an Aristophanic context sounds like an opposite of outlaw, or else—like 'Mother-in-Law—the embodiment of some unspecified sitcom joke). See further below, p. 229 with n. 41.

MN. Tell him to go to hell.
Instead, how about trying it with me?
EU. Well, in *that* case . . .

Mnesilochus' offer is duly accepted, although his attempt to carry himself off as a woman is doomed to failure (and the failure duly generates most of the subsequent action of the play). Euripides, one notes, never actually suggested that Mnesilochus should take the part. That—one might say—is because it won't work, and Euripides would be too clever to suggest it. Why, then, does the clever Euripides accept such an implausible offer at all? And why does the dumb and docile Mnesilochus suddenly thrust himself into the part in the first place?—a part which, while all goes well, he proceeds to perform with gusto and some considerable inventiveness. It is not an answer to say: 'the plot requires it.' This moment is itself part of the plot; and anyway that kind of answer only converts the first set of questions into a second set: why is it acceptable, on the level of what we call character, for the plot to 'require' it? In these various examples we seem to observe inconsistencies of behaviour in varying degrees on the part of the women, Euripides, and Mnesilochus. Why, and how, are such inconsistencies acceptable?

Consider again the women in *Thesmophoriazusae*. Their duality produces (or is produced by) not only inconsistencies of behaviour in the ordinary sense, but also inconsistencies of linguistic behaviour. There is a moment in the play when, after Mnesilochus in disguise has spoken up for Euripides (466–519), the women react furiously. One of them threatens, obscenely, to shave his (supposedly her) pussy (*χοῖρος*, 538), a threat to which Mnesilochus responds with understandable alarm ('Please, ladies, not my *pussy*!', 540). Up to this point the women have been fairly restrained in their language, not only in the devotional songs, with all their now familiar religiosities ('Come thou, mighty maiden . . . Come thou, lord of the sea . . .', 317 ff.), but in the dialogue too. The sudden use of the word 'pussy' represents, for them, a stylistic switch: the idiom suddenly changes, the level suddenly drops.

As so often in Aristophanes, we find ourselves confronted with the phenomenon of stylistic mobility and its discontinuous effects, but now by a new route and with a new question in mind: what are the implications of this discontinuity for the characters whose words engender it? Faced with the women's contribution to the play so far and asked to 'explain' this switch to obscene idiom, one might point to the particular speaker's anger, as if the change were explicable in terms of a real individual's real emotional reaction. Such a rationalizing explanation is certainly available for this passage *on its own*. But, as we know, stylistic switches abound in Aristophanes, and most of them are not explicable in such terms. One case in point, among many others, is a comparable vulgarism early on in the play, this time on the lips of Euripides. Mnesilochus, who is again the recipient of the obscenity, purports not to be able to remember who Agathon is. Euripides puts him wise (33–5):

MN. μῶν ὁ δασυπώγων;
EY. οὐχ ἑόρακας πώποτε;
MN. μὰ τὸν Δί' οὔπω γ' ὥστε κἀμέ γ' εἰδέναι.
EY. καὶ μὴν βεβίνηκας σύ γ', ἀλλ' οὐκ οἶσθ' ἴσως.

MN. The one with the thick beard?
EU. Haven't you seen him?
MN. I haven't—not consciously, anyway.
EU. Well, at least you must have shagged him—maybe not consciously.

Up to this point Euripides, like the women later, has spoken in a restrained idiom. His remarks to Mnesilochus have been equable in tone, and there is nothing now to suggest that his mood has changed. Nor is there anything in his characterization to come which would suggest that obscenity is a feature of his idiom, as it is, by contrast, of Mnesilochus'. This vulgarism, certainly, is hardly open to rationalization.[5]

[5] Regarding the tone of βινεῖν, H. D. Jocelyn, 'Attic *BINEIN* and English f . . .', *LCM* 5 (1980) 65–7, argues that (unlike e.g. English 'fuck') the word is not obscene, partly on the grounds of its distribution within Attic comedy (esp. its use by females), partly on the grounds of its supposed occurrence in a Solonian law (Hsch. s.v. βινεῖν = Solon, *Test. Vet.* 448 Martina). He suggests that the word, instead, had an 'intimate' tone. Against this: (i) the overwhelming occurrence of the word is in low literature (largely comic—cf. the representative citations in LSJ—but note also Arch. 152. 2, Hippon. 84. 16): if this (given the sense of the word) does not suggest obscenity, it is not clear what would. (ii) 'Intimacy' is not actually incompatible with obscenity: it is a known feature of current English (certainly British English) usage that the obscene word 'fuck' is used by some couples (including female members of couples) in intimate contexts, and one recalls D. H. Lawrence's thoughts in this general area (see 'A propos of *Lady Chatterley's Lover*', in D. H. Lawrence, *Phoenix II*, ed. W. Roberts and H. T. Moore (London

In Aristophanes the stylistic quality of a speaker's (or a singer's) words switches frequently and, often, drastically. In interpreting his plays, modern readers and, especially, modern critics tend to rationalize such switches, or (failing that) to explain them away as 'comic effect'—thus resorting to a tautology which in a sense points to the true explanation of the phenomenon and yet, in itself, explains nothing. The fact is that both our rationalizings and our ascriptions of 'comic effect' presuppose what is not the case: that, irrespective of any contrary indications, the speakers, and the singers, of Aristophanic comedy must ultimately conform to realist norms.

For a stylistic idiom to be compatible with realism, it must involve a range of expression which is *consistently* relatable to a vernacular language, a language of experience, a language of life. Either the idiom is felt to amount to a 'selection of the language really spoken by men', as Wordsworth called it;[6] or alternatively it involves a broadly consistent stylization, like (for instance) the stylization of Greek tragic dialogue, which does not constitute anything like a language of life, but is, nevertheless, fixed and conventionalized at a set, comprehensible distance from some hypothetical and more naturalistic idiom which *would* pass for a language of life *à la* Wordsworth. In the latter case, specifically colloquial vocabulary, phraseology, syntax, and so on, will tend to be excluded, not capriciously or opportunistically in one play or in one part of one play, but *throughout* the play or plays. And the same principle of consistency applies to the more conspicuous, if still limited, presence of archaisms, conventional tropes, and the other familiar features of an elevated language. This principle of consistency is not subverted (even though analysis is complicated), if the stability of a work is differential in kind: if there is the alternating distinction of idioms, 'natural' or stylized, for different sections or phases of the work that we discussed earlier—like the distinction between song and speech in Greek tragedy, or between narrative and direct speech in many novels,

1968) 514). (iii) The presence of an 'intimacy' in a law seems appreciably less likely (even) than that of an obscenity. (iv) But in any case the actual source of the 'Solonian' citation is as uncertain as its detail (on which Jocelyn himself remarks (67): 'this entry [in Hsch.] is obscure and has been much emended').

[6] Preface to *Lyrical Ballads*, ed. R. L. Brett and A. R. Jones (rev. edn., London 1965) 244 (1802 variant).

or between the direct speech of different characters in much narrative fiction and much drama too.

By contrast, Aristophanes' characteristic mobility of style makes for inconsistencies *within* a given speaker's range of idiom, from which it follows that the style in which his people express themselves is generally incompatible with any kind of realism. More fundamentally, as this consideration of style serves to suggest, the people of Aristophanes *per se* are not strictly containable within any realist understanding of human character at all. Their linguistic and their non-linguistic behaviour[7] may cohere, but in neither case on a realist premise. And as such, these beings are distinguishable from their counterparts in the central tradition of Western fiction, in drama or outside.

This whole non-Aristophanic tradition we may now simply call *the realist tradition*. It is the tradition within which 'l'effet du réel'[8] is not so much characteristic as ultimately decisive. In agreeing to call it 'realist', we are using 'realism' not (like many literary historians) as a period term,[9] but as a designation of 'a perennial mode of representing the world' in its 'consequential logic and circumstantiality', a mode which has no 'single style' and whose actual style, or styles, in any given age vary according to cultural norms, and whose 'dominance at any one time is a . . . cultural

[7] *Pace* the curious pretence (current among some literary theoreticians) that linguistic behaviour ('text') is everything. 'Outside of language there is neither self nor desire', says J. Frow, 'Spectacle binding: on character', *Poetics Today* 7 (1986) 238. In drama (which includes silent films and ballet), as in life (which subsumes deaf and dumb illiterates) this is self-evidently untrue. In the classical context cf. the welcome discussion by Wiles, 'Performance'.

[8] The phrase was coined by Roland Barthes in an essay itself entitled 'L'Effet du réel', in *Communications* 11 (1968) 84–9. For Barthes the stress is on 'effet' not on 'réel', because of the postmodern anxiety that literature should be seen as removed from reference (sc. to real life). However, the fact that all fictional characters (like everything in literature) are *constructed* apart from real life (which is what we mean by 'fictional') has no bearing on their capacity to evoke that outside reality: cf. G. D. Martin, *Language, Truth and Poetry* (Edinburgh 1975) 68–106, and Silk, 'Enactment'. Barthes effectively blurs the issue—as he does again in *S/Z* (Paris 1970) with his 'figure'/'discourse' distinction, which (helpfully) opposes any ascribing of *real* reality to fictional characters, but at the (regrettable) cost of making it difficult or impossible to distinguish realist and non-realist figures as we should. The succinct discussion of 'figure'/'discourse' by S. Goldhill, 'Character and action, representation and reading', in Pelling, *Characterization*, 100–27 at 111–14 (followed by Lada-Richards, *Dionysus*, 165, 216–17) does not confront the problem.

[9] Most commonly of nineteenth-century, as opposed to earlier, fiction, but also of 'modern', as opposed to 'ancient', fiction: so, e.g., among classicists, Sifakis, *Parabasis*, 7–14, esp. 9.

option.'[10] So defined, the realist tradition is the tradition canonized by Aristotle's theory and Menander's practice, and the tradition which reaches its fullest expression in the nineteenth-century novel. And so defined, the tradition includes instances of the two contrasting types of fiction, the narrative and the dramatic: narrative fiction, with (typically) its 'omniscient' narrator who can tell us about a character, as well as seeming to show us that character in action; and dramatic fiction, which presupposes the individual human presence of the actor—whose performance, furthermore, introduces a variable which (except in a marginal case like oral-epic recitation) has no equivalent in the narrative sphere. And yet, large and important though the differences between different manifestations of realism clearly are, even the difference between realist narrative and realist drama is not, for present purposes, to the point.

Within the realist tradition we encounter a wide variety of ways of representing fictional people. Sometimes we feel called on to comprehend these people as 'characters', sometimes to empathize with them as 'personalities'.[11] Some presentations seem to expand or diffuse single traits, some seem to produce 'rounded' characters. The presentation may impinge as two-dimensional or as three-dimensional; as more or as less inward-looking; as a matter of status at least as much as of temperament; as a matter of types or a matter of individuals. And interpreters may have good reason to draw attention to the differences between the presentations of (say) the Greek tragedians and Eugene O' Neill, or Euripides and his predecessors, or (most commonly) the modern Western novel and *its* predecessors.[12] But all such presentations have one thing in common. The people presented have what we may see as a constant relationship with 'reality'—with the world outside as

[10] J. P. Stern, *On Realism* (London 1973) 32, 28, 52, 79, 158. On the history of the term 'realism', see R. Wellek, 'The concept of realism in literary scholarship', *Neophilologus* 45 (1961) 1–20.

[11] C. Gill, 'The character-personality distinction', in Pelling, *Characterization*, 1–31.

[12] As (variously) J. P. Gould, 'Dramatic character and "human intelligibility" in Greek tragedy', *PCPS* 24 (1978) 43–67; J. Jones, *On Aristotle and Greek Tragedy* (London 1962) 239–79; I. Watt, *The Rise of the Novel* (London 1957) 9–34. On Greek tragedy see further the contrasting essays in Pelling, *Characterization*, by P. E. Easterling, 'Constructing character in Greek tragedy' (83–99), Goldhill, 'Character and action' (100–27), J. Griffin, 'Characterization in Euripides' (128–49).

we perceive it or might be presumed to perceive it—because (given the stability of the verbal idiom through which their being is projected) they are seen to stand at a constant distance from that real world.[13] They impinge as sentient beings, each with a tendency to be (in Aristotle's language) 'appropriate', 'lifelike', and 'consistent'[14]—and 'consistent', we may well think, is actually the decisive member of the series. At its most clear-cut this tradition produces figures in which we detect a wealth of recognizable detail, with each detail corresponding to some known or conceivable constituent of life, and each detail connectable with or continuous with some other—even *each* other—detail, and the product of the details a recognizable yet almost unique creation. Within this tradition we say, 'Medea says *this—that* tells us something about Medea', by which we mean that here is a new something to add to the continuum that we call 'Medea' and whose comprehensibility as such is already apparent.

It is within this tradition, and only within this tradition, that characters can be seen to do what we call 'develop', when the new something is of a particular, and particularly significant, kind.[15] Such development (it might be argued) implies a progression from one perceived state to another via shifts of emphasis between the identifiable details—perhaps like phonetic changes taking place via a continuum of allophones.[16] Within this tradition, development is possible, though most certainly not invariable or even usual: it is most characteristic of the nineteenth-century novel, though we seem to see it first attested in eighth-century BC epic, in the shape of Homer's Achilles.[17]

[13] Cf. Stern, *Realism*, 55. It is a familiar and obvious complication to any talk of 'reality' and the 'real' world that perceptions of realities vary, both between and within cultures, in response to which the twentieth century, beyond all others, has seen a series of intellectual challenges (mostly, broadly, postmodern: cf. above, p. 212 n. 8) to the very notion of 'reality' itself. For practical purposes, though, perceptions invited and focused by a work of literature (a process which significant literature of all ages has always involved: it is part of what we mean by calling literature itself 'challenging') are hardly affected. A more than usually comprehensive survey of the postmodern (etc.) positions in question is provided by Brooke-Rose, *Rhetoric*, 3–11.

[14] *Poet.* xv; see Halliwell, *Aristotle's Poetics*, 159–65.

[15] It is regrettably common to find the capacity 'to develop and change' virtually equated with 'character' *per se*, as by K. Newman, *Shakespeare's Rhetoric of Comic Character* (New York 1985) 1.

[16] On which see e.g. M. L. Samuels, *Linguistic Evolution* (Cambridge 1972) 126.

[17] See Silk, *Iliad*, 83–96.

Aristophanic Old Comedy does not properly belong to this tradition. You cannot, for instance, plausibly respond to Euripides' vulgarism by saying, 'Euripides says *this*—*that* tells us something about Euripides.' It tells us something about the given episode in the play and something about Aristophanes' mode of presenting his versions of human beings, but not strictly anything about a particular specimen of humanity. The same goes for (say) Dicaeopolis' sudden word-coinages or sudden bursts of paratragedy at the beginning of *Acharnians* or his oscillation between the tragic and a more immediate point of reference in his great self-apologia (497–9):

> *Condemn me not,* you in the audience,
> *If, whiles I am a beggar,* among us Athenians
> I talk affairs of state in a comedy.

In these passages, and in innumerable others like them, one figure in an Aristophanic play is the carrier for different, and—in realist terms—incompatible, linguistic idioms. What needs to be insisted on now is that such linguistic assemblages necessarily militate against our taking their carriers as realist figures in the sense given. Furthermore, it is not only discontinuities of stylistic register or tonal level which have this effect. Many jokes are precisely (as we say) 'out of character'—both in the sense that the particular kind of joke is less than 'appropriate' to the character in question and in the sense that any kind of joking seems inappropriate, coming from that character, at the moment in question. There are various reasons why Aristophanes (or we in the audience) might want to have Dionysus called 'son of Juice' in *Frogs* 22, but what possible reason could Dionysus himself have for representing himself—ostensibly to his slave—in this way and at this time? And the same is certainly true of all those many moments of 'metatheatrical' disruption that we tend to categorize as breaches of dramatic illusion, from Dicaeopolis' switches from character to actor (*Acharnians* 497)[18]—

> Condemn me not, you in the audience—

[18] And from actor to playwright, as at *Ach.* 502 (*οὐ γάρ με νῦν γε διαβαλεῖ Κλέων*: above, p. 40). For a different kind of categorization, see G. A. H. Chapman, 'Some notes on dramatic illusion in Aristophanes', *AJPh* 104 (1983) 1–23.

to Xanthias' query at the start of *Frogs* (1):

> Shall I tell them one of the usual jokes, master . . . ?

There are, it is true, characters in Aristophanic Old Comedy that seem to lend themselves better than others to a realist interpretation. Take Strepsiades in *Clouds*, up to his eyes in debt because of his family's extravagance. He is in many ways a type, a recognizable type, in opposition to his equally typical son Pheidippides. The son is a corruptible, extravagant young urban sophisticate (1399–1405):

ΦΕ. ὡς ἡδὺ καινοῖς πράγμασιν καὶ δεξιοῖς ὁμιλεῖν,
καὶ τῶν καθεστώτων νόμων ὑπερφρονεῖν δύνασθαι.
ἐγὼ γάρ, ὅτε μὲν ἱππικῇ τὸν νοῦν μόνῃ προσεῖχον,
οὐδ' ἂν τρί' εἰπεῖν ῥήμαθ' οἷός τ' ἦν πρὶν ἐξαμαρτεῖν.
νυνὶ δ', ἐπειδή μ' οὑτοσὶ τούτων ἔπαυσεν αὐτός,
γνώμαις δὲ λεπταῖς καὶ λόγοις ξύνειμι καὶ μερίμναις,
οἶμαι διδάξειν ὡς δίκαιον τὸν πατέρα κολάζειν.

PH. How nice to be *au fait* with clever and chic things,
And have the chance to sneer at traditional values!
When all that I could think about was racing,
I couldn't say two words without a howler.
But now that Socrates has put an end to all that,
And brought me round to subtlety and logic,
I think I'll prove it's right to hit your father.[19]

The father who duly falls victim to this assault is a thrifty, crude old peasant, scheming but not brainy, and deeply conservative:

> Once I had a charming rustic life . . .
> (43)
>
> Smelling of rough wine . . .
> (50)
>
> I'm so shook up inside I want to fart . . .
> (293)

Accordingly, his flirtation with the new order is merely opportunist—

[19] Translators (including myself at 'People', 157) offer 'I think I *can* prove'. Ph.'s proposition is actually more airily assertive.

If I can beat my debts
And make men think me
Bold, glib, confident, cavalier . . .
(443–5)—

and bound to be short-lived (1476–7):

ὡς ἐμαινόμην ἄρα,
ὅτ' ἐξέβαλλον τοὺς θεοὺς διὰ Σωκράτη.

How mad I was,
To cast the gods aside—for Socrates.

It is not difficult to list the leading characteristics of the two figures (in this instance they are inseparably matters of status and temperament), or to see how, with Strepsiades in particular, actions and words are aligned to each other: how they are evocative, that is, of various character-traits *as a continuum.* The old man's coarse language, for instance, is suggestive of an earthy background *and* of a certain intellectual mediocrity *and* of a fundamental antipathy to the Socratic Enlightenment. All three characteristics, accordingly, are shown to belong together, so that when Strepsiades, in bed and anxious to practise intellectualizing at Socrates' behest, is asked to come up with an idea (733–4)—

ΣΩ. *ἔχεις τι;*
ΣΤ. *μὰ Δί' οὐ δῆτ' ἔγωγ'.*
ΣΩ. *οὐδὲν πάνυ;*
ΣΤ. *οὐδέν γε, πλὴν ἢ τὸ πέος ἐν τῇ δεξιᾷ.*

SO. Got anything yet?
ST. Not yet.
SO. Nothing at all?
ST. Only a handful of cock—

we have no difficulty in construing *this* buffoonery as a natural corollary of *this* character's particular make-up.

Then again, Strepsiades has his individual features, from an indiscriminate fondness for diminutives—

Φειδιππίδη, Φειδιππίδιον
Pheidippides! Pheidippidesy!

ἴθι νυν κατάβηθ', ὦ Σωκρατίδιον, ὡς ἐμέ
Please, Socratesy, come down to my level![20]—

[20] *Nub.* 80, 237; so 132, 223, 746; cf. Sommerstein on 80.

to a kind of mean-spirited intransigence that once robbed him of due pleasure in his fancy wife (51–2)—

> She smells of perfume, powder, deep kissing,
> Extravagance—

and now allows him to derive an un-comedy-like satisfaction from the prospect of terminally confounding his enemies (1505–6):

> —*ἐγὼ δὲ κακοδαίμων γε κατακαυθήσομαι.*
> —*τί γὰρ μαθόντες τοὺς θεοὺς ὑβρίζετε;*
>
> —And what of me? I'll be burned alive!
> —So what made you do insult to the gods?[21]

Furthermore, Strepsiades even begins to develop. He learns from experience. He sees his past in a new perspective, and is therefore able to identify what went before as his mistake ('How mad I was', 1476), like (say) Cnemon in *Dyscolus* or Creon in *Antigone*.[22] These are real, if minimal instances of development. They are distinct, for instance, from the differential revelation of character we encounter in *Bacchae* with Pentheus, who begins as strident autocrat and ends as susceptible psychopath, but (we infer) was actually ('really') both all the time. The development of a Strepsiades, a Cnemon, or a Creon, of course, is slight compared with the development of an Isabel Archer:

> Madame Merle was already so present to her vision that her appearance in the flesh was like suddenly, and rather awfully, seeing a painted picture move. Isabel had been thinking all day of her falsity, her audacity, her ability, her probable suffering . . . She pretended not even to smile, and though Isabel saw that she was more than ever playing a part, it seemed to her that on the whole the wonderful woman had never been so natural.[23]

Such a complex response as Isabel's here, with its intricate mixture of positive and negative feelings, presupposes a fully explored personal history, which presupposes, in turn, a development over a substantial period of fictional time, even (as with James's novel) a period of years. Full development, one might say,

[21] Un-comedy-like, not in its harshness (one need think only of *Eq.* 976, *ἢν Κλέων ἀπόληται*) but in its moralizing religiosity: cf. below, pp. 352 ff. 1506 has a religious-archaic ring (and a tragic-compatible rhythm). On the 'burning alive' see below, p. 360 with n. 18.

[22] Men. *Dysc.* 713, Soph. *Ant.* 1272.

[23] Henry James, *The Portrait of a Lady*, ch. 52.

requires at least the time-span of a Shakespearean tragedy (or an *Iliad*)—the span sufficient, for instance, to show us a 'progress' like Macbeth's from a guilty recklessness ('come what come may', I. iii; 'If it were done when 'tis done, then 'twere well | It were done quickly', I. vii) to the several stages of moral dissolution that follow ('I am afraid to think what I have done', II. i; 'What man dare, I dare', III. iv; 'I have almost forgot the taste of fears', V. v). Greek tragedy (and Greek New Comedy too) tends, instead, to centre on an expanded moment of crisis and the magnification of an individual's response to it. Such patterns, nevertheless, are obviously conducive to the presentation of character-development, however embryonic; and it is symptomatic that they should be as generally uncharacteristic of Aristophanic comedy as they are characteristic of Greek tragedy.

The first clear approaches to the world of New Comedy, of course, are to be found in Aristophanes himself. The portrayal of Strepsiades and his son in *Clouds* is, perhaps, the fruit of an early, incomplete attempt at comic realist portrayal.[24] At all events, there is little sign of any immediate inclination on Aristophanes' part to repeat the experiment, nor of any tidy development towards a realist norm. As far as presentation of character is concerned, *Frogs* in 405 gives an impression not very different from *Acharnians* twenty years before, though the two extant plays from the fourth century make it clear that in this area, as in others, the establishment of realist norms is under way. The grumbling slave at the beginning of *Plutus*[25] belongs to the new ethos, as does a good deal of the depiction of ordinary men and women (albeit in a profoundly unordinary situation) in *Ecclesiazusae*.

Take, for instance, Blepyrus' interrogation of Praxagora when she eventually comes home with—inexplicably—his clothes. Here we have a coherently realist reference to a familiar situation, with suspicious husband and deceiving wife, though the deceit is not in fact at all what he assumes it to be (*Ecclesiazusae* 520–30):

ΒΛ. *αὔτη, πόθεν ἥκεις, Πραξαγόρα;*
ΠΡ. *τί δ', ὦ μέλε,*
σοι τοῦθ';
ΒΛ. *ὅ τι μοι τοῦτ' ἐστίν; ὡς εὐηθικῶς.*

[24] On the 'realism' of *Nub.*, see further below, pp. 357–8.
[25] Above, pp. 24–6.

ΠΡ. οὔ τοι παρά του μοιχοῦ γε φήσεις.

ΒΛ. οὐκ ἴσως

ἑνός γε.

ΠΡ. καὶ μὴν βασανίσαι τουτί γέ σοι

ἔξεστι.

ΒΛ. πῶς;

ΠΡ. εἰ τῆς κεφαλῆς ὄζω μύρου.

ΒΛ. τί δ'; οὐχὶ βινεῖται γυνὴ κἄνευ μύρου;

ΠΡ. οὐ δῆτα, τάλαν, ἔγωγε.

ΒΛ. πῶς οὖν ὄρθριον

ᾤχου σιωπῇ θοἰμάτιον λαβοῦσά μου;

ΠΡ. γυνή μέ τις νύκτωρ ἑταίρα καὶ φίλη

μετεπέμψατ' ὠδίνουσα.

ΒΛ. κᾆτ' οὐκ ἦν ἐμοὶ

φράσασαν ἰέναι;

B. Ah, Praxagora—and where have *you* been?

P. What's

It to you?

B. What's it to me? Stupid question![26]

P. Don't panic—not with another man.

B. Maybe

With more than one.

P. You can tell it's not

Like that.

B. How?

P. Do I smell of perfume?

B. Don't women ever get shagged without their perfume?

P. Not me, I'm sorry to say.

B. Well, what

Made you sneak out so early with my coat?

P. A woman, just a friend, in labour,

Sent for me in the night.

B. So why

Not tell me before you went?

Notwithstanding the possibility that an Aristophanic discontinuity may (even in late Aristophanes) be awaiting us at any moment, the excerpt smells realist through and through. The decisive factor for the diagnosis is not the ordinariness of the conversation

[26] Or perhaps εὐηθικῶς = 'how good-natured' (like our 'charming!'), used ironically. Not 'how simple can you get?' (Sommerstein), where 'simple' would have to mean *faux-naïve* to make sense. One can be ἀστεῖος καὶ εὐήθης at the same time (Pl. *Rep*. 349b).

or its ambience—though it would indeed be on such grounds that realism would commonly be ascribed to such a passage. It is, rather, the complete consistency of the particular ordinariness implied by the questions and answers and, correspondingly, of the relationship presupposed. The interest we are invited to take in the passage has a great deal to do with the Aristotelian line of thought: what would *such* a person do and say, how would *such* a person react, in this situation.[27] One notes the precision with which a restricted (essentially conversational) range of language, articulated in verse so intensively enjambed that the sense of formal parallelism is minimal, is used to plot the speakers' successive reactions and to convey the impression of a particular ongoing relationship and a particular interpersonal past behind the details of the encounter. One notes, in particular, the short step from his 'stupid' to her pre-emptive 'don't panic'; his irritable change of tack ('well, what made you . . . ?') after his failure to get any satisfaction from his foray into coarseness;[28] and the psychology of that coarseness itself, which in *this* passage—in marked contrast to our *Thesmophoriazusae* paradigm—readily suggests a speaker's *natural* exasperation and, behind it, a less-than-idyllic marriage lived on a less-than-heroic level of daily transactions.

Different though they may be from Praxagora and Blepyrus, most, if not all, of the characters in Aristophanes' earlier plays possess some semblance of realist continuity at least some of the time, and some of them (like Strepsiades) *might* be construed as belonging to the realist tradition *tout court*. Overall, however, these characters are better seen as belonging to an alternative mode of representation which we can call *recreative*, and whose distinctive and essential feature is discontinuity, linguistic or otherwise. The name 'recreative' is doubly appropriate: specifically, because Aristophanic people have (or are given) the capacity to recreate themselves anew; and generally, because the label tends to suggest that these people do enjoy some relationship with 'reality', but a less straightforward one than the mimetic relationship implied by 'realist' (we might provisionally say that 'recreative' suggests an alternative reality or else an alternative *to*

[27] Arist. *Poet.* IX, XV.

[28] He fails not least because her answer dryly implies his sexual inadequacy: cf. Sommerstein on 524–6.

reality as ordinarily perceived).[29] On the level of language, as we have seen, a mobile-discontinuous style is different in kind from a stable one. We can now add: that discontinuous style is analogous to discontinuous character, as well as one main cause of it; that there is a profound connection between stability (in whatever sphere) and realism; and that discontinuity in a literary work is a decisive indicator of non-realism wherever it occurs. In so far as character is concerned, we can also say, in particular, that just as a mobile-discontinuous style may well present a stable appearance for a given sequence, so recreative-discontinuous characters may seem to be operative on an equivalent premise to realist characters *for a time*. Yet sooner or later it will be apparent that the necessary consistency is lacking; and this lack will not impinge as some incidental or accidental omission, but as a characteristic and distinctive feature of discontinuous literature *per se*.[30]

[29] In 'People', 159–73, I called non-realist characterization 'imagist', a term with two advantages: it makes A's mode of presenting character sound distinctive (which it is), and it suggests the connection with an important technique associated, or associable, with discontinuous style. I now think these advantages are outweighed by two less helpful implications: that there is some special similarity between recreative character and imagery (this point was made to me by Christopher Pelling, editor of the *Characterization* volume, in which 'People' appeared), and that, in particular, the relation between recreative character and stability in characterization is somehow equivalent to the relation between the vehicle and tenor of an image (my own remarks in 'People', 159, tend to encourage this idea), with the result that stability (like a tenor) comes to seem a primary norm, even for A. That is not the case, and on this ground, above all, I prefer to withdraw 'imagist' as a general descriptive term—with due apologies to those who have thought it worth taking up (e.g. E. W. Handley, 'Aristophanes and the generation gap', in Sommerstein, *Tragedy, Comedy and the Polis*, 427). The association with images is now restricted to certain particular types of character (below, pp. 240 ff.).

[30] This theoretical distinction between realist and recreative-discontinuous characterization is my own. Various critics and theorists have suggested there is a tendency towards discontinuous characterization in *comedy in general*: e.g. Frye, *Anatomy*, 170; and notably Pirandello, who argues that serious writing 'composes' a character 'and will want to represent him as consistent in every action', whereas 'the humorist . . . will *decompose* the character . . . and . . . enjoys representing him in his incongruities' (*On Humor*, 143). Discontinuity in Aristophanic characterization has been discussed, but without what I take to be the necessary emphasis, e.g. by Dover, *Aristophanic Comedy*, 59–65. Remarkably, theories of character as a whole tend to ignore the fact that there is such a thing as discontinuous presentation at all. This is the case with such diverse and wide-ranging discussions as C. C. Walcutt, *Man's Changing Mask: Modes and Methods of Characterization in Fiction* (Minneapolis 1966); P. Hamon, 'Pour un statut sémiologique du personnage', in R. Barthes *et al.* (eds.), *Poétique du récit* (Paris 1977) 115–80; S. Freeman, 'Character in a coherent fiction', *Philosophy and Literature* 7 (1983) 196–212; Frow, 'Spectacle binding'; S. Chatman, 'Characters and narrators';

In other words, the various discontinuities that we began by glancing at in *Thesmophoriazusae* are all instances of the same fundamental discontinuous tendency: discontinuities between Mnesilochus the docile bumbler and Mnesilochus the inventive *poseur*, between clever Euripides and Euripides so witless that he accepts Mnesilochus' unlikely offer, between Euripides the well spoken and Euripides the suddenly obscene, between the women as pious worshippers and the same women as aggressive combatants of Euripides who (like Euripides himself) also turn suddenly obscene. And if, with such instances in mind but without realist preconceptions, we look back at Strepsiades in *Clouds*, we will readily find equivalents there too. Strepsiades may look like a realist figure much of the time, but on reflection we will probably agree that there is, for instance, no plausible continuum between the contemporary buffoonery of 'only a handful of cock' (734) and the deep and quite archaic earnestness of 'how mad I was | To cast the gods aside' (1476–7).[31] It is not that no single individual in real life could simultaneously house the contrasting qualities these two remarks imply, but that there is nothing—nothing at all—in the presentation of Strepsiades in the play that could explain the coexistence.

The continuous characters of the realist tradition do, or can, develop: they do, or can do, so by gradual movement between their particular traits. The recreative characters of Aristophanes are fundamentally different. They have the power to switch, to be transformed. That is: when they change, they change abruptly and, perhaps, entirely—like the women at the Thesmophoria, dropping their respectability and picking it up again; like the clever Euripides, abruptly accepting Mnesilochus' offer to help; or

U. Margolin, 'The doer and the deed: action as a basis for characterization in narrative'; C. Gill, 'The question of character and personality in Greek tragedy' (the last four essays in *Poetics Today* 7 (1986) 189–273); A. Sinfield, *Faultlines* (Oxford 1992) 52–79. Structuralist-semiotic attempts to 'dissolve' character into 'text' are no exception (see e.g. J. Weinsheimer, 'Theory of character: *Emma*', *Poetics Today* 1 (1980) 195); cf. Hamon, Margolin, Frow, *supra*: *all* character is simply subjected to a common reinterpretative principle. Margolin, however, briefly considers the phenomenon of texts (e.g. the *nouveau roman*) which frustrate expectations of 'a unified stable constellation' of '[character] traits or trait-clusters' (op. cit., 207). But it remains the case that 'no-one has yet succeeded in constructing a complete and coherent theory of character': M. Bal, *Narratology*, tr. C. van Boheemen (Toronto 1985) 80.

[31] On the archaic character of the latter sequence, cf. below, pp. 352–4.

like the stooge Mnesilochus, suddenly assuming the role of hero by making that offer. In short, the realist tradition, at its extreme, permits character-development, whereas the Aristophanic mode of representation involves, at *its* extreme, a binary principle: instead of development, it permits inversion or reversal. Recreative presentation, it will be gathered, allows for a merely sequential view of time. In the realist tradition, by contrast, time is perceived as a (literally) *con*sequential matter, as an Aristotelian process of events that follow the laws of 'probability or necessity'.[32]

The point about time is far-reaching. For the recreative character, things past of course exist and have a due significance, but it is, essentially, a symbolic significance. Consider the memory of time past with which the *Wasps* chorus confronts Philocleon, captive inside his own home (354–7):

ΧΟ. *μέμνησαι δῆθ' ὅτ' ἐπὶ στρατιᾶς κλέψας ποτὲ τοὺς ὀβελίσκους*
ἵεις σαυτὸν κατὰ τοῦ τείχους ταχέως, ὅτε Νάξος ἑάλω;
ΦΙ. *οἶδ'· ἀλλὰ τί τοῦτ'; οὐδὲν γὰρ τοῦτ' ἐστὶν ἐκείνῳ προσόμοιον.*
ἥβων γὰρ κἀδυνάμην κλέπτειν . . .

CH. Remember, in the army once, when Naxos fell,
Stealing skewers to get down the wall?
PH. I know, I know. But this is all so different:
I could steal then—I was young . . .

In realist terms, the evocation has an oddly take-it-or-leave-it quality: it is both vivid, in its (admittedly bizarre) specificity, and quite unverifiable, being so distant and distinct from anything else in Philocleon's immediate world. It is noteworthy that the more realist-looking Strepsiades in *Clouds* has a more realist-looking past to match, with reminiscences that relate directly to the family situation the action of the play is concerned with, from the fatal marriage which is the ultimate source of his debts (51–2)—

She smelled of perfume, powder, deep kissing,
Extravagance—

[32] Arist. *Poet.* VII–VIII. To dissociate Aristophanes and development is not to ascribe a non-developmental tendency to comedy as a whole, as Langer did in *Feeling and Form*, 335–6. Different again are the 'semantic reversals' which are reasonably taken to be a sign of inner 'psychic process' (i.e. of one form of realist characterization) in Shakespearean comedy by Newman, *Shakespeare's Rhetoric*, 11.

to the trivia of the son's early years, recollection of which will, he hopes, help to persuade Socrates to take him on as a pupil (877–9):

> *ἀμέλει, δίδασκε· θυμόσοφός ἐστιν φύσει.*
> *εὐθύς γε τοι παιδάριον ὂν τυννουτονὶ*
> *ἔπλαττεν ἔνδον οἰκίας ναῦς τ' ἔγλυφεν . . .*
>
> Don't worry—teach him: he's a gifted boy.
> When he was only, you know, really little,
> He used to make toy houses and carve boats . . .

In the recreative world, by contrast, the mundane details of ordinary life are as liable to change as the characters they are attached to. So Philocleon, it seems, has lost his teeth at some unspecified time in the past—but suddenly 'becomes' sufficiently toothful again to be able to gnaw right through a net his son has put over the house.[33] It is as if time exists effectively as multiples of momentary instants, each of which has an absolute, inviolate force, and within each of which the whole of life may be symbolically negotiated.

In any substantial work of realist fiction, narrative or dramatic, the characters will engage our interest—and convince us of their (as we like to call it) reality—chiefly through the revelation, or exploration, of their continuous selves; and such revelations or explorations are provided, above all, by their interactions with others. This is the case across the spectrum—from the elaborate engagements in a Henry James novel to (say) the stylized pairings of Sophocles' heroic Antigone with timid sister Ismene, with affronted autocrat Creon, with elusive chorus, and so on. In much realist writing, we feel able to discuss such interactions in terms of personal relationships, and to recognize their force and reality in (it may be) even a single charged moment. Take one such moment in Sophocles' *Oedipus Tyrannus* (726–7):

> *οἷόν μ' ἀκούσαντ' ἀρτίως ἔχει, γύναι,*
> *ψυχῆς πλάνημα κἀνακίνησις φρενῶν.*
>
> Lady, what restlessness of mind is on me,
> What wandering of thought, hearing these words.

When Oedipus says that to his wife, we do feel not only the continuum of past and present in this consciousness of memories,

[33] *Vesp.* 164–5, 367–71.

but also the vibration of a man's inner life with his woman. Along such lines, the confrontation of Praxagora and Blepyrus in *Ecclesiazusae* may betoken a 'real' (if limited and unedifying) relationship, but such is not the norm in the earlier comedies.[34] In *Peace*, Trygaeus, *en route* to heaven on his dung-beetle, has a touching exchange with his young daughter, followed by a quick word to the audience (146–53):

ΠΑ. ἐκεῖνο τήρει, μὴ σφαλεὶς καταρρυῇς
ἐντεῦθεν, εἶτα χωλὸς ὢν Εὐριπίδῃ
λόγον παράσχῃς καὶ τραγῳδία γένῃ.
ΤΡ. ἐμοὶ μελήσει ταῦτα γ'. ἀλλὰ χαίρετε.
ὑμεῖς δέ γ', ὑπὲρ ὧν τοὺς πόνους ἐγὼ πονῶ,
μὴ βδεῖτε μηδὲ χέζεθ' ἡμερῶν τριῶν·
ὡς εἰ μετέωρος οὗτος ὢν ὀσφρήσεται,
κατωκάρα ῥίψας με βουκολήσεται.

D. Mind you don't slip off and fall
All the way down and end up crippled,
And give Euripides ideas—and turn into a tragedy.
T. I'll watch myself. And to you all—farewell.
Now this heroic struggle is for you;
So please, no shitting or farting for the next three days,
In case the beetle gets a whiff in mid-air,
Dives to graze and throws me off head first.

We are surely in no danger of mistaking the temper of this confrontation. It is easier for an Aristophanic father to be transformed into a tragedy than to evince a personal relationship or any of the other possible corollaries of the realist continuum.

In Aristophanic Old Comedy we get used (whether we admit it or not) to reading the characters in largely behavioural terms: we concentrate on their words and actions at the expense of their minds and thoughts. In so far as they are discontinuous beings, can they actually be said to have minds and thoughts? In realist representation, characters are assumed to have minds and thoughts which work like those of real people in real life. Real people have experiences, whether *we* know about them or not; they have habits that imply responses to those experiences; and in general they have memories of their experiences. Fictional people,

[34] It is no coincidence that on the one occasion when we see a married couple at any length in the earlier plays, the Myrrhine–Cinesias scene at *Lys.* 845–979, feeling is located purely in the physical.

necessarily, have experiences only when we know that they do, and responses and memories only when these are made public in some way. Within this limitation, however, the characters of realist fiction impinge on us as sentient beings: so far as we see and know them, they act from their minds (experiences, responses, memories), and their behaviour is referable to their minds. The question arises: are we to make any such reference with recreative characters, and if so, when and why? Picture Mnesilochus taking his decision to help Euripides, and it seems obvious that such a character has a mental capacity. Think of Xanthias' anti-illusionary question to Dionysus at the start of *Frogs*, and it is hard to see what sort of experiences, responses, or memories such a being needs to be, or can be, credited with.

The fact is that, like the moments of time within which the recreative characters seem to live, the mentalities we seem to perceive in them have an instant quality. It is as if their particular actions or moments do imply minds or mental contexts, without, however, any corresponding presumption that the same mind or the same context will be implied at some other moment of time.[35] They have motives, they have feelings, which may be strong (think of Dicaeopolis or Dionysus), yet (from Dicaeopolis' hatred of the war to Dionysus' quest for a poet) these motives and feelings tend to lack any personal history—as those of Homer's Achilles or Molière's Monsieur Jourdain or Sophocles' Antigone or (needless to say) Henry James's Isabel Archer *or* (the significant exception) those of Strepsiades have a personal history.

With Strepsiades—married up, *therefore* in debt, *therefore* desperate, *therefore* willing to try even Socrates, *therefore* ready to exploit his own son—compare and contrast Dionysus and Dicaeopolis. When Dionysus sets off for Hades to fetch a dramatic poet—in the first instance, Euripides—and bring him back to Athens, his motive reflects a timeless Dionysiac interest in the issue (because Dionysus is a god of drama), but nothing in his own background, if background means contingent history. *He* wants a dead poet for the same reason as anyone would: because all the good ones are dead. And *he* wants Euripides, only because everyone wants Euripides: Euripides is the natural popular

[35] My provisional answer to a provisional question I posed in 'People', 171–2 (and to the comments on it by Pelling, *Characterization*, 252).

choice.[36] When Dicaeopolis takes the stage, brooding about his losses as a dispossessed Attic farmer, he (we must assume) is like any or all of the many real-life farmers of the 420s who were forced by war to seek refuge in the city (*Acharnians* 32–3):

> ἀποβλέπων εἰς τὸν ἀγρόν, εἰρήνης ἐρῶν,
> στυγῶν μὲν ἄστυ, τὸν δ' ἐμὸν δῆμον ποθῶν
>
> Looking out at the country, craving peace,
> Loathing the town, longing for my parish.

We know of no personal factor to help explain why he (unlike, say, the farmer Dercetes that we meet later in the play) has decided to *do* something about it—let alone any personal factor to help explain how *he* came to think of a one-man peace.[37]

Lysistrata, a different sort of peacemaker, is another revealing case. When she prepares to arbitrate between the warring Greeks, the chorus in her play salute her as 'bravest of all women' and call on her to summon up an impressive set of contrasting qualities (*Lysistrata* 1108–9):

> δεῖ δὴ νυνί σε γενέσθαι
> δεινήν, μαλακήν, ἀγαθήν, φαύλην, σεμνήν, ἀγανήν, πολύπειρον.
>
> Show yourself
> Fierce and gentle, noble and mean, strict and mellow,
> A woman of the world.

What kind of personal background must this woman have had that would make the possession of such a combination of capacities comprehensible?[38] The question has evidently occurred to Aristophanes himself. In Lysistrata's response, he makes her say (1124–7):

> ἐγὼ γυνὴ μέν εἰμι, νοῦς δ' ἔνεστί μοι.
> αὐτὴ δ' ἐμαυτῆς οὐ κακῶς γνώμης ἔχω,
> τοὺς δ' ἐκ πατρός τε καὶ γεραιτέρων λόγους
> πολλοὺς ἀκούσασ' οὐ μεμούσωμαι κακῶς.

[36] All the good poets dead: *Ran.* 71–97. Popular choice: *Ran.* 771–83, where Eur. is the first choice of even the majority in Hades.

[37] Dercetes, *Ach.* 1018–36. The arbitrariness of his decision on any 'personal' level by itself makes it clear why the kind of interpretation of Dic. offered by H. P. Foley, 'Tragedy and politics in Aristophanes' *Acharnians*', *JHS* 108 (1988) 33–47, is inappropriate (see e.g. Foley, ibid., 38, 'deliberately engages . . . ', and cf. below, pp. 296–7 n. 86).

[38] The interesting speculation that A based Lysistrata on a historical figure, a priestess Lysimache, has no bearing on the question: even if the speculation were convincing (cf. Henderson, *Lysistrata*, pp. xxxviii–xl), it is no part of the play.

I am a woman, but I have a mind.
I am not badly off for brains myself,
Nor am I badly schooled, for I have heard
My father talk with other older men.[39]

The evocation of domestic background, though slight, seems telling. Nevertheless, any fleeting impression that in realist fashion we are actually being told something—even something so slight—about our heroine is quickly dispelled by the realization these are, suddenly, tragic verses,[40] articulating (as it might be) the condition of some tragic Nausicaa and her memories of the sights and sounds of Alcinous' palace. It is in tragedy (*inter alia*) that characters have telling backgrounds; and if Lysistrata appears for a moment to have had one herself, we can only assume that it was in a separate tragic existence into which, recreatively, she has been—for an instant—transported.

It is, simply, characteristic that—in a realist sense—Aristophanes' recreative characters have no effective past. The paradigm here is Mnesilochus in *Thesmophoriazusae*. He is, unquestionably, a figure that—in realist terms, again—an audience knows very little about, with a background so tenuous that we do not even know (or frankly care) how he is related in family terms to Euripides.[41] Within the play, the few lines that purport to allude to his personal history are either inconsequentially unspecific, as with Euripides' instructions to him (1204–6),

σὺ δ' ὅπως ἀνδρικῶς,
ὅταν λυθῇς τάχιστα, φεύξει καὶ τενεῖς
ὡς τὴν γυναῖκα καὶ τὰ παιδί' οἴκαδε.

[39] Henderson ad loc. glosses 1125 as 'I am of an age to have a worthwhile opinion', but the Greek says nothing of any 'age'. Line 1126 surely implies conversation *between* father and elders, not two separate categories of talk (as if that were in any case likely).

[40] 1124 = Eur. fr. 483 (from *Wise Melanippe*). The source of 1125–7 ('quasi-tragic in rhythm and language': Henderson ad loc.) is unknown; cf. Rau, *Paratragodia*, 201.

[41] We have no reason to know that 'Mnesilochus' is his name, of course (above, p. 208 n. 4). The relationship to Euripides is referred to with the vague word κηδεστής ('relative by marriage') at *Thes.* 74, 210, 584, 1165. It should not be assumed that Mn. necessarily corresponded to a real relation of the real Eur., or (if he did) that the original audience would have known that and known who he 'really' was: cf. S. Halliwell, 'Aristophanic satire', in C. Rawson (ed.), *English Satire and the Satiric Tradition* (Oxford 1984) 6–20, and 'Comedy and publicity in the society of the polis', in Sommerstein, *Tragedy, Comedy and the Polis*, 321–40.

> And when you're free, run like a man and make
> Straight for your wife and kids at home,

or else explosively instantial, as with Euripides' *bon mot* about Agathon (35):

> Well, at least you must have shagged him—maybe not consciously.

And if Mnesilochus has no effective past, he has, likewise, no effective future. After half the play in captivity, he is now at last free to 'make straight for his wife and kids'. The very unrelatedness of this domestic detail to anything else we know of Mnesilochus, allied to its bland lack of specificity, does nothing to encourage us to envisage this character in continuing existence outside the play, and everything to put any such imaginative activity out of our heads.

Insistence on the common recreative status of a Mnesilochus, a Euripides, and a Dionysus (it might be objected) privileges the recreative/realist distinction at the expense of other significant categorizations which (it might be felt) in practice are liable to override it. Some of Aristophanes' characters—to begin at the pragmatic end—are of course historical figures. That is, they bear the names of, and some relation to, non-fictional individuals, usually, though not always, of Aristophanes' own day: Lamachus in *Acharnians*, Aeschylus and Euripides in *Frogs*, Agathon and Euripides in *Thesmophoriazusae*, the scientist Meton in *Birds*, Socrates in *Clouds*. Most of these figures are male—but then so are most of Aristophanes' characters (though much less markedly his choruses), especially in the earlier plays. Various other figures, in any event, bear a similar relation to beings from mythology and religion: Dionysus in *Frogs*, Iris, Prometheus, Poseidon, and Heracles in *Birds*. Some belong to a much-discussed category of allegory or personification. Many figures, often unnamed in their plays, are definable, at least up to a point, in terms of their status. One thinks of the various slaves and 'informers' (*sukophantai*), of the Spartan herald in *Lysistrata*, of the corpse in *Frogs*—and the women in *Thesmophoriazusae*. These (as our discussion has indicated) are not always distinguished from the seemingly separate category of chorus members, who likewise are sometimes named, but mostly not. Finally, we have the category to which most important figures belong: initiators of action. Many of these figures have special names, signifying some allegiance: Trygaeus ('Harvester'), Dicaeopolis ('Citizen Right'), Lysistrata ('Disbander of Armies'), the Sausage-Seller Agoracritus ('Chosen by the Assembly'),[42] Philocleon ('Love-Cleon), Bdelycleon ('Hate-Cleon').

As a matter of fact, these categories are imperfect, if only (though not only) because in practice they overlap or otherwise frustrate even their plain definition. 'Anonymous' status-defined figures may recall specific real-life individuals, as the two slaves who introduce *Knights* recall the generals Nicias and Demosthenes.[43] Initiators may have more ordinary names, like Strepsiades in *Clouds*—though his name is invested with significance (as 'Twister') during the play.[44] Alternatively, initiators may also be historical or mythological figures: Euripides in *Thesmophoriazusae*, Dionysus in *Frogs*. Then again, not only are various prominent figures resistant to classification, from the strictly anonymous Mnesilochus in *Thesmophoriazusae* to the Hoopoe in *Birds*; above all, as befits recreative figures, apparent status or allegiance may not be permanent: Philocleon has no Cleonic affiliation by the end of *Wasps*, while in *Clouds* the reformed—or rather *re*-formed—Strepsiades is no 'Twister' but quite straight.

It is true at least, though, that even these rough and ready categories do help to make it clear how Aristophanes' later practice changes. In *Ecclesiazusae* and *Plutus*—that is, in anticipation of the pattern familiar in New Comedy—the category of status-defined figures expands to include certain of the main characters, who are now invested with typical names, as for instance the slave Xanthias was in *Frogs*, and as now the old men Chremes and Blepyrus are in *Ecclesiazusae* and their counterpart Chremylus in *Plutus*. These latter figures are clearly types. So too, up to a point, are Strepsiades and Pheidippides in *Clouds*. And so too, one might say, are many of the status-defined figures in Aristophanic comedy in general, who (in accordance with their status) follow patterns of behaviour laid down by their defining

[42] Sausage-Seller's own interpretation of his name is different: *Eq.* 1258 (see Neil, Sommerstein, ad loc.).

[43] 'Recall', in the original performance, would obviously be partly dependent on the slaves' appearance, notably their masks. See variously: Bowie, *Aristophanes*, 55 n. 44; MacDowell, *Aristophanes and Athens*, 87–8; W. Kraus, *Aristophanes' politische Komödien* (Vienna 1985) 115–19.

[44] *Nub.* 434, 1455 (on which see below, p. 355). Cf. Dover, *Clouds*, pp. xxv–xxvi.

labels: the informers behave like informers, the women in *Thesmophoriazusae* like women, the frogs like . . . But here as elsewhere, the fact of recreativity makes a vital difference. The identification of a character as a type (or, equally, as its opposite, 'an individual') is a realist identification which begs the question—in respect of Strepsiades, the women, the frogs, even the informers. And we cannot properly ask what Aristophanes' characters are like 'apart from' their recreativity, because their recreativity affects all of their being (or beings). The question, 'are these characters individuals or types?', is eminently discussible in respect of Menander, and it is discussible in respect of Aristophanes the more his characterization approximates to the Menandrian-realist. It is, therefore, a more appropriate, and a more meaningful, question to ask of Chremes and Blepyrus in *Ecclesiazusae* than it is of Strepsiades in *Clouds*, and a still less revealing question to ask of Philocleon in *Wasps* than it is of Strepsiades. Philocleon, a very special and remarkable recreator, is, no doubt, both an individual and a type at different times, perhaps even at the same time, but that formula is not illuminating: the important thing is his capacity to recreate.

In this connection it is instructive to note that various interpreters of Aristophanes, from Süss to McLeish, have sought to identify his characters with a neo-Aristotelian set of character-types derived from the *Ethics* and elsewhere: notably the *eirôn* (the dry wit, who understates himself), the *alazôn* (the pretender, who overstates himself), the *bômolokhos* (the buffoon).[45] What these attempts show is that the 'types' cannot be consistently equated with Aristophanes' *characters*, but may be equated with their *functions*. Beyond a certain point, in other words, the analysis is bound to resemble a Proppian analysis of narrative functions,[46] in which a given function may be seen to be transferred from one

[45] Arist. *EN* 2. 7, 4. 7–8, *EE* 3. 7, *Rhet.* 3. 18: see W. Süss, *De Personarum Antiquae Comoediae Usu et Origine* (Bonn 1905) and 'Zur Komposition der altattischen Komödie', *Rh. M.* 63 (1908) 12–38; K. McLeish, *The Theatre of Aristophanes* (London 1980) 53–6, 74–5. The three types occur as a set in *Tract. Coisl.*: see Janko, *Aristotle on Comedy*, 39, 216–18, 242. The Greek word *eirôn* focuses on a quality close to our 'disingenuity' (cf. Dover on *Nub.* 445), but can hardly be translated in such terms.

[46] See V. Propp, *Morphology of the Folktale*, tr. L. Scott (Bloomington 1958; Russian original publ. 1928). The point emerges clearly from G. M. Sifakis, 'On the structure of Aristophanic comedy', *JHS* 112 (1992) 123–39: see e.g. 133–6, headed 'Bearers of functions, characters and types'.

character to another. So whereas Mnesilochus, for instance, begins *Thesmophoriazusae* as the buffoon, in the later stages of the play the buffoon's function is transferred from Mnesilochus to the Scythian, while Mnesilochus himself acts as a sort of 'dry wit' in his speech at the woman's assembly, when he catalogues the vices of the sex from (purportedly) a woman's point of view. The transferability of such 'functions', however, is largely, if not entirely, a corollary of recreativity. The application of these types to the discussion of Aristophanes, therefore, leaves a plausible realist interpretation of his characters as unattainable as ever.

Any critical placing of Aristophanes' treatment of character must take into account some fundamental comparative data: first, that he is by no means the only creative figure in the Western literary tradition whose style has mobile and discontinuous qualities; and correlatively, that the recreative features of a Dicaeopolis or a Mnesilochus are not unique to characters in Aristophanic comedy. From Aristophanes' own day to the beginning of the modernist age, realism of some kind does indeed seem to dominate fictional writing. Yet the Western world still offers illuminating parallels to his recreative mode.

More precisely: outside Aristophanes,[47] the best examples of recreative presentation seem either to belong to the modern avant-garde or to be naïve—perhaps in the ordinary sense of that word, or else in Schiller's sense, whereby (say) Homer is naïve, and the word tends to imply *early*.[48] We do indeed find hints of a recreative sensibility in Homer, especially in the *Iliad*, where (with the notable exception of Achilles) characters have fixed qualities which they either live up to or fail to live up to, and where the prospect of any such failure is felt as a threat to—because a reversal of?—personal integrity. So Hector, besought by Andromache to hold back from the fighting where he will risk his life and her future, grants the validity of her fears but points to the constraints of public opinion *and his own nature* (6. 441–6):

> *ἦ καὶ ἐμοὶ τάδε πάντα μέλει, γύναι· ἀλλὰ μάλ' αἰνῶς*
> *αἰδέομαι Τρῶας καὶ Τρῳάδας ἑλκεσιπέπλους,*

[47] As elsewhere, I put to one side the question of usage in other Old Comedy poets.

[48] Friedrich Schiller, *Über naive und sentimentalische Dichtung*. There are also some surprising counter-examples of sophisticated pre-modern recreativity: the Duke in Shakespeare's *Measure for Measure* is one.

> *αἴ κε κακὸς ὣς νόσφιν ἀλυσκάζω πολέμοιο·*
> *οὐδέ με θυμὸς ἄνωγεν, ἐπεὶ μάθον ἔμμεναι ἐσθλὸς*
> *αἰεὶ καὶ πρώτοισι μετὰ Τρώεσσι μάχεσθαι,*
> *ἀρνύμενος πατρός τε μέγα κλέος ἠδ' ἐμὸν αὐτοῦ.*
>
> Woman, this is on my mind like yours.
> But I have too much awe for the men of Troy
> And the long-robed Trojan women to skulk away
> From battle like a coward. Nor does my heart
> Bid me do that; no, I have learned
> Always to fight among the leading men of Troy
> And win great glory for me and my father.

'Yes,' says Hector in effect, 'you are right: I *will* be killed. But what else can I—*being me*—do? *Ich kann nicht anders*.'[49] His obstinacy, however, is prompted not by any sort of Lutheran conscience, but by a consciousness that cannot conceive of—and is not conceived in terms of—a flexible response.

In classical Greek drama as we have it, recreative figuration is much more characteristic of comedy than of tragedy; but the 'progress' of comedy (in the fourth century), as of tragedy (in the fifth), is clearly towards the realist mode. If one is prepared to extrapolate backwards from that tendency, it might be conjectured that early ('naïve'?) drama, tragedy as well as comedy, contained various recreative elements. One likely context would be the chorus—the stylized speaking or (especially) singing group, which both forms of drama eventually found to be incompatible with their aspirations towards realism, and sought to eliminate. The Aristophanic chorus, certainly, is—still?—markedly recreative. In no extant Aristophanic comedy, in fact, 'does the chorus have a consistent and unalterable dramatic character'.[50] The women in *Thesmophoriazusae*—in or out of the chorus—actually constitute a modest specimen of group variability. The *Clouds* chorus switch from being suspect deities of Socrates to traditional spirits of vengeance, while their counterparts in *Wasps* begin as creaky old men, turn into fierce wasps, and end as earnest commentators on the action. At the end of *Frogs* the chorus appear to be earnest and patriotic Athenians; at an earlier stage in the proceedings they were religious, and (literally) other-

[49] 'There is nothing else I can do.' The reference is to Luther's speech at the Diet of Worms, 18 Apr. 1521.

[50] Sifakis, *Parabasis*, 32.

worldly, zealots; and at a still earlier stage they were the frogs of the title.[51] The chorus in *Peace*, as one of the play's editors observes, actually has 'four or five distinguishable identities' in the space of five hundred lines.[52] But in tragedy too the identity of the chorus is often—in realist terms—elusive: the 'Theban elders' in *Antigone*, with their cosmic perception of 'wonders' and their worldly deference to King Creon, are a classic case in point.[53] Outside the chorus, the recreative presence is chiefly visible in the dramatic experiments of Euripides. His *Medea*, for instance, reveals *both* the progressive realist who explores the woman's inner agonies about killing her children *and* the avant-garde anti-realist who offers us her transfiguration from oppressed victim to divine agent of vengeance at the end. By contrast, even the notorious self-contradiction of an Antigone or the propensity of an Ajax to say 'what the situation demands' are to be identified as legitimate moments in a realist project to represent the confused overdetermination of life.[54]

Perhaps the simplest, and certainly the most naïve, type of recreative figuration is to be found in the fairy-tale. The ugly frog who changes into a handsome prince is a typical instance.[55] The character is represented as an unchanging being—except that it can go into binary reverse and become its own opposite. Compare the Aristophanic rejuvenation, as with the transformation of Demos from ugly old man to handsome younger man at the end

[51] An ongoing scholarly debate about whether the frog-chorus were visible or not (see Dover, *Frogs*, 56–7) tends to distract from the more fundamental question of whether there was a separate chorus here at all ('presumably the same choristers appeared in both roles', MacDowell, *Aristophanes and Athens*, 280).

[52] A. H. Sommerstein, *Aristophanes, Peace* (Warminster 1985), p. xviii.

[53] See Silk and Stern, *Nietzsche on Tragedy*, 267–8, and J. Gould, 'Tragedy and collective experience', in Silk, *Tragedy and the Tragic*, 217–43, at 241. The attempt (by e.g. G. Müller, *Sophocles: Antigone* (Heidelberg 1967)) to credit these Theban elders with a consistent, realist, Theban-elderly persona entails the administration of large, not to say fatal, doses of dramatic irony.

[54] Soph. *Ant.* 904–20 and *Aj.* 646–92. The complexities and varieties of Greek tragic presentation in many such cases have been admirably demarcated by recent critics (e.g. those cited above, p. 213 n. 12) in ways that help to make the general discrepancy with Aristophanic presentation unmistakable and attempts to assimilate the tragic and the Aristophanic (see e.g. M. Landfester, *Die Ritter des Aristophanes* (Amsterdam 1967) 22) unconvincing.

[55] Ancient equivalents would include some of the items discussed by K. J. Reckford, *Aristophanes' Old-and-New Comedy* (Chapel Hill 1987) 76–92 ('Wishing, hoping, and fairy tale'), e.g. the Aesopian fable of the cat and Aphrodite (ibid. 83).

of *Knights*.[56] Compare, too, similar transformations in surviving forms of traditional popular culture like the pantomime.

In our own age many writers, especially dramatists, have opened up the possibilities of recreative presentation in a more self-conscious, experimental way, by reacting against the whole realist tradition as no Greek of Aristophanes' day either needed to or could. Against familiar stabilities and traditional expectations of development the new age puts a series of challenging questions. Sometimes the challenge is mounted on behalf of what many would think of as a marginal artistic tendency—stream of consciousness, surrealism, the absurd. For Strindberg, it is associated with a neo-realist perception that modern people, 'living in a transitional era more hectic and hysterical' than earlier ages, are, and should be represented as, 'more vulnerable, . . . torn and divided'.[57] For Pirandello, questions give way to new answers: 'My drama lies entirely in this one thing . . . in my being conscious that each one of us believes himself to be a single person. But it's not true . . . each one of us is many persons.'[58] For Ionesco, the transformational principle has become a touchstone of dramatic propriety: 'I personally would like to bring a tortoise onto the stage, turn it into a racehorse, then into a hat, a song, a dragon, and a fountain of water.'[59]

Accompanying and often underlying these new positions is the rejection of the 'substantial unity of the soul' by influential thinkers like Nietzsche and Freud.[60] Marxist theory too produces its alternative to the realist tradition, above all in the work of Brecht. In *The Good Woman of Setzuan*, for instance, 'the "good woman" Shen Te assumes a mask of harsh oppressiveness and turns into the businessman Shui Ta, so that each of her twin personalities recalls the possibility of the other.'[61] As early as *The Threepenny Opera* (1928) Brecht is seen to be exploring norms of recreative figuration. At the final *peripeteia* of the drama, for instance, we find the arch-criminal, Macheath, suddenly snatched

[56] Below, p. 239 with n. 73.

[57] From Strindberg's preface to *Miss Julie* (1888), tr. E. M. Sprinchorn, in Dukore, *Dramatic Theory*, 567.

[58] The father's words in *Six Characters in Search of an Author* (1921), tr. F. May (London 1954) 25.

[59] *Notes and Counter-Notes*, 46.

[60] The phrase, 'substantial unity of the soul', is used—as a target—by T. S. Eliot in 'Tradition and the individual talent', 56.

[61] R. D. Gray, *Brecht* (London 1961) 66.

from the gallows by royal decree and raised to a peerage, abandoning his crude curses on the police and farewells to fellow criminals and lavatory attendants, in favour of the lofty operatic observation that the greater the need, the more imminent the rescue—this frog having become a prince after all.[62] And in this drama and others, Brecht, like Aristophanes before him, makes liberal use of discontinuous mechanisms to construct his characters, notably that anti-illusionist acknowledgement of the audience which ensures that realist continuity will be kept at a safe distance.[63] For Brecht, the premise of this and all other forms of discontinuity is the conviction that they militate against an audience's emotional involvement with the stage figures and elicit, instead, an 'alienated', critical-intellectual response to them and their actions—though, notoriously, many spectators of his drama have found little difficulty in nullifying this logic and the political intention behind it.[64] In Aristophanes, at all events—or so we shall suggest—this Brechtian version of the old antithesis between emotional and intellectual response is no more definitive than that other familiar association between intellectualization and the comic which his theory also, inevitably, recalls.[65]

More recent paradigms of recreation, beyond or within the realm of 'serious' art, range from the surreal switches, verbal and visual, of *Monty Python*[66] to the delicate extravagance of García Márquez's *One Hundred Years of Solitude.* From the relatively modest start of this extraordinary work—

[62] 'Die Mordgesellen, Abtrittsweiber, | Ich bitte sie, mir zu verzeihen. | Nicht so die Polizistenhunde'; 'Ja, ich fühle es, wenn die Not am grössten, ist die Hilfe am nächsten': Brecht, *Die Dreigroschenoper*, in Bertolt Brecht, *Versuche* I–IV (Berlin 1959) 217–18.

[63] A representative example from *Dreigroschenoper*: the address to the audience in the theatre by Macheath's rival Peachum, explaining the thinking behind the royal pardon for Macheath ('wir haben uns einen anderen Schluss ausgedacht'): Brecht, *Versuche* I–IV, 218.

[64] 'Despite Brecht's theoretical pronouncements, there are scenes of genuine dramatic intensity': Gray, *Brecht*, 92. Brecht's position is summed up in the famous 1930 chart of opposites: 'Dramatic Theatre . . . involves the spectator in stage action . . . One scene exists for another . . . Evolutionary inevitability . . . Epic Theatre . . . makes the spectator an observer . . . Each scene for itself . . . Jumps . . .': Bertolt Brecht, *Schriften zum Theater* (7 vols., Frankfurt 1963–4), ii. 117.

[65] Above, pp. 57–8.

[66] e.g. the transformation, in a late episode of the *Monty Python's Flying Circus* television series (7 Dec. 1972), of Mr Pither into the singer Clodagh Rogers, the revolutionary Leon Trotsky, etc.

from the narrow village of past times it changed into an active town with stores and workshops—

to its apocalyptic conclusion—

it was foreseen that the city of mirrors (or mirages) would be wiped out by the wind—

transformation seems to be the premise of the 'city' of Macondo, and of the people who live there—

Aureliano Triste told how he had seen her, changed into an apparition with leathery skin and a few golden threads on her skull—

to the point of seeming self-contradiction—

even when they were two worn-out old people they kept on blooming like little children and playing together like dogs—

as well as the point where imagery and 'actual' transformations meet:

she was shrinking, turning into a foetus, becoming mummified in life to the point that in her last months she was a cherry raisin lost inside her nightgown, and the arm that she always kept raised looked like the paw of a marimonda monkey . . . She looked like a newborn old woman.[67]

In this transformational world, very pertinently, the wiser characters have 'sensed the truth' about time:

that time also stumbled and had accidents and could therefore splinter and leave an eternalized fragment in a room.[68]

The diversity, sophistication, and richness of these modern experiments in recreative figuration suggests, if nothing else, that while we may argue for the superiority of realism, we cannot simply assume it. As John Gould reminds us in a celebrated discussion of tragic character, realist character in fiction—from Greek tragedy to Eugene O' Neill—is a construct, not a hidden pre-existing reality.[69] This is hardly to devalue realist characterization, since our sense of a human character in life,

[67] Gabriel García Márquez, *One Hundred Years of Solitude* (1967), tr. G. Rabassa (London 1970) 39, 422, 283, 345, 347–8.

[68] Ibid. 355.

[69] Gould, 'Dramatic character'. I should add that Gould is at pains to *contrast* Greek tragedy and O'Neill, and does not give them any common 'realist' label as I do.

arguably, must always be as much of a construct as a response to a hidden reality itself.[70] And certainly it does not justify us in describing realist characters as 'systems of rule-governed equivalences' or simply 'predications', as some theorists have done.[71] What it does, rather, is encourage us to see that the constructional quality of recreative figurations does not in itself invalidate their claim to serious attention.

The switches, the transformations, the reversals embodied in Aristophanic characters are—we may surely now agree—something more than incidental odd moments in otherwise tidy or homogeneous wholes. They represent a pervasive and essential fact of Aristophanic drama and, as such, may quite naturally constitute the most important part of a single character's presentation. Witness Philocleon in *Wasps*. That old man begins his play as a sort of caricature of Athenian legalism and finishes it as a sort of personification of the self-expressive life force, abusing, drinking, and dancing. At first he is helplessly 'pining' in captivity (317), confessedly a pitiable figure; by the end he is exuding total self-confidence, and 'much the most outrageous of them all' (1303). His reversal involves a peculiar personal rejuvenation—he is 'only young' (as he assures a flute-girl, somewhere between the drinking and the dancing), he has to wait for his meddlesome son to die before *he* can live life to the full (1352–5)[72]—and rejuvenations, of one kind or another, await old men at the end of various of the plays: Demos in *Knights* is again 'handsome' and 'as he once was' (1321, 1325); Trygaeus in *Peace*, when duly married to Opora, will be 'an old man, young again' (860–1); Aeschylus, in *Frogs*, not only old but dead, is to have new life to save his city in her hour of need (1500–1).[73] Needless to say, all these transformations—available only to recreative characters—

[70] Here, the persuasive force of revisionist arguments from the structuralist era remains strong: see e.g. E. Goffman, *The Presentation of Self in Everyday Life* (New York 1959); J. Lacan, *Ecrits* (Paris 1966).

[71] Esp. in the structuralist era, whence the two quoted formulations: Hamon, 'Pour un statut', 144; T. Todorov, *Grammaire du Décaméron* (The Hague 1969) 27–30.

[72] See further below, pp. 427–8.

[73] Not all interpreters see the *Eq.* rejuvenation as one, but see Silk, 'People', 166 n. 30, and S. D. Olson, 'The new Demos of Aristophanes' *Knights*', *Eranos* 88 (1990) 60–3. Philocleon's rejuvenation, of course, is not ceremonially acclaimed like the others, though it is acknowledged by at least one of his abused victims (*Vesp.* 1333; cf. MacDowell ad loc.).

are the climactic events, both for these fortunate figures and for the plays they dominate.

The transformational capacities of these characters are reminiscent of the powers of a poetic image. This equation—character : image—needs careful formulation, however, because a number of Aristophanes' characters invite comparison with images on quite different grounds. This is most obviously the case with the 'allegorical' conversion of abstractions into people—as with silent members of the *dramatis personae* like Opora (Summer) and Theoria (Holiday) in *Peace*, or, more full-bloodedly, with the representation of Right and Wrong as talking humans in *Clouds*.[74]

A comparable process is at work in the creation of some of the 'non-fictional' characters. Take Socrates in *Clouds*. This figure may or may not have traits comparable with those of the historical Socrates. What he certainly has is exaggerated traits—recondite scientific interests, pretensions to authority, spokesmanship of new deities, an indifferent attitude towards the two arguments, Right and Wrong—which collectively amount to a cartoon of the new intellectualism. But what sort of cartoon is it? Not the emblematic, metonymic kind (as Uncle Sam is a metonym for the USA or John Bull for England). Rather the metaphorical kind—like the lumbering cart-horse which the cartoonist Low regularly used to represent the Trades Union Congress in Britain between the wars, or the infant of tender years he once used to represent the human race in the new atomic age ('Baby play with nice ball?'). So in *Clouds* the new Enlightenment is personified as a mad scientist, called (for convenience) Socrates. So (more transparently) in *Knights* the relation between the people and their leading politicians is represented metaphorically as the relation between an old man (labelled Demos, as he might be in a modern cartoon) and his slaves, old and new.

Such representations are not in themselves recreative or incompatible with realism—in my sense; and, as such, they are to be distinguished from, for instance, Aristophanes' many representations of established human figures by means of sudden, one-off,

[74] The names of Peace's attendants are variously translated, but 'Holiday' has rightly caught on (e.g. Olson on *Pax* 523, Henderson in the new Loeb); 'Summer' is my own rendering of *Opôra* (and also what the Greek means: cf. Dunbar on *Av.* 709). On A's allegorizing abstractions, see Newiger, *Metapher und Allegorie*.

transformational images:[75] these, but not (in themselves) the allegories, embody recreative figuration and all its disruptive effects. A good example is the splendid image of Cleon the monster in *Wasps* (1031–5) and *Peace* (754–8)[76]—

> καὶ πρῶτον μὲν μάχομαι πάντων αὐτῷ τῷ καρχαρόδοντι,
> οὗ δεινόταται μὲν ἀπ' ὀφθαλμῶν Κύννης ἀκτῖνες ἔλαμπον . . .
>
> First I fought the Jag-Toothed One himself:
> Flashed from his eyes the Bitch-Star's awesome rays—

or indeed the less flamboyant, but no less telling, version presented by Sausage-Seller and Paphlagon-Cleon in *Knights*, when the two virtuosi offer master Demos conflicting oracles about the same monster (as Sausage-Seller thinks of him),

> ἐσφοιτῶν τ' ἐς τοὐπτάνιον λήσει σε κυνηδόν
>
> He'll sneak into thy kitchen like a dog
> (1033)

or protector (as Paphlagon sees himself):

> σῴζεσθαί σ' ἐκέλευ' ἱερὸν κύνα καρχαρόδοντα
>
> Quoth he: guard thou the holy Jag-Toothed dog.
> (1017)

In this *Knights* sequence, two quite different kinds of transformation are involved. Quite apart from the representation of Cleon as dog in the manner of the more elaborate image of *Wasps*, the two agonistic speakers are themselves transformed into something other—into walking-talking oracles, complete with all the phraseological paraphernalia of the genre (hexameter verse, sub-Homeric idiom, riddling expression)[77]—and so comprehensively that, instead of saying people are represented here as oracular voices, one might just as well say that two contrasting readings are represented (*re*-presented) as human agencies, just as Right and Wrong are in *Clouds*.

Whatever else he is, Euripides in *Thesmophoriazusae* is partly an elaborate, multi-transformational image of the kind under

[75] See above, pp. 123–4.

[76] Quoted here in the *Pax* version. See, in full, below, pp. 348–9.

[77] Features summed up in the phrase κύνα καρχαρόδοντα | for Cleon: cf. *Il.* 13.198 κυνῶν ὕπο καρχαροδόντων | (of real dogs). On the oracles in *Eq.* see further below, pp. 338–42.

discussion. For instance, despite his original disinclination to disguise himself, Euripides in fact goes through a series of disguises, the last of which is the disguise of the old madam. Why *that* disguise? Because Euripidean tragedy (in Aristophanes' eyes) is a new and potentially subversive kind of drama, fascinating but disturbing: lower in tone than the heroic tragedy of an earlier age (its heroes in rags were notorious), more seductive in its persuasive techniques.[78] This is all summed up in the representation of Euripides himself as an old hag bringing on a girl to seduce the forces of law and order (here the Scythian policeman) and thereby distracting and (literally) disarming them. More generally, the Euripides of this play is an image in the same sense: he is a personification of the 'real' Euripides' own plays. Among the other striking characteristics of those plays (as seen by Aristophanes) are melodramatic emotional moments, flashy ideas, modishly difficult thoughts, and a penchant for the unexpected. Accordingly, throughout this play the character Euripides is melodramatic ('today will tell | Whether Euripides shall live or die', 76–7), full of flashy ideas ('Brilliant and up to your best standard' (Mnesilochus) 93) given to modishly difficult thoughts ('All you're due to see must you not hear', 5), and, 'by introducing something new and clever' (1130), constantly doing the unexpected.[79] So comprehensive is the image, indeed, that in these respects Euripides might be taken for a figure belonging to the realist tradition. Irrespective of his relation to the historical Euripides or to the historical Euripides' plays (it might be said), his characterization endows him with the set and stable features of a real person, albeit a person comically stylized by its construction around a few limited traits. And given that unexpected behaviour is the prerogative of the discontinuous-recreative character, it might

[78] See e.g. *Ran.* 939–44, 954 (lowering the tone); 842, 1063 (rags); 771–6 (persuasion). The mode of transference seems to anticipate the technique of the (later) ancient biographers of Greek authors: 'the smallest hints of personality in conventional statements [in their works] could be developed into character traits [in their authors]' (M. R. Lefkowitz, *The Lives of the Greek Poets* (London 1981), p. ix). The attempt of some interpreters to see the madam disguise as emblematically 'comic' is gratuitous: cf. below, p. 322 n. 57.

[79] For these as characteristics of Euripidean drama, see (e.g.) *Ran.* 1331–63 (melodramatic moments and constant surprises: the Euripidean predisposition towards the unexpected is summed up in the word στρέφειν, 957); and 892–9 (modish thoughts and flashy ideas).

even be said that, in terms of his 'constantly doing the unexpected', what Aristophanes has done with Euripides is ingeniously convert his discontinuity into a real character-trait—as if one were to act on Aristotle's advice that an inconsistent character should be *consistently* inconsistent.[80] However, as our earlier discussion suggests, the point, in these Aristotelian terms, is that the Aristophanic Euripides, like recreative characters in general, is *inconsistently* inconsistent. Whatever his stable features, they still do not impinge as part of a realist whole.[81] If they did, we would find ourselves perplexed and resentful at his transformations, as we do not.

With Euripides' disguises still in mind, we may note a further connection between disguise and the recreative character. It is a sufficient, though not a necessary, condition of recreative figuration that it should involve figures whose external condition is decisive for their being. It follows that if such figures are disguised, they change.[82] In life we suppose that this is not true. In this kind of art, however, it has the appearance of truth—hence the wonderful repeated joke in the second half of *Thesmophoriazusae*, that by appearing to be Menelaus, Euripides can rescue Mnesilochus, if Mnesilochus appears to be Helen; and by appearing to be Perseus, Euripides can rescue Mnesilochus, if Mnesilochus appears to be Andromeda. Mnesilochus himself makes the principle explicit (1010–12):

> ἀνὴρ ἔοικεν οὐ προδώσειν, ἀλλά μοι
> σημεῖον ὑπεδήλωσε Περσεὺς ἐκδραμών,
> ὅτι δεῖ με γίγνεσθ' Ἀνδρομέδαν.
>
> My man won't let me down, after all—
> He just showed up as Perseus!—it was a sign
> For me to become Andromeda.

Role-playing and disguise, of course, often figure within the realist sphere. In Aristophanic comedy, however, they can claim a special significance.[83]

[80] Arist. *Poet.* xv.

[81] In 'People', 161–2, I suggested, with less qualification, that this kind of figure does *in part* belong to the realist sphere. Except in so far as *all* A's characters do so (in part), I now find that formulation misleading.

[82] However, the disguise need not involve a *visual* change for the transformation to count—as Mnesilochus does not change visually in the examples that follow.

[83] See further below, pp. 282 ff.

If Aristophanes' recreative characters do not possess continuity in the realist sense, this does not make them amorphous or incomprehensible, featureless or (above all) lifeless. For a start, most of the main figures, in particular, are animated by an intense gusto for living. Among the characteristic goals of this intensity, undeniably, are the primary satisfactions of food, drink, and sex, and indeed even in the three peace plays, *Acharnians*, *Peace*, and *Lysistrata*, the attainment of peace itself is realized in such terms, with partying and symbolic consummations. To many post-Aristophanic eyes, this is all part and parcel of comic 'degradation', the other side of which is the harsh ridicule reserved for 'real' historical individuals—and here at least that conventional category is a significant one, for, again, one can hardly deny that (with the revealing exception of fellow-writers, who, if satirized, are generally satirized without venom) there are few constraints on the abusive representations of public figures: the monster Cleon and the mad scientist Socrates are only the most lurid examples. Among politicians, in particular, 'bribery and corruption are constantly said to have been at work', while 'personal idiosyncrasies, especially social and sexual behaviour, are freely admitted to a kind of relevance by association.'[84] Yet it is more than some 'nostalgie de la boue' that impels us still to affirm the splendid exuberance of so many Aristophanic figures—including, indeed, some of those earmarked for abusive humiliation: Paphlagon-Cleon is a prime example.

Then again, the recreative characters can still have broad, even pre-eminent, qualities—and not just the 'typical' slaves or informers, but the main characters too. The heroine of *Lysistrata* is broadly noble, the Euripides of *Thesmophoriazusae* is broadly subtle. Above all, the characters tend to have an immediacy which reflects both their powers of mobile, instant behaviour and their author's characteristic instinct for the concrete and the sensuous. Right and Wrong, and Demos too, may be allegorical figures, but they are allegory made truly immediate in human shape. Indeed, it is when Aristophanes begins to give way to the interest in constructing realist figures that his people start to acquire a kind of flat transparency. The sober typicality of a Blepyrus or a Praxagora in *Ecclesiazusae* lacks the charge of their more recreative counterparts in earlier plays, but has

[84] Handley, 'Comedy', 378.

hardly yet gained much realist roundness or depth by way of compensation.

At their most charged, the recreative figures are not simply full of life: they are (as we aptly say) larger than life. Mnesilochus, for instance, has an extraordinary presence—or, one might prefer to say, a hundred different presences, from the baffled victim of Euripides' mystifications ('Amazing thing, intellectual conversation', 21) to the confident helper ('Tell him to go to hell. | Instead . . .', 211–12), from the colourful woman-speaker he becomes in Euripides' defence ('Three days we'd been married; we were in bed, | Husband asleep, and my boyfriend | —Took my virginity when I was seven— | Comes scratching at the door: he *wanted* me', 478–81) to his bewildering series of tragic personae ('Yea, I linger here, while Menelaus, | My ill-starred husband, never comes', 866–7). Each of these moments has its own absolute energy, and though they are linked by little more than that, there is assuredly a cumulative effect. The strange new whole gives something of a kaleidoscopic impression: we seem to have a rich sense of human possibility, and the range of human possibility, not in the realist terms of a finite individual, but in some other, beyond the individual altogether.

The kaleidoscopic whole compels our attention (no-one finds Mnesilochus boring), but we delight in it without any significant involvement. If we felt involved with Mnesilochus, we would surely be more awkwardly curious about his wife and children, his precise relationship to Euripides, his 'real' name.[85] Any such involvement is a realist phenomenon that presupposes a coherent and continuous figure (fictional or real), to whose coherence and continuity we can, as we say, 'relate'. It is not, though, that recreative character necessarily alienates us, as Brecht's theories of discontinuity suggest that it should—and in Aristophanes, perhaps, it never exactly alienates us at all. We do respond to Mnesilochus, but when we do, we respond, not as we ordinarily might, to a notional one man, nor to some eccentric or perverse equivalent of a notional one man, but to something altogether

[85] We would also be more put out than we are when important characters are removed from the action half way through their plays, as Euelpides is in *Av.* (846), Xanthias in *Ran.* (813), and (even in one of the semi-realist late plays) Praxagora in *Eccl.* (729). There is no counterpart to this pattern in 5th-cent. tragedy, where a character normally has to die (*vel sim.*) for this to happen (as with Sophocles' Antigone and Ajax).

larger: almost to what Bakhtin calls 'the entire world in its comic aspect'.[86] 'Larger than life', then, is a peculiarly apt phrase, and not least because it carries with it an impression of normative validity. The recreative character, at its most impressive, is not a poor relation of its realist counterpart, any more than comedy in general (with or without recreative characters) is, in any meaningful sense, secondary to 'serious', realist tragedy. It might indeed be argued that in Aristophanes, at least, various of the particular discontinuities that make the recreative characters what they are involve, precisely, an inversion of pre-existing realist norms, and often specific norms associated with tragic practice. When at *Peace* 146–8 (to recapitulate one of many examples) Trygaeus' daughter warns our hero not to fall off his beetle

> and end up crippled,
> And give Euripides ideas—and turn into a tragedy,

and the characteristic illusion-breaking metatheatrical reference reminds us that we are *not* in a tragedy, but in an Aristophanic comedy, where such references are a 'proper' part of a character's make-up, we might well agree that the non-tragic nature of this reference to tragedy constitutes a point *about* tragedy which, here, is part of *the* point. But this is only to say that we are back with *our* point: that recreativity is not in itself secondary to realism, nor comedy to tragedy, and that Aristophanes' willingness to promote any such sense of secondariness is specific and discussible in its own right.

Recreative figuration at its least impressive is represented by the anonymous miscellany of guises to be observed in the *Peace* chorus: it seems a high price to pay for freedom of utterance. For the recreative character at its most impressive, we should look more closely at Philocleon in *Wasps*. Here is a figure that is *par excellence* immediate, kaleidoscopic, larger than life, even by the standards of Mnesilochus in *Thesmophoriazusae*. Unlike Mnesilochus, we recall, Philocleon has a bit of a past (354–7),

> —Remember, in the army once, when Naxos fell,
> Stealing skewers to get down the wall?
> —I know, I know. But this is all so different:
> I could steal then—I was young . . .

[86] Above, p. 76.

but, like Mnesilochus, a purely notional future. He ends his play with a triumphant dance (1474–537), in which everyone in sight (like the bemused chorus) seems to be swept up.[87] This dancer—we know—is a very different creature from the caricature of the hopeless, fanatical juryman with which the play begins, while, more generally, the lawless Philocleon of the latter scenes is almost the binary opposite of the legalistic Philocleon of the first half of the play. But well before this change, inexplicable in realist terms, the striking, recreative nature of our hero has become apparent.

Though structurally one half of a contrasting pair, father and son, Philocleon is the central and dominant figure of the play. He is widely regarded as 'a triumph of characterization',[88] though perhaps not for the right reasons. His name—we know—is in itself allegorical. He is Philocleon, 'Love-Cleon', because he is a man addicted to jury service. In a litigious democracy like Athens, this means a man enamoured of his powers of decision-making and punishment—and it was Cleon, as spokesman of popular democracy, who championed the interests of jurymen, albeit (as Aristophanic comedy would have us believe) for his own ends. Philocleon's son, Bdelycleon, 'Hate-Cleon', tries and (in and after the agon) eventually succeeds in talking and tricking his father out of his addiction, after which the 'lover of Cleon' abandons his old life in favour of a new one: the allegory is confounded. All this is in the play. Yet it is not the whole play, nor even a suitable formula for the play. Philocleon does indeed find a new life, and allegory is indeed confounded; but the nature of the *life* and the *finding* and the *confounding* far exceed the logic of the formula, while, above all, Philocleon himself vastly exceeds it, both after and before his change of life. The formula implies that the play centres on the political-juridical system associated with Cleon and that, through the confounding, the play offers a direct critique of both Cleon and 'his' system. This is not so much untrue as misleading. It would be less misleading to say that the effective target of the critique is not *this* system, but politics, juridics, and system as such.[89]

[87] And everyone else (like the queue of angry citizens serving summonses on him, 1444–5) forgotten: cf. below, p. 271.

[88] A. W. Gomme, *More Essays in Greek History and Literature* (Oxford 1962) 79.

[89] See further below, pp. 369 ff., 431.

Though Philocleon is an old man, and though other Aristophanic plays feature old men as their central figures, he is significantly unlike any of them. Whatever else he is, he is uniquely *extreme*, and we soon become aware just how extreme he is. Unusually, we have a long description of him (67–133) before his actual entrance (144). As Xanthias, one of the household slaves, explains, Philocleon has finally driven his son to lock him in, because of an '*extraordinary* illness' (νόσον . . . ἀλλόκοτον, 71). The 'illness' is behavioural. As a juryman, Philocleon (89–90, 103–5)

στένει
ἢν μὴ 'πὶ τοῦ πρώτου καθίζηται ξύλου

. . . .

εὐθὺς δ' ἀπὸ δορπηστοῦ κέκραγεν ἐμβάδας,
κἄπειτ' ἐκεῖσ' ἐλθὼν προκαθεύδει πρῲ πάνυ,
ὥσπερ λεπὰς προσεχόμενος τῷ κίονι.

moans
Unless he's sitting on the front bench

. . . .

Straight after supper, yells for his shoes,
Goes off and sleeps down there with hours to spare,
Front of the court, stuck to the notice-board
Like a limpet.[90]

A few minutes later, we see this psychopathic figure in person, making the first of several attempts to escape his confinement (143–4):

ΒΔ. τί ποτ' ἄρ' ἡ κάπνη ψοφεῖ;
οὗτος, τίς εἶ σύ;
ΦΙ. καπνὸς ἔγωγ' ἐξέρχομαι.

BD. What's that noise in the chimney?
Oy, who are you?
PH. I'm smoke, on my way out.

His own self-descriptions are as extravagant as those offered by his slave. He must get out, he explains to Xanthias, or else a defendant is in danger of being acquitted (158–60):

ΞΑ. σὺ δὲ τοῦτο βαρέως ἂν φέροις;
ΦΙ. ὁ γὰρ θεὸς

[90] 'Notice-board' is κίονι ('pillar'): see MacDowell ad loc.

μαντευομένῳ μοὔχρησεν ἐν Δελφοῖς ποτε,
ὅταν τις ἐκφύγῃ μ' ἀποσκλῆναι τότε.

XA. Is that so bad?
PH. Look, I went to Delphi
To consult the oracle, and the god told me:
If any of my defendants ever get off,
I'll shrivel up.

Beside his father, Bdelycleon is a model of normality, yet even this normal son solemnly ascribes the most surprising propensities to the old man (139–41):

εἰς τὸν ἰπνὸν εἰσελήλυθεν
καὶ μυσπολεῖ τι καταδεδυκώς. ἀλλ' ἄθρει
κατὰ τῆς πυέλου τὸ τρῆμ' ὅπως μὴ 'κδύσεται.

He's into the kitchen, mousing along,
Hands and knees. And watch the sink,
In case he gets out down the plug-hole.[91]

The chorus consists of Philocleon's fellow-jurymen. When they come to pick him up on their way to court and then, after some deliberation, prepare to leave, he sings down plaintively to them from an upper window, a bit like a tragic version of a blues singer (317–22);

φίλοι, τήκομαι μὲν
πάλαι διὰ τῆς ὀπῆς
ὑμῶν ὄπ' ἀκούων.
ἀλλ'—οὐ γὰρ οἷός τ' εἴμ'
ἀίειν—τί ποιήσω;
τηροῦμαι δ' ὑπὸ τῶνδ', ἐπεὶ
βούλομαί γε πάλαι μεθ' ὑ-
μῶν ἐλθὼν ἐπὶ τοὺς καδί-
σκους κακόν τι ποιῆσαι.

How long, how long,
Have I been suffering!
At the window

[91] Up to a point, then, Bd. co-operates with his father's recreativity (cf. the co-operation of Euripides and Mnesilochus in *Thes.*: above, p. 243). Both Bd. and Ph. have engendered an extraordinary range of interpretations. The idea that Bd. is some sort of ideal-Aristophanic figure is put forward (incomprehensibly to me) by Russo, *Aristofane*, 194 (and in more detail by Reckford, *Old-and-New*, 254–5, 273–5). Interpretative versions of Ph. include the Freudian subject of G. Paduano, *Il giudice giudicato* (Bologna 1974). See further below, pp. 369 ff.

Hear your voices,
And I can't sing.

What can I do?
I'm being watched now,
And all I want is,
Be with you all,
Vote for mischief.[92]

'Vote for mischief' prompts one commentator to suggest that this is Philocleon's 'main pleasure in life'—as befits a functionary in a vicious system—whereas it would be more to the point to note the bland and almost Brechtian detachment of the remark.[93] It is not Philocleon's 'main pleasure in life', or else the compulsive and compelling dance he eventually sets in motion to envelop the play would be incomprehensible. '*Main* pleasure *in life*': this is realist talk, appropriate for an ordinarily continuous figure. But Philocleon, it is abundantly clear already, is anything but that: he is like a limpet; he is smoke in the chimney; he 'mouses along'; and now again he prays to Zeus to end his intolerable imprisonment by turning him into something, *anything* (323–31), even a stone (332–3):

ἢ δῆτα λίθον με ποίησον ἐφ' οὗ
τὰς χοιρίνας ἀριθμοῦσιν.

Make me the stone
They count the jury's votes on.

His juridical existence does indeed give him various small pleasures, some of them quaint, even touching, and (in themselves) easy to understand on a realist level. His family, it seems, are always after his jury pay, and he enjoys their performance. As he explains to his son (606–12):

ὅταν οἴκαδ' ἴω τὸν μισθὸν ἔχων, κἄπειθ' ἥκοντά με πάντες
ἀσπάζωνται διὰ τἀργύριον, καὶ πρῶτα μὲν ἡ θυγάτηρ με
ἀπονίζῃ καὶ τὼ πόδ' ἀλείφῃ καὶ προσκύψασα φιλήσῃ
καὶ παππίζουσ' ἅμα τῇ γλώττῃ τὸ τριώβολον ἐκκαλαμᾶται,
καὶ τὸ γύναιόν μ' ὑποθωπεῦσαν φυστὴν μᾶζαν προσενέγκῃ,

[92] Cf. 'How Long, How Long Blues' ('How long, how long, | Has that evenin' train been gone'): Leroy Carr, 1929.

[93] 'Main pleasure': Sommerstein ad loc. More sensitively, MacDowell ad loc.: 'the kind of explanation which would be used by an impartial critic more naturally than by himself'.

κἄπειτα καθεζομένη παρ' ἐμοὶ προσαναγκάζῃ—φάγε τουτί,
ἔντραγε τουτί. τούτοισιν ἐγὼ γάνυμαι . . .

I bring my wages home, and everyone's all
Over me. First my daughter bends down
To wash my feet, gives me a kiss, puts oil on me—
And all the while it's 'Daddy, this' and 'Daddy, that',
Her tongue's fishing the coppers out of me.[94]
As for the little woman, she sits there doting,
Forcing fancy pastry down my throat:
'Try this one—have a taste!' It's wonderful.

In a realist world, of course, Philocleon's 'my daughter' is presumably 'your sister', and Bdelycleon might expect to hear her name—but the realist logic is not operative, and we are not invited to make the connection. In a realist world, in any case, it would be disconcerting, to say the least, to find the juryman's relish for judging crimes (900)—

ὦ μιαρὸς οὗτος· ὡς δὲ καὶ κλέπτον βλέπει

What a villain he is—and such a thief's look—

coexisting with those pleasurable reminiscences of his own thieving villainies in what is actually—recreatively—another existence (357):

I could steal then—I was young.[95]

Most of the detail just considered belongs to Philocleon before Bdelycleon's agonistic triumph and the father's final agreement to abandon his obsession (1001–8). From this point, once suitably inducted by his well-meaning son, Philocleon becomes a seemingly hedonistic figure, who provokes the chorus' admiration for (1451–2)

οἷ μετέστη
ξηρῶν τρόπων καὶ βιοτῆς

how far he has come
From his dry ways and his style of life,

[94] Line 608 is figurative ('tongue' means words), not a moment of child–father eroticism; so, rightly, Sommerstein ad loc.

[95] Above, p. 224. It might well be pondered how far lines like 900 (above) likewise lend themselves to a sense of anomian relish in the crime, as well as in the condemnation. Cf. below, p. 415 n. 137.

and takes on anyone, his son included, who stands in his way. This is the Philocleon who steals the flute-girl (1345–6, 1368–9), mocks those who confront him with the law (1406), drinks and dances (1476–9). This huge transformation is rather like a switch from human perversity to an unleashing of animal spirits—and *animal* spirits (the *mot juste*, one can fairly say) constitute a very significant element in *Wasps* as a whole and a crucial element in Philocleon's own recreative make-up.

This is a play which begins with one slave's dream about eagles and snakes (15–17), and another's about sheep, whales, and crows (31–43), then moves on via a pantomime donkey (169–96) and a wasp chorus (223 ff.) to a dog-trial (835–994), and concludes, in Philocleon's dance finale, with a gathering of the crabs, in the form of the tragic poet Carcinus (*Karkinos* = 'crab') and his three sons (1501 ff.). And in this play, replete with animals, Philocleon is the master-animal, as befits his exceptional recreative powers.[96]

Our hero is indeed (as we have seen) in any case the beneficiary of an impressive scatter of transformations that have nothing to do with animals. On his first appearance he is, on his own admission, 'smoke' (*καπνός*, 144) and a little later, in imitation of Odysseus, 'No-man' (*οὖτις*, 184–5); in his darkest hour he prays to Zeus to make him, again, 'smoke' (324) or a 'voting stone' (332–3); and during the agon his own claim to possess powers over thunder and lightening like Zeus (619–27) prompts his son to convert the comparison into an ironic transformation and call him 'Father Zeus' himself (652).[97]

Yet even these impressive moments are as nothing compared to the tumultuous establishment of Philocleon's animal status, marked by an extraordinary sequence of direct comparisons, metaphors, and 'literal' transformations, accumulated in the earlier part of the play. Philocleon attaches himself to the court-house

[96] Typically—programmatically, almost—the opening snake promptly turns into a shield (18, cf. MacDowell ad loc.) and the eagle into Cleonymus (19). On the crabby end, see below, pp. 432–4. *Vesp.* also, of course, offers multiple-animal imagery for Cleon in the parabasis (1031–5). Interpreters of the play tend to minimize the importance of the menagerie. Exceptions include C. H. Whitman, *Aristophanes and the Comic Hero* (Cambridge, Mass. 1964) 162–5, and Bowie, *Aristophanes*, 79–80, 83.

[97] Specifically, *πάτερ ἡμέτερε Κρονίδη*. Other non-animal transformations for Ph. include the eccentric humans, *Προξενίδην* and *τὸν Σέλλου | τοῦτον τὸν ψευδαμάμαξυν* (325–6). Besides this, in the flute-girl scene, his sexual organ is a rope (1343) and the girl herself a torch (1372).

'notice board' like a limpet (λεπάς, 105). He comes home from court with his finger-nails full of wax like a bee (ὥσπερ μέλιττ' ἢ βομβυλιός, 107),[98] and 'honey-bee' is what his friends in the chorus call him (μελίττιον, 366). In his confinement he has to be watched 'like a cat that stole the meat' (γαλῆν κρέα κλέψασαν, 363). In his bids to escape, he hops up the wall of the house like a jackdaw (κολοιός, 129), he 'mouses along' in the kitchen (μυσπολεῖ, 140), he clings to the donkey like its foal (κλητῆρος . . . πωλίῳ, 189),[99] he is a mouse getting out of the roof (μῦς, 204–5)—or rather, not a mouse but a new species of 'roof-dweller' (ὀροφίας, 206),[100] which a 'literal' transformation at once converts into a bird. In Bdelycleon's words, 'the man's turning into a sparrow' (στροῦθος ἀνὴρ γίγνεται, 207)—and accordingly he calls for his hunting net and 'shoos' the bird back in (σοῦ σοῦ· πάλιν, σοῦ, 209). We have seen Mnesilochus, among others, transformed this 'literal' way (*Thesmophoriazusae* 1012)—

> It was a sign
> For me to become Andromeda—

and likewise Trygaeus cautioned *not* to get himself transformed this way (*Peace* 146–8):

> Mind you don't . . .
> . . . turn into a tragedy

It is in *Wasps* above all that we see such transformations take their place, alongside metaphors and comparisons, as contributory elements to the presentation of a major character and a major theme; and in the agon of *Wasps* this theme is summed up by Philocleon himself. With his own existence at the forefront of his mind, he points to the life of the juryman and asks, 'what *creature* is happier . . . or more awesome?' (τί γὰρ εὔδαιμον καὶ μακαριστὸν μᾶλλον . . . ἢ δεινότερον ζῷον, 550–1). And the whole sequence thus summed up actually begins, in similarly unspecified terms, in the first few lines of the play, when one slave asks the other (4):

[98] i.e. because the jurors had waxed tablets, on which they scratched a long line for a conviction, and Ph. always votes for a conviction (157–60, 999–1002)—and insists on scratching the long line on his fellow jurors' tablets too (106).

[99] A foal past its youth (παράβολος, 192): see MacDowell ad loc. (and on additional double meanings in 189 itself).

[100] Like a snake of that name: MacDowell ad loc.

ἆρ' οἶσθά γ' οἷον κνώδαλον φυλάττομεν;

You know what kind of *animal* we're guarding?

In the later part of the play there are a few verbal reminders of our hero's animality. According to a fellow-citizen, he has the stomach of a chicken (ἀλεκτρυόνος, 794); dining out, he misbehaves like a donkey (ὀνίδιον, 1306); and in his dance he identifies himself as the great tragedian of times past, Phrynichus, and in this persona 'cowers like a cock' (πτήσσει . . . ὥς τις ἀλέκτωρ, 1490). However, as that last instance shows, the verbal transformations have ceased to be predominantly animal. It is as if Philocleon began the play as an animal in words and is now an animal in action: there *is* a sort of continuity here, though hardly of a realist kind.

For, apart from anything else, the continuity subsumes not only Philocleon, in both or all of his phases, but the play as a whole, through *its* animal character. We are used to humans being animalized from Homer, especially in the similes of the *Iliad*, where the equation tends to carry with it a lowering of the human to animal. *Iliad* 16. 351–6:

οὗτοι ἄρ' ἡγεμόνες Δαναῶν ἕλον ἄνδρα ἕκαστος.
ὡς δὲ λύκοι ἄρνεσσιν ἐπέχραον ἢ ἐρίφοισι
σίνται, ὑπὲκ μήλων αἱρεύμενοι, αἵ τ' ἐν ὄρεσσι
ποιμένος ἀφραδίῃσι διέτμαγεν· οἱ δὲ ἰδόντες
αἶψα διαρπάζουσιν ἀνάλκιδα θυμὸν ἐχούσας·
ὣς Δαναοὶ Τρώεσσιν ἐπέχραον

So each Danaan captain killed his man.
As ravaging wolves fall on lambs or kids,
Picking out from the flock those that are left
Scattered on the hills by a shepherd's
Thoughtlessness, and on the spot
Snatch at the timid creatures where they sight them—
So Danaans fell on Trojans.

Heroes repeatedly likened to ravaging wolves and timid sheep are thereby simplified and in a sense reduced from their human complexity.[101]

In *Wasps* such an effect is not apparent. Instead, the variety of the transformations and their thematic kinship to the world of the

[101] Cf. Silk, *Iliad*, 71.

play as a whole create a different impression of diverse vitality and, in turn, a sense of the interrelatedness of all living beings, as the old man's strange touch confers on human life, with all its rules, a new vitality and spontaneity. At the heart of these relationships, Philocleon seems to transcend the bounds of an individual, as if he were indeed himself the centre of some larger organism. Perhaps, even, he is a kind of one-man community, as in fact at one point, eyeing the defendant in the dog-trial, he calls himself (917):

> οὐδὲν μετέδωκεν οὐδὲ τῷ κοινῷ γ', ἐμοί
>
> He gave me nothing—*me*, the community.

But that was Philocleon as, still, himself a political animal. Overall, and especially by the end of the play, he has transcended the political, including, of course, the political-allegorical implications of his name. In his person, it is as if the possibilities of life, not of a specified individual life (because he is 'larger than life' in *that* sense of 'life'), but of life itself, have been sensuously conveyed, which is to say that in his recreative figuration something of an inclusive vision is implicit. Here our experience is recast in a way that does nothing to enhance the understanding of human individuality or human relationships as we comprehend them in the realist traditions of thought and art. In lieu of realist perceptions, a new vision of life is created, which is certainly not that of Homer or the tragedians. However, it is a vision which—as the example of Philocleon shows—can claim its own validity.[102]

[102] Which is my answer to a challenging comment by Pelling, *Characterization*, 252, on my argument in 'People'. Picking up my examples of modern avant-garde figuration, Pelling suggests that Brecht, Strindberg, Pirandello 'present fragmented, discontinuous personalities [the *mot juste*?] . . . but they present that discontinuity as itself reflecting an important aspect of reality, either the reality of the individual figure or that of the fragmented world in which he lives', whereas the discontinuous characterization of A 'seems . . . less a refraction of reality than a flight from it'.

6

Causal Sequences and Other Patterns

> In the characters, just as in the structure of the action, always go for the necessary or the probable. When *x* says or does *y*, it must be necessary or else probable for *such* a person to say or do *such* a thing. Likewise it must be necessary or else probable that *this* should happen after *that* . . .

Aristotle's unambiguous declaration of principle (*Poetics* XV) conveniently—and ringingly—associates his requirements for tragic character with his specifications for the organic unity of the whole drama, conceived in terms of a unified and processive plot-structure (*muthos*). The *muthos* is the be-all and end-all, *arkhê* and *telos*; its unity is the play's unity; and the causal logic that determines the *muthos* is accordingly the be-all and end-all of the drama as a whole. *Poetics* VI: 'The action—that is, the *muthos*—is the goal of tragedy, and a goal is the most important thing of all. . . . The *muthos* is the first principle . . . of tragedy.' The formula for the requisite kind of unity is strict. The *muthos* 'should be constructed . . . around an action that is single, whole and complete' (*Poetics* XXIII), where 'single' and 'whole' and 'complete' imply an uncompromising causal sequence with 'beginning', 'middle', and 'end', wherein things happen 'because of', and not just 'after', the things that happen before them (*Poetics* VII, X).[1]

Aristophanes, transparently, does not do, or does not consistently do, the sort of thing Aristotle would have his tragic dramatists, and others,[2] do. Aristotelian norms, again and again, are found to be alien to Aristophanic practice. We have drawn

[1] In these passages, for the sake of English usage, I have translated as 'action' Aristotle's πράγματα (usually translated 'incidents) as well as πρᾶξις ('action' proper). M. Heath, *Unity in Greek Poetics* (Oxford 1989) 38–55, argues in effect that Aristotle's 'unity' is less 'organic' than has generally been supposed. For my purposes the supposition is as decisive as the fact—but in any case, fact is not obviously on Heath's side either (see e.g. comments by such reviewers as S. Halliwell, *JHS* 111 (1991) 230–1, and A. Ford, *Arion* 1.3 (1991) 137–43).

[2] The passage from *Poet.* XXIII, for instance, deals with epic.

attention to the significant link between Aristophanes' recreative figuration of character and his mobile style, both of them incompatible with the Aristotelian tradition. We now add a further link in the chain: just as Aristotle's requirements for dramatic organization belong with *his* kind of literature, so Aristophanes' organizational and structural priorities and alignments belong with *his*.

As with style and as with character, of course, Aristophanic plots (to defer the question of *other* organizational alignments)[3] are not all 'inconsequence'. It is not, indeed, that one element succeeds another like the allusions in Eliot's *Waste Land*, in a flurry of utter disconnection (426–8):

> *Quando fiam uti chelidon*—O swallow swallow
> *Le Prince d'Aquitaine à la tour abolie*
> These fragments I have shored against my ruins . . .

And though even that extreme instance is not to be dismissed as a possible reference point altogether, it is (of course) the case that the Aristophanic plot-line often gives an impression of realist continuity, because (of course) there are innumerable moments, or miniature sequences, of consequential action. *Thesmophoriazusae* again: Euripides is at a loss; *therefore* Mnesilochus makes his (admittedly surprising . . .) offer to infiltrate the women's gathering disguised as a woman; *therefore* (well . . .) Euripides accepts the offer; *therefore* Mnesilochus duly goes off to speak up for his kith and kin; *therefore* he is found out and taken prisoner; *therefore* Euripides has to conjure up some stratagem to get him free . . . In large part, this sequence *is* one of consequential action, and (of course) such sequences are not hard to find. Yet, as with style and as with character, the presence of discontinuities within the action (including the action just summarized) is impossible to ignore and, in the end, decisive.

Critics with Aristotelian expectations are (of course) aware that the master comedian fails to live up to them. They readily

[3] In this book 'plot' has its normal English sense, canonized for instance by E. M. Forster in his *Aspects of the Novel* (London 1927), where it signifies a causally determined sequence as opposed to a (mere) 'story', in which events have (merely) a chronological sequence. In recent narratological theory needless confusion has been induced by the anglicizing of the favourite Formalist opposition of 'fabula' (an abstracted order of events) and 'suzhet' (= an actual narrative sequence) as 'story' and 'plot', which, if anything, are the wrong way round.

acknowledge, for instance, 'looseness of structure' and 'weak endings', and in the latter stages of the plays, in particular, they find 'self-contained scenes' and, as likely as not, an absence of 'any genuinely new development'.[4] Of the *Acharnians* we hear:

> the essential issue, Dicaeopolis' achievement of his private peace and his success in persuading the chorus to agree with him, is settled halfway through the play: that is to say, the crisis of the play is located not at or near the end, but before the parabasis, and all that follows the parabasis (*a*) illustrates the consequences of the settlement of the issue and (*b*) at the end, pushes the consequences to the point of a noisy triumph without introducing any significant element of surprise. Each of the four illustrative episodes brings on new characters who serve a purpose in relation to that episode only.[5]

And then there are what impinge as causally unmotivated instances of 'a new turn' within a plot.[6] In *Frogs* Dionysus begins the play with a quest. By the end of the play a quest has been accomplished, but the quest accomplished is not the one Dionysus has before him at the outset. He begins with the purported object of bringing back Euripides from the underworld to remedy a shortage of good tragedians in Athens. He ends by bringing back Aeschylus as—seemingly—a potential source of moral enlightenment for the city. We are nowhere asked to suppose that Dionysus has rethought 'his ideas' on Athens' needs (indeed, it would be misleading to say that we are invited to *suppose* anything). We are simply presented, half way through the play, with an explanation given to Dionysus' servant by Pluto's servant about a dispute in Hades between Euripides and Aeschylus of which Dionysus is to be the judge—then with the dispute itself, with Dionysus' eventual decision in favour of Aeschylus, and finally with Dionysus' preparations to take Aeschylus back to earth at the end of the play. Critics, over the years, have reacted as if to 'two separate conceptions': perhaps it all goes to show that the play as we have it embodies an author's second thoughts? or may we, on the contrary, escape the problem by appeal to some quasi-causal principle of coherence—even

[4] R. G. Ussher, *Aristophanes, Ecclesiazusae* (Oxford 1973), p. xxxiv, and Dover, *Aristophanic Comedy*, 66.

[5] Dover, *Aristophanic Comedy*, 66.

[6] Dover, *Frogs*, 11.

perhaps a development within Dionysus' psyche (or at least within his perspective)—to compensate?[7]

If classical scholarship has been unduly deferential to Aristotelian principles of organic unity, to the detriment of Aristophanes and the appreciation of his comedy, a similar charge can be levelled at literary theory. In few if any other areas of theoretical debate has there been less willingness to confront fundamental questions, and this notwithstanding a mass of narratological enquiries into patterns, strategies, and perspectives.[8] Such investigations tend to assume norms of causally based organization; we need instead a problematizing of them. Yet if Aristophanes has no Aristotle to theorize on his behalf (and it is precisely for such reasons that *our* 'definition of comedy' needs to be so painstakingly constructed), we may at least take encouragement from the thrust of one sophisticated modern theory, in the shape of the parallel and avowedly anti-Aristotelian arguments of Bertolt Brecht. Specifically, as in our discussion of character, so now in

[7] Separate conceptions: e.g. T. Gelzer, *Der epirrhematische Agon bei Aristophanes* (Munich 1960) 26–31. Second thoughts: e.g. Russo, *Aristofane*, 313. Psychic development: C. P. Segal, 'The character and cults of Dionysus and the unity of the Frogs', *HSCP* 65 (1961) 212–15. Development within 'perspective': Lada-Richards, *Dionysus*, 220. Lada-Richards's argument in favour of such 'development' is conducted at length (op. cit. 216–325). Her rewarding analyses seem to me to constitute an admirably documented case for the proposition that Dionysus *switches*, but they do little or nothing for the idea of 'development' as such; e.g. (280–3) she herself shows Dionysus to be an 'amalgam of possible audience-responses' to the agon, while his *actual* responses during the agon simply oscillate between the 'shrewd' and the 'intellectually incompetent' (280); at one point (216–17) she explicitly defends the notion of Dionysiac 'development' against my concept of recreative (formerly 'imagist') character, though she acknowledges in advance (165 n. 12) that the 'development' might be interpreted (without psychological reference) as the 'logic of the narrative'. Cf. below, p. 367 with n. 31.

[8] Regarding the dramatic organization of A's dramas (theoretical perspectives apart), I have profited from many discussions, as different (from each other—and from my own) as Dover, *Aristophanic Comedy*; Russo, *Aristofane*; M. Landfester, *Handlungsverlauf und Komik in den frühen Komödien des Aristophanes* (Berlin 1977); P. Thiercy, *Aristophane: fiction et dramaturgie* (Paris 1986). For the current state of play in this area of theory, see e.g.: A. Z. Newton, *Narrated Ethics* (Cambridge, Mass. 1995); S. Onega and J. A. G. Landa (eds.), *Narratology* (Harlow 1996); K. Elam, *The Semiotics of Theatre and Drama* (London 1980), esp. 117–26; M. Pfister, *The Theory and Analysis of Drama*, tr. J. Halliday (Cambridge 1988) 196–245. Non-Aristotelian possibilities are acknowledged, if at all, in throw-away sentences (which are then duly ignored): 'we can, with some confidence, discuss . . . whether a plot is simple or complex, coherent or incoherent, whether it follows familiar models or contains unexpected twists' (J. Culler, *Structuralist Poetics* (London 1975) 206).

our investigation into dramatic structure and our underlying attempt to seek out the interrelationships between the various facets of Aristophanic comedy, a valuable point of reference is offered by Brecht's theoretical validation of his own theatrical practice.

As Brecht repeatedly urges us to see in his writings on the theatre, seemingly unrelated aspects of drama in fact hang together—above all, aspects of his own innovatory 'epic theatre' as against aspects of the traditional-dramatic, or 'Aristotelian', theatre. In particular he allows us to sense a connection between Aristotelian theatre's 'evolutionary' treatment of character and its 'linear development' of plot, as against the concern of his own epic theatre with 'jumps' and 'curves'. Traditional theatre means *growth*; his own means *montage*, where in place of a 'natural' whole, the individual events are tied together in such a way that 'the knots show'.[9] The 'natural' wholeness which Brecht rejects we may identify as a realist aspiration; and the coherence predicated of his iconoclastic drama has at least something in common with the non-realist coherence embodied in the drama of Aristophanes.

It is apparent that the 'jumps' associated with Aristophanes' characters and plots are not only related in kind: they may be the same thing. In *Thesmophoriazusae* the arbitrary 'decisions' of Mnesilochus and Euripides are also arbitrary turns of the plot. The switch of plot in *Frogs* involves, at the same time, an implicit switch on Dionysus' part which reflects, not that character's state of mind, but its recreative potential. The recreative transformation of the rejuvenated Demos in *Knights* involves a jump, indeed, to a kind of action which stands in a quite different relation to 'reality' than the kind represented by the rival campaigns for the soul of Demos that take up most of the play.

The problematic critical tendency to confront Aristophanes

[9] Brecht, *Schriften zum Theater*, ii. 117, vii. 67. The relevance of Brecht's theory to A's practice has been acknowledged by various scholars (see Silk, 'People', 46) and most recently by I. Lada-Richards, 'Estrangement or reincarnation? Performers and performance on the classical Athenian stage', *Arion* 5 (1997) 66–107. Before Brecht, Pirandello had briefly anticipated the connection between discontinuous character and discontinuous dramatic form: the 'decomposed' and 'incongruous' characters of 'the humorist' are related to 'all that is disorganized, unravelled and whimsical, all the digressions which can be seen in works of humor' (*On Humor*, 144–5).

with Aristotelian norms sometimes, as noted, leads to a search for crypto-causal, neo-Aristotelian 'solutions'. These are often associated with a wholly questionable insistence on making the plays more reassuringly like each other than in fact they are. The plays (we are assured) all focus on a central determinative 'comic hero' who . . . or they all centre on a 'Great Idea' which . . . or they all involve an 'elemental ground-plan' which . . .[10] That there are many similarities between the plays on the surface, and many deep affinities too, is hardly to be denied (and certainly not in this book), but the dangers of specious generalization are ever-present. The innocent-sounding proposition about the determinative hero, for instance, is applicable, more or less, to Dicaeopolis in *Acharnians*. Yet it is not applicable to *Wasps*, where most of the determinations belong to Bdelycleon but the centrality (and the true 'heroic' status) to Philocleon—or to *Knights*, where the determinative figure is, increasingly, Sausage-Seller, but the ultimate focus is Demos.

The neo-Aristotelianizing of Aristophanes comes in various guises. One of the more sophisticated models, but still one to be resisted, we have already flagged as a plausible one for *Plutus*—but, precisely, not for Aristophanic comedy as a whole. No, a man can't be turned into a beetle, but just suppose he were—what would happen?[11] Impossible premise, logical consequences: this pattern, or something of the kind, has been ascribed to Aristophanic Old Comedy, but rarely to any purpose. One commentator, for instance, detects in *Wasps* a mode of humour 'in which a situation or action is *developed logically* [my italics] to an absurd conclusion', because 'something which in real life would be an insuperable practical obstacle is disregarded', and in support of the formula offers an analysis of the dog-trial (764–1008): (*a*) Philocleon wants to try cases and his son wants him to stay at home, so (*b*) the obvious conclusion is that he should try cases at home; (*c*) cases tried at home must be for offences committed in the household; (*d*) the sort of offence committed in a household is the theft of food by a dog; therefore (*e*) a dog must be tried; naturally (*f*) his accuser must be another dog; so (*g*) the speech for the prosecution is

[10] See, respectively: Whitman, *Hero*; Sommerstein, *Acharnians*, 11 (following William Arrowsmith); Sifakis, 'Structure', 124.

[11] Above, p. 26 with n. 4.

made by a dog.[12] Calling this a movement 'from realism to fantasy', the sympathetic analyst adds: 'each stage of the development seems logical, and yet the conclusion is absurd, because Aristophanes has disregarded what would normally be an insuperable practical obstacle: dogs can't talk.'[13]

Elegant though the paraphrase may seem, its thrust is misplaced. At the risk of crushing Aristophanes' humour under a top-heavy scrutiny, let us analyse the analysis. As far as the suggested 'logic' is concerned, what we appear to have here, for a start, is a set of three conclusions (*b*), (*e*), (*g*), drawn from independent premises: (*b*) from (*a*); (*e*) from (*c*) (*d*); (*g*) from (*f*). That is: from the notion of trying cases at home (*b*), it does not follow that the cases 'must be for offences committed in the household' (*c*); nor, from the notion of trying a dog (*e*), does it follow that the accuser 'must be another dog' (*f*). Furthermore, there is no kind of equivalence between the items as a series. The three premises themselves differ drastically in (our indispensable concept) their perceptible distance from 'ordinary' reality, and so too do the three 'logical' relationships involved. 'Philocleon wants to try cases and his son wants him to stay at home': this is, in everyday terms, a relatively innocent and acceptable proposition. By contrast, the notion that 'cases tried at home must be for offences committed in the household' implies some exotic principle of homoeopathy, whereas—different again—the suggestion that the sort of 'offence' encountered in a household is the 'theft' of food by a dog is only acceptable as metaphor, while, finally, the proposition that 'his accuser must be another dog' defies all ordinary experience of reality, with metaphor or without. As for the three bits of logic: the third is almost a tautology (if a dog-accuser, therefore a dog prosecution-speech); the second is eventually, at least, comprehensible (if household offences . . . and if dog thefts . . ., therefore a dog-trial); but the first, as logic, works only by a kind of associative bluff, because 'trying cases at home' does not actually mean what would make 'ordinary' sense here (e.g. trying real cases by proxy), but what makes no ordinary sense (*playing* at trying cases). In this charming episode, lucidly analysed by the commentator, the constituent elements are seen

[12] D. M. MacDowell, *Aristophanes, Wasps* (Oxford 1971) 12–13 (associating A with the 'Theatre of the Absurd').

[13] Ibid.

to belong to quite various dimensions of 'reality' or 'unreality' or to offer us quite different relationships *vis-à-vis* the ordinary reality that we assume or know, love or hate.

Are there no determinative patterns that are characteristic of Aristophanic Old Comedy or at least (a more prudent version of the question) of Aristophanes' extant Old Comedies? For an audience, or a reader, any such pattern must be perceptible, even memorable, and there is indeed one such.[14] It is not, however, a pattern that an Aristotelian could make anything of. It is not necessarily a pattern of consequentially connected incidents, nor necessarily a consequential pattern, nor necessarily a pattern of incidents at all. It is best seen as a sequence of relational states between one interest or party—often, but not always, one focal individual—and the world at large. The pattern involves a series of five states or stages: *A* dissatisfaction, *B* quest, *C* conflict, *D* victory, *E* celebration. In some of the plays this is indeed a formula, however partial, for the plot, and in these cases one central hero, or one central hero along with others, stands at the centre of each phase. In *Birds* Peisetaerus is dissatisfied with Athens, therefore founds a new city, therefore comes into conflict with a series of antagonists (birds, men, then gods), with all of whom he comes to a triumphant accommodation, wherefore the final celebration. In *Acharnians*, similarly, Dicaeopolis is dissatisfied with the war, therefore goes in quest of peace, therefore comes into conflict with war-centred interests, over whom . . . So far as it goes, the schema fits four of the nine extant Old Comedies: *Acharnians*, *Peace*, *Birds*, *Lysistrata*. Furthermore, with some variations it fits the other five too. In *Knights* there is virtually no *E*. In *Wasps* *ABCD* belong to a different character from *E*: Bdelycleon is dissatisfied (etc.), but Philocleon has the final celebration. In *Clouds* *CD* are tangential to *AB*, and instead of *E* there is virtually a second *A*: Strepsiades' quest was to escape his debts; the conflict between Right and Wrong (*C*) is in a sense a consequence of that quest, and the victory of Wrong, *D*, a further consequence of *C*, but *CD* are not a solution to his problem; hence

[14] The schema is applicable to *Eccl.* and *Pl.* too, but those plays are not central to my concerns. Different versions of what is recognizably the schema proposed here may be found elsewhere: see e.g. Sommerstein, *Acharnians*, 11–13. A schema of the kind proposed by Sifakis, 'Structure', is not comparable: it may or may not have been significant at the compositional level, but is hardly operative as a perceptible reality.

instead of a final celebration, there is a second eruption of dissatisfaction on Strepsiades' part at Socrates' expense. In *Thesmophoriazusae*, more simply, there is no *DE*: no victory, no celebration. In *Frogs*, rather as in *Clouds*, though *E* is now operative, *CD* is again tangential to *AB*, in fact more obviously so: whereas the quest was to bring back Euripides, the conflict between Aeschylus and Euripides is not strictly a way of achieving that end, and indeed it results in a different end entirely, the victory of Aeschylus.

It will be granted that, variable or not, the pattern is a significant one, and that its contours are perceptible within any given play. It must be granted, equally, that even where there are visible causal links between its phases, the pattern is never a strictly Aristotelian-consequential sequence, if only because there is never a 'necessary' *therefore* between the conflict and the victory. On the contrary: it is characteristic that the victory is more or less arbitrary, and in one case, *Frogs*, it is actually presented as such. In *Frogs*, Aeschylus and Euripides compete to the death (or life), with Dionysus as judge. After six hundred lines of poetic disputation between the contestants, Dionysus, faithfully reflecting the balance of forces, can only say: 'I can't decide' (δυκρίτως γ' ἔχω, 1433). A minute later he does decide (1468):

> αἱρήσομαι γὰρ ὅνπερ ἡ ψυχὴ θέλει.
>
> Whom my soul doth desire, him will I choose.

The competition that precedes his choice is evidently—in an Aristotelian sense—incidental.[15] As with the transference from Bdelycleon to Philocleon in *Wasps*, and the tangentiality of conflict and victory to what precedes them in *Clouds* and *Frogs*, the overall schema is seen to be indifferent to causality. The pattern, one might say, is compatible with a broadly realist logic of motive and behaviour, but within the pattern one cannot predict how far such logic will be operative.

In any case, if the schema can accommodate causality, it can and does conceal causality-free zones in at least equal measure. As an abstraction, the schema operates on a level of paraphrase at which most of the least Aristotelian features of the plays are simply

[15] See further below, pp. 365–7.

eliminated. In the first place, the pattern tends to ignore the chorus and, not least, the choral parabasis. The parabasis is a prominent structural feature of the nine extant plays, and yet neither is it requisite for the pattern that there be one, nor—from the pattern—is there any way of telling where (or whether) it will occur.[16] Then again, the schema misses out large sequences of what, borrowing a phrase from Pirandello, we might call 'spoken action'.[17] At the beginning of *Frogs* (we recall) the 'action' consists of two elaborate verbal routines which can hardly be considered part of 'the plot' or its 'incidents', any more than they could be implicated in the given schema; yet these are the very stuff of Aristophanic comedy, and they have a specific thematic rationale within their play.[18] On a larger scale, what else but 'spoken action' is the long contest between the tragedians?—and this at least *does*, seemingly, belong in the schema and *is*, no doubt, also the substantial realization of that opening theme. But would it occur to us to call it 'action' at all, but for a tradition of neo-Aristotelian preoccupation with the causal continuum? And isn't it apparent how constricting and unrewarding it can be to confront Aristophanes with Aristotelian terms like 'action' and 'plot' at all?—and apparent, too, why plot summaries are so peculiarly unilluminating in his case? And isn't the thought of these questions, even, enough to suggest again, from a different point of reference, the un-Aristotelian expanses concealed behind, and within, the innocent-sounding sequence: dissatisfaction, quest, conflict . . .?

More simply, of course, there are also the much-discussed 'episodes', which tend to proliferate especially between the victory and the celebration, and which certainly slip out of sight in schematic paraphrase. Take *Birds*. Two Athenians have established *Nephelokokkugia*, or Cloudcuckooland, their utopia in the sky, and we are presented with a sequence of visitors to the new city (859 ff.). Each visitor makes a separate entrance; each has a different reason for coming; each says his bit; and each is promptly sent packing before the next one appears. First we see a priest, come to organize a sacrifice; then a Pindarizing poet, here to

[16] In the event, it sometimes occurs between *D* and *E*, as in *Ach.*, *Vesp.*, *Pax*. In *Eq.* and *Thes.*, it comes in the middle of *C* (and in *Av.* between phases of *C*); in *Nub.*, in the middle of *B*; in *Ran.*, between *B* and *C*. In *Lys.* it is actually part of *C*.

[17] See Elam, *Semiotics*, 126.

[18] *Ran.* 1–20, 21–32: above, pp. 26–9 and below, pp. 277–9.

celebrate the new world in fulsome verse; third, an oracle-monger with warnings for the city; then the scientist Meton with advice on town-planning; fifth, an inspector from Athens, come (evidently) to investigate a prospective new outpost of the Athenian empire; and sixth and last, a law-monger hoping to sell some brand-new laws. The whole breathless sequence is complete in under two hundred lines; it lasts perhaps fifteen minutes in performance. It is a cumulative sequence in the sense that each item adds something new, while the group of scenes as a performed entity would lend itself to an ascending sequence of theatrical pace and effect. As far as logical, or even simply chronological, sequence is concerned, however, various items could plausibly be interchanged.[19] The oracle-mongering, for instance, might well seem to imply a city yet to be founded; a poetic celebration (which here precedes it) might in itself point to a city whose foundation has already taken place. And as far as the rest of the play is concerned—if, by that, we mean the subsequent fate of the city and its citizens—any or even all of the items could have been eliminated altogether.

Above all, though, the schema tends to give a falsely 'realist' impression (to revert to our earlier terms of reference), because, as with the dog-trial in *Wasps*, the specifics that underlie the schematic abstractions need not belong to equivalent levels of reality. Take *Acharnians* and our 'dissatisfaction' and 'quest'. 'Dicaeopolis is dissatisfied with the war, therefore goes in quest of peace': sounds good. Yet this is a drastically reductive summary. Suppose we expand (and slightly rephrase) it to, for instance: 'a citizen is dissatisfied with the fact that his city is at war, therefore seeks to make a private peace.' This still reductive, but less reductive, paraphrase at once introduces a grossly non-realist element, not so much because 'private peace' is self-contradictory in the 'real' world, but because now there is an inconstant relation between the two sections of the paraphrase and any perceived reality behind them. 'A citizen is dissatisfied' is at one, nearer, distance, and '. . . private peace' is at another, further, distance. And this, on reflection, is so true of so many conjunctions in this play and in others, that the inappropriateness of reductive summary for Aristophanic drama, if not already apparent, becomes obvious.

[19] In semiotic terms, Aristophanic construction is often 'serial', rather than 'sequential': see e.g. Elam, *Semiotics*, 122.

Reductive summary as a tool of literary analysis was invented—needless to say?—by Aristotle.[20] It has its uses for realist fiction—for the *Odyssey*, for *Iphigenia in Tauris*, for Henry James; its usefulness for the viewer or critic of Aristophanes is very limited.

In confronting Aristophanic plots and patterns, practising Hellenists, one might have hoped, would have been more resistant to the influence of Aristotle on their presuppositions. It is, after all, no secret that in this area much Greek literature does not work according to Aristotelian *dicta*. From Homer to the late prose romances, Greek literature provides us with a great variety of instances and types, but two broadly distinct groups of composition. On the one side stand Homeric epic, tragedy, Menandrian comedy, Thucydidean history, and the philosophical treatise like Aristotle's. These works are all, *mutatis mutandis*, dominated by a principle of processive or otherwise systematic unity, such as Aristotle himself has taught us to call *organic* unity.[21] These are works where the part is, not just less than the whole, but subordinate to the whole, and where sequence is characteristically consequence, whether within the world of human action or within the sphere of abstract argument. On the other side, more or less, stand Hesiod, the Pindaric ode, Herodotus, the prose romances—and Aristophanic comedy. Here ideas and elements are liable to be organized according to principles of association and dissociation, and parts, though still surely parts of wholes, may often carry a more independent weight. All manner of qualifications come to mind, regarding particular members of both groups and, equally, the proper formulation of the contrast. The question of value, as between the two groups, is left open. Yet the contrast itself is surely beyond dispute.

On the non-Aristotelian side, Hesiod's *Works and Days* provides a simple and unsophisticated instance. At one point that poem consists of a sequence of otherwise diverse thoughts associated by 'the one idea . . . of preserving prosperity after you have earned it'; at another we find 'instruction on sailing' as a sort of 'natural supplement to instruction on agriculture'. Earlier

[20] With summaries of Eur. *IT* and Hom. *Od.* in *Poet.* XVII: cf. Sifakis, 'Structure', 124.

[21] A dramatic, or narrative, composition should be constructed like a living organism (ὥσπερ ζῷον ἓν ὅλον, *Poet.* XXIII): see Halliwell, *Poetics*, 96–9. The *Poetics* itself is in principle an 'Aristotelian' composition, albeit an imperfect specimen of unity in Aristotle's own sense: cf. Halliwell, ibid., 27–37.

on, Hesiod's 'arguments for *Dike* and for work' involve 'a succession of different formulations' made into 'an extended discourse' which 'reduces itself almost entirely to an alternation between *Dike prospers* and *Hybris is punished* or between the advantages of work and the disadvantages of idleness'.[22]

More illuminatingly, we might situate Aristophanic comedy within a more specific tradition of popular art, within and beyond the ancient world. It is demonstrably the case, though seldom acknowledged, that some of the salient features of popular art are constant over long periods, even over millennia. These include a liking for miniatures (jokes, riddles, proverbs, slogans, sound-bites) and for diffuse wholes, from Xenophon's *Ephesian Tale* to the modern soap opera—and especially for miniatures within diffuse wholes. Hence the quotable quote, the 'memorable moment ripped out of context'.[23] And hence the hit song, a notorious occasional phenomenon even in the high-art world of opera,[24] but an unashamed norm in the American musical, which in certain ways (we have already broached the thought) offers some intriguing parallels to an Aristophanic play. On the modern stage, or screen, 'musicals' in fact cover a wide spectrum from the 'loose' to the fully integrated.[25] The integrated end of the spectrum is occupied by art-musicals like the Bernstein–Sondheim *West Side Story* (1957). In this reworking of Shakespeare's *Romeo and Juliet*, the dramatic action forms a strict causal sequence,

[22] The quotations belong to M. L. West, *Hesiod, Works and Days* (Oxford 1978) 43–7, who attempts to explain the phenomena with reference to a theory of oral composition. The characterizations are good, but the attempted explanation is beside the point. Homeric poetry has at least as much to do with oral composition as Hesiodic poetry does, but (despite West's remarks on the subject, 43–4), the Homeric poems are essentially Aristotelian in organization, as Aristotle himself was the first to note (*Poet.* VIII). Other early epics were no doubt equally oral too, but (as Aristotle lamented) less unified than Homer's (*Poet.* XXIII). The late prose romances are entirely un-oral, but also less unified than Homer in Aristotelian terms.

[23] L. Zuidervaart, *Adorno's Aesthetic Theory* (Cambridge, Mass. 1991) 31, paraphrasing Adorno's dismissal of modern popular-classical music-listening habits, which Adorno (writing in 1938) saw as 'arrested at the infantile stage': 'Über den Fetischcharakter in der Musik und die Regression des Hörens', in Theodor Adorno, *Gesammelte Schriften*, ed. R. Tiedemann (23 vols., Frankfurt 1970–), xiv. 34. Cf. below, p. 414 with nn. 134–5.

[24] The famous allusion in *Don Giovanni* to 'Non più andrai' from *Figaro* attests both hit and quote together.

[25] On the distinction and its implications see G. Block, *Enchanted Evenings: The Broadway Musical from Show Boat to Sondheim* (New York 1997) 3, and *passim.*

while the music is not only organically related to the action but is itself organized as a coherent whole, complete with quasi-Wagnerian leitmotifs and orchestral commentary on the melodic line. At the loose extreme are the song-and-dance revues of the 1920s in which generally unrelated sketches and songs follow one another in non-narrative or, at most, loosely narrative sequence.[26] And in the middle come shows like the Gershwins' *Lady, Be Good!* (1924) with a story, but more or less detachable songs: the subsequent standard 'The Man I Love' was in and out of this Gershwin show, and others.[27]

This detachability is a distinctive, and for us a highly relevant, characteristic of the genre. *West Side Story* (and its like) apart, the glory of most musicals is that they make the great songs possible, as crystallized moments of shared poignancy or exuberance. Audiences know that, in films as in stage shows, while there may be a cumulative brio to the dramatic whole, any stretches of story in view at any given time are liable to be a pretext for the more or less self-sufficient musical bits in between. Yet audiences also know that in successful musicals of this type the detachable songs will still relate, in their own way, to the stuff of the drama. In the classic Warren–Dubin film *Forty-Second Street* (1933), the songs are clustered at the end and not one is directly related to the plot (or indeed to the characters, or choruses, who sing them). However, every song, and most obviously the title song, is *constructively related* to the film's theme ('putting on a Broadway show'). This, surely, is the kind of relationship that, say, the phallic song in *Acharnians* has with its play. Hunted down by the chorus on account of his shameful one-man peace, Dicaeopolis comes up with a one-man musicalization of Dionysiac ritual, and celebrates the joyful rhythms of peace-time in the name of the god of natural felicity, who is also the god of the dramatic festival ('putting on a Dionysus show . . .'?). In terms of probability or necessity, there is no need for the song, or its particular contents, to be a part of the play at all. Yet its dramatic relevance on a broad thematic level is as apparent as its redundancy in Aristotelian

[26] A case in point is the *Garrick Gaieties* revue of 1925, whence 'Manhattan' (above, p. 183).

[27] R. Lissauer, *Lissauer's Encyclopedia of Popular Music in America* (New York 1991) 544.

terms; and in this paradigm of popular art we have, equally, a model of Aristophanic composition in general.

The detachable song, in effect, takes place as an extended moment out of sequential time, and recreative construction of character, as we have noted, points in the same, momentary, direction. There is, surely, a profound connection between Aristotle's organic unity and the notion of time as a unified sequence. For Aristotle, for the whole realist tradition, in Lukács's words: 'to fulfil all the conditions of unity is actually to unify the past, the present, and the future.'[28] In Aristophanic comedy, time need not have this unified force. It follows that sequential events—events presented sequentially—may 'really' imply coexistence. This is clearly the case with the 'episodes'. They are like the items in a cumulative list.[29] A sequence like the visitors to the birds' new city is notionally, but only notionally, set on a progressive time-axis. Of course, a jump like the one implicit in Demos' rejuvenation could be said to (re)instate such an axis, but selectively and in reverse.

As usual, there are qualifications to be made. We have considered a sequence of relational states that, at a fairly rarified level of abstraction, is broadly characteristic of the plays: dissatisfaction, quest, conflict, victory, celebration. This is clearly a temporal sequence: the dissatisfaction must come before the quest, which must come before the conflict, and so on. We would seem, therefore, to be arguing that at a certain level of abstraction Aristophanic comedy is indeed structured on a time-axis, albeit not necessarily in 'ordinary' (that is, realist) consequential terms. It is actually (we might further suggest) only because this is the case that *any* consequential sequences are possible and comprehensible in this kind of drama. It is only because the underlying sequence from dissatisfaction to quest (and so on) is a temporal one that it can ever accommodate the apparatus of motivated continuity at all: Euripides is at a loss ('dissatisfied'), *therefore* Mnesilochus makes his offer . . . If, then, we say that Aristophanic comedy is outside any temporal order to the extent that it is discontinuous and non-realist, we must also say that in large part

[28] G. Lukács, *Soul and Form*, tr. A. Bostock (London 1974) 158.

[29] Cf. García Márquez, *One Hundred Years of Solitude*, 421: 'Melquíades had not put events in the order of man's conventional time, but had concentrated a century of daily episodes in such a way that they coexisted in one instant.'

it has accommodated itself to the logic of time—and that, no doubt, from the many clashes and discrepancies between this logic and its opposite a good deal of humour derives.

Aristophanic characters sometimes speak as if they knew what their realist counterparts could not *already* know. In *Lysistrata* an ambassador seems to know who Lysistrata is. 'We are not told how [he] knows', says a commentator, missing the point: the point is that the characters *and* the play, too, have no strictly coordinated past, of a kind that would invite the question to arise.[30] At the end of *Frogs*, Euripides appeals to Dionysus to fulfil an oath of which the audience, this time, knows nothing. A commentator is confused: 'Dionysus has not, within the play at least (and we are hardly justified in assuming off-stage conversations . . .), sworn by any gods to bring Euripides back to Athens.'[31] Rather, from the standpoint of this moment, Euripides' past and Dionysus' past are notional pasts, which can be recreated as occasion demands. Again, references to external time need not be co-ordinated. At *Wasps* 264–5 'the crops . . . need some rain'. This (says another commentator) 'implies that the season is early summer; on the other hand, the fact that Philocleon is provided with a fire and soup when judging in his domestic court (811–12) suggests that the weather is cold . . . Aristophanes is indifferent to consistency in such matters.'[32] It would be better to say that the indications of a time-axis are apparent, not real. We may, if we have realist yearnings, deplore the fact, but the fact is that time as a realist continuum is only operative when so presented. At the end of a play, for instance, it may well be inoperative. *Clouds*: 'Strepsiades revenges himself on Socrates by brute force, burning down the school; but he still has to live with his son and his creditors.'[33] Not so: there is no 'still', unless we are shown one. *Wasps*: Philocleon's dance ends the play, displacing (literally) the vengeful victims of his earlier escapades. Inappropriately, the realist mind is left wondering about the victims and their threats and what might happen tomorrow: 'by contrast with . . . *Wasps*, a New Comedy plot tidies everything up and discourages us from asking, as we leave the theatre, "and what happened *then*?"'.[34] In New

[30] *Lys.* 1086, with Henderson ad loc.

[31] *Ran.* 1469, with Stanford ad loc.

[32] Sommerstein on *Vesp.* 264–5, comparing *Thes.* 67 ('winter') and 80 ('early autumn').

[33] Dover, *Clouds*, p. xxiii.

[34] Dover, *Aristophanic Comedy*, 223; cf. above, p. 247.

Comedy, rather, precisely that sort of question *would* occur to the audience, and so would be anticipated and answered already. In *Wasps*, on the contrary, unless we are shown that there *is* to be a tomorrow—but a recreated tomorrow could be anything—there is no pressure to invent one.

If Aristophanes' construction of time is inclined to be distinctively non-realist, so too is his treatment of place—meaning the dramatic location of the moment. Here, though, commentators have found it easier to present the facts of the matter without realist preconceptions.[35] Early on in *Clouds* (138) Strepsiades explains that he lives a long way off in the country—and yet: 'for all dramatic purposes his house and that of Socrates [in the city] are treated as adjacent . . . In *Acharnians* . . . Dicaeopolis' house is in his own rural deme at 267, but apparently in the city for most of the rest of the play.'[36] In *Wasps*:

> at the beginning of the play the scene is the front of the house of Bdelycleon and Philocleon . . . When Philocleon is on his way home from the party, the scene may be in the agora (1372), though we are back in front of the house by the end of it (1444). Some passages have no particular location. And even if a location is clearly stated, the characters are at the same time actors performing in the theatre and can converse with the audience (54–135, 1497–500).[37]

These points are well made (and, *inter alia*, the relevance of 'breaches of the illusion' is apparent). Once more we see that the essence of Aristophanic discontinuity—now seen to subsume the whole spatio-temporal dimension—is that there is no single reality-distance (the Brechtian-sounding phrase is convenient, if clumsy) at which a play's own times and spaces are all operative. 'No particular location': this possibility, above all, contradicts the premise of a 'real setting' altogether.[38]

The contrast between Aristophanic norms and the realist continuities of plot, time, and place has further implications. Consider the opening of a representative work of realist drama, Sophocles' *Oedipus at Colonus* (Oedipus and Antigone, 1–19):

[35] Perhaps because Aristotle is so uninterested in place, even in 'unity of place', a principle of organic drama which, notoriously, was left to the Renaissance to formulate and enact: see e.g. M. Kommerell, *Lessing und Aristoteles* (Frankfurt 1940) 286–308.

[36] Sommerstein on *Nub.* 138.

[37] MacDowell, *Wasps*, 18–19.

[38] Cf. Silk, 'Space and solitude'.

ΟΙ. τέκνον τυφλοῦ γέροντος Ἀντιγόνη, τίνας
χώρους ἀφίγμεθ᾽ . . .
ΑΝ. πάτερ ταλαίπωρ᾽ Οἰδίπους, πύργοι μὲν οἳ
πόλιν στέφουσιν, ὡς ἀπ᾽ ὀμμάτων, πρόσω·
χῶρος δ᾽ ὅδ᾽ ἱερός . . .
οὗ κῶλα κάμψον τοῦδ᾽ ἐπ᾽ ἀξέστου πέτρου.

OED. Old man's, blind man's daughter, Antigone,
Where are we now? What land, what city? Who
Entertains the wandering Oedipus today?
. . . .
If you see anywhere where we might rest,
Public ground or sacred space,
Stop me and sit me down. We must know
Where we are. We are not of this place.
We need to ask and follow the instructions.
ANT. Wretched father Oedipus, I see
Towers that crown the city still far off.
But this is holy ground: that I can tell.
Here's, in abundance, laurel, olives, vines,
And flocks of nightingales within, sweet-singing,
And a rough stone here: sit down on it.

An obvious feature of this passage is its precise and powerful articulation of a scene. From these few lines we learn the identity of the speakers and their relationships (genealogical and moral), but beyond that we are invited into a particular moment in a particular myth and called on to involve ourselves in the realization of a specific locality, its texture and its sensuous particularities.[39] And even if we knew nothing of the myth or any legend concerning the site which the two travellers have reached, our impression would be much the same: a pre-existing world, *re*-constructed by a tightly organized progression of words—as a pre-existing face can be reconstructed in all its independent detail from eyewitness descriptions and an artist's image.

That impression is testimony to the distinctive power of Sophocles' realism, to which—let us call it back once more—the amiable opening of *Frogs* presents a drastic contrast:

[39] Not yet identified as Colonus, but already inferentially the legendary site of Oedipus' arrival in Athens. This aspect of the play, and the sense of localization at its start, has been much discussed. See most recently L. Edmunds, *Theatrical Space and Historical Place in Sophocles' Oedipus at Colonus* (Lanham 1996).

Shall I tell them one of the usual jokes . . .

. . . .

Yes, anything you like—except 'I'm all squeezy'

. . . .

So what was the point of my carrying all these . . .

. . . .

Well, how can you be carrying? You're being carried.

Our Xanthias and our Heraclean Dionysus are of course *en route* to Heracles himself—but the words have little enough bearing on the dramatic situation that is implicit in the costume and movement on stage.[40] Their situatedness in that situation is not just less overall than is the case with Sophocles' words: it is fitful, unpredictable, sometimes alluded to, sometimes obliterated. There is a paradox here. Tragedy deals with the less attached verities of universal myth, and yet makes sure its mythical world is presented in specifiable terms and palpable coherence. Aristophanes' comedy assumes the realities of a situated and specifiable present, and yet moves freely in or out of it, in a way that truly recreates it. By comparison with Sophocles' mythical domain, Aristophanes' generally more contemporaneous world is unstable. Xanthias and Dionysus, as they talk about squeezes and baggage-carrying (*Frogs* 1–34), are—like Antigone and Oedipus—going *somewhere*. That at least must be apparent from their visible movements on stage. In the original stage-setting, no doubt, it would also be apparent that the immediate somewhere is the door of a visible house, although the dialogue at first says nothing of it. However, there is no verbal indication of where all the talking is taking place; indeed, there is no verbal reference to place at all until Dionysus abruptly refers to the door once the discussion of baggage-carrying is complete (35). For all the immense sensuous appeal of, say, Dicaeopolis' evocation of the bustle of Athens, it is fair to say that even this bustling world is, in an inescapable sense, not *there* unless it is evoked, and, if there, still a world without inherent stability.

In Greek tragedy, as in realist fiction in general, we commonly find a fictive world *presupposed*. That is, the impression we have is of a pre-existing stable reality, appropriately and (in cases like *Oedipus at Colonus*) meticulously verbalized. At the beginning of

[40] See above, p. 28.

Acharnians, as Dicaeopolis contemplates the still empty Pnyx, we seem to be starting, at least, with a stable world: the world of politically conscious Athens, satirically adjusted perhaps, but to a seemingly specifiable degree. Yet by the time that Dicaeopolis (or his house) has been tacitly transported to his village in the country (267), the degree of apparent adjustment has changed drastically. This is not to say that the real world of politically conscious Athens has been mislaid or somehow pretended into non-existence, but that a world of a different kind is our immediate concern, a world which indeed relates urgently to politically conscious Athens, but which (to restate the point) has no stable relationship with it, because it is not (or does not imply) an external world of any equivalent kind.[41] The realization of any external world is not the inner goal of any Aristophanic play, and apart from short sequences (of which the opening of *Acharnians* is one) Aristophanes' undoubted genius for sensuous immediacy (to return to *that* point) is not generally available for such an end.

An essential property of an external world is its relationship to others. It has boundaries, and the more delineated it is, the clearer the boundaries, the distances, and the approaches involved, and the possibility of traffic with other worlds. Any relationship with other worlds implies the possibility of traffic between them. In the simplest kind of instance, the worlds are topographical, located in physical space, and the traffic involves physical motion. In this way the wandering Oedipus moves between the horrors of Thebes, which serve as backcloth to Sophocles' play, and the district of Colonus where he is to find a refuge. Traffic between such worlds involves process, and process is the life-blood of realist literature, serving its need for continuity, for subordination, for development, and frequently constituting its overt concern: *how* (in Sophocles) Oedipus finds peace, *how* (in Henry James) Isabel Archer finds herself caught up with Madame Merle, and *how* the relationship will develop. In Aristophanic comedy the operative significance of process is limited and at times even problematic. When priest, poet, and oracle-monger (and the

[41] Here postmodern formulae can be helpful. For example, 'the real referent "outside" the discourse which both fiction and realism presuppose has no function here as a non-literary, non-discursive anchoring point predating the text': Macherey and Balibar, 'Literature as an ideological form', 80 (though for A one needs to add 'no *assured*, or no *constant*, function').

rest) turn up in *Nephelokokkugia*, they turn up in episodic sequence, with no processive relationship between their visits. The sequence, in effect, is a list; and, as so often in Aristophanes' lists, the items are paratactically adjacent to each other, but not logically subordinated, one to another. Once again we acknowledge a visible and precise correspondence between Aristophanic style and the larger, organizational aspects of the drama.

In *Birds* we are not concerned with the process whereby we might plausibly get from priest to poet, or poet to oracle-monger, any more than we ask, '*how* can this switch have come about?', when Euripides accepts Mnesilochus' implausible offer in *Thesmophoriazusae*, or when the *Frogs* chorus cease to be frogs and become initiates, or cease to be initiates and become ordinary patriotic Athenians, or when in *Knights* Demos is rejuvenated, or when Dicaeopolis' physical being is transferred from town to country. And at the end of an Aristophanic comedy, we do *not* ask, 'and what happens *next*?', because the world we are momentarily acceding to has no guaranteed continuous existence outside itself: it does not necessarily imply any processive connection with a next stage.

The characteristic lack of concern for process shows itself at the heart of the Aristophanic plot, for instance in the way that great aspirations are realized. In three plays peace is achieved, and by grotesquely variable means. In *Acharnians* our hero gains the victory by making a private treaty, in *Peace* by rescuing the goddess after a flight to heaven on a dung beetle, in *Lysistrata* by fomenting a sex strike. Yet it is not the grotesqueness or the variability of the means that makes the attainment of peace in these plays so non-processive (and therefore so non-realist). It is the disinclination to articulate the means on each occasion. As any reader or spectator can confirm, it does not occur to us to reflect how *else* a sex-strike or a beetle-journey or a private peace might have turned out; whether the particular structure of incidents (as Aristotle would call it) that underlies each manoeuvre is the necessary one to achieve the goal; whether, indeed, the steps in the process are all set out. Rather, the very impertinence of thus getting from war to peace is a source of comic delight. Process, in any ordinary sense, is simply not at issue; and here at least Aristophanes is far removed from Brecht and his Marxist insistence on the logic of action, the consequences of behaviour, and, behind them, the (real or supposed) laws of social mechanisms and historical development. Brecht's theatre, in his own words, is

> . . . chiefly interested in the attitudes which people adopt towards one another, wherever they are socio-historically significant . . . It works out scenes where people adopt attitudes of such a sort that the social laws under which they are acting spring into sight. For that we need to find . . . such definitions of the relevant processes as can be used in order to intervene in the processes themselves . . . [Each] scene is played as a piece of history.[42]

What the author of *Frogs* and *Acharnians* is creating, or re-creating, is not quite diagnostic attitudes, enactments of social laws, or pieces of history.

If Aristophanes' dramatic constructions are not exemplars of causality, Marxian or Aristotelian, this does not make them arbitrary assemblages of miscellaneous items. Yet it is not simply intermittent or residual strings of causal continuity that hold them together. For a start, it is characteristic that, if not connected processively, the sections, incidents, and details of an Aristophanic play are associated thematically.[43] Like songs in the modern musical, they tend to carry a constructive relationship—though the nature of the construction, its apparent dramatic significance, and its seeming importance within the play are all variable. Contrast the essentially formal function of the thematic links between the beginning and end of *Peace* (*begins* with dung cakes, *ends* with wedding cakes), or the Dionysus–Xanthias 'feeds' at the start of *Frogs* (their opposition and their preoccupation with verbal routines prefiguring the great contest to come), with the definitive association between Philocleon and animals in *Wasps*.[44] Some plays are conspicuously richer than others in thematic material of a particular kind. In *Frogs* the same part of the prologue that prefigures the contest also introduces thoughts on the proper relationship between masters and slaves, with special

[42] From 'Über die Verwendung von Musik für ein episches Theater' (1935), tr. Willett, *Brecht on Theatre*, 86.

[43] 'Plot is but the temporal projection of thematic structures': Culler, *Poetics*, 224. One might consider the case for seeing (e.g.) the pseudo-sequentialities of *Av.* 859 ff. as 'thematic' (above, pp. 265–6).

[44] Cakes in *Pax*: μᾶζαν . . . κανθάρῳ, 1; πλακοῦντας ἔδεσθε, 1358; cf. Bowie, *Aristophanes*, 136–7, Whitman, *Hero*, 110. 'Feeds' in *Ran.*: above, pp. 31–2, 39. Philocleon and animals: above, pp. 252–5.

reference to topical happenings in Athens.[45] In the prologue we have (from Dionysus, 21–3)

> What an outrage, what impertinence,
> For me, Dionysus, son of—Juice,
> To struggle along on foot and let him ride . . .

and (from Xanthias, 33–4)

> why didn't I join the fleet?
> Then I could have told you where to go.

The theme recurs in the parabasis on the lips of the reflective chorus (693–4):

> *καὶ γὰρ αἰσχρόν ἐστι τοὺς μὲν ναυμαχήσαντας μίαν*
> *καὶ Πλαταιᾶς εὐθὺς εἶναι κἀντὶ δούλων δεσπότας.*

> What a disgrace that slaves who fight one battle
> Should be 'Plataeans', be masters, just like that.

Soon after this comes a short disputation on masters and slaves between Xanthias and a fellow-menial in the underworld (738–53). At the end of the play the theme surfaces again in Pluto's instructions to Aeschylus to (first, 1501) 'make our city safe' and (last, 1504 ff.) to tell miscellaneous public figures currently in positions of power to 'hurry on down' (i.e. die *now*) and (1509–11)—

> *κἂν μὴ ταχέως*
> *ἥκωσιν, ἐγὼ νὴ τὸν Ἀπόλλω*
> *στίξας αὐτοὺς καὶ ξυμποδίσας . . .*

> and if they don't,
> So help me Apollo, I'll give them
> A slave tattoo and chains . . .[46]

Implicit in the theme, presented so symmetrically within the play, is an argument: slaves (it seems) should not be masters, but some

[45] Above, p. 32. Contrast the use of a minor detail in one scene to anticipate the content of the next (*vel sim.*): see e.g. the *Ach.* example noted below, p. 282 n. 53.

[46] For the god of underworld darkness, Pluto, to swear by Apollo, god of heavenly light, is a surprise (and here a joke): one thinks, *per contra*, of the first simile in the *Iliad* (1. 47) where Apollo (dispensing plague) 'comes on like night'. As comm. (e.g. Dover ad loc.) note, Pluto here speaks like a slave-owner—though also like a god (*ἐγώ* + fut., 1514: M. S. Silk, 'Heracles and Greek tragedy', in I. McAuslan and P. Walcot (eds.), *Greek Tragedy* (Oxford 1993) 127–8, with n. 53).

'masters', perhaps, should be slaves . . . The theme in question (it also seems) is of marginal relevance to the main concerns of the play; that does not make the technique any less significant. In particular, it is worth noting the role of the choral parabasis in helping to carry the given motif. The Aristophanic parabasis has been called 'a prism through which the play's . . . themes are passed', and while this cannot stand as a formula for all the plays, it suggests, felicitously enough, the kind of constructive relationship the Aristophanic part is liable to have with its whole.[47]

As far as the parabasis itself is concerned, *Peace* offers a representative example, and a convenient one, in that we have discussed most of its contents separately already.[48] The parabasis of this play (729–818) is delivered while Trygaeus is on his way back to earth (by means suitably unexplained, but suitably divine: 720–8). The leader of the chorus (of, currently, farmers) begins by telling his comrades to give their tools to the stage-attendants (729–33); then offers the great praise of 'our director'—in the third person (734–53), then abruptly the first person (754–60)—for 'his'/'my' banishment of 'buffooneries' in favour of 'great' art, and the famous assault on Cleon, 'the Jag-Toothed One himself', in return for which 'I' deserve the public's support (760–74). There follows that astonishing *tour de force*, the choral song to the Muse, *pro*-peace and *contra*-Carcinus and 'my' other rivals (775–818). Everything here, transparently, is in thematic apposition to the play it belongs to—from the prayer for peace and the evocation

[47] The quotation comes from A. M. Bowie, 'The parabasis in Aristophanes: prolegomena, *Acharnians*', *CQ* 32 (1982) 29 (who, overemphatically, writes, 'the play's chief themes'). Cf. in *Ran.* again the ideologically loaded theme associated with the word-group γεν(ν)- represented esp. by γεννάδας, 'gentleman', and γενναῖος, 'noble', 'genuine'. Near the start of the play, Dionysus uses the adj. of Eur. and his verbal conceits (97), but later the two words are used more often and for more 'traditional' figures. After a reference to εὐγενεῖς citizens in the parabasis (727), Dionysus is γεννάδας at 739 and Aesch. at 997; γενναῖοι is then used of the traditional public (1011, 1014, 1019), of poets from Orpheus to Homer (1031), and finally of the respectable spectators 'corrupted' by Eur. (1050). Remarkably, γεννάδας in all occurs 5 times in *Ran.* and only 3 times in A's extant plays otherwise; γενναῖος (or -ως) 10 times in *Ran.*, 12 times otherwise. The theme is noted briefly, in a rather different spirit, by Goldhill, *Poet's Voice*, 204, and Lada-Richards, *Dionysus*, 284–5. On the elusiveness of the parabasis in A, Bowie, 'Parabasis', and Goldhill, *Poet's Voice*, 196–205, are sensitively attuned; T. K. Hubbard, *The Mask of Comedy: Aristophanes and the Intertextual Parabasis* (Ithaca 1991) makes the parabasis both more integrated and more 'autobiographical' than it is (and fails to problematize the 'auto').

[48] Above, pp. 46–8, 111–16, 146, 241.

of Cleon (its great emblematic opponent, now dead) to the talk of stage attendants, the director/poet, *his* other plays, his rivals in the competition for which *this* play is entered, and the presiding Muse.

The instances of the *Peace* parabasis and, before it, the *Frogs* prologue prompt the thought that thematic links tend to involve material generated by the chorus or else motifs 'innocently' introduced in the prologue. For instance, *Frogs* is not the only play whose content is loosely prefigured by an opening scene between squabbling characters. Consider Demos' two slaves in *Knights*, whimpering a duet of lamentation at their common plight, but the one eager for 'a way out', the other with 'no guts'.[49] Or heroic Lysistrata against her more pragmatic supporters in *Lysistrata*. Or thrifty father versus spendthrift son in *Clouds*. These cases, no doubt, vary in importance and (the same thing?) in adjacence to the subsequent conformations: in *Clouds*, above all, the vivid contrast of father and son is obviously most directly related to the battles to come. Yet in all these cases the modality of contrast has some thematic significance.

In so far as such thematic links are characteristic of Aristophanic drama, Aristophanic drama can be said to have its own characteristic unity: not Aristotelian-causal unity, but thematic unity. Any such claims, of course, for thematic unity and thematic significance raise the simple-sounding question: what counts as 'a theme'? It is, no doubt, an obstacle to the appreciation of the unity underlying Aristophanes' plays that his themes are often not identified as such at all—despite (or partly because of?) the fact that some of them recur from play to play. A case in point is the celebration of the poet (and the dismissal of his rivals) in the *Peace* parabasis just discussed. This kind of self-referential material is, of course, familiar enough in Aristophanes, especially (but not only) on the lips of the chorus. It may take the form of programmatic-sounding comment, like the weighing of 'great art' against 'buffooneries' in *Peace* (739–58). It may equally amount to more or less jovial abuse. A representative instance here is the treatment in *Acharnians* 1150–73 of one Antimachus, who as *khorêgos* once allegedly sponsored a chorus and failed to give due entertainment to its members. His reward (the *present*

[49] *Eq*. 9–10 (both), 11–12 (A), 17 (B). On the identity of the two, cf. above, p. 231 with n. 43.

chorus hope) will be to have a dog steal his own dinner one day, and then have some drunk assault him in the dark one night and for him to (1168–73) . . .

> ὁ δὲ λίθον λαβεῖν
> βουλόμενος ἐν σκότῳ λάβοι
> τῇ χειρὶ πέλεθον ἀρτίως κεχεσμένον·
> ἐπᾴξειεν δ' ἔχων τὸν μάρμαρον,
> κἄπειθ' ἁμαρτὼν βάλοι Κρατῖνον.
>
> Feel for a stone in the pitch black,
> Pick up a turd he just shat,
> Charge with his gleaming brickbat,
> And miss, and hit Cratinus.

The short song (of which these are the closing lines) is 'a choral interlude', says one commentator; 'a satiric chanson, entirely outside the action of the piece', says another.[50] If we insist on privileging 'the action', this will very likely be our response, and the song is indeed, no doubt, a good example of the action- or plot-detachable song—from which, however, it does not follow that it *is* detached, thematically at least. Its thematic connection is not difficult. Dicaeopolis is off to dine and party with the priest of Dionysus (1085–93), by which celebration his victory will be rewarded and symbolically confirmed. The celebration betokens victory for Dicaeopolis in the play, for the chorus as (now) his allies in the play—and for the chorus as performers and the poet Aristophanes himself, if victory is his (therefore theirs) in the dramatic competition. Just as, in the lofty Pindaric epinician, there is a symbolic meeting between the athletic victory celebrated and the poet's own achievement as celebrator—between the 'swift chariot' of a victorious Hieron and the 'chariot of the Muses'[51]—so in the less exclusive art-world of Aristophanes now, the poet's and the hero's competitive fortunes seem to converge. And mindful of dinner, and in anticipation of Dicaeopolis' final celebration, the chorus duly recall a notional/notorious occasion when dinner (customarily provided for performers by the *khorêgos*) was denied and the whole institutionalized competition, and with it the hope of victory, threatened.[52] The choral curses on such enemies of the

[50] Representively, Sommerstein and Starkie ad loc.
[51] Pind. *Ol.* 1. 110: see e.g. Gerber ad loc.
[52] On the *khorêgos*, see above, p. 7. Whether the occasion was notional or

institution (and the hope) finally fall, as if by some ritualized joke, on Cratinus, Aristophanes' fellow-poet and rival in this very competition, who threatens the hope (though not the institution)—that is, this particular celebratory alignment of poet, hero, and chorus.[53]

In this book we have made much of transformations: characters 'become', 'turn into', suddenly appear 'as', what (before the transformation) they were not. These moments of becoming are not just mechanisms of discontinuity—significant though that function certainly is. In several plays they constitute another, recurring, theme for our attention. Think of *Wasps* and Philocleon's animal spirits. Or think of *Thesmophoriazusae*, that drama of shifting *personae*, disguises, and imitations, where transformation—stylistic and other—is not (as in *Wasps*) especially associated with any one character in the play, but is certainly a recurring focus of attention in its own right. This is a play in which the playwright Agathon becomes his characters, because (149–50)

> *χρὴ γὰρ ποιητὴν ἄνδρα πρὸς τὰ δράματα*
> *ἃ δεῖ ποιεῖν, πρὸς ταῦτα τοὺς τρόπους ἔχειν*
>
> A dramatist must tailor his life-style
> To the dramatic task in hand,

while Mnesilochus, with Agathon's aid, but with no such artistic aim in view, becomes a woman (266–7):

> *ἀνὴρ μὲν ἡμῖν οὑτοσὶ καὶ δὴ γυνὴ*
> *τό γ' εἶδος*
>
> We're there! The man's a real woman
> To look at—

on which basis alone is he able to join the women worshippers. Duly uncovered and taken prisoner, Mnesilochus casts around for an escape. His first attempt involves seizing a hostage, in the shape of a baby belonging to one of the women, only to find, on inspection, that (733–4) 'the baby's turned | Into a flask of

notorious hardly matters, nor would it to the original audience (though that audience might have known which it was). Cf. above, p. 229 n. 41.

[53] On the 425 competition, see above, p. 19. There is further thematic material in the passage discussed. The harsh satire on Antimachus includes a physical assault on him (1166–7) and his unsuccessful counter-attack (1168–73)—as if in anticipation of the description of Lamachus the wounded general that at once follows (1174–89).

wine' (*ἀσκὸς ἐγένεθ' ἡ κόρη | οἴνου πλέως*), which the women have brought for their own diversion: no escape results. Desperate to send word to Euripides, he recalls a trick used in the latter's *Palamedes*, where a message was dispatched by sea, written on an oar (771–3):

> *ἀλλ' οὐ πάρεισιν αἱ πλάται.*
> *πόθεν οὖν γένοιντ' ἄν μοι πλάται; πόθεν; πόθεν;*
> *τί δ' ἄν, εἰ ταδὶ τἀγάλματ' ἀντὶ τῶν πλατῶν . . .*
>
> But there's no oars here.
> What can I do for oars? What can I do?
> Suppose I use these tablets as the oars . . .

There follow the two great transformational episodes, in which hope of escape again beckons: Helen–Menelaus and Andromeda–Perseus, the first recalling Euripides' recent *Helen* and the second another notable Euripidean drama, *Andromeda*.[54] In both cases Mnesilochus 'is' (still) a she and in both cases transformational phraseology is in the foreground. Guarded by one of the women, he has an idea (850):

> *ἐγᾦδα· τὴν καινὴν Ἑλένην μιμήσομαι*
>
> I know what—I'll play his new Helen.

The woman's rejoinder is scornful (862): 'Turning into a woman *again*?' (*αὖθις αὖ γίγνει γυνή;*). The new Helen is shortly joined by 'her' Menelaus (Euripides), and it is when their transformational double-act—inexplicably—fails that Euripides, now, initiates a second—equally unsuccessful—tragic transformation, though it is still Mnesilochus who announces the parts (1011–12):

> He just showed up as Perseus!—it was a sign
> For me to become Andromeda.[55]

Failures as rescue-attempts though they may be, these two scenes, particularly the first, serve to acquaint us with a whole portfolio of transformational poses, involving tragic quotations and adaptations (855),

[54] Rau, *Paratragodia*, 53–89.
[55] Above, p. 243. Here, as often, the 'becoming' is articulated through the verb *γίγνεσθαι*.

> *Νείλου μὲν αἵδε καλλιπάρθενοι ῥοαί*
>
> These are the virgin waters of the Nile

a hypertragic recognition/welcome-home duet (909–14),

> —*Ἑλένῃ σ' ὁμοίαν δὴ μάλιστ' εἶδον, γύναι*
>
> . . . .
>
> —*ὦ χρόνιος ἐλθὼν σῆς δάμαρτος ἐσχάρας,*
> *λαβέ με λαβέ με, πόσι . . .*
>
> —Lady, I see in you the very look of Helen
>
> . . . .
>
> —O come at long last to your wife's deep fire,
> Husband, take me, take me . . .[56]

and some spirited attempts on the part of the woman guard to restore 'normality'. When 'Menelaus' asks (896),

> *ξένη, τίς ἡ γραῦς ἡ κακορροθοῦσά σε;*
>
> And who is this old woman that reviles you?

and his 'Helen' answers, mythologically (897),

> *αὕτη Θεονόη Πρωτέως*
>
> Proteus' daughter, Theonoe

she resists the attempt to have herself transformed as well and counters—in substance and style—*de*transformationally (897–9):

> *μὰ τὼ θεώ,*
> *εἰ μὴ Κρίτυλλά γ' Ἀντιθέου Γαργηττόθεν·*
> *σὺ δ' εἶ πανοῦργος.*
>
> For god's sake,
> I'm Critylla from Gargettus, my dad's Antitheus,
> And you're a crook.

The transformational role-playing in the play is completed by a weird series of presences. The more obvious include Agathon's

[56] *ἐσχάρας* in 912 as codd. (with ingenious obscene innuendo in place of the original Euripidean *ἐς χέρας*: Sommerstein ad loc., Henderson, *Maculate Muse*, 143). Hypertragic, partly because *ἐσχάρας* produces a poetic 'terminal accusative' (V. Bers, *Greek Poetic Syntax in the Classical Age* (New Haven 1984) 62–85), partly because of the metrical switch from (*ὦ* . . .) iambic trimeters to (*λαβέ* . . .) dochmiacs (the quintessential tragic metre: West, *Greek Metre*, 108), with emotive repetitions in Euripidean lyric manner (cf. above, p. 165 n. 9).

servant acting out his master's high-style preciosities as a religious votary (39–42),[57]

> *εὔφημος πᾶς ἔστω λαός,*
> *στόμα συγκλῄσας· ἐπιδημεῖ γὰρ*
> *θίασος Μουσῶν ἔνδον μελάθρων*
> *τῶν δεσποσύνων μελοποιῶν.*
>
> Host, be silent! Lips, be sealed!
> Deep within my master's halls
> The Muses' throng has come to pay a visit
> Melodious.

Then there is the cross-dressing effeminate Cleisthenes, come to warn the women of the presence of an intruder. The new arrival announces himself in the masculine; he is given his male name;[58] and he is sufficiently still a man for the women to exclude him peremptorily when the cross-examination of Mnesilochus threatens to reveal the mysteries of the women's Thesmophoria in his presence (627–8). He is, however, properly introduced, by the chorus, 'in character' (571–2):

> *παύσασθε λοιδορούμεναι· καὶ γὰρ γυνή τις ἡμῖν*
> *ἐσπουδακυῖα προστρέχει . . .*
>
> Stop bickering! Look, there's a woman
> Running up this way . . .

Then there are the women themselves. Their festival, the Thesmophoria, was an all-women's institution at Athens, whose tone was one of abstention and continence, as ritual expression of which the women were strictly separated from their men. In the play this ritual separateness is duly stressed (the taboo that Mnesilochus is violating by his male presence depends on it), but is additionally reinterpreted to give the women an imitation-male-democratic council and assembly, with all the due procedures to match (372–6):

> *ἄκουε πᾶσ'. ἔδοξε τῇ βουλῇ τάδε*
> *τῇ τῶν γυναικῶν· Τιμόκλει' ἐπεστάτει,*
> *Λύσιλλ' ἐγραμμάτευεν, εἶπε Σωστράτη·*
> *ἐκκλησίαν ποιεῖν ἕωθεν τῇ μέσῃ*
> *τῶν Θεσμοφορίων . . .*

[57] Notwithstanding a hint of prosaic self-deflation in 'pay a visit': ἐπιδημ-εύω and -ιος are Homeric, but ἐπιδημ-έω is not attested in pre-Hellenistic verse (despite its religiose connotations: cf. Williams on Call. *h. Ap.* 13).

[58] Masc.: *φίλος* 575 etc., *ἀκούσας* 577 etc. Male name: *Κλείσθενες* 634.

Oyez, oyez. At a meeting of the women's council, held under the chairpersonship of Timoclea, it was proposed by Sostrata that an assembly be held on the morning of the second day of the Thesmophoria . . . Signed Lysilla, Secretary . . .[59]

After all of which intensive playing of roles, Euripides' final transformation, as old madam Artemisia, is almost sedate.

In *Thesmophoriazusae* transformations constitute a major theme, which is also, to some extent (as in Mnesilochus' disguise as a woman), part of 'the plot', while greatly exceeding it. The same is true in *Birds*, where, however, the transformations are more systematic, if also more homogeneous. In *Birds* the dissident Athenian Peisetaerus, aided and abetted by his friend Euelpides, finds himself opposing not only his former city, by abandoning it, but the whole order of the universe, by challenging the power of heaven. Persuading the birds to take advantage of their intermediate position between gods and men by establishing their own city in the sky, and having now 'become' a bird himself, he takes over command of the city and thereby of all things, first as chief official (*arkhôn*, 1123), and eventually as supreme ruler (*turannos*, 1708) and new Zeus (1748–53). This apotheosis is plausibly seen as the climactic instance of a 'subversion . . . of the established hierarchy of the universe . . . men are spoken of as birds, gods as birds or as men, birds as men or as gods'.[60] At the heart of this 'subversion' is a principle incidentally articulated by Peisetaerus to an Athenian informer anxious to become a bird in the manner of Peisetaerus himself (1436–9):

ΣΥΚ. ὦ δαιμόνιε, μὴ νουθέτει μ', ἀλλὰ πτέρου.
ΠΕΙ. νῦν τοι λέγων πτερῶ σε.
ΣΥΚ. καὶ πῶς ἂν λόγοις
ἄνδρα πτερώσειας σύ;
ΠΕΙ. πάντες τοι λόγοις
ἀναπτεροῦνται.

INF. Don't tell me off, friend, please. Just give me wings.
PEI. I'm doing it now with words.

[59] The Greek is in verse, but is more appropriately rendered in prose (unusually, there is a bit of prose not long before, 295–311). On the democratic-procedural cast of the passage, see Sommerstein on 372–9.

[60] A. H. Sommerstein, *Aristophanes, Birds* (Warminster 1987) 3.

INF. Give a man wings
With words? How can you do that?
PEI. Words
Make everyone fly.

This is then explained with reference to a series of punning jokes: words can make you feel *high*[61] . . . and so on. Not all the transformations in the play work through puns, but (by contrast with the actual disguising that is so much in evidence in *Thesmophoriazusae*) most of them are primarily and essentially verbal—though the theme does indeed get under way with a 'real' transformation. Tereus the Hoopoe had been a man and 'become a bird' (ὄρνις ἐγένετο, 16), as had his bird-servant (72–3). Peisetaerus, with Euelpides in search of the Hoopoe, duly claims to be a bird himself ('*We're* not men . . .', 64–5). After a long series of more or less untranslatable jokes centred on the status and identification of such changelings,[62] we embark on the second phase of transformation, in which birds are recreated as gods—provided that (in Protagorean fashion) men think of them as gods. Initially surprised (571),

> καὶ πῶς ἡμᾶς νομιοῦσι θεοὺς ἄνθρωποι κοὐχὶ κολοιούς;
>
> And how are men to think of us as gods, and not as jackdaws?

the birds are persuaded by Peisetaerus (586–7) that

> ἢν δ' ἡγῶνται σὲ θεόν, σὲ βίον, σὲ δὲ Γῆν, σὲ Κρόνον, σὲ Ποσειδῶ,
> ἀγάθ' αὐτοῖσιν πάντα παρέσται
>
> If men see you as God, Life, Earth, Cronus, Poseidon,
> All good things can be theirs,

after which their transformation becomes a matter of assertion (716):

[61] *Av.* 1447: ὑπὸ . . . λόγων ὁ νοῦς . . . μετεωρίζεται. The verb is to be taken as standard usage of mental excitement (not 'metaph.', *pace* Dunbar ad loc.) on the strength of (from 5th cent. BC) Hegem. Parod. 1. 1 p. 42 Brandt and (from 4th cent. BC) Demosth. 13. 12, together with the rare derivative μετεωρισμός, Hp. *Acut. Sp.* 14 (and cf. LSJ s.v. μετέωρος III): on the lexicographical logic here, see Silk, *Interaction*, 27–56, esp. 40–1 and (on the evidential value of derivatives) 29–31, 48.

[62] Anticipated already at 57–9, where the Hoopoe is summoned first by the human παῖ, then by the quasi-avian ἐποποῖ.

ἐσμὲν δ' ὑμῖν Ἄμμων, Δελφοί, Δωδώνη, Φοῖβος Ἀπόλλων.

We're your Ammon, Delphi, Dodona, we're your Phoebus Apollo.

The Greek for 'bird' (*ornis*) is also the Greek for 'omen', and given the significant part played by omens in Greek religion, the birds are able to point to the verbal coincidence as proof of their own divine status:[63] they are assuredly man's 'prophetic Apollo' (722). This established, Peisetaerus can call them simply 'the new gods' (τοῖσι καινοῖσιν θεοῖς, 848).[64] The old gods, conversely, are now on a par with mere men, and hence, by due transformational procedures, may be said to *be* men, and goddesses women. Athena, martial protectress of Athens, is now merely (830-1)

θεὸς γυνὴ γεγονυῖα πανοπλίαν
ἕστηκ' ἔχουσα . . .

a goddess, turned woman with
A suit of armour on . . .

So far, transformations impinge as enactments of each of the play's successive phases. Eventually they seem rather to combine in a hectic crescendo. A young man comes in warbling a song from Sophocles, 'O, to be an eagle' (γενοίμαν αἰετός . . ., 1337); Basileia—'Sovereignty' of heaven, and (as such) sought by Peisetaerus as symbol of his new dominion—is only 'a woman' (γυναικός, 1639);[65] birds (in Peisetaerus' blunt words to the erstwhile deity Iris) are 'men's gods now' (ὄρνιθες ἀνθρώποισι νῦν εἰσιν θεοί, 1236), while Iris herself is treated not as a god (ποίοις θεοῖς, 'what gods?', 1233), but as a woman who can be threatened with rape (1253–6) or indeed as a bird who can be 'shooed' away (οὐκ ἀποσοβήσεις; 1258). Peisetaerus, finally, completes the circle in his own person. Now transformationally a bird, he demands Zeus' sceptre 'for us birds again' (ἡμῖν τοῖσιν ὄρνισιν πάλιν, 1600),[66] and in the last line of the play is duly acclaimed as 'god supreme' (δαιμόνων ὑπέρτατε, 1765).[67] The man-become-bird has become

[63] The 'proof' culminates in a series of transformational equations: ξύμβολον ὄρνιν, φωνὴν ὄρνιν, θεράποντ' ὄρνιν, ὄνον ὄρνιν (721).

[64] τοῖς καινοῖς θεοῖς again at 862, τοῖς πτερίνοις θεοῖς at 903.

[65] With 1337 cf. 978–9, 987–8, 1380. On Basileia see below, p. 407 n. 119.

[66] 'Again' presupposes the birds' cosmological claims to primal authority set out at 685–703.

[67] For good measure, Peisetaerus at one point adds to the tally of cumulative transformations by seeming to offer to make Heracles τύραννον ὀρνίθων (1673)—but, as it turns out, only by sleight of word (see Sommerstein ad loc.).

bird-become-god,[68] while—almost passing without comment in this welter of transformations—his marriage to divine Basileia carries with it an implicit rejuvenation. The 'old man' he once was (γέρων ὤν, 1256) now has a share in 'youth' (τῆς ὥρας, 1723).[69] Up to and including this final resolution, certainly, the transformational themes of the play are orchestrated to a remarkable degree.

The almost schematic quality of the 'logic' of the transformational phases in *Birds* is unusual. There is indeed often a schematic tendency in the organization of the plays, but of a rather different kind. What tends to be involved is a pattern of mutually defining emblems. The most obvious and familiar pattern is antithesis, and this tends to be articulated in the concrete metonymic form of conflicting individuals or groups. Thus we have: in *Frogs*, literary tradition versus experimental modernity (Aeschylus versus Euripides); in *Clouds*, educational sophistication versus unsophistication (Socrates versus Strepsiades); in *Acharnians*, war versus peace (Lamachus versus Dicaeopolis); in *Lysistrata*, the same antithesis, this time articulated as men versus women. Such configurations have a better claim than either plot or process to be counted as the 'first principle' of the dramas they belong to. They are often more significant than the characters who embody them, while the plots constructed around them tend to be

[68] *Pace* some critics (e.g. Sommerstein, *Birds*, 3), there is no implication that the (other) birds and Peisetaerus are in different categories, or that he is exploiting them. Simply, *they* make *him*, and *he* makes *them*, special. At 1707–8 a herald pronounces the γένος of birds as τρισμακάριον and Peis. as τὸν τύραννον, and in effect pronounces them τρισμακάριοι *because* he is τύραννος. Likewise the chorus at 1725 sees his marriage as μακαριστόν for the city. The point is amplified at 1726–8 and enforced at 1731–42 through the analogy of ('orthodox') divine marriage. It is not just that Peis. is *marrying into* divinity or power: he is conferring them on the community (ἀστοῖς καὶ βασιλεῦσιν: Pind. *Pyth.* 1. 68). *Inter alia* the fact that on the brink of power (1579–693) Peis. 'is preparing birds for the table in precisely the manner he so strongly criticized in 531–8' (Sommerstein, loc. cit.) has no realist-logical significance: the joke is at the expense of such logic, not at the expense of 'the birds' themselves.

[69] And also in 'looks' (τοῦ κάλλους), though the text is doubted by some (see Dunbar ad loc.). Dunbar on 1723 seeks to ascribe the ὥρα and the κάλλος of 1723 exclusively to Basileia, but (*a*) the reference of the words is open in the Greek (simply, '*what* youth! *what* beauty!'); (*b*) Peis. has already been praised for his new appearance (1709–12); (*c*) in that praise, *his* looks *and* Basileia's are explictly conjoined (he is παμφαής, 1709; she has κάλλος, 1713); (*d*) the same conjunction is irresistibly suggested by the envelopment of the open-ended ὥρα and κάλλος between the masculines of 1721 (μάκαρα) and 1725 (γήμας).

pretexts rather than ends; and unlike those characters and those plots, they are open to immediate enforcement from the wealth of parallel structures, balances and contrasts, which characterize Aristophanic writing—from the stylistic unit to the parabasis—at all levels.[70]

When the configuration involves an opposition, as in the cases cited, dramatic movement consists in the juxtaposition of the coordinates, as if in some kind of ritual confrontation, and the effective imposition of one coordinate on the domain of the other. In this way tradition is imposed on modernity in *Frogs*, unsophistication on sophistication in *Clouds*, peace on war in *Acharnians* and *Lysistrata*. However, the emblems are not abstract coordinates, nor are their confrontations abstract. Accordingly, the imposition is represented physically. In *Lysistrata* the sexes fight hand to hand, but in the eventual settlement 'man stands by wife and wife by man again' (1275–6). Physicalization tends to be at its most graphic at a play's end. At the end of *Acharnians*, peace is translated into a physical banquet from which Lamachus, embodiment of war, is excluded; in *Clouds*, Strepsiades physically destroys the edifice that Socrates had created; in *Frogs*, Aeschylus physically leaves the underworld for the coveted return to earth, where Euripides had hoped to go. In all such cases, Aristophanes' ultimate concern is to present a physical enactment of the imposition and, more lavishly, of the central confrontation on which the imposition depends. This means, *inter alia*, ensuring that the presentation of the confronted emblems is compatible with a decisive judgement of value, even if (as usual) that judgement does not rest on any logical demonstration. Any such demonstration would focus attention on the process whereby one member of the duo supplants the other and the imposition takes effect—a process of supplanting and effecting that would (we recall) involve transaction between recognizably pre-existing worlds. One thinks again of the typically realist-Aristotelian process of verbal transaction and implicit understanding whereby Oedipus comes to occupy the pre-existing external world of Colonus, or the process of suffering and learning whereby he

[70] Parallelism in the stylistic unit: above, pp. 126 ff., 165–6. In the parabasis, see e.g. Handley, 'Comedy', 106–8, Pickard-Cambridge, *Dithyramb*, 194–9, 213–28. Parallelism in the parabasis (as also in the agon) is closely associated with the syzygy (below, p. 292 n. 75).

attains a state of grace *vis-à-vis* his past in another external world, in and around Thebes.

Aristophanes is not primarily interested in presenting any pre-existing external worlds (we come back to this point). His new worlds are recreated. When (as in the cases noted) these worlds are antithetical, they are presented not in processive relationship, but as opposing tableaux, richly elaborated, where the elaboration conveys their mutual exclusivity. It is characteristic of such oppositions that specific points of contrast from all the far-flung corners of experience are presented in unacknowledged series, as if (though in themselves unpredictable) to be ticked off, like items in a list. So in *Frogs*, where Aeschylus and Euripides embody the opposition, we are offered a series of contrasts in everything from religious affiliation to verbal style. Aeschylus swears by the traditional powers of nature (886),

> Δήμητερ, ἡ θρέψασα τὴν ἐμὴν φρένα
>
> O Demeter, wet-nurse of my soul,

Euripides, by the deities of the new intelligentsia (892):

> αἰθήρ, ἐμὸν βόσκημα, καὶ γλώττης στρόφιγξ . . .
>
> O Aether, my pasture, O Hinge of the Tongue.

Aeschylus recommends himself in concrete images evocative of traditional ideals (1016),

> . . . πνέοντας δόρυ καὶ λόγχας καὶ λευκολόφους τρυφαλείας . . .
>
> . . . real heroes, breathing spear and lances, helms white-crested . . .

Euripides in intellectual conceits redolent of modern preoccupations (942),

> ἐπυλλίοις καὶ περιπάτοις καὶ τευτλίοισι λευκοῖς
>
> A diet of sound-bites, exercises, raw vegetables.[71]

[71] A discontinuous list of three distinctive items. 'Sound-bites', because of Eur.'s supposed addiction to gnomic generalization (below, p. 416): ἐπύλλια here (and presumably also, *pace* comm., in its other two occurrences, *Ach.* 398, *Pax* 532) is not 'versicles' (LSJ, meaninglessly: are Euripidean verses shorter than the usual?), but the diminutive of ἔπος, 'saying, proverb' (LSJ s.v. I. 5), a much better-established sense than LSJ's two citations would suggest (Hdt. 7. 51 τὸ παλαιὸν ἔπος, Ar. *Av.* 507 (of a supposed proverb)): cf. e.g. Pind. fr. 35b (of the phrase μηδὲν ἄγαν), Soph. *Ant.* 621 (κλεινὸν ἔπος), Anaxarchus 1 Diels–Kranz (ἔπος

Such antithetical patterns are common, not invariable. There is one already in the early *Banqueters* (427 BC), which (as the few surviving fragments and testimonia show us) portrayed an old man with two sons, Decent and Dirty (ὁ σώφρων and ὁ καταπύγων), the one brought up on Homer, the other on rhetoric;[72] and the pattern is maintained, beyond *Frogs*, in the two surviving late plays.[73] Yet sometimes antithesis is subsumed or even supplanted, notably in *Thesmophoriazusae*, where (contrary to a fashionable misreading) a latent opposition between men and women, apparent in the pseudo-polemics of the parabasis, is not made operative beyond a superficial level, and, instead, a more complex series of patterns helps to define the play as a whole.[74] The antithetical pattern is, nevertheless, characteristic.

It is characteristic, above all, that the emblematic antitheses, where these occur, are articulated on a one-against-one basis in more or less stylized structures. The agon is the most obvious of these structures; and, with its elaborate 'syzygy'-pattern of opposing songs and speeches in formal debate,[75] its relationship to the great antitheses might seem obvious as well. Nevertheless, it is misleading to ascribe to the agon any decisive relationship with these central antithetical patterns, let alone with Aristophanic drama as a whole. In *Wasps* the agon proves to be quite tangential to the ultimate movement of the play. In *Acharnians* there is a debate centred on a notable speech by Dicaeopolis, but there is no precisely formalized agon. *Thesmophoriazusae* has a comparable speech by Mnesilochus, but again there is no formalized agon, and this is a play without a central antithesis anyway. Conversely, in

as the outcome of πολυμαθίη). περιπάτοις: both medical exercise and an allusion to Euripidean stage movement (see Sommerstein ad loc.). 'Raw vegetables' (lit. 'white beet'): both a purgative and an allusion to the canard about Eur.'s mother (see Dover on 942–3).

[72] See *PCG* iii. 2. 123, *testim.* vi (= *Nub.* 529 with schol.), with frs. 205, 233.

[73] In *Eccl.* political malaise, embodied in male agedness and its traditional politics, is challenged by a new communism fostered by the men's younger womenfolk, while in *Pl.* benevolent old man Wealth and 'tragic' woman Poverty (423–4) confront one another in A's last surviving agon.

[74] See below, pp. 320 ff.

[75] The iambic or epirrhematic syzygy is, essentially, a four-part ABAB pattern, within which AA respond in sung form and BB in the form of speech or recitative: Handley, 'Comedy', 106–10, offers a helpful overview. Such structures, highly characteristic of A's Old Comedies, are especially (but not exclusively) associated with the agon and the parabasis: see the analyses in Pickard-Cambridge, *Dithyramb*, 213–28. On the formal features of the agon, see esp. Gelzer, *Agon*.

Birds (which again has no clear antithesis at its centre) and *Lysistrata* (which does), there is a formal agon, though no true debate, because one speaker (Peisetaerus, Lysistrata) dominates the proceedings largely or entirely. In *Knights*, there is not one formal agon, but two—but then, in this play, most of what happens is contest, formal or informal, anyhow.

A central antithesis is realized by the overall organization of a play, not by any single set-piece. The extended example of *Acharnians*—a play with a straightforward antithetical basis, but no agon—should make the point clear. In this play the opposition, peace against war, is already implicit in Dicaeopolis' opening speech (1–42), where war is the unwelcome status quo—unwelcome especially to the countryman, 'Loathing the town, longing for my parish' (33)—and the peace-lover's receding hopes that the Assembly will discuss peace are bound to be frustrated, because (26–7) 'as for peace, | They couldn't give a damn.' The immediate *they* of this accusation are the presidents of the Assembly, but it soon becomes clear that any spokesman for peace will find himself in confrontation with a multitude of *them*, some of them active embodiments of war, some obstacles to peace by complicity or inertia. Within a few minutes, a couple of the latter make successive appearances in the first two of a long series of adversarial scenes: Dicaeopolis versus . . . The two scenes, moreover, have an obvious parallelism. An ambassador sent, years before, to the king of Persia to get money for the war effort returns with 'the King's Eye', who communicates the futility of the enterprise in pidgin Greek (100–25); another ambassador, Theorus, returns from the king of Thrace with a body of mercenaries who show their true colours by stealing Dicaeopolis' shopping (163–74).[76] Before these two episodes comes a short scene in which a divine peace-maker Amphitheus is expelled from the Assembly (45–58); between them, an even shorter one in which Dicaeopolis sends Amphitheus off to Sparta to procure a one-man peace (128–33); after them, another (175–203) in which Amphitheus returns with treaties and warnings about the resentment of the old Acharnian countrymen of the chorus (183):

> σπονδὰς φέρεις τῶν ἀμπέλων τετμημένων;
>
> Our vines are cut down, and you've made a deal?

[76] Cf. Sommerstein on *Ach.* 164.

The foreign imposter scenes, then, are framed within a larger pattern of contrasting alternations.

Oppositional content, oppostional form: this intensity of antithesis is maintained for the rest of the play, albeit the forms (and, so to speak, the contents) are not always the same. The third Amphitheus scene is followed by a quite new contrast of performative set-pieces: on the one side (204–40), the entrance of the angry chorus, seeking out the traitor Dicaeopolis; on the other (241–79), our hero's phallic ritual with wife and daughter in celebration of peace; both scenes combine speech (or, in the chorus's case, recitative) and song. The chorus and Dicaeopolis now meet in protracted open opposition (280–392), much of it articulated in precise parallelism.[77] Two one-off sequences follow. The first (393–488), between Dicaeopolis (in search of oratorical weaponry) and Euripides (the man to provide it), is not in itself, except on the most trivial level, confrontational (if only because, as Dicaeopolis' arms-supplier, Euripides is on the same side); the second (496–556) is Dicaeopolis' speech in defence of peace. The chorus' response to the speech (557–71) is to split into antithetical halves, for and against, at which point Lamachus appears, as the full embodiment of war and the ethos of war in opposition to Dicaeopolis; it is from this point that the emblematic opposition is translated into two contrasting individuals, albeit one—Dicaeopolis—is given more time and more words to make the position he embodies known. After a stylized debate between the two (572–625),[78] Lamachus withdraws to carry on the war, and the chorus pronounce themselves convinced by Dicaeopolis' arguments and deliver the parabasis (626–718) with much talk (and song) of topicalities, beginning with the poet's career ('Ever since our director . . .', 628) and ending with the troubles of the aged (717–18):

> *κἀξελαύνειν χρὴ τὸ λοιπόν—κἂν φύγῃ τις ζημιοῦν—*
> *τὸν γέροντα τῷ γέροντι, τὸν νέον δὲ τῷ νέῳ*
>
> In future, like should exclude like: so let the old
> Deal with the old in court—and young, the young.

[77] Including, *inter alia*, a chiastic ABBA sequence (ode 284–301, epirrhema 302–18, antepirrhema 319–34, antode 335–46) between 284 and 346 (Pickard-Cambridge, *Dithyramb*, 212).

[78] Part of an iambic syzygy that Pickard-Cambridge (*Dithyramb*, 213) calls a 'quasi-agon'.

These details have a characteristic relevance to the themes of the play: the veteran chorus members, and Dicaeopolis himself, are representatives of 'the old',[79] while 'our director' goes on to claim to offer guidance to the city, as Dicaeopolis, on the play's behalf, just has ('Comedy has a sense of duty too', 500). Other items touched on during the parabasis have a more direct relationship to the play's antithetical basis: from Cleon and tricky foreigners (warmongers and accomplices of warmongers: 659–60, 634–40) to the music of the countryside (the songs of peace: 673–4).

This parabasis as a whole—substantial, striking, rhapsodically relevant to the play as a whole—effectively divides the play in half at the moment of decision in favour of peace. The two halves thus created, then, themselves constitute a contrasting pair: up to this point a world of struggle, and from now on a world of fulfilment. Demonstrating and enacting its special status, furthermore, the parabasis introduces a new and quite distinctive mood and quality of feeling, in its lament for 'the old'[80]—while conversely its characteristic responsional syzygy-construction enacts the definitive antithetical thrust of the play in formal terms. This central section of the drama is, therefore, in every sense the centre of the drama.

The relationship between the two main sections of the play, created by the parabasis that divides them, is now schematically enforced by a parallel disposition of minor characters. The *struggle* began with a short sequence of exotic travellers, from the King's Eye to the Thracian mercenaries confronted by Dicaeopolis; the *fulfilment* begins with a short sequence of regional figures seeking out Dicaeopolis, who, now at peace, has set up his private trading-area (719–28). The visitors, from Megara (729–835) and Thebes (860–958), have their visits complicated by a pair of Athenian trouble-makers (an informer and one Nicarchus)—as the earlier scenes were complicated by the two rogue ambassadors.[81] Another rich sequence of oppositional moments culminates in the final

[79] e.g. the chorus are γέροντας at 222; Dic. is addressed as γέρον at 397. On the age of a γέρων, cf. M. S. Silk, 'Nestor, Amphitryon, Philocleon, Cephalus: the language of old men in Greek literature from Homer to Menander', in F. De Martino and A. H. Sommerstein (eds.), *Lo spettacolo delle voci* (2 pts., Bari 1995), ii. 166.

[80] See above, pp. 198 ff.

[81] Amphitheus (the 'immortal', 47), from the earlier part of the play, has no direct counterpart in the second half, except for the miracle-worker Dicaeopolis himself.

tableau of words (1190–227) in which Dicaeopolis and Lamachus act out the alternatives they embody in the minutest stylistic detail ('Boys, get me up'—'Girls, get it up': 1214 ff.).[82] That particular detail is in fact part of the climax of a most elaborate parallelization: a messenger summons Lamachus to war (1073 ff.), another messenger summons Dicaeopolis to a Dionysiac feast (1085 ff.); Lamachus' slave brings out the wherewithal to arm his master, Dicaeopolis' slave brings out the delicacies to feed his master (1097 ff.). The victory of peace is articulated by paratactic accumulation; one is reminded irresistibly of the now familiar paratactic list of blessings on the stylistic level.

Striking moments *en route* to this closing sequence include parallel personifications of 'war' (πόλεμος, 979 ff. and 'reconciliation' (διαλλαγή, 989 ff.) in matching subsections of the 'second parabasis',[83] and symmetrical scenes in which Dicaeopolis refuses to share peace with a fellow-farmer Dercetes (1018–36), but does offer a share to a bride and groom (1048–66). The juxtaposition, musically enforced within a syzygy,[84] carries a clear judgemental implication. As the first speech in the play proposes (and the proposal is never questioned), war is being maintained by the stubbornness or inertia of the male citizen-body. As a woman, the bride is 'not to blame for the war' (1062),[85] and the bridegroom, at first rebuffed (1054–5), can sample peace with her. Short as it is, this scene serves to point the interpretation of the one before it: as a citizen, Dercetes has been one of the stubborn or the inert, and no reward is due to him. Representatively, then, structural organization plays its part in determining the meaning of the action and conveying that meaning in dramatic terms. And the whole rich complex of balances and contrasts, parallels and symmetries, that the play embodies does precisely this on a larger scale. The alternative worlds of war and peace are thereby interpreted and the alternative conveyed—and the manifold details of the play, including such particularities of 'plot' and also 'character' as are fairly ascribed to it, serve this end.[86]

[82] Above, p. 125.

[83] *Vel sim.*: cf. Bowie, 'Parabasis', 34 n. 38, and (on the concept in general) P. Totaro, *Le seconde parabasi di Aristofane* (Stuttgart 1999).

[84] See Pickard-Cambridge, *Dithyramb*, 214.

[85] τοῦ πολέμου τ' οὐκ αἰτία, with αἰτία Blaydes's conj. (accepted by Coulon and others) for codd. ἀξία. Either way, the point is broadly the same.

[86] It should be obvious why it is (to say the least) inappropriate to see Dic. as 'a

It is worth stressing—to turn the argument back for a moment—that both the kind of determinative organization just discussed and the intensive patterning that seems 'naturally' to accompany it have their counterpart at the level of structures on a smaller scale. If we scrutinize the movement of a passage like *Knights* 1164 ff. (Paphlagon and Sausage-Seller),

> —A chair for you: I got in first
> —You missed the table: I got in firster . . .[87]

it becomes clear that the progress of a dialogue (or it might equally be a song, or speech, or a section of recitative) may be determined by the 'logic' of parallelism. If Paphlagon says *this*, Sausage-Seller may say *that*; had Paphlagon not said *this*, Sausage-Seller might not now be saying *that*; had Sausage-Seller not been due to say *that*, then Paphlagon might not have said *this*; and, generally, had Paphlagon and Sausage-Seller not been participants in (or constructors of) a parallel series, their particular contributions might have taken a different tack altogether. And as for the intense patterning that the overall organization of *Acharnians* depends on, this has *its* counterpart, and more, on the musical level in the characteristic syzygy-structures of parabasis and agon.[88] And it is by now abundantly apparent that the fullness and relative precision of such correspondences finds no equivalent in the construction of the plot. On the contrary: the discontinuities that abound on the stylistic level find *their* counterpart as much in the construction of Aristophanes' dramatic fictions as in the representation of the beings who people them.

At the level of overall organization, there is one other significant set of patterns: reversal and inversion. Given the interconnectedness of elements in Aristophanic comedy, there is an obvious temptation to posit some intimate connection between reversal/inversion, on the one hand, and the favoured antitheticality (combined with the instinct for transformation), on the other,

selfish and solipsistic hero' (Bowie, 'Parabasis', 40) or 'a fantasy of total selfishness' (Dover, *Aristophanic Comedy*, 88): cf. the sensible discussion (with bibliog.) in MacDowell, *Aristophanes and Athens*, 75–7. That view in any case grossly ignores the representative status of Dic. beyond the individual: see above, p. 228 with n. 37, and cf. below, pp. 406–9.

[87] Above, pp. 127–8.
[88] Above, p. 292 with n. 75.

but there is no necessary connection.[89] In *Thesmophoriazusae* reversals and inversions abound, but there is no significant antithesis in the play;[90] the same might be said of *Birds*, with its essentially triangular configuration of birds, men, and gods, and the various reversals of role between members of the three orders. Conversely, a play may have its central antithetical basis, but no inversion or reversal to speak of, unless it be simply the common comic 'change from unhappiness to happiness' on the part of the leading player or players:[91] witness *Acharnians* and *Peace*. In *Clouds*, on the other hand, the reversal of Strepsiades and Pheidippides from respective enthusiast and sceptic towards the new Socratic Enlightenment to the opposite is crucial to the revenge of the old (Strepsiades) on the new (Socrates) in the final development of the play, but then this is an unusual play in which there *is* development, and the alignment of opposites and inversions/reversals is—organically—related to that.[92] In *Wasps*, where the generations are again involved, the familiar pattern of behaviour whereby the young resist the orthodoxies of their elders (witness, of course, the end of *Clouds*) is inverted, so that the son Bdelycleon labours in vain to reduce his father to order, the recreative corollary of which is that the old man *becomes* 'young' in his own right: 'I'm only young, you see' (νέος γάρ εἰμι, 1355). Here, though, the antithetical basis of the earlier part of the play (pro- and anti-Cleon) has faded from view, and this inversion belongs to a different, and richer, configuration.[93]

From *Clouds* to *Birds* to *Lysistrata*, many of these inversions and reversals imply inverting and reversing assumed power-relationships between the dominant and the dominated. This is oddly apparent in *Thesmophoriazusae*, where 'dominant and dominated' means 'men and women', but the play itself is *not* 'about' men-versus-women[94]—and roles are *still*, repeatedly, reversed. The upshot is a peculiarly autonomous weight to each instance of reversal—that is, to the scenes or moments when the women

[89] Critics are often sloppy and assume one: I myself have been guilty of such sloppiness in 'People', 170–1.

[90] See below, pp. 320 ff.

[91] The 'change' is not, of course, invariable: above, pp. 58–9. The phrase is Aristotle's (e.g. *Poet.* VII, implicitly applied to comedy at *Poet.* XIII, 1453^{a}12–14, 30–8).

[92] See above, pp. 216–19, and below, pp. 352–65.

[93] See below, pp. 369–75, 425–35.

[94] See below, pp. 320 ff.

take a decision in their Assembly, when Mnesilochus is taken prisoner by them (he at once seeks, unsuccessfully, to restore stereotypical power-relations by kidnapping their 'baby'), when the weak 'man' Cleisthenes is put down by the strong women ('stand aside—I'll do the interrogating', 626), when Euripides is forced to come to terms with them. In this connection, one is forcibly reminded of Bakhtin's vivid image of the medieval carnival as inverted counter-culture to the civil and ecclesiastical establishment. Everywhere we meet (in his words) 'the relativity of prevailing truths and authorities . . . the peculiar logic of the "inside out"'.[95]

Yet for all its brilliance, Bakhtin's carnival model is not, in this connection, a helpful point of reference. Aristophanic comedy presents us with rich patterns of juxtaposition and confrontation, but not indeed with any uniform pattern of inversions such as Bakhtin ascribes to the carnival—nor indeed with the kind of universal dissolution of boundaries and categories that he finds there.[96] Aristophanes' plays are not so remorseless, even in their recreation of pre-existing categories. They are not so uniform, not so formulaic. They are too free. As constructions, they are not shapeless assemblages of thematic elements in constructive relationships—any more than they are either plotless unwholes or exemplars of the perfect Aristotelian-organic plot. 'Perfection of plot', said Edgar Allen Poe, 'is unattainable in fact, because Man is the constructor. The plots of God are perfect. The Universe is a Plot of God.'[97] If Aristophanic comedy has no interest in the perfect plot, neither does it show much hankering after perfection of any kind—and least of all (given its comic integrity) the mysterious perfection of a God-driven universe.

[95] Bakhtin, *Rabelais*, 11. On inversions in *Thes.*, cf. Zeitlin, *Playing the Other*, 375–416.

[96] This is one overwhelming reason for finding in Bakhtin theoretical food for thought (cf. above, p. 76), rather than a specific model, for (e.g.) Old Comedy. For other reasons, see below p. 307 and, in more detail, the lucid discussion by Goldhill, *Poet's Voice*, 176–88. Compare and contrast, further: W. Rösler, 'Michail Bachtin und die Karnevalskultur im antiken Griechenland', *QUCC* 23 (1986) 25–44; A. T. Edwards, 'Historicizing the popular grotesque: Bakhtin's *Rabelais* and Attic Old Comedy', in R. Scodel (ed.), *Theater and Society in the Classical World* (Ann Arbor 1993) 89–117; P. von Moellendorff, *Grundlagen einer Ästhetik der alten Komödie: Untersuchungen zu Aristophanes und Michail Bachtin* (Tübingen 1995).

[97] *The Complete Works of Edgar Allen Poe*, ed. J. A. Harrison (New York 1902), xvi. 10.

By this reversion to the theoretical perspectives of our earlier discussions, we have reached a point in the argument already approached by other routes earlier in the chapter. God-driven universes and power-relationships, comic competitions and external worlds, dissatisfaction and celebration: these are among the issues raised by any consequential discussion of Aristophanes. It is time we turned to the question of 'issues'.

7

Serious Issues and 'Serious Comedy'

Aristophanic comedy, of course, has its visible loyalties and animosities. In a very obvious way (for instance), *Clouds* mounts a harsh attack on Socrates (or the character called Socrates) and *Knights* on Cleon (in the guise of the character called Paphlagon), while from *Acharnians* to *Lysistrata* peace is repeatedly represented as triumphant over war, as (in *Frogs*) the old-generation Aeschylus is represented as triumphant over the newer-generation Euripides.

This cluster of seeming choices is summed up at the end of *Knights*, where the rejuvenated Demos is described by the chorus (1331–2) as 'resplendent in his old-time costume' and 'smelling not of voting-shells'—associated with the processes of new democracy—'but of peace', and then greeted thus (1333–4):

> *χαῖρ', ὦ βασιλεῦ τῶν Ἑλλήνων· καί σοι ξυγχαίρομεν ἡμεῖς·*
> *τῆς γὰρ πόλεως ἄξια πράττεις καὶ τοῦ 'ν Μαραθῶνι τροπαίου.*
>
> All hail, king of Hellenes!
> Worthy now of our city
> And our Marathon trophy—
> Your joy is our joy.

Detaching oneself from this charming rhetoric, one notes, amidst a cluster of seeming choices, a cluster of seeming paradoxes: an apolitical ideal of a *polis*, a *dêmos* in power and restored to its full vigour but distancing itself from its own processes, a cheer for peace *now* but also for a great war *then*.

Within the range of seeming choices, the old-time ideal world is commonly associated with rural tradition; and, correlatively, old men and farmers (often, like Dicaeopolis or Strepsiades, the same people) tend to be on the winning side—as, or as if, the simple, true, natural centre of Attic strength and health—despite the slowness and clumsiness of a Strepsiades in the event. If this natural simplicity seems to be threatened on one side by war (and particularly by a war that imprisons the countryman in the city, 'longing for his parish'),[1] it can also be seen to be under threat from modernity in the form of the new Enlightenment (as Strepsiades, or his son, is from Socrates) or equally in the form of the new radical democracy (as Philocleon is from the ideal Cleon of his name): the loyalties and the animosities have, if nothing else, a tidy shape.

At a fundamental level, assuredly, one may find in the presentation of 'the natural', in the vitality of Dicaeopolis' phallic song, in the glorious ingenuity of the contest in *Frogs*, a kind of Lawrentian afirmation, an exuberance for its own sake, an amoral joy, 'beyond good and evil', in being alive. Yet even here total consistency is lacking—and in any case where does this amoralism (to which we shall return) leave the choices, especially the political choices, in view?[2]

The spirit and the significance of the specific loyalties and the specific animosities is much contested. For one interpreter, Aristophanes (along with other Old Comedy poets) shows implicit sympathy for one reading of Athens and its political life by 'consistently and one-sidedly champion[ing] the position of the "best"'—that is, the conservative opponents of radical democrats like Cleon; for another, Aristophanes' 'exaltation of the "good old days"', represented by his depreciation of contemporary politicians and others, is no more than 'comic opportunism'.[3]

In confronting these views of Aristophanes and the texts they seek to explain, we are faced with a set of urgent and much-discussed questions which have repeatedly impinged on our enquiry, but which, perhaps, we have so far seemed content to hint at but also to dodge. Any dodging, as a matter of fact, has

[1] *Ach.* 33: above, p. 228.

[2] 'Lawrentian': see e.g. 'Why the novel matters' (1923), in *Selected Literary Criticism*, 102–18. 'Beyond good and evil': the phrase that Nietzsche was to use as title of his *Jenseits von Gut und Böse* (1886) he first anticipated in 1872 in *The Birth of Tragedy*, III, to characterize the spirit of Greek religion. On the 'loyalties and animosities' in general see e.g. D. F. Sutton, *Self and Society in Aristophanes* (Washington, DC 1980) 1–54; Ehrenberg, *People*, 253–359.

[3] J. Henderson, 'The *demos* and the comic competition', in J. J. Winkler and F. I. Zeitlin (eds.), *Nothing to Do With Dionysos?* (Princeton 1990) 271–313, at 284, and M. Heath, *Political Comedy in Aristophanes* (Göttingen 1987) 23. Much of the modern discursive literature on A focuses on, or circles around, this debate; see most recently the essays in Dobrov, *City* (which include a restatement by Heath, 'Aristophanes and the discourse of politics', 230–49) and, for a survey of views, Bremer, 'Aristophanes', 127–34.

been by way of a tactical postponement. The urgent and much-discussed questions are questions of some delicacy, which are best approached when the ground has been properly prepared. In this light, the foregoing hints will (one may hope) turn out to have been not evasive but preparatory.

At the centre of the questions is the word 'serious', and the question: is Aristophanic comedy serious? To an Aristotelian it is tragedy—for instance and pre-eminently—that has 'serious concerns' (*ta spoudaia*), whereas comedy is all about 'the amusing', 'the laughable' (*to geloion*).[4] In *Frogs* (389–90) Aristophanes' own chorus invokes precisely the same antithesis, but begs permission

> καὶ πολλὰ μὲν γελοῖά μ' εἰ-
> πεῖν, πολλὰ δὲ σπουδαῖα
>
> To say much that's amusing
> And much that's serious.

We have already confronted the Aristotelian oppositional principle in connection with tragedy and comedy *per se*, and in that same theoretical connection Aristophanes' stated aspiration too. What are we to make of it now as a formula for Aristophanic comedy itself?—or rather (given that there is no problem in agreeing that Aristophanic comedy does 'say much that's amusing') what are we to make of the proposition that Aristophanic comedy has something (even 'much') about it that makes it reasonable to associate it with the magic word, 'serious'?

If one thinks of the notorious portrayals of Cleon or Socrates (which led to prosecutions of the poet or, conversely, the public figure), or again of the positive praises of peace, one might well imagine that the first question should be, not '*is* Aristophanic comedy serious?', but '*how*, or *how far*, is it serious?'. And of course one might well recall that the expression of a serious-sounding aspiration in *Frogs* is far from the only one in the plays. After all, as early as *Acharnians* (499–500) Aristophanes purports to be seeking a dispensation to 'talk affairs of state in a comedy', because 'comedy has a sense of duty too'. Yet notwithstanding the existence, the profusion even, of such serious-sounding claims and, likewise, such serious-sounding elements within the plays, it may indeed seem difficult (if our argument so far is convincing) to

[4] *Poet.* IV, 1448^{b}33–7. See above, p. 53.

ascribe *real* seriousness to a brand of comedy full of seeming paradoxes, in which realities may be emblematic and plots pretexts, where there is precious little interest in process, and where Aristophanes' characters and their actions are at inconstant distances from, and their recreative world has no stable relationship with, the horrors and wonders of contemporary Athens.

In Aristophanic criticism, seriousness (in line with Dicaeopolis' protestations in *Acharnians*) is generally discussed in connection with Athenian politics. As a point of departure, then, let us look at two representative, contrasting, discussions that associate Aristophanic seriousness with the political life of contemporary Athens. The first is a 1987 essay by Malcolm Heath, called *Political Comedy in Aristophanes*. For Heath, Aristophanic comedy is 'a form of entertainment',[5] and it is so on the grounds that the plays are largely lacking in seriousness in the political arena. Heath takes issue with—among many others—de Ste Croix, who famously ascribed to Aristophanes a political stance in favour of the traditional established order and against all threats to this establishment, whether intellectual (like Socrates') or political (like Cleon's). Aristophanes (de Ste Croix concluded) 'used many of his plays (even while they of course remained primarily comedies) as vehicles for the expression of serious political views'.[6] Though Heath's position is very different from this, his terms of reference are similar. Against de Ste Croix he sets up a series of counter-arguments. In the attack on Socrates in *Clouds*, de Ste Croix had detected 'an intent to influence opinion' against Socrates; Heath argues, to the contrary, that external evidence, like the favourable representation of Aristophanes in Plato's *Symposium*, suggests that the comic poet was 'on amicable terms with Socrates', and concludes that Aristophanes is unlikely to have had any such 'intent'.[7] Turning to *Knights*, Heath considers the massively unfavourable treatment of Paphlagon-Cleon. The play, he notes, won first prize in 424, only a few weeks before Cleon himself was to win a public vote of confidence in the form of election to the post of general (*stratêgos*); and his

[5] Heath, *Comedy*, 27.

[6] G. E. M. de Ste Croix, *The Origins of the Peloponnesian War* (London 1972) 356.

[7] Heath, *Comedy*, 9–12. As my central concern is not with Heath but with A, I have included a representative, but not a complete, set of his arguments; the same goes for my account of Henderson, below, pp. 306 ff.

inference is that the theatre audience (as representative of the city as were the electors, and presumably, in part, the same people) must have compartmentalized their response to this comedy from their response to Athenian politics, as (by implication) Aristophanes himself must have supposed they would. Whatever else it may be, then, *Knights* is not a call to action.

Reviewing the quest for peace in *Acharnians*, Heath ponders Dicaeopolis' long speech—that speech in which comedy's 'sense of duty *too*' is so memorably asserted—and concludes that any 'seriousness' here is devalued by a 'farrago of jokes', not least the 'preposterous' account of the origins of the war (which Dicaeopolis traces back to the kidnappings of prostitutes by rival gangs of Athenians and Megarians).[8] *Acharnians* and other plays, of course, have a parabasis in which the chorus purports to address, counsel, criticize, the writer's public in the writer's persona — or, as Heath puts it, the author assumes 'the role of adviser'.[9] This role, however, he sees as generally a comic pose—it is not evidence of 'serious intent'—though he admits, as an exception, the parabasis of *Frogs* (686 ff.):

> τὸν ἱερὸν χορὸν δίκαιόν ἐστι χρηστὰ τῇ πόλει
> ξυμπαραινεῖν καὶ διδάσκειν. πρῶτον οὖν ἡμῖν δοκεῖ
> ἐξισῶσαι τοὺς πολίτας κἀφελεῖν τὰ δείματα·
> κεἴ τις ἥμαρτε σφαλείς τι Φρυνίχου παλαίσμασιν,
> ἐγγενέσθαι φημὶ χρῆναι τοῖς ὀλισθοῦσιν τότε
> αἰτίαν ἐκθεῖσι λῦσαι τὰς πρότερον ἁμαρτίας.
> εἶτ' ἄτιμόν φημι χρῆναι μηδέν' εἶν' ἐν τῇ πόλει . . .
>
> Chorus has a sacred right and duty
> To teach and give our city good advice.
> Ours is:
> End the terror! Equal rights for citizens!
> Those led astray by Phrynichus did wrong.
> Now, though, let them be allowed to make
> Atonement. No citizen should have his rights
> Taken away . . .

In this piece of 'good advice' (for which, indeed, Aristophanes is said to have been honoured by 'our city'),[10] the most striking feature is the proposal of an amnesty for the supporters of the oligarchic faction of 411. The parabasis (Heath suggests) betokens

[8] *Ach.* 524 ff. (see below, p. 347): Heath, *Comedy*, 16–18.
[9] Heath, *Comedy*, 19.
[10] See e.g. Dover, *Frogs*, 73–5.

'serious intent' on two grounds: it is 'jokeless', and it offers a practicable policy. However, he can detect no kinship in this respect between the parabasis and its play as a whole. By the application of his two principles on a larger scale, he decides that 'the action of *Frogs* is a comic fantasy that Aristophanes has not tried to co-ordinate with the apparently serious advice of its parabasis'.[11]

Heath's conclusion follows. Whether positive or negative, Aristophanic comedy as a whole has only a 'tenuous attachment to reality': 'political reality is taken up by the poet and subjected to the ignominious transformations of poetic fantasy. But the product of the fantasizing process did not and was not intended to have a reciprocal effect on political reality; comedy had no designs on the political life from which it departed, and in that sense was not political.'[12] This relationship (Heath redefines it pragmatically as 'an amiable and bantering intimacy between poet and audience') precluded, for instance, any seriously critical stance on the author's part, so that in place of an independent appraisal of experience (in line with 'certain traditional concepts of the poet's role'), the plays are attuned to 'the prejudices and expectations of the majority of Aristophanes' audience'—that is, to the interests of the *dêmos*, who thereby exercise a tacit control over the comic drama.[13] Heath's general position is clear-cut: even the harshest 'abuse of individuals' that we find in *Knights* or *Clouds* represents a 'form of entertainment'; and in these and other plays of Aristophanes, seriousness (or 'serious intent') is rare or non-existent *tout court*.[14]

Contrast, but also compare, the discussion by Jeffrey Henderson of 'the *dêmos* and the comic competition' (1990).[15] It is Henderson's contention that the poets of the Old Comedy, and Aristophanes in particular, had a politically significant, culturally sanctioned function as licensed jester on behalf of the *dêmos* and the democracy of Athens. Henderson's starting-point is those programmatic-sounding words in *Frogs*—'much that's amusing | And much that's serious'—which he takes as representative evidence for the proposition that Old Comedy was 'both artistic and political' and that the comic poets were public voices who could,

[11] Heath, *Comedy*, 21.
[12] Ibid. 23, 42.
[13] Ibid. 42, 40.
[14] Ibid. 27, 16, 20, 41.
[15] Henderson, '*Demos*', 271–313.

indeed were expected to, comment on and seek to influence 'public thinking about matters of major [i.e. public] importance', and so specifically and even uniquely that they should now be seen (in Henderson's memorable phrase) as 'the constituent intellectuals of the *dêmos*'. In support of his proposition, Henderson cites ancient evidence (from the so-called 'Old Oligarch', a late fifth-century anti-democratic pamphleteer, and others), and notes: that the comic poets 'argue vehemently . . . about the most important and divisive issues of the day'; that 'the positions they advocate or denounce represent those of actual groups'; that 'their techniques of persuasion and abuse are practically identical with those used in political and forensic disputes'; that Old Comic satire is neither neutral nor indiscriminate ('the poets show systematic bias in their choice of people and policies to satirize or not to satirize'); and that the impact of Old Comedy reflects its given function—and here Henderson (like others before him) points to the decrees defining the limits of comic outspokenness, the lawsuits brought against Aristophanes by Cleon, the crown conferred on the poet for his 'advice' in the *Frogs* parabasis, and the fateful consequences of his portrayal of Socrates.[16]

What Henderson proposes is that Old Comedy had a mediating role between the establishment and the people, and that modern scepticism about such a role is due to the difficulty we have in associating 'humour' and 'seriousness' in the necessary way—however, 'the problem is not to distinguish humour and seriousness, but rather to analyse the dynamics of comic persuasion.'[17] At this point Henderson appeals to carnival, as depicted by Bakhtin, but by way of a significant contrast. Unlike carnival, the comic voice of medieval counter-culture, Old Comedy shows solidarity with the official culture of fifth-century Athens, not least in its negative treatment of radical politicians such as Cleon and its tacit support of the contemporary representatives of a more traditional leadership: 'those who claim that the comic poets were mere humorists must explain why they consistently and one-sidedly championed the position of "the best". Like Thucydides they refrain from criticizing [the conservative leader] Nicias . . . [and] they explain away, play down or even omit to mention the victories . . . achieved by the new politicians.' All in all, the comic festivals are 'not carnival, but civic business'.[18]

[16] Ibid. 272–3. [17] Ibid. 272–4. [18] Ibid. 274–5, 284, 286.

In his characterization of contemporary comedy (Old Comedy), the Old Oligarch speaks of the comic poets' habits of 'ridicule' (*kômôidein*) and 'abuse' (*kakôs legein*):[19] '[The Athenians] do not allow [the comic poets to] ridicule or abuse the *dêmos*' (κωμῳδεῖν δ' αὖ καὶ κακῶς λέγειν τὸν μὲν δῆμον οὐκ ἐῶσιν). Turning to the comic treatment of prominent individual members of the community, Henderson formulates a distinction, based on this pairing, between 'jesting' ridicule and 'serious' abuse. He further relates the two terms of the distinction to the 'amusing' and the 'serious' of the *Frogs*, and duly finds both represented in Aristophanes' plays, where they correspond to contrasting intentions: 'abuse was identified not so much by its source or its content as by its intended effect', where the intention is 'malicious' or 'hostile'; the absence of any such intention points to 'jesting' humour.[20] Thus, Aristophanes' attacks on Cleon and Socrates are (in Henderson's view) specimens of 'serious', because 'hostile', abuse, whereas the treatment of Lamachus in *Acharnians* is humorous and 'not hostile'.[21]

All in all, Henderson concludes, Old Comedy was institutionalized by the *dêmos* as a 'yearly unofficial review' of the current establishment.[22] In addition, though, Old Comedy had a positive function too. Its 'grotesquely exaggerated and caricatured' image of Athens and Athenian life also offers 'ideal goals', and 'the comic hero' himself 'represents the ideal society', without challenge to the 'constitutional structure of democracy' or the 'inherent rightness of the *dêmos*' rule'.[23] In this sense 'serious intention' is expressed throughout Old Comedy, and the job of the comic poet is to articulate and reveal in comic form 'the social currents running beneath the surface of public and official discourse'.[24]

As they stand, both of these arguments—Henderson's and Heath's—seem to me fundamentally flawed, valuable and thought-provoking though various of their formulations are. And much as the two interpreters disagree—in approach and perspectives, as well as conclusions—they do in fact share a series of problematic assumptions, to which the flaws in question may be traced.

In the first place, they both assume that seriousness in Aris-

[19] Ps.-Xen. *Ath.* 2. 18.
[20] Henderson, '*Demos*', 285, 299–301, 303–4.
[21] Ibid. 304–7.
[22] Ibid. 307.
[23] Ibid. 308–11.
[24] Ibid. 312–13.

tophanic comedy is dependent on, and referable to, the poet's intentions ('malicious', 'hostile', or whatever), *despite* the fact that the comedy is what we do have and the intentions are what we don't have, *despite* the fact that works of art do not in practice necessarily correspond to their creators' intentions (where these *are* available), *despite* . . ., *despite* . . ., *despite* . . .[25]

Secondly, and relatedly, interpretation of Aristophanic plays and their claims to seriousness is made to depend on externals: on what the Old Oligarch says about contemporary comedy (Henderson), or the way Plato represents Aristophanes and Socrates (Heath), or what Cleon, or the city, did to or for Aristophanes in response to his plays (both). This is a bit like trying to decide whether a vehicle is or isn't a car (it might be a van, a lorry, a coach), on the basis of whether it turns up at a car-park: a more sensible course might be to take a closer look at the vehicle. In Henderson's case, in particular, the preoccupation with externals (from the Old Oligarch to the comic competition) facilitates a tacit equation between Aristophanic drama and all Old Comedy (for which Aristophanic drama merely provides most of the extant evidence). This is, or may be, like equating Italy, or France, or Germany, or Britain, with Europe.[26]

Third: the two interpreters assume that seriousness is better (more desirable, more valuable, more praiseworthy) than non-seriousness. They may or may not be right: it depends what their 'seriousness' is.

Fourth: they incline to assume that seriousness and humour

[25] See above, p. 42 with n. 1. In Heath's case, intentionalism is a credo: *Comedy*, 7–8, and (in more detail) *Poetics*, 31–2, 44–7.

[26] At one point ('*Demos*', 293) Henderson qualifies his position, but elsewhere tends to ignore his own qualification. Heath and Henderson also show a correlative tendency to assume a homogeneous audience (despite occasional qualifications, like 'the majority of Aristophanes' audience': Heath, *Comedy*, 40). This is bizarre. Modern audiences in lively societies are rarely homogeneous, and it is not obvious why their ancient equivalents should have been so. In particular, it seems improbable that—say—Nicias and Cleon, the young Plato and the young Isocrates, the old Euripides and the older Sophocles, would have had shared responses—and improbable too that in a society informed by *their* divergent ideas and *their* divergent aspirations, an otherwise volatile collection of humbler fellow-spectators would have been any different. Cf. the sensible remarks by C. Segal, 'Catharsis, audience, and closure in Greek tragedy', in Silk, *Tragedy and the Tragic*, 171 n. 36, and Lada-Richards, *Dionysus*, 11: most versions of contemporary reader-response/reception theory (on which cf. Lada-Richards, loc. cit.) are predicated on this datum. Authors too can be inconstant in their interpretative responses to their own work: cf., on A himself, Dover, *Clouds*, p. lvi.

come in separate packages. Henderson indeed, at one point, seems to insist that this need not be so ('the problem is not to distinguish humour and seriousness'), while his closing thoughts on the Old Comic playwrights as articulators of the attitudes ('the social currents') of the *dêmos* point the same way. However, central to his discussion is the dichotomy between 'jesting' and 'abuse', 'artistic and political', which proclaims separation as a main presupposition of his whole argument. And in Heath, despite a single acknowledgement, in passing, that 'serious points can be conveyed in comic guise',[27] the imprint of the dichotomy is pervasive, so that, for instance, the *Frogs* parabasis *must* be serious because of its alleged jokelessness, and the rest of *Frogs* (and Aristophanes' 'political' comedy in general) non-serious, because of its evident jokefulness.[28]

Fifth, and above all: the two interpreters are in tacit agreement that we know what seriousness is and why it matters, and that the challenge is to decide whether Aristophanes does, or does not, have it. This is surely wrong. The challenge is, precisely, to decide what seriousness is and why it matters. Our first task must be to scrutinize the notion of seriousness *per se*.

The oddity of never discussing seriousness, but forever appealing to it, emerges with a certain piquancy from Henderson's account of comedy and the *dêmos*. For Henderson, Old Comedy has a serious aspect—but what makes it serious is actually quite unclear. Is it serious because of Old Comic abuse (as opposed to Old Comic jesting)? If so, an Aristophanic comedy is only serious some of the time (the abusive part of the time). Alternatively, is Old Comedy serious by virtue of its capacity (formulated in Henderson's closing words) to mediate 'the social currents running beneath the surface of public and official discourse'? If so, all Aristophanic Old Comedies must be serious in their entirety. However, if it is to this formula that Old Comic seriousness must be referred, it is surely not a very decisive seriousness. For it is not only Old Comedy in the fifth century BC that mediates 'the social currents'. Surely most, perhaps ultimately all, literature in all

[27] *Comedy*, 15.

[28] See esp. *Comedy*, 18–21. Despite his comments on the jokeless parabasis of *Ran.*, Heath quotes with evident approval a naïve 'axiom' enunciated by de Ste Croix that the comedian 'must always be funny' (*Comedy*, 39: de Ste Croix, *Origins*, 357). What implications that might have for (the composer of) a jokeless parabasis, we are not told.

periods of all cultures does just this. Claims can be, have been, made even for such unprestigious literary forms as the thriller, and for such despised literary modes as pornography, that they bring to the surface contemporary configurations of thought or feeling, tensions, fears, or desires, that would otherwise be unexpressed. If Aristophanic comedy is serious only in so far as it mediates (or 'reveals', in Henderson's own words) 'the social currents', then it is no more 'serious' than most, or all, of the world's literature, past or present, good, bad, or indifferent; and in that case this is not in itself a kind of seriousness worth debating, and any claim for Aristophanic seriousness loses its distinctive point.[29]

At this juncture, however, one notes that Henderson's closing formula is followed by a short, additional reformulation which, though at a tangent to his overall argument, is nicely calculated to point the way forward. The passage, with this additional element, runs:

> Who can plot the course and effect of the social currents running beneath the surface of public and official discourse? It was for the comic poets to reveal them, to give them the powerful and memorable airing that only the comic context allowed.[30]

If seriousness implies not only 'revelations', but also 'powerful and memorable airings', then we are indeed dealing with a different order of seriousness, and a kind of seriousness surely more worth serious consideration—and more worth having. Pornography and thrillers have nothing powerful or memorable to them—or if they do, we incline to call them something more weighty, like 'erotic novels' or 'film noir'. Yet if Aristophanic comedy does have this kind of seriousness, we should certainly feel some surprise if it turns out to be no more weighty than a container of 'jesting' and 'abuse'. That is: seriousness is not some

[29] The same goes for many comparable formulae for the social role of Greek drama. Take e.g. Goldhill, *Poet's Voice*, 174: 'the public space of the festival becomes not merely the arena for a contest between poets, but also for the contestation of the values, attitudes and beliefs of the citizens.' The 'contestation' bit sounds good—until one reflects: replace 'citizens' by 'public', and of what public art (dramatic or other) in what age is this *not* true? Even with opiate pap-art, there must always be such a 'contestation'. Across the spectrum of the world's public art, 'contestation' will vary in explicitness, in quality, in intensity—but hardly in kind.

[30] Henderson, '*Demos*', 313.

easily encapsulated commodity; it does have something to do with evaluation; but it is a variable, in terms both of its nature and its degree. We can distinguish between the seriousness of a Jane Austen and a Brecht, an Alexander Pope and a García Márquez, a Virgil and a Euripides—just as in ordinary parlance we can, and do, speak of someone or something as *more* or *less* serious than someone or something else.

'Ordinary parlance' is itself as good a ground as any on which to take our initial stand. Let us—in full awareness of our own earlier arguments—consider the ordinary usage of the English word 'serious'. Heath, Henderson, and many others (I suggest) confuse, or equate, three different senses of the word:[31] serious meaning 'sober', serious meaning 'honest', serious meaning 'substantial'.

Serious: sober. 'A good portrait . . . must be either serious or smirking, or it's no portrait at all' (Dickens, *Nicholas Nickelby*, ch. 10). We say: 'his voice suddenly became serious.' 'Serious' in any such context implies dignity, solemnity, formality; its opposite is 'jokey' or 'humorous'. A letter on official stationery is serious in this sense: irrespective of its particular contents, its formality demands respect. Seriousness of this kind is very much a Greek value: it underlies the traditional privileging (so apparent in Aristotle) of epic and tragedy over comedy, and 'serious' in this sense undeniably corresponds to an area covered by Aristotle's word *spoudaios* in *Poetics* IV and elsewhere. Is Aristophanes often serious in this sense? Clearly not. The *Clouds* chorus's praise of Athens and the joke-free advice in the parabasis of *Frogs* do offer this kind of seriousness,[32] and these passages are untypical. They are also, as pieces of achieved literature, relatively unimpressive.

Serious: honest. 'The accent of high seriousness, born of absolute sincerity, is what gives to such . . . criticism of life as Dante's its power. Is this accent felt in the passages which I have been quoting from Burns? Surely not; surely, if our sense is quick, we must perceive we have not in those passages a voice from the very inmost soul of the genuine Burns' (Matthew Arnold, 'The

[31] One could no doubt conduct similar manoeuvres with equivalent words in other languages, but I leave that to those more qualified to judge. In my own searches, for quotations and orientations, I have consulted *OED* among other dictionaries. The categorizations of *OED* (I have to report) seem, by comparison with those of more modest rivals (notably the new Collins), incomplete and confused.

[32] i.e. *Nub.* 298–313 and *Ran.* 686–705.

Study of Poetry', 1880).[33] We say: 'is this a serious proposal of marriage?' The voice that 'suddenly became serious' is judged to be so by virtue of its external qualities; the marriage-proposal that is taken to be 'serious' is so taken by virtue of a judgement about the proposer's inner disposition, essentially his (or her) intentions. This kind of seriousness is opposite to 'pretending' or 'posing'. In Greek antiquity, it was not given any unqualified value. Homer's Achilles values it ('hateful to me as the gates of Hades is that man who hides one thing in his mind and says another'), whereas Homer's wily Odysseus is presented as a master of such 'hateful' duplicity; and as between these rival paradigms, later authorities do not take up an entirely consistent position.[34] The Achillean ideal of personal integrity is of prime concern, certainly, to early Christians, to (much later) the makers of Protestant Europe, and (later still) to the thinkers and writers of Romanticism, in which era a new inwardness engenders a notable literary-critical version of the ideal, called 'sincerity', together with the related literary-interpretative procedure (shared, as we have noted, by Heath and Henderson) of intentionalism.[35]

In life, it is clear enough why sincerity should normally be accounted a virtue. In elective politicians, to take one particular instance, we value not only the ability to get things done, and the judgement that guides them towards one course of action rather than another, but also the honesty that encourages us to trust, where we cannot judge, that the proposed course of action is right (and not, for instance, merely self-serving), and indeed what that proposed course of action is in the first place. It has never been very clear how such a virtue might bear on literary judgements, given that in literature (dramatic or other) 'courses of action' in the ordinary sense are not usually 'proposed' at all[36]—though this

[33] Matthew Arnold, *Essays in Criticism*, ed. K. Allott (London 1964) 257.

[34] *Il.* 9. 312–13. For the pervasive Greek tolerance towards Odyssean wiliness, see M. Detienne and J.-P. Vernant, *Les Ruses de l'intelligence. La mètis des Grecs* (Paris 1974).

[35] On the strongly (though not uniquely) Romantic affinities of intentionalism, see Silk, *Interaction*, 59–63, 233–5. Heath's attempt (*Poetics*, 46) to deny the link misses the point. There is no doubt that pre-Romantics (including ancients) sometimes ascribe intentions to authors. What they do not do (except rarely, as with Plato: Silk, *Interaction*, 234) is make Heath's mistake of supposing that acceptable interpretations in some way depend on the intentions ascribed.

[36] Except e.g. for literature in the Marxist tradition. In Kantian and post-Kantian aesthetics, of course, the whole conception of literature and art as a whole precludes any such proposal.

does not seem to deter Henderson and, particularly, Heath from pursuing such a criterion: as far as Heath is concerned, for instance, the 'serious intent' of the *Frogs* parabasis is suggested not only by its 'jokelessness', but by the fact that it offers a 'practicable policy'.[37]

'Serious', meaning 'honest', opposite to 'posing': is Aristophanes ever 'serious' in this sense? For the reason given, the answer—as also its relevance to any sensitive interpretation of Aristophanes' plays—must be elusive. All one can say for sure is that if *posing* threatens to disqualify literature from this kind of seriousness, then most of Aristophanic drama must indeed be disqualified several times over. With all its characteristic discontinuities and its shifting stances and distances, most of Aristophanes is (whatever else it may be) poses, large and small. Consider only the *Peace* parabasis, where Aristophanes has his chorus declare that (734–5)

> χρῆν μὲν τύπτειν τοὺς ῥαβδούχους, εἴ τις κωμῳδοποιητὴς
> αὑτὸν ἐπῄνει πρὸς τὸ θέατρον παραβὰς ἐν τοῖς ἀναπαίστοις
>
> Really the ushers ought to have him flogged,
> A comic poet who has himself praised
> In the theatre, in the parabasis, in the anapaests—

as—in the theatre, in the parabasis, and indeed in these very anapaests—Aristophanes promptly goes on to do, before going on to criticize his rivals for exploiting the same broad comedy that he exploits himself.[38] Or recall that compound persona—author, character, disguiser, actor—that introduces Dicaeopolis' great oration on behalf of peace (*Acharnians* 497 ff.):

> Condemn me not, you in the audience,
> If, whiles I am a beggar, among us Athenians
> I talk affairs of state in a comedy . . .[39]

On one front (one inclines to agree), if Aristophanes can be so insistent on talking about 'talking affairs of state', Heath and Henderson are entitled to test him; on another, the prospects of successfully doing so with only the touchstone of sincerity, disguised as 'seriousness', to hand, seem more unpromising than ever.

[37] Heath, *Comedy*, 19–21.
[38] *Pax* 739–47: cf. Sommerstein's notes ad loc.
[39] Above, pp. 39–41.

Serious: substantial. 'Drama is made serious by the degree in which it gives the nourishment, not very easy to define, on which our imaginations live' (J. M. Synge).[40] We say: 'she is the only serious candidate'; 'this is a deeply serious contribution to the understanding of Aristophanes'. 'Serious' in this sense implies a judgement that something or someone—though not necessarily our *favourite* something or someone (we speak of a 'serious accident' and a 'serious illness')—is weighty or impressive: its opposite is 'trivial'. When Aristotle (*Poetics* VI) refers to tragedy's 'serious action' (*praxis spoudaia*), he invokes this kind of seriousness. In a letter to a friend in 1817, the poet Keats, musing on 'genius and the heart', on 'worldly happiness', on 'the holiness of the heart's affections and the truth of imagination', writes: 'if a sparrow come before my window, I take part in its existence and pick about the gravel.'[41] That remark is impressive and arresting. It may be jocular in tone; it may even have been written with (so to speak) tongue in cheek; yet we can see it as profoundly serious. Conversely, the choral praise of Athens in *Clouds*, trite and uneventful as it is, is properly seen as a far less serious piece of writing, for all its evident solemnity of tone and however honourably meant. However, is Aristophanes generally serious in the quite distinct third sense of the word? It must be plain that our answer is: surely so.

We are beginnng to make headway. We can say, in the first place, that the whole discussion of 'seriousness in Aristophanes' is bound to be complicated by the fact that there are different kinds of seriousness, especially if one of them is problematic in its own right. Then again, in practical applications, the categories of seriousness overlap. Something may be serious in all three senses—like (it may be) 'serious music' or a 'serious newspaper'. Or in any two of the senses, but not the third: a 'serious relationship' between two people calls for something substantial (shared attitudes and interests) and something honest (commitment), but hardly sober formality. Or just in one—like . . . Aristophanic comedy?

Eccentric logic and confusion of categories are common enough occurrences, even in the most sophisticated discourse. When the categories in question are crossed by single words, these errors are doubtless harder than ever to avoid or to detect, and some kind of

[40] Above p. 60 with n. 55.

[41] Letter to B. Bailey, 22 Nov. 1817.

tacit transference across the categories is all too possible. Such confusion (to restate our earlier argument once more) afflicts Aristotle, for whom seriousness is confronted under the heading of the word *spoudaios*. This word can mean 'serious' in the sense of 'sober', and is then opposite to *geloios*, 'amusing'. Yet it can equally mean 'serious' in the sense of 'substantial', and is then opposite to *phaulos*, 'trivial', 'inferior'. Substantial things, of course, normally count for more than trivial things; it does not follow that sober things (like tragedy) count for more than amusing things (like comedy). Through tacit transference across the categories, Aristotle in effect assumes that it does follow.[42]

A comparable confusion and transference of value can now be seen to afflict Heath and Henderson, and doubly so. In the first place, they seek to transfer to serious–sober the value appropriate to serious–substantial: hence the exaggerated interest in the joke-free parabasis of *Frogs* and in Aristophanic 'abuse' (as against Aristophanic 'jesting'). But then again they contrive an alternative conflation of serious–substantial and serious–honest, and hence require of Aristophanic comedy that, when dealing with politics, it should cultivate a kind of political commitment that one would expect of, and indeed (under the heading of serious–honest) require of, a democratic politician. At which point, one may well feel entitled to wonder precisely why it is that these—and many other—modern scholars are so concerned with the specifically political aspect of Aristophanic comedy at all.

Let us take these points one by one. Regarding the overvaluation of Aristophanic sobriety—by Aristophanes, perhaps, as well as by Heath and Henderson—more needs to be said, but not yet.

Regarding commitment: there is of course such a thing as a successful work of literature centred on an uncompromising ideological attachment (Dante's *Commedia* and Lucretius' *De Rerum Natura* are two notable instances), and also such a thing as a successful writer who is politically *engagé* (like Brecht), and from Solon to Havel there have been sundry instances, even, of worthwhile writer-politicians and worthwhile literature as political activity. Experienced readers, though, distinguish attachment (irrespective of one's attitude to the attachment in question) from missionary activity ('we hate art that has a palpable design upon us', said Keats).[43] And there is the cautionary tale of the old and

[42] Above, pp. 53, 80–1.

[43] Letter to J. H. Reynolds, 3 Feb. 1818.

born-again Tolstoy, oblivious of the fact that the supremely Christian Dante could choose the non-Christian Virgil as his guide, dismissing most of the world's art, including his own, because now all art must be 'Christian art' with a specific 'task' ('to establish brotherly union among men').[44] And in the century Tolstoy lived on into, there are inumerable instances of unedifying literature explicitly serving the interests of totalitarian régimes, on the political left or right.

Take the single instance of Ezra Pound's *Cantos*, much of which espouses (in an admittedly eccentric version) a specific political creed, the dismal and destructive Fascism of the inter-war (and early war) years. Pound's commitment, its genuineness, and its relationship with an only too specifiable programme of political action have never been doubted. Criticism of a work as vast, as (in some ways) hermetic, and as (in many ways) disparate as the *Cantos* is not a straightforward matter. But are we, even for a moment, to consider the idea that, by virtue of its political commitment, the *Cantos* has a kind of 'serious' value it would otherwise lack? The ascription of any such positive value on any such grounds to Aristophanes is hardly less absurd. And, in case the bracketing with Pound seems surprising, one might recall that famous prize-winning advice to restore the rights of the oligarchic revolutionaries in *Frogs*—and add that the jury is still out on the degree to which the advice, in 405 BC, helped to facilitate the establishment, and with it the grim excesses, of the Thirty Tyrants, the following year.[45] No doubt Aristophanes was not the sole advocate of the ill-fated plan, and no doubt he 'meant well', and no doubt stern moral judgements on long-dead writers have a certain irredeemable quaintness to them. Nevertheless, before Aristophanes is credited with any kind of 'seriousness' because of this episode, one must, as for Pound, set out a different case. Alongside the points made, let us add that the advice in the parabasis is exceptionally loosely connected with the rest of its play. In any ordinary (even ordinary-Aristophanic) sense, it does not arise out of the play or restate any of its themes, but is (as

[44] The closing words of *What is Art?* (1898).

[45] See: W. G. Arnott, 'A lesson from the Frogs', *G&R* 38 (1991) 18–23; Dover, *Frogs*, 73–6; MacDowell, *Aristophanes and Athens*, 299–300; Goldhill, *Poet's Voice*, 203. I am grateful to Simon Hornblower for helpful discussion of this issue.

Heath, for one, properly insists) isolated from it:[46] it is, in a straightforward sense, gratuitous. Accordingly, might we not think it profoundly irresponsible and *unserious* for a writer who has the public ear, yet is in no way politically accountable, to take advantage of his position to offer such advice in this gratuitous way?

Mindful of such complications, let us turn to the final question raised: why the emphasis on Aristophanic politics at all? It is not enough to say: aren't most of Aristophanes' Old Comedies about politics, one way or another? It depends what 'about' means: see below . . . The answer, rather, lies in a cluster of reasons. Interpreters are, as usual, predisposed to follow Aristotle, and his privileging of 'serious action', by themselves privileging drama that at least seems to foreground politics (which for most of us, if not always for Aristotle, is very much a 'serious' thing).[47] And then, Aristophanes' own words on Aristophanes, from *Frogs* to *Wasps* to *Acharnians*, do encourage us to pay special heed to (as it might be) advice about the exiles or the battle with Cleon or, generally, 'affairs of state'. And then again, a number of ancient testimonies external to Aristophanes, from the Old Oligarch onwards, undoubtedly put a certain stress on this aspect of Old Comedy in general and Aristophanes in particular. As the ancient Life of Aristophanes has it: 'there is also a story that when the tyrant Dionysius wanted to find out about the way politics [*politeia*] worked in Athens, Plato sent him a copy of Aristophanes and advised him to do it by studying the plays.'[48]

Testimonies *external* to Aristophanes: in a sense all these grounds for privileging politics in Aristophanic comedy have something external about them. The ideas of Aristotle, the Old Oligarch, and the Aristophanic *Vita* are obviously external to the plays themselves, while Aristophanes' 'own words', in or out of a parabasis, inevitably have an elusive status in a kind of proprietorial no man's land. Involvement in the political life of Athens is, of course, precisely what Old Comedy as a whole is famous for, in contradistinction (not least) to the kinds of comedy that succeeded it. It does not follow that politics was central to all

[46] Heath, *Comedy*, 20–1. 'Isolated', unless we count the γεν(ν)- theme: above, p. 279 n. 47.

[47] In *Poetics*, notoriously, Aristotle effectively ignores the political aspect of drama: E. Hall, 'Is there a *polis* in Aristotle's *Poetics*?', in Silk, *Tragedy and the Tragic*, 295–309.

[48] *Vit. Aristoph.*: *PCG* iii. 2. 3, 42–5.

Old Comedy (in fact, we think we know it was not),[49] and it is now high time that we broached the thought, heretical as it may seem, that Aristophanic comedy, whether or not politically 'serious' (in the Heath–Henderson sense), is not as *deeply* concerned with politics as it is widely taken to be, and that its ultimate claim to seriousness lies elsewhere. And what will decide the question is what must decide all questions about the interpretation of Aristophanes: not external 'evidence', but the plays themselves, as achieved entities (again, see below . . .).

If political engagement does not in itself make literature more serious (are Pound's *Cantos*, with all their dreary Fascism, *thereby* more serious than Eliot's *Four Quartets*?), likewise merely being 'about' politics does not in itself (by some kind of osmosis?) make literature more serious: is Sophocles' *Trachiniae* (which is not, in any obvious sense, about politics) less serious than *Antigone* (which, most would say, is)? 'About' (let us agree) is reductive, and a great deal depends on what one reduces *to*: hence its bluntness as a tool for our (or any) investigation. Think of the Keats letter and the poet's description of his taking part in the 'existence' of his sparrow and 'picking about the gravel'. What is that bit of Keats's letter *about*? If we say, 'sparrows and gravel', that sounds trivial; if we say, 'poetic empathy', it sounds more substantial. Is *Lysistrata* ('about' peace and war) more serious than *Thesmophoriazusae* ('about' an old man dressing up as a woman)? Or is *Thesmophoriazusae* ('about' tragedy and . . .) more serious than *Lysistrata* ('about' a sex strike).[50]

We propose, in effect, to recentre the issue of Aristophanic seriousness. We shall do so in an awareness of the many problems, theoretical and practical, posed by consideration of seriousness as a whole. *Inter alia*, we may hope thereby to avoid any unacknowledged transference of properties or values from one kind of seriousness to another, whether this involves the equation of 'humorous' and 'trivial' summed up in the phrase 'mere humorists'—or the patronizing ascription of 'fantasy' to a text which may or may not be in some sense political, but which cannot be readily

[49] e.g. it was apparently not in the Crates/Pherecrates tradition: above, p. 51.

[50] On *Thes.* see below, pp. 320 ff. A classic instance of insensitive reduction was perpetrated by Tolstoy to do down his own *Anna Karenina*: 'how an officer fell in love with a married woman'. See e.g. F. R. Leavis, *Anna Karenina and Other Essays* (London 1973) 31–2.

translated into political action—or the strange logic by which a politically orientated joke-free zone becomes *ipso facto* politically serious (because sober, therefore honest).

How does Aristophanic seriousness work? What does it look like? Our earlier discussions have provided various paradigms for our consideration, from the massively imposing (and richly comic) presentation of the peace–war antithesis in *Acharnians* to Philocleon's transcending of (what else but?) political normalities in *Wasps*. Before we return to the overtly political, and to these and other points of reference, let us take another look at a further model, *Thesmophoriazusae*, a play with no overt political content and indeed (apart from the presence of Euripides and Agathon) with very little topical reference of any kind.[51] This comedy, which we have offered as a paradigm of discontinuous character and transformational moments, is perhaps Aristophanes' most brilliant play, yet, at the same time, perhaps not an unqualified success. The problem with the play is symptomatized by the practical difficulty that faces anyone staging it: what to do with the anticlimax at the end? That end, indeed, serves to focus attention on the problem, though the problem goes deeper.

Like *Lysistrata* from the same year, *Thesmophoriazusae* is often loosely read as a play centred on an opposition between men and women (and inevitably the play has much to say to anyone interested in male/female power relationships in antiquity). But though borne out superficially by the confrontation between two men (Euripides and his stooge, Mnesilochus) and the women at their festival, the reading is a misreading.[52] In the first place: though Mnesilochus is, in one obvious sense, a typical man, *l'homme moyen sensuel*, his master Euripides, who is the source of the confrontation, is not. Then again: the women, though intermittently defined, or self-defined, in contradistinction to men, notably in the parabasis (801–2)—

[51] In obvious contrast to *Lys.*, staged in the same year, 411. The two Eur. plays that count for most in *Thes.*, *Helen* (see *Thes.* 850–928) and *Andromeda* (*Thes.* 1009–135), were topical in the sense that they both date from the year before, 412.

[52] The most sophisticated version of the position is F. I. Zeitlin, 'Travesties of gender and genre in Aristophanes' *Thesmophoriazousae*', in Zeitlin, *Playing the Other*, 375–416. In a chapter headed 'Men as women', L. K. Taaffe, *Aristophanes and Women* (London 1993) 74–102, discusses the play more closely than the antithesis implies, yet remains bound to it. I committed myself to the same misreading at 'People', 170.

βάσανον δῶμεν, πότεροι χείρους· ἡμεῖς μὲν γάρ φαμεν ὑμᾶς,
ὑμεῖς δ' ἡμᾶς

Let's test which sex is worse: we say it's you,
You us—

are at odds with Euripides (and Mnesilochus), but not with men as such. Indeed not, for they are assisted (and Mnesilochus opposed) by two more men, the magistrate and the Scythian, and one half-man ('Dear ladies, my own kin', 574), Cleisthenes. And again: the women are not presented as schematic opposites of men, in the way that (say) Lamachus (with his warrior existence) is presented as schematic opposite of Dicaeopolis (with his recovered life of rural peace) in *Acharnians*: they are happy to play at being men in their version of the male *ekklêsia*; they share one of Euripides' defining attitudes, a capacity for high-style verse; and at the end of the play they come to an accommodation with Euripides himself without any fundamental transformation on their part, or indeed on his part either.

Unlike *Acharnians* or *Knights*, *Lysistrata* or *Frogs*, the play is simply not organized antithetically: it has no agon, and no proper winner or loser, but only a compromise. There is indeed a kind of antithesis between two opposed caricatures of the women: a hostile story of female depravity ascribed to Euripides and presented, on his behalf, by Mnesilochus; and a positive story of women's purity and propriety implicit in their hymns and explicit in their own parabasis ('The loom, the rod, the basket, safe in our hands', 821–2). In practice, though, there is an equilibrium between the two caricatures which is never resolved. The caricatures themselves, obviously, belong to a particular conflict embodied in the play, which is a conflict on more than one level. The women's concern to take action against Euripides for a perceived affront to their sex leads to a second affront in the shape of Mnesilochus' infiltration into their festival. In effect, the second affront is a 'degraded'—and more degrading—equivalent of the first: Euripides' creation of a figure like Phaedra purportedly undermines the sense of female dignity on an aesthetic-intellectual level, as Mnesilochus' violation of the segregated solemnities of the Thesmophoria undermines it on a straightforward physical level.[53] But none of this makes the opposition, so far

[53] Eur.'s portrayals of Phaedra (in two separate *Hippolytus* plays) become, for A,

as it exists, the centre, let alone the organizing principle, of the play.

A different, but equally unhelpful, misreading of *Thesmophoriazusae* is that Euripides is an enemy—*our enemy* — and a figure, accordingly, belittled by the play. In point of fact, Euripides is not belittled in any extant play by Aristophanes, notwithstanding some amusement at his expense in *Acharnians* and his eventual defeat in the contest with Aeschylus in *Frogs*; and he is certainly not belittled here. He is indeed depicted as Enlightenment Man, with all the ambivalent associations that such an appellation carries;[54] and on this account his ingenuities and their subversive potential are writ large in the play; but during the action he does little or nothing that could imply any questioning of his stature. He is not, for instance, precious and degenerate like the effeminate Agathon (191–2):[55]

> . . . εὐπρόσωπος, λευκός, ἐξυρημένος,
> γυναικόφωνος, ἁπαλός, εὐπρεπὴς ἰδεῖν
>
> Pretty, fresh face, clean-shaven, pale, soft skin,
> Woman's voice.

Nor is he some kind of failure.[56] His attempts to rescue Mnesilochus by tragic quotations may come to nothing, but the one who suffers for it is Mnesilochus, not himself. He may not be a glorious quester like Dicaeopolis, but he does work things out eventually, dealing with the Scythian, not indeed by tragic quotations, but still by a piece of theatrical-Euripidean disguise.[57] In particular, his distinctive ingenuity is vindicated. That ingenuity may be

a paradigm of dramatized immorality: *Thes.* 153 (see Sommerstein ad loc.) 497, 546–7 (where Ph. is an archetypal γυνὴ πονηρά), *Ran.* 1043 (where Φαίδρας are πόρνας).

[54] Below, pp. 324–6.

[55] See further p. 326 n. 64 below.

[56] 'A dreadful failure in this play': Whitman, *Hero*, 218. Cf. below, p. 332 n. 75, *inter alia*.

[57] i.e. as madam. Bowie, *Aristophanes*, 219–25, makes a case for the interesting idea that *Thes.* proposes the superiority of comedy over tragedy but without doing down Eur. himself. However, there is less to be said for his suggestion (ibid. 224) that Eur. abandons 'tragic stratagems in favour of disguise as a comic bawd with a dancing girl'. All Eur.'s stratagems, in A, are equally 'comic'; a madam ('bawd'), though a strikingly low figure, is not in fifth-century terms as distinctively comedic a stereotype as in later Greek comedy; and in this last scene, symptomatically, Eur. impinges as almost a 'straight' figure (and markedly more so than the satirical target he was in the opening scene).

frustrated for much of the play, but not because it is spurious. Euripides is thwarted *despite* his ingenuity; and in the end his ingenuity wins through.[58]

The common ground of these two misreadings is the desire to find in the play a confrontational pattern at the deepest level, whereas the actual conflict, however we define it, is surely implicated in a larger and less tidy pattern. The most important element in this pattern is poetry; and though it is of course Euripides' poetry that provokes the women into conflict with him, poetry itself is not an element of the confrontation. The play is full of poetry: Agathon's, Euripides'—and the women's, for they are themselves poeticizers by virtue of their devotional hymns. Closer to a deep confrontational element is religion. Euripides (in his Enlightenment persona) is presented as a sceptic of traditional religion, the women as upholders of orthodox piety. The women, of course, have come together to celebrate the traditional rites of the Thesmophoria; their whole collective identity is thus based on religion. By giving them a skin of wine, a conspiracy, and a certain preoccupation with sexuality, Aristophanes has indeed introduced an element of not especially pious self-indulgence into the traditional austerities of the ritual.[59] More fundamentally, though, he has given the whole festival a wider significance in strictly religious terms.

The Thesmophoria was a festival in honour of the goddess Demeter and her daughter Persephone. Accordingly, when Mnesilochus joins the women in disguise, he makes sure to acknowledge only the right deities (284–7):

> . . . τὴν κίστην καθελοῦ, κᾆτ' ἔξελε
> τὰ πόπαν', ὅπως λαβοῦσα θύσω ταῖν θεαῖν.
> δέσποινα πολυτίμητε Δήμητερ φίλη
> καὶ Φερρέφαττα . . .[60]

[58] Again, there is nothing in *Thes.* about the 'bankrupcy of contemporary tragedy' (Whitman, *Hero*, 217). Even in *Ran.*, except for one, late, assertion (1491–5: below, p. 366), there is no suggestion that Euripidean tragedy is bankrupt. In *Thes.* Eur. is the great master of tragic tricks, whose innovations, for instance, are never derided as Agathon's are derided by Mnesilochus (59–62, 130–72).

[59] Notwithstanding an element of female *aiskhrologia* at the festival: W. Burkert, *Greek Religion*, tr. J. Raffan (Oxford 1985) 242–6. On the self-indulgences, see *Thes.* 733–4 (wineskin) 372–9 etc. (conspiracy) 340–6 etc. (sex).

[60] Text as Sommerstein.

> . . . put the basket down and take
> The round cakes out, so I can sacrifice
> To the two goddesses. Mistress, dear queen Demeter,
> And you, Persephone . . .

Quite unexpectedly, however, the women themselves show no disposition to confine their worship to the two goddesses: on the contrary, they celebrate the Olympian pantheon as a whole. Their several devotional hymns mention Demeter or the two goddesses occasionally, but their first one begins by invoking the whole 'race of the gods' (*θεῶν γένος*, 312), and goes on to celebrate Zeus, Apollo, Athena, Artemis, Poseidon, and others. In similar vein, their last hymn begins with Pallas (1136), before eventually looking to the two 'mistresses of the Thesmophoria' (1156), while the long choral section at 947–1000 begins with 'the two' (948), turns explicitly to the 'race of the Olympians' (*γένος Ὀλυμπίων θεῶν*, 960), and ends, at length, with Dionysus (987–1000). Without actually contradicting the Demetrian presuppositions of the festival, Aristophanes has converted it into a symbol of orthodox religion as a whole, and thereby has made the women embodiments of religion *tout court* in a more representative way than one would have thought possible with the participants in a very particular and unusual festival for an essentially chthonic goddess.[61]

Euripides (on the other side) has no truck with ordinary religious devotions. His preference is for new sophisticated belief or no religion at all. Hardly have we encountered him on his way to Agathon's house than we find him baffling Mnesilochus with an account of Aether, the primal creative source of sight and hearing (14–18), while later he swears by Aether in preference to any ordinary god (272–4). Like Socrates in *Clouds*, then, he cultivates peculiar deities of an avant-garde intellectual provenance[62]—or, alternatively, he believes in no gods at all. Such, at least, is the complaint of the market-woman who sells myrtle for use in religious sacrifices (450–2):

[61] On chthonic Demeter, see e.g. Burkert, *Religon*, 159–61, 244. A's 'reinterpretation' of Demetrian religion, though no doubt reflecting the Greek (male) belief that women's religiosity is special ('in religion . . . we women play the greatest part', Eur. *Mel. Des.*: p. 123, 12–13 *TGFS*), is as remarkable in its way as his 'reinterpretation' of Socrates as the representative sophist (above, p. 240), but strangely passed over by critics: M. Habash, 'The odd Thesmophoria of Aristophanes' *Thesmophoriazusae*', *GRBS* 38 (1997) 19–40, is a rare exception.

[62] See below, p. 359.

νῦν δ' οὗτος ἐν ταῖσιν τραγῳδίαις ποιῶν
τοὺς ἄνδρας ἀναπέπεικεν οὐκ εἶναι θεούς·
ὥστ' οὐκέτ' ἐμπολῶμεν οὐδ' εἰς ἥμισυ.

And now *he* turns up with his tragedies,
Makes people think there aren't any gods—
And my trade's down half what it used to be.

Yet if Euripides' depiction as the unbelieving modern intellectual puts him into direct opposition with these representatives of religious orthodoxy, it has to be said that, apart from the myrtle-seller's personalized complaint, this term of opposition is not made explicit elsewhere in the play. Furthermore, his irreligion is subsumed under a larger intellecual-Enlightenment persona, which is not in the same way antithetical to the women's collective *raison d'être*. Like *Frogs*, the play begins with two travellers on a journey to a house—in this case, Agathon's. Mnesilochus, the one traveller, wearily asks Euripides, the other, where they might be going. The immediate result (and again one thinks of *Frogs*) is an elaborate verbal routine in the shape of a bizarre quibble. This time, though, the bizarre quibble (on the lips of Euripides) clearly tells us something about its speaker (5–14):

ΕΥ. ἀλλ' οὐκ ἀκούειν δεῖ σε πάνθ', ὅσ' αὐτίκα
ὄψει παρεστώς.
ΜΝ. πῶς λέγεις; αὖθις φράσον.
οὐ δεῖ μ' ἀκούειν;
ΕΥ. οὐ ἅ γ' ἂν μέλλῃς ὁρᾶν.
ΜΝ. οὐδ' ἆρ' ὁρᾶν δεῖ μ';
ΕΥ. οὐχ ἅ γ' ἂν ἀκούειν δέῃ.
ΜΝ. πῶς μοι παραινεῖς; δεξιῶς μέντοι λέγεις.
οὐ φῂς σὺ χρῆναί μ' οὔτ' ἀκούειν οὔθ' ὁρᾶν;
ΕΥ. χωρὶς γὰρ αὐτοῖν ἑκατέρου 'στὶν ἡ φύσις.
ΜΝ. τοῦ μήτ' ἀκούειν μήθ' ὁρᾶν;
ΕΥ. εὖ ἴσθ' ὅτι.
ΜΝ. πῶς χωρίς;
ΕΥ. οὕτω ταῦτα διεκρίθη τότε.
Αἰθὴρ γὰρ ὅτε . . .

EUR. Ah: all you're due to see must you not hear.
MN. You what? Say it again: I mustn't hear?
EUR. Not what you're due to see.
MN. But I can't see?

EUR. Not what you're due to hear.
MN. It's too clever
For me: mustn't hear, mustn't see?
EUR. Bear in mind that in the scheme of things
The concepts are quite differentiated.
MN. What—not hearing and not seeing?
EUR. Indeed.
MN. Differentiated?
EUR. And separate.
It all began with *Aether* . . .[63]

The effect of these linguistic acrobatics, then, is to establish, at the outset, Euripides' Enlightenment persona (sharply etched against Mnesilochus' clumsy incomprehension), in association with which his irreligion (*vel sim.*) is little more than an attendant detail. Enlightenment Man surfaces again when Euripides reveals his plan to deal with the women by persuading Agathon (*Ἀγάθωνα πεῖσαι*, 88) to smuggle himself into their assembly to speak in his defence (*λέξονθ' ὑπὲρ ἐμοῦ*, 91): his problem will be solved by recourse to the Enlightenment techniques of persuasion and argument. But it is only when this first plan fails, and a second plan (Mnesilochus as replacement for Agathon) is failing too (with Mnesilochus under arrest), that Euripides is forced to run through the full range of his Enlightenment ingenuity in search of a guise and a pose to set his suffering assistant free.[64]

[63] Eur.'s *ὁρᾶν* and *ἀκούειν* are bathetically 'explained' at 26–9: *ὁρᾷς τὸ θύριον τοῦτο; . . . ἄκουε . . . ἐνταῦθ' Ἀγάθων*. The philosophizing at 11 (*χωρὶς γάρ*) is not an 'answer' to 10, though it picks up (by way of pretext) the continuing possibility of a disjunctive, rather than a conjunctive, pairing of the two verbs.

[64] Contrast, then, Eur.'s intellectual modernism with Agathon's: the latter's modernist affinities are not intellectual but (as is clear from his own composition and his servant's, *Thes.* 101 ff., 39 ff.) New Dithyrambic: B. Zimmermann, *Dithyrambos. Geschichte einer Gattung* (Göttingen 1992) 124, and id., 'Critica ed imitazione: la nuova musica nelle commedie di Aristofane', in B. Gentili and R. Pretagostini (eds.), *La musica in Grecia* (Rome 1988) 199–204. The suggestion made by (e.g.) Henderson, *Maculate Muse*, 88, that Agathon symbolizes 'the emasculated art of contemporary tragedy, invented by Euripides', misrepresents A's treatment of both writers. The only basis for a link between the two is Eur.'s emollient remark about Agathon, *ἐγὼ τοιοῦτος ἦ | ὢν τηλικοῦτος, ἡνίκ' ἠρχόμην ποιεῖν*, and Mnesilochus' comment, *μὰ τὸν Δί', οὐ ζηλῶ σε τῆς παιδεύσεως* (173–4)—all of which is no more consequential than Agathon's servant's dig at Mnesilochus, *ἦ που νέος γ' ὢν ἦσθ' ὑβριστής, ὦ γέρον* (63), to which, indeed, 174 (on which see Sommerstein ad loc.) is a kind of delayed response. That the Agathon *scene*, with all its poetry, thematically prefigures the later Euripidean scenes with *theirs*, is

If we turn to Euripides' actual offence against the women, we encounter a surprising lack of definition about the precise charges. Euripides' own version is that they accuse him of slander in his plays (*τραγῳδῶ καὶ κακῶς αὐτὰς λέγω*, 85) on grounds unspecified.[65] From their own words in assembly, we gather that there are several 'slanders'.[66] Euripides, it seems, is forever (392–4) . . .

> *τὰς μοιχοτύπας, τὰς ἀνδρεραστρίας καλῶν,*
> *τὰς οἰνοπίπας, τὰς προδότιδας, τὰς λάλους,*
> *τὰς οὐδὲν ὑγιές, τὰς μέγ' ἀνδράσιν κακόν*[67]
>
> Calling us whores and nymphomaniacs,
> Lushes, back-stabbers, big-mouths—
> Real rubbish, trouble for husbands.

The distracting hints of bathos in the second line may or may not encourage us to take the accusations 'seriously', but all in all we are left to infer that the central and most damaging imputation is that of sexual licentiousness. When Mnesilochus mounts his defence, he does so on the grounds that Euripides has not so much misstated the case against women but understated it, and his sequence of choice anecdotes concentrates on sexual misdemeanours ('Three days married, we were, and my boyfriend pays a visit . . .', 478 ff.), while his representative instance of Euripides' portrayal of women is the love-crazed Phaedra in *Hippolytus* (497–8).

This impresssion is confirmed by the argument that follows between Mnesilochus and one of the women. Both accept as common ground (546–50) that a Euripidean woman will always be a 'bad' woman, a Phaedra or a Melanippe, and never a faithful Penelope.[68] And even though the argument still allows for sundry allegations of a different kind, from petty household thefts to murder (555–63), the impression remains: a special association is presupposed between women and sexuality.[69] However, there is

obvious—and quite a different matter: it prefigures the women's scenes with *their* poetry in equal measure.

[65] Sim. *μέλλουσί μ' . . . ἀπολεῖν . . . ὅτι κακῶς αὐτὰς λέγω* (181–2).

[66] The women feel they are *προπηλακιζομένας . . . ὑπὸ Εὐ. . . . καὶ πολλὰ καὶ παντοῖ' ἀκουούσας κακά* (386–8); cf. 787–8 (in the parabasis).

[67] Text as Sommerstein.

[68] Whether Melanippe was actually a 'bad' woman (she was raped by a god) is another matter: cf. Sommerstein ad loc.

[69] In itself, a conventional Greek—male—assumption: witness the mythic claim

no intimation within the play that Euripides—like, maybe, Phaedra's Hippolytus—might be an opponent of sexuality itself; the women's association with sexuality is apparent, but apparently non-confrontational.

In default of any further definition, we are left with a kind of dramatic rhapsody on three jostling themes, where the themes in question are three large components of Aristophanic, or rather Attic, sensibility: poetry, religion, sexuality. These three are presented, almost, as coordinates in some larger pattern. It is, almost, as if Aristophanes fancies a glimpse into some primal unity within which the three components—now sundered?—belonged together, as they do (for instance), and effortlessly, in Sappho's poetic tribute to the goddess of love, the best part of two centuries before (fr. 1. 1–5):

> ποικιλόθρον' ἀθανάτ' Ἀφρόδιτα,
> παῖ Δίος δολόπλοκε, λίσσομαί σε,
> μή μ' ἄσαισι μηδ' ὀνίαισι δάμνα,
> πότνια, θῦμον,
>
> ἀλλὰ τυίδ' ἔλθ' . . .
>
> Rich-throned immortal Aphrodite,
> Cunning child of Zeus, I beg you
> Not to crush my heart, Lady,
> With ache and anguish,
>
> But come . . .

Almost and *almost*: because at no stage in the play is this larger pattern suitably enforced. It could hardly be so, given that at no stage is any one of the three items identified schematically; nor is anything made of the connections between Euripides and the women as poet and poeticizers, or (beyond the myrtle-seller's speech) between the women as upholders of religion and Euripides as sceptic. Indeed, if the three presences are perceptible as such, it is because they remain constant points of reference while their embodiments shift, thanks to the role-playing that is such a feature of the play. For not only are the women exponents of poetry, albeit in a muted kind of way, by virtue of their devotional

of Tiresias (who had experienced life as both man and woman) that women enjoyed sex nine times more than men (Hes. fr. 275), or simply the fact that sex was the province of a female deity, Aphrodite (hence called τὰ Ἀφροδίσια); see in general N. Loraux, *Les Enfants d'Athèna* (Paris 1981) 157–96.

lyrics. More surprisingly, Euripides eventually aligns himself with female sexuality. As his final impersonation, after playing two romantic male leads, Menelaus and Perseus, he becomes the old madam whose protegée seduces the Scythian. Not long before, and more surprisingly still, perhaps, he aligns himself with religion too by playing god as part of his rescue attempts for Mnesilochus. In becoming Perseus, Euripides is turning himself into a son of a god, a combatant of gods, and a hero with a cult at Athens.[70] Another bit of ingenuity on Euripides' part, furthermore, duly signals Perseus-Euripides' claim to some sort of divine status. Euripides has (he assures Mnesilochus) 'countless means', or *mêkhanai*, at his disposal (927), and, as Perseus, he duly makes his entrance on the *mêkhanê*, the stage 'machine' raised above the ordinary performing space[71] and associated with the appearance of gods.[72] In the stage

[70] Perseus is the son of Danae and Zeus, and combatant of Medusa. The legend that he actually killed his half-brother Dionysus is probably Hellenistic, but Perseus is already seen fighting the maenads on 6th-cent. vases, and the later story reflects the existing stature of its subject: T. Gantz, *Early Greek Myth* (Baltimore 1993) 299–311. For the cult at Athens see Paus. 2. 18. 1.

[71] For the original production this is doubted by some (e.g. Rau, *Paratragodia*, 67), though not by those who have studied the matter most closely (notably Taplin, n. 72 below). Euripides-Perseus enters *ταχεῖ πεδίλῳ διὰ μέσου . . . αἰθέρος | τέμνων κέλευθον* (1099–100). The natural interpretation of these words is in any case that he enters on the *mêkhanê*, and the word play surely confirms it. The word play itself (which I have not seen noted before) actually involves a longer set of passages. Before the paratragic rescue attempts begin, the captive Mnesilochus appeals desperately for some unspecified *μηχανὴ σωτηρίας* (765). It is after his unsuccessful bid as Menelaus that Euripides gives Mnesilochus his assurance that he has *μυρίαι . . . μηχαναί* at his disposal (927). When even this Perseus-epiphany *on* one of these 'means' leads nowhere, he announces again his determination to find *ἄλλην τινὰ | τούτῳ πρέπουσαν μηχανήν* (1131–2). The whole set reads like an orchestrated sequence, especially as these uses of the word are the only ones in the play, except for an innocent 'means' near the beginning (87).

[72] This last point is controversial. The use of the *mêkhanê* at this period is considered concisely but fully by Taplin (*Stagecraft*, 443–7), who sees no reason to doubt that here in *Thes.*, and in other plays, A uses the *mêkhanê* and that for Perseus' equivalent arrival in *Andromeda* Eur. did the same. Taplin notes that the *mêkhanê* 'was conventionally used for [divine] epiphanies in the 4th cent., and it soon became proverbial' (ibid. 444). After reviewing the evidence, however, he thinks it 'far from sure that in the 5th cent. the *θεὸς ἀπὸ μηχανῆς* was in fact *ἀπὸ μηχανῆς*' (ibid. 445), which would mean that the divine associations of the contrivance were not yet established. However, once one grants (*a*) that the *mêkhanê* was available to and used by the tragedians of the late 5th cent., and (*b*) that it was proverbial for divine epiphanies a generation later (the earliest evidence is in Plato: ibid. 444 n. 5), it seems artificial not to relate these data to (*c*) the fact that in late 5th-cent. tragedy divine epiphanies become very common (for a list see ibid. 444–5), and thus infer, on admittedly circumstantial evidence, that the connection was already established.

symbolism (and the proleptic pun) the poet's new quasi-divine status is made manifest.

These realignments of Euripides and female sexuality, Euripides and traditional religion, might seem to dovetail nicely together. Indeed, one might even glimpse, in the conjunction, a specific symbolic sequence just before and just after the bargain between Euripides and the women is struck. *His* appearance in a divine guise (1108–34) is followed by *their* final performance in the likeness of hymn-singing poets (1136–59), while the bargain (1160–75) is sealed when *his* last ingenious manoeuvre for dealing with the Scythian (1176–209) involves sexual deception as, and by, a woman. And if these realignments, based on particular exchanges of role, help make the three coordinates (almost) into true presences (almost), so too does the cumulative effect of the role-playing. With so much shifting and exchanging, it is inevitable that the profile of the individual identities is lowered—even beyond what would be expected of an 'ordinarily' discontinuous Aristophanic play—while the profile of the alignments that, between them, they create is raised.

And yet, in the end, the pattern of coordinates, symbolic sequences, alignments and realignments comes to nothing. The play moves to its reconciliation, but it is hardly a reconstitution of Sappho's primal unity. The reconciliation involves a compromise: the women acknowledge that poetry (in the shape of Euripides) is not their inevitable enemy; Euripides, that female sexuality need not be his target and, tacitly, that (with the Thesmophoria still in progress, on its middle day) the rituals of religion, as vested in the women, shall proceed in due order and without further violation. This compromise has no psychological significance for Euripides or the women; and, in particular, there is nothing of a conversion on either side: not one of these figures, in truth, is enough of a person to have a conversion. Nor is the compromise presented as a piece of mature wisdom about the conduct of life. In fact, no intellectual consideration is raised at all. On an intellectual level (to be blunt), the actual stuff of the compromise is disconcertingly trivial: *he* will leave them ('women') alone in future; *they* will let the old man go and (by implication) leave *him* alone too, on pain of having their husbands told about their conspiracy;[73] and the whole

[73] *ἃ νῦν ὑποικουρεῖτε*, 1168. The context might seem to allow the additional implication that Eur. will make public the whole truth about the women's sexual

negotiation is over in ten lines (1160–70), with one loose end—how to deal with the Scythian—as the only obstacle to Mnesilochus' freedom. What we are offered, then, is a mechanical realignment, which (at most) derives an impressionistic plausibility from the blurring of distinctions which the accumulated role-playing has engendered.

As a resolution of a pattern, this is less than adequate. What is a resolution that rests on so little except impressionistic gestures? The role-playing gives the reconciliation a measure of plausibility; it does nothing to make it satisfying. Negatively, indeed, poetry and sexuality and religion, like their elusive human embodiments, are all now free of threat; but there is no equivalent positive image to point to. In pragmatic terms, the solution is not *realized*: its various elements are not decisively related, one to another—the women's hymnal poetry to Euripides' poetry, their religion to his brief identification with the divine. In the end, one has room to wonder whether Euripides is accepted by the women in his particularity or as representative of poetry in general: is he *this* (anti-woman) poet or *any* (anti-woman) poet? And the fact that the doubt can still arise is a sign that not only the resolution, but the pattern itself is, after all, in question. Here, at least, Aristophanes' 'mutually defining emblems' are insufficiently worked out; perhaps significantly, no clear sense of value arises from their configuration; one way or another, their full realization is hardly attempted and certainly not achieved.

Might one argue that Aristophanes is simply unable to do more with such a pattern? It is instructive to ask why. Whatever else, the problem must be partly one of abstract expression. A fuller articulation, perhaps, would call for a degree of abstraction alien to the sensuous norms of Aristophanes' comedy. And indeed one has only to remember Aristophanes' distance—even in his religiose lyrics—from those ethical generalizations ('gnomic banalities') through which his tragic counterparts so often tease out their positions,[74] to imagine how uncongenial such an undertaking might be. There are, of course, ways and means of accommodating abstraction; and to a writer who can dramatize Right and

and other subterfuges, which (given the women's response) would then imply that they acknowledge it as the truth; but nothing is said explicitly of this, and νῦν tells against it.

[74] The phrase is Dover's: above, p. 203.

Wrong (*Clouds*), or Demos (*Knights*), or War and Peace (*Peace*), the three given entities would not necessarily present insoluble problems. The doubt persists, none the less: Aristophanes would find their fuller articulation and their resolution incompatible with his comedy.

A second and more specific difficulty, it may be, is the question of idiom. Whatever else the undertaking might involve, it would surely involve some coordination of the mobile (but partly paratragic) *lexis* of the Aristophanic Euripides with the consistently elevated poetic-religious language of the women's lyrics. Yet it is not at all apparent how this could be done, because where the one is infinitely—comically—adaptable, the other presupposes a conventional solemnity from which a bridge to the Protean comic is hard to imagine. If (one might say) the goal is reconciliation, what can hardly be reconciled is the version of poetry in the devotional lyrics and the one in Euripides' comic ingenuities.

As if by way of acknowledgement that the maze of alignments and realignments offers no way out, the impressionistic pattern is allowed to lapse in favour of another. Poetry is still to the fore and, with it, role-playing. Like poetry, role-playing is everywhere in *Thesmophoriazusae*, and the principal role-players—in particular, Euripides, Mnesilochus, and the women—all, in their different ways, poeticize. This is, no doubt, a strangely assorted group of poeticizers, but whereas there is no sense of any overall common ground between the specimens of poetry that they produce, in a different perspective their 'authors' are all indeed felt to be as one. All these role-playing poeticizers are Athenian, and all share in the reconciliation at the end. One figure, the Scythian, is excluded from the reconciliation; and very conspicuously, the Scythian is not Athenian, plays no roles, and does not poeticize. Far from taking wing to the realms of poetry, he has an earth-bound language which is not even proper Greek, but a kind of pidgin;[75] and it is the very grossness of this contrast in the final scenes that serves to evoke—*per contra*—a pattern of solidarity, at least of Attic solidarity, after all.

Yet the revised pattern carries a sharper and more surprising

[75] Cf. Colvin, *Dialect*, 290–1. The Scythian is also stupid, as only a foreigner can be, and (dialect apart) irredeemably inarticulate—therefore the opposite of Eur., supremely clever and profoundly articulate. Accordingly, the discomfiture of the Scythian is the final vindication of Eur. himself.

implication. Throughout the action, from the effusions of Agathon to Euripides' final disguise, the stage has been full of role-playing; at the very end, there is none. This end is also, of course, quite unlike the end of so many Aristophanic comedies, which close expansively on a *kômos*. Plays as different as *Birds* and *Acharnians*, *Wasps* and *Lysistrata*, show us stage figures putting the symbolic seal on their success, and making it our success, with a grand gesture of collective celebration: a banquet, a wedding, a communal dance and song. The end of this play, though affirming solidarity, does so in a minimalist way: it is not expansive but reductive. Having played his last role, Euripides is able to free Mnesilochus, and both leave the stage. Only the Scythian is left, briefly, with the chorus. There is no more playing of roles; the Scythian goes off; then the women go off. The roles are all played out, and the stage empties. It is as if to say: take role-playing away, and nothing is left[76]—an impressive and disconcerting image indeed.

What does this reading of *Thesmophoriazusae* tell us about Aristophanes as a serious writer? We may note, first of all, how readily he follows a form of organization in which antithesis, though available, plays no major part. There is some sort of conflict, there is dislocation, and eventually there is reconciliation; but the dislocation is not presented as an antithesis which the reconciliation (in the event, a surprisingly matter-of-fact reconciliation) might resolve. We are aware how strong Aristophanes' instinct is for oppositional patterns. On this evidence we might well conclude that, strong as it is, that instinct is ultimately subordinate to the instinct for reconciliation.

It is instructive, again, to see that, though away from the political arena, Aristophanes seems—again instinctively—to evoke and configure big issues, without, in the end, carrying the configuration through. The role-playing theme, in the end, arguably makes a *point*: could this be said of the other issues that are so prominent in the play? If we think back to our original coordinates, we must agree that we are hardly the wiser (*mot juste*) about religion or sexuality: *inter alia*, both are—conventionally—

[76] In *Thes.* at least, the text gives no grounds for the speculation, sometimes entertained by A's comm., that an original lyric may have been lost. Certainly no *kômos* could ever have stood here: there is nothing left to celebrate and no one left (for the chorus?) to celebrate it with.

assigned to women, and reassigned indecisively. Nor are we any the wiser about Euripides. We are not, for instance, even required to let it cross our minds whether there might be a question or two about the *real* Euripides: are we to conclude that the real Euripides' presentation of women is (or is not) justified? equally, does that presentation actually involve a prejudicial view of women at all? The play does not engage our minds like this; though hugely intellectual in one way, it is not intellectual in this way; and here it is symptomatic that one feels uneasy about using a word like 'point' even in connection with the undoubted meaning, and meaningfulness, of the role-playing theme.

Though a limiting judgement is implicit in these conclusions, they do not constitute a depreciation of Aristophanes' play. For also implicit in them is an indication of where his true and extraordinary strengths lie, and a provisional formula for the way he treats issues, including political issues, elsewhere. Aristophanic comedy does not articulate the abstract in the intellectual way that 'points' implies. War or peace, sexuality or religion or role-playing: Aristophanes does not explore such issues intellectually. He re-forms them on the ground in front of us, refocuses them,[77] recreates them. 'Points', disembodied abstractions, are alien, just as the disembodied intellectualizing of a Socrates is alien—and when first sighted (at *Clouds* 218), the disembodied intellectual, Socrates, is appropriately up in the air.

At the opposite end of the spectrum from *Thesmophoriazusae*, consider *Knights*, a play where issues, political issues indeed, are unmistakable. On a crude reading, those issues and the play as a whole are co-extensive: Demos (the people of Athens) is in thrall to his unscrupulous slave Paphlagon (Cleon), and the two 'good' slaves in Demos' household conjure up a champion who can 'free' their master and return him to an attitude of political responsibility ('I'm so ashamed of all my past mistakes', 1355). Yet in that very formulation of responsibility an irreducible irresponsibility is implicit—irresponsibility on Aristophanes' part towards his own 'serious' issues. Demos is so stupid and so gullible that the only way Paphlagon can be displaced is if he is *re*placed by a man (Sausage-Seller) who surpasses him in those very qualities that

[77] For the 'eyes' of our mind ('exprimit et oculis mentis ostendit', Quintil. 8. 3. 62: the terms are those in which the ancient rhetoricians proclaim the virtues of vivid presentation).

make Cleon such a menace. In the eventual happy ending, however, Sausage-Seller is turned into an honest adviser, Paphlagon into a humble Sausage-Seller himself, and Demos is restored to his former glories. And Demos, now 'ashamed' of all his 'past mistakes' is duly consoled by Sausuage-Seller (1356–7):

> *ἀλλ' οὐ σὺ τούτων αἴτιος—μὴ φροντίσῃς—*
> *ἀλλ' οἵ σε ταῦτ' ἐξηπάτων.*
>
> You're not to blame—don't think about it:
> It was those who tricked you.

If Demos could 'think about it', though, he might well reflect that this consolation is only available to him because the speaker of the consoling words (Sausage-Seller) has triumphed, and that Sausage-Seller's triumph (whence his right and opportunity to console) is due solely to his own special pre-eminence in tricking Demos, and that this pre-eminence, in turn, is due to Sausage-Seller's marvellous low qualities, the formulation of which early in the play permits a characteristic series of satirical jabs, like (180–1)

> *δι' αὐτὸ γάρ τοι τοῦτο καὶ γίγνει μέγας,*
> *ὁτιὴ πονηρὸς κἀξ ἀγορᾶς εἶ καὶ θρασύς*
>
> This very thing guarantees your greatness—
> Your bad breeding, your market-training, your insolence

and (191–3)

> *ἡ δημαγωγία γὰρ οὐ πρὸς μουσικοῦ*
> *ἔτ' ἐστιν ἀνδρὸς οὐδὲ χρηστοῦ τοὺς τρόπους,*
> *ἀλλ' εἰς ἀμαθῆ καὶ βδελυρόν.*
>
> Public office isn't a job for an educated man,
> Not now, or a man of good character:
> It needs someone who's ignorant and disgusting.

The satirical critique is presented as a critique of Paphlagon-Cleon, but Sausage-Seller's successful use of Paphlagon-Cleon's own despised qualities ('This rogue has met another, | Whose rogueries go much further', 683–5), necessarily puts a question mark against the critique of Paphlagon-Cleon himself.

The problem is not that Sausage-Seller has eventually to be made into a 'proper' moral hero[78] in order to make his moral

[78] Complete with new name Agoracritus, lit. 'Chosen by the Assembly', but

point, nor that he has to be converted into an honest counsellor of state by the characteristic non-realist means of recreativity: non-realism and recreativity are perfectly compatible with political seriousness (witness Brecht).[79] Again, Aristophanes' antipathy to Cleon (a 'national hero' at the time)[80] need not be doubted, nor indeed his correlative loyalty to the ideal of a traditional Athens when public office was *not* in the hands of the 'ignorant and disgusting' and when the values of Marathon—whatever that might mean—held sway. The problem is that this loyalty is nowhere enacted, and only lightly presented at all, and the antipathy, though pervasive, is subordinate to an exhilarating projection of a Punch-and-Judy confrontation whose remarkable virtuosity dominates the action. Paphlagon is an abusive and unctuous villain; his opponent is an abusive and unctuous villain; and their opposition, however, problematic in moral-political terms, is massively productive of an immensely enjoyable contest of ripe abuse and appalling unctuousness, from the more sophisticated (1166–9)—

PAPH. I offer you a barley-cake,
Made of flour we won that day in Pylos.
S.-S. And I've got finger-bread for you,
Breadfulled by Our Lady's ivory finger[81]—

to the less (364–5):

ΑΛ. ἐγὼ δὲ βυνήσω γέ σου τὸν πρωκτὸν ἀντὶ φύσκης.
ΠΑ. ἐγὼ δὲ γ' ἐξέλξω σε τῆς πυγῆς θύραζε κύβδα.[82]

S.-S. I'll stuff your arse-hole like a sausage skin.
PAPH. I'll drag you by the butt and tip you out.

This extravagant exercise in competitive odiousness takes up most of the play (273–1252). While it lasts, it is in effect an end in itself:

interpreted (with 'degrading' re-etymology) by Sausage-Seller himself as 'Used to arguments in the Market' (1257–8).

[79] NB that there is no question of some kind of higher deception on this character's part, as if he were like Dionysus in *Bacchae* (or the chorus in *Clouds*)—pretending to be one thing, then finally revealing his new powers. Even as late as 752–5 (οἴμοι κακοδαίμων), Sausage-Seller is still an 'ordinary' player in the game. By 1321 (τὸν Δῆμον . . . καλὸν . . . πεποίηκα) he is a recreated and indeed (literally) recreative wonder-worker.

[80] A. H. Sommerstein, *Aristophanes, Knights* (Warminster 1981) 2.

[81] Above, pp. 127–8.

[82] Text as Sommerstein.

it is so sublimely appalling that one hardly wants it to end. Organized antithetically, as, given the equivalence and kinship of the two agonists, it can be, it thus reveals why Paphlagon's opponent simply had to be equivalent, akin, *and*, accordingly, subversive of the moral-political 'point'. When all is said and done, the modal exuberance—the astonishing game of abusive and unctuous verbalizing—counts for more than the moral-political argument it purports to serve.

In the course of the long contest, some argumentative blows, inevitably, are struck—the very representation of Paphlagon-Cleon as a villainous slave being chief among them. But the argumentative possibilities are never explored as the modal possibilities are. These modal explorations are what *Knights*, in the truest sense, is 'about', and their articulation, of course, presupposes their author's predisposition towards, and immense skill in operating, that battery of stylistic techniques that come under the heading of parallel structures.

The plausibility of this interpretation becomes the more apparent when we acknowledge that there is still more modal exploration in *Knights*. As so often, there is a substantial paratragic element, represented variously by the charming high-style song of praise (551 ff.),

> ἵππι' ἄναξ Πόσειδον, ᾧ . . .
>
> Poseidon, Lord of horses, who . . .[83]

by Sausage-Seller's jovial appropriation of a tragic messenger's set speech to report his own triumph in the *boulê* (637–40),

> νῦν μοι θράσος καὶ γλῶτταν εὔπορον δότε
> φωνήν τ' ἀναιδῆ. ταῦτα φροντίζοντί μοι
> ἐκ δεξιᾶς ἐπέπαρδε καταπύγων ἀνήρ.
> κἀγὼ προσέκυσα . . .
>
> 'Grant me now courage, a resourceful tongue,
> A shameless voice.' And as I prayed, some arsehole
> Farts on the right-hand side, and I bow low
> To the happy omen . . .

and by a deflating use of the grand manner to record the moment of Paphlagon's final collapse. Oedipus-like, he pursues the

[83] On the lyric see Silk, 'Lyric poet', 144 n. 138.

interrogation of one whose revelations must mean his own undoing. In this remarkable sequence, declamatory asides and exclamations alternate with bathetic questions—and with answers which themselves oscillate between the bathetic and the grand (1240–8):

ΠΑ. ὦ Φοῖβ' Ἄπολλον Λύκιε, τί ποτέ μ' ἐργάσει;
τέχνην δὲ τίνα ποτ' εἶχες ἐξανδρούμενος;
ΑΛ. ἠλλαντοπώλουν καί τι καὶ βινεσκόμην.
ΠΑ. οἴμοι κακοδαίμων· οὐκέτ' οὐδέν εἰμ' ἐγώ.
λεπτή τις ἐλπίς ἐστ' ἐφ' ἧς ὀχούμεθα.
καί μοι τοσοῦτον εἰπέ· πότερον ἐν ἀγορᾷ
ἠλλαντοπώλεις ἐτεὸν ἢ 'πὶ ταῖς πύλαις;
ΑΛ. ἐπὶ ταῖς πύλαισιν, οὗ τὸ τάριχος ὤνιον.
ΠΑ. οἴμοι, πέπρακται τοῦ θεοῦ τὸ θέσφατον.

PAPH. Lycian Apollo, what willst thou with me?
When you were growing up, what was your trade?
S.-S. Rent-boy I was, yea, and sausage-seller.
PAPH. Dear god, is this the end of Paphlagon?
Just one last hope keeps us still afloat.
So tell me this: was it the agora
Where you sold sausages, or at the city gates?
S.-S. The city gates, where salt fish is for sale.
PAPH. No, no! God's oracle has come to pass![84]

It would be misleading, though, to claim that these varieties of paratragedy are in any substantial way orchestrated to form a coherent presence, as they are in *Thesmophoriazusae*. In *Knights* we might say that they amount to something more than a mere scatter of stylistic effects, but something less than a fully identifiable mode. There is, by contrast, one other identifiable mode in the play, as readily identifiable as it is unexpected. When Paphlagon acknowledges 'God's oracle', he is attaching his fall to what one interpreter has dubbed 'parachresmody',[85] the art of imitation oracles. Partly with satirical reference to the superstitions of contemporary Athens, mock oracles occur here and there in Aristophanes' plays, but in *Knights*, uniquely, a 'parachresmic' mode is established in its own right. Within the action of the play

[84] 'Oedipus-like': cf. Soph. *OT* 1147–85 and Rau, *Paratragodia*, 170–2. 'Grand manner': see e.g. Neil on 1242. In 1243 the English alludes to Edward G. Robinson's famous declamatory death-line in the film *Little Caesar* (1930).

[85] Jeffrey Henderson in an unpublished paper (his own term is '*parachrêsmôidia*').

its rationale is that Demos' new slave, Paphlagon, finds, or invents, oracles to persuade his master to follow his own bidding (61):

> *ᾄδει δὲ χρησμούς· ὁ δὲ γέρων σιβυλλιᾷ.*
>
> He chants oracles: the old man's Sibyl-crazy.

Paphlagon, however, is known to have a special oracle which he keeps secret, which Demos' good slaves contrive to steal (115–17), and which turns out to contain the formula for his own destruction (127–43). Like most Greek oracles, this one is composed of quasi-epic dactylic hexameters, with diction, dialect, and idiom to match, and is suitably Delphic in character. One of the good slaves himself refers to its (196)

> . . . *ποικίλως πως καὶ σοφῶς ᾐνιγμένος*
>
> Intricate and subtle riddling language.

The Delphic message begins (197),

> *ἀλλ' ὁπόταν μάρψῃ βυρσαίετος ἀγκυλοχήλης* . . .
>
> Yea, when a crook-taloned eagle of leather shall snatch . . .

which is duly explained as a prophecy of a messianic Sausage-Seller—explained, indeed, as such to the great deliverer himself, who, 'as if by providence' (147), has just made his appearance.

An oracle stands at the head of the play, then, and an allusion back to the oracle at its dénouement. In the meantime, we are periodically reminded that while Paphlagon has the elaborate cunning of his oracles, Sausage-Seller matches him, and indeed outdoes him, in 'intricate subtlety'.[86] And we note the way the chorus slips momentarily into a dactylic cast of words when proclaiming the new Messiah (328–9),

> *ἀλλ' ἐφάνη γὰρ ἀνὴρ ἕτερος πολὺ*
> *σοῦ μιαρώτερος, ὥστε με χαίρειν*
>
> Someone's turned up at last, who's
> Still more slimy than you are:
> I'm delighted

[86] Paphlagon earns a *ποικίλος* at 758, Sausage-Seller *ποικίλως* and *σοφῶς* at 459 and 421, and *δόλοισι ποικίλοις* at 685–6.

as also when inveighing against the old trickster's corruptions (402–3):

> *ὦ περὶ πάντ' ἐπὶ πᾶσί τε πράγμασι*
> *δωροδόκοισιν ἐπ' ἄνθεσιν ἵζων*
>
> Minding everyone's business,
> Perched on bribery's blossoms
> Like an insect.[87]

Then again, we find Paphlagon apppealing to an oracle (*τοῖς λογίοισιν*, 797) in which Demos is promised that his empire will stretch even into Arcadia. The anapaestic metre of his words readily permits a momentary allusion to the rhythms, as well as the phraseology, of Delphi (797–8):

> . . . *Ἑλλήνων ἄρξῃ πάντων* . . .
> . . . *δεῖ ποτ' ἐν Ἀρκαδίᾳ πεντωβόλου ἡλιάσασθαι.*
>
> . . . Lord of all Hellenes . . .
> . . . shall in Arcadia soon be on juries for great gain.[88]

Well before the final phase of the contest and Sausage-Seller's victory, these hints of parachresmody come to startling fruition when the contestants agree to duel with oracles for Demos' favour (960–72). In the course of the episode that follows, the duellists take turns to offer a series of rival oracles, each in suitable form and more or less suitable idiom and accompanied by suitable interpretations. Paphlagon begins (1014–20):

> *ἄκουε δή νυν καὶ πρόσεχε τὸν νοῦν ἐμοί·*
> *φράζευ, Ἐρεχθεΐδη, λογίων ὁδόν, ἥν σοι Ἀπόλλων*
> *ἴαχεν ἐξ ἀδύτοιο διὰ τριπόδων ἐριτίμων.*
> *σῴζεσθαί σ' ἐκέλευ' ἱερὸν κύνα καρχαρόδοντα,*
> *ὃς πρὸ σέθεν χάσκων καὶ ὑπὲρ σοῦ δεινὰ κεκραγὼς*
> *σοὶ μισθὸν ποριεῖ. κἂν μὴ δρᾷ ταῦτ', ἀπολεῖται·*
> *πολλοὶ γάρ μίσει σφε κατακρώζουσι κολοιοί.*[89]

[87] The phraseology evokes—and harshly clashes with the tone of—traditional 'praise-poetry' imagery like Alcm. 3. 72 *χάρις ἐπὶ . . . χαίταισιν ἵσδει*, Pind. *Nem.* 7. 53 *τὰ τέρπν' ἄνθε' Ἀφροδίσια* and *Pyth.* 10. 53–4 *ἐγκωμίων γὰρ ἄωτος ὕμνων | ἐπ' ἄλλοτ' ἄλλον ὥτε μέλισσα θύνει λόγον*. The two couplets (*ἀλλ'* . . . and *ὦ* . . .) are metrically responsive: Parker, *Songs*, 164–5.

[88] Cf. the sound and sentiment of e.g. the supposedly 6th–5th-cent. BC oracles ap. Hdt. 1. 66. 1 *ἐν Ἀρκαδίῃ . . . Τεγέην ποσσίκροτον ὀρχήσασθαι* | and Diod. Sic. 8. 29 *Κυρήνης | εὐρείης ἄρχειν* . . .: H. W. Parke and D. E. W. Wormell, *The Delphic Oracle*, ii (Oxford 1956), nos. 31 and 71.

[89] Text as Sommerstein in 1019. After 1014 (an iambic trimeter) the hexameters

Okay, listen to me and pay attention:
'Son of Erechtheus, mark well the prophecy which Lord Apollo
Uttered deep in his shrine, from priceless tripod delivered.
Keep thou safe the dog (he bids thee), the Jag-Toothed One, holy
Open-mouth yapper and fearsome barker on thy behalf.
Dog thy pay will provide, and if he fails, he's done for;
Yea, for many the jackdaws that croak him down and detest him.'

Like many old men in Aristophanes, Demos is not quick on the uptake, and in plain, and plaintive, iambics asks for a commentary (1022):

τί γάρ ἐστ' Ἐρεχθεῖ καὶ κολοιοῖς καὶ κυνί;

What's with Erechtheus, jackdaws, and the dog?

Paphlagon (in the same metre) interprets (1023–4):

ἐγὼ μέν εἰμ' ὁ κύων· πρὸ σοῦ γὰρ ἀπύω·
σοὶ δ' εἶπε σῴζεσθαι 'μ' ὁ Φοῖβος τὸν κύνα.

I am the dog: you see, I bark for you.
He's telling you, look after the dog—that's me.

And so it goes on with a counter-oracle from Sausage-Seller (1030):

φράζευ, Ἐρεχθεΐδη, κύνα Κέρβερον ἀνδραποδιστήν . . .

Son of Erechtheus, mark well a kidnapping Cerberus Hell-Hound . . .

In these alternations of oracular quotation and ordinary iambic verse commentary, the spotlight is of course on the oracles. Yet soon (in good discontinuous-recreative fashion) the distinction begins to break down, and the oracular mode takes over. In place of the predictable alternation, the contestants, as if under the influence of their quotations, actually start declaiming in parachresmic dactyls on their own account—

ΠΑ. *μὴ πείθου· φθονεραὶ γὰρ ἐπικρώζουσι κορῶναι*

PAPH. Trust not those words: crows that are croaking against me are jealous

(1051)

. . . .

begin in impressively allusive style: cf. e.g. *φράζεο δή, Σπάρτη* . . . and *αὐδῶ Ἐρεχεΐδῃσιν* . . . (the beginnings of two oracles, ap. Xen. *HG* 3. 3. 3 and Dem. 21. 51, from 5th and 4th cents. BC: Parke-Wormell, *Oracle*, nos. 112. 1 and 282. 1).

ΑΛ. *τοῦτό γέ τοι Παφλαγὼν παρεκινδύνευσε μεθυσθείς*

S.-S. Thus did Paphlagon dare in a moment of drunken bravado (1054)[90]—

until eventually even the bemused Demos finds himself joining in (1059):

ΠΑ. *ἔστι Πύλος πρὸ Πύλοιο—*

ΔΗ. *τί τοῦτο λέγει, πρὸ Πύλοιο;*

PAPH. Pylos comes before Pylos—

DEM. What's all this about, 'before Pylos'?

By which stage in the proceedings the dominance of mode seems complete.[91] It is not that the issues have melted away, as they do in *Thesmophoriazusae*. Rather, they have assumed the status of a pretext and have ceased to be—if they ever were—the point.

Let us restate: 'the issues' in *Knights* never were, never could have been, 'the point'; and the non-realist character of Aristophanic comedy, and this comedy in particular, shows why. It is certainly possible for drama that is non-realist in prominent aspects to make issues central and to foreground their centrality. Consider, once again, our paradigm of Brecht and *The Threepenny Opera*. That musical drama, as we have seen, exhibits non-realist discontinuities on various levels, which culminate in the bizarre pardoning of the despised and condemned Macheath and his elevation to the aristocracy. However, this abrupt recreation, suitably announced by the King's messenger, is not quite (literally not quite) the end of the story. The *Opera*, with all its bizarre moments, has continually violated the norms of any known external reality—and yet it has still somehow preserved a sense of a stable world which is available for reference if ever the instabilities so vividly dramatized are themselves reversed. Just such a reversal follows the arrival of the messenger and his exciting news. Macheath's erstwhile rival Peachum announces 'a chorale for the poorest of the poor, whose difficult life you [the performers] have portrayed today', and adds: 'you see, in real life the King's messengers hardly ever come, and those who get kicked

[90] Rogers's translation, whose verve here one can only admire.

[91] By a process of transformation ultimately akin to that whereby in *Thes.* Mnesilochus and Eur. become Euripidean characters. Demos does it again at 1069 and 1082.

kick back.'[92] One can argue that the reversal is arbitrary (as arbitrary as the happy ending it has just displaced), but one does not feel that 'the message' the reversal carries has been imposed.

In *Knights* there is no equivalent to this configuration of the non-realist and the real. Is it that Aristophanes recreates issues, like so much else, and that what he does not do with his issues (but what Brecht, it may be, somehow achieves with his) is keep their presentation at a constant distance from a perceived reality? Suppose we seek to convert the issues of *Knights* into a series of equivalently 'real' propositions. We might end up with (for instance):

(*a*) The current leadership of Athens is self-seeking and cynical.
(*b*) The *dêmos* of Athens is gullible when faced with persuasive popular leaders.
(*c*) The Athenian aristocracy (as represented by the *Knights* of the chorus) is not self-seeking, and might be expected to help the *dêmos* change its leadership.
(*d*) An *utterly* self-seeking and cynical new leadership might turn out to be an improvement on the present *relatively* self-seeking and cynical leadership.

Of these propositions, (*a*) and (*b*) presuppose a pessimistic view of human nature, or of *homo politicus*, in the light of Athenian experience;[93] and (*c*) an optimistic view of human nature (or . . .);[94] whereas (*d*) bypasses human nature and politics, as known in the big world, altogether.

It is not, then, that (in Heath's words) Aristophanic comedy shows a 'tenuous attachment to reality',[95] but that in its response to political (and other) issues it operates, as it does elsewhere, at a shifting distance from the—from any—given. Anyone inclined to doubt this conclusion might profitably consider, for instance,

[92] '. . . singt den Choral der Ärmsten der Armen, deren schwieriges Leben ihr heute dargestellt habt, denn in Wirklichkeit ist gerade ihr Ende schlimm. Die reitenden Boten des Königs kommen sehr selten, und die getreten werden, treten wieder': Brecht, *Versuche I–IV*, 218. Cf. above, pp. 236–7.

[93] (*a*) and (*b*) are compatible with what, in other contexts, we might indeed think of as political 'realism': cf. Stern, *Realism*, 40.

[94] See *Eq*. 576–80. The hope, at this point, is for a 'sentimental unity of classes against Cleon': Dover, *Aristophanic Comedy*, 99.

[95] Heath, *Comedy*, 23.

translating the elusive 'issues' of *Knights* into the more readily analysed sphere of character portrayal. Take Paphlagon. Sometimes he is a politician, expressing (however selectively) views that his Cleonic counterpart in real Athens might not have disowned—

> *ἐγὼ μὲν οὖν αὐτίκα μάλ' εἰς βουλὴν ἰὼν*
> *ὑμῶν ἁπάντων τὰς ξυνωμοσίας ἐρῶ*
>
> No—I'm off to the Council this minute
> To tell them about your conspiracies
> (475–6)—

or else a politician, but not one talking like a 'real' Cleon, but one articulating the logic (or realpolitik) of his position in an expressionist manner half-way between a Thucydidean speaker and one in Brecht—

> *ἐγὼ δ' ἔκλεπτον ἐπ' ἀγαθῷ γε τῇ πόλει*
>
> But when I stole, it was for the city's good
> (1226)[96]—

or else a politician recreated as imitation tragic hero—

> No, no! God's oracle has come to pass
> (1248)—

or as creative oracle-monger—

> Son of Erechtheus . . .
> (1015)—

or, of course, as foul-mouthed slave:

> I'll drag you by the butt . . .
> (365).

Quite simply: the Cleon that might be judged to underlie these differing characterizations is, all in all, too various to grasp as an independent reality, and the motivation to hold on to that reality wanes the more we respond to the exuberant richness of the whole.

[96] 'Sometimes . . . it is through speeches that [Thucydides'] people (like Alcibiades at Sparta) give themselves away': S. Hornblower, *Thucydides* (London 1987) 69. 'The epic theatre is chiefly interested in the attitudes which people adopt towards one another, wherever they are socio-historically significant . . . In the epic theatre it is perfectly possible for a character to explain himself': dicta by Brecht in 1935, tr. Willett, *Brecht on Theatre*, 86, 83.

It might be argued, furthermore, that inconstant distance is written into the basic allegory of a play where politicians, like Paphlagon-Cleon, are represented as slaves, and the people as their master. The politicians are individuals, and are represented still as individuals. The people, represented likewise as an individual, is actually a group. A recreative world that can accommodate a pairing of a Xanthias and a Dionysus—a man-slave and a god-master—can cheerfully accommodate such a configuration too; but a discrepancy remains. This discrepancy is concealed, but not resolved, by the metonymic sleight of making the Demos individual an old man, on the unstated pretext that many of Cleon's supporters in the *dêmos* were (like Philocleon and the chorus in *Wasps*) indeed old men. To see the members of a group as one individual is inevitably to see them at a much greater distance, at which any differences between those individual members come to seem insignificant. Yet the hypothetical spectrum of differences between the actual individual members of the Athenian *dêmos* would hardly have been less than the given differences between Demos' various 'slaves' in the play. Then again, the fate of Paphlagon-Cleon, according to the play, is first to ride high, then eventually to be brought low—both of which conditions 'make sense' for the real individual alluded to—whereas the fate of Demos, according to the play, is first to be tricked, as either an individual or a group might be, but then eventually to be rejuvenated. In recreative terms, this still 'makes sense' for an individual; what might it mean for a group?

We can only repeat our earlier conclusion with a new emphasis. It is characteristic of Aristophanic comedy that, assuming (as it does) Athens' known and specifiable present, and yet moving freely and recreatively in and out of it (as it does), it tends to destabilize that contemporary world and its issues, in the very act of drawing attention to them. Furthermore, those issues may include what we have conventionally identified as Aristophanes' loyalties and animosities; and the presentation of Paphlagon-Cleon in *Knights* is a case in point. It should be added, too, that even if the loyalties/animosities themselves retain, at least, a consistent value within a given play, they do not necessarily retain it across different plays. Peace is the unquestioned desirable goal in *Acharnians*, *Peace*, and *Lysistrata*; in *Birds*, on the other hand, war seems to be fine as a means to an end, while in *Frogs*, not only does the war seem to be accepted as a fact of life, but Lamachus, the very figure who in *Acharnians* was the emblem of undesirable war, is now a convenient symbol of traditional value himself.[97] Again, if one of the grounds for animosity against the Socrates of *Clouds* is his disdain for traditional religion, it is an obvious rejoinder that the Aristophanes of *Frogs* can himself present his own patron deity Dionysus as a buffoon, and the Aristophanes of *Birds* even show the whole Olympian pantheon dispossessed and Iris, their messenger, threatened with physical assault and sexual violence without any hint of retribution.[98]

The lesson of *Knights*, the lesson of *Thesmophoriazusae*, and seemingly the common implication of these various inconstancies, is all one: public issues are not avoided; they are sought; yet they are sought as a kind of pretext or precondition. This book is not written on intentionalist premises, and does not place any decisive significance on the alignment of its interpretations with suppositions about Aristophanes' own ideas on the matter. Nevertheless, it is of obvious interest to glance back at some of his seemingly programmatic utterances on comedy and note, not only (once again) how elusive such utterances can be, but also how readily compatible they are with our interpretation.

Pride of place may be given to Dicaeopolis' insistence on 'talking affairs of state in a comedy' (*Acharnians* 499). In the general context of a defence of peace in time of war, this suggests a direct engagement with issues such as any 'constituent intellectual of the *dêmos*' would be proud of. In its specific context, however, the talking is rather different. On the lips of a uniquely composite figure, kitted out with Euripidean rags and Euripidean words, who in the next line refers even to 'comedy' through a distracting comic coinage ('trygedy'), these words do not have the effect of foregrounding issues. What they push into the foreground is the sublime ingenuity that has made this moment possible: here at least the effect of art is *not* to conceal, but to proclaim, itself.[99] And

[97] *Ran.* 1039–42.

[98] Cf. Ehrenberg, *People*, 263–8. Irrespective of one's estimation of Dionysus by the end of *Ran.* (cf. above, p. 259 n. 7), there is no doubt that he is a buffoon for most of the play.

[99] Compare and contrast the classical principle, 'ars est celare artem' (see e.g. J. F. D'Alton, *Roman Literary Theory and Criticism* (London 1931) 133–4) and the Jakobsonian principle that the 'poetic function' promotes 'the palpability of signs' (R. Jakobson, 'Closing statement: linguistics and poetics', in T. A. Sebeok (ed.), *Style in Language* (Cambridge, Mass. 1960) 356).

from a 'constituent intellectual' standpoint, what follows is no better—the marvellously grotesque account of the origin of the Peloponnesian War (*Acharnians* 524–31):

> *πόρνην δὲ Σιμαίθαν ἰόντες Μεγαράδε*
> *νεανίαι 'κκλέπτουσι μεθυσοκότταβοι·*
> *κᾆθ' οἱ Μεγαρῆς ὀδύναις πεφυσιγγωμένοι*
> *ἀντεξέκλεψαν Ἀσπασίας πόρνα δύο·*
> *κἀντεῦθεν ἀρχὴ τοῦ πολέμου κατερράγη*
> *Ἕλλησι πᾶσιν ἐκ τριῶν λαικαστριῶν.*
> *ἐντεῦθεν ὀργῇ Περικλέης οὐλύμπιος*
> *ἤστραπτ', ἐβρόντα, ξυνεκύκα τὴν Ἑλλάδα . . .*
>
> Some young sportsmen took a trip to Megara
> And kidnapped a local prostitute, Simaetha;
> And the Megarians, garlicked sore,
> Grabbed two of Aspasia's prostitutes in revenge.
> And that was what brought war
> Bursting down on Greece: three slags.
> Then in his wrath Olympian Pericles
> Lightened, thundered, stirred Greece up . . .[100]

Suffice it to say that no contemporary witness to the war, and no modern student of Thucydides and our other testimony to it, could react to this amazing sequence in any straightforward way.[101] On the one hand, it contains elements of dispassionate, almost Homeric, even-handedness as between the warring parties, which could, if desired, be translated, as if part of an allegory, into 'ordinary' political terms. On the other hand, the main ingredients are not thus reducible, nor do they even, in themselves, point in a single direction. The whore-thefts correspond to nothing in late fifth-century history, though to much in Herodotean and, before that, Homeric mythological narrative:[102] remarkably, they both

[100] My transl. does little justice to the amazing three-word line 525, to the power of the verb-images (*πεφυσιγγωμένοι, κατερράγη, ἤστραπτ'*, etc.), or indeed to the force of clashes of register (e.g. between coarse lexicon and tragic-compatible rhythm in 529).

[101] Which did not stop later historians 'taking it seriously': cf. esp. Plut. *Per.* 24. 3, 30. 4.

[102] With a bit of help from Cratinus' *Dionysalexandrus* (cf. Handley, 'Comedy', 126). Discussion of (esp.) the Herodotean affinities (sc. to Hdt. 1. 1–5) is bedevilled by the supposition that what must be in question here is specific allusion (or not) and 'parody' (or not): see (respectively) Edmunds, '*Acharnians*', 13, and MacDowell, *Aristophanes and Athens*, 62–3. The generic timbre of A's 'history' is what counts.

magnify and degrade the causes of the war. 'Olympian Pericles', possibly reducible, but essentially alluding to a comic stereotype,[103] maintains the epic presence, but, given the violent tonal switch from 'slags' to Olympus, carries forward the degrading effect so powerfully that our rational attention to the degraded subject—the outbreak of war—must again be strictly secondary to the glorious defamiliarizing shock. Though called into being by 'the issues' as ordinarily understood, therefore, comedy's 'sense of duty' recreates them, not exactly beyond recognition, but almost beyond any occasion for reflection.

And consider again the celebration in the *Wasps* parabasis of Aristophanes' attack on Cleon, with his claim to be a 'deliverer from evil' and a 'cleanser of the land' (ἀλεξίκακον τῆς χώρας τῆσδε καθαρτήν, 1043), and then its more explicit restatement in *Peace* (748–52):

> τοιαῦτ' ἀφελὼν κακὰ καὶ φόρτον καὶ βωμολοχεύματ' ἀγεννῆ,
> ἐποίησε τέχνην μεγάλην ἡμῖν κἀπύργωσ' οἰκοδομήσας
> ἔπεσιν μεγάλοις καὶ διανοίαις καὶ σκώμμασιν οὐκ ἀγοραίοις,
> οὐκ ἰδιώτας ἀνθρωπίσκους κωμῳδῶν οὐδὲ γυναῖκας,
> ἀλλ' Ἡρακλέους ὀργήν τιν' ἔχων τοῖσι μεγίστοις ἐπεχείρει . . .
>
> By getting rid of poor, lowbrow buffooneries—

'buffooneries' like hungry Heracleses and tricky slaves—

> Our art he has made great and built it up
> To towering dimensions with great lines,
> Ideas, jokes not everyday. Not ordinary
> Private men and women has he satirized,
> But like a Heracles tackled the great ones . . .

At which point the memoir moves into the first person (754–60):

> καὶ πρῶτον μὲν μάχομαι πάντων αὐτῷ τῷ καρχαρόδοντι,
> οὗ δεινόταται μὲν ἀπ' ὀφθαλμῶν Κύννης ἀκτῖνες ἔλαμπον,
> ἑκατὸν δὲ κύκλῳ κεφαλαὶ κολάκων οἰμωξομένων ἐλιχμῶντο
> περὶ τὴν κεφαλήν, φωνὴν δ' εἶχεν χαράδρας ὄλεθρον τετοκυίας,
> φώκης δ' ὀσμήν, Λαμίας δ' ὄρχεις ἀπλύτους, πρωκτὸν δὲ καμήλου.
> τοιοῦτον ἰδὼν τέρας οὐ κατέδεισ', ἀλλ' ὑπὲρ ὑμῶν πολεμίζων
> ἀντεῖχον ἀεὶ καὶ τῶν ἄλλων νήσων.
>
> First I fought the Jag-Toothed one himself:
> Flashed from his eyes the Bitch-Star's awesome rays;

[103] See Cratin. 73 *PCG* (with Kassel and Austin's note ad loc.).

Licked round his head a hundred flatterers' heads;
His was a cataract's annihilating roar,
A seal's smell, Lamia's unwashed balls, a camel's arse.
Square at the fiend I looked: I stood my ground,
Battling for the empire and for you.[104]

We have stressed the elusiveness of Aristophanes' claims.[105] In the context now of a discussion of 'seriousness' and 'issues' and, especially, political 'issues', we can only amplify that impression. In particular we may note that while the poet claims credit for the way he stood up to Cleon, and also claims to have made 'our art'—the art of comedy—'great', the two claims are only loosely attached. It is not, it seems, on the basis of any big satirical stand that 'our art' has been made 'great', but on the basis of Aristophanes' writing ('great lines'). At this point, one notes, too, that 'great' is writ large in Aristophanes' claims in general—'our art' is now 'great', his writing is 'great', and his opponents are 'great' (in fact, 'great*est*': *μεγίστοις*, 752): it is as if the greatness of his satirical opponents is presented as a symptom of the great art, rather than its essence. 'Great'—and special: Cleon is special, just as Aristophanes' writing is special. 'Jokes not everyday' and 'not ordinary | Private men and women': a juxtaposition of two negatives makes the point. In this passage the literary claim is both sharper and stronger than the political-satirical claim; the literary claim, in fact, subsumes the other; and the space given to the magnificent image of Cleon the monster (repeated from *Wasps*) confirms and enacts the point.

The great satire is a means, not an end. If Aristophanes writes here as a public servant, it is as servant of the Muses. This does not mean that Aristophanic comedy loses its claim to be serious. It does mean that the seriousness it ultimately aspires to—which will be confronted in our final chapter—is not the kind generally ascribed, or denied, to it.

[104] See above, pp. 46–7. [105] Ibid.

8
Mode, Meaning, and Assessment

Aristophanes lays claim to sophistication, to originality, above all to seriousness. He does so, not despite his humour, let alone by virtue of his occasional humourless moments, but on the strength of his humour.

The servant of the comic Muse lays claim to *sophia*, as poets in Greece traditionally had. He speaks for, or to, the community—and not only the immediate community, but the community of listeners, watchers, or readers in the future—as poets had spoken since Homer.[1]

Aristophanes' claim, in effect, is that his comic poetry possesses authority; and this protestation of authority (to restate once more) lies at the heart of his long engagement with tragedy and his near obsession with exploring the limits of comic appropriation of tragedy. It is a premise of *Frogs* that the contemporary community in distress must turn to a tragic writer for its salvation—

> *Αἰσχύλε, χώρει,*
> *καὶ σῷζε πόλιν τὴν ἡμετέραν*
>
> Aeschylus, go your way,
> And save our nation
> (*Frogs* 1500–1)—

as it is a premise of *Acharnians* that tragedy, in the shape of Euripidean properties (poetic and theatrical), can help Dicaeopolis talk a sceptical public round to the cause of peace. Tragedy, it seems, has a status all its own, but (if Aristophanes' endeavour can be realized) *not* all its own—'because comedy too has its authority', as one might plausibly, on reflection, paraphrase Dicaeopolis' famous line (*Acharnians* 500).

[1] On *sophia*, cf. above, p. 46 n. 11, p. 48 n. 19. The poet's claim to speak to posterity begins with Helen's admission that she and Paris are *ἀοίδιμοι ἐσσομένοισι* (*Il.* 6. 358). Among a host of subsequent acknowledgements is A's decision to rewrite, and republish, *Clouds*.

It is apparent from our earlier analysis of Aristophanes' lyrics that for him tragedy represents the highest poetic use of words. Occasionally, as in the *parodos* of *Clouds* ('Clouds everlasting . . .', 275 ff.), he attempts to use tragic language continuously like a tragedian, but to do so is to compromise the essential range and discontinuity of his style. On the whole, therefore, even when words used are tragic words, he resists any such attempt. What he does in general is use tragedy to help create a series of new *paratragic* verbal modes, each of which involves some version of a tragic co-presence, and may sometimes (though usually it does not) involve the satirical technique we call parody.[2] Let us think back to Mnesilochus impersonating one of Euripides' heroines,

> O come at long last to your wife's deep fire,

or the compound of low and high so characteristic of Aristophanes' lyrics, the 'low lyric *plus*', where the *plus* derives from a tragic matrix,

> Sun will shine as never when
> On immigrant and citizen
> The day Cleon drops dead,

or the familiar collision of a *plus* with a *low* on which so much of Aristophanes' discontinuity depends,

> Felicity among the blest.
> Mind you, if Carcinus turns up . . .

or (*pianissimo*) the comic power yet poignancy of Dicaeopolis alone in the assembly,

> And as for peace,
> They couldn't give a damn. O City city,

where, without any disruption, the tragic evocation is seen to enlarge the tone of Dicaeopolis' lament.[3] Modally distinct as these

[2] Cf. above, p. 39 n. 30. On the concept of a co-presence, see Silk, 'Paratragedy', 496–7, 502. The distinction between paratragedy and parody of tragedy is essential: paratragedy is 'the cover term for all of comedy's intertextual dependence on tragedy, some of which is parodic, but some is not', whereas parody is 'any kind of distorting representation of an original, which in the present context will be a tragic original' (ibid. 479); for the ramifications of the distinction, see ibid. 478–504.

[3] Respectively: *Thes.* 912 (above, p. 284), *Eq.* 973–6 (above, pp. 187–9), *Pax* 779–82 (above, pp. 111–13), *Ach.* 26–7 (above, pp. 36–7). Cf. Silk, 'Paratragedy', 497–8.

passages clearly are, they have in common not only a paratragic resonance, but the fact that in all of them the resonance serves to inform the comic here-and-now and not (as parodic allusion does) to redirect our attention to an absent satirical target.

If, for Aristophanes, tragedy connotes authority, one would expect to find immediate tonal confirmation in at least some of his diverse paratragic usages. This (we can now see) is indeed what we find in, for instance, the commanding tone of the denunciation of Cleon ('Sun will shine') and more strongly in the enlarged tone of Dicaeopolis' 'O City city'. The association of the authoritative and the tragic is perhaps most decisively confirmed, however, by a remarkable passage near the end of *Clouds* (1452–62). Strepsiades and the chorus:[4]

ΣΤ. *ταυτὶ δι' ὑμᾶς, ὦ Νεφέλαι, πέπονθ' ἐγώ,*
ὑμῖν ἀναθεὶς ἅπαντα τἀμὰ πράγματα.
ΧΟ. *αὐτὸς μὲν οὖν σαυτῷ σὺ τούτων αἴτιος,*
στρέψας σεαυτὸν εἰς πονηρὰ πράγματα.
ΣΤ. *τί δῆτα ταῦτ' οὔ μοι τότ' ἠγορεύετε,*
ἀλλ' ἄνδρ' ἄγροικον καὶ γέροντ' ἐπήρατε;
ΧΟ. *ἡμεῖς ποιοῦμεν ταῦθ' ἑκάστοθ', ὅντιν' ἂν*
γνῶμεν πονηρῶν ὄντ' ἐραστὴν πραγμάτων,
ἕως ἂν αὐτὸν ἐμβάλωμεν εἰς κακόν,
ὅπως ἂν εἰδῇ τοὺς θεοὺς δεδοικέναι.
ΣΤ. *ὤμοι, πονηρά γ', ὦ Νεφέλαι, δίκαια δέ.*

STR. It's your fault, Clouds, this happened to me:
I put my whole life in your hands.
CHO. No: you are responsible. You took the steps,
Strepsiades, down to iniquity.
STR. So why not tell me that before,
Instead of leading an old countryman astray?
CHO. This is the way we always treat a man
We find enamoured of iniquity.
We drop him into trouble:
That way he learns to fear the gods.
STR. A cruel lesson, Clouds, but just.

Pheidippides, freshly inducted into the new arts of sophistic amoralism, has threatened to give his mother a beating and prepares to argue the right to do so. Strepsiades, having engineered

[4] Text as Dover. My account of this passage closely follows that in Silk, 'Paratragedy', 498–502.

his son's philosophical training for his own unworthy ends, is brought to his senses. He points his finger at the Clouds: *they* are responsible. And with this allusion to responsibility comes an evocation of a well-known world of late archaic and early classical ideology, whose watchwords are *suffering*, *responsibility*, *god*, *justice*, *punishment*, *delusion*, *recognition . . . too late*. This nexus of ideas dominates (for instance) Creon's anguished exchange with the chorus in *Antigone* 1270–4:

ΧΟ. οἴμ' ὡς ἔοικας ὀψὲ τὴν δίκην ἰδεῖν.
ΚΡ. οἴμοι,
ἔχω μαθὼν δείλαιος· ἐν δ' ἐμῷ κάρᾳ
θεὸς τότ' ἄρα τότε με μέγα βάρος ἔχων
ἔπαισεν, ἐν δ' ἔσεισεν ἀγρίαις ὁδοῖς.

CHO. Too late, it seems, you have seen justice.
CRE. Now, now, sadly I recognize what happened:
A god brought a great weight down on my head,
Struck me and shook me into crime.

Likewise, it underlies (for instance) Herodotus' presentation of Croesus (1. 87. 3):

Κροῖσε, τίς σε ἀνθρώπων ἀνέγνωσε ἐπὶ γῆν τὴν ἐμὴν στρατευσάμενον πολέμιον ἀντὶ φίλου ἐμοὶ καταστῆναι; ὁ δὲ εἶπε· ὦ βασιλεῦ, ἐγὼ ταῦτα ἔπρηξα τῇ σῇ μὲν εὐδαιμονίῃ, τῇ ἐμεωυτοῦ δὲ κακοδαιμονίῃ· αἴτιος δὲ τούτων ἐγένετο ὁ Ἑλλήνων θεὸς ἐπάρας ἐμὲ στρατεύεσθαι.

'Croesus, who was it persuaded you to march against my country and make yourself my enemy instead of my friend?' And Croesus answered: 'It was I who did these things, my Lord, to your gain and my loss; but the god of the Greeks is reponsible: he led me on to march.'

But then, a little later (1. 91. 6):

. . . *συνέγνω ἑωυτοῦ εἶναι τὴν ἁμαρτάδα καὶ οὐ τοῦ θεοῦ.*

. . . he recognized it was he who had gone wrong, and not the god.

As Herodotus' articulation reminds us, this is by no means an exclusively tragic nexus, but it is, of course, one that Attic tragedy makes peculiarly its own in *Antigone* and many other plays.[5]

No (says Aristophanes' chorus), Strepsiades himself is responsible: he chose his wickedness for himself. And why, then, did they

[5] Cf. Silk, 'Tragic language', 469–70. One may add the non-tragic Cnemon to the list (above, p. 218).

not tell him all this *at the time*? Why was he left, like a Creon (or a Croesus), to see it all too late? It seems that these choral deities led him on in his delusion (ἐπήρατε, precisely as a god led Croesus on in his: θεὸς ἐπάρας ἐμέ). True enough (say the chorus), but it was done for a purpose: the gods drive men on, so men can learn the hard way, as Creon learned. And Strepsiades is convinced. Like Cadmus in *Bacchae*, another (though, so to speak, later) tragic sufferer, he acknowledges that the punishment, however harsh, is just (πονηρά γε . . . δίκαια δέ)—or, as Cadmus was to put it (*Bacchae* 1249–50):

> ὡς ὁ θεὸς ἡμᾶς ἐνδίκως μὲν ἀλλ' ἄγαν
> . . . ἀπώλεσ' . . .
>
> Justly, but too much, the god has ruined us . . .

However late, a sinner like Strepsiades must learn his cruel lesson. In the words of the vengeful god of Bacchae (1345):

> ὄψ' ἐμάθεθ' ἡμᾶς, ὅτε δ' ἐχρῆν οὐκ ᾔδετε.
>
> Too late you knew me: when you ought, you knew me not.

In the remarkable exchange between contrite Strepsiades and vengeful Clouds, a generalized tragic coloration is spread over the passage, so that not only do we have no sense of a particular tragic *locus*, or a particular tragedy or tragedian,[6] but—most unusually—the paratragedy does not impinge as a sudden change of key. There is no effect of suddenness at all, but rather one of concealed modulation into a new hybrid that establishes itself unannounced and without advertisement.

The prerequisite for this noteworthy effect is the exclusion of any operative collision on the stylistic level. The means to this end are several. In the first place, the passsage exhibits a wholly untypical restraint in expression, which in Aristophanic comedy is generally so unrestrainedly mobile, forever switching to and from word play, obscenities, accumulations, metaphors, jokes, and discontinuities of all kinds. Here all such exuberance is absent; in fact, all humour is absent; and even an apparent exception like the punning metaphor in 1455 (*strepsas*: 'steps, |

[6] Rau, *Paratragodia*, 173–5, following Newiger, *Metapher und Allegorie*, 67–8, talks of an Aeschylean 'theodicy' here; likewise, more hesitantly, Segal, 'Cloud-chorus', 143, 158. There is nothing so distractingly specific and in phraseological terms nothing particularly Aeschylean at all.

Strepsiades')[7] serves rather, once again, to evoke a *tragic* menace—because (with a wholly appropriate imprecision) the usage carries a certain suggestion of the fatal, *fateful*, name, the *nomen omen*, that had, or would, implicate such figures as Aeschylus' Helen (*helenaus*: 'shipwrecker'), Sophocles' Aias (*aiai*: 'alas'), Euripides' Pentheus (*penthos*: 'grief').[8] Rhythmical restraint, too, plays an important part here.[9] Then again, the phraseology and idiom of the passage is, for the most part, neutral and neither distinguishably tragic nor Aristophanic: the language mostly comes from the common ground of both.[10] Non-tragic phraseology and idiom is restricted to a few minor items,[11] while,

[7] The best I can do with the Greek: *strepsas*, in effect, is '*twisting* your way to evil and thus living out your name, *Twister*'. 1454–5 has also a strange—and very unexuberant—intensifying clustering of echoic pronominal forms (*αὐτός, σαυτῷ, τούτων, σεαυτόν*), on which cf. Silk, 'Authority', 24–5.

[8] *Agam.* 687–8 (cf. Fraenkel ad loc.), *Aj.* 430–1, *Bacch.* 507–8. The *nomen omen* is not exclusively tragic (see e.g. W. B. Stanford, *Ambiguity in Greek Literature* (Oxford 1939) 34–8 and 184, index s.v.), but characteristically so. On 'appropriate imprecision', cf. F. R. Leavis, *Education and the University* (London 1948) 77: 'the inimitable mark of the poet . . . is his ability to control realization to the precise degree appropriate.' On the special tragic significance of 'the name', see Silk, 'Tragic language', 465–96.

[9] Though the sequence 1452–62 contains at least three sets of untragic anapaests (1452 and 1462, fourth foot; 1453, second; also 1458, fifth, with codd. *ὅταν τινά*: *ὅντιν' ἄν*, read above, is Porson's emendation) and two breaches of Porson's Law (1454, 1459). Dover (on 1458) and Sommerstein (on 1452–64) note the approximation to tragic rhythm, but fail to note the extent of these exceptions. Anapaests, esp. in proper names, occur increasingly in late 5th-cent. tragic trimeters, and Euripidean trimeters in particular (see e.g. West, *Greek Metre*, 81–2), but their appearance, esp. their avoidable and concentrated appearance, is still uncharacteristic of tragedy as such.

[10] Into this category fall such expressions as *ἅπαντα τἀμά* (1453): see e.g. Soph. *Aj.* 132 *ἅπαντα τἀνθρώπεια* and *OC* 1613 *πάντα τἀμά*, Ar. *Thes.* 262 *τἀμὰ ταυτί* and 591 *τἄλλ' ἅπανθ'*, notwithstanding a baffling error in LSJ s.v. *ἐμός*: 'contr. with the Art., *οὑμός* . . . *τἀμά*, Trag. (not Com.)'; fuller details on (*ἅ*)*πας* in B. L. Gildersleeve, *Syntax of Classical Greek*, ii (New York 1911) 304–16. Again, *πονηρὰ πράγματα* (1455): see e.g. Eur. fr. 1027. 1 Nauck *πραγμάτων αἰσχρῶν*, Thuc. 7. 48 *πονηρὰ τὰ πράγματα*, Ar. *Vesp.* 1496 *μανικὰ π.* and *Av.* 1472 *δεινὰ π.* Again, *ἠγορεύετε* (1456) is standard Greek from Homer onwards: see LSJ s.v. Again, *ἐπήρατε* (1457): Ar. *Nub.* 42 *ἥτις με γῆμ' ἐπῆρε τὴν σὴν μητέρα*, Pherecr. 156.1 *PCG* *εἰκῇ μ' ἐπῆρας*, and (tragic and ominous) Soph. *OT* 1328 (*τίς σ' ἐπῆρε δαιμόνων*), Eur. *Or.* 285–6. Again, *ἐραστήν* (1459): Ar. *Pax* 191, Amphis Com. 15. 3 *PCG*, Pl. *Phdr.* 253d, Soph. *OT* 601, Hdt. 3. 53. Again, *ὅπως ἄν* + subj. of purpose (1461): Aesch. *Cho.* 580, Soph. *El.* 41, Ar. *Ach.* 444 and *Vesp.* 178, Pl. *Smp.* 199a (see further Goodwin, *Moods and Tenses*, 117).

[11] *ταυτί* (1452): deictic *-ί* never in tragedy, ubiquitous in comedy (Ar. *Nub.* 8 etc.). *ἄγροικον* (1457), alien to 5th-cent. high poetry, incl. tragedy; common in comedy and prose: Ar. *Ach.* 371 (+ 16 other examples in O. J. Todd, *Index Aristophaneus* (Cambridge 1932), s.v.), Eup. 222. 2 *PCG*, Xen. *Mem.* 3. 13. 1,

conversely, any touches that might impinge as distinctly tragic are avoided.[12] There is simply no discontinuity here. On the contrary, something half-suggestive of tragic pain and tragic dénouement seems to have overtaken its victim by an—as befits a tragic event—inexorable development. This extraordinary effect marks the climax of an extraordinary play. The passage evokes the world of tragedy by methods that are something like tragic methods, and behind its persuasive commitment is an implicit understanding that at such a moment only tragedy and the tragic will do. The evocation creates sombre mood, divine presence, but (above all) authority: as if to say, if tragic, *therefore* beyond dispute.

Not all of Aristophanes' diverse modes look to tragedy. Some are constructed within what one might reasonably see as the popular domain: low lyric, obscenity, abuse. Some, again, appropriate other media or genres besides the tragic: the 'parachresmody' of *Knights* is a case in point.[13] Yet it is apparent that a high proportion of Aristophanes' modal experiments derive from tragic sources, just as it is clear that the outcomes of these experiments are usually humorous, irrespective of whether the source material seems in itself 'natural' for comedy (because popular, like abuse) or (like tragedy) not. Of the non-humorous exceptions, most, if not all, are from a tragic matrix, and the most striking of these are in *Clouds*: the chorus's entrance-song, which we have analysed as a less than successful piece of high-style pastiche, and the much more impressive moment of Strepsiades' awakening, which we have just considered. More impressive—but still, in Aristophanic terms, a high-risk endeavour, eschewing as it does the main resources in the poet's creative armoury.

Arist. *EN* 1128^{a}9, Thphr. *Char.* 4. ἑκάστοτε (1458), likewise: Ar. *Nub.* 617 (+ 22 other examples in Todd, op. cit., s.v.), Antipho 6. 13, Thuc. 1. 68, Hp. *Aer.* 5. ἐμβάλωμεν (1460), in its given idiom, likewise: Antipho 3. 4. 10 ἡμᾶς εἰς μὴ προσηκούσας συμφορὰς ἐμβάλητε, Pl. *Phlb.* 20a, Aeschin. 3. 79, Ar. *Ach.* 679, Aristophon 6. 5 *PCG*, Hp. *Morb.* 4. 54 (p. 598, 14 Littré).

[12] With the possible exception of στρέψας (σεαυτόν), whose status is hard to determine. The only close parallel for the idiom is Eur. *Supp.* 412–13 [πόλιν] πρὸς κέρδος ἴδιον . . . στρέφει. Less closely, cf. Soph. *Ichn.* 230 Radt and Ar. *Thes.* 1128 (=Eur. fr. 139 Nauck, but perhaps not conclusively paratragic itself: cf. Rau, *Paratragodia*, 88).

[13] On 'parachresmody', see above, p. 338. Freely experimental though A is, there are modal experiments, where tragedy is *not* involved, which he seems not to favour. The use of prose is one—though one which (according to schol. *Eq.* 941: see Sommerstein ad loc.) A's rival Eupolis did favour.

Clouds is a play that Aristophanes invites us to think of as different. Witness the parabasis of *Wasps* (1044–7),

> *πέρυσιν καταπρούδοτε καινοτάτας σπείραντ' αὐτὸν διανοίας,*
> *ἃς ὑπὸ τοῦ μὴ γνῶναι καθαρῶς ὑμεῖς ἐποιήσατ' ἀναλδεῖς.*
> *καίτοι σπένδων πόλλ' ἐπὶ πολλοῖς ὄμνυσιν τὸν Διόνυσον*
> *μὴ πώποτ' ἀμείνον' ἔπη τούτων κωμῳδικὰ μηδέν' ἀκοῦσαι . . .*
>
> Last year you let him down. Brand-new ideas he planted;
> They didn't take—you couldn't understand them.
> By Dionysus, though, by every last
> Drop of sacrificial wine, he swears:
> Better comic poetry was never heard . . .

and then the revised parabasis of *Clouds* itself (521–4):

> *ὡς ὑμᾶς ἡγούμενος εἶναι θεατὰς δεξιοὺς*
> *καὶ ταύτην σοφώτατ' ἔχειν τῶν ἐμῶν κωμῳδιῶν,*
> *πρώτους ἠξίωσ' ἀναγεῦσ' ὑμᾶς, ἣ παρέσχε μοι*
> *ἔργον πλεῖστον . . .*
>
> Taking you for a sophisticated audience
> And this for the most intellectual of my plays,
> I thought to give you the first taste; it gave me
> A lot of work . . .

Aristophanes' very insistence on revising the play is revealing. In a society where not only does drama presuppose performance, but a single performance is the norm, to revise a play with no guarantee of another staging—and the revised play never was staged—indicates the special importance his 'brand-new ideas' had for him. And the most brand-new of these ideas, we propose, is the idea of an authoritative comic drama whose authority derives from tragedy.[14]

Of all Aristophanes' Old Comedies, *Clouds* is the least discontinuous, the most processive, the most Aristotelian: it is the

[14] Most modern readings of A agree that his comedies 'consistently maintain a playful disrespect towards tragedy' (B. Heiden, 'Tragedy and comedy in the *Frogs* of Aristophanes', *Ramus* 20 (1991) 95–111, at 96). Contrast such admirable formulations (albeit not necessarily developed as I would propose) as: 'by linking his comedy and Euripidean tragedy . . . he claims for it the moral authority, literary prestige, and latitude that audiences have always given to [genres like tragedy]' (H. P. Foley, 'Tragedy and politics in Aristophanes' *Acharnians*', *JHS* 108 (1988) 33–47 at 43); 'a kind of bid for comedy to stand on a civic pedestal beside that of tragedy' (Taplin, 'Comedy and the tragic', 198, on *Ran.*). It is none the less true that A is not *solemn* about tragedy and tragedians, not even about the Sophocles that he declines to 'degrade' in *Ran.* (76–82): cf. *Pax* 695–9.

play whose characters and plot are closest to the models of realism and organic unity. It is also the only one of his surviving fifth-century plays in which 'issues' are and remain unremittingly central, right up to the very end of the play. It is the most moralizing of his plays, and one whose humour is largely satirical and negative, and where, indeed, humour itself is eventually almost displaced. It is a play whose end, in any case, is signally lacking in the kind of festive celebration we associate with Aristophanes. According to our reading of Aristophanes, the play is much the least Aristophanic.

The satire of *Clouds* is directed against the new sophistic Enlightenment personified as 'Socrates', who is presented as a savant equipped with disciples and his own seat of learning, the *phrontistêrion* or Brain-House. The aspects of the new movement satirized in the play include atheism (or at least unconventional religion) and scientific enquiry; they centre, above all, on persuasion as an end in itself. Old Strepsiades seeks salvation from his worldly woes, essentially financial troubles, in Socrates' intellectual method; and what attracts him to Socrates is the supposition that the method includes the power to persuade by argument and, therefore, the power to argue a way out of debt. This argumentative power, which he seeks first for his son, then for himself, then for his son again, is vividly dramatized as the two Arguments (*Logoi*), Right and Wrong, which are literally given house-room by Socrates and which can between them argue either side of a case; the same power is also referred to under such headings as *glôtta*, the 'tongue' with which the new disciple will wage his war (419), and *peithô*, the 'persuasion' which Pheidippides, now Socratized, will eventually use to out-talk his father (1398). The power is amoral. It enables a speaker 'to triumph, whether his cause is just or unjust' (99). That was precisely what the old man had counted on all along, and it is only when the amoral power is turned against himself that he is shaken into his 'tragic' recognition. This approximation to development, operative both for Strepsiades and for the play as a whole, ensures that the given configuration of ideas, actions, and characters impinges as a nexus of 'issues' in the true sense. Hence its dramatic plausibility—and hence, once again, its peculiar alienness to Aristophanes' own customary norms.

Not the least alien feature of the play is its moralizing. Where

Dicaeopolis' phallic song representatively celebrates a life-enhancing amoralism, *Clouds* rests on 'a moral framework . . . as stark as that of an evangelical tract'.[15] And closely associated with this 'moral framework' is the play's aberrant kind of religiosity. The religion of Dicaeopolis' phallic song ('Oh, Mister Prick') impinges as a buoyant expression of natural instincts. The devotional hymns in *Thesmophoriazusae* ('Pallas, lover of the dance . . .'), conventional and restrained though they may be, nevertheless achieve a conventional propriety which—at the very least—poses no problems for the tone and direction of the play as a whole. In *Clouds*, uniquely, problems do arise, and they arise because the vengeful choral divinities emerge, eventually, as remote, awesome beings, morally distinct from ordinary humanity—so remote, indeed, that one senses in them a spiritual, even metaphysical, power with which comedy, rooted in the human and the material, cannot readily engage. The phallic song and the devotional hymns serve to affirm material humanity or to invest it, briefly, with a conventional cultic grace; the morally operative Clouds, in the end, threaten to diminish it by their contrastive spirituality. The force of this threat, furthermore, is enhanced at the climactic end of the play by a striking configuration of religiosities which are remote, not only from 'ordinary' Aristophanic religion, but from the abstracted world of sophistic divinities we first encountered. As first presented by Socrates, the 'Clouds everlasting' (275) were the purveyors of 'reason, argument, and thought' (*γνώμην καὶ διάλεξιν καὶ νοῦν*, 317), who belonged to a new holy trinity of abstractions, 'Void, Clouds, and Tongue' (*τὸ Χάος . . . καὶ τὰς Νεφέλας καὶ τὴν Γλῶτταν*, 424), behind whom was a supreme abstraction, the celestial 'Whirl' (*Δῖνος*), replacing Zeus (379–81)—all duly identified, with the aid of disembodied reason, by Socrates in his temple of abstraction, the Brain-House. The vengeful Clouds who eventually reveal their concern that the wrongdoer should 'learn to fear the gods' (1461) at once inspire Strepsiades to reaffirm the rule of Zeus and deny the outlandish Whirl (1468–74), then to pray to Hermes for advice (1478–82).[16]

[15] Dover, *Aristophanic Comedy*, 112. On the moralizing in *Nub.* there is much of value in Whitman, *Hero*, 119–43.

[16] In Greek religious ideology, Hermes is a mediator between human and divine and a peculiarly approachable god: *πᾶσι δ' ὅ γε θνητοῖσι καὶ ἀθανάτοισιν ὁμιλεῖ* *h. Herm.* 576, cf. *Il.* 24. 334–5. See in general L. Kahn, *Hermes passe ou les ambiguités de la communication* (Paris 1978).

The advice he purports to hear is to burn down the Brain-House, and in taking it he now acts as agent of divine vengeance himself,[17] threatening—and, for all we know, acting out—a sentence of death on Socrates and his fellow-deviants and finally reaffirming the religious order as he does so.[18]

With this climactic development in mind, arresting and disturbing as it is, we can at last suggest a particular, underlying, reason why Aristophanes should have taken so much trouble to suppress his stylistic instincts in the *parodos* of the play—beyond, that is, the general appeal of high-style lyrics attested in *Thesmophoriazusae* and elsewhere. His compositional dilemma is that he wishes to present Socrates' new deities as bogus and yet also to flag their religiosity. More precisely, his composition tends to privilege the play's stark climax, the persuasive force of which depends partly on its lack of corrective humour. In this largely developmental and processive play, it seems to follow that the Clouds, who end as humourless beings, must begin as humourless beings. They cannot, however, begin as the sinister, 'tragic', humourless beings that they eventually are seen to be, but 'tragic' and humourless they must be. The inert pastiche of the *parodos* is the result, and its deficiencies bring home the problematic nature of the whole enterprise. For an extraordinary experiment in hybrid 'Aristotelian' drama, for a glimpse of 'tragic' authority, Aristophanes has repressed his stylistic and modal instincts, his humour, his affirmations.[19]

[17] As has been noted by A. Köhnken, 'Der Wolken-Chor des Aristophanes', *Hermes* 108 (1980) 154–69 at 165, the point is enforced by a pair of phraseological echoes in Strepsiades' closing words. The Clouds' tragic-religious persona is crystallized in 1460–1 *ἕως ἂν αὐτὸν ἐμβάλωμεν εἰς κακόν, | ὅπως ἂν εἰδῇ τοὺς θεοὺς δεδοικέναι*. The first of these lines is recalled by Strepsiades' exhortation to his slave, *ἕως ἂν αὐτοῖς ἐμβάλῃς τὴν οἰκίαν* (1489), the second by his very last words of all, *μάλιστα δ' εἰδὼς τοὺς θεοὺς ὡς ἠδίκουν* (1509).

[18] So M. Nussbaum, 'Aristophanes and Socrates on learning practical wisdom', *YCS* 26 (1980) 78. The idea that there is, or is about to be, a death at the end of the play was argued for by E. C. Kopff, '*Nubes* 1493 ff.: was Socrates murdered?', *GRBS* 18 (1977) 113–22, and against by F. D. Harvey, '*Nubes* 1493 ff.: was Socrates murdered?', *GRBS* 22 (1981) 339–43, and M. Davies, 'Popular justice and the end of Aristophanes' *Clouds*', *Hermes* 118 (1990) 237–42—whose suggestion that the image of a burning house implies exile rather than death seems to rest on very little in the way of Greek evidence and nothing at all within *Nub.* itself. Certainly Socrates' last word, *ἀποπνιγήσομαι*, is a straightforward cue to the imminence of death: *οἵ δέ μιν ἀπέπνιξαν καὶ ἔπειτα ἔθαψαν*, Hdt. 2. 169. 3.

[19] Various attempts have been made to explain away the shift of the chorus from sophistic deities to agents of divine justice (most recently by Bowie, *Aristophanes*,

Let *us* affirm, at once, that an author has every right to experiment, to create hybrids, to be Aristotelian—as we have the right, indeed the duty, to assess the results. And a properly critical assessment of *Clouds* will point to other specific deficiencies in the play that are distinguishable from, but relatable to, those under review. Aristophanes' problem, in a sense, is that he is playing not to his strengths but to his weaknesses, because Aristotelian drama requires a degree of co-ordination which he is unable to achieve. Strepsiades, for instance, does approximate to a realist developmental figure—and yet does also retain various of the discontinuous propensities of Aristophanes' 'normal' characters.[20] Then again, a moral drama should be coherently moral; *Clouds* is not, constructed though it is on a powerful set of oppositions, with unmistakable moral implications. The problem here is that the versions of opposition, or their moral implications, are not fully aligned.

The first version is set out early on by Strepsiades, recalling his fateful marriage and the aromas of his wedding-night, when *he* went to bed (50)

> Smelling of rough wine, dried figs, sheep's wool, abundance

and (51–2)

> *She* smelled of perfume, powder, deep kissing,
> Extravagance, bingeing, love-goddesses.[21]

The passage sets up two alternative worlds on the premise of the 'conservative' ideology so prominent, and yet so elusive, within

124–30), but without proper reference to the quality of the writing (in either guise); the shift (it must be stressed) is no problem on the level of recreation, but on the realist level that is so surprisingly prominent in the play (cf. on Strepsiades, below, p. 362). Throughout this discussion I prefer to avoid any engagement with two much-discussed questions: why did *Nub.* fail in performance in 423? and to what extent is it possible to identify revisions within our version of the play? The task as I see it is to establish a considered view of the play we possess, not to speculate about historical possibilities. The comparative 'failure' of *Nub.* as I would read it may or may not have anything to do with its rejection by the first audience, while the evidence we have concerning the differences between the first and the existing play is both meagre and difficult: see Dover, *Clouds*, pp. lxxx–xcviii. *Inter alia*, two ancient sources (Hyp. 1, p. 1 Dover, and schol. *Nub.* 543) seem to say that no burning-down was involved in version one, but, as Dover notes (*Clouds*, p. xciii), this 'neither excludes nor fortifies the possibility that the first version ended with some act of violence against Socrates and his school'.

[20] Above, p. 223.

[21] Above, p. 147.

the plays as a whole: traditional country, rough but healthy, and innovating town, refined but degenerate. The contrast is morally loaded, in favour of the country, if only because it is under the urban wife's influence that the young Pheidippides is corrupted and incurs the debts which drive his father into the arms of Socrates (60–77). The imprint of the contrast, with its moral tinge intact, is felt more or less throughout the play, and not least at the end, when rough but healthy Strepsiades turns the tables on refined but degenerate Socratism. However, it is only in this closing phase that the moral tinge is translated into a full-blooded contrast between good and evil—and the 'good' confronts the 'evil' in a violent and, prospectively, criminal act. In terms of the individual character Strepsiades, the paradox defies explanation. It is (one might say) convincing enough that this embodiment of material man should deflate the forces of abstract and esoteric thought, perhaps even by violence—just as he brought the deflating effect of stylistic violence to greet the Clouds themselves, in their first—abstract-esoteric—embodiment (267):[22]

> Oh please, let me wrap myself up or I'll get all soaked.

What is unconvincing, and even arbitrary, is that this same materializer should be allowed—in a now largely Aristotelian play—to recreate himself as a religious being of the most austere and morally uncompromising kind.

Moral misalignment is no less apparent earlier in the play, at the point where the opposition is translated into the *Logoi*, Right and Wrong. Here, Right is traditional and Wrong modern, but though Wrong is essentially unscrupulous, Right (oddly bad-tempered and strikingly 'obsessed with boys' genitals')[23] is not entirely edifying himself. More important, this version of the opposition is fundamentally flawed in that both *Logoi*, Right as well as Wrong, live in Socrates' Brain-House and hence should be equally suspect to a traditionalist as equally the product of a new degeneracy—or if not, then the new degeneracy is not wholly degenerate after all.

One might attempt an intellectual rationalization of these

[22] Above, pp. 168–9.

[23] Dover, *Clouds*, p. lxiv. It is misleading, though, to imply, as Dover does (ibid. lvii–lxvi), that the *Logoi* are degraded equally: Right is *mostly* scrupulous, on his given terms, and *inter alia* voices the charming rural vignette at 1005–8.

contradictions in terms of innocence and corruption. Strepsiades, both as would-be customer of the Socratic and as its criminal destroyer, is an innocent, whose only response to degeneracy is corrupted compliance with it—or corrupted violence against it; and Right too has in some sense, perhaps, been taken over by Socrates. More grandly, we may argue—taking a tip from the young Nietzsche—that this great comic observer sees the portentous cultural developments all around him as a destructive dissociation, and represents the sundered whole as two degraded parts: material man become obtuse tradition, thinking man become cynical modernity.[24] Yet no such allegorical reading is *enacted* by the play as a whole (if only, though not only, because the alignments are drastically inexact), and whether any of this might have been envisaged by the author is beside the point: works of art do, or should, 'enact their moral valuations'.[25] At the heart of *Clouds* there is a moral incoherence of which Aristophanes may be aware (*hence* his revisions?), but which he is unable to resolve. Behind this strangest of comedies, dissociation is an operative issue; in artistic, dramatic, comic terms, it is hardly confronted.

We can still, without disparagement, congratulate the humorist on the boldness of his experiment. He has tried out a new type of satiric-comic morality play, and *en route*, under tragic influence, explores the possibility of a new set of hybrid modes to match—or perhaps the tragic inspiration and the glimpse of the hybrid modes come first, and the new comic pattern follows. Either way, though, the experiment is bound to fail—by Aristophanes' own standards as set out elsewhere and as still operative, however contradictorily, within *Clouds* itself. Contradiction is apparent not only at the heart of the play's moralizing but, of course, between that moralizing (in its final, harsh version, above all) and the characteristic humour represented early on by (say) Strepsiades' vision

[24] Nietzsche, *Birth of Tragedy*, XII–XV (on 'Socratism'); in XIII Nietzsche refers to the 'profound instincts' ('die tiefen Instinkte') of A in presenting Socrates as he does. Cf. above, pp. 11–13, and contrast Dover, *Aristophanic Comedy*, 113: 'it is difficult for the modern reader to understand how a writer so sensitive and subtle as Aristophanes could have taken the field with such vigour on the side of the philistines against that spirit of systematic, rational inquiry which we regard as an essential ingredient of civilization.' I note that Plato, so mindful of A's treatment of his master Socrates, chooses to ascribe to A a vision of humanity as a split whole, albeit of a rather different kind: *Smp.* 189c–193d.

[25] Leavis: below, p. 423.

of himself as supreme persuader, a vision richly and deliciously articulated in accumulative imagery (446–9):

> a mint of lies,
> A coiner of phrases, a smooth lawyer,
> A tablet of stone, a drum, fox, needle's eye,
> A lash . . . [26]

The stern religiosity of the play's end presents an incompatible reading of life, and if *Clouds* leaves a peculiarly sour after-taste behind it, it is not because the satire of Socrates is so harsh (though it is harsh), nor even because Strepsiades' alternative response is so harsh (though again it is), but because Strepsiades' touches of mockery at his moment of victory remind us, cruelly, of the Aristophanic humour that, under pressure from the play's 'tragic' logic, has now been squeezed out.

Like (say) *Acharnians*, *Clouds* closes with a tableau of opposites, but the mood could hardly be more different. Strepsiades on the roof of the Brain-House sets fire to its rafters, and Socrates, choking, calls out in confusion. On his first appearance—to us and to Strepsiades—Socrates, high in a basket, had (literally) talked down to the other in a mixture of the portentous and the quaintly prosaic (225):

> ἀεροβατῶ καὶ περιφρονῶ τὸν ἥλιον.
>
> I'm an aerobat examining the sun.[27]

Finally triumphant, his negator Strepsiades now throws the same words back (1503), but given the combination of religiosity and violence, the situation is truly (one might well say) beyond a joke. This harsh climax displaces the celebration and the 'happy end' that are characteristic of Aristophanic comedy and comedy as a whole. It is indeed as if Aristophanes is suppressing his own instincts to the point of undermining his own medium. His experiment is one which the freedom of comedy allows him to

[26] Above, pp. 100–1.

[27] Translators of the line tend to misrepresent its tone: '(*Tragically*) I tread the air . . .', Starkie. -βατέω compounds (of which this seems to be the first attested) are not 'tragic': the next earliest attestation is ὀνοβατέω, Xen. *Eq*. 5. 8 ('get a mare covered by an ass'). Contrast Socrates' lofty ὦ 'φήμερε in 223, evoking Pindar's ἐπάμεροι (*Pyth*. 8. 95: above, p. 201) and (for us) also Plato's ἐφήμεροι (*Rep*. 617d: above, p. 105).

conduct, but one which comes close to subverting comedy—and, with it, that distinctive freedom—altogether.

Whatever else it achieves or fails to achieve, *Clouds* has the incidental merit of suggesting—*per contra*—still more than we have hitherto been able to articulate about the coherence of the essential Aristophanes. That coherence we have sought to distinguish from the quite different kind of unity associated with Aristotelian norms. What we have now seen is an apparent relationship between those norms and moralism, while, conversely, all the stylistic exuberance and all the discontinuities that we have acclaimed as Aristophanic would seem to have a prospective relationship with his humour: in large part, no doubt, they *are* his humour. Furthermore: if the moralizing of *Clouds* seems, on reflection, to consort easily with the play's satirical element, then here is one of several signs that, in the final analysis, however much Aristophanes may be celebrated as a comic satirist, he is what he is, not so much because his comedy is satirical, as because his satire is comic. *Clouds* is a deeply satirical play. Under the name of 'Socrates' it ridicules a rich and revolutionary complex of ideas and experiments, and in pursuit of its satirical target it is even prepared to turn its back on humour. Were *Clouds* a typical play, one might well conclude that Aristophanic comedy could most plausibly be credited with 'seriousness' on the grounds of its accommodation with sobriety. It is not a typical play, and the case for Aristophanes' seriousness can and should be made on more significant grounds associated with humour, not with its absence.

The problems that are so central to *Clouds* are not, indeed, unique to it. In particular, a comparable moralism, but of a more restricted kind, is visible in *Frogs*, a play constructed on a superficially equivalent opposition between the rival tragedians, 'traditional' Aeschylus and 'modern' Euripides. The opposition is articulated in a long contest between the two, for most of which the audience is clearly invited to see the contestants as on a par. The contestants begin as parallel caricatures, the one all manic inspiration, the other all sharp talk (*μανία* : *ὀξύλαλος*, 815–16). Six hundred lines later, after some significant points of contrast, some deft satire, and some charming silliness,[28] the pair are still so

[28] Respectively, e.g.: public heroism versus private passion, 1039–44; the critique of lyrics, 1248–364; the froth about prologues, 1119–247.

meticulously aligned that their judge, Dionysus, is reduced to exclaiming (1433):

> *νὴ τὸν Δία τὸν σωτῆρα, δυσκρίτως γ' ἔχω.*
>
> I swear by Zeus our saviour, I can't decide.

Then, however, and only then, things change. Without a word of explanation from Dionysus, but with a rush of words from the god Pluto and the chorus, we are suddenly asked to see one contestant as an impressive and worthy winner, the other as an unimpressive and unworthy loser, and the impressiveness and the worth are, it seems, essentially moral. The winner, Aeschylus, has not only a 'consummate intelligence' (*ξύνεσιν ἠκριβωμένην*, 1483); he is a source of *good* for his fellow-citizens and others (*ἐπ' ἀγαθῷ μὲν τοῖς πολίταις* . . ., 1487 ff.), because he has 'good advice' to give which will 'save the city' (*σῷζε πόλιν τὴν ἡμετέραν* | *γνώμαις ἀγαθαῖς*, 1501–2). On the other side, Euripides is abruptly—and symptomatically—branded a 'Socratic' (*Σωκράτει* | *παρακαθημένον λαλεῖν*, 1491–2), who has 'rejected culture' (*ἀποβαλόντα μουσικήν*, 1493) and 'stripped tragic art of its greatness' (*τά τε μέγιστα παραλιπόντα* | *τῆς τραγῳδικῆς τέχνης*, 1494–5) in favour of 'theory' (*σεμνοῖσιν λόγοισιν*, 1496) and 'useless nit-picking' (*σκαριφησμοῖσι λήρων*, 1497);[29] and when Aeschylus adds further and flatter insults to the list ('criminal . . . lier . . . buffoon': *πανοῦργος* . . . *ψευδολόγος* . . . *βωμολόχος*, 1520–1), no one contradicts him—as indeed none of these praises of Aeschylus and abuses of Euripides are contradicted.

The pretext, or at least the occasion, for this moral denunciation is the final round in the competition, when the competitors offer Athens, close to defeat in war, advice in her hour of need (1420–3). Whether Dionysus' decision is actually precipitated by their advice is unclear, but given that the grounds for the decision are not argued or even stated, it hardly matters.[30] The moral conclusion is, in the truest sense, arbitrary in either case. It is neither a plausible 'development' on the part of Dionysus nor implicit in

[29] On *μουσική* in 1493 cf. Lada-Richards, *Dionysus*, 225–7, and on 'theory' (1496) cf. Dover, *Frogs*, 21.

[30] Asked, *κρίνοις ἄν* (1467), Dionysus simply 'decides', *αἱρήσομαι* . . . *ὅνπερ ἡ ψυχὴ θέλει* (1468). From 1420 the contestants are concerned with ethical-political questions: first, Alcibiades (1422–32); second, the city's 'salvation' (1435–66). It is after the Alcibiades section that Dionysus declares his inability to reach a decision, which leaves one little the wiser (*sic*) when he does announce it.

the earlier action, and while such discontinuity is of course, *qua* discontinuity, as Aristophanic as it could possibly be—and Dionysus is as entitled as anyone to a recreative switch—in its moral assertiveness the final denunciation is simply alien.[31] It is true that the earlier part of the contest contains moments when issues of moral import are raised in a way calculated to make us aware of their moralism. Above all, there are the moments when the tragedians agree that tragedy educates ('we make men better citizens', 'adults have poets to instruct them').[32] However, the very fact that the tragedians agree on the principle removes it from the competitive sphere. Up until the final round of the contest, they take up a good deal of time disagreeing on—among much else—whether the other lives up to the educative ideal or not, and since it is precisely on the basis of this lengthy disagreement that Dionysus professes himself unable to decide, the non-moral premise of the contest before the dénouement is more, not less, apparent.[33]

If *Frogs* has its inappropriate moral end—its final forced injection of *Moraline*, as Nietzsche called it[34]—it remains true that only in *Clouds* is moralism dominant, just as *Clouds*, arguably, is the only one of the nine Old Comedies of which we can truly say that satire is at its heart. Satire is essentially moral—and negative. Its essence is a sense of 'contradiction between actuality and the

[31] On the essential equality of the contest and the arbitrariness of the decision, cf. Goldhill, *Poet's Voice*, 211–19, Bowie, *Aristophanes*, 246–51, and (despite a problematic 'Gorgianic' perspective) G. B. Walsh, *The Varieties of Enchantment* (Chapel Hill 1984) 80–97. The arbitrariness was acknowledged in later antiquity: see esp. Hyp. 1 (*a*) 27 in Dover, *Frogs*, 114 (κρίνας παρὰ προσδοκίαν ὁ Διόνυσος). It is esp. apparent, in that Dionysus uses 'Euripidean sophistry' to declare the decision (ἡ γλῶττ' ὀμώμοκ', Αἰσχύλον δ' αἱρήσομαι, 1471: above, p. 31 n. 10). For attempts to argue dramatic (even organic) sense into the decision, see esp.: Segal, 'Dionysus and the unity of the *Frogs*', 207–42; H. Erbse 'Dionysos' Schiedsspruch in den Fröschen des Aristophanes', in K. Vourveris and A. Skiadas (eds.), *Δώρημα Hans Diller zum 70. Geburtstag* (Athens 1975) 45–60; and most recently, Lada-Richards, *Dionysus*, 216–325 (who proposes that Dionysus' decision follows his 'initiation' and, in effect, polis-ization). Cf. my comments on *Ran.* above, pp. 258–9 with n. 7 and p. 264.

[32] Respectively Eur. (βελτίους . . . ποιοῦμεν | τοὺς ἀνθρώπους ἐν ταῖς πόλεσιν, 1008–9) and Aesch. (τοῖσιν . . . ἡβῶσι ποιηταί [sc. διδάσκαλοι], 1055: cf. above, p. 48 with n. 17).

[33] The γεν(ν)- theme in *Ran.* (above, p. 279 n. 47) is not used consistently enough or decisively enough to affect the point, notwithstanding the theme's strong moral connotations.

[34] *Antichrist* 1. 2.

ideal':[35] the feeling that the world is like *this*, whereas it could and should be something else; the more that something else is specified and delineated, the more the negative satire will be counterbalanced by a compensatory positive;[36] but the satiric element is, in itself, negative. The world as it is has avoidable deficiencies, and these are held up to ridicule. Satire invites, and perhaps promotes, dissatisfaction. In this sense, all Aristophanes' plays include some satire, but only in *Clouds* is satire dominant, because only here is dissatisfaction as such—symptomatized by the final, violent *coup de théâtre*—victorious.

Despite its end, *Frogs* does not leave us with the sense that Euripides should never have existed. *Acharnians* satirizes Lamachus, as well as others, but we do not come away with the sense that war itself is unacceptable *per se*—or Lamachus either, humiliated though he is. The primary impetus of *Acharnians* in any case is not hostility—to Lamachus or to any other figure—but celebration: an impetus revealed in its full glory once its conditions (the institution of peace) have been met. *Acharnians* is targeted on peace and celebrates peace. *Clouds* is targeted on the new Enlightenment and enacts its negation through a powerful satirical representation. *Clouds* therefore is exclusive in a way that is not true of *Acharnians*, nor even of *Knights*, where Paphlagon-Cleon's perverse genius is celebrated, as much as satirized, in so far as his perverted qualities, raised to a still higher (or lower) level, are embodied in Sausage-Seller and his glorious victory.[37] In *Thesmophoriazusae*, more representatively, the portrayal of Agathon, we might say, is largely satirical, largely negative: Agathon is effeminate and precious; his new production (which we see and hear in rehearsal, 101–29) is less than captivating. But Agathon is only incidental to the play—unlike Euripides, whose representation, though itself satirical in part (witness the treatment of his verbal 'nit-picking' in the opening scene), is quite other overall. 'Euripides is not as he should be' is hardly the implication of the ingenious manoeuvres with Euripidean poetry in the rescue attempts or of the cool compromise at the end of the play.[38]

[35] Schiller, *Naive and Sentimental Poetry*: *Sämtliche Werke*, xii. 193.

[36] Cf. F. R. Leavis's classic discussion of Swift's 'habitually critical attitude' and the 'negative emotions he specializes in', in *The Common Pursuit* (London 1958) 74.

[37] In *Vesp.* too Cleon is not entirely excluded; he survives, after all, in the name of the triumphant Philocleon.

[38] Nit-picking (*Thes.* 1–21): above, pp. 325–6. Overall: above, pp. 322–34.

The point is surely beyond dispute. Though Aristophanes' plays are full of undesirable people and undesirable practices which are satirically treated as unacceptable blots on the comic scene, only in *Clouds* is satire truly dominant, and it is (let us suggest) largely because of a misplacing and an overvaluation of this play within the Aristophanic canon that Aristophanes has so closely been identified with satire at all.[39] *Clouds* remains an extreme and extraordinary, but unrepresentative, experiment, which is in various ways marginal, and even alien, to Aristophanic Old Comedy as a whole.

At the opposite end of the spectrum from *Clouds* is *Wasps*, a play extreme only in the sense that it embodies most fully the Aristophanic qualities we have sought to define in this book. Where *Clouds* is negative and exclusive, *Wasps* is positive and inclusive; where *Clouds* is critical, *Wasps* celebrates; and where *Clouds* gives way to satire, *Wasps* goes beyond satire to an all-consuming humour: modally, as otherwise, the two plays present a remarkable contrast. *Wasps* has a 'hero' who is morally outrageous, but (or and) who wins: a recreative figure, presented to us (as we have seen) with sensuous immediacy and impinging, not as the mere representative of a political stance that his name suggests, but as an embodiment of human possibility beyond the representative. Like, say, Dicaeopolis in *Acharnians*. Philocleon belongs to the Athenian *dêmos*, at a particular time and in a particular place, yet like Dicaeopolis he talks, and acts, not so much *to* the *dêmos* as *before* the *dêmos*:

> Condemn me not, you in the audience,
> If, whiles I am a beggar, among us Athenians
> I talk . . . [40]

Philocleon is rooted in his political present, yet transcends it. For this transcending, it is of the essence that he should remain, as he does, a public and an essentially communal figure, with none of the inner life of so many tragic heroes (or even of Strepsiades). His

[39] Plato, no doubt, has played a part here, by (rightly or wrongly) perpetuating the idea that A and *Nub.* had some determinative effect on the fate of his master Socrates: *Ap.* 19b–d. Looking back to the Henderson–Heath argument, one might with hindsight say that Henderson has offered a satisfying formula for the sociological significance of Aristophanic (Old Comic) satire—but does not properly consider what part such satire has in the plays.

[40] *Ach.* 497–9: above, pp. 39 ff..

strength presupposes the community; it is not the strength of the isolated or the marginal.[41] To readers with Aristotelian or moral expectations, the triumph of this recreative figure is a problem.[42] Anyone who has followed the argument of this book will rather be prepared to see his victory as an enhancement of life in the broadest and deepest sense of that elusive word. Just as the phallic song in *Acharnians* implies a new comic vision that contradicts existing categories of articulated response, low and high, and invites us to see the enhanced low as a new normative standard, so Philocleon offers a recreation of experience that challenges the categories of political existence.

Wasps cannot be understood, of course, without reference to the circumstances of the Athenian legal system and the astonishing political significance of the lawcourts in the late fifth century. At the centre of this system were large juries of citizens, often poor and old, paid to serve, and empowered to convict or acquit even the wealthiest and most powerful individuals of the day, at no personal risk (there were no appeals against conviction, and no juryman could be called to account for any verdict). It is a premise of *Wasps* that in the Athens of 422 such powerful individuals might pose a threat to the supremacy of Cleon; that the old jurymen were of special interest to Cleon as potential instruments against those few individuals who stood in his way; that Cleon increased their daily pay to ensure their loyalty to him; that, by playing on their envy, Cleon encouraged them to condemn—'sting'—the powerful few who were, or might be, his opponents; that, in short, some trials involved the victimization of the few through the manipulation of the many.

The 'stingers' in *Wasps*—the chorus of old jurymen and that most zealous 'Cleon-lover', Philocleon—are all persuaded, during the course of the play, that their faith in Cleon is misplaced. It falls to 'Cleon-hater', Bdelycleon, to do the persuading, by

[41] Cf. at this point the argument in Silk, 'Space and solitude'.

[42] Cf. Dover, *Aristophanic Comedy*, 125–6: 'recent commentators have remarked on the sympathy and affection which [Philocleon] evokes in the spectator and in the reader. I admit that he evokes mine: and yet I remain astonished at the hidden strength of antinomian sentiment which that sympathy and affection imply.' Sutton, *Self*, 83–91, takes refuge from his own distaste for the triumphs of 'unbridled egotism' (ibid. 88) by exploring the possible relevance of the Adlerian 'omnipotence fantasy', but does at least acknowledge the stature of the 'comic hero' in *Vesp.* and elsewhere; contrast e.g. K. C. Sidwell, 'Was Philocleon cured?', *C&M* 41 (1990) 9–32.

arguing, in formal contest with his father, that the old jurors are indeed the victims of manipulation. Philocleon, who supposes that jurymen possess a power 'equal to that of any king' (*οὐδεμιᾶς ἥττων . . . βασιλείας*, 548–9), and that he and his kind 'rule the world' (*ἄρχω τῶν ἁπάντων*, 518), is duly, if painfully, convinced that, on the contrary, their manipulation by Cleon is a fact, and one which shows up this 'lordship' as slavery (*δουλεία*, 682) in disguise. To a historian of Cleonic Athens the persuasiveness of this argument may not be easy to gauge,[43] but to an admirer of Aristophanes the question is rendered inconsequential by what follows. Philocleon's 'conversion' is not like Strepsiades', whose response is to destroy the individual and the cause he so lately espoused. If Strepsiades' conversion has the lineaments of a tragic reversal—concentrated, sombre, and violent in its implications—Philocleon's has a different character, a different tone, and very different consequences in every way.

It is symptomatic that where Strepsiades' conversion impinges on us as harsh and sour, Philocleon's leans towards paratragedy of the most robustly hilarious kind. At the start of the confrontation with his son, he declares (523):

> *ἢν γὰρ ἡττηθῶ λέγων σου, περιπεσοῦμαι τῷ ξίφει.*
>
> If I lose in debate, I'll fall on my sword.

When the realization of defeat is duly upon him, he proposes to fulfil his promise—with what turns out to be, not the smooth and sinister hybrid elevation of the moment of *peripeteia* in *Clouds*, but a typically bizarre juxtaposition of the tragic and the mundane colloquial (756–9):

> *σπεῦδ', ὦ ψυχή—ποῦ μοι ψυχή;*
> *πάρες, ὦ σκιερά—μὰ τὸν Ἡρακλέα,*
> *μή νυν ἔτ' ἐγὼ 'ν τοῖσι δικασταῖς*
> *κλέπτοντα Κλέωνα λάβοιμι.*

[43] On the historicity, or otherwise, of this picture of Athenian law in action, see e.g. R. J. Bonner and G. Smith, *The Administration of Justice from Homer to Aristotle* (2 vols., Chicago 1930–8) i. 231–2, 248, ii. 22–5, and M. Ostwald, *From Popular Sovereignty to the Sovereignty of Law* (Berkeley 1986) 231–6. Whatever else may be true, it is certainly true that, within two generations of this play, something very like Bdelycleon's argument seems to have become the small change of political debate: see e.g. Dem. 3. 31–3.

> [*Raises his sword, the point towards him*]
> Speed thou, my soul!
> [*Attempts to run through his sword, but misses, entangling the weapon in the folds of his cloak*]
> Soul, where are you?
> Let pass, thou shade-y—
> [*Gives up*] Heracles!
> Let's hope I never have to sit in court
> And help convict
> Cleon of embezzlement.[44]

A literal-minded ('Aristotelian') reader might wonder whether that last delicious joke implies Cleon's criminality or Philocleon's reluctance to acknowledge it. The Aristophanic point is rather that the very imprecision of the joke (which makes it *sound* as if Cleon is already presumed guilty, without actually saying so),[45] and its place in a sudden blur of tones and registers, gives notice that comic exuberance is re-establishing itself, and not focused hostility of the kind we have studied in *Clouds*. Satire is of course present, but is transformed by being subsumed within a larger, and larger-spirited, whole.

The same pattern is visible in the scene that follows, when the son's campaign to liberate his father from a continuing obsession with legal proceedings engenders the great dog-trial, in which the dog Labes is tried for stealing Sicilian cheese. With filial patience, Bdelycleon organizes a harmless miniature trial at home, but exploits it as a way of turning his father into an acquitter (the satirical point that the old jurymen prefer convicting is still operative, and indeed as the trial begins Philocleon rubs his hands at the prospect of a condemnation, 893–8). The trial proceeds in a sublime parody (*sic*) of Athenian legal procedure, reaching its comic climax when Bdelycleon, on behalf of the defendant, brings on the defendant's children—his puppies—to whimper for him and melt the jury's heart (975–84). Meanwhile a transparent political allegory is acted out: the Greek for *dog* recalls the Greek for *Cleon* (*kuôn*: *Kleôn*); the defendant (the dog Labes)

[44] Stage directions based on Sommerstein ad loc. The passage relies on the use of two unrelated quotations, the second of which has no actual connection with a σκιά ('soul', 'phantom') at all; see MacDowell ad loc. and, in more detail, Rau, *Paratragodia*, 153–4.

[45] 'Sound' is the *mot juste*: the suggestion is enforced by the alliterative link in κλέπτοντα Κλέωνα.

evokes an opponent of Cleon's (Laches), himself accused of embezzlement in Sicily. And yet, as before, politics and satire dissolve into the rich humour which dominates the scene. Tricked into an acquittal, Philocleon is distraught. In lines tinged with the paratragic once again, he bemoans his predicament (999),

> *πῶς οὖν ἐμαυτῷ τοῦτ' ἐγὼ ξυνείσομαι;*
>
> How shall I square this with my conscience now?

and calls on the gods to hear his justification (1002):

> *ἄκων γὰρ αὔτ' ἔδρασα κοὐ τοὐμοῦ τρόπου*
>
> Against my nature I did this, against my will![46]

As if to still any doubts about the superseding of political satire, Bdelycleon at once points to a fresh field of interest for his father's, and our, pleasure: he promises a new life for the old man, a life of gentlemanly sophistication (all 'dinners, parties, shows', 1005). Abandoning his tragic pose as suddenly as he had taken it on, Philocleon accepts the offer ('right, then', 1008), from which point the action of the play allows the satirical only a very subordinate place indeed. The Cleon-hating son, who is so eager to convert his father to his own sophisticated way of thinking and living, fails dismally. The father *is* talked out of his legal pro-Cleonic obsessions, but he is *not* talked into the conventions of polite society. He goes to a party, and turns out to be a 'confounded nuisance' (*ἀτηρότατον . . . κακόν,* 1299) and 'far and away the most drunk and disorderly there' (*τῶν ξυνόντων πολὺ παροινικώτατος,* 1300). The slave Xanthias explains (1304–6):

> *εὐθὺς γὰρ ὡς ἐνέπλητο πολλῶν κἀγαθῶν,*
> *ἀνήλατ', ἐσκίρτα, 'πεπόρδει, κατεγέλα,*
> *ὥσπερ καχρύων ὀνίδιον εὐωχημένον.*[47]

[46] For both lines, note the tragic-compatible vocabulary, idiom, and rhythm, and with their general shape/orientation cf. e.g. (for 999) *πῶς οὖν παλαιὰ παρὰ νεωτέρας μάθω;* (Aesch. *Cho.* 171), *τὰ πίστ' ἐμαυτῷ τοῦ θράσους παρέξομαι* (Eur. *Pho.* 268), and (for 1002) *ἑκὼν ἑκὼν ἥμαρτον· οὐκ ἀρνήσομαι* ('Aesch.' *Prom.* 266), *ἄκων γὰρ ὤλεσάς νιν* (Eur. *Hipp.* 1433), *ἀλλὰ θατέρου τρόπου* (Eur. *Med.* 808). As elsewhere, comm. and others (preoccupied with specific tragic allusions) ignore these subtler paratragic gestures.

[47] Text as MacDowell.

So once he's had his fill, off he goes,
Jumping, skipping, farting, making fun,
Like a donkey on a feed of corn.

Here the exuberant accumulation of verbs, as much as the animal comparison that follows, sums up the relish for living that reveals the erstwhile puritan and zealot of the law as a great-humoured law-breaker. This recreated Philocleon treats anyone in his path to insult and assault, and responds with renewed abuse to threats of legal redress (1332–40, 1406–41). He makes off with a flute girl, and after she is taken off him by his son, compensates by initiating the astonishing dance competition with which the play ends. This dance duly brings the theatrical proceedings to an end, at the expense of all thoughts of summonses and quotidian formality. By this point, all legal, political, practical, realities have disappeared from the play, as they have from its extravagant hero, and any sense of satire with them. It is as if the satire were the opening term of a *Priamel*: *there*, and real enough, especially at the time, but ultimately a foil for a mode of artistic response that operates at a deeper, elemental, existential, level. In the same spirit, indeed, one might almost reinterpret the relationship between rational Bdelycleon and extravagant Philocleon themselves—as one between the consistent rationality of the realist and the unpredictable extravagance of the recreative.

With hindsight, a new significance may be claimed for the slogans exchanged, like two boxers' blows, by worldly-realist son and expansive-recreative father: 'you're really a slave' (*δουλεύων λέληθας*, 517)—'me a slave? I rule the world' (*παῦε δουλείαν λέγων—| ὅστις ἄρχω τῶν ἁπάντων*, 517–18). The rival claims, perhaps, seem not so much contradictory, as alternative readings: the first, self-evident in the political-satirical perspective; the second, a prospect of Philocleon as he will be in his transfigured existence. It is an existence (we might reflect) which is incomprehensible to the chorus, once the old man's partners in legalist zealotry, now themselves recreated as uncomprehending 'ordinary men', who almost to the end maintain a well-meaning but fatuous expectation that Philocleon will learn his lesson—and conform. Commending Bdelycleon not only for his 'filial devotion' but also for his 'wisdom' (*φιλοπατρίαν καὶ σοφίαν*, 1465), they predict that the old man will switch to 'a life of comfort and luxury' (*τὸ τρυφῶν καὶ μαλακόν*, 1455), but add (1456–61):

τάχα δ' ἂν ἴσως οὐκ ἐθέλοι·
τὸ γὰρ ἀποστῆναι χαλεπὸν
φύσεως, ἣν ἔχοι τις ἀεί.
καίτοι πολλοὶ ταῦτ' ἔπαθον·
ξυνόντες γνώμαις ἑτέρων
μετεβάλοντο τοὺς τρόπους.[48]

But maybe he won't want to:
It's hard to change your nature.
But then again it happens—
You mix with new ideas,
You change your way of life.

The utter irrelevance of these banalities to Philocleon's actual inclinations, and the total inappropriateness of their everyday tone to Philocleon's vast excess, only serve to underline his distance—his existential distance—from worldly-realist, political-satirical norms, like those of the reformed chorus and the sensible (if not exactly 'wise') Bdelycleon.

* * *

Comedy and the existential: this improbable nexus, prompted by consideration of Aristophanes' literary modes and the modal subtlety of *Wasps*, is of some significance for the understanding of Aristophanic comedy and comedy *tout court*. One very special mode or quality of literature, which remains to be considered, has a particular relationship to this nexus: *pathos*. And it is no coincidence that *Wasps* is the play which, more than any other, reveals Aristophanes' disposition towards, and capacity to achieve, this special quality, just as it is the Aristophanic play which, more than any other, allows us to comprehend the improbable nexus itself.[49]

What is pathos as a constituent quality—or mode—of literature? A useful starting-point is provided by Northrop Frye's *Anatomy of Criticism*. Frye suggests we recategorize Western literature. Among his new categories is the 'low mimetic', represented very prominently in, for instance, the nineteenth-century realist novel. Frye sees the hero of the 'low mimetic mode' as one of us, such that we respond to a sense of his common humanity. Without fully

[48] Text as MacDowell.
[49] The discussion that follows (pp. 375–403, and again 418–29) incorporates a modified version of parts of Silk, 'Pathos'.

formalizing a relationship between pathos and the 'low mimetic', Frye relates pathos distinctively to this type of literature and to its hero, and comments:

> pathos presents its hero as isolated by a weakness which appeals to our sympathy because it is on our own level of experience. I speak of a hero, but the central figure of pathos is often a woman or a child . . . we have a whole procession of pathetic female sacrifices in English low mimetic fiction from Clarissa Harlowe to Hardy's Tess and James' Daisy Miller.

He does not define pathos, but suggests it has 'a close relation to the sensational reflex of tears', and adds: 'pathos is increased by the inarticulateness of the victim. The death of an animal is usually pathetic, and so is the catastrophe of defective intelligence that is frequent in modern American literature.'[50]

Pathos, in Frye's sense of the word, is a literary correlate of pity. It is the quality Simonides was famous for. Catullus spoke of 'Simonides' tears'; Dionysius pointed to his gift for arousing pity (τὸ οἰκτίζεσθαι) by avoiding the grand style and concentrating on an appeal to the emotions (μὴ μεγαλοπρεπῶς ἀλλὰ παθητικῶς); the *Life of Aeschylus* explains that 'Aeschylus was defeated by Simonides in competition for an elegy on the victims of Marathon, and elegy, of course, largely involves the delicacy associated with the rousing of sympathetic emotion' (τῆς περὶ τὸ συμπαθὲς λεπτότητος); and Quintilian, after remarking on Simonides' simplicity and directness and charm (*tenuis . . . sermone proprio et iucunditate quadam*), adds that his great strength was his power of moving his reader to pity (*praecipua tamen eius in commovenda miseratione virtus*).[51] Quintilian points to the pity as if it were separate from the simplicity and the directness and the charm. This is mistaken, as a glance at the Danae fragment shows:[52]

[50] Frye, *Anatomy*, 38.

[51] Cat. 38. 8; D. Hal. *de Imit.* (ii. 205 U-R, *Opusc.*: on the sense of παθητικός, cf. below, p. 381); *Vit. Aesch.* in *Biog. Gr. Min.* p. 119 Westermann; Quintil. *Inst.* 10. 1. 64.

[52] Simon. 38 *PMG* (but reading Schneidewin's μιν in 3); for fuller discussion, see Silk, 'Pathos', 79. My transl. takes the liberty of offering, in the phrase 'little one', a portmanteau of the two phrases ὦ τέκος ('child', 7) and λεπτὸν . . . οὖας ('little . . . ear', 20, not quoted here), in order to keep the essential tone of ὦ . . . πόνον in the Greek.

ὅτε λάρνακι
ἐν δαιδαλέᾳ
ἄνεμός τε μιν πνέων
κινηθεῖσά τε λίμνα δείματι
ἔρειπεν, οὐκ ἀδιάντοισι παρειαῖς
ἀμφί τε Περσέι βάλλε φίλαν χέρα
εἶπέν τ'· ὦ τέκος οἷον ἔχω πόνον·
σὺ δ' ἀωτεῖς, γαλαθηνῷ
δ' ἤθεϊ κνοώσσεις
ἐν ἀτερπέι δούρατι χαλκεογόμφῳ . . .

Fraught inside the carven chest,
Wind blowing, wave stirring, Danae
Broke: cheeks wet, arms round her child,
'We are in trouble, little one', she says, 'and you,
On brass-nailed timber drear,
Sleeping, sucking . . .'

As Frye says, a 'hero', isolated by weakness, is often a woman or a child. Here we have both, and both are sympathetic in their weakness. Mother and child drift helplessly at sea, and if Danae is weak, the baby Perseus is weaker still. From the part of the poem that survives it is apparent that the situation is made specific by external detail. More precisely, our eyes are directed to the scene but are kept moving from the external focus to the internal: from the chest and the elements outside to the mother's perspective of the sleeping child. That is, we keep switching from the objective element of the scene to the meaning of each element as the mother perceives it: danger and innocence. And what is especially striking about the passage is a parallel alternation between elaborate lyric style and Simonides' famous simplicity and delicacy. The external is presented in ornate diction: 'carven chest', 'brass-nailed timber drear'. The internal is set out in the simplest language available: 'in trouble'. But this stylistic contrast is not merely striking: it is clearly the mechanism by which the emotional character of the passage is realized. The elaborate lyric phraseology both sets the scene and keeps us at a distance: the simplicities close the distance and bring us face to face with the emotional reality which the external specifics of the given situation imply. As many ancient theorists noted, the rousing of sympathetic emotion calls for linguistic simplicity.[53]

[53] παθητικὴ . . . λέξις, ἐὰν . . . ἐλεεινὰ [λέγηται], ταπεινῶς [λέγοντος]: Arist. *Rhet.* 3. 7. 3. Cf. e.g.: 'Longinus', *Subl.* 8.2; Longin. *Rhet.* 1. 2. 216 Spengel–Hammer;

Compare Thomas Hardy's 'After a Journey':

> Hereto I come to view a voiceless ghost;
> Whither, O whither will its whim now draw me?
> Up the cliff, down, till I'm lonely, lost,
> And the unseen waters' ejaculations awe me.
> Where you will next be there's no knowing,
> Facing round about me everywhere,
>   With your nut-coloured hair,
> And gray eyes, and rose-flush coming and going.
>
> Yes: I have re-entered your olden haunts at last;
> Through the years, through the dead scenes I have tracked you;
> What have you now found to say of our past—
> Scanned across the dark space wherein I have lacked you?
> Summer gave us sweets, but autumn wrought division?
> Things were not lastly as firstly well
>   With us twain, you tell?
> But all's closed now, despite Time's derision.
>
> I see what you are doing: you are leading me on
> To the spots we knew when we haunted here together,
> The waterfall, above which the mist-bow shone
> At the then fair hour in the then fair weather,
> And the cave just under, with a voice still so hollow
> That it seems to call out to me from forty years ago,
>   When you were all aglow,
> And not the thin ghost that I now frailly follow!
>
> Ignorant of what there is flitting here to see,
> The waked birds preen and the seals flop lazily;
> Soon you will have, Dear, to vanish from me,
> For the stars close their shutters and the dawn whitens hazily.
> Trust me, I mind not, though Life lours,
> The bringing me here; nay, bring me here again!
>   I am just the same as when
> Our days were a joy, and our paths through flowers.

Set in a dramatic present, the poem shows us its author, haunted by the memory, and more than the memory, of his dead wife, revisiting the scenes of their courtship. Emotion is inherent in the situation: the living seeking the dead in a half-world of memories

Hor. *AP* 95–8; Quintil. *Inst.* 9. 3. 102, 11. 1. 49. Likewise, Lessing, *Hamburgische Dramaturgie*, 59; Johnson, *Lives*, i. 112 ('passion runs not after remote allusions'); and many modern authorities since.

both of a wronged relationship and of a happiness before the wrong, the latter made more poignant by the simple fact that the wrong can never be righted.

The poem begins with a specific setting and Hardy's distinctive and distancing idiom—

> Hereto I come to view a voiceless ghost . . .
> And the unseen waters' ejaculations awe me—

and ends with the language and emotion of proximity:

> I am just the same as when
> Our days were a joy, and our paths through flowers.

Within the poem the same pattern keeps recurring. In stanza 1, we move from the 'unseen waters' ejaculations' to *you*, 'coming and going'; in stanza 3, from the 'mist-bow' to 'you were all aglow'; above all, in stanza 4, from 'The waked birds preen and the seals flop lazily' to 'bring me here again! | I am just the same as when . . .' If the last few lines of the poem had survived as an isolated fragment, their obvious emotion would probably strike us as sentimental. The same might well be said of our response to the Simonides, if we only had the lines, '. . . arms round her child, | "We are in trouble, little one" . . .' In both cases, however, the emotion is presented as a logical development of a situation. Both situations are, potentially, highly emotive: a helpless mother and child, a love that was and absence that is—and '*was* versus *is*', '*once* but *now*', is a particularly powerful stimulant. But in both cases the linguistic organization, and especially the linguistic switches discussed, shape the emotion to a different, and higher, end.

So far, our discussion has in effect identified pathos, the literary quality, with the group of sympathetic-identificatory responses which (no doubt under Aristotle's influence) critics have, for centuries, considered together under the name of pity.[54] However, while this identification is assumed by Northrop Frye and others,[55] and while it seems to be permitted by the Simonides

[54] i.e. because of his inclusive use of the word ἔλεος in his definition of the tragic affect, *Poet.* VI: *δι' ἐλέου καὶ φόβου περαίνουσα τὴν τῶν τοιούτων παθημάτων κάθαρσιν*, 1449b27–8.

[55] So the nurse's emotive grieving in *Medea* 20–36 earns the description, 'a passage of pure Euripidean style and pathos', from P. Pucci, *The Violence of Pity in Euripides' Medea* (Cornell 1980) 46. See further (e.g.) J. Griffin, *Homer on Life and*

example, it is surely not permitted by the Hardy. 'After a Journey' is a poem for whose quality 'pathos' is the entirely appropriate word, but a poem to which a response involving pity is not called for. In the Simonides, there are two available human objects of pity, and pity is the more naturally evoked because one of the pitiable objects is engaged in pitying the other. In the Hardy, there is no one to pity: not the ghost, who is dead and (unlike a Virgilian Dido) beyond pity; nor indeed the authorial 'I', whose dispassion and understanding (both shown in his truly self-effacing concentration on the 'thin ghost' as is, and woman as was) simply remove him from consideration as a pitiable figure. It is pity, let us say, that requires a specific pitiable object with what Frye calls 'a weakness which appeals to our sympathy'. Here there is none, and yet there is pathos *in the situation*. With hindsight, we can take this to include not only the man's search, the 'dark space' and the 'division', but also the power to make the past into art. That is, the pathos depends not on any weakness, as such, but on a vulnerability and the defiant understanding of it. 'It is not suffering in itself that is pathetic', wrote Schiller, 'but only the resistance opposed to suffering.'[56]

Pathos is a concept requiring precise formulation. In educated modern usage, it is taken to be (a little vaguely) 'that quality in speech, writing, music, or artistic representation . . . which excites a feeling of pity or sadness' or (a little more vaguely) the 'power of stirring tender or melancholy emotion'.[57] This conception of pathos arises in the later eighteenth century as a convergence of various developments in Western attitudes to ethics and art.[58] These include a growing emphasis on the idea that all literature,

Death (Oxford 1980) 103–44, and J. de Romilly, *L'Evolution du pathétique d'Eschyle à Euripide* (Paris 1961), *passim*. These three important, and very different, discussions agree in using 'pathos' (as I would say, indiscriminately) for passages productive of 'pity' and evocative of what I call pathos, for passages evocative of pathos without producing 'pity', and for passages productive of 'pity' but not evocative of pathos.

[56] Friedrich Schiller, *Über das Pathetische* (1793): *Sämtliche Werke*, xi. 252.

[57] *OED* s.v. 1, a.

[58] I know of no comprehensive treatment of the subject: in recent years affective criticism has been spurned by theorists and even historians of theory. Much relevant material can be found in R. Wellek, *A History of Modern Criticism, 1750–1950* (4 vols., London 1955) i–ii, and other such surveys. On Greek (rather than modern) *pathos*, there are valuable comments in Heath, *Poetics*, 10–11 n. 10, and T. Gould, *The Ancient Quarrel between Poetry and Philosophy* (Princeton 1990) *passim*.

especially poetry, is or should be emotionally affecting, as (more traditionally) oratory had been required to be; so, according to Dennis in 1701, 'passion . . . is the characteristical mark of poetry, and consequently must be everywhere'.[59] Then there is a penchant for fellow-feeling and altruism, very obvious in eighteenth-century experiments with so-called 'serious drama' and 'sentimental comedy', and equally apparent in literary theory, where the newly esteemed feelings are often subsumed under the heading of 'sympathy' or associated with more familiar terms like 'pity'. Lessing's conversion of Aristotle's *katharsis* into a prescription for pity as an end in itself ('tragedy must extend our capacity for feeling pity')[60] is, in this sense, representative. The upshot is that a focus on strong, primary emotions (Dennis's 'passion') rapidly gives way to a closer concern with the subtler sympathetic responses and the literary quality, or qualities, that evoke them. 'Pathos' becomes a characteristic name for these literary qualities, as it had previously been a possible name for the primary emotions. Regarding the terminology involved: the Greek words *pathos* and *pathêtikos* had meant (among many other things) 'emotion' and 'emotive'; Greek *pathos* may, at times, overlap with modern 'pathos', but never actually means the same;[61] and Greek usage is maintained, in transliteration, by writers of Dennis's time, including Dennis himself, whose assertion that 'passion . . . is the characteristical mark of poetry' is conveniently followed by the corollary, 'wherever a discourse is not pathetic, there it is prosaic'. In contrast, the process of semantic-conceptual development has clearly taken place by 1815, when we find Coleridge considering some of the literary 'excellencies' of his friend Wordsworth in terms of a 'mild and philosophic pathos'. Coleridge's formulation, thought through with exceptional clarity, is valuable both as a gloss on our discussion so far and for the assistance it promises to give to our discussion still to come. Coleridge comments on a

[59] In *The Advancement and Reformation of Poetry: The Critical Works of John Dennis*, ed. E. N. Hooker (Baltimore 1939) i. 215.

[60] Gotthold Ephraim Lessing, *Sämtliche Werke*, ed. K. Lachmann and F. Muncker (24 vols., Leipzig 1886–1924) xvii. 66.

[61] Cic. *Orat.* 37. 128: 'Graeci . . . παθητικὸν nominant, quo perturbantur animi et concitantur.'

meditative pathos, a union of deep and subtle thought with sensibility; a sympathy with man as man; the sympathy indeed of a contemplator, rather than a fellow-sufferer . . . but of a contemplator from whose view no difference of rank conceals the sameness of the nature . . . The superscription and the image of the Creator still remain legible to him under the dark lines with which guilt or calamity had cancelled or crossbarred it.[62]

Old usages are not always superseded by new ones; and some of the elusiveness associated with 'pathos' is no doubt due to the occasional survival of the word's earlier reference as an undertone to sophisticated English usage even in our own day,[63] the more so because the equivalent terms in other Western languages are sometimes much more ambivalent. Schiller's important essay 'Über das Pathetische', for instance, deals as much with *pathos* in the Greek sense as with 'pathos' in the English. One important corollary is that his Graeco-Germanic *pathos* is liable to imply a greater intensity of feeling.[64] 'Pathos' in our sense presupposes the 'contemplator's' emotional subtlety and restraint: the subtlety and restraint associated, for instance, with early Greek epitaphs and with the still earlier 'obituaries' in the *Iliad*.[65] Any such subtlety and restraint tends to be overwhelmed by strong, primary emotion—by 'the violent gestures and wild cries of passionate woe which are admitted in Greek tragedy',[66] by grief, by pity. Is this not, after all, the emotional reality of the Simonides poem? The ancient critics (though hardly assisted by lacking the modern conceptual category of pathos) were not entirely wrong about his 'Danae'. Its undoubted pathos is accompanied by, and overlaid by, evocations of pity for its two hapless subjects.

[62] Samuel Taylor Coleridge, *Biographia Literaria*, ed. G. Watson (corr. edn., London 1965) 270.

[63] e.g. Frye, *Anatomy*, 217: 'pathos, though it seems a gentler and more relaxed mood than tragedy, is even more terrifying.'

[64] Cf. the comment by D. Breazeale, *Philosophy and Truth: Selections from Nietzsche's Notebooks of the Early 1870s* (New Jersey 1979) 61: 'The German word *Pathos* is much more common than its English cognate. In addition to the ordinary sense of the English word, it also means "vehemence", "ardour", "solemnity" and "fervour". Nietzsche often uses the word in a manner which recalls the original Greek contrast between *ethos* . . . and *pathos*.' And cf. n. 156 below.

[65] Cf. Griffin, *Homer*, 141–2.

[66] Ibid. 142. The Greeks' own emotional responses to their tragedies were certainly strong (cf. W. B. Stanford, *Greek Tragedy and the Emotions* (London 1983) 2–7), and correspondingly their vocabulary of pity subsumes a variety of feelings, or patterns of behaviour, of a 'visceral intensity' (ibid. 23): see briefly Stanford, ibid. 23–5, and in detail W. Burkert, *Zum altgriechischen Mitleidsbegriff* (Erlangen 1955).

The Hardy poem is a clearer example of pathos than the Simonides, and it shows that pathos requires a context. If pathos depends on a '*once* but *now*', we must have a sense of the 'once' as well as the 'now'. Simonides' pathos, albeit overlaid, does likewise develop from a clearly defined setting. It follows that a work may begin emotively (as do various Greek tragedies), but not pathetically. Contrast the logic of pity. Pity can be instantaneous: a person in a weak condition may be pitiable, irrespective of the background to that particular instance of the condition. And equally, distinguish pathos from sentimentality. Take, as a textbook case, Lewis Carroll's verses prefixed to *Through the Looking Glass*. Stanza 1:

> A tale begun in other days,
> When summer suns were glowing—
> A simple chime, that served to time
> The rhythm of our rowing—
> Whose echoes live in memory yet,
> Though envious years would say 'forget' . . .

The all-too-evident emotion is attached to the familiar '*once* but *now*' rhythm, and to nothing else. Substantial context is non-existent. There is not even enough of a context for us to have any idea (without extraneous biographical aids) who the 'we', referred to in line 4, might be, and whether the 'rowing' and the 'chime' are literal or not. A little more is forthcoming from stanza 2—

> Without, the frost, the blinding snow,
> The storm-wind's moody madness—
> Within, the firelight's ruddy glow,
> And childhood's nest of gladness.
> The magic words shall hold thee fast:
> Thou shalt not heed the raving blast—

yielding us a *now* consisting of wintry weather (outside) and a 'nest of gladness' (inside), for which the 'summer suns' of the earlier stanza (plus or minus the chime and the rowing) represent the required *once*. Hazy and unlocalized as it is, this is all we get by way of a specific context. Stanza 3 completes the effusion with a series of generalized clichés—

> And though the shadow of a sigh
> May tremble through the story,

For 'happy summer days' gone by,
A vanish'd summer glory—
It shall not touch with breath of bale
The pleasance of our fairy-tale—

and with a 'shadow of a sigh' ourselves, we acknowledge that the little piece has returned to its emotive base.

Sentimentality involves an indulgence in feelings whose colour or intensity is in excess of the situation from which they purport to arise.[67] It invites an audience's (or author's) enjoyment in the sensation of feeling which one would think inappropriate in a corresponding situation in life. The sentimentalist reader's (or writer's) emotions are imprecise because they are not properly located: there are no adequate specifics for them to be placed and given precision by. In Eliot's phrase, they lack an 'objective correlative'.[68] In slightly different terms, I. A. Richards noted that a sentimental response tends to 'confine itself to one aspect only of the many that the situation can present' or else to 'substitute for it a factitious, illusory situation'[69]—as Lewis Carroll's response obviously does when he evokes the 'happy summer days' of childhood. Richards went on to psychologize the phenomenon:

> most . . . sentimental fixations and distortions of feelings are the result of inhibitions . . . If a man can only think of his childhood as a lost heaven, it is probably because he is afraid to think of its other aspects . . . As a rule the source of such inhibitions is some painfulness attaching to the aspect of life that we refuse to contemplate. The sentimental response moves in to replace this aspect by some other aspect more pleasant to contemplate.[70]

As Richards suggests, sentimentality is painless; and it is painless because it is uncritical and easy. It is easily achieved, it elicits feelings which are easily stirred, and (inevitably) it involves easy language. The language through which Hardy establishes his

[67] The principle was first grasped by 'Longinus': compare his disparagement of *πάθος ἄκαιρον* (*Subl.* 3. 5) with his praise of Sappho's *συμβαίνοντα παθήματα ἐκ τῶν παρεπομένων* (10. 1).

[68] In 'Hamlet and his problems': Eliot, *The Sacred Wood*, 100. Cf. F. R. Leavis's discussion of Tennyson's 'Tears, Idle Tears', in *A Selection from Scrutiny* (2 vols., Cambridge 1968), i. 217, and his comments on the lack of a 'justifying situation' in Cory's 'Heraclitus', ibid. 211.

[69] Richards, *Practical Criticism*, 261.

[70] Ibid. 267.

context (to take the clear contrast) defamiliarizes: it is arresting, even abrasive. Its surprising collocations ('mist-bow', 'seals flop lazily') and oscillations between the archaic ('whither'), the colloquial ('I'm'), and the ostensibly prosaic ('ejaculations') disconcert us into a decisive realization of the situation it deals with.[71] Sentimentality involves the opposite: the language is inert, and reveals nothing, because, strictly speaking, there is nothing but the only too visible emotion to reveal. And then, sentimentality dwells on something pleasant, albeit, perhaps, pleasantly melancholy. Again contrast Hardy, who contemplates not only the lost 'paths through flowers' and the 'sweets' of summer, but the 'division' of autumn, the present where 'Life lours', and the omnipresent fact of 'Time's derision'.

The sentimentalist likes to indulge himself at the expense of the weak (who have no comeback) and to convert the harmlessness of their condition into a passive virtue. This is what Carroll does when he allows his preface to represent childhood as 'a lost heaven', in marked contrast to the story that is to follow, and without reference either to childhood's unpalatable pettinesses or to its developing potential for adulthood. With such cases in mind, we should surely query Frye's association of child-heroes with pathos, and indeed his further associations of pathos with 'the inarticulateness of the victim', 'the death of an animal', and 'the catastrophe of defective intelligence': are these not rather contexts more congenial to sentimentality? Needless to say, there are also unsentimental ways of being preoccupied with childhood (and the rest). What is distinctive about sentimentality in its treatment of such subjects is that it uses them as a pretext for emotional indulgence. The purported objects of the emotion are therefore strictly objects of exploitation, and 'objects' is clearly the *mot juste*.

In all these respects sentimentality in art is difficult, if not impossible, to distinguish from sentimentality in life: Richards's analysis surely makes this clear. Here at least sentimentality belongs with pity and the other relatable sympathetic emotions. The versions of pity that we feel for (say) Sophocles' Neoptolemus or Shakespeare's Duncan are akin to the feelings we have for those who are ill-used or vulnerable in life: a measure of sympathetic identification, along with a certain distance which implies our

[71] Cf. (*mutatis mutandis*) the ancient principle, τὸ ἐκ τῆς ἐναργείας πάθος (Demetr. *Eloc.* 214).

respect for the individuality of the other,[72] and almost certainly a moral sense of the ill-used as both worthy of our feeling and yet (sign of distance again) necessarily below us. There are, of course, important distinctions too, notably that the 'relationship' of pitier to pitied in art is one-way, which means, among other things, that our everyday selves are not at risk of a reaction from the object of our pity. 'The movement of our melancholy passions is pleasant', wrote Edward Young in the heyday of Enlightenment sympathy, 'when ourselves are safe.'[73] And it is characteristic of a sentimental response in life, as well as in art, to choose, precisely, situations where ourselves *will be* safe. For all that, the point stands: these emotional responses are familiar to us from the experience of life as ordinarily lived.

Pathos is different. It is essentially an aesthetic quality, and if we find it in life, it is by extension of a response we have learned from the experience of art. In particular, pathos lacks the moral basis which is characteristic of the life-emotions. If we see someone suffering, we may feel pity for the victim of misfortune, even if we know nothing about the background of the misfortune or the victim himself; but we will feel more pity, or will pity more keenly, if we know the victim to be suffering unjustly.[74] And where sentimentality is concerned, it is usually a precondition of emotion that the purported object of the feeling is innocent: hence the peculiar suitability of young children or animals. It is possible to sentimentalize a criminal, but only by glossing over the crime: a simple case of sentimental partiality. Yet pathos is not dependent on such considerations. A classic moment in *Macbeth* offers a clear demonstration of the principle. Macbeth and Seyton (v. v):

M. What is that noise?
S. It is the cry of women, my good lord.
M. I have almost forgot the taste of fears.
The time has been my senses would have cool'd
To hear a night-shriek, and my fell of hair
Would at a dismal treatise rouse and stir
As life were in't. I have supp'd full with horrors;

[72] Cf. Rousseau's account of pity, in *Emile* and elsewhere, and the probing discussion by Jacques Derrida, *De la grammatologie* (Paris 1967) 243–72 (esp. 269–72).

[73] *Conjectures upon Original Composition* (1759), ed. E. Morley (Manchester 1918) 41.

[74] δεῖ γὰρ ἐπὶ . . . τοῖς ἀναξίως πράττουσι . . . ἐλεεῖν, Arist. *Rhet.* 2. 9. 2.

Direness, familiar to my slaughterous thoughts,
Cannot once start me. Wherefore was that cry?

S. The Queen, my lord, is dead.

M. She should have died hereafter;
There would have been a time for such a word.
To-morrow, and to-morrow, and to-morrow,
Creeps in this petty pace from day to day
To the last syllable of recorded time,
And all our yesterdays have lighted fools
The way to dusty death. Out, out, brief candle!
Life's but a walking shadow . . .

There is no question of our pitying—let alone sentimentalizing—Macbeth in the loss of his wife, as we have pitied the wronged Duncan. If nothing else, the reminder of Macbeth's, and Lady Macbeth's, 'slaughters', interposes a moral obstacle to our pity; and his own cold impartiality makes it difficult, even at such a moment of intense loss, to see him as a victim one might pity at all. Yet the conclusive generalities about life that this climactic moment calls forth themselves call forth an unmistakable pathos, by a process of sublimation as yet unexplained, and notwithstanding the moral disqualification of their speaker and our distance from him.

The sentimentalist distorts the purported object into a pleasant, perhaps pleasantly melancholy, version of itself and identifies, sympathetically but uncritically, with the new creation, inviting the reader, in turn, to do the same. Any distance between self and object would expose the object and bring the distortion into view. It follows that sentimentality is at risk from laughter. Laughter can be sympathetic, but it can only be fully identificatory in the context of mass hysteria. Normally, laughter involves sufficient distance for the laugher to be aware of his (or her) independent existence as something apart from the object of his laughter and for him to have a sense of an independent reality that he is laughing at or laughing with. Accordingly, laughter and sentimentality are unlikely to be compatible: many filmgoers' feelings of discomfort about some of Chaplin's less successful experiments are relevant here.

On the other hand, some distance is requisite for pity, as already explained. And distance of a quite different order is requisite for our response to pathos. As with pity, there must be a solid reality through which emotion may be localized, but pathos invites, besides, what Coleridge rightly saw as a *contemplative* response: a response to Hardy's resistance and to Macbeth's dispassion and to the understanding of vulnerability which both personae are made to voice.

Pathos requires distance, but not total distance. Accordingly, we do not expect to find pathos in contexts of aggression or negation—in the form of unqualified (or 'unsubsumed') abuse or obscenity or satire—where an object is viewed, at best with detachment, at worst with hostility, but always with total self-possession and entirely from the outside.[75] Such modes of expression entail a barrier between a *me* and a *him*, *her*, or *them*, as unmistakably as sentimentality calls for an uncritical identification of the two.

Pathos, as distinct from the aggressive as it is from the sentimental, requires distance together with what the logic of this argument might suggest was some measure of identification. Our *Macbeth* example, however, tells strongly against such a conclusion as it stands. And with our various paradigms before us, and this one in particular, we should keep Coleridge's 'contemplation' firmly in mind. For in this example there is no one that we might identify with, while there is, certainly, much to contemplate. What we are in fact contemplating, and what our distance is enabling us to contemplate, is related to the fictional person, Macbeth, but is not actually a personal *him* at all. If one pities, in response to life or to literature, one must pity a person, or some equivalent. Pathos may involve focusing on an individual person, but the focus then seems to be on the person *as representative of something beyond the personal.* When we experience pathos, we do feel a sympathetic understanding, not with or of any individual person, but with or of some play of ideas, some intimation, grounded, perhaps, in an individual person, yet pointing beyond that ground.

There is a great deal of abuse, obscenity, and satire in Aristophanes, but all such negativity is generally subsumed within a

[75] In the light of Richards's thoughts on inhibition as the hidden correlate of sentimentality, the relation between obscenity, in particular, and sentimentality can be summed up in a formula. Obscenity presupposes violation of a taboo (normally sexual or scatological: Henderson, *Maculate Muse*, 2), i.e. an assault on inhibition; obscenity and sentimentality are, as such, incompatible.

more comprehensive and broadly positive attitude which communicates itself as such to the reader. *Hence* the exhilaration associated with the inventive contest of abuse in *Knights*; *hence* the sense of exuberance engendered by the phallic song in *Acharnians*—and by the triumph of Dicaeopolis in general; and *hence*, to take our most recent example, the fact that in *Wasps* the repeated movement from satire on legal procedure and politics to paratragic delight does not impinge as an escape from something 'heavy' to something 'light', but as a 'natural' movement between one expression of Aristophanic humour and another. And among the expressions of Aristophanic humour which cannot coexist with unqualified ('unsubsumed') abuse, obscenity, or satire is pathos, such as we find (for instance) at *Wasps* 1051–70:

ἀλλὰ τὸ λοιπὸν τῶν ποιητῶν,
ὦ δαιμόνιοι, τοὺς ζητοῦντας
καινόν τι λέγειν κἀξευρίσκειν
στέργετε μᾶλλον καὶ θεραπεύετε,
καὶ τὰ νοήματα σῴζεσθ' αὐτῶν 1055
εἰσβάλλετέ τ' εἰς τὰς κιβωτοὺς
μετὰ τῶν μήλων. κἂν ταῦτα ποιῆθ',
ὑμῖν δι' ἔτους τῶν ἱματίων
ὀζήσει δεξιότητος.

ὦ πάλαι ποτ' ὄντες ἡμεῖς ἄλκιμοι μὲν ἐν χοροῖς, 1060
ἄλκιμοι δ' ἐν μάχαις,
καὶ κατ' αὐτὸ τοῦτο μόνον ἄνδρες ἀλκιμώτατοι.
πρίν ποτ' ἦν, πρὶν ταῦτα· νῦν δ'
οἴχεται, κύκνου τε πολιώτεραι δὴ
αἵδ' ἐπανθοῦσιν τρίχες. 1065
ἀλλὰ κἀκ τῶν λειψάνων δεῖ
τῶνδε ῥώμην νεανικὴν σχεῖν·
ὡς ἐγὼ τοὐμὸν νομίζω
γῆρας εἶναι κρεῖττον ἢ πολ-
λῶν κικίννους νεανιῶν καὶ
σχῆμα κεὐρυπρωκτίαν. 1070

Love and cherish writers who
Try to say something new.
With your kept clothes keep their wit
Safe with citron. In a bit
Everything you wear will be
Scented with ingenuity.

Hard in the dance,
Hard in war, once,
So hard *here*, once.

Now grayer than a swan,
Hair gone:
Done with—and yet
Even this skeleton
Can hold a young man's energy
And prove that age can beat the younger set:
All kiss-curls, style, and sodomy.[76]

The chorus of elderly dicasts have been on stage for some 800 lines. We have seen them in the fantastic guise of wasps in support of the beleaguered Philocleon. We have just now had them address us, ostensibly as the author's spokesmen, in the parabasis. We saw them first, represented very plainly as old men creaking at the joints (230 ff.), but only after an altogether more alarming pen-picture from Bdelycleon (223–7):

τὸ γένος ἤν τις ὀργίσῃ
τὸ τῶν γερόντων, ἔσθ' ὅμοιον σφηκιᾷ.
ἔχουσι γὰρ καὶ κέντρον ἐκ τῆς ὀσφύος
ὀξύτατον, ᾧ κεντοῦσι, καὶ κεκραγότες
πηδῶσι καὶ βάλλουσιν ὥσπερ φέψαλοι.

Get at these pensioners, and you stir up
A wasps' nest: they've got stings in their backside
So sharp, they crack, jump, stab like sparks.

The reality, as the chorus now enter and speak, is rather different (230–9):

χώρει, πρόβαιν' ἐρρωμένως. ὦ Κωμία, βραδύνεις.
μὰ τὸν Δί' οὐ μέντοι πρὸ τοῦ γ', ἀλλ' ἦσθ' ἱμὰς κύνειος·
νυνὶ δὲ κρείττων ἐστί σου Χαρινάδης βαδίζειν.
ὦ Στρυμόδωρε Κονθυλεῦ, βέλτιστε συνδικαστῶν,
Εὐεργίδης ἆρ' ἐστί που 'νταῦθ', ἢ Χάβης ὁ Φλυεύς;
πάρεσθ' ὃ δὴ λοιπόν γ' ἔτ' ἐστίν, ἀππαπαῖ παπαιάξ,
ἥβης ἐκείνης, ἡνίκ' ἐν Βυζαντίῳ ξυνῆμεν
φρουροῦντ' ἐγώ τε καὶ σύ· κᾆτα περιπατοῦντε νύκτωρ
τῆς ἀρτοπώλιδος λαθόντ' ἐκλέψαμεν τὸν ὅλμον,
κᾆθ' ἥψομεν τοῦ κορκόρου κατασχίσαντες αὐτόν.

[76] 1062: text as MacDowell, with Bentley's ἀλκιμώτατοι for the μαχιμώτατοι of codd. For the use of 'hard' (in the dance) in 1060, cf. *OED* s.v. A. IV. 19, as in Kingsley (1860), 'the hardest rider for many a mile round'.

Come on, quick march, keep at it. Cómias, you're lagging.
Once you didn't use to: you were a real dog-leash.
Chárinádes can outwalk you now. Strymodórus,
Can you see Euérgides or Chábes anywhere?
So—this is all that's left, is it, of us young men,
When we were at Byzantium on guard,
You and I?—that night we took a walk, nicked
The baking-woman's bowl, chopped it up
For firewood, boiled our porridge in it.[77]

Wistfully recalling their youth, the old men, overheard, are anything but frightening. The awed characterization that precedes their entry directs our attention to it and to them. What duly confronts us is not exactly the squad of redoubtable fighters that Bdelycleon led us to expect. Instead, we have a version of the '*once* but *now*', attached to one passing hint of past glory,[78] but then very unsentimentally grounded in the specifics of Byzantium and distanced, practically out of reach of any sympathetic response, by the take-it-or-leave-it memory of mundane fiddling in days gone by: almost as in Macbeth's speech, there is no one for us to identify with. The plain style of their leader's words, meanwhile, and the apparent lack of any joking either from or at the chorus contrasts with the established comic context sufficiently to prepare us for what is, eventually, to follow and to leave us now with a kind of suspended understanding.[79]

It is in the middle of the parabasis, with the chorus momentarily in a state of seeming solitude,[80] that the theme first announced in the *parodos* suddenly, and more pointedly, recurs. The recurrence is sudden, because (as, *mutatis mutandis*, in the Hardy) there is a strong and unexpected switch, as the chorus leave their amiable disquisition on Aristophanes' own poetic

[77] With stress-markers (not 'accents') on the proper names in the transl. Greek text as MacDowell.

[78] For the transl. of 236 ('When . . . guard'), cf. the grand manner of Marlowe's 'And ride in triumph through Persepolis' (*Tamburlaine the Great*, Part I, II. v). The Greek (a 'comic' iambic tetrameter catalectic) begins with an iambic trimeter (*ἥβης . . . Βυζαντίῳ*), where idiom (note the absence of def. art. with *ἐκείνης*) and rhythm are impeccably tragic-compatible.

[79] MacDowell's comments ad loc. ('combines pathos and gentle amusement in a manner similar to some scenes in Chekhov') are admirably in the right direction, if a shade too explicit. On the lack of jokes: the first is at 243 ('three days' supply of anger').

[80] *Seeming*: they have the audience to talk, or sing, to. See further Silk, 'Space and solitude'.

talents (a witty demonstration of Aristophanic wit) to demonstrate them more decisively by reverting to dramatic character, but now in song and, for a moment, on a higher stylistic level.[81] And the effect is more pointed, because the '*once* but *now*' theme is more than incidental, while its emotional significance is given exquisite expression in the lingering quality of the repetitions, 'hard . . . hard', 'once . . . once' (*ἄλκιμοι* . . . *ἄλκιμοι* . . . *πρίν* . . . *πρίν* . . .).[82] Emotion (one should add) is deftly qualified by the euphemism in 1062, which yet avoids compromising the tone: 'So hard *here*' (*καὶ κατ' αὐτὸ τοῦτο μόνον ἄνδρες ἀλκιμώτατοι* (*indicating their phalli*)).[83] The emotional quality of the passage is in any case far removed from identificatory emotiveness: the chorus as we have known them since the *parodos* (our necessary context) have been too intermittently grotesque for that. And yet—or, rather, *and therefore* —there is every justification for sensing in these lines a moment of pure pathos, as pure as (dare one say?) we found in the Hardy or the Shakespeare, notwithstanding the obvious differences between pathos in its comic and its non-comic versions. One of these differences emerges as the old wasps continue their song: we who were strong are now weak . . . but still a hell of a lot stronger than the youth of today with their tasteless fashions and their nasty sexual habits. The pathos, then, having abruptly appeared (or, as we may feel with hindsight, reappeared) makes way, with equal abruptness, for satire and obscenity and, in general, anti-pathetic aggression. The mood is swiftly established and as swiftly subverted.[84]

Northrop Frye's 'pathos' (in his 'low mimetic' mode) is associated with women and children, among others. Clearly, the subjects of pathos (in his sense) are likely to be various, both in 'low mimetic' fiction and elsewhere. The tragic mimesis of Euripides' *Heracles*, for instance, contains a varied series of figures more or less pathetic (in Frye's sense), from the elderly Amphitryon to Heracles' hapless wife and young children and Heracles

[81] Cf. Silk, 'Lyric poet', 143 n. 136.

[82] Cf. MacDowell ad loc. (*Wasps*, 270).

[83] Stage direction Sommerstein's.

[84] The *Vesp.* passages have close equivalents in *Ach.* There too we find a decrepit chorus making its entrance lamenting its former strength (208 ff.) and a parabasis song in which that opening note is intensified (692 ff.: above, pp. 198–200). There, though, there is a measure of organic development towards the pathetic, and the pathos, when it comes, is less pure: see, in detail, Silk, 'Pathos', 90.

himself. It is striking, then, that Aristophanes' pathos—in our sense of the word—is specifically and exclusively associated with old men, their past youth, their losses, their complaints. This is the case not only in *Wasps*, but in *Acharnians*, *Lysistrata*, and elsewhere.[85] In fact, the pattern, old men looking back, is so much a feature of the Aristophanic landscape that Aristophanes can write his own parody of it. At *Ecclesiazusae* 214 ff., Praxagora is practising her forthcoming speech at the Assembly, when she will be disguised as a man, but speaking in favour of women's rule. On their behalf she points to their record in upholding the old traditions in a pure and uncorrupted way. Her chief resource is a catalogue of mock-emotive one-liners, each one ending with the same evocative phrase, 'the way they once did': *ὥσπερ καὶ πρὸ τοῦ*. The list begins innocently enough (221),

> *καθήμεναι φρύγουσιν ὥσπερ καὶ πρὸ τοῦ*
>
> They sit and cook, the way they once did

but soon turns to subversive satire (224),

> *τοὺς ἄνδρας ἐπιτρίβουσιν ὥσπερ καὶ πρὸ τοῦ*
>
> They ruin husbands, the way they once did

and finds suitable closure in obscenity (228):

> *βινούμεναι χαίρουσιν ὥσπερ καὶ πρὸ τοῦ*
>
> They love a shag, the way they once did.

Here the characteristic *locus* of Aristophanic pathos is evoked as a target for comic parody in its own right.[86]

The Aristophanic evocations of old men looking back to a past youth are wont to involve allusion, not so much to any likely past,

[85] For *Ach.* see esp. n. 84 above (and cf. below, p. 398 n. 101) and, for *Lys.*, Silk, 'Pathos', 90–3, 95–6.

[86] For a fuller discussion of this passage, see Silk, 'Pathos', 93–4. In *Eccl.* the women as a group specifically try to be *old* men (*ᾄδουσαι μέλος πρεσβυτικόν τι*, 277–8). Their own mock-*parodos* (289 ff.) trembles on the brink of mock-pathos, but despite another *πρὸ τοῦ* (300) and a self-heroizing allusion (303–4), never quite gets there. The phrase *πρὸ τοῦ* (one should note) is not restricted to pathetic or pathos-related contexts. Even aged choreutae can use it without any such feeling (as *Pax* 1312), and the phrase can figure in a series of a quite different kind (as *Thes.* 398, 410, 418, 424). Conversely, there is at least one attested instance of nostalgic *πρὸ τοῦ* in Old Comedy outside A: Eupol. 219 *PCG*.

nor to any sentimentalized past, but to a great heroic past—when they stood on guard at Byzantium or fought at Marathon or Salamis or even earlier, a hundred years ago, in the days of Hippias and Cleomenes.[87] The tendency to defy ordinary chronology in these passages must have been even more evident in first performance than it is to us. What are we to make of it? Part of the effect is to provide a humorous characterization of the old soldier ('Old men forget . . . | But he'll remember with advantages').[88] But the effect goes beyond a joke. The heroics serve to intensify the contrast, the familiar '*once* but *now*', on which pathos seems so often to depend, and act as an oblique signal that though these men may be anonymous (more or less), as well as comic, their pathos matters and deserves our ('serious'?) contemplation. It is worth remarking that other writers, especially orators, invoke those great days too, and that their invocations, emotive as they may be, tend to be very different in orientation and mood. 'The Greeks of old', says Demosthenes in the *Third Philippic*, 'were as eager for freedom as we are for slavery. There was something then, there *was*, which no longer exists . . . It was something which animated Greece *en masse*, something which triumphed over all the wealth of Persia: it was our ancestors' *distaste for corruption*.'[89] The orator strives to rouse his audience to action, not to any complex feeling involving contemplation. Greek orators indeed sometimes strive to stir the sympathetic emotions, and that goal is never more apparent than when the speaker in the Athenian courts brings on his children to rouse a jury's sympathy—the practice which Aristophanes himself parodies with the puppies of the criminal dog Labes in *Wasps*. But pathos belongs to the aesthetic sphere, as practical oratory never fully does. Accordingly pathos, strictly understood, is not in the normal oratorical repertoire, and the orators' appeals to the battles of the past have only a superficial similarity to those of Aristophanes.

[87] Respectively, *Vesp.* 236, *Ach.* 697–8, *Ach.* 214 (cf. Sommerstein ad loc.), *Lys.* 665 and 273–82 (ditto). There is another self-heroizing allusion by the semichorus (of women, disguised as old men) in *Eccl.* 303–4, where the ref. to Myronides points to the battle of Oenophyta (but the passage is not pathos-related—cf. n. 86 above; likewise *Vesp.* 1098). Marathon is also evoked on behalf of old Demos at *Eq.* 781, by old men at *Lys.* 285 (see Henderson ad loc.), and perhaps at fr. 429 *PCG* (*Merchant Ships*): see Kassel–Austin ad loc.

[88] *Henry V*, IV. iii; one notes how in the Cleomenes passage two days of history have grown into six years of recollection (*Lys.* 280: Hdt. 5. 72. 2).

[89] Dem 9. 36–7.

The pathetic potential of men's old age for Aristophanes is amply attested. The instances cited so far have been largely drawn from the semi-anonymous world of his choruses. We also find there explicit statements which are not in themselves evocative of pathos, but serve to confirm his preoccupation, notably *Peace* 335–6:

> Better, happier, fartier, laughier,
> Freed of that shield,
> Than if I'd sloughed my old age off.[90]

The speaker (chorus-leader) acclaims peace more—even—than he would a hypothetical escape from old age: one gathers that old age is the pre-eminent symbol of vulnerability. There are, again, passages striking for their sympathetic references to individuals, like the parabasis of *Knights* with its *philanthrôpia* towards the old comic poets, especially Magnes and Cratinus (519–33). Above all, various of Aristophanes' main characters are themselves old men, with pathos, therefore, latent in their representation. One thinks back to Dicaeopolis, for whom the war means exile from the countryside, but (*Acharnians* 26–7)—

> as for peace,
> They couldn't give a damn. O City city—

and the distinctive tone of that passage is at last fully open to explanation.[91] And one thinks again of *Clouds* 1456–7—

> So why not tell me that before,
> Instead of leading an old countryman astray?—

where, as if by inversion, the *once*, and not its loss, is a matter of regret.[92] But these are hints only. The most fully realized instance is the representation of Philocleon in *Wasps*, to which we shall return, in due course, once more.

Arguably, there are no cases of Aristophanic pathos, strictly understood, which are not associated with old men. Other triggers produce other responses. Pitiable childhood, for instance, is treated as an opportunity for ripe effects of (often paratragic) incongruity—from the weeping puppies in *Wasps* to the 'baby'-snatching in *Thesmophoriazusae*, from the sex-starved Cinesias in

[90] Above, p. 133.
[91] Above, pp. 33–7. Dicaeopolis is explicitly a γέρων (above, p. 295 n. 79).
[92] Cf. also old Demos at his moment of contrition: *Eq.* 1354–5.

Lysistrata, declaiming on behalf of his bereft foreskin, 'as if it were a motherless daughter', to the desperate Megarian and his daughters in *Acharnians* ('Would you rather be sold, or starve?'—'Be sold, be sold!')—but never for pathos.[93]

More significant for our purposes are Aristophanes' versions of the tragic reunion or 'home at last' scene—

> O dearest light . . .
> O voice, you have come? . . .
>
> O much-missed day[94]—

which vary from the inspirationally quaint, like the lip-smacking Dicaeopolis' call to a Theban eel (*Acharnians* 885–6),

> ὦ φιλτάτη σὺ καὶ πάλαι ποθουμένη,
> ἦλθες ποθεινὴ μὲν τρυγῳδικοῖς χοροῖς . . .
>
> O dearest one, much missed
> By choruses in comedy, you have come . . .

to the true and extraordinary *locus* of pathos, *Peace* 582–600, already considered in part and worth reconsidering now in full:[95]

> χαῖρε χαῖρ'· ὡς ἀσμένοισιν ἦλθες ἡμῖν, φιλτάτη·
> σῷ γὰρ ἐδάμην πόθῳ
> δαιμόνια βουλόμενος 585
> εἰς ἀγρὸν ἀνερπύσαι.
> ἦσθα γὰρ μέγιστον ἡμῖν κέρδος, ὦ ποθουμένη,
> πᾶσιν ὁπόσοι γεωρ-
> γὸν βίον ἐτρίβομεν· 590
> καὶ μόνη γὰρ ὠφέλεις.
> πολλὰ γὰρ ἐπάσχομεν
> πρίν ποτ' ἐπὶ σοῦ γλυκέα
> κἀδάπανα καὶ φίλα·
> τοῖς ἀγροίκοισιν γὰρ ἦσθα χίδρα καὶ σωτηρία. 595
> ὥστε σὲ τά τ' ἀμπέλια
> καὶ τὰ νέα συκίδια
> τἄλλα θ' ὁπόσ' ἐστὶ φυτὰ
> προσγελάσεται λαβόντ' ἄσμενα. 600

[93] *Vesp.* 976–81, *Thes.* 689–761, *Lys.* 954–8 (where ταυτηνί is the ψωλήν of 979), *Ach.* 733–5. On these and other relevant passages, see Silk, 'Pathos', 95–8 (where, however, the generalization of the term 'parody' is not helpful: cf. above, p. 351 n. 2).

[94] Soph. *El.* 1224–5, Eur. *Hel.* 623: above, p. 196.

[95] Above, pp. 196–7. For fuller discussion of the tragic pattern and related passages (*Av.* 676–80, *Thes.* 912–13, and esp. *Pax* 551–9), see Silk, 'Pathos', 98–101.

> You're come, dear lady: missed you, we did, yes,
> Direly, wanting to repossess
> My land. Lady much-missed, you helped us live,
> When you, and no one else, did give
> Us farmers much—
> Sweet, cost-free, welcome—once, in time of peace.
> To country-folk you meant oats and salvation.
> So now vine, figlet, all the plants, touch
> You and smile in glad acclamation.

In an earlier chapter, we discussed the intimate tone of this lyric, its equation of emotive tragic one-to-one relationship and a community's 'love' of peace, and the way the tragic resonance serves to revalue the paraphernalia of rural life upwards.[96] All these remarkable features of the writing, we can now see, contribute to the exploration of a strange, new version of contemplative-humorous pathos, which centres, as so often, on the emotional rhythm of a '*once* but *now*'. Like Dicaeopolis with his eel, the chorus begin their greeting to their returning goddess with a statement of mode and a defining allusion to the paratragic. But this chorus, being a chorus of old countrymen,[97] has an old countryman's memory of peaceful country life as it once was, and as the chorus invoke their memories, the idioms of paratragedy ('. . . come, dear . . . missed . . . missed . . .') disappear. In their place, a switch to plain language ('us farmers', 'cost-free') triggers that distinctive Aristophanic pathos, crystallizing here around the phrase πρίν ποτ' ἐπὶ σοῦ, 'once, in your time', meaning 'once, in time of peace'. If there is an external resonance here, it is—disconcerting as it may seem—from that most pathetic moment in early Greek literature, when the bright star of Hector is about to be snuffed out, as Achilles chases him past the springs of Scamander and the washing tanks where the women of Troy used to wash their clothes,

> τὸ πρὶν ἐπ' εἰρήνης, πρὶν ἐλθεῖν υἷας Ἀχαιῶν.
>
> Once, in time of peace, before the Achaeans came.[98]

[96] Above, pp. 196–7.

[97] Notwithstanding complications about the 'character' of this chorus (above, p. 235), its γῆρας (336) does not seem to change during the play.

[98] *Il.* 22. 156. On the pathos of this passage, see Silk, *Iliad*, 65–6, and 'Pathos', 104–5.

But any such evocation lasts only a moment. Our concern is the gains of peace, characteristically summed up as 'oats and salvation', and through this paradigmatic phrase (comic concrete, 'tragic' abstract),[99] we modulate to a most delicate and unexpected humour, with the vision of the young plants smiling on their old benefactress, before the closing 'glad' (ἄσμενα) deftly restores the context of reunion.[100] Given humour of such delicacy, pathos, however restrained, can survive. Pathos and humour converge, in fact, on the charming diminutive συκίδια ('figlet').[101]

The choral song is humorous, but moving as well, despite the customarily extravagant context, which on this occasion subsumes an improbable clutch of deities: Hermes, Peace, and her two well-endowed female attendants. That such grotesque contexts can permit pathos as well as, and even alongside, humour is one of Aristophanes' remarkable achievements. And the achievement is only possible because of his ability to make his grotesque recreated worlds believable, as comic entities, and to articulate them in terms derived from even a source so potentially distracting as tragedy, without destroying their autonomy.[102]

This complex achievement is sufficiently remarkable to warrant consideration of parallels, by way of corroboration. There are indeed few available. One, close but slighter than the Aristophanic, involves the comic verse of Victorian England: specifically, Edward Lear's use of Tennyson in 'The Courtship of the Yonghy-Bonghy-Bò'. The particular Tennysonian original that seems to be mainly at work in Lear's piece is 'The Lady of Shalott', which begins with a depiction of Arthurian Camelot:

[99] Above, pp. 205–6.

[100] ἄσμενα (600) specifically recalls ἀσμένοισιν (583).

[101] Seemingly coined from σῦκον for this passage, but prepared by the parallel, familiar form ἀμπέλια (596–7), which is attested both in earlier A (*Ach.* 512) and in plain prose (Hp. *Mul.* 1. 78 and *Nat. Mul.* 109). In effect, συκ. is the beginning of the miniature image (smiling plants) and ἀμπ. makes it interactive (pivotal to the vehicle in parallel structure: Silk, *Interaction*, 89–93). With *Pax* 596–7 cf. a touch of pathos in embryo at *Ach.* 996–7 (νέα μοσχίδια . . . γέρων) and the comments by Parker, *Songs*, 16–17.

[102] In the corresponding passage of 'Pathos' (p. 101), I spoke of grotesque 'fantasy-worlds'—infelicitously, as I now think: cf. above, pp. 190–1. Coexistence of pathos with the grotesque may, in original performance, obviously have involved coexistence with the *physical* grotesque (phallus etc.: above, p. 8, with n. 15), *passim*.

On either side the river lie
Long fields of barley and of rye,
That clothe the wold and meet the sky;
And through the field the road runs by
  To many-towered Camelot;
And up and down the people go,
Gazing where the lilies blow
Round an island there below,
  The island of Shalott . . .
Four gray walls, and four gray towers,
Overlook a space of flowers,
And the silent isle imbowers
  The Lady of Shalott.

After a sad sequence of events, in which the Lady's hopes of romance are shown to be cursed, and she dies, the poem ends:

Lancelot mused a little space;
He said, 'She has a lovely face;
God in his mercy lend her grace,
  The Lady of Shalott.'

Lear's poem evokes Tennyson's rhythm, his incantatory repetitions, some of his phraseology, his theme of lost romance, and the emotion to go with it. The emotion is transplanted, however, into the grotesque setting of the fabulous Coast of Coromandel, where the might-have-been romantic pair are the Lady Jingly Jones, busy with her milk-white hens of Dorking, and the Yonghy-Bonghy-Bò himself, whose defining features are his tiny body, large head, and honourable intentions. The poem begins:

On the Coast of Coromandel
Where the early pumpkins blow,
In the middle of the woods
Lived the Yonghy-Bonghy-Bò.
Two old chairs, and half a candle,
One old jug without a handle,
These were all his worldly goods:
In the middle of the woods,
These were all the worldly goods,
Of the Yonghy-Bonghy-Bò,
Of the Yonghy-Bonghy-Bò.

Here we note, in particular, Lear's 'Where the early pumpkins blow' against Tennyson's 'Gazing where the lilies blow', and

Lear's 'Two old chairs, and half a candle' against Tennyson's 'Four gray walls, and four gray towers'.[103] Lear's poem, however, is clearly not any kind of satirical parody. His allusions are not concentrated enough for that, and in any case they become fainter as the poem proceeds. What Lear is doing, wittingly or not, is using Tennysonian idiom, as the dominant idiom of mid-nineteenth-century English verse,[104] to help create his own bizarre composite, which is, for the most part, ludicrously more remote than anything in Tennyson ('Lived the Yonghy-Bonghy-Bò'), but sometimes considerably more solid ('Two old chairs, and half a candle'). The presence of Tennyson is strong enough to carry with it the melancholy tone which is so characteristic of his writing. Yet it is Lear's very un-Tennysonian switch to the solid, but potentially sad, particularity of the 'two old chairs' that begins to focus the melancholy and activate it as a faint, transmuted pathos in its own right. Once established, and despite intermittent lurches towards the sentimental, the mode is precariously maintained, through Lear's eccentric hybrid idiom—

> 'Your proposal comes too late,
> Mr Yonghy-Bonghy-Bò!
> I would be your wife most gladly!'
> (Here she twirled her fingers madly)
> 'But in England I've a mate!'—

up to the inevitable end:

> From the Coast of Coromandel
> Did that Lady never go . . .
>
> On that little heap of stones
> To her Dorking Hens she moans
> For the Yonghy-Bonghy-Bò.

In so far as Lear succeeds in avoiding a descent into sentimentality, even at the end, it is because of the distancing effect of

[103] Lear's opening rhythm and rhyme, as well as the contents of the second line, may themselves have influenced another Tennysonian poem, 'Frater Ave Atque Vale': 'Row us out from Desenzano, to your Sirmione row! . . . There beneath the Roman ruin where the purple flowers grow' (cf. n. 104 below). There are, no doubt, additional influences on Lear's own composition (Longfellow's 'By the shore of Gitche Gumee'—'The Song of Hiawatha', 1855—for one).

[104] 'The Lady of Shalott' was published in 1832, Lear's poem (written originally as a song) in 1877. 'Frater Ave Atque Vale' (n. 103 above) dates from 1880 (publ. 1883).

'Dorking Hens' and the hero's ubiquitous name, against which background the simple word 'never' acquires a curious finality. And in so far as pathos is not simply swamped by cruder emotion, it may be said that Lear's pathos exists as much *because of* the grotesque aspects of his piece as in spite of them. The point is equally applicable to Aristophanes.

It also needs to be said that the scale of achievement represented by Greek tragedy compared with Tennyson's poem is, no doubt, roughly equivalent to that represented by Aristophanes compared with Edward Lear's. And that the very precariousness of Lear's miniature triumph serves to point up the scope of Aristophanes' success.

* * *

Aristophanes' perpetual agon with tragedy produces a multitude of allusions and recreations of material and form. Through it he achieves both a measure of self-definition and, ultimately, an assertion of his own independence. In the instances under review he shows the power to use disparate materials, including tragic originals, to create something hugely comic, yet also productive of pathos; and the pathos created is wholly distinct from anything associated with tragedy.

Greek tragedy appeals predominantly to the primary sympathetic emotions ('pity'). Evocations of pity are not characteristic of Aristophanic comedy—though weak and ill-used characters abound there—and for two reasons. The first is Aristophanes' exploitation of satire and other modes of distance; the second is the discontinuities of comic action and reaction which make us less able, and less inclined, to put ourselves in a character's place ('identification'). Tragedy's emotional power presupposes the continuity which modern audiences and readers, in the wake of Aristotle, find so characteristic of the genre. This continuity (we hope to have established) is a matter both of cumulative-logical construction and of style. The more or less continuous stylization of tragic language, on the one hand, and tragedy's dramatic continuity, on the other, are ultimately one continuity; equally, the discontinuities of action in Aristophanic comedy are correlative to those stylistic discontinuities which we have discussed at length and whose association with pathos we have noted.

Greek tragedy undoubtedly generates pathos. But the powerful continuities of tragedy are not, in themselves, conducive to pathos and are, on the contrary, hospitable to the stronger, primary emotions. This is especially obvious in respect of characters who suffer unjustly. We pity the blighted Cadmus in *Bacchae*, the helpless children in *Medea*, the anguished Neoptolemus in *Philoctetes*, and pathos in the strict sense is not registered as a part of our response, or not distinctively so. In so far as Shakepearean tragedy is more inclined to discontinuity than its Attic counterpart, it presents greater opportunities for pathos. And correspondingly, pathos may be much more readily recognizable in Greek tragedy at its less characteristic moments of discontinuity. Consider, for instance, the poignant moment in *Choephori* when Clytemnestra pleads to Orestes for her life, as mother to son, and the confident avenger, poised to kill her, startles us by hesitating, by turning back to the hitherto mute Pylades for advice—and to our complete surprise Pylades speaks (899–900):

ΟΡ. Πυλάδη, τί δράσω; μητέρ' αἰδεσθῶ κτανεῖν;
ΠΥ. ποῦ δαὶ τὸ λοιπὸν Λοξίου μαντεύματα . . . ;

OR. Pylades, what do I do? Am I to spare my mother?
PYL. Apollo's oracles—what becomes of them . . . ?

The sincerity of Clytemnestra's appeal is beside the point. Orestes' reaction attests its power; and the dislocation that results has a sudden, sublime, arresting effect, through which we seem to feel the collision of two lives as a moment out of ordinary lived time, 'at the still point of the turning world'. Identification in the ordinary sense is not available to us: this is true pathos.[105]

Such discontinuities are perhaps less characteristic of tragedy than of any of the other main poetic genres.[106] Greek tragedy does, of course, favour a pattern whereby dramatic specifics make way for melancholy general truth. Take, for instance, the junction in Sophocles' *Oedipus Tyrannus* between Oedipus' desolate cry (1184–5),

> . . . πέφασμαι φύς τ' ἀφ' ὧν οὐ χρῆν, ξὺν οἷς τ'
> οὐ χρῆν ὁμιλῶν, οὕς τέ μ' οὐκ ἔδει κτανών.
>
> Shown up! I am son, consort, killer of those
> I must not, must not, never should have been.

[105] Cf. Silk, 'Tragic language', 474–5.
[106] Cf. Silk, 'Pathos', 104–5, on *Il.* 22 and Pind. *Isth.* 7.

and the chorus's declaration of universal truth (1186–8):

> ἰὼ γενεαὶ βροτῶν,
> ὡς ὑμᾶς ἴσα καὶ τὸ μη-
> δὲν ζώσας ἐναριθμῶ.
>
> O mortal generations,
> How close to nothing are your lives:
> Make audit.[107]

But such tragic shifts from particular to general are most marked when, as here, they are predictable shifts from speech to choral song. These shifts are stylized—they are a function, of course, of the stylized differential stability that is a feature of Greek tragedy—and the pathos they provoke is like a stylized, therefore less urgent, equivalent of the quality we have been endeavouring to define.

Aristophanic pathos (it must be plain) is quite distinct from anything in tragedy. It may involve the appropriation of material that once belonged to tragedy, but it is not itself derived from tragedy. Given its intimate connection with discontinuity, that most Aristophanic of mechanisms, it should be seen not as some alien growth in a comic environment, but as natural to Aristophanes. From its relationship with pathos, meanwhile, it follows that discontinuity itself is more than a disruptive force. Disruptive it certainly is—by virtue of the explosion we associate with the image, the switch of style, the instant obscenity, the unpredicted appeal to the audience, the sudden joke. Yet it is also constructive.

Discontinuity defamiliarizes. As such (to borrow the vogue language of the 1960s) it is a part, not just of Aristophanes' medium: it is a part, and a significant part, of his message. In this characteristic usage a comic vision is implicit: a vision founded on the defamiliar, on a surprising perception of life, on surprise itself. Comedy in general tends to work through surprise: here as elsewhere we confront the thought that Aristophanic comedy represents the comic in an unusually pure form. The comic vision of Aristophanes is not without its disturbing quality (think of the end of *Thesmophoriazusae* or the premise of *Knights*), but (outside *Clouds*) it is generally a positive vision. It is in the first instance a vision of unlimited possibility, and in this it is diametrically opposed to the New Comic tradition, with all its

[107] See further Silk, 'Tragic language', 484–8.

restriction, its generic specificity, its characteristic closing-down. The explorations of mode discussed earlier in this chapter constitute, by themselves, a radical opening-up of possibility: this is certainly part of the vision enacted by Aristophanes' comedy.

At one extreme the vision subsumes the celebration of coincidence—the random pun, the opportunist joke. Coincidence, though, is commonly too random for Aristophanes: there is nothing random about his modal experimentation, his thematic unity, or his sensuous control. More centrally, the vision proclaims what Dürrenmatt called an 'unformed world',[108] alternative versions of which are created, or recreated, with an abundant energy in play after play. It is an unformed world, none of whose alternative versions (to the despair of those who hope to tie Aristophanes to serious–sincere attitudes of a real-political kind) can claim to be wholly definitive. It is an open-ended world, whose ends are foreclosed by the realist-Aristotelian-Bergsonian comedy of the next century, where more or less ordinary characters aspire to lives of expediency, moderation, and conformity to pre-existing norms: 'how to do your life some good', 'there's no pleasure in excess'.[109] The Aristophanic vision of an unformed world does, up to a point, subsume the concern of the ordinary man with everyday 'frustrations, discomforts and longing for a better life',[110] just as, up to a point, it subsumes the public preoccupation of the *dêmos* with war and peace, fashionable educators and leaders. But its dreams—even on the level of a better life and preoccupation with mistrusted leaders—go beyond either, grounded as they may be in both (*Knights* 164–8):

> —Of all these thou shalt be the lord
> And of the market, harbours, Pnyx:
> Walk over Council, prune the generals,
> Lock them up, string them up, get it up in the Prytaneum.
> —Who, me?[111]

The little man who craves revenge on the 'them' that have (he thinks) exploited him or kept him down may have his prejudices reinforced by Dicaeopolis' contempt for ambassadors

[108] Above, p. 92.
[109] Ar. *Pl.* 38 *τῷ βίῳ τοῦτ' αὐτὸ νομίσας ξυμφέρειν*, Alexis 256 *PCG τὰ πέριττα μισῶ· τοῖς ὑπερβάλλουσι γὰρ | τέρψις μὲν οὐκ ἔνεστι.*
[110] Handley, 'Comedy', 377.
[111] Above, pp. 153–4.

and informers; he will perhaps be surprised by the idea of a private peace. *L'homme moyen sensuel* may well find something 'natural' in the physicality of Dicaeopolis' phallic song, but could hardly have the same response to its hybrid mode. The private peace and the hybrid mode upset preconceived notions of low and high, us and them, and thereby challenge the very categories of the ordinary man's perception. Above all, the placing—and even displacing—of the political, in *Wasps* in particular, constitutes such a challenge. It is easy to imagine 'the ordinary man' relating, as of right, to the allegory in Philocleon's name; harder to imagine him taking as read the way Philocleon goes beyond his name in his heightened existence at the end of the play.

It is not that Aristophanes celebrates free spirits, exactly—as if Dicaeopolis and Philocleon were put forward as individual role-models: they are, for better and worse, not 'individual' in the necessary sense, and what is celebrated is, rather, free *spirit* as such. Nor is it that the unformed worlds—by contrast with the realism of later comedy—are essentially escapist or utopian: they are no more escapist than the mythic worlds of tragedy, and (though there is indeed more to say about the worlds constructed in *Peace* and *Birds* and, later, *Ecclesiazusae*) Aristophanic comedy is not given over to any utopian rejection of the here-and-now.[112] The here-and-now is not rejected but subsumed.

From Paphlagon-Cleon in *Knights* to Right in *Clouds* to (yes) Aeschylus in *Frogs*, Aristophanic individuals are in obvious ways deformed and degraded—but the *possibility* they represent is celebrated—even the possibility represented by Paphlagon-Cleon, which has its immortal tribute both in the appalling exuberance of the contest with Sausage-Seller and (since the 'qualities' of the two are so kindred) in the appalling triumph of Sausage-Seller himself. The character Paphlagon, of course, is himself excluded from the characters and chorus who do the eventual celebrating within the play, condemned as he is to ply the lonely trade of his erstwhile rival, Sausage-Seller, at the symbolic margin of the community, the city gates (*Knights*

[112] On the utopian in A, compare and contrast: Sutton, *Self*, 55–68, 83–92; B. Zimmermann, 'Utopisches und Utopie in den Komödien des Aristophanes', *WüJbb* 9 (1983) 57–77; and the essays in Dobrov, *City*, esp. the thoughtful discussion by D. Konstan, 'The Greek polis and its negations', 3–22.

1398–401);[113] and yet—almost by a kind of Hegelian synthesis—the energy he represents is retained. If any Aristophanic characters and what they stand for (besides the special case of Socrates in *Clouds*) are utterly excluded, it is the 'agelasts', the interferers, like the informers in *Acharnians*, who are bent on reining back the expansive spirits in their pursuit of possibility.[114]

At this point the lesson of *Thesmophoriazusae* takes on a new significance, perhaps: the pull towards reconciliation is stronger than the instinct for division. Once again we can see why Aristophanes is not likely to end up as a 'serious' political writer: he lacks, not only a consistent solidarity, but (more particularly and more obviously) any consistent or comprehensive sense of an Other, against which the solidarity can be defined. In the twentieth century, with his eye on the dramatic audience as well as the drama itself, Brecht articulates the issue with his peculiar combination of clarity and extremity:[115]

> In calling for a direct impact, the aesthetics of the day call for an impact that flattens out all social and other distinctions between individuals. . . . A collective entity is created in the auditorium for the duration of the entertainment, on the basis of the 'common humanity' shared by all spectators alike. [Brechtian drama] . . . is not interested in the establishment of such an entity. It divides its audience.

Brechtian epic theatre *is*, quintessentially, political theatre, and politics *is* division, in Greece or anywhere else.[116] Aristophanic satire, like all satire, is in principle divisive: one figure, or one group, is satirized; another (made explicit or not) is exempt; and we are invited to side with the exempt. This is the solidarity of the part, as opposed to other parts, the group as opposed to other groups; the joke, as we say, is within the family, and those outside are excluded from it.

This, ultimately, is not the spirit of Aristophanic comedy,

[113] Cf. Bowie, *Aristophanes*, 53, and Silk, 'Space and solitude'.

[114] 'The typical Aristophanic antagonist is a kill-joy, whom Rabelais and Meredith have termed the agelast': Sutton, *Self*, 51. 'Typical', however, is overstated—and one should note in particular that authority-figures are sometimes ridiculed (like most of the visitors, human or divine, to the birds' new city in *Av.*), sometimes not (like the magistrate in *Thes.* and the commissioner in *Lys.*).

[115] Brecht, *Versuche* V-VIII, 237 : from notes on *Die Mutter* (1933). In the original, 'for the duration of the entertainment ('für die Dauer des Kunstgenusses') is emphasized.

[116] *ἕτερον γὰρ συμμαχία καὶ πόλις*, Arist. *Pol.* 1261^{a}24–5.

which does project a sense of solidarity, but solidarity of a more elusive—and open—kind. When Dicaeopolis cries out 'O City city' (*Acharnians* 27), solidarity is co-extensive with the community of Athens, in which spirit even—or especially?—Dionysus can become a god with a distinctly Attic mission (*Frogs* 1418–19):

> ἐγὼ κατῆλθον ἐπὶ ποιητήν. τοῦ χάριν;
> ἵν' ἡ πόλις σωθεῖσα τοὺς χοροὺς ἄγῃ.
>
> I came down for a poet, to save the city
> And its dramatic festivals.[117]

Yet the instances of *Peace* and, above all, *Lysistrata*, where in the end Spartans and Athenians combine in pan-Hellenic celebration, show that Aristophanic solidarity is not limited to Athens—and it is noteworthy that even in *Acharnians*, where Megarians and Boeotians are not exactly treated as Dicaeopolis' next of kin, they are nevertheless treated with more respect than most men of Athens, from General Lamachus to farmer Dercetes, who turned their backs on peace.[118] In *Birds*, at the other extreme, Athenian man ends up as lord and master of Sovereignty, and hence notional ruler of the universe[119]—within which scheme of things Athens and Greece as a whole must be subsumed in fact, but in effect seem to be bypassed.

Even the Aristophanic agon, which seems to build division into the plays, is not all it seems. Here too division is not decisive: it is an essentially provisional state of affairs, and most obviously where the agon takes place between the questing individual and the chorus, as in *Acharnians* and *Birds*. Here the chorus initially represents an opposition to the individual which, left to itself, would use violence against him, but which agrees first to debate and then to be persuaded.[120] However grotesque the terms of

[117] With attribution of the lines (sc. entirely to Dionysus) as Dover. On the 'especially' Dionysiac aspect of the lines, cf. Lada-Richards, *Dionysus*, 220.

[118] The most revealing instance of all is the farmer, who, though a fellow-worker of Dicaeopolis, is denied a 'drop of peace' (1033–5), implicitly for this reason: cf. Dicaeopolis' comments on the bride (1061–2) and see above, p. 296. Megarians and Boeotians: cf. MacDowell, *Aristophanes and Athens*, 71–5. Panhellenism in *Pax*: A. C. Cassio, *Commedia e partecipazione* (Naples 1985) 139–45.

[119] 'Sovereignty', i.e. *Basileia*—whether Βασίλεια or Βασιλεία: see Bowie, *Aristophanes*, 163–5; MacDowell, *Aristophanes and Athens*, 217–18; Dunbar on *Av.* 1531–6.

[120] Persuasion is of the essence: see e.g. *Ach.* 626 μεταπείθει, *Av.* 460 ἀναπείσων (text as Dunbar, q.v.).

debate, the existence of this pattern is significant. It is as if, when one party defeats the other, the losing party is in a ritual sense included and, if not validated, at least recognized.

All in all, as far as solidarity is concerned, the comedy of Aristophanes is a world away from Brecht's divisive drama and (here at least) closer to Bakhtin's carnival, which opens up the prospect of a solidarity 'universal in scope', beyond all hierarchies, divisiveness, and negativity.[121] Aristophanic comedy does of course have its negativities, its divisive satire, its contests, its exclusions, its insistence on boundaries (if only, and always, the boundaries of the festival competition) that preclude any universal dissolution. And yet it too opens up the prospect of an open solidarity. The unformed world is an open world, pregnant with possibility. The prerequisite is an open interest: the kind of interest that satire is too dismissive to encompass—the kind of interest that is both (in Coleridge's idiom) 'contemplative' and even (in Pirandello's) 'perplexed'.[122] The Aristophanic vision requires possibility to be left open and not to be closed down prematurely. Hence, for instance, a curious characteristic of the agon, where a Paphlagon-Cleon and a Sausage-Seller compete in pursuit of verbal supremacy. In Greek oratorical practice the assumption is that the opening speaker has an advantage—yet in the Aristophanic agon the opening speaker usually loses.[123] Why so? Because (perhaps) the opening represents the established, the given, the actual, and the characteristic movement within Aristophanes' comic logic is for the actual to be modified into the possible. The 'interest'—including the 'perplexed interest'—that Pirandello saw as the very heart of humour was, for Pirandello, vested in individuals. With Aristophanes this is not so. Initiatory speech and activity is, necessarily, embodied in individuals, but the 'interest' is in their words and actions: the configurations of possibility in which they participate. The baffled Commissioner in *Lysistrata*, faced with the heroine's powers of argument and imagery, perhaps constitutes a rare exception:[124] here is a Pirandelloesque 'perplexity' transferred to a character. Elsewhere, and

[121] Above, p. 76. 'Closer to carnival': notwithstanding the differences (above, p. 299 with n. 96).

[122] Above, pp. 76 (Pirandello) and 381–2 (Coleridge).

[123] See Sommerstein on *Nub.* 941.

[124] *Lys.* 387–613: cf. my discussion of 587–99 in 'Pathos', 95–6.

in general, the 'interest' is articulated in terms that—to say it once more—subsume but go beyond the individual.

Only in *Clouds* are the horizons of seeming possibility—demarcated here between the outlandish Socrates and the modestly grotesque Strepsiades—drastically shrunk. The openness denied in *Clouds* is the openness enacted everywhere—by the victories of the second speaker, by ubiquitous recreative imagery, by the final image of role-playing in *Thesmophoriazusae*: the drama, and the *dramatis personae*, can become *this* or *this* or *this* or—only take away the becoming, and no more possibility, therefore no more drama, is left.

The possibility of becoming may be seen as one of the two principal co-ordinates of Aristophanes' comic vision; the other is the necessity of connecting. If possibility is associable with Aristophanes' penchant for the defamiliar, connection is to be related to his deep instinct for the particular, the concrete, the immediate: the physical delights of food, drink, and sex; the stylistic accumulations of diversities and the sensuousness of sound and image; the physicalities of traditional rural Athens; all the experiential rituals and rhythms that Dicaeopolis yearns for as he sits 'longing for his parish' (*Acharnians* 33), everything he conjures up in the phallic song, everything in sight or in store as the chorus finally hail him 'and his wineskin' (1234) at that supreme moment of converging celebrations—for Dicaeopolis in the play, for the performers and the poet himself in the ritual competition.

It is Pirandello, again, who warns us against ascribing to 'the humorist' the abstracted concentration that characterizes 'art in general' and its quest to make life 'reasonable' and 'coherent'.[125] Aristophanes is not abstract, indeed not—in any dissociated sense of rationality—'reasonable'. His primary responses, certainly, are to the here-and-now, the particular in time and place—however much an Aristophanic particular is liable to recreate the here-and-now and to embody a larger reference, and however much an Aristophanic world will frustrate any expectation of a stable relationship with the pre-existing world to which its connections belong.

Aristophanic comedy's essential connection is, of course, with a pre-existing Athens and its citizens' collective memory—of

[125] Above, p. 95.

Marathon, of country life, of the festival institutions and their traditional celebratory resonances. The natural repositories of memory are the old—which, in an essentially male-dominated society, means old men. *Hence* the special suitability of old men both for the choruses and the casts of Aristophanic drama,[126] in whom—and *only* in whom—the special quality of pathos is embodied. Unlike the comedy of manners, from Menander onwards, Aristophanes does not celebrate youth and youthfulness, celebratory though Aristophanic comedy is. Instead he has his old men look back to it—

> And prove that age can beat the younger set:
> All kiss-curls, style, and sodomy[127]—

and return to it in triumphant rejuvenation. By rejuvenating the old—embodiments of tradition, but also emblems of decline and exhaustion—Aristophanes affirms connection and possibility together.

The formula, connection and possibility, helps to shed further light on the problematic end of *Frogs* and the wholly problematic *Clouds*. In both plays the two co-ordinates have been dissociated and opposed. In *Frogs* the contesting parties, the solution to whose contest seems so arbitrary, are all but direct embodiments, Aeschylus of connection, Euripides of possibility. It is as if Aristophanes has allowed himself—in a spirit of wholly admirable humorous 'interest'—to construct the antithesis on this basis, only to demonstrate precisely the schematic equivalence that the comic Dionysus acknowledges—

> I swear by Zeus our saviour, I can't decide[128]—

but then obliterates that interest by denying the equivalence in the final imposition of one co-ordinate on the other. In *Clouds*, more drastically, possibility is vested in a satirical caricature (Socrates), connection in an old countryman (Strepsiades), initially passive and generally inept. As we have argued, a conceivable allegorical reading (thinking man versus material man, cynical modernity

[126] There are, no doubt, other reasons on other levels, including the satirist's suspicion of any innovation—against which the elderly are always likely antagonists: cf. E. W. Handley, 'Aristophanes and the generation gap', in Sommerstein, *Tragedy, Comedy and the Polis*, 417–30.

[127] *Vesp.* 1068–70: above, pp. 389 ff.

[128] *Ran.* 1433: above, p. 366.

versus obtuse tradition) is hardly justified.[129] Instead, we should frankly admit the negativity of both portrayals and the consequent closing-down of 'interest', in the sense in which we are using the word.

In both plays possibility is equated with modernity and eventually dismissed by association with the negative implications of the equation. In contenting himself with that equation and those implications, Aristophanes (we are now in a position to see) is doing his creative intelligence less than justice. In an age of cultural transition and experiment, a composite movement like the new Enlightenment is no doubt fair game for satirical treatment:

> *τοῦτον τὸν ἄνδρ' ἢ βιβλίον διέφθορεν*
> *ἢ Πρόδικος ἢ τῶν ἀδολεσχῶν εἷς γέ τις*
>
> He's done for:
> It was a book that did it; maybe Prodicus;
> One of the chattering classes anyway.[130]

More fundamentally, the dissociation that is implicit in an astonishingly accelerated development of the life of the mind—a dissociation, in effect, between traditional connections and new possibilities—is indeed fraught with problems for a 'whole' response to life, as well as opportunities for new thought and new art. But (or and) Aristophanes is himself implicated in the new. For all that his breadth and immediacy of response to existing art and life may reveal him as a marvellous product of, or advertisement for, experiential unity, he is also an innovator whose very commitment to (for instance) radical experimentation with new modes affirms his modernity. In flatly condemning the new Enlightenment, he is condemning not only some of the most impressive features of the age—from the sophistic to the tragic[131]—but also partly condemning himself; and the paradox is writ large in *Clouds*, which invents a novel mode of drama to convince us of the dangers of novelty, as it is in the arbitrary end of *Frogs*, whose author summarily dismisses, as if beneath consideration, the Euripides on whom he has lavished half a creative

[129] Above, p. 363.
[130] Ar. fr. 506 *PCG* (*Fryers*).
[131] *Inter alia*, it is possible and even plausible to argue that in certain respects the sophists and the tragic poets 'engaged in a shared investigation': H. P. Foley, *Helios* 15 (1988) 66 (in a review of Goldhill, *Reading Greek Tragedy*).

lifetime of considered interest. The *interested* treatment of Euripides in *Thesmophoriazusae*—more ambivalent and more open by far—surely betokens a less dissociated and therefore more fully intelligent and honourable response than the crude simplification of *Clouds* or the opportunism of *Frogs*. *Thesmophoriazusae* is a more 'serious' play—in at least one sense of that word—than the other two.

* * *

Aristophanes' great achievement carries with it limitations, which any responsible assessment must acknowledge. In the first place, we have to note the less productive implications of his discontinuity. On the structural level, discontinuity precludes most of the potential advantages of Aristotelian processive literature—taken for granted by readers of realist writing in all cultures—in terms of development and consequence. The question marks one finds it necessary to put against the very different dénouements of *Knights*, *Thesmophoriazusae*, and *Frogs* illustrate the problem. On a smaller scale—but correlative to the opportunism that helps to engender the final scene in *Frogs*—we have occasions when, for lack of any overriding principle of progressive organization, thematic links are unenforced or momentary exuberance given its head in a hit-or-miss spirit. The result is that, even in the best plays, there are—simply—bits that don't work.

The parabasis, irreducibly unpredictable, provides various examples of material barely integrated or humour that misfires. The inflated and largely inconsequential parabatics of *Thesmophoriazusae* spring to mind. The women of the chorus offer a general apologia for their sex and a selective critique of men (785–845). *Inter alia*, men ride in style at public expense, whereas a woman who helped herself to public money would make sure she repaid it—with a basketful of wheat she'd stolen from her husband (811–13). And though the play is *not* 'men against women' in any significant sense, that last joke, uneventful enough by any standards, is made the foil for some ponderous abuse (814–18),

> ἀλλ' ἡμεῖς ἂν πολλοὺς τούτων
> ἀποδείξαιμεν ταῦτα ποιοῦντας . . .

But this is a true description of you.
Are ye not gluttonous, vulgar, perverse,
Kidnappers, housebreakers, footpads and worse?

after which the chorus resume the defence of the sisterhood (819–20):

καὶ μὲν δή που καὶ τὰ πατρῷά γε
χείρους ἡμῶν εἰσιν σῴζειν . . .

And we in domestic economy too
Are thriftier, shiftier, wiser than you . . .[132]

A writer's inspiration can flag at any time. It is much more likely to do so, perhaps, when a passing idea is not subject to the challenges that the logic of 'organic unity' creates.

Again, the ramifications of discontinuity and non-realism at all levels ensure that value is projected through configurations of mode, pattern, style, not through the exploration of individuals or issues as generally understood. Our finding is that, outside *Clouds* (where the limitations are of a different kind), the treatment of 'issues' is erratic or transmuted, while the kind of human interest we value in Homer and the nineteenth-century novel, in Chekhov and—on a more restricted stage—Menander, is generally absent. Diverse and endlessly impressive as carriers of humour though they are, Aristophanes' recreative characters have little in the way of personality, relationships, or psychological life. If we need fictional characters to identify with and grow with, we should look elsewhere.

Above all, the tension between the popular basis of Aristophanes' comedy and its sophisticated practices (and not least the appropriation of the tragic) has its consequences. As our study of the song-lyrics has shown, the popular is not, in itself, the successful, and (songs apart) it is easy enough to compile a list of popular-sounding, and less than overwhelming, elements which survive more or less unchanged in their dramatic setting: low slapstick, the simpler kinds of obscenity and abuse, 'Megarian humour', the kinds of comic business derided—and exploited—by our poet himself.[133] Here at least is something of the 'ordinary man's vision'—and its limitations.

[132] Text as Sommerstein, transl. as Rogers (whose take-it-or-leave-it, light-verse jolliness seems ideal here).

[133] *Vesp.* 57–61; cf. above, p. 47 n. 12.

Popular art and its limitations in the modern age have been subjected to a sharp critique in Marxian terms by Theodor Adorno. For Adorno modern popular art is a monolith of commercial manipulation in which artistic value and critical perspective are subordinate to commercial success: an art which conditions its listeners (Adorno's main focus is popular music) to accept endless versions of the same, the status quo, the undeveloped rudiment, the atomistic (separate melodies, fragments, 'effects').[134] Adorno makes no claim to be generalizing about (and barely acknowledges) popular art in earlier cultures, and some of the features he lists are distinctively modern and certainly un-Aristophanic—not least the lack of a critical centre. What is of interest for us, though, and particularly in the light of our own analogy between Aristophanes' songs and the (best) products of Tin Pan Alley and Broadway, is how much is the same: the atomism most obviously.[135] Indeed, if for 'commercial success' we substitute success in the comic competition, we have, no doubt, a convenient formula for the immediate rationale of some of the most repetitive, and least consequential, features of Greek comedy, Aristophanic and other.

Yet it is almost always misleading to attach the word 'popular', or its associations, to Aristophanic comedy without qualification. Comedy as a whole is characteristically 'closer to life' than other media or other genres,[136] and Aristophanes himself needs his access to 'the people' and the life of 'the people', just as he feeds on topical issues. But characteristically too the popular elements are combined with others to form a new, and more sophisticated, whole (*Wasps* 65–6):

> ὑμῶν μὲν αὐτῶν οὐχὶ δεξιώτερον,
> κωμῳδίας δὲ φορτικῆς σοφώτερον.
>
> No more sophisticated than *you* are yourselves,
> But more artistic than low comedy.

And here the trouble, as well as the opportunity, begins. The new elements are largely derived from tragedy and ultimately inspired

[134] See esp. Adorno's essay, 'Über den Fetischcharakter in der Musik', 24–6, 34, 46–7.

[135] Above, pp. 268–70. It must follow that Adorno's insistence on associating modern popular art with capitalism loses much of its force, once any kinship with pre-modern art is established.

[136] Above, pp. 91, 95.

by the ideal of authority evoked by tragedy. As such, it is all too easy for problems of accommodation to arise, most obviously when the popular suddenly surfaces in a sophisticated setting (our example from the parabasis in *Thesmophoriazusae* is a case in point)[137] and when the pull of the tragic model is too strong, as it is in the cases of tragic pastiche in the lyrics.

The problems inherent in Aristophanes' appropriation of tragedy have of course their highest profile in *Clouds*. The construction, the ideology, the texture, the whole conception of the play, seem to imply a craving for a tragic respectability and dignity which popular comedy can hardly satisfy. The unanswered question about the relation of comedy to tragedy is raised here in its sharpest form—but in a pragmatic sense answered, soon enough, by what the handbooks call the fourth-century convergence of Old Comedy and Euripidean tragedy. In Menander we see that convergence complete—by which point the possibility that there might be (might have been) some other answer to the question has ceased to matter.

It is not the argument of this book that Aristophanes has no limitations, but that these are the corollaries of his huge virtues, which deserve more admiration and a more informed understanding than they have hitherto had, and that within his overall achievement tragedy is a crucial factor—for ill, but also, and largely, for good. Not only is tragedy the source of so many of his experiments, modal and other; it also provides the essential perspective and point of reference against which Aristophanic comedy asks to be placed. It is arguable that only tragedy, sphere of the universal, could have provided the stimulus to construct a comic vision beyond the demotic and the everyday.

In the light of this argument, we must once more, and more confidently than before, affirm the centrality of Euripides: the writer for whom generic conventions become a laboratory and 'genre' invites 'transgression'; the writer whose experiments (from

[137] A more complex example involves the awkward questions raised by the assimilation of the questing individual, comic-heroic embodiment of possibility, to the popular figure of the trickster (embodiment of *mêtis*: see in general Detienne and Vernant, *Les Ruses*). The energy of (say) a Philocleon in *Vesp.* transcends awkward moral questions (albeit not for all audiences/readers: above, p. 370 with n. 42)—but what of (say) a less vibrant figure like Peisetaerus in *Av.*? 'Idiot,' says Poseidon to Heracles, 'don't you see he's tricked you all along?' (*Av.* 1641): how do *we* respond to this tricky 'he'?

the treatment of the recognition scene in *Electra* to the depth-psychologizing of Pentheus in *Bacchae*) serve both to challenge previous practice and to raise the issues involved to the level of full consciousness; the writer impelled by the intellectual explorations of the age to invent a new kind of 'dramatized debate in sophistic terms and strategies'.[138] This is the writer who clearly meant more to Aristophanes than any other. It was Aristophanes' older contemporary Cratinus (fr. 342) who suggested a link between Euripides as writer and Aristophanes himself, by conjuring up a vignette of a modish artist-intellectual:

> *ὑπολεπτολόγος, γνωμιδιώκτης, εὐριπιδαριστοφανίζων*
>
> Micro-intellectualist, mega-sloganist, Eurip-Aristophanist.

The ancient commentator who quotes the words claims that 'Aristophanes was ridiculed for satirizing Euripides and yet copying him'.[139] The line comes across as more of a tease than a critical *aperçu*. Nevertheless, it serves to situate Euripides firmly at the centre of new Enlightenment preoccupations—and Aristophanes with him. And the three big coined words, deftly concocted to suggest the tone of the new movement, also evoke its pretensions and the critical self-consciousness that underlies them.

It is not, though, that under Euripidean influence Aristophanes devotes his career to a quest for some kind of comitragedy (as Euripides is sometimes seen as inventor of a kind of tragicomedy). The apparent goal is humorous drama with tragedy-derived authority, but with the comic vision intact. As Aristophanes' own protestations seem to confirm, his *œuvre* represents a protracted series of experiments, with (it would seem) Euripides a model experimenter, but not a model for the particular experiments themselves.[140] Only occasionally, and above all in *Clouds*,

[138] See Goldhill, *Reading Greek Tragedy* (222–64), whence the quoted phrases (244, chapter title, 'Genre and transgression', and 238).

[139] *Ἀριστοφάνης δ' ὁ κωμῳδοποιὸς . . . ἐκωμῳδεῖτο . . . ἐπὶ τῷ σκώπτειν μὲν Εὐριπίδην μιμεῖσθαι δ' αὐτόν*: schol. Areth. (B) Pl. *Ap.* 19c (= *PCG* iii. 2. 6, test. 3). The scholiast goes on to quote Ar. fr. 488 *PCG*, a frag. as elusive in context as in detail.

[140] Cf. above, p. 52. The A–Eur. relationship is seldom acknowledged. Recent exceptions include: R. Friedrich, 'Euripidaristophanizein and Nietzschesokratizein', *Dionysius* 4 (1980) 5–36 (who sees A as critical of Euripidean tragedy but under its influence); E. Bobrick, 'The tyranny of roles: playacting and privilege in Aristophanes' *Thesmophoriazusae*', in Dobrov, *City*, 177–97 (who, at 193, speaks of A's 'genuine affinity for Euripides'); and H. J. Tschiedel, 'Aristophanes und

does Aristophanes attempt to write *like* tragedy, or *like* some tragedy-based hybrid, and then (as *Clouds* shows) the attempt involves a threat to humour, or at least his humour, as such. Even in *Clouds* he does not attempt to construct a stable hybrid. That step, which in effect marks the end of Old Comedy, seems to have been taken by the time of *Plutus*, and the relative stability of that play signals that the experiments have come to an end.

It might therefore be said, by way of qualification to our earlier thesis, that Aristophanes can, after all, be credited with one consistent, sustained, 'serious interest' in every sense of the word: his own medium. His relish for 'explaining' his comedy (in the parabasis and elsewhere), for depicting and appropriating Euripides, for so often proclaiming a relationship with tragedy by the use of tragic elements in new contexts and configurations: all this betokens an intense interest in self-definition, for which Euripides—paradigm of the self-conscious experimenter—provides a model. And yet implicit in self-consciouness is dissociation, *therefore* this Euripidean model must be problematic, and *therefore* (if for no other reason) the rejection of Euripides in *Frogs*. At which point in the argument we might well conclude that this rejection is the most significant part of the play's moralized outcome, and not the fact that the beneficiary should be Aeschylus.

The special relationship Aristophanes has with Euripides prompts one further line of thought. At the end of *Frogs*, Euripides is castigated as an associate of Socrates ('sitting down with Socrates and talking', 1491–2), and the same is suggested elsewhere.[141] If these correlations count for anything, the possibility must be entertained that Aristophanes' hostility to the new Enlightenment in *Clouds* is testimony to an awareness of his own implication in the movement and an attempt to exorcise it.[142] Such a violent rejection of self is duly translated into violence on stage—at Socrates' expense.

* * *

Euripides: zu Herkunft und Absicht der Weiberkomödien', *GB* 11 (1984) 29–49 (who argues that A's women heroines show the influence of Eur.).

[141] Above, p. 366. Cf. Ar. fr. 392 *PCG*.

[142] Cf. Bowie, *Aristophanes*, 133.

Aristophanes' use of tragedy is a symptom of the boundless freedom of Aristophanic art. Humour (says Ionesco) *is* freedom,[143] and, utterly beyond the capacity of the social drama that is to succeed it, Aristophanic comedy is free to explore its own limits, even to the point of its own subversion. In this display of freedom, we will find that comic pathos (once again) has a decisive significance, because it can be seen to bring Aristophanes even to the point of confronting the comic impossible: existential intimations, metaphysical constructions, of reality.[144] Only in the final resolution of *Clouds* does he ever make a direct attempt on the forbidden peak, and at the cost of humour: the existential-metaphysical *is* the comic impossible. Yet the authoritative model of tragedy, where that impossible is at home, encourages, perhaps, the aspiration to find some equivalent to the existential-metaphysical in truly comic terms. How can this be done? The question requires us to pick up the theoretical argument about pathos where we left it before.

Aristophanic pathos (to recapitulate and restate), whether or not inspired by the tragic example, is distinct from it. In Aristophanes, pathos is made possible by the discontinuity so characteristic of his work, and exemplifications of pathos outside comedy bear out the association. Not the least significant of these are moments when (as it might be) dramatic specifics collapse into the melancholy general truth. Pathos does not always involve a switch from particular to general, but it does involve an embodied truth, sympathetically presented, which goes beyond any particular, any individual. Our discussion of moments of pathos in (for instance) *Macbeth*—

> She should have died hereafter;
> There would have been a time for such a word.
> To-morrow, and to-morrow, and to-morrow,
> Creeps in this petty pace from day to day—

points to a process of 'sublimation' beyond the individual and the individual's moral qualifications, or disqualifications, for sympathy. We are not concerned with moral principles that transcend

[143] Above, p. 92.

[144] For this surprising argument I derive (again: cf. above, p. 363 n. 24) modest encouragement from Plato, whose presentation of A in *Symposium* gives us not a political satirist, compulsive parodist, or casual entertainer, but a creative inventor of myths about life.

the individual. We are, however, concerned—beyond morality—with the existential, and hence, inevitably, with metaphysics. Coleridge, discussing Wordsworth's pathos, points to the sympathy of a *contemplator* 'from whose view no difference of rank conceals the sameness of the nature', and goes on to invoke the 'superscription and image of the Creator'.[145] The specific religiosity of that formula is unhelpful, but the instinct, which it reveals, to seek the meaning of pathos in the metaphysical, demands our attention.

It is apparent that pathos, or something very like pathos, is sometimes associated with statements of the human condition: 'O mortal generations', 'Tomorrow, and tomorrow, and tomorrow'. Such statements make more or less explicit what, in other versions of pathos, is ultimately implied. They centre on the fact of the individual's transience and mortality, his[146] vulnerability to time, his vulnerability as an essential fact arising from his being sited in time, his subjection not merely to the contingent and (in principle) avoidable misfortunes of ordinary life—becoming poor, becoming disabled, becoming isolated from others—but to the fundamental necessity of *becoming* as such, his being finite and subject to the laws of finitude. This predicament may be conventionally acknowledged by any individual. It is confronted directly, perhaps, only by favoured individuals at enhanced moments, perhaps moments of solitude, perhaps seemingly supernaturally enhanced moments, such as, assuredly, we do not associate with Aristophanes, but find, for instance, in the final chapter of the modern classic by García Márquez:[147]

> Aureliano had never been more lucid in any act of his life as when he forgot about his dead ones and the pain of his dead ones and nailed up the doors and windows again with Fernanda's crossed boards, so as not to be disturbed by any temptations of the world, for he knew then that his fate was written in Melquiádes' parchments . . . It was the history of the family, written by Melquiádes, down to the most trivial details, one hundred years ahead of time . . . Impatient to know his own origin, Aureliano skipped ahead. Then the wind began, warm, incipient, full of voices from the past . . . and he began to decipher the instant that he was

[145] Above, pp. 381–2.

[146] My use of the masculine hereabouts reflects both the cultural assumptions of the theorists under discussion and the realities of A's theatre—not (e.g.) any assumption about the masculinity of pathos *per se*.

[147] *One Hundred Years of Solitude*, 420–2; see further Silk, 'Space and solitude'.

living, deciphering it as he lived it, prophesying himself in the act of deciphering the last page of the parchments, as if he were looking into a speaking mirror. Then he skipped again to anticipate the predictions and ascertain the date and circumstances of his death. Before reaching the final line, however, he had already understood that he would never leave that room, for it was foreseen that the city of mirrors (or mirages) would be wiped out by the wind and exiled from the memory of man at the precise moment when Aureliano Babilonia would finish deciphering the parchments . . .

The fundamental necessity of *becoming*: this predicament is a familiar premise of a hundred metaphysical systems, Greek and other, countless common intuitions, and various religions, from the elaborate intellectual systems of the East to the fertility religion from which Attic comedy is widely taken to have derived. In these diverse contexts it is commonly associated with a complementary conception of that which does *not* become, some inclusive infinite to which all individuals ultimately belong—at which point (as with Coleridge's 'image of the Creator') one crosses the line into the metaphysical, and it is hardly possible to find any words which do not imply commitment to a particular metaphysical or religious system of belief. In the schematic neo-Platonism of the poet Shelley, for instance, 'the one remains, the many change and pass.'[148] 'The one remains', it *is*, whereas 'the many' individal reflexes or embodiments of that unity and infinity 'change and pass': they *become*. In Kierkegaard's version of the predicament, humanity, living in its transience and finitude, yet in some sense partaking of the infinite, sees itself as embodying a contradiction, 'this tremendous contradiction, that the eternal becomes'.[149] Such a contradiction is a problem beyond the power of its subjects to solve, but a problem which—we may say—impinges on the 'contemplative' disposition required to create or comprehend pathos.

Pathos in literature implies an intimation or apprehension of the existential which, when accounted for in abstract language, is commonly, if not inevitably, mediated in metaphysical terms. We may readily agree that much literature, and comedy above all, is extremely poor soil for abstractions, especially metaphysical ones; that not all instances of pathos (and maybe very few in comedy) *in themselves* prompt such apparently lofty thoughts; and that there

[148] Shelley, 'Adonais', st. 52.

[149] Kierkegaard, *Postscript*, 76.

is certainly no specific metaphysical gesture that one is required to make, no specific metaphysical concept that one is required to accommodate, in order to acknowledge and respond to pathos. Even so, it seems impossible to account fully for pathos, if we resist what for convenience may be called its existential, and therefore metaphysical, affinities.[150]

The humorist capable of pathos is to be distinguished from the creator of pure ridicule or pure satire. Whereas the satirist, in particular, offers a critique of one or other worldly problem that afflicts the individual or the group and the prospect or potentiality of a worldly solution, or at least worldly alternative, to it, the humorist is capable of seeing all individuals and all existence as inherently problematic: 'the humorist', says Kierkegaard, 'smiles sadly at existence in time with its breathless haste and illusory decision.'[151] Even if Aristophanes in some moods may be taken for a pure ridiculer or satirist, his pathos by itself reveals a larger perspective and a deeper vision. Unlike Sophocles or Shakespeare—or Kafka—the humorist, however, does not continue to look down the depths to the point where the 'contradiction' seems distractingly painful. 'The humorist', says Kierkegaard, 'comprehends the profundity of the situation, but at the same moment it occurs to him that it is doubtless not worthwhile to attempt an explanation': he 'revokes its essential significance for the existing individual', and this 'revocation' is the moment of humour, or, in Kierkegaard's own words, 'this revocation is the jest.'[152] We have reached this point before;[153] we can now go further. Whatever plausibility Kierkegaard's theory in its precise form may or may not have within his philosophy as a whole, we propose one modification, with which it would seem to shed more light on humour in general and comic pathos in particular. The comic writer sees (it may be) the essential contradiction—but also, and in the same degree, contemplates alternatives to it. Even here, perhaps, he retains what Pirandello called the 'feeling of the

[150] The argument that follows (which modifies that in Silk, 'Pathos'), though conducted largely through Kierkegaard, makes use of insights from Jean Paul and from Pirandello (partly responding to Jean Paul). See e.g. Pirandello, *On Humor*, 16, interpreting humour as 'a philosophical laughter mixed with pain because it stems from the comparison between the small finite world and the infinite idea' (cf. ibid. 108)—which, following Jean Paul, he contrasts with 'vulgar satire'.

[151] Kierkegaard, *Postscript*, 242.

[152] Ibid. 401, 404.

[153] Above, p. 87.

opposite'[154]—and declines to privilege the painful implications of contradiction. He declines to accept that painful implications are *the* truth, the *only* truth, and leaves open the possibility that alternatives, however absurd, *even if* absurd, *especially if* absurd, may be true, or true in a sense, or true too; and if this version of 'the world in its comic aspect' seems to be objectionably relativist, the comic writer can only contemplate a humorous response to *that* response too.[155] As far as potential pain is concerned, the comic writer senses, but—yes—revokes the pain 'for the existing individual', and with it revokes any terms which might evoke the pain directly. Accordingly, comic pathos, however disconcerting, is not painful; and however strongly articulated, it is embodied in finite human lives, without overt reference to anything beyond them. So it is with Aristophanes. Nevertheless, it remains the case that the human lives in which Aristophanes finds pathos are those of old men whose youth has gone for ever. These old men may have their particular topical grievances, but they are not people with purely soluble problems and purely contingent misfortunes—'as if an existing individual would be happy if such and such misfortunes were not there' (Kierkegaard again).[156]

All pathos seems to represent an articulation of the same small set of existential themes, which may be more or less explicit, more or less disguised. In comedy the disguise is heaviest, and clues to what lies behind it may be as modest as Edward Lear's one word 'never':

> From the Coast of Coromandel
> Did that Lady never go . . .

Among our other examples, Hardy's

> I am just the same as when
> Our days were a joy, and our paths through flowers[157]

[154] Above, p. 76.

[155] My 'answer' to the questions posed above, pp. 87–8. On absurdity, see, rather differently, Nietzsche, *Birth of Tragedy*, VII. 'The world in its comic aspect' is Bakhtin: above, p. 76.

[156] *Postscript*, 401. To dispel any possible misconception about my use of Kierkegaard, he has his own thoughts on 'pathos'—including a distinction between 'aesthetic pathos' and 'existential pathos' (ibid. 386–98)—which have little or no direct bearing on my immediate concerns. *Inter alia*, his 'pathos' seems to have too much to do with Greek 'suffering' to be very helpful here.

[157] Above, pp. 400–1 and 378. In 'Pathos', from this point in the argument, I inadvertently converted Hardy's 'just' into 'still' ('I am still the same'). I am

may be taken as a paradigm of the pathetic defiance of 'becoming', just as '*once* but *now*' is a common formula for its acknowledgement. And if we recall the breakthrough into another dimension of feeling and significance that suggests itself as the effect of the mother–son confrontation in *Choephori* ('At the still point of the turning world'), we seem to have, not only a corroboration of the existential sense, but an image of the realization of such a sense in language: an image of the means as well as the effect.

The existential is not easily translated into words. In particular, and paradoxically, it cannot be adequately expressed, but only *described*, in the metaphysical abstractions through which it is commonly mediated. Kierkegaard, speaking in metaphysical abstractions himself, makes the point: 'because abstract thought is *sub specie aeterni*, it ignores the concrete and the temporal, the existential process, the predicament of the existing individual'; 'abstract thought is wont to speak of contradiction . . . although by abstracting from existence and from existing it removes the difficulty and the contradiction'.[158] The point is relatable to the principle enunciated in a quite different connection by F. R. Leavis, responding to Samuel Johnson's criticism of Shakespeare. 'Shakespeare', said Johnson, '. . . seems to write without any moral purpose . . . his precepts drop casually from him; he makes no just distribution of good or evil, nor is always careful to show in the virtuous a disapprobation of the wicked.' 'Johnson', says Leavis, 'cannot understand that works of art *enact* their moral valuations. It is not enough that Shakespeare, on the evidence of his works, "thinks" (and feels) morally: for Johnson a moral judgement that isn't *stated* isn't there.'[159]

To apply Leavis's principle to the present case: the writer sensitive, not merely to the contingent accidents of existence among which we live, but to its necessities, must enact his existential valuation in order to express it. But how is this to be done? Conveying the contingent accidents of existence is hard enough: it is what most writers spend their energies striving to do.

grateful to Guy Lee (who drew my attention to the slip) for the suggestion that in so doing I 'improved' on Hardy, but feel obliged, none the less, to restore Hardy's text.

[158] *Postscript*, 267, 314.

[159] Raleigh, *Johnson on Shakespeare*, 20–1; Leavis, *The Common Pursuit*, 110–11.

A stylized acknowledgement of the necessities of existence is presented by much Greek tragedy ('O mortal generations') and, less forcibly, by a multitude of explicit statements from Hesiod's account of the ages of man to Gray's *Elegy*. But stylization means a stable, consistent idiom which (as postmodernists are fond of saying about language as a whole) constitutes, in itself, its own barrier against the experience of the truths or perceptions it seeks to encompass. We do in fact live among contingencies, in the turning world. Hence any experience of necessities at the 'still point' is only possible in what Nietzsche once called 'moments of sudden illumination';[160] and their expression in words, their experiential articulation, may be achieved, in turn, through sudden moments of arrest and defamiliarizing estrangement which carry with them the sense of a breakthrough into another experiential world which, here, may be experienced as a world beyond the contingent. Hence the characteristic association between pathos and the mechanism of discontinuity. To restate our earlier point: wholly continuous, stable, processive, cumulative literature, dramatic or non-dramatic, will tend to sustain its vulnerable individuals with powerful feelings of identificatory sympathy ('pity'), and to that extent it will tend to sustain them *as* vulnerable individuals in the world of contingency to which pity and individuals belong. The effect may be what Racine called a 'tristesse majesteuse': it will not be pathos in our sense.[161]

Discontinuity, it seems, can effect a breakthrough to another world beyond the contingent, from where the human predicament can be confronted;[162] but short of threatening its own existence (as in *Clouds*), comedy cannot confront any human predicament, unless by simultaneously turning to an alternative, less painful,

[160] 'Über das Pathos der Wahrheit' (1872): Nietzsche, *Werke*, iii. 2. 249.

[161] Preface to *Bérénice* (1670): 'Ce n'est point une nécessité qu'il y ait du sang et des morts dans une tragédie; il suffit que l'action en soit grande, que les acteurs en soient héroïques, que les passions y soient excitées, et que tout s'y ressente de cette tristesse majestueuse qui fait tout le plaisir de la tragédie.' ('There is no need to have blood and deaths in a tragedy; it is enough that the action be grand, the characters heroic, the passions roused, and everything have the feeling of that majestic sadness which constitutes all the pleasure of tragedy.')

[162] Though there are other enacting mechanisms for pathos, notably differential understanding, esp. familiar in the form of dramatic irony: see Silk, 'Pathos', 108–9, and (for a wider context) cf. the discussions by T. G. Rosenmeyer, 'Ironies in serious drama', and N. J. Lowe, 'Tragic and Homeric ironies', in Silk, *Tragedy and the Tragic*, 497–519, 520–33.

reading of the human condition. Yet comedy admits pathos. Comic pathos, then, is comedy's indirect acknowledgement that there is a human predicament of which its own terms of reference preclude any direct expression.

It follows that the association of comedy and pathos is not contradictory but essential. That conclusion becomes the more plausible when we recall (from Aristophanes, and from the lesser instance of Edward Lear) that pathos may exist as much because of, as in spite of, those grotesqueries which are so characteristic of full-blooded comedy, yet, on the face of it, so inimical to the pathetic. And the conclusion may be enforced by an unstated implication of our earlier discussions. While pathos hints, pessimistically enough, at predicaments and vulnerabilities, it is (unlike occasions for pity?) never depressing. Whether because of the contemplative element in the response it calls forth, or the defiance it so often invites us to contemplate, or the 'sudden illumination' it produces, pathos embodies what Nietzsche called 'pessimism of *strength*';[163] hence the affirmative note that is rightly associated with all comedy is not impaired.

It is once again in *Wasps* that these arguments receive their due confirmation and particularization: in that most exuberant of Aristophanes' comedies, where discontinuity and recreativity play so large a part; where politics and satire are subsumed (like the 'Cleon' in Philocleon's name) within a larger, more comprehensive, even universal, perspective; where the necessity of connecting is acknowledged in Philocleon's Athenian preoccupations, but where the possibility of becoming is celebrated in everything that goes beyond them; where the tragic ingredients of new hybrids help to open up the 'interest', not (as in *Clouds*) to close it down; where the comic poet's sensitivity to pathos is most evident and the purest comedy the result.

Like other comedies, *Wasps* has an old chorus which is the focus for pathos. Like other comedies, it also has an old 'hero'. And as in other comedies, this old hero is the beneficiary of an amazing rejuvenation. What makes *Wasps* different from any other Aristophanic comedy is that the pathos associated with the old chorus is coordinated with, and in fact counterpointed against,

[163] In his 'Versuch einer Selbstkritik', prefaced to the 1886 edition of *Die Geburt der Tragödie*: see Silk and Stern, *Nietzsche on Tragedy*, 438 (index, s.v. 'pessimism').

the rejuvenation of the old hero in such a way that each serves as a kind of informative context for the other.[164] It is not that Philocleon, the old hero of *Wasps*, is himself a focus for pathos: on the contrary. It is rather that the grotesque terms of his portrayal, within which his rejuvenation is subsumed, permit a fantasia on the theme of transience which would not be possible from the old chorus alone and which serves as a productive contrast to the presentation of their old age.

Philocleon and the chorus are aligned in age and sympathies: they are 'fellow-jurymen' (266) and 'friends' (317). And like the chorus, Philocleon is poor, physically weak, and presumed to be sexually impotent.[165] He and they, however, do not constitute a group. They are in effect two versions of a single entity: one named version, which is all grotesque excess and near-manic energy, and one, more or less anonymous, which is much closer to moderate normality. The difference is apparent by the time of their first encounter (by which time we have seen *his* bizarre attempts at escape as well as *their* creaking joints), and not least from what each has to say of, and to, the other. Philocleon is a prisoner in his own house, and his fellows, on their way to court, have been speculating about his non-appearance (266–89): has he lost his shoes? has he had an accident? is he ill? Their characterization of him and his likely mishap is humorous, but ordinary enough in its circumstantiality and its moderate, sympathetic tone. By contrast, his own account of himself, when he does appear, is in a musical extravaganza ('How long, how long . . .', 317–33), full of desperation and excess ('Thundering Zeus, turn me to smoke', 323–4).[166] Despite the chorus's additional persona as wasps, this distinction is effectively maintained throughout the play. Thus, after the agon, it is the chorus who comment mildly on Bdelycleon's good sense and express the hope that Philocleon too will become 'sensible' (σωφρονεῖ, 748), whereas Philocleon himself is caught in his paroxysm of melodramatic heroics ('Speed thou, my soul! Soul, where are you?', 756).[167] And later,

[164] The closest parallel is in *Pax*, which has both its old chorus and its old Trygaeus who becomes 'young' (860–1)—but where no equivalent coordination between the two is established.

[165] His poverty, e.g. 564–5; theirs, 300–2. His weakness, e.g. 165, 356–7; theirs, e.g. 230–7. His and their impotence, 739–40, 1062–3, 1343–4 (and see MacDowell and Sommerstein ad locc.).

[166] Above, pp. 161 and 249–52.

[167] Above, pp. 371–2.

while his son is literally carrying him away from physical encounters with flute-girls and innocent bystanders, the chorus are still nodding and shaking their heads at the situation—whose extravagance, indeed, seems quite unrelatable to their amiably prosaic assessment of it ('What a piece of luck for him . . . But maybe . . . But then again . . .', 1450–61).[168]

The chorus, meanwhile, have been vehicles for pathos—'Hard in war, once' (1061)[169]—as Philocleon, with his restless energy and the grotesque excess that informs all his actions, has not. And he, meanwhile, has emerged from his defeat in the agon as a rejuvenated figure. With his sheer amoral energy, he resists his son's endeavours to fit him for the polite society of 'sophisticated gentlemen' (1175), and begins to seem more of a life-force than a man subject to the relativities of time and circumstance. And yet he is still a man, and an old man, with a tiresomely conventional son and an old man's presumed impotence, for all his eagerness to make the most of his flute-girl. That erotic encounter produces the most explicit statement of the rejuvenation motif and, at the same time, an inimitable joke about existence itself. Whereas the old chorus embodies pathos and therefore cannot (without evoking real pain) pursue any existential questions, glorious and grotesque Philocleon, who does not suffer from pathos, can and does (1351–6):

> *ἐὰν γένῃ δὲ μὴ κακὴ νυνὶ γυνή,*
> *ἐγώ σ', ἐπειδὰν οὑμὸς υἱὸς ἀποθάνῃ,*
> *λυσάμενος ἕξω παλλακήν, ὦ χοιρίον.*
> *νῦν δ' οὐ κρατῶ πω τῶν ἐμαυτοῦ χρημάτων·*
> *νέος γάρ εἰμι. καὶ φυλάττομαι σφόδρα·*
> *τὸ γὰρ ὑίδιον τηρεῖ με . . .*
>
> You be a real good girl now, pussy,
> And when my son dies, I tell you what,
> I'll ransom you: you can be my private whore.
> I don't control my own estate just yet.
> I'm only young, you see, and my boy's
> So protective: he keeps an eye on me.

He is 'only young', *neos*.[170] As *neos*, he defies the laws of existence. Yet even as *neos*, he is caught in these laws, because, being *neos*, he

[168] Cf. Sommerstein ad loc. As at 273–84 the chorus offer a series of mutually exclusive possibilities, none of which is in fact correct: cf. above, pp. 374–5.

[169] Above, pp. 389–92.

[170] As one of his victims acknowledges (he is a *νεανίας*, 'young man', 1333).

is subject to another set of contingencies: he has his youngers and betters to rein him in. He is still a man, then, like the chorus; but then they, equally, are men like him; and in the final demonstration of their relationship, he and they, the two versions of one entity, converge. They join in a glorious dance, sublimely irrelevant to any of the worldly concerns of the play and calculated, in fact, to deny whatever remains of its worldly logic. That denial, however, seems to affirm the comic-existential theme. In support of Philocleon's boast that with the old dances of Thespis' time he can make the new generation of dancers look like 'old Cronuses' (1476–81), *all* the old men end the play dancing together (1535–7). Their dance is a Terpsichorean equivalent of the old soldier's commemoration: an expression of old men's nostalgia, with memories heroized in recall. And yet it is also a final, defiant inversion of the laws of transience which those memories epitomize: a deeply comic projection of survival and enactment of life grasped, recreatively, in the moment. The convergence is complete.

According to Northrop Frye, 'the basis [of pathos] is the exclusion of an individual from a group, [which is] the deepest fear in ourselves that we possess.'[171] Not so. In *Wasps* the old chorus, who are a focus for pathos, are themselves a group and are not excluded, or at risk of exclusion, from any larger group, or indeed from society as a whole. On the other hand, Philocleon, who by his outrageous behaviour actually excludes himself from society as a whole, is not a focus for pathos, but for its inverse. Clearly, the pathos associated with the chorus is inexplicable in Frye's terms. It presupposes an acknowledgement, albeit a disguised acknowledgement, of their *in*clusion in the painful necessities of existence; in a deeper disguise, that acknowledgement finds expression in the joyous excess of old, but rejuvenated, Philocleon; and the final acknowledgement is made when the two disguises come together as one in the dance. This eventual convergence is an affirmation, and what Kierkegaard would have us call a 'revocation', on a grand, comic scale. Yet pathos is not evaded or destroyed, but converted into a last defiant display of comic possibility. 'I am just the same as when', says Hardy, and

[171] Frye, *Anatomy*, 217. Contrast Kierkegaard's opposition between 'the security of social continuity' and 'the elusiveness of existence [which] isolates me whenever I apprehend it' (*Postscript*, 76).

the pathos is in his impossible act of defiance. Philocleon's dance is that act's comic equivalent.

* * *

By Kierkegaard's canons, Aristophanes, in the final analysis, is escapist. Aristophanes does in a sense revoke—he revokes suffering—but only in a sense, and only as much as (say) Euripides' *Trojan Women* or Kafka's *Castle* revoke celebration. Aristophanes' drama would be more escapist, perhaps, if it stayed closer to its worldly roots and forebore to travel to the remotest realms of possibility: if it contented itself, perhaps, with a realist response to the rich texture of the Athens of its day, in place of its extraordinary enactment of an immanent freedom of being. More escapist and no closer to any truth, perhaps. Thinking back to the questions of realism and comic truth that we raised at an earlier stage of this book, let us now propose that realisms, of whatever sort or provenance, and whether more or less impressive realisms, are not prior testimony to any truth, such that comic constructions like Aristophanes' are derivative of them. Aristophanes' constructions are no more derivative of realist portrayals than the comic is secondary to the tragic, however loudly Aristophanes himself may appeal to tragedy as if it were. Indeed, to vary Pirandello's phrase for once, the 'surprised (and surprising) interest'—the characteristic comic vision—that is associated with Aristophanes' constructions sounds (for what it may be worth) more like a primary, autonomous response to experiential reality than one might expect to find in the more orderly world of much realist presentation.

Aristophanes' comic constructions have their own primary integrity, and the nature and scope of their coherence shows it. Again and again we have felt obliged to seek out new formulations and new categories for that coherence (so different from any realist-Aristotelian unity) of style and structure, mode and character—and vision. It is (we suggest) a coherence founded on a generous apprehension of possibilities and connections, a coherence which bids us welcome, not to intellectual figuration or psychological insight, but to radical openness to life.

We can leave the last word to that play which, of all Aristophanes' plays, best demonstrates these qualities. *Wasps* again:

Hard in the dance,
Hard in war, once,
So hard *here*, once . . .

We recall the old wasps' lament at the very end of the play when old Philocleon (so hard *here*, once) attempts to make off with his flute-girl and then ends up (hard in the dance) beating—as he hopes—'the younger set', a magnificent, grotesque, weirdly rejuvenated figure, the master-animal in a play alive with animals, affirming energy. Poetry (said Ezra Pound) is language 'highly energized', and the energy the comic hero affirms (formerly given over to politics and law) is now translated into song and dance—in Greek terms, lyric poetry—with Philocleon in his final recreative role as performer-poet.[172]

Philocleon is an old man who, by comic possibility, is young again, and therefore sings and dances with all the energy of youth, as if to prove that

An aged man is but a paltry thing,
. . . unless
Soul clap its hands and sing,

which is not Aristophanes but Yeats; and Yeats's great poem, 'Sailing to Byzantium', to which these lines belong, provides an apt commentary on the comic poetry of *Wasps*. Like Aristophanes and his Philocleon, Yeats and his aged man are haunted by the ever-present reminders of youth,

The young
In one another's arms, birds in the trees—
Those dying generations—at *their* song,[173]

but unlike Aristophanes and his Philocleon, Yeats and his aged man are tormented by these reminders and dream of a deliverance from the vanished world of youth into the permanent stillness of eternity, symbolized by 'the holy city of Byzantium'. Their quest is to be 'out of nature', like the gold in a 'gold mosaic'. Nature is youth and therefore age and death. The aged man is a 'dying

[172] *Literary Essays of Ezra Pound*, ed. T. S. Eliot (London 1954) 49. For a rejection of the quotidian world in favour of poetry, cf. in miniature *Pax* 775 ff., where it is war, not politics, that is rejected (*Μοῦσα . . . πολέμους ἀπωσαμένη*: above, pp. 111 ff.), and where talk of rival artists likewise accompanies celebration.

[173] My italics.

animal', who seeks to be gathered 'into the artifice of eternity'. The song that beckons, then, is not the song of life, but a deathless alternative to 'that sensual music'.

Such is not the song that Philocleon sings. *This* animal is far from being 'a dying animal'. *His* eternity is a dance and song that subsumes sensuality, and the triumph of that dance and song is itself a triumph over the limitations of age and its apprehension of mortality. Byzantium is a symbolic confine of the mind. Philocleon rejects all confines: the confines of his house when his son imprisons him there, the confines of acceptable behaviour imposed on him when he loses the political argument, and the confines he once gloried in: the rules of law. Amazingly, indeed, in a culture so bound up with rules and (especially) law—a notoriously litigious culture for which 'the role of the lawcourts and the law . . . the general publishing and discussion of laws, the equality of citizens before the law, the citizens' part in the adjudication of cases, the citizens' duty to uphold the city's laws . . . are major topics in the discussion of the growth of democracy and democratic ideology'[174]—Aristophanes sets his Philocleon free from all these confines, and leaves him to dance the dance of life, and sing its song, without any limitations.

Philocleon's dance is a strange dance, and for several reasons: because it is not the solo effort that his newly antinomian activities might have led us to expect, but a competition; because Philocleon is an unlikely dancer on any reckoning; because the dancing turns out to be tragic dancing; and because, whereas his supposed rivals in the competition are contemporaries, the dancing that he aspires to emulate turns out to belong to the earliest of all known tragedians, Thespis (1477–81):[175]

> περιχαρὴς τῷ πράγματι
> ὀρχούμενος τῆς νυκτὸς οὐδὲν παύεται
> τἀρχαῖ' ἐκεῖν' οἷς Θέσπις ἠγωνίζετο·
> καὶ τοὺς τραγῳδούς φησιν ἀποδείξειν Κρόνους
> τοὺς νῦν διορχησάμενος ὀλίγον ὕστερον.

> He's in such rapture
> He's danced non-stop all night
> Old steps that Thespis used in competition.

[174] Goldhill, *Reading Greek Tragedy*, 34.

[175] Into the mixture Philocleon also stirs something else from another, not quite so early tragedian, Phrynichus (*Vesp.* 1490: see MacDowell ad loc.).

> He says he'll have a dancing contest with the new
> Tragic artistes and show them up as Cronuses.

Thespis takes us back to the very foundation of Attic tragedy, and the beginning of the institutionalized dramatic festivals, when the tragic poet was also his own performer. In a spirit of inclusiveness, as well as of self-assertive rivalry, Philocleon summons up the modern Thespians to match his efforts, who duly arrive (1500–11) in the shape of the sons of the contemporary tragedian Carcinus (himself celebrated as naval commander as well as tragic poet),[176] who now in turn puts in a personal appearance at the very end (1532–3). The latter's name, *Karkinos*, meant 'crab', and his nickname (in acknowledgement of his naval achievements) was *thalattios*, 'Sea Lord', quoted here (1519), but in incongruously high-style form,[177] then amiably translated still higher to Poseidon's cult title, 'Master of the Seas' (ποντομέδων ἄναξ, 1532). Thanks to comic recreation, they are all now tragic performers (*tragôidoi*, 1480), who, without any limiting resolution of their competition, lead the chorus off still dancing—with, apparently, Philocleon, the sons of Carcinus, Carcinus himself, and chorus too, all united as, or with, the *comic* troupe, *khoros trugôidôn*, on which phrase (1537) the play ends. 'Throw your leg up to heaven' (ῥῖπτε σκέλος οὐράνιον, 1530), sing the chorus, and all no doubt do just that; but there is no danger of any leg hitting a metaphysical heaven by mistake, because the dance, however tragic in origin, is no longer tragic in orientation, but subsumed within the comic domain.

Tragôidoi and *trugôidoi*: these two words, which point to tragedy and to comedy under the comic appellation that sums up comedy's consciousness of tragedy, frame the closing song and dance.[178] Like the rest of the play, the scene is full of animals, so that Philocleon (himself the animal essence of the play as a whole) is confronted with 'crab' Carcinus and his sons, who are three more crabs (1507). One of these comes on like a 'scorpion or spider',[179] then all three together—now crabs, now dancing

[176] See MacDowell, Sommerstein ad loc. This is the same Carcinus who is subsequently mocked at *Pax* 781 ff. (above, p. 113).

[177] θαλασσίοιο (text as MacDowell, q.v.) with traditional literary -σσ- and epic-poetic -οιο. For the nickname cf. Pl. Com. 143 *PCG*, and see MacDowell on *Vesp.* 1501.

[178] On *trugôid-* see above, p. 41. On the final song (and dance) (1518–37), see Parker, *Songs*, 256–61.

[179] So Henderson (new Loeb), q.v.

birds—become 'a reel of wrens' (1513),[180] 'shrimps' brothers' (1522), and in a last, almost excruciating moment of punning exuberance, 'threeshes' (1534).[181] From this rush of image and movement emerges the play's final vision of comic hybridity, one that is richly allusive both to the topical life of Athens and to the tragic-poetic tradition that for Aristophanes connotes the authoritative ideal. Inspired by drink (1476) and music (1477),[182] Philocleon declaims in a suitably impossible procession of sub-tragic and demotic Greek—in that hugely intensified version of popular idiomatic resources that characterizes Aristophanic expression—from the moment he makes his appearance in this scene (1482),

> τίς ἐπ' αὐλείοισι θύραις θάσσει;
>
> Who coucheth at the outer gate?[183]

through a running commentary he gives on his own performance (1488–9, 1492),

> οἷον μυκτὴρ μυκᾶται καὶ
> σφόνδυλος ἀχεῖ
>
> . . . .
>
> πρωκτὸς χάσκει
>
> Back cracks,
> Nostril doth roar,
>
> . . .
>
> Arse yawns[184]

to his last utterance of all (1515), in which he looks ahead to a victory dinner of boiled crab (because the play is still all animals,

[180] The Greek is ὀρχίλων, 'wrens', with (in this context) a connotation of ὀρχεῖσθαι, 'dance': so Sommerstein (following schol.).

[181] τριόρχοις, 'buzzards', re-etymologized *ad hoc* as from τρεῖς, 'three' and (again: n. 180 above) ὀρχεῖσθαι, 'dance'. This detail and the writing of the scene as a whole are oddly slighted by MacDowell ad loc. (and *Wasps*, 329). On the animalian end, cf. Bowie, *Aristophanes*, 95–6.

[182] νὴ τὸν Διόνυσον, as the slave who tells us about the drink and the music aptly begins (1474): the music is played on the Dionysiac *aulos* (1477).

[183] Pure high-style: Rau, *Paratragodia*, 155.

[184] In 1488–9 the absence of any def. art. and the presence of the 'Doric' alpha in ἀχεῖ are high-style; everything else is ordinary enough, though not actually low (μυκτήρ and σφόνδυλος are, *inter alia*, standard medical terms in the Hippocratic corpus: LSJ s.vv.). In 1492 πρωκτός is low; χάσκει is alien to Attic prose, but common in epic and later verse (though not esp. tragic verse) and Ionic prose (LSJ s.v.); the two words are clearly spoken (sung) by Ph. (so MacDowell).

and with or without a win in the dance contest, there may be a win and a celebration in the comic competition):

ἅλμην κύκα τούτοισιν, ἢν ἐγὼ κρατῶ
Mix a marinade, in case I win.[185]

Perhaps (being hard in the dance) he may win—but there is no foreclosing, and possibility is left open.

In their own way, the dance, the impossibly hybrid Greek, the comic enactment (in comic anticipation) of dramatic victory, all celebrate the connection, the cultural continuum, for which Dionysus in *Frogs*—comic god in search of tragic poet—was so concerned (1419):

save the city
And its dramatic festivals.[186]

That concern in *Frogs*, of course, presupposes Athens' desperate state near the end of the war. Years earlier in the same conflict, Aristophanes had characterized his city as a 'land supreme in war *and poets* and power' (πολέμῳ τε καὶ ποιηταῖς δυνάμει θ' ὑπερφερούσης . . . χώρας, *Knights* 583–5), where the characteristically intrusive force of that 'and poets' isolates and frees the phrase from its political surroundings, just as its presence in the list connects it to them.[187] In *Wasps*, now, in that same connective yet free and open-minded spirit, the comic poet attaches poetry to its Athenian context and, in the act of attachment, sets it free.

Philocleon's dance is tragic in provenance, animal in spirit, richly allusive in the range of reference it calls up—and only comedy, through its freedom and recreative power, could encompass such diversity. Like Philocleon's words in this scene, the words of the chorus range over the stylistic spectrum, from the high-poetic ('Master of the Seas', 1532) down to the comedic low, on which level they bring the play to its close. The last word of all is *trugôidoi*, that rich and ripe formation by which Aristophanic comedy asserts its relationship to the tragic genre and yet its

[185] Transl. after van Daele (Budé). These last words (spoken) are free of high-style features—as if Philocleon's whole final utterance were designed to mimic the contours of a hybrid Aristophanic lyric, starting high and dipping low (above, pp. 189–90).

[186] Above, p. 407.

[187] Cf. the lists discussed above, pp. 152–6.

autonomy from the tragic, its own institutional and rural-traditional connections and equally its right to look where it pleases, whether near or impossibly far, for its reference and its recreation. In the very act of closure the exuberant compound proclaims the openness of comic possibility, yet does so through the specificities, the necessary connections, between Aristophanes and his Athens.

In these assertions and these proclamations lies Aristophanes' claim to comic seriousness and his ultimate significance as a comic poet. *Wasps* is not perfect comedy: there is no such thing. But it is as pure comedy as anything could be, as close as anything could be to definitive comedy, and in its final moment the definition of comedy is implicit.

Bibliography of Abbreviated Works

In the notes above, certain standard editions and works of reference are referred to in abbreviated form, thus:

Biog. Gr. Min.	A. Westermann (ed.), *Biographi Graeci Minores* (Brunswick 1845)
CEG	P. A. Hansen (ed.), *Carmina Epigraphica Graeca* (Berlin 1983–9)
CGF	G. Kaibel (ed.), *Comicorum Graecorum Fragmenta* (Berlin 1899)
FGH	F. Jacoby (ed.), *Fragmente der griechischen Historiker* (Berlin and Leiden 1923–)
IEG	M. L. West (ed.), *Iambi et Elegi Graeci*[2] (Oxford 1989–92)
LSJ	H. G. Liddell and R. Scott, *A Greek-English Lexicon*[9], rev. H. S. Jones (Oxford 1925–40)
LSJ, *Supp.*	P. G. W. Glare (ed.), *Greek-English Lexicon, Revised Supplement* (Oxford 1996)
OCD[3]	S. Hornblower and A. Spawforth (eds.), *The Oxford Classical Dictionary*[3] (Oxford 1996)
OED	*The Oxford English Dictionary*[2] (Oxford 1989), prep. J. A. Simpson and E. S. C. Weiner
PCG	R. Kassel and C. Austin (eds.), *Poetae Comici Graeci* (Berlin 1983–)
PLF	E. Lobel and D. L. Page (eds.), *Poetarum Lesbiorum Fragmenta* (Oxford 1955)
PMG	D. L. Page (ed.), *Poetae Melici Graeci* (Oxford 1962)
RE	A. Pauly, G. Wissowa, and W. Kroll (eds.), *Real-Encyclopädie der klassischen Altertumswissenschaft* (Stuttgart 1893–)
TGF	B. Snell, R. Kannicht, and S. Radt (eds.), *Tragicorum Graecorum Fragmenta* (Göttingen 1971–)
TGFS	J. Diggle (ed.), *Tragicorum Graecorum Fragmenta Selecta* (Oxford 1998)

* * *

The bibliography that follows lists works of (mostly) secondary literature which are cited more than once, and therefore referred to in abbreviated form, in the notes of one or more of the chapters of the book. Standard commentaries (referred to by the commentator's name) are not included unless confusion might otherwise result.

ADORNO, T., 'Über den Fetischcharakter in der Musik und die Regression des Hörens', in Theodor Adorno, *Gesammelte Schriften*, ed. R. Tiedemann (23 vols., Frankfurt 1970–), xiv. 14–50.

ALLEN, W., *Getting Even* (London 1973).

ARNOTT, W. G., 'Comic openings', *Drama* 2 (1993) 14–32.

BAKHTIN, M., *Rabelais and His World*, tr. H. Iswolsky (Cambridge, Mass. 1968).

BAUDELAIRE, C., 'De l'essence du rire', in *Curiosités esthétiques*, ed. H. Lemaitre (Paris 1962) 241–63.

BOWIE, A. M., 'The parabasis in Aristophanes: prolegomena, *Acharnians*', *CQ* 32 (1982) 27–40.

——*Aristophanes: Myth, Ritual and Comedy* (Cambridge 1993).

BRECHT, B., *Versuche* (Berlin 1959).

——*Schriften zum Theater* (7 vols., Frankfurt 1963–4).

BREMER, J. M., 'Aristophanes on his own Poetry', *Entr. Hardt* 38 (1993) 125–65.

BROOKE-ROSE, C., *A Rhetoric of the Unreal* (Cambridge 1981).

BURKERT, W., *Greek Religion*, tr. J. Raffan (Oxford 1985).

COLVIN, S. C., *Dialect in Aristophanes and the Politics of Language in Ancient Greek Literature* (Oxford 1999).

COULON V. (ed.) and VAN DAELE, H. (tr.), *Aristophane* (Paris 1923–30).

CSAPO, E., and SLATER, W. J., *The Context of Ancient Drama* (Ann Arbor 1995).

CULLER, J., *Structuralist Poetics* (London 1975).

DALE, A. M., *The Lyric Metres of Greek Drama*^{2} (Cambridge 1968).

——*Collected Papers* (Cambridge 1969).

D'ALTON, J. F., *Roman Literary Theory and Criticism* (London 1931).

DERRIDA, J., *De la grammatologie* (Paris 1967).

DETIENNE, M., and VERNANT, J.-P., *Les Ruses de l'intelligence. La mètis des Grecs* (Paris 1974).

DOBROV, G. W. (ed.), *The City as Comedy* (Chapel Hill 1997).

DOVER, K. J., *Aristophanes, Clouds* (Oxford 1968).

——*Aristophanic Comedy* (London 1972).

——*Greek and the Greeks* (Oxford 1987).

——*Aristophanes, Frogs* (Oxford 1993).

DUKORE, B. F. (ed.), *Dramatic Theory and Criticism* (New York 1974).

DÜRRENMATT, F., *Theater-Schriften und Reden*, ed. E. Brock-Sulzer (Zurich 1966).

EDMUNDS, L., 'Aristophanes' *Acharnians*', *YCS* 26 (1980) 1–41.

EHRENBERG, V., *The People of Aristophanes*[2] (Oxford 1951).

ELAM, K., *The Semiotics of Theatre and Drama* (London 1980).

ELIOT, T. S., *The Sacred Wood* (London 1920).

—— 'Tradition and the individual talent', in *The Sacred Wood*, 47–59.

ELSE, G. F., *The Origin and Early Form of Greek Tragedy* (Cambridge, Mass. 1965).

FOLEY, H. P., 'Tragedy and politics in Aristophanes' *Acharnians*', *JHS* 108 (1988) 33–47.

FOWLER, A., *Kinds of Literature* (Oxford 1982).

FREUD, S., *Jokes and their Relation to the Unconscious*, tr. J. Strachey, Penguin Freud Library, vi, ed. A. Richards (Harmondsworth 1976).

—— *Group Psychology and the Analysis of the Ego*, tr. J. Strachey, Penguin Freud Library, xii, ed. A. Richards (Harmondsworth 1985) 95–178.

—— 'Humour', tr. J. Strachey, Penguin Freud Library, xiv, ed. A. Dickson (Harmondsworth 1985) 425–33.

FROW, J., 'Spectacle binding: on character', *Poetics Today* 7 (1986) 227–50.

FRYE, N., *Anatomy of Criticism* (Princeton 1957).

GEISSLER, P., *Chronologie der altattischen Komödie*[2] (Zurich 1969).

GELZER, T., *Der epirrhematische Agon bei Aristophanes* (Munich 1960).

GOFFMAN, E., *Frame Analysis* (New York 1974).

GOLDHILL, S., *Reading Greek Tragedy* (Cambridge 1986).

—— *The Poet's Voice* (Cambridge 1991).

GOLDSMITH, O., *The Miscellaneous Works of Oliver Goldsmith* (London 1806).

GOODWIN, W. W., *Syntax of the Moods and Tenses of the Greek Verb* (rev. edn., London 1929).

GRIFFIN, J., *Homer on Life and Death* (Oxford 1980).

HALLIWELL, S., *Aristotle's Poetics* (London 1986).

HAMON, P., 'Pour un statut sémiologique du personnage', in R. Barthes *et al.* (eds.), *Poétique du récit* (Paris 1977) 115–80.

HANDLEY, E. W., 'Comedy', in P. E. Easterling and B. M. W. Knox (eds.), *The Cambridge History of Classical Literature*, i: *Greek Literature* (Cambridge 1985) 355–425.

HEATH, M., *The Poetics of Greek Tragedy* (London 1987).

—— *Political Comedy in Aristophanes* (Göttingen 1987).

HENDERSON, J., *Aristophanes: Lysistrata* (Oxford 1987).

—— The *demos* and the comic competition', in J. J. Winkler and F. I. Zeitlin (eds.), *Nothing to Do with Dionysos?* (Princeton 1990) 271–313.

HENDERSON, J., *The Maculate Muse: Obscene Language in Attic Comedy*[2] (Oxford 1991).

——(ed. and tr.), *Aristophanes*, Loeb Classical Library (Cambridge, Mass. 1998–).

HERRICK, M. T., *Comic Theory in the Sixteenth Century* (Urbana 1964).

IONESCO, E., *Notes and Counter-Notes*, tr. D. Watson (London 1967).

JANKO, R., *Aristotle on Comedy* (London 1984).

JEAN PAUL, *Sämtliche Werke*, ed. E. Berend (Weimar 1935).

JOHNSON, S., *Lives of the English Poets*, ed. A. Waugh (London 1906).

KIERKEGAARD, S., *Concluding Unscientific Postscript*, tr. D. F. Swanson and W. Lowrie (Princeton 1941).

KOESTLER, A., *The Act of Creation* (London 1964).

KUGELMEIER, C., *Reflexe früher und zeitgenössischer Lyrik in der alten attischen Komödie* (Stuttgart 1996).

LADA-RICHARDS, I., *Initiating Dionysus: Ritual and Theatre in Aristophanes' Frogs* (Oxford 1999).

LANGER, S., *Feeling and Form* (New York 1953).

LAWRENCE, D. H., *Selected Literary Criticism*, ed. A. Beal (London 1956).

LEAVIS, F. R., *The Common Pursuit* (London 1958).

LÓPEZ EIRE, A., *La lengua coloquial de la comedia aristofánica* (Murcia 1996).

LYONS, J., *Semantics* (2 vols., Cambridge 1977).

MACDOWELL, D. M., *Aristophanes, Wasps* (Oxford 1971).

——*Aristophanes and Athens* (Oxford 1995).

MCMAHON, A. P., 'Seven questions on Aristotelian definitions of tragedy and comedy', *HSCP* 40 (1929) 97–198.

MACHEREY, P., and BALIBAR, E., 'Literature as an ideological form', in R. Young (ed.), *Untying the Text* (London 1981) 79–99.

MÁRQUEZ, G. G., *One Hundred Years of Solitude*, tr. G. Rabassa (London 1970).

——*Love in the Time of Cholera*, tr. E. Grossman (New York 1988).

MATHEWS, G., 'Aristophanes' "high" lyrics reconsidered', *Maia* 49 (1997) 1–42.

MOULTON, C., *Aristophanic Poetry* (Göttingen 1981).

NEWIGER, H.-J., *Metapher und Allegorie. Studien zu Aristophanes* (Munich 1957).

NEWMAN, K., *Shakespeare's Rhetoric of Comic Character* (New York 1985).

PARKE, H. W., and WORMELL, D. E. W., *The Delphic Oracle* (Oxford 1956).

PARKER, L. P. E., *The Songs of Aristophanes* (Oxford 1997).

PELLING, C. B. R. (ed.), *Characterization and Individuality in Greek Literature* (Oxford 1990).

PICKARD-CAMBRIDGE, A. W., *Dithyramb, Tragedy and Comedy*², rev. T. B. L. Webster (Oxford 1962).
—— *The Dramatic Festivals of Athens*², rev. J. Gould and D. M. Lewis (corr. edn., Oxford 1988).
PIRANDELLO, L., *On Humor*, tr. A. Illiano and D. P. Testa (Chapel Hill 1974).
PRATO, C., 'I metri lirici di Aristofane', *Dioniso* 57 (1987) 203–44.
RALEIGH, W. (ed.), *Johnson on Shakespeare* (rev. edn., Oxford 1925).
RAU, P., *Paratragodia* (Munich 1967).
RECKFORD, K. J., *Aristophanes' Old-and-New Comedy* (Chapel Hill 1987).
RICHARDS, H., *Aristophanes and Others* (London 1909).
RICHARDS, I. A., *Practical Criticism* (London 1929).
ROGERS, B. B. (ed. and tr.), *The Comedies of Aristophanes* (11 vols., London 1902–15).
ROSEN, R., *Old Comedy and the Iambographic Tradition* (Atlanta 1988).
RUSSO, C. F., *Aristofane autore di teatro*² (Florence 1984).
STE CROIX, G. E. M. DE, *The Origins of the Peloponnesian War* (London 1972).
SCHILLER, F., *Sämtliche Werke*, ed. E. von den Hellen *et al.* (16 vols., Stuttgart 1904–5).
SCHWYZER, E., *Griechische Grammatik*² (Munich 1959–71).
SEGAL, C. P., 'The character and cults of Dionysus and the unity of the *Frogs*', *HSCP* 65 (1961) 207–42.
—— 'Aristophanes' cloud-chorus', *Arethusa* 2 (1969) 143–61.
SEIDENSTICKER, B., *Palintonos Harmonia* (Göttingen 1982).
SIFAKIS, G. M., *Parabasis and Animal Choruses* (London 1971).
—— 'On the structure of Aristophanic comedy', *JHS* 112 (1992) 123–39.
SILK, M. S., *Interaction in Poetic Imagery* (Cambridge 1974).
—— 'Aristophanes as a lyric poet', *YCS* 26 (1980) 99–151.
—— 'LSJ and the problem of poetic archaism: from meanings to iconyms', *CQ* 33 (1983) 303-30.
—— *Homer, The Iliad* (Cambridge 1987).
—— 'The autonomy of comedy', *Comparative Criticism* 10 (1988) 3–37.
—— 'Pathos in Aristophanes', *BICS* 34 (1988) 78–111.
—— 'The people of Aristophanes', in Pelling, *Characterization*, 150–73.
—— 'Aristophanic paratragedy', in Sommerstein, *Tragedy, Comedy and the Polis*, 477–504.
—— 'The "six parts of tragedy" in Aristotle's *Poetics*', *PCPS* 40 (1994) 108–15.
—— 'Language, poetry and enactment', *Dialogos* 2 (1995) 109–32.
—— (ed.), *Tragedy and the Tragic: Greek Theatre and Beyond* (Oxford 1996).

SILK, M. S., 'Tragic language: the Greek tragedians and Shakespeare', in Silk, *Tragedy and the Tragic*, 458–96.

—— 'Style, voice and authority in the choruses of Greek drama', *Drama* 7 (1999) 1–26.

—— 'Pindar meets Plato: theory, language, value, and the classics', in S. J. Harrison (ed.), *Texts, Ideas, and the Classics* (Oxford, forthcoming).

—— 'Space and solitude in Aristophanes', *Pallas* 55 (2001), forthcoming.

—— 'Aristophanes versus the rest: comic poetry in Old Comedy', in D. Harvey and J. Wilkins (eds.), *The Rivals of Aristophanes*, forthcoming.

—— and STERN, J. P., *Nietzsche on Tragedy* (Cambridge 1981).

SOMMERSTEIN, A. H., *Aristophanes: Acharnians*[2] (Warminster 1984).

—— *et al.* (eds.), *Tragedy, Comedy and the Polis* (Bari 1993).

STANFORD, W. B., *Aeschylus in his Style* (Dublin 1942).

—— *Aristophanes, The Frogs* (London 1963).

STARKIE, W. J. M., *The Acharnians of Aristophanes* (London 1909).

STERN, J. P., *On Realism* (London 1973).

STYAN, J. L., *The Dark Comedy* (Cambridge 1968).

SUTTON, D. F., *Self and Society in Aristophanes* (Washington, DC 1980).

SYPHER, W. (ed.), *Comedy* (New York 1956).

SZEMERÉNYI, O., 'The origins of Roman drama and Greek tragedy', *Hermes* 103 (1975) 300–32.

TAILLARDAT, J., *Les Images d'Aristophane*[2] (Paris 1965).

TAPLIN, O., *The Stagecraft of Aeschylus* (Oxford 1977).

—— 'Tragedy and trugedy', *CQ* 33 (1983) 331–3.

—— 'Fifth-century tragedy and comedy: a *synkrisis*', *JHS* 106 (1986) 163–74.

—— 'Comedy and the tragic', in Silk, *Tragedy and the Tragic*, 188–202.

WEST, M. L., *Greek Metre* (Oxford 1982).

WHITMAN, C. H., *Aristophanes and the Comic Hero* (Cambridge, Mass. 1964).

WILES, D., 'Reading Greek performance', *G&R* 34 (1987) 136–51.

—— *The Masks of Menander* (Cambridge 1991).

WILKINSON, L. P., *Golden Latin Artistry* (Cambridge 1963).

WILLETT, J. (ed.), *Brecht on Theatre* (New York 1964).

ZANKER, G., *Realism in Alexandrian Poetry* (London 1987).

ZEITLIN, F., *Playing the Other* (Chicago 1996).

ZIMMERMANN, B., *Untersuchungen zur Form und dramatischen Technik der Aristophanischen Komödien* (3 vols., Königstein and Frankfurt 1984–7).

Index of Aristophanic Passages

This index lists discussions of specified extant plays by Aristophanes and specified passages from those plays. For discussions of other authors and of Aristophanic fragments, see General Index. It should be noted that, in the case of overlapping or sequential passages, compendious references have often been used. Thus the reference to *Ach.* 263–79 subsumes discussions of (e.g.) 271–5 (on p. 122), 276–9 (on p. 123), 267 (on p. 272), as well as the whole sequence, 263–79 itself (on pp. 181–7).

General Index

Full lists of discussions of, and references to, extant plays by Aristophanes will be found in Index of Aristophanic Passages; here only a few particular discussions are listed. Where no ambiguity results, various post-classical authors and authorities are cited by surname alone. An asterisk before an italicized item (as **agroikos*) indicates a lexicographical or similar discussion of a Greek word.